Edited and designed by
Time Out Guides Limited
Universal House
251 Tottenham Court Road
London W1T 7AB
Tel + 44 (0)20 7813 3000
Fax + 44 (0)20 7813 6001
Email guides@timeout.com
www.timeout.com

Editorial

Editor Christi Daugherty
Deputy Editor Laura Martz, Peter Watts
Consultant Editor Michael Depp
Listings Editor Alexis Green Averbuck
Proofreader Marion Moisy
Indexer Jonathan Cox

Editorial/Managing Director Peter Fiennes
Series Editor Ruth Jarvis
Deputy Series Editor Lesley McCave
Guides Co-ordinator Anna Norman
Accountant Sarah Bostock

Design

Art Director Mandy Martin
Acting Art Director Scott Moore
Acting Art Editor Tracey Ridgewell
Senior Designer Averil Sinnott
Designers Astrid Kogler, Sam Lands
Digital Imaging Dan Conway
Ad Make-up Charlotte Blythe

Picture Desk

Picture Editor Kerri Littlefield
Deputy Picture Editor Kit Burnet
Picture Researcher Alex Ortiz
Picture Desk Trainee Bella Wood

Advertising

Sales Director Mark Phillips
International Sales Manager Ross Canadé
International Sales Executive Simon Davies
Advertising Sales (New Orleans) OffBeat
Advertising Assistant Lucy Butler

Marketing

Marketing Manager Mandy Martinez
US Publicity & Marketing Associate Rosella Albanese

Production

Guides Production Director Mark Lamond
Production Controller Samantha Furniss

Time Out Group

Chairman Tony Elliott
Managing Director Mike Hardwick
Group Financial Director Richard Waterlow
Group Commercial Director Lesley Gill
Group Marketing Director Christine Cort
Group General Manager Nichola Coulthard
Group Art Director John Oakey
Online Managing Director David Pepper

Contributors:

Introduction Christi Daugherty. **History** Will Coviello (*A walk through black history* Colleen McMillar). **New Orleans Today** Harriet Swift (*A Streetcar named road chaos* Christi Daugherty). **Mardi Gras** Will Coviello. **Literary New Orleans** Michael Depp. **Accommodation** Harriet Swift. **Sightseeing** Will Coviello (CBD & Warehouse District, *Doing the strip*), Christi Daugherty (Introduction, French Quarter, *Walk this way French Quarter, Cities of the dead*), Sharon Donovan (*Taking the Longue Vue*), Russell McCulley (Marigny & Bywater, Lower Garden District), Colleen McMillar (*The Irish Channel*), Alex Rawls (Tremé), Christine Richard (Mid-City), Harriet Swift (Garden District & Uptown, *Walk this way Garden District, You can always pray, Audubon Zoo, Getting Inside*). **Museums** Erik Bookhardt. **Guided Tours** Harriet Swift (*Nature just around the corner* Russell McCulley. **Restaurants** Michael Depp. **Coffeeshops & Cafés** Michael Depp. **Bars** French Quarter, CBD, Lower Garden District, Bywater (Christi Daugherty, David Lee Simmons), Uptown, Marigny (Michael Depp), Mid-City (Christine Richard), *How to drink in the French Quarter* Christi Daugherty. **Shops & Services** Jyl Benson (*Be nice or leave* Michael Depp). **Festivals & Events** Christi Daugherty, Sharon Donovan (*Jazz Fest* Alex Rawls). **Children** Jyl Benson. **Film** David Lee Simmons. **Galleries** Erik Bookhardt (*Hot shops, Encouraging art* Alexis Green Averbuck). **Gay & Lesbian** Russell McCulley. **Music** Alex Rawls (*When the saints go marching in* Colleen McMillar). **Performing Arts** Christi Daugherty, Sharon Donovan. **Sport & Fitness** Alex Rawls. **Trips Out of Town** Will Coviello (*Courir du Mardi Gras*), Christi Daugherty (Getting Started), Colleen McMillar (Cajun Country), Christine Richard (Beaches, Plantation Country), Harriet Swift (*This isn't Tara*). **Directory** Alexis Green Averbuck (Getting Around), Harriet Swift (Resources A-Z).

The Editor would like to thank: Jack Jewers (for everything), Myra Marguerite 'Cissy' Burson (for her endless patience), Martha and Joe Daugherty, Mila Martins, Ros Sales, Ismay Atkins, Jyl Benson, Bonnie Warren, Simone Rathlé, Patti Nickel, Celeste Wilson, the staff at the New Orleans Convention and Visitors Bureau, especially Beverly Gianna and Christine DeCuir.

Alamo Rent A Car supplied Christi Daugherty's rental car in New Orleans (reservations 08705 994000/www.Alamo.co.uk).

Maps J.S. Graphics (john@jsgraphics.co.uk)

Photography by Amanda Edwards except: pages 3, 11, 172, 200, 208, 227 Paul Avis; pages 6, 10, 12, 32, 213 AKG; page 103 Corbis; pages 23, 26, 28, 53, 74, 178 Louisiana/New Orleans Tourist Board; pages 187, 188 Pictorial Press; page 223 Getty Images; page 69 Christi Daugherty. The following images were provided by the featured establishments/artists pages 19, 35, 40, 45, 48, 50, 97, 99, 183, 194, 215, 225, 239.

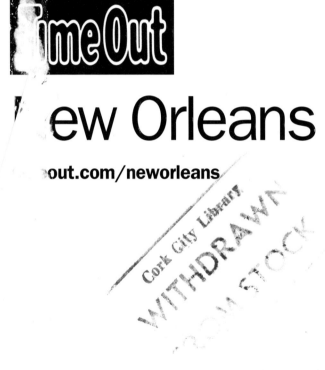

TimeOut

ew Orleans

out.com/neworleans

Published by Time Out Guides Ltd, a wholly owned subsidiary of Time Out Group Ltd.
Time Out and the Time Out logo are trademarks of Time Out Group Ltd.

© **Time Out Group Ltd 2005**
Previous editions 1998, 2000

10 9 8 7 6 5 4 3 2 1

New Orleans 3rd edition (0-140-29413-9) first published in Great Britain in 2003 by the Penguin Group
This edition published in Great Britain in 2005 by Ebury Publishing
Ebury Publishing is a division of The Random House Group Ltd,
20 Vauxhall Bridge Road, London SW1V 2SA

Random House Australia Pty Limited 20 Alfred Street, Milsons Point, Sydney, New South Wales 2061, Australia
Random House New Zealand Limited 18 Poland Road, Glenfield, Auckland 10, New Zealand
Random House South Africa (Pty) Limited Endulini, 5A Jubilee Road, Parktown 2193, South Africa

Random House UK Limited Reg. No. 954009

Distributed in USA by Publishers Group West
1700 Fourth Street, Berkeley, California 94710

Distributed in Canada by Penguin Canada Ltd
10 Alcorn Avenue, Toronto, Ontario, Canada M4V 3B2

For further distribution details, see www.timeout.com

ISBN 1-904978-84-3

A CIP catalogue record for this book is available from the British Library

Colour reprographics by Icon, Crowne House, 56-58 Southwark Street, London SE1 1UN

Printed and bound in Germany by Appl
Papers used by Ebury Publishing are natural, recyclable products made from wood grown in sustainable forests

Contents

Introduction   2

In Context

History   6
New Orleans Today   18
Mardi Gras   22
Literary New Orleans   29

Accommodation

Accommodation   36

Sightseeing

Introduction   54
The French Quarter & Around   56
Faubourg Marigny & Bywater   69
CBD & the Warehouse District   72
Uptown   77
Tremé & Mid-City   89
Museums   96
Guided Tours   101

Eat, Drink, Shop

Restaurants   106
Coffeeshops & Cafés   130
Bars   134
Shops & Services   148

Arts & Entertainment

Festivals & Events   176
Children   182
Film   186
Galleries   190
Gay & Lesbian   197
Music   202
The Performing Arts   215
Sport & Fitness   219

Trips Out of Town

Getting Started   228
Plantation Country   229
Cajun Country   235
Beaches   241

Directory

Getting Around   248
Resources A-Z   252

Further Reference   262
Index   264
Advertisers' Index   270

Maps

Trips Out of Town   272
Greater New Orleans   275
Uptown   276
Mid-City   278
Garden District & CBD   279
Transport   280
French Quarter   282
Street Index   283

Introduction

New Orleans has a lot to live up to. It is known alternately as one of the world's: biggest party towns, most historical cities and most exotic places. It's seen as mysterious, dangerous, exciting… You don't quite know what to expect the first time you come here, but you know it's going to be different.

Everybody has a moment on their first trip here – a brief flash of realisation – when they discover that they love New Orleans. It could be passing the kids tapping for change in the French Quarter, or hearing a gospel singer's voice rise out of the dark on Royal Street. Or it could be as simple as overhearing a comment from a wizened shoeshine man in Jackson Square, as he calls for business: 'Shoeshine, shoeshine, shoe… Oh, don't you know those tennis shoes give me the blues?'

Maybe your moment will come during one of those afternoon thundershowers that pour down on the city out of nowhere on hot summer days. One minute the sun is shining, the next minute the rain is coming down in buckets and you're trapped under a balcony with a dozen strangers, waiting for it to break. As you watch the steam rise off the hot pavement in the pouring rain, and you discover that heat has a smell, you just might think, 'This is what I came here for'.

Not everybody has that moment, of course. The writer Nora Ephron sneered that this is one of the country's 'most ingrown, self-obsessed cities'. And, that is partly true. But it's also impressively unsympathetic, and tends to make everybody bristle. It seems to take a certain kind of person to dislike New Orleans. To see only the dirt and none of the glory; only the poverty and none of the richness. For there are different kinds of wealth. And different kinds of beauty.

To dislike New Orleans – nah, that's just plain wrong. But to be unsure of her, well, that's common. The writer Andrei Codrescu once wrote that the city 'is Blanche DuBois, and that mix of knowledge, denial, hunger and experience is precisely what makes her so attractive to outsiders. Those who are not outsiders and who know her only too well have mixed feelings'.

But before you can be jaded by New Orleans, you must first fall in love with her. You must learn as Tennessee Williams did, that there is something about this city that gets under your skin. He wrote: 'Don't you just love those long rainy afternoons in New Orleans when an hour isn't just an hour, but a little piece of eternity dropped into your hands, and who knows what to do with it?'

ABOUT THE TIME OUT CITY GUIDES

The *Time Out New Orleans Guide* is one of an expanding series of Time Out City Guides produced by the people behind London and New York's successful listings magazines. Our guides are all written and updated by resident experts who have striven to provide you with all the up-to-date information you'll need to explore New Orleans.

THE LOWDOWN ON THE LISTINGS

Above all, we've tried to make this book as useful as possible. To that end, all the addresses, telephone numbers and websites, as well as transport information, opening times, admission prices and credit card details, are included. Wherever possible, we've also provided details about facilities, services and events. All of this information was checked locally and was correct at the time we went to press. However, businesses open and close every day, so before you go out of your way, we would advise you to phone and check opening times.

While every effort has been made to ensure the accuracy of the information contained here, the publishers cannot accept responsibility for any errors it may contain.

PRICES AND PAYMENT

Prices throughout this guide are given in US dollars ($). The prices we've supplied should be treated as guidelines, though, not as gospel. If you find that they vary wildly from those we've quoted, please write and let us know. We aim to give the best advice possible, so we want to know if you've been badly treated or overcharged, or if (as we hope) you've been pleasantly surprised.

We have noted whether venues take major credit cards: American Express (**AmEx**), Diners Club (**DC**), Discover (**Disc**), MasterCard (**MC**) and Visa (**V**). Many businesses will also accept other cards, including Switch or Delta. Most shops, restaurants and attractions accept dollar travellers' cheques issued by major financial institutions.

THE LIE OF THE LAND

We've divided the city up as the locals know it, into smaller neighbourhoods, to make it easier for you to handle. All our addresses include cross streets, to help you find your way around more easily. All our maps are in the back of the book, and map references included in each central New Orleans listing indicate the page and square on which the address will be found (street maps start on page 276).

TELEPHONE NUMBERS

The area code for New Orleans is 504. All telephone numbers given in this guide take this code unless otherwise stated. For more information on phone codes, dialling and call charges, *see p259*.

Advertisers

We would like to stress that no establishment is included in this guide because it has advertised in any of our publications, and no payment of any kind has influenced any review. The opinions given in this book are those of Time Out writers and are entirely independent.

ESSENTIAL INFORMATION

For all the practical information you'll need for visiting the city – including visa and customs information, advice on facilities for the disabled, emergency telephone numbers and medical services – turn to the **Directory** chapter. You'll find it at the back of this guide, starting on page 248.

If you have any questions once you arrive in New Orleans, and you cannot find the answers in this book, contact the **New Orleans Convention and Visitors' Bureau** (566 5011/1-800 672 6124/www.neworleanscvb.com), or stop by its helpful French Quarter office at 529 St Ann Street, at Jackson Square.

LET US KNOW WHAT YOU THINK

We hope you enjoy the *Time Out New Orleans Guide*, and we'd like to know what you think of it. We welcome tips for places that you believe we should include in future editions and take notice of your criticism of our choices. There's a reader's reply card at the back of this book, or you can email us at guides@timeout.com.

> There is an online version of this guide, and guides to more than 35 international cities, at **www.timeout.com**.

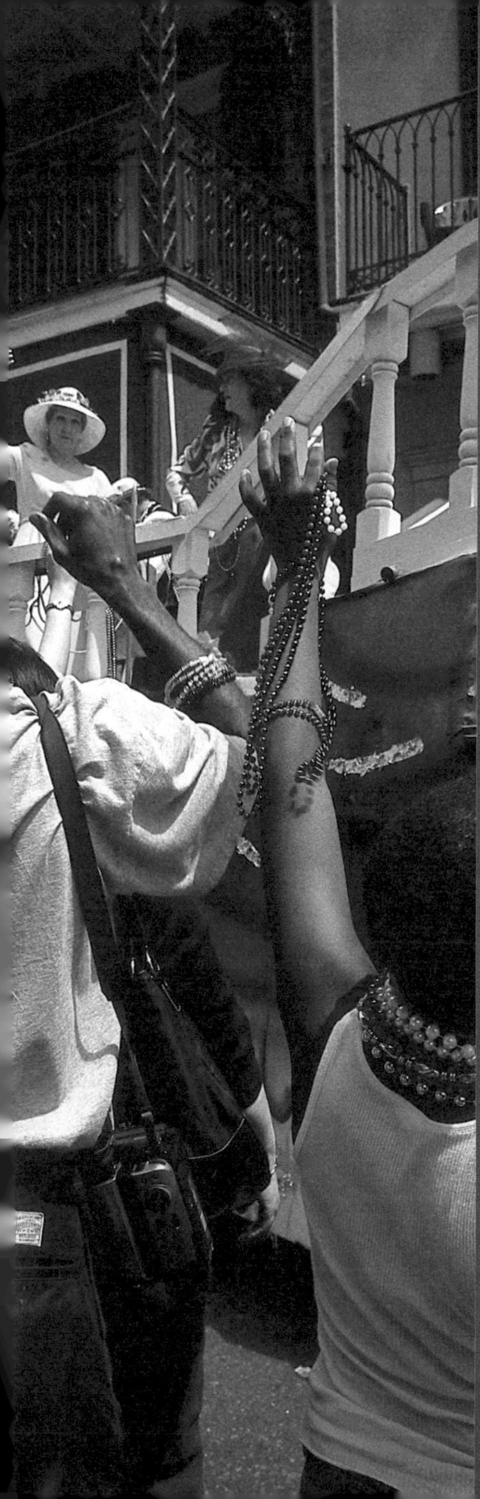

In Context

History 6
New Orleans Today 18
Mardi Gras 22
Literary New Orleans 29

Features

Pretty Baby 9
A walk through black history 10
Quadroon balls 17
A streetcar named road chaos 21
How it started 25
A brief word of advice 26
Future Mardi Gras dates 28

The Battle of New Orleans.

History

On Mardi Gras day in 1699, a French explorer stumbled upon a swamp settlement. The rest, as they say, is history.

In April 1803, President Thomas Jefferson's emissaries secured the Louisiana Purchase for the United States and, in so doing, put the nation on course for becoming a global power. The territory stretched from the object of Jefferson's desire, the port of New Orleans, as far north as the Rocky Mountains. For less than four cents an acre, Jefferson had doubled the size of the country.

But the last thing he wanted to do was tell the American people. In the North, not many people were excited about making the people of the Louisiana Territory into fully fledged citizens. They knew the western border of their young country was populated with roughnecks, sailors, illiterate and free-wheeling frontiersmen, gamblers, prostitutes and shady riverboat people who plied the Mississippi.

Add to that the foreign allegiances of New Orleans and the prospects of Caribbean revolutions bubbling up in southern Louisiana, and there was considerable fear that they wouldn't be able to rule the new territory at all. Jefferson waited until the Fourth of July to sell the idea to Americans as a great step forward for the nation. Approval of the deal in Congress was not unanimous.

Americans simply didn't feel the same connection to Louisiana that Europeans did. In many ways, they still don't. New Orleans and Louisiana were treasures the European powers desperately wanted but could not afford to keep. And so it was the Americans who saw New Orleans reach the pinnacle of success that France and Spain had foreseen, and then go into decline.

New Orleans remains the least American of US cities, and one of the most fascinating. The hardships of creating a city in a swamp and the long distance from overseeing capitals allowed New Orleans to develop an extraordinary personality all its own.

The city sometimes seems to have more romantic mythology than an actual history. Much of its culture bubbled up from the street, like jazz and Mardi Gras. And, frankly, some of what you hear around here simply isn't true. But real New Orleans history is, on its own, strange and outrageous enough that fiction could hardly make it more entertaining.

A LONG TIME AGO ON A CONTINENT FAR, FAR AWAY

In 1492, Columbus' discovery of the New World set the European powers scrambling. Though the continent was already occupied when Columbus arrived, it didn't stop the Spanish claiming Florida and parts of Central and South America. The French took Canada and discovered a bounty in fur trade. The British colonised the East Coast. But the Europeans didn't dominate South Louisiana from the get-go, as they did other American colonies. It was just too hard to get here.

'Iberville named the spot Pointe du Mardi Gras, and celebrated as he knew the French were doing in Paris.'

The lives of Native Americans are little mentioned in the history of New Orleans, but this is mainly because so many historians overlooked an important part of the early colony's workings. Nomadic hunting tribes had lived in Louisiana for between 8,000 and 10,000 years before the French arrived. By 2000 BC, different tribal groups had made permanent encampments, developing complex societies and leaving behind evidence of utilitarian and ceremonial pottery. By the time the first Europeans showed up, there were many groups living in the marshy lowlands of the Delta.

Spaniard Hernando de Soto reached the Mississippi River in 1540, but it was René-Robert Cavelier, Sieur de la Salle, who claimed Louisiana for France in 1682. Early exploration took its toll, though – De Soto died of fever and De la Salle was killed by his own men before they themselves died, either of starvation, exposure or in battles with Indians.

Over the years, Native American tribes struggled against the French, allied with them at times, and were ultimately defeated by them.

Still, the natives quickly became enmeshed in the colony's trade economy. During the 1700s they traded with the Europeans, usually on their own terms. But in 1729, a massacre of French settlers in what is now Natchez, Mississippi, left New Orleans' Europeans paralysed with fear. Plans were drawn up to build a wall around the city, and work began before the panic subsided and the settlers lost interest in the project. The city was left with a deep ditch on one side, which filled with water and created a mosquito problem.

HIGH START-UP COSTS

In the 1690s, French King Louis XIV sent a capable leader to set up the colony. Pierre Le Moyne, Sieur de Iberville, was a naval hero from French Canada. Accompanied by his younger brother Jean Baptiste Le Moyne, Sieur de Bienville, he and his group set up in Mobile Bay, in what is now Alabama, and explored the coast and inland waters. In what New Orleanians now view as their city's true beginning, Iberville and his crew arrived 60 miles below the current city on Mardi Gras day in 1699. He named the spot Pointe du Mardi Gras, and they celebrated as they knew the French were doing back in Paris.

For nearly two decades, the colony was a money pit. There was no silver here as there had been in Mexico, and no furs as there had been in Canada. Instead, the French built forts to deal with incursions by the Spanish and raids by the Native Americans. The coastal areas were swampy and sandy – difficult to walk through, let alone cultivate. Frenchmen refused to move there, and to make things more complicated, Iberville was called away to fight the British in the Caribbean, where he died of yellow fever.

Aged just 21, Bienville assumed control of the colony. He governed it fairly well, but by 1712 the French government wanted out. It looked to a rich countryman to develop Louisiana. Antoine Crozat took over, issuing orders from the comfort of Versailles, and by 1716 he had lost a fortune on the project.

THE GREATEST SCAM EVER

Ruling as regent for the young Louis XV, the Duke of Orleans looked for a new developer. He turned to renowned gambler and financier John Law. In a plan to develop Louisiana as a stock venture, the Scotsman created the Company of the West and backed it with the Banque Générale de France. The bank issued paper money, a new financial concept at the time. After a recession hit Europe, Law was put in charge of all France's finances. He absorbed the Company of the West into the Company of

Reading books is one way of looking at history, but when you come to The National D-Day Museum and you meet veterans who greet you at the door, who are standing throughout the galleries, it's a different way of doing things. This museum understands that there's always another story to be told, and it honors the common American, the person you'd never read about in any text book.

Will Hales
High School Senior

the Indies and backed it with the new Royal Bank of France. Fuelled by Law's talk of gold and silver in the colony, Frenchmen drove the colony's stock price sky-high, often paying on credit or with paper money from the bank. The term 'millionaire' was coined before the bubble burst, leaving French finances in ruins.

Meanwhile, the city of Nouvelle Orleans was being founded in the Louisiana colony. A site the Native Americans had used as a narrow bridge through the swamps between the river and Lake Pontchartrain was selected. A military-style street grid was set up (which is why the French Quarter's strict right angles don't resemble the layout of European cities). Law named the settlement after the Duke, and its streets after royal relatives. The early colony was populated by French Canadian sailors, French marines, and petty thieves, prostitutes and debtors released from French jails.

Never having visited Louisiana, Law nonetheless thought he detected potential in the area, but he surely also knew of its severe

faults. The state was a swamp infested with disease-carrying mosquitoes and surrounded by occasionally hostile natives. Still, Law concentrated on selling it in Europe. He promised Europeans they'd find gold and silver all but lying on the ground, and a workforce of Native Americans eager to labour for free. Germans migrated to the colony in droves, settling west of New Orleans along the river. Lesser French and Spanish gentry also bought Law's sales pitch and moved to New Orleans.

Law imported African slaves from the Senegambian region in large numbers. (In fact, black people would comprise half the population of Louisiana until well after the Civil War.) Because establishing the colony was such a struggle, slaves were not only allowed but encouraged to use skills such as brick-making and ironwork. They also maintained their own religion, later to fuse with Catholicism and become Vodou (or, in the Hollywood spelling, 'Voodoo'). It's worth

Pretty baby

Prostitution has always had a place in New Orleans, and Storyville was its most famous address. This red-light district, which no longer exists, was the city's sin centre in the late 19th and early 20th centuries.

Ironically, Storyville was born out of an attempt at progressive reform. Sidney Story, a city councilman, thought containing and regulating prostitution would help clean up the city. He succeeded in getting brothels out of many neighbourhoods, but he also inadvertently created a centre for vice and the beginning of sexual tourism.

In 1897, when Story's ordinance was passed, the blocks between Canal and Basin streets and Claiborne Avenue, which he chose for his red-light district, were largely residential. By 1917, when the US Navy demanded that it be shut down – threatening to close the local naval base otherwise – Storyville was wall-to-wall brothels and saloons. The name was the hookers' lasting and embarrassing tribute to the councilman.

Storyville harboured grand bordellos bedecked in velvet and brocade as well as mean streets full of crib girls who hired bare rooms by the night to ply their trade. Madams like Lulu White erected castles of prostitution. Most of the profits came from liquor. Bribes kept policemen and politicians compliant.

The district was advertised all over the country, and the allure of interracial sex was one of its major draws. A railway station close to the district brought out-of-town visitors virtually to the brothels' doorsteps. Quadroon women – the products of relationships between white men and free women of colour (*see p17,* **Quadroon balls**) – were particularly sought after. Directories were published listing prostitutes by race, and plenty of dark-haired white women claimed to be of mixed race.

In the parlours of the bordellos, early jazz musicians played for clients awaiting their turns. One of the most famous of these piano-playing 'professors' was Jelly Roll Morton, who later claimed to have played at Lulu White's Mahogany Hall for 15 years. It was in the whorehouses and saloons of Storyville that jazz came of age.

Little is left of the neighbourhood now. Storyville was torn down in the 1930s and replaced with public housing. Only three of its buildings survive, none of them well enough preserved to be likely to get landmark status. The best accounts of Storyville come from jazz musicians, and the best record of the women who worked there is provided in the extraordinary photographic portraits by EJ Bellocq, which can be found in books in virtually all bookstores in New Orleans.

A walk through black history

The African-American experience in New Orleans has been unique, largely owing to the city's French and Spanish past. In many ways, though, this fact is rarely recognised.

The **Gallier House** museum at 1132 Royal Street (*see p63*), has highlighted the city's complicated racial history in an acclaimed new tour. It is one of the few mainstream facilities to have done so.

Now a museum, the well-preserved house was designed by James Gallier Jr, one of New Orleans' most noted architects, as his family home. From the 1850s, he lived in the house with his wife, their four daughters, and their four slaves.

The Galliers had three female slaves and one male slave; they lived in separate quarters attached to the main house and furnished with hand-me-down pieces.

Slave ownership, while not uncommon, required considerable financial means. In New Orleans, slightly more than 37 per cent of families owned slaves.

After the first slaves arrived in New Orleans in 1719, the French government introduced laws outlining the rights and responsibilities of slave owners, slaves and free people of colour – policies known as the 'Code Noir'. Slaves could not be freed without government approval. By custom, slaves worked from sunrise to sunset.

The Emancipation Proclamation freed slaves throughout the Confederacy in 1863. By the time of the 1870 census, none of the Galliers' former slaves was living on the property.

The **African-American Experience Tour** of Gallier House is an excellent way to explore the city's 'other history'. Guides detail the slaves' daily responsibilities, describe what New Orleans was like at the time, and give a different perspective on the history of black people in New Orleans.

The tour is offered daily in February, Black History Month in the US. The rest of the year, it's available to groups of at least 10 people by appointment, or to individuals as time permits.

noting that the French Code Noir governing slaveholding was fairly liberal by comparison to similar laws in British colonies: it allowed slaves to retain their culture, gave them Sundays off and prohibited slave owners from breaking up families.

During the first four years of Law's control, the colony's population grew from 400 to 8,000. But his venture could not last long. Built on air, the company went bust by the early 1720s, unable to back up the paper money it had invented. Law eventually fled to France, where he died in obscurity.

SIN CITY

By the 1740s, Nouvelle Orleans had a new governor, and things in the city had stabilised. Society balls became a part of the culture, and masked ones became popular, though they were not yet associated with Mardi Gras. New Orleans was still a rough frontier port with a largely illiterate population, and visitors were already starting to comment on the city's pronounced fondness for drinking, dancing, gambling and vice of all sorts.

European descendants born in the colony were called Creoles. Later, people of African and Caribbean descent were also called Creoles, especially in Cajun country, to the west of New Orleans. After the Civil War, the term often referred to people of mixed race. Locals generally go by context to understand which is meant.

BURN, BABY, BURN

After the French lost the French and Indian War (also called the Seven Years War), they ceded Canada to Britain. They transferred Louisiana to Spain purely to keep it out of British hands. Content with having France out of North America, Britain left Spain alone with the challenge of governing the complex and rebellious Louisiana territory.

The announcement of Spanish rule was not popular in the colony. The first Spanish governor, a scientist named Antonio de Ulloa, got off to a bad start by failing to visit New Orleans for a year after his arrival in Louisiana, preferring to administer the colony from a small outpost down the river. No great wave of Spanish immigration followed, and the citizens of New Orleans resisted the Spanish leaders to the point of mounting an outright insurrection in 1768. Ulloa departed, and the Spanish dispatched General Alejandro O'Reilly along with a force of 2,000 soldiers. O'Reilly eventually executed six rebel leaders, earning himself the enduring nickname 'Bloody O'Reilly'. He was, however, the first of several fairly competent and effective

Spanish administrators. Immigration to the colony flourished, though not many of those coming in were Spanish.

The greatest legacy left by the Spanish was the architecture of the French Quarter, which they rebuilt after almost the entire city burned to the ground – twice. The first blaze started on Good Friday in 1788, when flames from votive candles on a makeshift altar spread to a wooden wall and took off. According to local lore, the priests at St Louis Cathedral refused to ring the warning bell to call for firefighters because it was a holy day. So the cathedral burned down, along with virtually every other structure in town. The Spanish architects who rebuilt the city designed structures with flat roofs and interior courtyards – features typical of their home country. In 1794, another massive fire destroyed 200 buildings. Whatever French colonial architecture had made it through the first fire was lost to the second. This time, the Spanish rebuilt using less wood and more brick-between-posts construction, which was less inflammable, and covered everything in stucco for coolness. Architecturally speaking, then, 'the French Quarter' is a fairly major misnomer.

BARGAIN OF THE CENTURY

By the late 1700s, New Orleans again found itself the focus of colonial manoeuvring. Spain had held the territory peaceably for years, but control of the Mississippi was becoming an issue. Jefferson knew that New Orleans would be a crucial port as Americans moved west. The best way to get raw materials in and out of the central US was always going to be the Mississippi River, and its mouth was the port of New Orleans. Control New Orleans, and you controlled America.

Spain had never really been able to afford to challenge the Americans during the years when it had held the Louisiana Territory, but France was a different story. Jefferson believed it had the money and the will to take on the fledgling nation, and perhaps to win. In a letter to the US Ambassador to France, Robert Livingston, Jefferson wrote, 'The day that France takes possession of New Orleans fixes the sentence which is to restrain her forever within her low water mark. It seals the union of two nations who in conjunction can maintain exclusive possession of the ocean. From that moment we must marry ourselves to the British fleet and nation.'

Napoleon acquired Louisiana through a secret treaty with Spain in 1800. Fortunately for Jefferson, though, France's colony in St Domingue (now Haiti) chose that moment to

The **French Quarter**, 1926.

rebel. Toussaint l'Overture led a successful revolt, decimating subsequent detachments of French troops. Louisiana had been intended as a bread-basket for feeding St Domingue's lucrative sugar plantations; without the sugar profits, it was suddenly less useful. Napoleon needed cash to fight his European wars, and he knew he wouldn't be able to defend the colony if he wanted to. In 1803, Jefferson offered to buy New Orleans; Napoleon surprised him by agreeing to sell the entire French colony for $15 million. For that price, Jefferson acquired the central section of North America, from New Orleans north to Canada and west to the Rockies.

BRAWLERS, DUELLERS AND PIRATES

With the deal struck, Jefferson dispatched William CC Claiborne to govern New Orleans. He knew there was no other American city quite like it. French was the most common spoken language. There were many educated free people of colour, some of whom owned large plantations and hundreds of slaves, blurring racial lines in a way that had never been seen before (and has rarely been seen since). The Creoles were fond of dancing, drinking and gambling. They were not fond of Americans, and in the early years they weren't certain the territory would remain under American control. Considering themselves Europeans, they would even have welcomed back the Spanish, but in their hearts they hoped Napoleon would return to his dream of a western empire.

Soon, feuding between French and Americans in New Orleans boiled over everywhere – there were even fights at public dances, where Claiborne was forced to intervene, ordering an alternating schedule of waltzes and French quadrilles. Down at the docks, American traders and boat workers caroused and brawled openly with Creoles.

No one better illustrates the lawlessness of the times than the notorious pirate Jean Lafitte, who made a fortune plundering Caribbean shipping from his base near New Orleans. Lafitte and his band of 'Baratarians' also operated a massive illegal slave trade out of the swamps and bayous south of the city. In an effort to stop the pirate, Claiborne put a $500 bounty on his head. Lafitte, in turn, announced a much larger bounty on the governor's head. The struggle between the two eventually came to involve General Andrew Jackson, who was mounting a ragtag team of volunteers to defend the colonies from the British, who were already invading the northern section of the US in the War of 1812. Nobody knew the waterways of southern Louisiana like Lafitte, and Jackson found that he had no choice but to ask for the pirate's help. And so Jean Lafitte, for at least a short while, became a legitimate member of New Orleans society.

BATTLE OF NEW ORLEANS

The War of 1812 went badly for the US for some time. By 1814, British troops had marched on Washington and burned the White House. Around the same time, British ships were sailing for the Gulf of Mexico, under orders to take New Orleans. Jackson had been sent to protect the city with virtually no trained troops at all. He wasn't sure he would have the Creoles' support, but he set to work assembling a force anyway. Word of the impending battle brought in volunteers from all over the wild, woolly territory. Trappers, explorers and wanderers showed up, clad in buckskin and carrying their own weapons, to offer Jackson their help.

In December 1814, his volunteers skirmished with the British, first losing five boats in a battle on water but later executing a daring and successful raid on a British encampment just before Christmas. Another battle on New Year's Day 1815 cost the British twice as many casualties as the Americans suffered, and dealt a tremendous blow to the British troops' morale.

Jackson's greatest strategic success was in gaining time to set up a defence. While the British regrouped, he chose an area of what is now Chalmette, just downriver from New Orleans, for his defensive line. It was a brilliant decision. The British force of 6,000 had to approach head-on, sandwiched between river and swamp. For this battle, Jackson united the forces of New Orleans: units of free black men, volunteers from Tennessee and Kentucky, Choctaw Indians and Lafitte's Baratarians. On 8 January 1815, this unlikely army slaughtered more than 2,000 British soldiers and their leader, General Edward Pakenham, while suffering only 71 losses themselves. It was a humiliating defeat for the British, but the ultimate irony was that it occurred after the war had technically ended. The Americans and the British had signed a peace treaty in Belgium, ending the conflict, but word had not reached the generals in New Orleans.

The War of 1812 was the last time that a European power contested its old colonies on US soil. But it had an added symbolic significance: the multicultural force that defended New Orleans foreshadowed the melting pot the nation was to become.

THE YANKS MOVE IN

After the war, Americans flooded into New Orleans and, in essence, built a city of their own. Feeling unwelcome in the French-speaking quadrant (thus the name 'French Quarter'), they settled across Canal Street, creating the 'American sector'. There, they created little sub-cities – Lafayette, which had its own port, was centred in what is now the Garden District.

But technology soon shortened the distance between the French and American sectors. The St Charles Avenue streetcar line was built for commuters in 1831. By 1852, most of the municipalities had been absorbed into New Orleans, and the centre of political power shifted. City Hall was moved from the Cabildo (see p66) in the Creole-dominated French Quarter to Gallier Hall (see p72) in the American sector.

> ### 'Steamships loaded with cotton looked like floating pyramids; sometimes their smokestacks set fire to the cargo, igniting the pyres.'

Immigration also continued steadily, particularly in the form of refugees from the war in St Domingue. More free people of colour and slaves joined the city's Creole mix. When the Americans took over, slaves retained the relatively favourable Code Noir privileges they had had under the French system. Thus, they were allowed to gather in Congo Square on Sundays to dance and play music. This tradition became crucial to the development of music of New Orleans. An African dance, the *bamboula*, was a courtship ritual sometimes performed there; according to historians, its rhythm is essentially the same as that found in New Orleans 'second line' jazz (see p213 **When the saints go marching in**).

NO IRISH, NO DOGS
It was around this time that New Orleans was coming into its golden age, with steamships and trade bringing in serious wealth. After the first steamship arrived in 1812, commerce exploded. In the early part of the 19th century, shipping on the Mississippi River created more millionaires in the Delta than lived in New York. Steamships loaded with cotton looked like floating pyramids; sometimes, cinders from their smokestacks set fire to the cargo, igniting massive pyres. Mark Twain was among the men seduced by the adventurous life aboard the riverboats. He romanticised the river world and was one of the first American writers to mythologise New Orleans as an exotic oasis at the end of the Mississippi.

In the years leading up to the Civil War, two of the city's biggest problems were fires and epidemics. The fires did nothing to restrain the city's booming economy, but a series of disease outbreaks during the 1850s took thousands of lives in New Orleans. Yellow fever, cholera and tuberculosis all killed residents in great numbers, and the city was regularly placed under quarantine.

The growing need for labourers affected the city's ethnic make-up. Irish immigrants fleeing the potato famine were lured to New Orleans in the 1830s to help dig the New Basin Canal; more than 8,000 of them lost their lives to yellow fever and cholera before the canal was completed in 1838 (see p82 **The Irish Channel**). So desperate were these Irish workers that they literally competed with slaves for work. They also suffered intense discrimination. By the 1850s, the anti-Catholic, anti-immigrant 'Know-Nothing Party' seized control of the city, as much by violence and intimidation as by voting, and New Orleans was divided along ethnic lines for some time.

VOODOO HOODOO
By the mid 19th century, Catholicism was heavily entrenched in New Orleans. French and Spanish Creoles had already established a local diocese. With the arrival of the Irish, a second diocese was created in the American sector, with St Patrick's Cathedral (see p74) as its base. African-American Creoles built a third major church, St Augustine's, in the Tremé. Also growing in the city, though, was the influence of voodoo, which fused African beliefs with elements of Catholicism.

'Voodoo queen' Marie Laveau ascended to a position of prominence and power in the mid 1830s. She went to mass every day and reigned as a counsellor and adviser well into the 1870s. Even Queen Victoria is said to have sought her help. Laveau, also a herbalist, nurse and hairdresser, gained the confidences of many in Creole society. She was spiritually and politically influential, and many feared her.

Laveau profited from the lurid accounts of voodoo practices, charging white people $10 to watch drumming and snake-dance rituals. Potions were sold in pharmacies to many people who did not openly embrace voodoo. The legendary Love Potion No.9 was one of the many concoctions that could be bought discreetly over the counter.

PARTY TOWN
When it came to culture, throughout the antebellum period, New Orleans rivalled America's largest cities. The city may have been a rambunctious port town, but its Creole residents loved opera, theatre and public dances. Talented local painters

Creole cottages like **Madame John's Legacy** once dominated the Quarter. *See p62.*

emerged, and photography was introduced in 1839, only months after the first successful commercial process was perfected in Paris. The naturalist and illustrator John James Audubon spent a couple of years during the 1820s in New Orleans and south Louisiana, working on his guide to North American birds. He lived on Dauphine Street.

It was during this time that Mardi Gras took hold. Masking at Mardi Gras had been common before the Louisiana Purchase, but the new American government had outlawed it. The anti-masking rules weren't regularly enforced, though, and were eventually repealed. On Mardi Gras day, 1839, a crowd of marchers pushed the first float through the streets. In the 1840s, Carnival was threatened by violence and the throwing of everything from bags of flour to bricks, but by 1857 American businessmen got interested in reviving Mardi Gras and created the first parading 'krewe'. For more on **Mardi Gras**, *see pp22-8*.

WELCOME TO THE OCCUPATION

New Orleans, unlike the rest of the South, had much to gain by staying in the Union, but it was heavily entrenched in the politics of the Civil War and couldn't avoid getting involved. Though many free people of colour lived in the city, New Orleans was still the largest slave trading centre in the South. The issue of race was to dominate Louisiana politics for another century and more.

After the Civil War broke out, New Orleans was one of the first southern cities to fall to the Union (in 1862). The city's memory of the war focuses on its years of occupation by Union troops. Particularly despised in local memory is General Benjamin F Butler, who was in charge of the city during the war. He gained the loathing of the people by publicly executing a man who had desecrated a Union flag. The outraged ladies of New Orleans responded with a sort of gentlewomen's rebellion, emptying chamber pots onto Union soldiers from open windows, treating them with contempt in the street, and – perhaps most unforgivably to Butler – refusing to talk to them, let alone go out with them. In revenge, the general decreed that any woman caught disrespecting a Union soldier would be arrested and jailed as a prostitute. His outrageous decision was the subject of heated debate as far afield as Washington and London.

New Orleans stayed occupied until the Civil War ended in 1865, and afterwards, it stayed under Reconstruction longer than any other Southern city. The last Union soldier did not leave until 1877.

FABLES OF THE RECONSTRUCTION

The political aftermath of the Civil War took a far worse toll on New Orleans than the fighting ever had. The state's politics were overhauled – African-Americans were enfranchised during Reconstruction by carpetbaggers and northern governors, and then disenfranchised again by local politics and violence.

Racial politics here had already been complex before the war, with educated free people of colour and mixed-race Creoles essentially part of the upper class. After the war, the traditional Southern black–white divide became more dominant here, putting the pre-war free people of colour in a precarious position. The Unification Movement arose in the 1870s to call for racial power sharing, but not enough parties were willing to compromise any of their own interests to make the movement work. Instead, the self-proclaimed 'White League' formed, and the subsequent upheaval resulted in a race riot at the bottom of Canal Street in 1874. White League troops numbering more than 8,400 faced half as many Metropolitan police. A gun battle left 33 men dead, and federal troops had to restore order.

> **'In the 1890s, in dancehalls along Perdido and South Rampart streets, players like Buddy Bolden began making a sultry new form of music, influenced by ragtime and blues.'**

By the end of the 19th century, a new group had joined the mix: a wave of Italian migrants, many from Sicily, who had come to do farm work. They spread through the region and soon dominated the French Market and the docks. By the beginning of the 20th century, the French Quarter had been dubbed 'Little Palermo'. Once again, anti-immigrant hysteria led to social unrest. In 1891, Chief of Police David Hennessey was fatally shot by a still-unknown assailant. Italian immigrants were rounded up and taken to jail. People taunted Italians with the line 'Who killa da chief?' After a newspaper editorial exhorted citizens to take hold of the city's future, a mob descended on the jail, where the doors had been left open and the guards had disappeared. The mob killed 11 of the men inside, in the largest mass lynching in the state's history.

THE BIRTH OF JAZZ

In the face of discrimination, the African-American population banded together. Denied insurance, they created benevolent societies to pay for members' medical care and funerals. These were followed by 'social aid and pleasure clubs', which established and carried on the tradition of jazz funerals accompanied by marching brass bands. Large numbers of these societies still exist and hold celebratory parades Uptown and in Tremé, usually after church on Sundays.

The birth of jazz is one of New Orleans' greatest claims to fame. Jazz has no known parents; musicians seem to have left it on the city's doorstep one morning after the clubs closed. In the 1890s, in the dancehalls along Perdido and South Rampart streets, players like Buddy Bolden began making a sultry new music, influenced by elements including ragtime and blues. Over the next 20 years this style evolved into jazz. So many forces and individuals came together in the making of jazz – largely thanks to New Orleans' unique racial blend – that it's difficult to determine its exact history. But if there was a moment that sealed the city's destiny as the cradle of jazz, it was the birth of Louis Armstrong in 1900. Born into poverty, he learned to play cornet (a kind of trumpet) in the Colored Waifs' Home, where he'd been placed after being caught firing a pistol on New Year's Eve. He went on to play with greats like King Oliver and became famous at a young age. Eventually Armstrong followed Oliver to Chicago; by then jazz had become well established here. New Orleanian Nick LaRocca made the first commercial jazz recording here in 1917.

THE STRUGGLE

At no time in the 20th century did New Orleans ever regain its previous status as the most powerful city in the South. All of Louisiana gradually lapsed into a deep and abiding poverty virtually unparalleled elsewhere in the US. Plagued by corruption and essentially still agrarian, the state fell woefully behind in the industrial age. New Orleans, with its port and tourist trade, eventually became the lifeboat in Louisiana's sea of poverty. But no single city can carry an entire state, and the sheer depth of the state's economic crisis ultimately dragged the city down with it. Politically and economically, New Orleans waned, even as its fame grew.

In the 1950s and 1960s, civil rights and desegregation dominated the local headlines. Since Reconstruction, African-Americans had seen their rights, even the ability to vote, eroded through 'Jim Crow' segregation laws. Now they fought to get them back. In one of the era's most poignant moments, a quiet little girl named Ruby Bridges was escorted into an integrated classroom in New Orleans as an angry white mob screamed at her. Though state schools were integrated, 'white flight' to private schools and suburbs soon reimposed racial distance. Today, central New Orleans is more than 75 per cent African American, while the suburbs are majority white.

DOIN' BIDNESS, LOUISIANA STYLE

Industrialisation happened slowly and belatedly in Louisiana, but when it did arrive, it hit like a ton of bricks. It wasn't until the 1960s and 1970s that the oil business boomed here. When it did, it was like a bubble that ballooned up with thrilling beauty and promise and then burst. Oil exploration in the Gulf of Mexico was centred on the port of New Orleans, sparking a feverish period of construction that gave rise to the

Quadroon balls

Before the Civil War, quadroon balls were a common rite of passage for many rich New Orleans men. 'Quadroons' were upper-class women of mixed race. Elegant and well-educated, they were seen as exotic and exciting. The balls, which were held at the **Quadroon Ballroom** off Royal Street (see p62), were designed to bring together quadroons and wealthy white landowners in a kind of high-stakes dating game.

Some men were just looking for mistresses at the balls. But others took women as de facto wives, in a practice known as *plaçage*. A man would provide for a woman and her mother (who had to approve the arrangement). He was expected to support her, and she was expected to be faithful to him. Any resulting children were considered legitimate and could inherit. Daughters were 'married' off at quadroon balls after they came of age.

The balls took place secretly before 1805, and publicly thereafter, until racial politics and the Civil War made them impossible. They're still one of the most scandalous, romanticised and fictionalised parts of the city's history, as well as the most obvious facet of its tradition of flouting racial taboos.

skyscraper skyline visible today. It all ended in the 1980s, when OPEC brought oil prices down, crushing the local petrochemical industry, which had chosen the wrong time to expand. Through the 1980s, the Fortune 500 firms departed the skyscrapers; some stayed vacant for years. Today, only Entergy is still headquartered here.

'If, one day, New Orleans' tourism bubble bursts, the city will have amused itself to death. What a way to go.'

During the oil boom, the chemical industry, too, discovered Louisiana. Vast, polluting factories sprouted like fungi along the river from the Gulf to Baton Rouge; health fears brought the sobriquet 'Cancer Corridor'. Since the 1970s, the state has been at the bottom of all national environmental and health rankings.

AND THE BANDS PLAYED ON

Even as the state's economy faltered, New Orleans gave birth to one cultural phenomenon after another, and its worldwide fame grew. After jazz came rock 'n' roll and R&B. In the 1950s, Fats Domino and New Orleans R&B ruled the national charts. In the late 1960s and 1970s, New Orleans funk drew international attention. The general musical renaissance spawned Jazz Fest in 1970, even as local musicians like the Marsalis family members took jazz in new directions.

But the city was creating more than music. Even in its worst days, artists and writers flocked here, lured by the sunny weather, European feel, *laissez les bons temps rouler* attitude, low rents and love of booze, gambling and sin. Over the years, writers like William Faulkner, Tennessee Williams and Truman Capote joined Walker Percy and Sherwood Anderson here. As they wrote about the city, as the musicians sang about it and the painters painted it, tourism exploded. Now everybody seems to want a piece of New Orleans. More than 10 million tourists visit the little city by the river each year. Its glittering convention centre is half a mile long and growing. Hotels account for virtually all new construction downtown, and almost every ex-oil company skyscraper has been converted into one.

If, one day, the tourism bubble finally bursts, overdeveloped, overexposed and overdone, New Orleans will have amused itself to death. But what a way to go. The writer Lafcadio Hearn, who spent a decade here during the post-Reconstruction hard times, wrote, 'It would be better to live here in sackcloth and ashes than to own the entire state of Ohio.'

New Orleans Today

A new mayor, a new basketball team – what could possibly go wrong?

New Orleans has been built upon a site that only the madness of commercial lust could ever have tempted men to occupy.
Illustrated London News, 1853

New Orleans is a region of architectural decrepitude where an ancient and foreign seeming domestic life in the second storeys overhangs the ruins of former commercial prosperity, and upon everything has settled a long sabbath of decay.
George Washington Cable, late 19th century

There is an attitude to anything new in New Orleans of 'We be here before you got to government, and we be here after you leave.' Now the 'We Bes' are learning something new.
Mayor Ray Nagin, 2003

With the dawning of the 21st century, New Orleans entered its fifth century, blinking hard. The last decades of the 20th century had been devastating for the city, as its primary economic engine, the oil business, went bust in the 1980s and a horrific criminal culture took root in the 1990s. Crime and economic struggles define most American cities, but New Orleans was awash in bad news. Its population had dropped by almost 14 per cent during the 1980s and 1990s, down to 484,674. The city as a whole ranked as one of the country's poorest and least literate, with 28 per cent of residents living in poverty and almost a quarter having never finished high school. If that wasn't enough, the city has gradually been sinking into the swamp, as it slowly loses its natural barriers to hurricanes with the disappearance of the south Louisiana wetlands. Scientists estimate that a direct hit on New Orleans by a Category 4 or 5 hurricane would put the French Quarter under 20 feet of water and kill 100,000 people.

With New Orleans losing residents by the thousands, death by hurricane hanging over its head and its public institutions barely hanging on, how did the city's elected leaders propose to pull the city out of its black hole and push it toward greatness?

By getting it a basketball team.

Years before, New Orleans had built a multi-million-dollar basketball arena to tempt a pro team, but so far it had only been able to use it for rock concerts and minor league hockey games. It wasn't enough that the city already

18 Time Out New Orleans

had a perennially losing, under-capitalised pro football team, the Saints: the power brokers were adamant that it needed a National Basketball Association team, too. Aside from a handful of indignant, well-reasoned letters to the local newspaper, the city as a whole backed the idea. Pouring municipal money into obtaining a pro franchise was thought to be a brilliant move.

And so, in 2001, a cross-section of New Orleans' political, economic and celebrity powers formed a 'leadership team'. They went after one of the lamest NBA teams on record, the Vancouver (British Columbia) Grizzlies. Even with such a low goal, New Orleans lost to Memphis in the bidding war for the team. Undaunted, the scouting party bravely announced that they had learned a lot from this sad defeat and would continue moving forward. In 2002, the group showed that it had indeed learned how it was done, landing the Charlotte (North Carolina) Hornets; another losing team the previous owner city couldn't wait to get off its hands.

It's typical of New Orleans to look to entertainment as the way to solve problems. And the problems, from the very beginning, have been enormous. If you build a city in a disease-infested swamp alongside a river that frequently floods, it's hard to know where to start totting up the disadvantages. Yet through yellow fever epidemics, floods, war and poverty, New Orleans has always found a way to amuse itself. And the entertainments have been so brilliant that they've drawn millions of others to the swamp city. Given such a historical context, why not try to untangle poverty, bad schools and a low tax base with basketball?

After a disconcerting stint in the early 1990s as the murder capital of the US, New Orleans got a grip on crime in the late 1990s. Marc Morial, a young, vigorous mayor and son of New Orleans' first black mayor, Dutch Morial) got a handle on crime thanks to a strong police chief, Richard Pennington. The forward momentum began to wind down in Morial's second term (1998-2002), though, and the administration showed signs that the old-fashioned patronage machine was still at work. Though limited by law to two consecutive terms, Morial launched an impressive power grab for a third in 2001, unleashing a high-powered, well-financed campaign to have the law changed. When that was defeated in a city election, he convinced the previously nonpolitical Pennington to run for mayor.

With Pennington ahead in the polls, it looked like the mayor's office would stay in the Morial family. Then something amazing happened. A dark horse entered the race and

won. Ray Nagin, a 46-year-old cable television executive, swept to the front with a combination of straight talk, easy humour and an ability to keep his eye on the ball.

Nagin came from a blue-collar African-American family in Algiers, rather than the aristocratic Creole background of the Morials and most of the city's previous black mayors. He'd climbed the corporate ladder in the competitive cable business by dint of will and talent. He had college degrees, a stable marriage, children and an annual salary of more than $400,000. The city was impressed, if only because it's rare to find a politician in New Orleans who knows how to make a living outside the shadow of City Hall.

The first months of Nagin's term bore a whiff of *Mr Smith Goes to Washington*, as the well-intentioned naïf tried to apply common sense to a Byzantine political labyrinth. He made some splashy attempts at curtailing New Orleans' legendary corruption, such as the arrest of

The answer to everything: basketball.

dozens of taxi drivers who had allegedly been licensed through bribes and the high-profile dismissal of entrenched department heads. None of the early dust-ups led to sustained legal action. But New Orleans – always up for a good show anyway – didn't mind the theatrics, as Nagin was having an effect on key quality-of-life issues. He actually kept a promise to fill more than 60,000 potholes on the city's decrepit old streets. And city government finally went online.

In his willingness to take on 'the way things have always been here', Nagin won a reputation as a stand-up guy. He personally cancelled a number of big-bucks contracts the departing Morial administration had handed out to its relatives and friends. When the contractees howled that Nagin had no legal authority to do that, his reaction was basically 'So sue me.' Not eager to defend their cash cow deals in court, the Morialistas withdrew to the sidelines.

While some tout Nagin as a 'reform' mayor, he represents a decidedly New Orleans version of reform. His administration's first crisis was the abrupt departure of its chief administrative officer, Kimberly Williamson, an African-American woman with a reputation as a stickler for rules, procedures and fiscal responsibility. The public panicked, worried that she was leaving because Nagin didn't want someone with her morality around.

'In New Orleans, a reputation as a non-drinking, humourless Bible-thumper is worse than corruption or bribery.'

Williamson herself calmed the fears, indignantly telling reporters that the 'inner circle' disliked her because she saw after-work cocktail gatherings as a waste of time. The inner circle leaked to the press that not only was Williams anti-cocktail, she was constantly preaching to people and pressuring them to attend her church. Mutterings of 'too Baptist' did the rounds. In New Orleans, a reputation as a non-drinking, humourless Bible thumper is a far worse stain than corruption or bribery. The people sided with the mayor on that one.

As low as New Orleans ranks on many indexes of city desirability, it rates equally high on others. The city routinely tops national polls as the favourite city of travellers, the best place for dining, the best for honeymoons and even one of the best for low-income bohemians. Even with all of its problems, New Orleans continues to attract a steady stream of bright, accomplished new residents, drawn to its rich culture and relaxed pace. Census information

indicates that the city gets an unusually high influx of under-35s from places like New York, California and Washington state, where you'd think people would have plenty of options. Anecdotal research shows that newcomers from New York, San Francisco and Seattle are attracted by the city's grand apartments that rent for as little as $500 and by the easy availability of cheap space for art studios.

The flip side of the city's slow-moving, welcoming atmosphere is that it often loses those bright pennies after a while. Even native sons and daughters eventually feel compelled to shake the Mississippi River mud off their feet and make it in 'the real world'. Louis Armstrong said as much, without actually coming out and calling New Orleans lacking, in his autobiography. He mused, 'I'm always wondering if it would have been best in my life if I'd stayed like I was in New Orleans, having a ball. I was very much contented just to be around and play – I wonder if I would have enjoyed that better than all this big mucky-muck travelling all over the world.'

In a wily way, Armstrong was pointing out his own energy and ambition, noting that he had had not just the talent but the will to leave New Orleans and become a star. It's a familiar story. Sidney Bechet, Louis Prima, Wynton Marsalis, Branford Marsalis, Dr John and Harry Connick Jr are just a few of those who have left town like Armstrong to find their destinies.

The remarkable feature of New Orleans is the way its essential nature endures in the face of everything American society throws at it. Music, Mardi Gras, parades, food and parties are the lifeblood of the city. In many tourist destinations, the good times are a pantomime put on for paying guests, but here, if the tourist trade dried up tomorrow, Mardi Gras, Jazz Fest, second line parades, street parties and all-night French Quarter bars would carry on just as they do now. The city is a world unto itself, and that's one of the reason people love it so much. It is what it is.

When a new schools superintendent came to New Orleans in 2002, he suggested that some schools might stay open during Mardi Gras week. Nobody paid any attention to him. Later, he was interviewed on Mardi Gras Day, wearing beads, sitting in a viewing stand on St Charles Avenue. He was clearly amazed by the all-encompassing spectacle unfolding in front of him, throughout the city and its suburbs, and out into the countryside.

'I just had no idea,' he said, as bands and floats and walking parades passed by in front of gaily attired cheering crowds on the bright winter's morning. 'I didn't know there was anything like this in America'.

A streetcar named road chaos

Since 2001, visitors to New Orleans could be forgiven for wondering just what the hell is going on in its roadworks department. For months, even years, some of the city's busiest streets have been closed – poof! Disappeared. Dug up and shut down.

Canal Street, Carrollton Avenue, Claiborne, Napoleon, Interstate 10… the list goes on and on. The work has disrupted bus routes, truncated streetcar lines, chipped away at taxi drivers' always limited goodwill, rendered maps instantly obsolete and generally driven everyone a little crazy. The Big Easy? Hardly. Try the Big Pain in the Butt.

The situation is the result of a convergence of factors, almost none of which, funnily enough, involve the roads themselves. In Uptown, a massive project to improve the city's drainage system (it just keeps on flooding up there) has kept parts of North Claiborne and Napoleon avenues closed for years. But the big project, as far as just about everyone's concerned, is the one that's closed Canal Street and Carrollton Avenue for years. This is the first step in the expansion of the streetcar line to encompass much more of the city. When complete, it will make transport in the city cleaner, simpler and more efficient.

And besides, streetcars are just pretty.

The finished line will run down Canal Street to Carrollton Avenue in Mid-City, and then down Carrollton all the way from City Park to St Charles Avenue in Uptown, where it will connect with the St Charles streetcar line. The Canal Street section should be complete by the end of 2003, though work on the Carrollton section may continue into 2004.

With luck this is just the beginning, though, as negotiations are already underway to bring back the fabled Desire streetcar line. While its resurrection may be years away, if it does come to pass, the line will run from Canal Street to Desire Street in the Ninth Ward. For most tourists, it'll just make for a nice photo (there's not much to see down there), but for locals, it'll be a lifesaver.

The city of New Orleans was once laced by streetcar lines. As you walk on Royal Street in the Quarter, or on Baronne Street Uptown, or here and there around town, you'll come across old segments of track that show just how extensive the network once was. Between 1924 and 1965, virtually all of it was torn up, after city officials decided that the automobile was destined to replace old-fashioned trolley cars. Of course, the second they decided this, it became a self-fulfilling prophecy – fewer streetcars meant more people had to buy cars, and the future was set.

But this never really became a true car town. The streetcar line on St Charles Avenue never stopped running, and it never lost its popularity. Today, it's used as much by locals – downtown professionals heading to work, kids in school uniforms – as by tourists. Over time, city administrators noticed this, and before long it became apparent that streetcars were cheaper and cleaner to operate than buses. And so it was that, using hundreds of millions of federal dollars, work began on the new streetcar project in 1998. By 2003, it felt like half the city had been dug up.

So as you sit steaming in traffic, stymied by another closed street, or staring hopelessly at a map trying to figure out another route Uptown (take Tchoupitoulas Street – it's the locals' shortcut) or to Mid-City (use Esplanade Avenue or Bienville Street), remember that what those concrete barricades and bright orange pylons really mean is that the next time you come back to New Orleans, you'll be able to smoothly glide almost anywhere worth going in a picturesque streetcar for a buck fifty. And smile.

Mardi Gras

Welcome to the biggest free party on Earth.

It's hard to believe what people will do for a strand of cheap plastic beads. They'll beg, jump up and down and scream at guys in shiny clown suits and opera masks. They'll grab them away from pretty women and small children. Flash their breasts or drop their trousers on a public street in front of thousands of strangers.

We can almost guarantee that you would do the same. Pictures and stories of Mardi Gras do no justice to the actual experience of getting sucked into it. When you're packed in among the hundreds of thousands of celebrants and the beads are flying, you'll go native. You'll do whatever it takes. At Mardi Gras, the strange customs, weird symbolism and flowing alcohol conspire to create a primal logic that's hard not to follow and pointless to resist.

New Orleanians have been doing it for more than 250 years. Long before the beads arrived, bizarre traditions drove Mardi Gras. The absurdity now culminates on Fat Tuesday with a citywide collage of spectacles. After his selection as Rex, King of Carnival, one of the city's leading male citizens will likely sink more than $100,000 into the sequined short tunic, yellow beard and tights he'll wear sitting on his rolling papier-mâché throne. The parades are full of faux royalty and mounted officers, who look like a mix of Renaissance nobility and Ku Klux Klan members. And if you think that's weird, consider the African-American krewe of Zulu – whose members wear blackface, afro wigs and grass skirts as they parade St Charles Avenue, mocking the most demeaning minstrel show stereotypes. In some of the city's poorest neighbourhoods, black men march dressed in a sort of exaggerated parody of Native American Indians, in neon-coloured plumage.

The official height of Carnival is the 12 days before Ash Wednesday. All the major parades fall in this period, which encompasses Fat Tuesday and the preceding two weekends. The size and intensity of festivities build until Fat Tuesday's ultimate release.

For visitors, it's all nothing more or less than the greatest free show on Earth.

WHAT TO EXPECT

The whole Carnival celebration revolves around private groups called 'krewes'. These social groups – made up largely of local businessmen and women – have been around since the first float parade was staged in 1857 by a group of rich guys calling themselves the Mystick Krewe of Comus (*see p25* **How it started***). While Mardi Gras was celebrated in New Orleans before then, it was done only with street parties and drinking. Comus changed everything by painting a big wagon, lighting it with torches and dragging it through the streets.

The idea took off, and within a few years there were many groups calling themselves krewes, claiming that their memberships were secret (which is why krewe members still wear masks), and competing to have the most beautiful floats and the most popular parades.

'It is permissible for a woman to subtly flash her breasts at a float.'

Today, more than 60 krewes conduct their own parades between Twelfth Night and Ash Wednesday, and all the parades feature the same basic elements. Generally, the krewe's 'royalty' (a king and queen, and occasionally dukes and duchesses) appear first, along with a few cars carrying krewe officers (although in more traditional krewes the officers ride on horseback). The king and queen ride on floats that are essentially rolling thrones. None of them can be counted on for many beads. The king and queen are in such absurdly elaborate costumes they can hardly move, much less throw – sometimes their robes are literally nailed to the float. So they feebly toss a strand of beads every block or two. Everybody claps politely and waits for the real floats to come by.

Luckily, they're right behind. The best are the big double-decker floats, filled with masked riders throwing armloads of beads. These are generally alternated with funky New Orleans high school marching bands, mounted riding groups, 'dance' teams from the suburbs and the occasional military band. Traditional parades also feature *flambeaux,* which are men carrying gas torches on their backs. Once, these were all that lit the way for the floats.

With its ancient oak trees and stately mansions, St Charles Avenue is the most beautiful parade route. Most of the parades make their way down it from Napoleon to the edge of the French Quarter. No krewes parade in the French Quarter. That ended in the 1960s, when the crowds simply got too big. Virtually all parades end on Canal Street these days.

WHO ARE THESE KREWES, ANYWAY?

Each krewe has its own distinct personality. The 'old-line' krewes – including **Comus**, **Momus**, **Proteus** and **Rex** – were formed between 1857 and 1872. Today, Rex's parade features some of Carnival's most beautiful floats, decorated with paper flowers in very traditional style. The biggest krewes – **Rex**, **Zulu**, **Bacchus**, **Orpheus** and **Endymion** – put on large, extravagant parades with celebrity riders. Their floats are embellished with flashing lights, neon and fibre optics.

Much of this is due to the influence of the krewe of **Bacchus**, which always puts on one of the best parades. It formed in 1969 and instituted the trend for having a celebrity king, and started a trinket-throwing arms race. Their floats grew ever larger, with upper decks and multiple trailers.

In 1974 **Endymion** formed and quickly became one of the biggest krewes; its parade, which is always held on the Saturday night before Fat Tuesday, is legendary.

Harry Connick Jr formed **Orpheus** in 1993, and the celebrity connection meant that it was one of the biggest and brightest krewes from the start. Its parades are always particularly bead heavy, and its floats are celebrity central.

A Mardi Gras Indian costume.

How it started

As long as there has been a New Orleans, there has been Mardi Gras. It is one of history's little synchronicities that French explorers first landed on Louisiana soil on Mardi Gras day in 1699. So the first Europeans ever to set foot in the state celebrated Mardi Gras here.

In the 1740s, the state's French governor instituted weekly balls in New Orleans. The first masked balls were held soon after that, although those weren't associated purely with Carnival.

The celebration grew as the years passed, both within the white population and the black. But in 1781, when the city was under Spanish rule, a law was passed forbidding blacks and Native Americans to mask during Carnival.

Despite governmental efforts to restrict festivities to the white upper classes, by the early 1800s masking on Fat Tuesday had grown common, and Mardi Gras was a popular public celebration.

The Creoles (descendants of the French and Spanish) started Carnival, but it was the Americans who formed the Mistick Krewe of Comus in 1857 who first really put it on its current course. One night that year they chose a theme from the poetry of Milton, and paraded with two floats lit by men carrying torches. The city was charmed by the pageantry and the novelty of the idea. Soon it had spread. After the Civil War (1861-5), several more krewes formed, including the Twelfth Night Revelers in 1870. At their second ball, they started the king cake tradition, in which a bean or tiny baby figurine was baked in a cake; whoever found it in their slice was said to be king or queen for the day. In 1872, when Russian Grand Duke Alexis Romanoff came to Carnival, Rex formed in his honour, and staged the first daytime parade.

By then, the Mardi Gras mould was set. For the next century, Carnival was ruled by krewes, some of which paraded and others of which only held masked balls. More sprouted up throughout the 20th century, the most notable being Zulu, the first African-American krewe, which started parading in 1909 in parody of the all-white krewe of Rex. In its first parade, the Zulu king wore a lard can crown and carried a banana stalk sceptre.

Some krewes are more political than others. The krewe of **Saturn** and the tiny **Krewe du Vieux** are both political in nature, and their themes and floats reflect that bent. They tend to take up political and social issues and mock the famous and infamous in their parades.

There are several all-women krewes, including the **Krewe of Muses**. This is one of Carnival's most exciting new group, and its purple beads are greatly sought after.

Sadly, the highly secretive **Comus** – the first proper krewe – no longer parades. It quit parading in the 1990s, after new city ordinances were enacted forbidding segregation among Mardi Gras krewes. It still exists, though, and the traditional meeting of the courts of Rex and Comus is broadcast on local public television (WYES, channel 12) on Mardi Gras night. It makes for a very bizarre scene – portly middle-aged masked men dressed like Shakespearian characters and nubile, 18-year-old 'queens' toasting each other with golden chalices – and is well worth catching if you have stumbled back to your hotel room in time.

THROW ME SOMETHING, MISTER

During Carnival, people tend to walk around so buried in plastic bead necklaces that they look like technicolour Mr T's. Unless they've cheated and bought the beads (so *very* tacky), they've caught them when they were thrown from a float during a parade. Anything tossed by a krewe from a float is called a 'throw'. Today, they're virtually all plastic beads, along with a few other objects. And they are a ubiquitous part of Mardi Gras. But it wasn't always so. Throws only became a regular part of the parades in the 1920s. The first prized beads were Czech glass necklaces thrown in the years just before World War II.

Traditionally, by the way, little kids attempt to catch the attention of krewe members by shouting 'Throw me something, mister!' Here are some things to look for:

● When it comes to **beads**, these days, the bigger and gaudier the better. Long 'pearls' (strands of large white plastic beads) are coveted, while colourful medallion beads, bearing the krewe's insignia, are getting more and more elaborate.
● Painted Zulu **coconuts** are the most rare and coveted prizes of Mardi Gras. They are handed to select spectators by Zulu riders.
● Cheap plastic krewe **cups,** with gaudy insignias and themes, became ubiquitous throws in the early 1980s.
● Rex started throwing aluminium coins featuring its insignia and theme in 1959, and they were immediately dubbed '**doubloons**'.

A brief word of advice

Mardi Gras is one of the world's most misunderstood holidays, shrouded in myth and rumour. If you've never done Mardi Gras before, here are a few tips that could help to ensure that you have a good time.

● Mardi Gras is generally safe. Police and state troopers are out in force. Most arrests are for public urination and lewdness, though police try to be tolerant. Fighting or posing any threat to others, on the other hand, will get you arrested quicker than you can say 'He started it!'

● In the midst of drinking and good times, be wary of sudden, eager friends. Do not get in a car with a kindly stranger you meet on Bourbon Street, even if he says he knows of a great club or party a short drive away.

● If you want to flash some flesh, or generally do things you wouldn't do back home, stick to Bourbon Street. It is a world unto itself.

● Stunt drinking is not advised. Mardi Gras is a marathon, not a sprint. Pace yourself. Passing out in the Quarter is so uncool, and you'll only wake up in jail.

● During parades, the city becomes difficult to navigate, as major streets shut down for hours. Wear comfortable shoes and prepare to walk everywhere. Use public transport when possible, as parking is a nightmare. If you have to get to the airport, leave plenty of time if parades are rolling. The words 'I got stuck behind a parade' will not get you a free airplane ticket in this town.

● Mardi Gras is the worst time to eat out in New Orleans. Most good restaurants close on Fat Tuesday. Many restaurants downtown and in the French Quarter dumb down or severely restrict their menus at the height of Carnival. Head Uptown or to Mid City for a good meal.

● Mardi Gras is good for kids. Bourbon Street isn't. Families will enjoy watching parades everywhere except downtown.

● Along with stuffed animals and toys, the seat of a pair of **knickers** is an easy place to print a logo, so these have become popular throws as well. Along the route, it is generally customary to wear them on your head.

HOW TO MAKE OUT LIKE A BANDIT

The most common way to get booty off of the floats is to make eye contact with krewe members as they pass, smile, wave subtly or to say something banal like, 'Happy Mardi Gras!' Wearing a costume or bright wig always improves your chances. Of course, if you want to get down and dirty, those with no conscience stand near ladders set up by parents for their little children, or by pretty young women, and intercept everything thrown their way (girls can't catch, and kids have little hands).

In the CBD (and generally only there) it is permissible for a woman to subtly flash her breasts at a float, *as long as there are no children nearby*. She is guaranteed to be buried in beads if she does, however, the men around her will probably nab them all because, as you know, girls can't catch.

SHOW US YOUR TITS

On the same topic, these days, there are two Mardi Gras, really. One features traditional parades downtown and on St Charles Avenue. This one draws families with kids, and lots of locals who stand on the same piece of grass every year, looking for their friends on the floats who will bury them in a mountain of cheap plastic beads.

The other one is Bourbon Street.

This is as much about the uninitiated making the most of their own expectations as it is about New Orleans' libertine brand of fun. Take away the Quarter's distinctive architecture, and, during Carnival, this could be a student spring break town almost anywhere. Whether that's a good or bad thing, of course, depends on your own personal taste.

Bourbon Street is by no means only for tourists, but during Carnival it's dominated by them, and a fairly recent custom. Flashing for beads is a Bourbon Street game immortalised in amateur videos, like Mantra Entertainment's *Girls Gone Wild* series. These days it's also on the internet, as playboy.com is now a Carnival regular, with Playmates and 'Cyber Girls' staging their own flashing exhibitions from Bourbon Street balconies on the final weekend.

Although it seems like it's been around forever, flashing for beads only became common in the 1980s. It's had many effects on Carnival, but its main impact has been fuelling the market for ever bigger and gaudier beads. Simple supply and demand sets the exchange rate, as groups

of drunken men spend hours milling about the street and dangling strands from balconies, hoping for a girl to lift her top. The deal is this: guy on balcony/girl on street (or the reverse). He offers flashy beads (bigger breasts mean bigger beads; it ain't fair but this is Mardi Gras), they negotiate, usually in sign language, for the even bigger beads he wears around his neck. Eventually, if she is amenable, he holds the strand of beads of her choice out, she lifts her top, he drops (or throws upward) the beads. She, or her friends, catch them. The deal is done. Happy Mardi Gras. Please drive through.

Believe it or not, this is a legitimate barter arrangement, and if the bead thrower shirks on it, he can find himself getting beaten up by outraged passers-by who know the rules. It is not unknown for New Orleans police officers to order a man who changes his mind about handing over the beads to do it or face jail (disturbing the peace, if you please).

On Mardi Gras day itself (Fat Tuesday), the flashing tends to go both ways. You're likely to see more naked dicks wandering around Bourbon Street that day than you might ever see in your life otherwise. Unfortunately (for men), so many guys are so eager to 'drop trou', that girls rarely find it necessary to hand over any beads at all.

> ### 'Frankly, most locals never go to a Mardi Gras ball. Why should they?'

During the final Mardi Gras weekend, flashing is as common as dirt (downtown *only* – don't try this Uptown), and more extreme acts are also sometimes performed for beads on both straight and gay blocks of Bourbon Street. Some are as innocent as kissing, some are not innocent at all. But keep in mind that sex acts on the street are illegal – and even flashing right in front of a cop can be a bad idea if he's in a mood. Pick your time, and try to have some common sense. You do *not* want to go to jail during Mardi Gras.

WELCOME TO PARTY GRAS

The whole Carnival season is a whirlwind of parades and parties; private social groups are behind most, so don't expect to be invited to a ball if you're just here for a few days. Invitations are sought after and tend to go to locals and friends of locals. Still, there's plenty on tap for the general public, and, frankly, most locals never go to a Mardi Gras ball in their lives. Why should they, when the party on the street is so good? On the third Saturday before Fat Tuesday, the **Krewe du Vieux** gets the party going in the French Quarter. The style of the parade harks back to past parades with mule-drawn floats rolling through the streets of the historic district. The krewe's vision of satire makes theirs the raunchiest parade of the season, combining sexual innuendo with a healthy disrespect for local institutions, including City Hall and the school board.

On the Sunday of the first weekend, Mardi Gras goes to the dogs. The **Mistick Krewe of Barkus** was started as a parody of old-line krewes by a group of gay men and their dogs. It has since grown into a suburbanites' pet festival and fundraiser benefiting local animal shelters. Most of the 1,000 canines and their escorts will be in fancy dress; those at the beginning of the parade will be sporting the most outrageous costumes.

The madcap **MOMS Ball** always takes place on the Saturday before Fat Tuesday, generally at Blaine Kern's Mardi Gras World. For more than 30 years, this party has been an exhibitionist's dream come true. Fancy dress – particularly the skimpy kind – is encouraged: if you aren't wearing it you may be asked at the door to forgo clothing altogether. The party starts late and runs later. Check local listings for specifics.

On Lundi Gras – Fat Monday – there are two main events at the Riverfront. Zulu holds an all-day party in Woldenberg Park, near Canal Place Shopping Center. They announce their royalty and parade figures, such as the Big Shot and Witch Doctor, to the crowd and krewe members over the course of the afternoon. At 6pm Rex, the King of Carnival, arrives at Spanish Plaza by Coast Guard cutter. Then the Mayor of New Orleans issues a proclamation granting him reign over the city on Mardi Gras Day. In a new tradition, as part of this event, Rex and King Zulu greet each other, symbolically breaking down the walls of segregation that traditionally divided the black and white krewes. The free festivities include fireworks and concerts on the riverfront.

One of the best celebrations is held 24 hours later. The annual **gathering of the drummers** on Frenchmen Street in the Marigny has been going on since the early 1990s. Percussionists – sometimes dozens of them – gather just outside the French Quarter before sunset on Mardi Gras day to beat out a tribal rhythm as hundreds gather in the street to dance. The convergence brings by all the walking human art you could imagine – people on stilts, people eating fire, people in and out of costume dancing like lunatics. It is one of the best of the new Mardi Gras traditions, and one that you generally will not find listed anywhere.

MEDIA GRAS

As any trip on the web will show, the mysteries of Mardi Gras are increasingly well documented on the internet. Everything from naked girls to blokes wandering around with cups of booze have their own sites. The best websites include mardigras.com, mardigrasdigest.com and mardigrasneworleans.com. All of these keep tabs on Carnival news and provide links.

Mardi Gras is well covered by the local print media. Two annual publications, *Mardi Gras Magazine* and *Arthur Hardy's Mardi Gras Guide*, are devoted to Carnival and can be found just about everywhere in town.

The Times-Picayune, the local newspaper, publishes daily parade guides. The free local weekly, *Gambit*, also publishes an excellent guide to Mardi Gras parades and events, including a breakdown of throws, parties and numbers of floats. Local television and radio broadcasts alerts when parades are delayed or cancelled because of weather.

Future Mardi Gras dates

24 February 2004
8 February 2005
28 February 2006
20 February 2007

Literary New Orleans

'There is just something about New Orleans that makes writers happy'. Andrei Codrescu

Why do writers gravitate towards a city? Partially because their peers are there, partly because they want to be part of a movement-in-the-making; they feed off of the atmosphere, the way that history and a people can texture a place with both conflicts and contradictions. Writers also tend to go where it's cheap, and where the booze flows without restriction. Paris in the 1920s? Sure, it was Paris, but, man, did the dollar go a long way over there back then.

Those same factors explain the astonishing literary depth in New Orleans. Granted, many of those who comprise the city's history were just passing through (**Walt Whitman**, **Mark Twain**, **O Henry** and **Jack Kerouac** were a few) but others came to be so inextricably linked with the city – **Tennessee Williams**, **Truman Capote**, **Lillian Hellman** and **Walker Percy** among them – that they raised its literary profile on the world stage. Stanley Kowalski's bellowing cry, 'Stella!' became as widely known a cultural reference as Mona

Lisa's smile. And the more gothic, twisted and humid New Orleans' prose became, the more readers and writers became intrigued with it.

Of course, all that atmosphere also attracts the melodramatic and the hacks. For every crafter of apt, alluring descriptions of the French Quarter, there are dozens of cliché-peddling hucksters. For every 'I Saw in Louisiana a Live Oak Growing', there is at least one 'Ode to the Crawfish'.

New Orleans' relevance on the writing landscape has swelled and receded. There have been high points – **Sherwood Anderson's** salon at the Pontalba Apartments in Jackson Square, Capote's and Williams' respective residencies – but there are many whose literary reputations have faded into the dimmest obscurity, surviving only in footnotes and scholars' dusty bookshelves. Most recently, the city has reclaimed some of the footing it had lost since the mid-20th century as Pulitzer Prize winners and other canonical-writers-in-the-making have made New Orleans their home.

EARLY DAYS

The first major figure to kick-start a local literary movement was arguably **George Washington Cable** (1844-1925), whose portraits of Creole life were part of a local-colour movement across the country. Cable earned a national reputation among his contemporaries with works like *The Grandissimes* and *The Creoles of Louisiana*. He also kept a long-running literary salon in his home – **Oscar Wilde** (1854-1900) popped in after an unpopular lecture at the grand French Opera House in 1882.

Cable spurred the career of another notable early writer, **Grace King** (1852-1931), who had a salon of her own and who began to write based on her distaste for Cable's portraits. Her works include *Balcony Stories* and *New Orleans: The Place and the People*. King and Cable remained locked in an adversarial tango; they're largely unread today, and it's best to leave them in each other's angry company.

More canonically hardy is **Kate Chopin** (1851-1904), who had been relegated to the local-colour dustbin until feminists retrofitted her as a hero for her bold and masterly *The Awakening* (1889). The novel, about a young Creole wife chafing against the strictures of her society, is particularly memorable for its protagonist's drastic final action. Don't expect to visit Grand Isle and see the Hamptons of the Bayou that Chopin knew, though – a hurricane long ago wiped away most of the history and landscape, leaving only a thread of land.

A last noteworthy figure in this first wave was **Lafcadio Hearn** (1850-1904), a Greek-Irish journalist born in the Greek Isles who spent a decade chronicling French Quarter life, and whose work has recently seen a revival of interest. His best-known book is a collection of Creole proverbs, *Gombo Zherbes* (1885). Hearn eventually departed for a trip to Japan and other peculiar adventures.

LITERARY DRIVE-BYS

Two better-known writers, **Mark Twain** and **O Henry**, both claimed to have received their professional christening, so to speak, here, though neither story has ever been verified.

Twain, né Samuel Clemens (1835-1910), spent his early years as a riverboat pilot (between 1857 and 1861) in and around New Orleans; it was then, he said, that he picked up his pen-name. He returned in 1882 to gather material for chapters which later appeared in his book *Life on the Mississippi*.

Henry (1862-1910), born William Sidney Porter, came to the city under somewhat less hospitable circumstances, having chosen it as a hide-out when embezzlement charges forced

him out of Austin, Texas, in 1894. Several of his short stories, including 'Cherchez la Femme', were later set here. Although he was only passing through town en route to a longer-term escape in Honduras, the story goes that he was in a bar here when a patron called out, 'Oh, Henry – another of the same!' and a pen-name was born. Then again, he also said that he picked it up from a local society newspaper, so the truth is anyone's guess. Who'd believe a convicted felon anyway? (Henry eventually did a five-year stint in Ohio.)

Though he didn't change his name here, **Walt Whitman** (1819-1892) did live in New Orleans for a few months in 1848 and wrote sketches for a local newspaper. He later composed the poem 'I Saw in Louisiana A Live Oak Growing' about his time here. In a later reminiscence, he memorably noted his frequent visits to the French Market in the Quarter, where 'I nearly always on these occasions got a delicious cup of coffee with a biscuit, for my breakfast, from the immense shining copper kettle of a great Creole mulatto woman (I believe she weigh'd 230 pounds). I have never had such coffee since.'

SHERWOOD MAKES THE SCENE

Yet all that was prelude to the first real literary events of merit in New Orleans – the arrival of **Sherwood Anderson** and the brief but vibrant life of the *Double Dealer*. In response to fussy critic HL Mencken's grumblings about the South as an intellectual cesspit, Albert Goldstein and Julius Weis Friend founded the *Double Dealer* in 1920 in the French Quarter. It was conceived as an ambitious literary magazine for young comers, and it fulfilled its promise (though reports of New Orleans as 'the Greenwich Village of the South' might have been somewhat exaggerated). Writers like Hart Crane, Robert Penn Warren, Ernest Hemingway, Ezra Pound and Thornton Wilder were among its many notable contributors.

> ### 'There is something left in this people here that makes them like one another.' Sherwood Anderson

But perhaps the best-known among them was Anderson (1876-1941), who arrived in New Orleans in 1922, his reputation already cemented with the publication of *Winesburg, Ohio*. Cheap rents in the still-undiscovered Quarter were a major draw, and Anderson and his wife, Elizabeth, took up residence in the Pontalba Apartments on Jackson Square (**Katherine Anne Porter** would also live there in 1937). There, he played host to many writers visiting the city, including **Edna St Vincent Millay**, **W Somerset Maugham** and **Ring Lardner**. His Saturday night dinners became the stuff of local legend.

More significantly, Anderson became an important advocate for New Orleans' literary relevance. His short story about New Orleans, 'A Meeting South', appeared in the legendary *Dial,* but the real clincher was 'New Orleans, the *Double Dealer* and the Modern Movement in America', written, of course, for the *Double Dealer.* In it, he professes his love for life in the 'old city here, on the lip of America', where '(f)rom my window, as I sit writing, I see the tangled mass of the roofs of old buildings. There are old galleries with beautiful hand-wrought railings, on which the people of the houses can walk above the street, or over which the housewife can lean in the morning to call the vegetable man pushing his cart along the roadway below.'

With unabashed enthusiasm for New Orleans, he continues, 'There is something left in this people here that makes them like one another, that leads to constant outbursts of the spirit of play, that keeps them from being too confoundedly serious about death and the ballot and reform and other less important things in life.' All of which leads him to conclude, 'Just why it isn't the winter home of every sensitive artist in America, who can raise enough money to get here, I do not know.'

One bright spark who heard the call was **William Faulkner** (1897-1962). Then a poet drawn by Anderson's example, he spent six months between 1924 and 1925 in a Pirate's Alley apartment just off Jackson Square; it is now home to a bookshop which bears his name (*see p158*). Faulkner, whose literary career was young then, made frequent boozy visits to Anderson's apartment; the elder writer would hold court and Faulkner would listen. He later described his transition from poet to novelist in this way: 'Met man named Sherwood Anderson. Said, "Why not write novels? Maybe won't have to work." Did. *Soldier's Pay.* Did. *Mosquitoes…* Own and operate own typewriter.'

This time in New Orleans was relatively prolific for Faulkner, who wrote his first novel, *Soldier's Pay,* while living in the Pirate's Alley apartment. He also wrote a series of sketches of French Quarterites for the *Times-Picayune* and the *Double Dealer* which were later collected in *New Orleans Sketches.* Along with his house-mate, **William Spratling** (1900-1967), Faulkner compiled a series of caricatures called *Sherwood Anderson and Other Famous Creoles;* the introduction, penned by Faulkner, mocked the elder writer's style.

He celebrated signing the contract for his second novel, another French Quarter satire called *Mosquitoes,* with a lavish party at **Galatoire's Restaurant** (*see p111*). The novel's florid descriptions of Jackson Square illustrate an ambitious writer revving up his style; his protagonist 'peered out across an undimensional feathered square, across stenciled palms and Andrew Jackson in childish effigy bestriding the terrific arrested plunge of his curly balanced horse, toward the long unemphasis of the Pontalba building and the three spires of the cathedral graduated by perspective, pure and slumbrous beneath the decadent languor of August and evening.' In this dusky square, 'Pontalba and cathedral were cut from black paper and pasted flat on a green sky; above them taller palms were fixed in black and soundless explosions.'

Faulkner left New Orleans quickly enough, but it remains significant as the place where he made the transition from poet to novelist with those early works. A local organisation, the Faulkner Society, continues to commemorate his time here with year-round literary events and the Faulkner Words & Music Festival every December (*see p179*).

'New Orleans streets have long, lonesome perspectives…' Truman Capote

The *Double Dealer,* for its part, ceased publication after just five-and-a-half years. Anderson departed New Orleans after 1925. Prior to that, in 1920, **F Scott Fitzgerald** had spent several months here working on his first novel, *This Side of Paradise,* in an apparently unwelcome separation from his future wife, Zelda. **John Dos Passos** stopped through for a month in 1924 while working on his seminal *Manhattan Transfer.* A few years later, in 1928 and again in 1929, **Zora Neale Hurston** was in town conducting folkloric research on local subjects, including Marie Laveau, the results of which were published in *Mules and Men.*

THE BIG BANG

The 1930s were a quieter decade for literary New Orleans, except for the presence of **Lyle Saxon**, an author and preservationist who headed the local Works Progress Administration project and later authored the folklore collection *Gumbo Ya Ya,* which remains in print.

In the 1940s, things got kicking again. Writer **Truman Capote** (1924-1984), who was born at the local Touro Infirmary while his parents were staying at the Monteleone Hotel, returned

Tennessee Williams wanted to die in New Orleans. *See p33.*

to New Orleans in 1945 to write *Other Voices, Other Rooms* as well as a number of his best short stories. The famously gin-soaked, debauched and diminutive playwright fit in well in the city. He kept company in the city's gay demi-monde whenever he wasn't prowling the town with photographer **Henri Cartier Bresson** looking for stories for profiles of the city for the magazine *Harper's Bazaar.* Capote's essay 'New Orleans (1946)' evokes the French

Quarter of the time, and shows his ambivalence for it: 'New Orleans streets have long, lonesome perspectives; in empty hours their atmosphere is like Chirico, and things innocent ordinarily (a face behind the slanted light of shutters, nuns moving in the distance, a fat dark arm lolling lopsidedly out some window, a lonely black boy squatting in an alley, blowing soap bubbles and watching sadly as they rise to burst), acquire qualities of violence.'

Like Capote, **Lillian Hellman** (1905-1984) was born here; she spent her first five years at a Prytania Street boarding house run by her two aunts, and moved to New York in 1911 when her father's business here failed. She travelled between the two cities until her teen years; the memories she acquired lend enormous texture to her memoir *An Unfinished Woman,* which recounts the dramas of the boarding-house tenants, the fig tree where she hid and read, and her first stabs at rebellion. Hellman was later known for her plays *The Children's Hour, The Little Foxes* and *Toys in the Attic,* but *An Unfinished Woman* reinforces her ties to the city more than any of her other work.

'The air was so sweet in New Orleans it seemed to come in soft bandanas...'
Jack Kerouac

And then there was Tennessee. If no other writer had ever passed through or alighted here, **Tennessee Williams** (1911-1983) alone would suffice to give this city a permanent place on the canonical landscape. Williams, a Mississippi native raised in St Louis, first came to New Orleans in the late 1930s. Nomadic by nature, he moved frequently (especially back to New York and Key West), but during his frequent tenures here he produced some of his best work. Among them was *A Streetcar Named Desire,* a Pulitzer Prize-winning play that rendered the French Quarter and its downtown environs in a humid, dreamy and terrifying haze of sexuality, desperation, hypermasculinity and lilting, devastated womanhood. At last, New Orleans had a bona fide classic on its hands – a work conceived in and about it rendered with complete mastery by an author at the top of his craft.

Williams wrote the play at 632 St Peter Street in the French Quarter, in an 1842 house that survives today. The streetcar whose name he borrowed, alas, does not.

In New Orleans, Williams was liberated by the city's thriving gay culture, which he said conflicted with his relatively puritanical upbringing in a way 'I've probably never ceased exploiting.' He wrote many other works about New Orleans, and another of his Pulitzer-winning plays, *Cat on a Hot Tin Roof,* is set in the nearby Mississippi Delta.

Williams' last permanent residence in New Orleans was at 1014 Dumaine Street, where he hoped eventually to die in his beloved brass bed (but didn't). By then a fixture at numerous local restaurants and bars (some of which still

proudly claim the attachment), he whiled away his declining time working on other, minor plays and his memoirs.

In the late 1940s, New Orleans also had a brush with the Beat movement. **William Burroughs** (1914-1997) and his wife, Joan, spent part of 1948 and 1949 across the Mississippi River in Algiers Point (at 509 Wagner Street, for devotees). Burroughs was a habitué of the heroin trade scene at Lee Circle, and found himself taking the ferry back and forth daily to nourish his expensive habit, ultimately taking a role on the supply as well as the demand side.

Jack Kerouac and his travelling buddy **Neal Cassady** visited Burroughs in 1949 en route to San Francisco, though their drug-fuelled stop was cut short when Burroughs refused to lend Kerouac money. Nevertheless, the visit was immortalised in a passage in Kerouac's *On the Road,* in which the protagonist and Dean Moriarty (Cassady) pay a visit to Old Bull Lee, the novel's Burroughs surrogate. Kerouac writes, 'The air was so sweet in New Orleans it seemed to come in soft bandanas; and you could smell the river and really smell the people, and mud, and molasses, and every kind of tropical exhalation with your nose suddenly removed from the dry ices of a Northern winter.'

LITERARY ESTABLISHMENT
Those who came on to the scene from the 1960s onward were a little less blustery and hyperbolic than their predecessors, but the quieter literary life that they nurtured has lingered nonetheless.

An exception to this general trend was poet **Charles Bukowski** (1920-1994), who had a brush with the infamous Jim Crow laws almost immediately upon his first arrival here in 1942. Seeing the white poet make his way to the back of a city bus, the conductor, as one of the South's sterling preservers of separatism, soon informed him of the error of his ways. Still, Bukowski remained in the city for a bit longer, throwing together some fantasy stories as an escape from the tedious jobs that he temporarily held while he was here.

Bukowski's connection to the city was re-established when Jon and Gypsy Lou Webb came to town and started *Outsider* magazine in 1960. Though it only lasted for four issues, each was memorable in its way, with work by poets like **Lawrence Ferlinghetti, Allen Ginsberg** and Bukowski, to whose work a major section of one issue was devoted. The Webbs later published several volumes of Bukowski's poetry, including *Crucifix in a Deathbed,* which he wrote while staying here again in 1965.

Less notorious than the legendarily hard-drinking (and -living) Bukowski, **Shirley Ann Grau**, a native New Orleanian, nonetheless came into her own as a novelist in the mid 1960s, winning a Pulitzer Prize for her 1965 work *The Keepers of the House.*

Walker Percy (1960-1990), a non-practising physician who had houses both Uptown and across Lake Pontchartrain in the suburban town of Covington, won a National Book Award in 1962 for his debut novel, *The Moviegoer,* an examination of faith set in contemporary New Orleans. Percy eventually taught at Loyola University, where his students included future writers like **Tim Gautreaux, Valerie Martin** and **Sheila Bosworth**.

Percy was later instrumental in bringing the astonishing works of **John Kennedy Toole** (1937-1969) to light. Toole, a native New Orleanian, was the quintessential product of the city's social peculiarities (which range from unusually intrusive parental relationships to a sometimes ferociously defensive provinciality). At the same time, he was an acerbic social critic of them. His posthumously published novel, *A Confederacy of Dunces,* remains the most accurate, biting and desperately hilarious work about the city that has ever been written.

Unfortunately, Toole, who wrote the book during a stint in the army and held itinerant teaching posts thereafter, became despondent when he couldn't find a publisher and killed himself in 1969. His mother, whose legendary perseverance locals still discuss with a shudder, pursued her son's dream for him, and finally found an advocate for the novel in Percy. She begged him to read it, and when he finally did, he, too, became its champion. *A Confederacy of Dunces* was finally published in 1980, and won the Pulitzer Prize the next year, beating out one of Percy's own novels.

In the louder realm of mass-market fiction, Anne Rice made the city a goth magnet in 1976 with the publication of *Interview with the Vampire.* The fevered devotion that the novel (and the subsequent film and many sequels and spin-offs) has inspired is difficult to overstate. Suffice it to say that Rice's home in the Garden District (or at least the gates in front) might soon be added to the list of the nation's most visited attractions, perhaps just slightly behind one of the lesser Disney parks.

In the past couple of decades the city has seen other heavyweights, from **Ellen Gilchrist**, who won the National Book Award for *Victory Over Japan* in 1984, to Pulitzer Prize-winning poet **Yusef Komunyakaa.**

Robert Olen Butler, who gave voice to the scores of displaced Vietnamese living at the city's periphery (they were brought here by

Catholic charities at the height of the war in the 1970s), won the Pulitzer for *A Good Scent from a Strange Mountain* in 1993. **Richard Ford**, who has lived in New Orleans on and off for more than a decade, won a Pulitzer and a PEN/Faulkner Award for *Independence Day,* the first novel to earn both distinctions. New Orleans, though, has been largely absent in his work (and muted when it does appear) – which is actually refreshing. The 'I live and write here, but don't start looking for odes to the French Quarter in my work' ethos is still something of a novelty here, alas.

Heavy-hitting popular historian **Stephen Ambrose** (1936-2002) had strong ties to the city until his recent death. The author of such bestsellers as *D-Day, Undaunted Courage* and *Citizen Soldiers* was for many years a professor at the University of New Orleans, where he founded its Eisenhower Center for American Studies; his mantle has since been taken up by rising young turk **Douglas Brinkley**. A fixture of the TV news and public radio punditry and the author of several of his own ambitious works (which, like Ambrose's, have successfully crossed over to popular audiences), Brinkley is following in Ambrose's footsteps, he directs the Eisenhower Center and continues to draw national attention to its efforts.

Meanwhile, journalists **Walter Isaacson, Nicholas Lemann** and **Michael Lewis** have all sprung to growing eminence from New Orleans roots, while Transylvanian transplant **Andrei Codrescu**, who can regularly be heard in commentaries on National Public Radio, lends a Draculean drawl to the French Quarter. His fiction, which includes *Messiah,* is frequently set in the city.

At the same time, some of the city's darker depths are being mined further by other emerging voices – horror writer **Poppy Z Brite** (who also enjoys the dubious distinction of being rocker Courtney Love's biographer) and fiction writers including **John Biguenet** and **Dean Paschal** are among them.

While no one has yet supplanted Tennessee Williams for sheer arresting literary power vis-à-vis New Orleans, the city remains a decidedly writerly destination, an invigorating little patch of difference surrounded by otherwise fallow fields of American sameness. The still relatively low cost of living here draws in the up-and-comers, while allowing those who have become established to live like minor royalty. Sure, New Orleans still lends itself to hackery – those clichés of 'the mighty Mississippi' and the 'rich gumbo' of New Orleans life that come all too easily. But the real thing keeps emerging here, too. And the city's most interesting chapters may have yet to be written.

Accommodation

Accommodation   36

Features
When too much is not enough   37
The boutique clique   45
Top five bargain hotels   51

Accommodation

Remember, in the end, it's just a bedroom.

Despite the fact that hotels are the lifeblood of New Orleans' top industry, local hoteliers have a laid-back attitude about the whole thing. It's a kind of hubris, as if they're thinking, 'What the hell. They'll come no matter what.' So in a city with 30,000 hotel rooms – and more opening all the time – it's just not as easy as it should be to find a good hotel. To put it simply: service, cleanliness, management and efficiency aren't always what you'd hope for here, and rarely will you find all four in one place.

Still, if you approach hotels as you should approach the city itself – with humour and flexibility – you'll find a good place to stay. On a positive note, you often get a lot for your money here, especially in the off season.

WHERE TO STAY

Let's get the **French Quarter** out of the way to start with. Most first-time visitors want to stay there, perhaps in fear that they won't find the rest of the city as interesting. Festive though the Quarter is, keep in mind that you'll pay for the privilege. Rooms here usually cost at least 20 per cent more than comparable rooms elsewhere. They're also smaller (most are in historic buildings that can't be enlarged or significantly altered). In addition, the whole blasé factor is highest here – the desk clerks, housekeepers and even managers often take the attitude that if you don't want the room because it's dirty, the tap drips or the air-conditioning doesn't work, there are others who'll snap it up. There are exceptions, of course – top-flight hotels like the **Ritz Carlton** (see p39) and the **Soniat House** (see p39) pride themselves on service. But if money's an object, unfortunately, you'll have to take your chances.

The hot new zone for affordable hotels is the **Faubourg Marigny**, just beyond the Quarter. In the last few years B&Bs have taken off here, and many of the area's Greek Revival villas, Creole cottages and Victorian mansions have been redone for paying guests. The **Royal Street Courtyard** (see p44) and **Claiborne Mansion** (see p43) are prime examples. Marigny has some of the best extras in town: architecturally significant houses presided over by managers full of enthusiasm, five minutes' walk from the Quarter.

On the other side of the French Quarter, across Canal Street, is the **Central Business District**, home of the city's business hotels.

Most chains have an outpost here, and you can find good weekend deals. This is also where the boutique hotels are: the **International House** and **Loft 523** (for both, see p47). While it's true that boutique bargains are thin on the ground, for your money you will get great design and lots of yummy bath products.

The **Garden District** and **Uptown** have fewer hotels. Wealthy residents in the prime neighbourhoods discourage (read: fight tooth and nail against) B&Bs, although their numbers are increasing. It's almost inevitable that in an area filled with gorgeous, many-roomed mansions that cost a fortune to maintain, the idea of turning some into guesthouses should prove attractive. One on lovely St Charles Avenue was converted into the gracious, if a bit tattered, **Columns Hotel** (see p49).

MARDI GRAS, JAZZ FEST & SPECIAL EVENTS

Unsurprisingly, hotel rates jump for Mardi Gras, Jazz Fest and for what hoteliers label 'special events' (anything from the Super Bowl to a minor street festival). There's no way around this profiteering, so if you have plans to come at one of these times, book as early as possible. A year in advance is not unusual for Mardi Gras, but you should be all right with three to six months. Book a room even if you're not sure you're coming; better to lose the deposit than to end up sleeping in the car.

Most deals are to be had during the summer, which is New Orleans' low season. Come at that time and you'll understand why, as from mid-May to the first Monday of September the sticky, tropical heat wilts the tourism market.

KEEP IN MIND

● Hotel bills include the city's 13 per cent tax, plus a $1, $2, or $3 a night 'occupancy fee'. B&Bs are not subject to the tax.
● Parking will be a problem if you're staying downtown. Most places have valet service or some kind of parking arrangement, but it can cost as much as $28 per day. If a hotel offers parking, quiz the reservation staff closely on what it will really mean for your wallet.
● Hotels look at phone calls as manna from heaven, shooting fish in a barrel and… well, other metaphors about making easy money. They charge for local calls and even for toll-free calls. Check the policy before you pick up the phone.

● New Orleans is behind the curve on disabled access, but it isn't really its fault. The city's historic buildings have kept the city barrier-friendly instead of barrier-free. If you need disabled access, choose a new hotel or one that's been recently renovated.

● Always bargain when booking a room. Hotels are loath to admit they charge anything besides the rack rate, but in reality hardly anyone pays the posted rates. Check online, call 1-800 numbers and talk to different reservations clerks, and you'll almost always find a better deal.

● Illegal guesthouses – mostly flats and spare rooms rented out by individuals without city licences – are widespread and often advertised on the internet. While these places can be clean and comfortable, and offer good deals, be very careful. The best rule is to never stay anywhere that hasn't been recommended to you by a former guest. Otherwise, take your business elsewhere.

ABOUT THE LISTINGS
Unless otherwise stated, all the places listed have air-conditioning and phones and do not include breakfast in their rates. Rooms prices were accurate at press time but may fluctuate wildly according to the season, special events and the convention trade.

French Quarter

Deluxe

Hotel Maison de Ville & the Audubon Cottages
727 Toulouse Street, at Royal Street, New Orleans, LA 70130 (561 5858/1-800 634 1600/fax 528 9939/www.maisondeville.com). Bus 3 Vieux Carré. **Rates** (incl continental breakfast) $245-$260 single; $395 suite; $625 cottage. **Credit** AmEx, DC, Disc, MC, V. **Map** p282 B2.

Maison de Ville is like a quiet, self-contained planet one block (but a whole world) away from the raucous cacophony of Bourbon Street. This elegant, quiet little hotel is a confection of deep Oriental carpets, antique furniture and soothing colours. It has two distinct parts: Maison de Ville features a townhouse, former slave quarters, courtyard and carriage house on Toulouse Street, while the seven small, self-sufficient Audubon Cottages occupy a peaceful, private enclosure a few blocks away on Dauphine. At Maison de Ville, the rooms are on the small side but decorated and maintained with great care. At the cottages (artist John James Audubon lived and worked in No.1 during his New Orleans stay), the rooms are larger and the furnishings grander. Another perk is the hotel restaurant, the Bistro at

Accommodation

When too much is not enough

There's luxury and then there's *luxury*. Any big chain hotel can give you big beds, pricey soaps, room service and deep carpets. But for that extra edge of absolute indulgence, when you're ready to give up any pretence of responsibility and max out the credit card, burn through next month's mortgage and enjoy absolutely every minute of it, here are the places to go.

Audubon Cottages
If Tennessee Williams had written happy endings, this is where Blanche DuBois would have spent her days. *See p37.*

Maison Orleans at Ritz-Carlton
A room here resembles a Hollywood vision of how rich people live, with working fireplaces, plush couches and a personal butler. *See p39.*

Soniat House
Pause for a nanosecond at Soniat House (pictured) and a staff member will be at your side: 'Is there anything you need? May I help, suggest, listen, carry something?' How we miss them. *See p39.*

Maison de Ville – which is one of the city's best (*see p108*). Children under 12 are allowed in the cottages but not in the main hotel.
Hotel services *Bar. Concierge. Laundry. No-smoking rooms. Parking (valet). Restaurant. Swimming pool.* **Room services** *Dataport. Minibar. Room service (11.30am-10pm). TV: cable/VCR.*

Ritz-Carlton Hotel

921 Canal Street, at Dauphine Street, New Orleans, LA 70112 (524 1331/1-800 241 3333/fax 670 2864/www.ritz-carlton.com). Canal Streetcar/bus 3 Vieux Carré. **Rates** $99-$395 single/double; $545 suite. **Credit** AmEx, DC, Disc, MC, V. **Map** p282 A1.
Anyone walking into the luxurious Ritz-Carlton for the first time might assume this stately hotel had been here for ages. It's a mistake the Ritz is happy to encourage. The beaux arts building (formerly a department store and Canal Street landmark) has been lavishly remade into a hotel of the grandest sort. Public areas and guest rooms are filled with antiques and awash in layers of fabric, marble, gilt and cut flowers. The Ritz standard has been rigorously applied to all aspects of the hotel, including the world class Victor's restaurant (*see p120*), one of the best spas in the country, and a jazz room (French Qurater Bar, *see p136*) that books exciting, contemporary players instead of the usual hotel-bar ensemble. Best of all, it bucks the local 'Later, darlin'' attitude with staff who are attentive and prompt. It is oddly designed as three hotels in one; they have separate names but the same facilities. The largest is the Ritz-Carlton; the most extravagant is the Maison Orleans, all of whose 75 rooms have butlers (670 2900; rates $109-$495); and the Iberville Suites, which offers many of the same amenities as the Ritz-Carlton at half the price (523 2400; rates $89-$295).
Hotel services *Bar. Beauty salon. Business services. Concierge. Disabled: adapted rooms. No-smoking rooms. Parking (valet). Restaurants. Spa.* **Room services** *Dataport. Hairdryer. Iron. Minibar. Room service (24hrs). Turndown. TV: cable/VCR.*

Royal Sonesta Hotel

300 Bourbon Street, at Bienville Street, New Orleans, LA 70130 (586 0300/1-800 766 3782/fax 586 0335/www.royalsonestano.com). St Charles or Canal Streetcar/bus 3 Vieux Carré. **Rates** (incl continental breakfast) $289-$409 single/double; $479-$1,500 suite. **Credit** AmEx, DC, Disc, MC, V. **Map** p282 B2.
Although it covers almost a block, has more than 500 rooms and opens onto rowdy Bourbon Street, the Sonesta has the feel of a small village. It's a friendly, interesting place run by a small army of staff. Within the sprawling space are bars, restaurants, shops and meeting rooms, all with the lively ebb and flow of a crossroads hotel. Most of its rooms are attractive, with amenities and a courtyard view.
Hotel services *Babysitting. Bars. Business services. Concierge. Courtyard. Disabled: adapted rooms (10). Gift shop. Gym. Laundry. No-smoking rooms. Parking. Restaurants. Swimming pool.* **Room services** *Dataport. Minibar. Room service (7am-2am). Safe. TV: cable. Voicemail.*

Soniat House

1133 Chartres Street, between Ursulines & Governor Nicholls streets, New Orleans, LA 70116 (522 0570/1-800 544 8808/fax 522 7208/www.soniathouse.com). Bus 3 Vieux Carré. **Rates** $195-$295 single/double; $425 one-bedroom suite; $625 two-bedroom suite. **Credit** AmEx, MC, V. **Map** p282 C2.
You have to look hard to find this hotel, as it blends so perfectly into the private, neutral facades of peaceful lower Chartres Street. For those who can afford to slip through its anonymous doors, down the flagstone carriageway and up the curving staircases to the lacy ironwork balconies, it's well worth the hunt. Soniat House is contained within two 1830s Creole townhouses that face each other across Chartres Street. Both are rambling structures with lush, romantic courtyards. The 33 rooms and suites are all tastefully decorated in soothing colours, with French, English and Louisiana antiques, art and antiquarian books. Best of all, the hotel's hallmark is exquisite service from a low-key, affable staff. Please note that, as in many hotels converted from old buildings, room sizes vary wildly.
Hotel services *Bar. Concierge. Courtyard. Laundry. No-smoking rooms. Parking (valet/ $19 per night).* **Room services** *Dataport. Turndown. TV: cable.*

W Hotel French Quarter

316 Chartres Street, at Iberville Street, New Orleans, LA 70130 (581 1200/1-877 946 8357/fax 522 2910/www.whotels.com). Canal Streetcar/bus 3 Vieux Carré. **Rates** $129-$750. **Credit** AmEx, DC, Disc, MC, V. **Map** p282 A2.
This building has been a small hotel for ages but was recently purchased and done over by the upscale W chain recently. The upgrade was quite a success, offering a sleekness and contemporary style not often seen in New Orleans, much less in the French Quarter. Rooms are on the small side, but this works well with W's trademark minimalist style. Most important are the beds: fabulous rafts piled high with down comforters, thick pillows, soft sheets and luxurious pillow-top mattresses. W makes a fuss about its beds, and for once, the hype is accurate. The restaurant, Bacco, is also one of the city's best for pasta (*see p113*).
Hotel services *Concierge. Gym (off site). No-smoking rooms. Parking (valet). Restaurant. Swimming pool (outdoor).* **Room services** *Dataport. Minibar. Room service (7am-10pm). TV: cable/DVD/pay movies/VCR.*

High-end

Bienville House

320 Decatur Street, at Bienville Street, New Orleans, LA 70130 (529 2345/1-800 535 7836/fax 525 6079/www.bienvillehouse.com). Canal Streetcar/bus 3 Vieux Carré, 55 Elysian Fields. **Rates** (incl continental breakfast) $130-$335 single/double; $425 and up suite. **Credit** AmEx, DC, Disc, MC, V. **Map** p282 B3.

The pretty **Le Richelieu Hotel**. *See 41.*

As one of the newest hotels in the Quarter, Bienville House offers the convenience and amenities many travellers think are standard until they check into an old-school New Orleans hotel. Built within the shell of a 19th-century warehouse, it has kept its vintage exterior, but the interior has been completely restructured. The rooms were built to be accessible for the disabled, and all are wired for computers, faxes, cable and other high-tech necessities. The small lobby is a squeeze to get in and out of, but the hotel is home to a good restaurant, Gamay Bistro.
Hotel services *Bar. Business services. Concierge. Disabled: adapted rooms. Laundry. No-smoking floors. Parking (valet). Restaurant. Swimming pool.* **Room services** *Dataport. Iron. TV: cable.*

Hotel Provincial

1024 Chartres Street, at Ursulines Street, New Orleans, LA 70116 (581 4995/1-800 535 7922/fax 581 1018/www.hotelprovincial.com). Bus 3 Vieux Carré. **Rates** from $79 single/double; $259 suite. **Credit** AmEx, DC, Disc, MC, V. **Map** p282 C2.
The family-owned Provincial is a favourite among frequent visitors, including many businesspeople, who usually avoid the French Quarter. Unlike many Quarter hotels, it has ample business facilities, on-site parking and plenty of meeting rooms. Two storeys of rooms encircle its pleasant courtyards, which have been converted to include a swimming pool. The 105 rooms are spacious and decorated in a neo-Victorian style. The hotel also boasts a stylish Asian-fusion restaurant with the most ridiculous name in New Orleans: Stella!
Hotel services *Bar. Business services. Concierge. Disabled: adapted rooms. Laundry. No-smoking rooms. Parking. Restaurants. Swimming pool.* **Room services** *Dataport. Hairdryer. Iron. TV: cable. Voicemail.*

Hotel Ste Helene

508 Chartres Street, at St Louis Street, New Orleans, LA 70130 (522 5014/1-800 348 3388/fax 523 7140/www.melrosegroup.com). Bus 3 Vieux Carré. **Rates** (incl continental breakfast) $149-$215 single/double; $225-$350 suite. **Credit** AmEx, DC, Disc, MC, V. **Map** p282 B2.

Despite the fact that it doesn't get much more central than this, there's a serene ambience about the Ste Helene that makes it an ideal retreat after busy days and nights. It's tucked into Chartres Street next to the Napoleon House, a couple of minutes from Jackson Square, the bars of Bourbon Street and the shops of Royal Street. There are 26 rooms on three floors, many overlooking the inner courtyard. Rooms are pleasantly decorated, but some are on the dark side (which, on the other hand, could be useful after a late, cocktail-infused night).
Hotel services *Concierge. Disabled: adapted rooms. No-smoking rooms. Swimming pool.* **Room services** *Dataport. Hairdryer. Iron. TV: cable.*

Lafitte Guesthouse

1003 Bourbon Street, at St Philip Street, New Orleans, LA 70116 (581 2678/1-800 331 7971/fax 581 2677/www.lafitteguesthouse.com). Bus 3 Vieux Carré. **Rates** (incl continental breakfast) $99-$229 single/double. **Credit** AmEx, DC, Disc, MC, V. **Map** p282 C2.
Staying at the Lafitte lets visitors in on a New Orleans secret: just beyond the brash bars and strip clubs, Bourbon Street is one of the loveliest residential streets in the city. This 1849 Creole townhouse on the residential section of Bourbon has been sensitively retooled as a small hotel. Liberally sprinkled among the 14 rooms are luxurian half-tester beds, fireplaces, claw-footed bathtubs and private balconies. There's an early evening wine-and-hors-d'oeuvres gathering for guests in the parlour.
Hotel services *Concierge. No-smoking rooms. Parking ($15 per day).* **Room services** *Dataport. Hairdryer. Iron. TV: cable.*

Monteleone Hotel

214 Royal Street, at Iberville Street, New Orleans, LA 70130 (523 3341/1-800 535 9595/fax 528 1019/ www.hotelmonteleone.com). Canal Streetcar/ bus 3 Vieux Carré. **Rates** $145-$450 single/double; $350-$3,000 suite. **Credit** AmEx, DC, Disc, MC, V. **Map** p282 A2.
The Monteleone first opened in 1886, and along with the Fairmont (*see p44*) it's one of the city's two grandest old hotels. Its marble-and-gilt lobby, with

an enormous grandfather clock and a perpetual retro-European feel, as if you've stepped into a Humphrey Bogart World War II film, is an excellent place to people-watch. The Carousel Bar (*see p135*) is vainglorious. The rooms were renovated in 2002 to the tune of $25 million, and it shows. The decor is elegant and not as chintzy as it once was, with thick curtains, fine linens and granite-and-marble baths. There are 600 rooms here, but you'd never know it – the valet in the parking garage is likely to remember which car is yours from the first day. The only negative is that room service is a bit slow and not as gracious as you might hope, but that's a small quibble about a fabulous hotel.

Hotel services *Babysitting. Bars. Beauty salon. Business services. Concierge. Disabled: adapted rooms. Gym. Laundry (valet). No-smoking rooms. Parking. Restaurants (3). Swimming pool.* **Room services** *Dataport. Hairdryer. Iron. Minibar. Phone lines (2). Room service (6am-11pm). Safe. Turndown (on request). TV: cable.*

Olivier House Hotel

828 Toulouse Street, at Bourbon Street, New Orleans, LA 70112 (525 8456/1-866 525 9748/ fax 529 2006/ www.olivierhouse.com). Bus 3 Vieux Carré. **Rates** $110-$145 single/double; $165-$250 suite; $350 cottage. **Credit** AmEx, DC, MC, V. **Map** p282 B2.

The Olivier House Hotel starts in an 1836 Creole townhouse and spreads out to include several buildings at the back and side. It's a magic castle of a place, ranging from tiny rooms with one bed and not much else to the garden room (a renovated stable) and a self-contained cottage that resembles a Victorian doll's house. The Danner family has run the hotel for decades, creating a relaxed atmosphere where even pets are welcome. Rooms are decorated with a mixture of antiques and flea-market finds.

Hotel services *Babysitting. Concierge. Computer with internet. Disabled: adapted room (1). Laundry. No-smoking rooms. Parking (free). Pets allowed. Swimming pool.* **Room services** *Hairdryer. Iron. Kitchenette (most rooms). Minibar. Room service (8.30am-9.30pm). TV: cable.*

Prince Conti Hotel

830 Conti Street, at Bourbon Street, New Orleans, LA 70112 (529 4172/1-800 366 2743/fax 581 3802/www.princecontihotel.com). Bus 3 Vieux Carré. **Rates** $69-$179 single/double; $229-$325 suite. **Credit** AmEx, DC, Disc, MC, V. **Map** p282 B2.

The 1950s are alive and well at the Prince Conti, where splendid Martinis are served in the bar (the Bombay Club, *see p135*) and the standards of service and comfort have never changed. All 53 rooms are furnished with antiques (some, like canopy beds, more impressive than others). Rooms vary in size, and bathrooms can be on the small side. The staff tend to be long-term, making for a smooth, friendly operation, which is saying a lot in laissez-faire New Orleans. The Conti attracts an older, sedate clientele, making it a good choice if you're looking for a rare quiet hotel in the Quarter.

Hotel services *Bar. Business services. Concierge. Disabled: adapted rooms. Parking (valet, $20). Restaurant. Safe.* **Room services** *Dataport. Hairdryer. Iron. Newspaper. Room service. TV: cable.*

Le Richelieu Hotel

1234 Chartres Street, at Barracks Street, New Orleans, LA 70116 (529 2492/1-800 535 9653/fax 524 8179/www.lerichelieuhotel.com). Bus 3 Vieux Carré, 48 Esplanade. **Rates** $85-$170 single; $95-$180 double; $200-$475 suites. **Credit** AmEx, DC, Disc, MC, V. **Map** p282 D2.

In 1977, Paul McCartney and his family took over one entire floor of Le Richelieu and stayed for two months while he was recording in New Orleans. Today the hotel seems frozen at that time, which is fine with its corps of international fans, who like its easygoing pace, long-term staff and modest rates. If you're driving, this hotel is a real French Quarter bargain because of its large, free parking lot. There are some vintage pieces in the rooms and suites, but mostly you'll find standard hotel furniture built more for durability and comfort than for looks.

Hotel services *Babysitting. Bar. Concierge. Free local phone calls. Laundry. Parking (free). Restaurant. Swimming pool.* **Room services** *Dataport. Hairdryer. Iron. Refrigerator. Room service. Turndown (on request). TV: DVD/satellite/ VCR. Voicemail.*

Mid-range

Chateau Hotel

1001 Chartres Street, at St Philip Street, New Orleans, LA 70116 (524 9636/fax 525 2989/ www.chateauhotel.com). Bus 3 Vieux Carré. **Rates** (incl continental breakfast) $99-$139 single; $109-$159 double; $159-$209 suite. **Credit** AmEx, DC, Disc, MC, V. **Map** p282 C2.

This is a modest hotel with a devoted following; guests return year after year, and staff make a point of getting to know them personally. The open-air bar set in the middle of the courtyard, just a few steps from the pool, sets the tone for the place, as it seems to encourage guests to mingle, have a drink and get comfortable. The hotel is within a few blocks of the French Market and Jackson Square but sits on a quiet corner of Chartres. The rooms are comfortable, if not fancy, and are decked out in vaguely Victorian fabrics and accessories. It's a lovely old building, so many rooms have exposed brick and beams.

Hotel services *Bar. Concierge. Parking (free). Swimming pool.* **Room services** *Dataport. Hairdryer. Iron. Radio. TV: cable.*

Cornstalk Hotel

915 Royal Street, at St Philip Street, New Orleans, LA 70116 (523 1515/fax 522 5558/www.travel guides.com/bb/cornstalk). Bus 3 Vieux Carré. **Rates** (incl continental breakfast) $75-$185. **Credit** AmEx, MC, V. **Map** p282 C2.

The hotel is named after its famous fence, an ornate ironwork one with yellow ears of corn popping out of thick, dark-green stalks. The hotel is equally

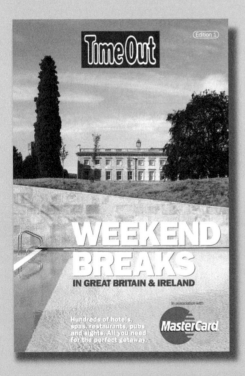

idiosyncratic, with 14 guest rooms shoehorned into an 1840s house. Some are comically small, especially for two people, but all have private baths and are well appointed with antiques. The hotel has a spacious porch overlooking Royal Street, and has the relaxed ambience of a family home.
Hotel services *Concierge. Parking (limited).* **Room services** *Dataport. Hairdryer. Iron. TV: cable.*

Hotel St Marie

827 Toulouse Street, at Bourbon Street, New Orleans, LA 70112 (561 8951/1-800 366 2743/fax 571 2802/www.hotelstmarie.com). Bus 3 Vieux Carré. **Rates** $69-$199 single/double; $129-$279 suite. **Credit** AmEx, DC, Disc, MC, V. **Map** p282 B2.
The St Marie, like its sister hotels the Prince Conti and the Place d'Armes, is a quiet, mild-mannered place which has built up a solid reputation for comfort and service at reasonable rates. With 100 rooms and six suites, it has all the Quarter requisites: tropical courtyard, swimming pool, balconies. The rooms are more furnished than decorated, but they're more than adequate for visitors who don't plan to do much more here than sleep. The rooms facing the courtyard are sunnier and quieter than those overlooking Toulouse Street.
Hotel services *Bar. Business services. Disabled: adapted rooms (3). Laundry. Parking (valet, $20 per night). Restaurant. Swimming pool.* **Room services** *Dataport. Hairdryer. Iron. Room service (7am-11pm). TV: cable.*

Hotel Villa Convento

616 Ursulines Street, at Chartres Street, New Orleans, LA 70116 (522 1793/fax 524 1902/www.villaconvento.com). Bus 3 Vieux Carré. **Rates** (incl continental breakfast) $99-$125 single/double; $109-$175 suite. **Credit** AmEx, Disc, MC, V. **Map** p282 C2.
The Villa Convento is exactly what good small inns used to be: a family-run place that offers clean, comfortable rooms at a modest price, run by a group of friendly, helpful people. The Campo family has owned the hotel since 1981, and they still imbue it with their knowledge and enthusiasm. It has the feel of an old-fashioned boarding house, with long hallways and staircases leading off in several directions (in the 1960s, it was a rooming house, and singer Jimmy Buffett was a resident). Some of the rooms on the upper floors have balconies with views of the Quarter, and these are the best spots. The hotel does not allow children over 10.
Hotel services *Courtyard. Free local calls.* **Room services** *TV: cable.*

Place d'Armes

625 St Ann Street, at Chartres Street, New Orleans, LA 70116 (524 4531/1-800 366 2743/fax 571 3803/www.placedarmes.com). Bus 3 Vieux Carré. **Rates** (incl continental breakfast) $69-$219. **Credit** AmEx, DC, Disc, MC, V. **Map** p282 C2.
This unpretentious hotel is the closest you can get to Jackson Square – just a few steps from the heart of the Quarter. It doesn't have a strong personality,

but with its location it doesn't need one. Inside are attractive, clean rooms, a lovely, spacious courtyard and a tiny stab at a swimming pool. It might not be dazzling, but this is still one of the best values in the city, if only for its excellent location.
Hotel services *Concierge. Parking (valet, $20). Swimming pool.* **Room services** *Dataport. Hairdryer. Iron. TV: cable.*

Ursuline Guest House

708 Ursulines Street, at Royal Street, New Orleans, LA 70116 (525 8509/1-800 654 2351/fax 525 8408). Bus 3 Vieux Carré. **Rates** (incl continental breakfast) $85-$125 single/double. **Credit** AmEx, MC, V. **Map** p282 C2.
There are only 13 rooms in this adults-only hotel in a quiet stretch of the French Quarter. Most of the rooms open on to the pleasant courtyard, where the spa bath purrs softly behind the greenery. The dark, quiet rooms are good places to recover from one too many drinks and a bit too much dancing. Or you could opt for some hair of the dog, as complimentary drinks are served to guests each evening. It has a large gay clientele, but straight couples enjoy its easygoing, child-free atmosphere too.
Hotel services *Disabled: adapted rooms (2). Jacuzzi. No-smoking rooms. Parking (limited).* **Room services** *TV: cable.*

Faubourg Marigny & Bywater

High-end

Claiborne Mansion

2111 Dauphine Street, between Frenchmen Street & Elysian Fields Avenue, New Orleans, LA 70116 (949 7327/fax 949 0388/www.claibornemansion.com). Bus 3 Vieux Carré, 5 Marigny/Bywater, 48 Esplanade. **Rates** (incl continental breakfast) $112 single/double; $300 suite. **Credit** AmEx, MC, V. **Map** p277 G6.
From the outside, the Claiborne Mansion still looks like the private estate it was for more than 100 years. The neo-classical townhouse was built in the 1850s by the son of the first American governor of Louisiana, William CC Claiborne. Besides the main house, the inn includes a cottage (favoured by actress Sandra Bullock) and an extensive garden. The rooms have been intelligently re-imagined as a contemporary version of antebellum luxury, with rich fabrics, curtained beds and spacious marble baths. The location is ideal, across the street from Washington Square Park and a block from the music clubs, bars and restaurants of Frenchmen Street. Owner Cleo Pelleteri, a New Orleans native, offers sound advice on how to negotiate the city.
Hotel services *Concierge. Laundry (valet). No-smoking rooms. Parking (limited). Pets (some) allowed. Swimming pool.* **Room services** *Dataport. Hairdryer. Iron. Turndown. TV: cable/VCR. Voicemail.*

Elysian Fields Inn

930 Elysian Fields Avenue, at Burgundy Street, New Orleans, LA 70117 (948 9420/1-866 948 9420/fax 948 0053/www.elysianfieldsinn.com). Bus 3 Vieux Carré, 5 Marigny/Bywater. **Rates** (incl continental breakfast) $95-$175 single/double. **Credit** AmEx, Disc, MC. **Map** p277 G6.

Strategically placed between two of the city's most popular gay bars, Kim's 940 and The Phoenix (for both, *see p198*), the new Elysian Fields Inn is a comfortable place for all travellers. It was to Elysian Fields that Blanche Dubois was directed to when she took the streetcar named Desire; these days, the No.82 bus will have to suffice. Unusually for a B&B, this inn is accessible for the disabled.

Hotel services *Concierge. Disabled: fully accessible. Full kitchen (self-service). Computer with online access. No-smoking rooms. Parking (free).* **Room services** *CD player. Dataport. Iron. Turndown. TV: cable/DVD/VCR. Voicemail & free local calls.*

The Frenchmen Hotel

417 Frenchmen Street, at Decatur Street, New Orleans, LA 70116 (948 2166/1-800 831 1781/fax 948 2258/www.frenchmenhotel.com). Riverfront Streetcar/bus 3 Vieux Carré, 5 Marigny/Bywater. **Rates** (incl continental breakfast) $59-$109 single/double; $89-$199 suite. **Credit** AmEx, Disc, MC, V. **Map** p282 D3.

One of the few hotels in Marigny's B&B-land, this is a sleepy, old-fashioned kind of place in a fabulous location – just across the street from the French Quarter and right on the doorstep of Frenchmen Street. The hotel encompasses two 19th-century townhouses connected by a green and shady courtyard with a tiny swimming pool. Rooms are not spectacular, but are unfussy and utilitarian.

Hotel services *Jacuzzi. No-smoking rooms. Parking (limited, free). Swimming pool.* **Room services** *Dataport. Hairdryer. Iron. TV: cable.*

Royal Street Courtyard

2438 Royal Street, at Spain Street, New Orleans, LA 70117 (943 6818/1-888 846 4004/fax 945 1212/email Royalctyd@aol.com). Bus 3 Vieux Carré, 5 Marigny/Bywater. **Rates** (incl continental breakfast) $55-135 single/double. **Credit** Disc, MC, V. **Map** p277 H6.

Among guests at this B&B, the inviting veranda is the most popular spot, even more so than the leafy walled courtyard. On the front porch, big, comfortable rocking chairs look out on to Royal Street, where it seems as if most of the city's colourful characters must pass by sooner or later. The 1844 Italianate villa has only nine rooms, and all are furnished with brass beds, four-posters, armoires, local art and decorated in soft colours. There are some minor drawbacks – some private baths are across the hall from their rooms, and there's a steep staircase – but these are more than equalled by the location, five minutes' walk from Frenchmen Street and the Quarter. No children under 16 are allowed.

Hotel services *Jacuzzi. No-smoking rooms.* **Room services** *TV: cable/VCR.*

Sun Oak Bed & Breakfast

2020 Burgundy Street, at Frenchmen Street, New Orleans, LA 70116 (tel/fax 945 0322/ www.sunoaknola.com). Bus 3 Vieux Carré, 55 Elysian Fields. **Rates** (incl continental breakfast) $75-$200 single/double (2-night minimum). **No credit cards. Map** p277 G6.

When the term 'Creole' came into vogue a few years ago, almost everything in New Orleans was renamed Creole something-or-other. Architecture professor Eugene Cizek and artist Lloyd Sensat know the difference between the bandwagon and the genuine, and they're happy to share the knowledge along with their meticulously restored Creole cottage. There are only two guest rooms (each with a private bath) in the small compound, which also includes two lush hidden gardens. Cizek and Sensat have used antiques and historic mementoes to great effect throughout the building.

Hotel services *Cooking facilities. Garden. No-smoking rooms. Parking (free).* **Room services** *Iron. TV.*

Budget

Mazant Guesthouse

906 Mazant Street, at Burgundy Street, New Orleans, LA 70117 (944 2662). Bus 5 Marigny/Bywater. **Rates** $29-$44 single/double. **No credit cards.**

When Americans who stay here call the laid-back Mazant 'European', they don't really mean it in an entirely complimentary sense. The rambling, two-storey house is a warren of odd-sized rooms and shared bathrooms, and few attempts have been made to disguise its shabbiness. It has the feel of a 1960s communal house (albeit a cheerfully amiable one). Guests like to gather in the downstairs parlour/dining room/kitchen and on the upstairs balcony, swapping stories and trading drinking tips. If you're visiting during hot weather, be advised that only the bedrooms are air-conditioned. Five of the 11 rooms have private baths; none have phones.

Hotel services *Garden. Kitchen. No-smoking rooms. Parking (free). Payphone.* **Room services** *TV: cable.*

CBD & Warehouse District

Deluxe

Fairmont Hotel

123 Baronne Street, at Canal Street, New Orleans, LA 70112 (529 7111/1-800 441 1414/fax 529 4775/www.fairmont.com). St Charles or Canal Streetcar/bus 3 Vieux Carré. **Rates** High season $175-$335 single/double. Low season $120-$260 single/double. **Credit** AmEx, DC, Disc, MC, V. **Map** p282 A1.

Once New Orleans' reigning grand hotel, the Fairmont remains outstanding, although it has been eclipsed over the years by more modern competitors.

The boutique clique

With designers' names stamped all over them, the city's three boutique hotels are the most un-New Orleans of New Orleans hotels. **International House**, **Loft 523** and the **W** all exude a kind of sophistication the rest of the city neither has nor covets. They create a strange, almost uncomfortable juxtaposition of New York style in a European city in the deep South. Locals view them with a combination of amusement, bemusement and a touch of envy. The younger generation of the chattering classes hang out in their stunningly trendy bars – and each hotel has one – with their holidaying Northern counterparts, as if hoping that some of that Yankee attitude will rub off on them. But others tend to avoid these bars like the plague. 'Trying too hard,' they sneer.

There is no question that these hotels divide people like few others in the city. Some love them; some hate them. And, frankly, they're not for everybody. The **W** (see p48) is the kind of place where the big bookshelves in the designed-to-death lobby are filled with tomes – all wrapped in blank paper covers. Who cares what the titles are or who wrote them? They're just part of the look. But the rooms are plush, its Whiskey Blue bar is famous, and the gorgeous rooftop pool has real grass and stepping stones.

Loft 523 (see p47), the most recent addition to the boutique clique, is in a converted parking garage downtown, and it takes the design ethos to the point of no return. The rooms have cold concrete floors, chilly painted brick walls and furniture so minimal it's almost invisible. This is serial killer chic. Even the guests are minimalised; with just 18 rooms, spread over multiple floors, it's possible to spend days here without seeing anyone but the desk clerk.

The nameless bar on the ground floor is the ultimate in design-above-everything, with glass masks on the wall glowing in different colours which change so subtly you almost wonder if you've imagined it.

Around the corner, **International House** (pictured), owned and run by the same people as Loft 523, has the warmest ambience of the three (see p47). It's decorated in creamy fabrics and muted colours throughout, and it has charming traditions like changing to 'summer dress' in the late spring – overnight, all the furnishings are covered in clean white

linen, light fixtures are altered and everything changed ever so slightly. Guests go to bed in one hotel and wake in another. Similarly, the bar, Loa (which is named after a voodoo goddess), is the least pretentious of the boutique bars, though it still admires its own cheekbones (see p142).

In the end, not all boutique hotels are made the same. While there's an element of snobbery to all of them, some are less cliquey than others. But all promise (and deliver) things like added staff attention, special touches (pricey bath products, Egyptian cotton sheets, thick bathrobes) and a beautiful, unusual look. Whether they're worth the money is up to you.

Coldly beautiful,
Loft 523. See p47.

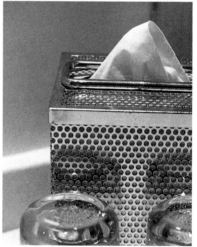

Many regulars have a soft spot for the place they still call 'The Roosevelt' (its name in its glory years). A favourite of raffish ex-governor Huey Long, it was the model for Arthur Hailey's great pulp novel *Hotel*. It dates from 1893, and no modern hotel – boutique or otherwise – can begin to think about equaling its grandeur. Its long, sweeping lobby is one of the city's true wonders, and it stretches all the way from University Place to Baronne Street. The Fairmont has some of the problems you'll find in many historic hotels – some sections seem to be under con-

stant renovation, and some of the rooms can be on the small side, but one cocktail in the Sazerac Bar (*see p142*), one of the world's great watering holes, and you'll forget to complain.

Hotel services Bar. Beauty salon. Business services. Concierge. Disabled: adapted rooms. Gym. Laundry. No-smoking floors. Parking (valet). Restaurants. Swimming pool. Tennis courts. *Room services* Dataport. Fax (some rooms). Iron. Minibar. Phone lines (multiple). Room service (24hrs). Turndown. TV: cable. Voicemail.

International House

221 Camp Street, at Gravier Street, New Orleans,
LA 70130 (553 9550/1-800 633 5770/fax 200
6532/www.ihhotel.com). Bus 3 Vieux Carré,
11 Magazine. **Rates** $89-$319 single/double.
Credit AmEx, DC, Disc, MC, V. **Map** p279 C1.
When it opened in 1999, this was the only boutique
hotel in New Orleans. The brainchild of *wunderkind*
developer Sean Cummings, it brought the concept
of sophisticated hotels to a city that desperately
needed them. With creamy colours, clean lines and
not a frill to be seen, it's a calming, modern,
California kind of a place (the check-in staff have
names like 'Sunshine' – we kid you not). The best
trendy bar (if there is such a thing) in town, Loa (*see
p142*) is just off the lobby and brings in the trust-
fund crowd nightly. Rooms are large and simply
designed, with CD players, wide windows, deep
bathtubs and Aveda products lined up invitingly
alongside brushed-steel sinks. Not too cool to be
welcoming, this place hits just the right note.
Hotel services *Bar. Concierge. Disabled: adapted
rooms. Gym. Laundry (valet). No-smoking rooms.
Parking ($25). Restaurant.* **Room services** *CD
player. Dataport. Iron. Minibar. Room service
(6am-11pm). Turndown. TV: cable.*

Loft 523

*523 Gravier Street, between Camp & Magazine
streets, New Orleans, LA 70130 (200 6523/1-800
633 5770/fax 200 6532/www.loft523.com). Bus 3
Vieux Carré, 11 Magazine.* **Rates** $249-549
single/double. **Credit** AmEx, DC, Disc, MC, V.
Map p279 C1.
When he opened this ultra-boutique hotel in 2002,
Sean Cummings went as minimalist as you can go
without eliminating furniture altogether. Around the
corner from International House, this place has all
the warmth and charm of the parking garage it once
was: concrete floors, big bare pillars and stark spot-
lighting conspire to create a chilly mood. The 18 big,
empty rooms are dominated by large televisions and
CD players. The bathrooms are fabulous, with
Italian marble bathtubs, open showers with multiple shower heads and Aveda products; the stacks of
white towels provide the only soft touch in the building. The walls seem soundproofed to the point where
nobody can hear you scream. Designed within an
inch of its life, this place will appeal to a certain segment of the hotel population. You know who you are.
Hotel services *Bar. Concierge. Disabled: adapted
rooms. Laundry (valet). No-smoking rooms. Parking
($25).* **Room services** *CD player. Iron. Minibar.
Room service (6am-11pm). Turndown. TV: cable.*

High-end

Le Cirque Hotel

*2 Lee Circle, at St Charles Avenue, New Orleans,
LA 70130 (962 0900/1-888 487 8782/fax 962
0901/www.hotellecirque.com). St Charles Streetcar.*
Rates $59-$299. **Credit** AmEx, DC, Disc, MC, V.
Map p279 B2.

Lee Circle is a stripped-down urban space with a
dark past that's been lost to changing times, and
nothing symbolises its evolving identity as much as
this sleek hotel, whose curved, modern façade vies
with the statue of General Robert E Lee as the
circle's dominant element. Le Cirque is at the edge
of the trendy Warehouse District and close to a number of museums, including the dynamic new Ogden
Museum of Southern Art. The rooms have a
contemporary look, and many have enormous baths.
The well-regarded Lee Circle Restaurant takes up
most of the ground floor, while nearby the brilliant
Circle Bar makes a de facto hotel bar (*see p141*).
Hotel services *Bar. Business services. Concierge.
Disabled: adapted rooms. Laundry (valet). No-
smoking rooms. Parking (valet). Restaurant.*
Room services *Dataport. Hairdryer. Iron. Minibar.
Room service (7am-11pm). Safe. Turndown. TV:
cable/VCR.*

Hotel Monaco

*333 St Charles Avenue, at Poydras Street, New
Orleans, LA 70130 (561 0010/1-866 561 0010/
fax 561 0036/www.monaco-neworleans.com).
St Charles Streetcar.* **Rates** $150-$355 single/
double; $355-$1,800 suite. **Credit** AmEx, DC, Disc,
MC, V. **Map** p279 C1.
The Egyptian theme here has nothing to do with
New Orleans, but its over-the-top implementation is
pure Big Easy. This 1926 high-rise began life as a
Masonic temple that also contained office space.
Then, in 2001 the Monaco group (part of the San
Francisco-based Kimpton boutique chain) spent $34
million turning it into a hotel. The entrance is a swirl
of romance and colour, with an elaborately tiled
barrel-vaulted ceiling. The lobby is all but hidden
behind diaphanous, tent-like drapes and African art.
Guest rooms echo the sheik-on-the-bayou theme,
with raffia headboards, boldly striped patterns, rustic lamps and plush chairs. The early evening drinks
party in the lobby is always well attended; even non-
guests try to slip in for the fun. The restaurant,
Cobalt, is as famous for its classic American food as
for its hot bar scene (*see p119*).
Hotel services *Bar. Business services. Concierge.
Gym. Laundry. No-smoking rooms. Parking (valet).
Restaurant. Safe. Pets allowed ($50 deposit).* **Room
services** *Dataport. Iron. Minibar. Phone lines
(multiple). Room service (24hrs). TV: cable/VCR.
Voicemail.*

Le Pavilion Hotel

*833 Poydras Street, at Baronne Street, New Orleans,
LA 70112 (581 3111/1-800 535 9095/fax 522
5543/www.lepavilion.com). St Charles Streetcar.*
Rates $119-$475 single/double; $400-$1695 suite.
Credit AmEx, DC, Disc, MC, V. **Map** p279 B1.
Le Pavilion carries on the tradition of the grand
hotel, despite guests who insist on wearing T-shirts
and tank tops in the sumptuous lobby, which is,
itself, something of a local landmark: brides pay
steep fees just to be photographed here, regardless
of where their weddings were actually held. Almost
a block long, it has masses of gilt, marble, flowers

The **Hotel Monaco** – it's more exotic than it looks. *See p47.*

and chandeliers the size of ponies. Single guest rooms can be on the small side, but almost all are furnished with antiques and art. Evenings are enlivened by one of the city's most whimsical hotel traditions: a late-night buffet of peanut butter-and-jam sandwiches is wheeled out on silver platters, accompanied by pitchers of cold milk. The restaurant, the Crystal Room, is an overlooked gem. The glam rooftop swimming pool is another treat.
Hotel services *Bar. Business services. Concierge. Gym. Disabled: adapted rooms (4). Laundry. No-smoking rooms. Parking (valet, $25). Restaurants. Swimming pool.* **Room services** *Dataport. Iron. Minibar. Room service (24hrs). Turndown. TV: cable.*

St James Hotel
330 Magazine Street, at Gravier Street, New Orleans, LA 70130 (304 4000/1-800 273 1889/ fax 304 4444/www.decaturhotels.com). Bus 11 Magazine. **Rates** $59-$499 single/double.
Credit AmEx, Disc, DC, MC, V. **Map** p279 C1.
The St James is famous as the home of Cuvee (*see p119*), one of the city's new wave of haute cuisine restaurants. Guests at the hotel get a leg-up on reservations, which is no small perk. This fairly new hotel is housed in a 19th-century building. It's located in the CBD, where most things go quiet after 5pm, but several restaurants are within walking distance, and the hotel has easy access to public transport. This is a good base for business travellers.
Hotel services *Business services. Disabled: adapted room (1). Gym. No-smoking rooms. Parking (valet). Restaurant. Swimming pool.* **Room services** *Dataport. Hairdryer. Iron. TV: cable.*

W Hotel
333 Poydras Street, at S Peters Street, New Orleans, LA 70130 (525 9444/1-800 622 5953/fax 581 7179/www.whotels.com). Bus 3 Vieux Carré, 10 Tchoupitoulas. **Rates** $129-$350 single/double; $250-$800 suite. **Credit** AmEx, DC, MC, V. **Map** p279 C1.

Urbane, attractive and oh-so-trendy, the W is like a little piece of Manhattan in downtown New Orleans. The lobby is a hipster's Disneyland, with a 'hidden' Martini bar, the ridiculously cosmopolitan Whiskey Blue bar (*see p142*), Asian-inspired floral statements, a library of books carefully wrapped in blank jackets, and plenty of seating. Up above, the rooftop pool has a real lawn, stepping stones and private cabanas equipped for laptops and phones. The service is some of the best in the city, but the attitude factor is high as well. Rooms are lovely, and the beds as comfortable as they're rumoured to be.
Hotel services *Bar. Concierge. Disabled: adapted rooms. Fitness centre. Laundry. No-smoking rooms. Parking (valet). Restaurant. Spa. Swimming pool.*
Room services *Dataport. Iron. Minibar. Room service. Safe. Turndown. TV: cable/VCR. Voicemail.*

Garden District & Uptown

High-end

Hubbard Mansion
3535 St Charles Avenue, between Delachaise & Foucher streets, New Orleans, LA 70115 (897 3535/fax 899 8827/www.hubbardmansion.com). St Charles Streetcar. **Rates** (incl continental breakfast) $129-$200 single/double; $235 suite.
Credit AmEx, Disc, MC, V. **Map** pp276-7 D/E9.
Most people never realise this imposing Greek Revival-style building is actually a 21st-century addition to St Charles Avenue. Sitting majestically behind an ironwork fence, Rose and Don Hubbard's two-storey columned house blends in perfectly. Private rooms open on to a central hallway which ends at the elegant dining room. The house is furnished with 19th-century antiques, most of them unearthed somewhere in Louisiana. This place is ideal for Mardi Gras, as most of the major parades pass right outside. The Hubbards are an African-

American couple who were major players in New Orleans' legendary political scene, so they have more than a few stories to tell about the city.
Hotel services Disabled: adapted rooms. Laundry (self-service). No-smoking rooms. Parking ($12).
Room services Dataport. Hairdryer. Iron. Jacuzzi bath. TV: cable/VCR.

McKendrick-Breaux House Bed & Breakfast

1474 Magazine Street, at Race Street, New Orleans, LA 70130 (586 1700/1-888 570 1700/fax 522 7138/www.mckendrick-breaux.com). Bus 11 Magazine. **Rates** (incl continental breakfast) $145-$195 single/double. **Credit** AmEx, MC, V. **Map** p279 B3.
The main rooms of the McKendrick-Breaux House are splendid compositions rich in texture, colour and history. The interior of this 1860 Greek Revival townhouse has been carefully restored. Special touches can be found throughout, from the cut flowers and huge, claw-footed bathtubs down to the pretty garden. Owner Eddie Breaux, a passionate preservationist, lives on-site and is happy to talk about how he rescued the house from the wrecking ball. The B&B is on an up-and-coming section of Magazine Street fairly close to downtown and a short bus ride from the shopping further along. Guests should take a taxi or drive at night.
Hotel services Courtyard. Jacuzzi. Laundry. No-smoking rooms. Parking (free). **Room services** *Dataport. Hairdryer. Iron. TV: cable. Voicemail.*

Mid-range

Avenue Plaza Hotel

2111 St Charles Avenue, at Jackson Street, New Orleans, LA 70130 (566 1212/1-800 535 9575/fax 525 6899/www.avenueplazahotel.com). St Charles Streetcar. **Rates** $109-$299 suite. **Credit** AmEx, DC, MC, V. **Map** p279 B3.
Locals know all about this hotel's excellent Mackie Shilstone Pro Spa (*see p226*), and its clientele, mostly business travellers, are drawn partly by the fact that they can join in the action at the plush gym whenever they wish. Each of the 256 suites features a full (if small) kitchen; a 'junior suite' is basically really a big room with kitchen alcove and bathroom. If you're on the road a lot and fancy boiling your own egg after a good workout, this place could be for you.
Hotel services Babysitting. Bar. Beauty salon. Business services. Café. Concierge. Disabled: adapted rooms. Gym. Jacuzzi. Laundry. No-smoking floors. Parking (valet). Spa. Swimming pool. **Room services** *Kitchenette. TV: cable. Voicemail.*

The Chimes Bed & Breakfast

1146 Constantinople Street, at Coliseum Street, New Orleans, LA 70115 (488 4640/1-800 729 4640/fax 488 4639/www.chimesbandb.com). St Charles Streetcar/bus 11 Magazine. **Rates** (incl breakfast) $89-$135 suite. **Credit** AmEx, MC, V. **Map** p276 D9.
Jill Abbyad runs the Chimes like an extension of her family home, serving up a delicious breakfast,

encouraging questions and generally pampering her guests. A stay at this casually stylish Uptown pad is like a visit with old friends. Jill, her husband, Charles, and their two children live in the main house, across a brick courtyard from the five guest suites. The house is a short walk from St Charles Avenue and Magazine Street and provides a restful retreat from the frantic fun of the city. All rooms have private baths and phones.
Hotel services Courtyard. No smoking. **Room Services** *Dataport. Hairdryer. Iron. Turndown (on request). TV: cable/VCR. Voicemail.*

Columns Hotel

3811 St Charles Avenue, between Peniston & General Taylor streets, New Orleans, LA 70115 (899 9308/1-800 445 9308/fax 899 8170/www.thecolumns.com). St Charles Streetcar. **Rates** (incl breakfast) $110-$180 single/double. **Credit** AmEx, MC, V. **Map** p276 D9.
You might recognise this place – every film made in New Orleans seems to have a scene on its spacious veranda overlooking St Charles Avenue. In the film *Pretty Baby*, the 1883 Italianate mansion did duty as Brooke Shields' and Susan Sarandon's bordello home. But it's not just the celeb credentials that make this hotel a favourite with guests. Couples seeking romance love its 19th-century elegance, stained glass, sweeping staircases and glowing mahogany woodwork. Rooms come in various sizes, and most are furnished with 19th-century pieces. Six have shared bathrooms.
Hotel services Bar. Library. No-smoking rooms. Restaurant. TV room. **Room services** *Newspaper. TV (2).*

Hampton Inn Garden District

3626 St Charles Avenue, at Foucher Street, New Orleans, LA 70115 (899 9990/1-800 426 7866/fax 899 9908/www.hamptoninn.com). St Charles Streetcar. **Rates** (incl continental breakfast) $99-$159 single/double; $139-$250 suite. **Credit** AmEx, DC, MC, V. **Map** p276 D9.
If you're looking for a modern hotel in the Garden District, this chain hotel isn't a bad bet. It's sensitively designed to fit into the landscape, with all the amenities many older hotels lack inside. It was built to be virtually barrier-free, and parking has also been given consideration. Guest rooms are impersonal but comfortable. A narrow lap pool is wedged into a small but appealing courtyard.
Hotel services Disabled: adapted rooms (5). Free local calls. No-smoking rooms. Parking. Swimming pool. **Room services** *TV: cable. Voicemail.*

Budget

Marquette House

2253 Carondelet Street, at Jackson Avenue, New Orleans, LA 70130 (523 3014/fax 529 5933/email: HINeworlns@aol.com). St Charles Streetcar. **Rates** *Dormitory* $17 members; $20 non-members. *Apartments* $50 members; $53 non-members. **Credit** MC, V. **Map** p279 B3.

McKendrick-Breaux House.
See p49.

This is New Orleans' oldest and most popular hostel, and the nearest thing to a wholesome youth centre that can be found in the city. It's a compound of dormitory buildings and apartments, the latter representing some of the most outstanding value accommodation in town. Housed in a two-storey plantation-style building, the apartments feature kitchenettes, several beds and sitting areas. There are plenty of backpackers here, but a good many of the regular guests are greying baby boomers taking advantage of the bargain. The atmosphere is generally friendly, but mutterings are sometimes heard that staff can be less than accommodating. *Hotel services Computer with internet. Cooking facilities. Locker storage. No-smoking dormitories. Parking ($5). Payphone.* **Room services** *Kitchenettes (apartments only). No phone (dormitories).*

Old World Inn

1330 Prytania Street, at Thalia Street, New Orleans, LA 70130 (566 1330/fax 566 1074/ www.oldworldinn.com). St Charles Streetcar. **Rates** $55-$95 single/double. **Credit** Disc, MC, V. **Map** p279 B2.

This charmingly shabby inn in the Lower Garden District is friendly, low-key and low-tech. The inn's long-time owners sold it in 2003, but it has remained essentially the same, with eclectic antique furnishings and a determinedly old-world attitude. There are no telephones, TVs or radios in the basic but pleasant rooms. Guests will even find it difficult to get permission to plug in hairdryers or other electrical equipment for fear of overloading the 100-year-old building's stretched resources. It's altogether a very pleasant place; without all that electronica, its quiet, and guests gather in the evening in the sitting room to talk over cocktails or coffee. Given the handy location, it is one of the city's best bargains. One break in the old-world ambience: no smoking is allowed anywhere in the hotel. *Hotel services No-smoking rooms. Restaurant.* **Room services** *No phone.*

St Charles Guesthouse

1748 Prytania Street, between Felicity & Polymnia streets, New Orleans, LA 70130 (523 6556/fax 522 6340/www.stcharlesguesthouse.com). St Charles Streetcar. **Rates** (incl continental breakfast) $35 backpacker room; $45-$65 double with shared bath; $65-$95 double with private bath. **Credit** AmEx, MC, V. **Map** p279 B2.

Sure, it's not actually on St Charles Avenue, but that just makes Denis Hilton's rambling guesthouse more of a find. Rates are modest, rooms are comfortable and the atmosphere is genuinely friendly. The soft-spoken Hilton is a steady and welcome presence, chatting with guests, taking detailed phone messages and quietly making arrangements for any special needs. His philosophy is that guests are here to see New Orleans, not to watch television or keep up with the office, so there are no telephones or TVs in the rooms. (He does, however, make arrangements for plugging laptops into a phone line). Europeans return year after year, often starting out as students in the clean but spartan backpacker rooms and moving up as they can afford it to rooms with creature comforts like double beds, old-fashioned tiled bathrooms and air-conditioning. A courtyard pool keeps things cool, and there's a barbecue grill. Highly recommended. *Hotel services Fax machine. Library. No-smoking rooms. Payphone. Swimming pool.* **Room services** *No air-conditioning (backpacker rooms). No phone.*

St Charles Inn

3636 St Charles Avenue, at Foucher Street, New Orleans, LA 70115 (899 8888/1-800 489 9908/fax 899 9908/www.stcharlesinn.com). St Charles Streetcar. **Rates** (incl continental breakfast) $75 single; $100 double. **Credit** AmEx, DC, Disc, MC, V. **Map** p276 D9.

On beautiful St Charles Avenue, this hotel is an ugly duckling among the swans. But with great rates and clean rooms, who cares about looks? Situated right on the streetcar line, it's a throwback to the big-box hotels of the 1970s, without the frills. There's a restaurant downstairs, the plain rooms offer sturdy beds and furniture and clean tiled bathrooms, and there's ample parking. Basically, this is a handy place to sleep, change clothes and store your stuff. **Hotel services** *Bar. Café. Disabled: adapted room. No-smoking rooms. Parking (free).* **Room services** *Dataport. Hairdryer. Iron. TV: cable.*

St Vincent's Guesthouse

1507 Magazine Street, at Race Street, New Orleans, LA 70130 (566 1515/fax 566 1518/ www.stvincentsguesthouse.com). Bus 11 Magazine. **Rates** (incl breakfast) $59-$89. **Credit** AmEx, DC, Disc, MC, V. **Map** p279 B3.

This former Catholic orphanage's rows of small rooms are ideal for budget travellers and backpackers. The little rooms are simply furnished, but unlike those in hostels, they are equipped with TVs and phones. A courtyard and large swimming pool are two of its best features. It is fully accessible for guests in wheelchairs, with elevators, wide-door bathrooms and exterior ramps. **Hotel services** *Disabled: adapted rooms (2). Elevator. Internet access. No-smoking rooms. Parking (free). Swimming pool.* **Room services** *TV.*

Mid-City

High-end

Degas House Bed & Breakfast

2306 Esplanade Avenue, at North Tonti Street, New Orleans, LA 70119 (821 5009/1-800 755 6730/fax 821 0870/www.degashouse.com). Bus 48 Esplanade. **Rates** (incl continental breakfast) $125-$250 single/double. **Credit** MC, V. **Map** p278 F5.

In 1872-3, the French painter Edgar Degas visited his mother's Creole family, the Mussons, in New Orleans for several months and stayed in this, their 1852 Italianate mansion. Now a B&B – and a sort of mini-shrine to Degas – the house has seven bedrooms on two floors, all with private baths (one has

a Jacuzzi). The rooms are furnished with period pieces, but in a minimalist style; you'll find no cosy clutter here. Prints and reproductions of Degas' work are everywhere in the building. Although the original house was divided into two in the early 20th century, it's still possible to see the rooms Degas used as backdrops for the handful of paintings he completed while in New Orleans. **Hotel services** *Concierge. No-smoking rooms. Parking (free).* **Room services** *Dataport. Hairdryer. Iron. Turndown. TV: cable.*

Mid-range

Cotton Brokers Houses Bed & Breakfast

Benachi House, 2257 Bayou Road, at Esplanade Avenue, New Orleans, LA 70119; Esplanade Villa Bed & Breakfast, 2216 Esplanade Avenue, at Bayou Road, New Orleans, LA 70119 (525 7040/1-800 308 7040/fax 525 9760/www.nolabb.com). Bus 48 Esplanade. **Rates** (incl breakfast) *Benachi House* $105-$125 single/double. *Esplanade Villa* $125-$135 suite. **Credit** AmEx, DC, Disc, MC, V. **Map** p278 F5.

The Benachi is one of the city's most famous antebellum houses; it's rich in history and remarkable for its architecture and interior. With four guest rooms, it's a mini-estate within the city, consisting of a 1858 Greek Revival mansion on a vast, landscaped lot with a carriage house, patio and gazebo. Restoring the house was a labour of love for attorney and preservation expert James Derbes. When he opened it as a B&B, there was so much demand that he turned his skills to an 1880s-era building across Esplanade Avenue. The 1880 Esplanade Villa has five suites, each with a parlour and Victorian bathroom, complete with claw-footed tub. Guests at both breakfast at Benachi. A prime place for Jazz Fest – the Fair Grounds are a five-minute walk away. **Hotel services** *Laundry (self-service). No-smoking rooms. Parking (free).* **Room services** *TV: cable.*

Top five
Bargain hotels

Chateau Hotel
This low-key French Quarter treasure has attentive staff, a great location and a happy vibe for as little as $99. You can stroll to Jackson Square or Bourbon Street in a few minutes, or just stay and mingle at its pleasant open-air bar. *See p41.*

Chimes Bed & Breakfast
This Uptown B&B gives you a fabulous breakfast and a courtyard room for under $100 a night. And the owners make it feel like you're staying with old friends. *See p49.*

Cornstalk Hotel
One of the most famous sights in the Quarter is this old-fashioned guesthouse, where some rooms go for under $100. *See p41.*

Marquette House
Sure, the city's premier hostel has cheap dorm rooms, but the real bargain is the funky apartments at $50 a night. *See p49.*

Mazant House
Rooms start at $29 at this place, which is perfect for those who yearn to live in a 1960s commune. *See p44.*

India House – it beats working.

Budget

India House

124 South Lopez Street, at Canal Street, New Orleans, LA 70119 (821 1904/fax 821 2299/ www.indiahousehostel.com). Canal Streetcar/bus 41 Canal. **Rates** (plus $5 key deposit) $15 dormitory; from $35 double. **Breakfast** $3.50. **Credit** MC, V. **Map** p276-7 D/E6.

People who walk in the door of India House, a loose-limbed hostel in a marginal neighbourhood off Canal Street, have immediate and sharply varied reactions to this colourful place. Either they throw down their backpacks, stretch out on the couch and think, 'I'm home!' or they streak out the door and run screaming to the nearest chain motel. Sure, this shabby but welcoming old house isn't for everyone, but a steady stream of twentysomething backpackers, budget travellers and international tourists fall in love with its communal, hard-partying atmosphere. There are dorm facilities (co-ed and single sex) and modest private cabins. There's a small but pleasant courtyard pool where guests can mingle and share their stories about Nepal and surfing in Indonesia. As you would imagine, group parties are a regular feature here. It can all get very friendly, which can be good or horrible, depending on your own personal point of view. It's all just a little too rowdy for some. Public transport is just around the corner on Canal Street, but visitors should be careful when travelling alone or late at night.

Hotel services *Cooking facilities (24hrs). Laundry. Parking (free). Payphone. Swimming pool. TV room: cable.* **Room services** *No phone.*

Reservation services

There are several reservation services in town that specialise in providing a helping hand in negotiating the city's hotel maze. They charge the hotels and B&Bs for bookings, so travellers get free advice and help. If you need further information and guidance, it's a good idea to contact the **New Orleans Convention and Visitors Bureau** (566 5011).

Bed & Breakfast and Beyond

3115 Napoleon Avenue, at Claiborne Avenue, Uptown, New Orleans, LA 70125 (896 9977/1-800 886 3709/fax 896 2482/www.nolabandb.com). Bus 24 Napoleon. **Open** 8am-10pm daily. **Map** p276 D8.

Maggie Shimon takes pride in her highly personalised service that promises to match travellers to the perfect B&Bs for their holidays. Regular customers swear that her instincts are perfect. She also deals with other visitor requests, including booking tours and special events.

New Orleans Bed & Breakfast and Accommodations

Suite 208, 671 Rosa Avenue, Metairie, LA 70182 (838 0071/1-888 240 0070/www.neworleans bandb.com). **Open** 9am-5pm Mon-Fri.

Owner Sara-Margaret Brown represents more than 200 hosts in the area, and can recommend houses, apartments and condos for travellers who are less interested in staying in hotels, and would rather have the chance to live like locals. Also, because of her extensive offerings, she often has vacancies.

Sightseeing

Introduction	54
The French Quarter & Around	56
Faubourg Marigny & Bywater	69
CBD & the Warehouse District	72
Uptown	77
Tremé & Mid-City	89
Museums	96
Guided Tours	101

Features

Walk this way French Quarter	60
Doing the strip	65
You can always pray	71
The American Sector	75
Audubon Zoo...	78
Getting inside	81
The Irish Channel	82
Walk this way Garden District	84
Taking the Longue Vue	90
Cities of the dead	94
'Southern art' is not an oxymoron	97
A sculptural garden of Eden	99
Nature just around the corner	103

Introduction

Welcome to the City that Care Forgot – you may find it hard to leave.

Most people who visit New Orleans remember their first glimpses of the city from the back of a taxi – through the disappointment of the suburbs to that first sight of the low-slung French Quarter, dark and gloomy at the edge of a bright, modern downtown, looking somehow dangerous and immortal. Looking just as it should. Those who drive into the Quarter remember trying to find the damned thing amid New Orleans' confusing morass of one-way streets, poorly signed interstate exits and skyscraper hotels. When the Quarter finally appears before them, it feels like victory just to have found it at all.

It's no surprise that so many visitors spend virtually all their time within the 20-block-square area of the Quarter, but it's a bit of a shame. For they miss the grand old oaks that arch across St Charles Avenue, as if to protect it from the sun. They miss the vast mansions of the Garden District, which grow younger as you move away from downtown, so that passing through the neighbourhood is like moving through the years. And they miss the shady blocks of Esplanade Avenue leading down to the surprise of the waters of Bayou St John. They miss the rambling cemeteries that stretch for miles through Mid-City, the vast expanse of City Park, and long afternoons spent sipping iced coffee under a pecan tree and watching the world go by.

But, in the end, everybody has their own New Orleans. And whether yours is in the French Quarter, or up in the Riverbend, there is much to experience. Welcome to it. Enjoy your time, however brief, exploring the City that Care Forgot.

FINDING YOUR WAY AROUND

For reasons hard to fathom, New Orleans feels much bigger than it is. In reality, this is a fairly small town. The problem is that it's built into a sharp curve in the Mississippi River, which means that its streets undulate like the river. It is somehow appropriate that getting a sense of direction here is virtually impossible. For example, the 'West Bank' is actually on the east side of the river. There is no north, no south – a compass will not help you. It gives you a fabulous sense of disorientation – if you don't mind that sort of thing – to realise that, quite simply, in New Orleans you never really know where you're going.

Luckily, the locals sorted out a system years ago, whereby all things are pointed out in relation to the one constant with which this town always lives: the Mississippi River. So directions are given as 'towards the river' or 'away from the river'. The river is the easiest thing to find on any map, so if you orient yourself to it and follow those directions, you'll eventually find your way around.

Starting in the **French Quarter**, whose simple grid of streets you'll find the easiest part of town to navigate, and keeping the river to your left, you can easily make your way downtown. **Canal Street** marks the end of the Quarter and the beginning of the **CBD**.

At Canal Street, to add to the confusion, all the French Quarter streets switch over to their 'American' names. Bourbon Street becomes Carondelet, Chartres Street becomes Camp, Royal Street becomes St Charles Avenue. Any of these will take you through the **Lower Garden District**, which is gritty and busy, then to the **Garden District** proper, which is green and leafy and filled with mansions, and then on to **Uptown**, where the mansions give way to Tulane and Loyola universities and the quiet of Audubon Park. **St Charles Avenue**, the most beautiful path to Uptown, ends at the junction with Carrollton Avenue.

Mid-City is just as easy to find. **Esplanade Avenue** demarcates the opposite edge of the Quarter from Canal Street. It runs all the way up to City Park, where it ends at the junction of Carrollton Avenue. Heading left on Carrollton from here will take you in a loop to St Charles Avenue in Uptown, which would, in turn, bring you back to the French Quarter, and deposit you gently on Royal Street.

See? It's easy.

By 2004, the Canal Streetcar will make essentially this same loop easy for the carless, and once that happens it will surely be the best way to travel. Until then, whether by bus, car, streetcar or your own two feet, get moving. After all, you might only be here once, and what if you missed something?

► For more on **getting around New Orleans**, see pp248-51. For **guided tours**, see pp101-4. For information on **safety**, see p258.

The French Quarter & Around

Quite simply one of the most exhilarating neighbourhoods on Earth.

This is it. The be all and end all. The goose that laid the golden egg. This is the New Orleans people already know long before they ever arrive, and the one that 10 million people travel thousands of miles to see each year. It is called the Vieux Carré (or 'Old Square') by almost nobody these days except some pretentious, overpaid artist types with posh flats down near Esplanade Avenue, but that is what the French called it back in their day. 'French Quarter' is a much better name for it anyway. 'French Quarter' implies Moulin Rouge and sexy girls and grifters trying to take your cash, artists and musicians on street corners and no clocks anywhere to tell you how much time you've wasted or how much money or how many brain cells. And that's the whole idea.

There is no first thing most people notice about the Quarter. Instead, they're hit by a sensory overload that sends them staggering to the nearest bar, where they can try to get their bearings. First there's the look of the place – frilly wrought iron that drips and swirls off the big balconies that are bursting with flowers. There are tantalising glimpses of southern outdoor living – of ceiling fans and rocking chairs, of chilled glasses on tiny cocktail tables in shady courtyards glimpsed through metal bars. There are the sun-faded colours of the buildings, with their wooden shutters propped open in the morning then closed against the heat of the afternoon. There's the vivid green of the trees, the bright pinks and reds of the bougainvillaea and petunias. Then there's the noise – the Cajun and zydeco and blues pouring from the open doors of bars and shops; trumpet and guitar played on corners; soulful voices rising from beneath balconies; the N'awlins drawls of the horse-drawn carriage drivers making up stories to entertain their passengers; the rough laughter of the strippers hanging out the doors of the grimy joints on Bourbon Street; and the never-ending tap-tap-tappity-tap from the kids with bottle-caps glued to their shoes tapping for change on every street. But most of all, there are the smells – vats of spicy food and gallons of spilled beer, the sticky sweet smell of cocktails and the sharp tang of boiled crawfish all melding in the musty heat to create an overwhelming scent that is unforgettable.

Yes, this is the French Quarter – one of the world's best-known neighbourhoods. And it's famous for a reason. So get yourself ready for anything, and dive on in.

WHY IT DOESN'T LOOK FRENCH

One thing you might notice right away is that despite its name, the Quarter (as the locals call it) actually has a colonial Spanish look. That's because a great fire destroyed nearly all of the city in 1788, about 20 years after the French had ceded the place to Spain. The Spanish, having seen how quickly the fire spread through the wooden settlement, rebuilt it using wood only for the frames, with brick walls and everything coated in layers of stucco. They chose wrought iron instead of wood for the balconies because wood rots too fast in the suffocating humidity.

GETTING STARTED

The Quarter is a village: its street pattern, thirteen blocks wide and six blocks deep, is just as Adrien de Pauger designed it in 1722, four years after the French established a little settlement in the bend of the Mississippi. Because of that, it's easily walkable and best experienced on foot. If travelling by car, your

> 'They left the party and walked towards the French Market through the brick and cobbled streets. They passed the rows of stucco buildings that had once been the homes of the French and Spanish aristocracy, and which were now gutted and remodeled into bars, whorehouses, tattoo parlors, burlesque theaters, upper-class restaurants, and nightclubs that catered to homosexuals. They could hear the loud music of Bourbon and the noise of the people on the sidewalk and the spielers in front of the bars calling in the tourists who did not know or care who had built the Quarter.'
> James Lee Burke, *Half of Paradise*

Flag-waving the French Quarter way.

first act should be to park in one of the garages on Decatur Street at the Canal Street end of the Quarter. On-street parking is for residents only and towed cars are a major form of income for the city of New Orleans. If you're travelling by streetcar, with a nod to the vagaries of the ongoing construction project (see p21), the line usually ends on Canal Street near Bourbon Street, right at the edge of the Quarter.

Most people start at Canal Street and work their way in. The best part of the Quarter is the centre, with the edges largely residential and devoid of major attractions, so start heading towards the action.

Bourbon Street

For most people, the first stop is the city's best known street. It is not named after the Kentucky whiskey but after the French royal family, although rarely has a name been so inadvertently appropriate. Bourbon Street is a boozy neon-lit parade of wall-to-wall sleaze, with sex shops, strip bars, stores full of tourist tat and takeaway daiquiri stands. Decoration is supplied by pictures of naked women and lighted beer signs. It is smelly, dirty and cacophonous. But, nonetheless, it can be, when you are in the right mood and with the right group of people, a lot of fun.

Most of the sex shops are on the first four blocks, and most are fairly cheesy with a 1950s attitude toward sex. There's **Larry Flynt's Hustler Club** and **Big Daddy's**, which advertises its strippers with a kitschy pair of fishnet-clad plastic legs swinging out of a wall over the pavement.

Beyond the sex strip, things get a little more family-oriented, with pricey tourist trap restaurants (an exception is **Galatoire's**, one of the city's best restaurants; see p111), lots more souvenir shops and bar after bar after bar. Most bars do not have a cover charge, but instead make it up in their drink prices. In some, your first drink will be ruinously expensive, say $15, which incorporates a de facto cover charge, and all subsequent drinks relatively reasonably priced. In general, it's a good idea to ask what the prices are before committing yourself to buying a cocktail, because once you've ordered it, you're paying for it.

Bourbon is closed to traffic every evening, except at the intersections with cross-streets where cars creep cautiously through the crowds of drunks carrying plastic cups of booze on their all-night pub crawls. Bars and stores leave their doors open virtually all of the time, so you can check out a place without going inside. Many of the restaurants and bars lined up along Bourbon Street have touts outside trying to lure

OUR HISTORY LESSONS
— COME WITH A SOUNDTRACK.

Louisiana Purchase
1803 — 2003
BICENTENNIAL

EVERYTHING'S JAZZIER IN LOUISIANA.
Come see what we mean at the Louisiana Purchase Bicentennial
Celebration. Come learn about the greatest real estate deal in
history with special events and exhibits all year long, all across
the state. And, while you're at it, take in a little deep sea fishing, see a Mardi Gras
parade, and decide who makes the best gumbo in the state. For your FREE
Louisiana Tour Guide, visit our Web site or call 1-800-879-4978.

Louisiana
Come As You Are. *Leave Different.*®
www.LouisianaTravel.com

in the passing crowd. While they can be entertaining, to put it mildly, it is generally a good idea not to believe them.

The street has segregated itself along lines of sexual orientation – the first seven blocks (up to Orleans Street) are filled with straight bars, pubs and restaurants, while the next two blocks hold mostly gay venues, including the biggest gay bars in the city: the **Bourbon Pub** and **Oz** (*see pp197-8*). On both sides of the dividing line, though, the zeitgeist is the same – it's all about sex and booze.

Most of the side-streets leading up to Bourbon have the same philosophy. The most festive is St Peter Street, home to **Pat O'Brien's** (*see p139*) famous for its massive and lethal hurricane cocktails (a few kinds of fruit juice and a whole lot of rum). Two doors down is the old **Tabary Theatre** (732 St Peter Street), best known as 'Le Spectacle'. Built in 1791, this was the first Spanish theatre in the US. Just a few steps from here is **Preservation Hall**, with its perennial band of octogenarians playing trad jazz to a reverential crowd. There are no reservations or advance tickets, so the visitors have to queue for the chance to spend a few minutes inside watching the old guys play; most think it's worth the wait (*see also p205*).

Back on Bourbon and beyond the gay sector, the street becomes residential. The mood here is more subdued and, beyond the simple beauty of the overall architecture, there are only a handful of places of any interest to tourists. That said, the best bar on Bourbon Street is down here at No.941, in a building that looks like it's going to tumble down at any moment. **Lafitte's Blacksmith Shop** (*see p137*) will probably outlive all of us, though. The exact date the building was constructed is not known, but it is believed to have been built the decade before the 1788 fire, which would make it one of the oldest Creole cottages in the city. Its name comes from the widespread belief that the building was once home to the family of the pirate, Jean Lafitte, and that the family ran a blacksmithing shop in the front section, while selling his illegally gained booty out of the back. The veracity of this is not known.

North of Bourbon Street

Heading north off Bourbon Street and away from the river, the two streets parallel to Bourbon are Dauphine and Burgundy. While these are perfectly pleasant with some fine hotels and restaurants, they are mostly quiet, residential areas with few sights. Head instead for cross-streets St Louis or Conti. On St Louis Street is the **Hermann-Grima Historic House**, a museum house restored to its full

1830s glory (*see below*). On Conti Street is the spectacularly cheesy **Musée Conti Wax Museum of Louisiana** (*see below*).

After Dauphine and Burgundy, Rampart Street forms the down-at-the-heel border of the French Quarter. Back in the 19th century, this was the beginning of Storyville and of the city's jazz culture. That is all long gone, but in recent years an effort has been made to restore its jazz heritage, and so it is home to two of the city's best jazz bars: the **Funky Butt** and **Donna's Bar & Grill** (*for both, see p202*). These are the places to go if you came here to see local jazz.

Hermann-Grima Historic House

818-20 St Louis Street, between Bourbon & Dauphine Streets (525 5661). Bus 3 Vieux Carré, 57 Franklin. **Open** *Tours* every hour 10am-3.30pm Mon-Fri. **Admission** $6; $5 concessions; free under-8s. **Credit** AmEx, MC, V. **Map** p282 B2. Take from this what you will: the best part of this house museum is its fully working 1830s kitchen. Every Thursday, from October until May, volunteers cook a meal using the tools, foods and methods that would have been available at the time.

Musée Conti Wax Museum of Louisiana

917 Conti Street, at Dauphine Street (525 2605/www.get-waxed.com). Bus 3 Vieux Carré, 57 Franklin. **Open** 10am-5.30pm Mon-Sat; noon-5.30pm Sun. **Admission** $6.75; $5.75 concessions. **Credit** AmEx, MC, V. **Map** p282 B1/2. Somewhat anachronistic, the wax museum comprises a labyrinth of dimly lit hallways bordered by kitsch tableaux played out by waxen mannequins. Opened in 1964, it has a few rather dated displays – including the visit of the Duke and Duchess of Windsor to Mardi Gras in the mid-1950s. But the exhibits have been kept in good shape and part of the fun is stepping back in time to an earlier sensibility. The museum has recently added a display devoted to earlier history, with figures of Napoleon, the pirate Jean Lafitte and the Baroness Pontalba.

Royal Street & around

Running parallel to Bourbon towards the river, Royal Street is a different world. If Bourbon is a street of bars, this is a street of shops. From end to end it is lined with antiques stores gleaming with dark wood and silver, art shops filled with paintings and sculptures, and jewellery stores with everything from fine estate jewellery to cheap glass baubles. There are bars here, but fewer of them, and they tend to be more local.

The elegant nature of Royal Street can be traced back to its 19th-century heritage as the city's banking district. The buildings at Nos.334, 343, 403 and 417 Royal were all once among the biggest banks in the area. The one at No.343 was designed by the great-grandfather

Walk this way French Quarter

Duration 35 minutes or two hours (depending how long you spend in the bar).

The Quarter is so small and easily traversed that you can get very familiar with it in just a long weekend. Still, a good walking plan will get you started and once you know your way around, you can find your own favourite areas to hang out. Here's a quick walking guide to help you explore the architectural highs and Bourbon Street lows that the upper French Quarter has to offer.

Walk into the Quarter on **Bourbon Street** from Canal Street, and make your way through the dark, dank section before it all goes touristy. This is the workaday French Quarter, but it turns, right about the time you pass the venerable Creole restaurant **Galatoire's** (No.209) – the top restaurant of New Orleans society, law and politics – into a red-light district. Here you'll find the palace of nudity that is **Larry Flynt's Hustler Club** at No.225, owned by the titular king of sleaze. From here there's just one porn emporium after another until you reach that great-uncle of local stripping: **Big Daddy's** (No.522). This is a divey burlesque house with plastic legs clad in high heels swinging out of the wall over the pavement.

Lesson in the wonders of breast implants now over, walk past Bourbon's assorted music bars, souvenir shops and tourist restaurants and turn right on St Louis Street.

About a block down on your left is the **Omni Royal Orleans Hotel** (No.621). You can rest a spell in the cool of its grand lobby, or ascend its rooftop bar for a spectacular view of the city. At the intersection of St Louis and Chartres Streets, the fabulously dilapidated building facing you – and out of which you just might hear classical music blaring – is **Napoleon House**, one of the city's best historic bar/restaurants. If you choose to stop here for a Pimm's Cup or to dally over a beer, a po-boy and a cup of gumbo, who could blame you?

When you're ready to move on, turn left on to Chartres, and you'll pass a series of small boutiques and shops on your right, and the arse end of the Omni on your left. Take a quick left on Toulouse Street and wander past its odds and ends to Royal Street, where you should turn right again to see the most beautiful wrought-iron balconies in the city. The building at No.640, near the corner with St Peter is the **Maison LeMonnier**, which has been half-jokingly described as the city's 'first skyscraper', as it was the first to rise to three storeys. It was built in 1811, and you can see where the original owners had their initials, 'YLM', worked into the wrought iron.

Behind the cathedral, you should see a little pedestrian alleyway passing a small green park that contains a large statue of Jesus. This is **Pirates Alley**, and down it you will

of the painter Edgar Degas, whose family was prominent in 19th-century New Orleans, while the structure at 417 Royal Street – now **Brennan's Restaurant** (*see p111*) – was originally the Banque de Louisiane, which is why there is a 'LB' in its wrought-iron railing.

Down the block from Brennan's, at 437 Royal Street, is the site of one of the most significant discoveries ever made in the city – nay, the world. For it was here in the 1790s that a pharmacist named AA Peychaud concocted a mixture he called 'bitters', blended it with cognac and created the first mixed drink. Peychaud created his potion in an egg cup, or *coquetier* in French, and the new drink became known as a 'cocktail' among Americans.

The grand edifice that takes up a solid block across the street from Brennan's is the Louisiana State **Supreme Court Building**, or it will be if the renovation work is ever finished. The building has been empty for the best part of a

decade now, while an achingly slow effort has been underway to convert it into the state's highest court. At some point it may actually be completed. An entire block of Spanish/French buildings was knocked down to build this ode to Victorian grandeur in 1912.

The first eight blocks of Royal Street contain some of the grandest Spanish townhouses and the one at No.533 is a particularly good example. **Merieult House** was built in 1792, and today it is the home of the **Historic New Orleans Collection**, an excellent museum and research centre dedicated to the history of the city (*see p97*). In addition to the museum itself, guided tours are available around the carefully restored upper floors of the house and the courtyard. Or you could skip their entirely and head straight for its gift shop to buy yourself a little present.

Down the street at No.621 is the **President Zachary Taylor House**, where the man who was called 'Old Rough and Ready' for his find the erstwhile home of **William Faulkner**. Here he wrote his first novel, *Soldier's Pay*, in 1925, after coming to New Orleans as a poet. The building, once a French colonial prison, has since been turned into a popular and friendly bookshop dedicated to Faulkner.

Following Pirates Alley to its end brings you into the ruckus of **Jackson Square**, with its mimes, musicians and mentalists. You can get your tarot cards read here or, if that's all hocus-pocus to you, visit one of its historic buildings or just watch the crowds.

Spend as long as you wish among the weirdos and tourists, and wander through its museums, then head directly across the square to Decatur Street, where this walk will end. The canopied café across Decatur from Jackson Square is **Café du Monde**, famed for its *beignets* (heavy fried doughnuts without holes) and *café au lait*. Virtually nothing else is on the menu, but a half hour here, in the shade of the canopy as the breeze wafts off the river, is critical to making any visit to New Orleans complete.

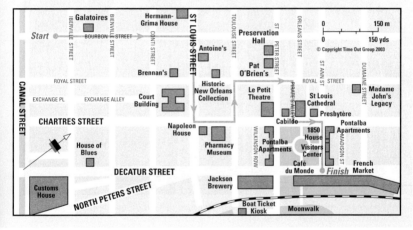

exploits in the Mexican War often stayed with his daughter's family in the 1840s. He was elected US president in 1848.

A few steps off Royal on St Louis Street is **Antoine's Restaurant** with its rabbit warren of dining rooms. One of the city's best-known restaurants, it has been operated by the same family since 1840 (*see p109*).

The wrought-iron balconies along Royal are among the best in the city. One of the prettiest, with its pattern of oak boughs and acorns, is on **Labranche House** at 700 Royal Street at the corner of St Peter. The house was built in 1840, and the distinctive iron decoration was added in 1850. It is now the busy **Royal Café**, which, while very touristy, is not a bad place to have lunch and watch the world go by. This block of Royal Street (between St Peter and Orleans) is particularly colourful and lively, and almost always has bands playing in the street and mimes in impossibly elaborate outfits.

Two blocks further along (towards Esplanade Avenue), the thick, elaborate fence at No.915 is one of the city's rare 'cornstalk fences'. These massive cast-iron creations were outrageously expensive in the 18th and 19th centuries, so were seen as an indication of great wealth.

As you pass along behind **St Louis Cathedral** you'll see a small garden that contains a memorial to those who fell victim to yellow fever in the 18th and 19th centuries. Carried by mosquitoes, it was one of the many deadly diseases that wiped out early residents. This is **St Anthony's Close**, and its main feature is a snowy white statue of a robed Christ with uplifted arms, but this was not always a holy place; it was the city's duelling ground before the church sanctified it.

Between Royal and Bourbon streets on Orleans Street, is the site where the old **Orleans Ballroom** once stood. This is where elegant 19th-century galas were held to introduce

Royal Café: the frilliest of them all
See p61.

wealthy white gentlemen to single women of
colour who could become their de facto wives.
Even though interracial marriage was illegal
at that time, such arrangements were always
common in New Orleans. To get around the law,
the marriage of a white man to a mixed-race
woman was called *plaçage*, and thus their
children were not considered illegitimate. The
ballroom was dubbed the **Quadroon Ballroom**,
and was in steady use until it burned down in
1816. It was rebuilt, and has been carefully
incorporated into the design of the building
that is now the Bourbon Orleans Hotel (717
Orleans Street). Ascend the grand staircase
and you might be able to peer inside.

A few blocks down Royal Street on Dumaine
Street is the drab green structure known as
Madame John's Legacy (632 Dumaine). It's
not much to look at compared to some of its
glitzier neighbours, but its very plainness is its
attraction. The raised Creole cottage dates from
1726, making it one of the oldest buildings in
New Orleans and a rare example of early French
colonial architecture. The house provides a

dramatic example of how the French Quarter
might have looked had fire never destroyed it,
and the Spanish not rebuilt it to their own more
flamboyant tastes (*see p63*).

Down Dumaine from Madame John's Legacy
is the **New Orleans Historic Voodoo
Museum**. The French Quarter has a number
of self-proclaimed 'voodoo stores' and you
can even buy voodoo dolls in souvenir shops,
but this is the real deal in that it is run by
practitioners of voodoo. The people inside
are quite serious about voodoo as a spiritual
belief, and voodoo ceremonies are occasionally
held in the upstairs rooms. It is as educational
as you make it – the more questions you ask,
the more you will learn (*see p63*).

Back on Royal Street, as you head towards
Esplanade Avenue you'll pass two other famous
houses. At No.1132 is **Gallier House** (*see p63*),
built by architect James Gallier Jr as his family
home. Gallier was among the most respected
architects of his time, and the house contains
interesting innovations, including one of the
first indoor plumbing systems in New Orleans.

Two doors down, at the corner of Governor Nicholls Street, is the **Lalaurie House** (1140 Royal Street), the most famous haunted house in the city. The structure was built by Louis McCarty in 1831 and given to his daughter, Marie Delphine McCarty Lalaurie. According to local lore, Madame Lalaurie was a twisted type, who took pleasure in torturing her slaves. Neighbours, it is said, sometimes heard screams and moans coming from the building. Then, on 10 April 1834, a fire broke out and when they arrived to put out the blaze, the fire department found starving, wounded slaves shackled and held in cages. Some, it is said, had even been mutilated in bizarre medical experiments. When word spread, an angry mob besieged the house and Madame Lalaurie was forced to flee the country. It is said that if you walk by the house on a quiet night, you can still hear the ghosts of the slaves crying for help. Understandably, the house is a regular stop on the city's ghost tours.

Gallier House

1132 Royal Street, between Governor Nicholls & Ursulines Streets (525 5661). Bus 3 Vieux Carré, 48 Esplanade, 55 Elysian Fields, 81 Almonaster, 82 Desire. **Open** *Tours* every hour 10am-3.30pm Mon-Fri. **Admission** $6; $5 concessions; free under-8s. **Credit** AmEx, MC, V. **Map** p282 D2.

James Gallier Jr, son of pivotal New Orleans architect James Gallier Sr, designed this side-hall, Italianate townhouse. The house has been carefully restored and furnished in the style of an upper-middle-class family of the 1860s. Furnishings change with the seasons, with slip covers and Japanese matting added in summer and Christmas decorations in the winter. (*See also p10,* **A walk through black history**.)

Madame John's Legacy

632 Dumaine Street, at Royal Street (568 6968/ http://lsm.crt.state.la.us/). Bus 3 Vieux Carré, 55 Elysian Fields, 81 Almonaster, 82 Desire. **Open** 9am-5pm Tue-Sun. **Admission** $3; $2 concessions; free under-12s. **Credit** MC, V. **Map** p282 C2.

Its longevity renders this one of the most architecturally and historically significant structures in Louisiana. But it was a writer that gave it enduring fame and a mysterious name. George Washington Cable, a 19th-century essayist and novelist who was one of the great myth-makers of New Orleans, used the house in his novella, *Madame John's Legacy*, the story of how a quadroon mistress used her inheritance from her white lover. The building dates from 1726 (later than the French Colonial period) although what stands now is reportedly a faithful replica of the original structure, which was destroyed in a fire in 1788. A raised structure, with a deep gallery and thin columns, it is the only remaining French Quarter dwelling that echoes plantation structures from the same period. It is now the property of the Louisiana State Museum and has been respectfully restored, right down to the original, olive-coloured trim paint. Rather than a historic house museum, it is used as a gallery and display space.

New Orleans Historic Voodoo Museum

724 Dumaine Street, at Royal Street (523 7685/www.voodoomuseum.com). Bus 3 Vieux Carré, 55 Elysian Fields, 81 Almonaster, 82 Desire. **Open** 10am-8pm daily. **Admission** $7; $3.50-$5.50 concessions; free under-5s. **Credit** AmEx, Disc, MC, V. **Map** p282 C2.

Dedicated to the art and spiritualism of voodoo, this museum has dual purposes – to educate and to practise. So, the front room has the usual oils and powders and voodoo-related knick-knacks, but you can also tour the voodoo altars, learn about what is involved in the rites, and even have a gris-gris (a protection talisman) made by a voodoo priest or priestess. If you're interested in the process, and they

Do-do that voodoo at the **Voodoo Museum**.

believe your interest is genuine, staff may invite you to witness a voodoo ceremony conducted on the premises – but only the most serious will be so lucky. A new branch at 217 N Peters Street (522 5223) concentrates on contemporary voodoo practices. Both offer entertaining tours of St Louis Cemetery No.1.

Chartres Street & Jackson Square

Chartres Street (pronounced 'charters'), which runs parallel to Royal Street, is less easily definable than Royal or Bourbon. Its mixture of upscale galleries, shops, bars, restaurants and flats are interrupted only by the raucous tourist circus of Jackson Square. It is quietest at the two extremes: at Canal Street its balcony-shaded blocks hide a series of bars, some restaurants and tourist-oriented shops. In the lower Quarter, near Esplanade Avenue, it becomes a residential stretch of flats with lush balcony gardens and temptingly shady private courtyards you can see through the gates.

At No.410, across from the Supreme Court building (see p60) is a gorgeously renovated 19th-century police station. It still holds a portion of the French Quarter police division, along with the **Williams Research Center**. The latest project of the ever admirable Historic New Orleans Collection (see p97), this is a museum/library hybrid. It often has fascinating

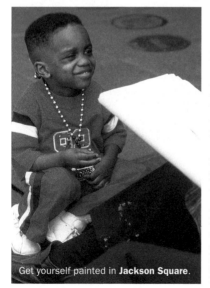
Get yourself painted in **Jackson Square**.

displays of historic objects, documents and art. Admission is free and knowledge is priceless.

Less than a block away at No.500 stands the exquisitely decaying bar/restaurant called **Napoleon House**. Greatly admired for its picturesque antebellum interior and known for its sometimes deafening classical music, this is another of the city's mythological drinking dens. Its name comes from the local lore that in a fit of French loyalty, its owner built the place in 1814 as a residence for Napoleon, should he ever manage to escape from his island prison. Allegedly, some hot-blooded locals were even brewing up a plan to spring the general from St Helena before he died. How true this is, we will never know. But it makes a lovely story.

Just down the way, you can hear **Jackson Square** before you can see it. If the French Quarter has a fulcrum upon which it all balances, this is it. Because this is where its musicians, priests, historians, artists, grifters and tourists all gather in a teeming, noisy, pretty green square that was created in 1721 as a military practice field. Originally called the Place d'Armes, it was renamed in 1848 in memory of General Andrew Jackson, who led a ragtag group of volunteers to victory against the British in 1815 in the Battle of New Orleans (see p13). Jackson went on to be the seventh president of the US, served two terms and was enormously popular. His likeness jauntily doffs its hat atop a rearing horse in the centre of the square. When created by the sculptor Clark Mills in the mid-19th century, this was the first statue in the world in which a horse had more than one hoof off the base. In a deliciously cruel move, the Union soldiers who occupied the city during the Civil War ordered the base inscribed with the words that remain there today: 'The Union must and shall be preserved'.

Throughout the day, Jackson Square is filled with street performers, musicians and mimes. The cast changes constantly, but you can usually find a troupe of gymnasts performing astounding feats, magicians spinning trickery and comedians riffing off the crowds while balancing on ladders or unicycles.

The red brick buildings draped in delicate filigreed wrought iron on either side of the square are the **Pontalba Buildings**, credited by many historians as the first apartment buildings in the US. They were completed in 1850 by the Baroness Micaela Almonester de Pontalba, who also brought in the square's thick, wrought-iron fences, and, in 1856, had the greenery at the centre landscaped in the sun pattern favoured in Paris as an homage to Louis XIV, the Sun King. In a piece of charming self-aggrandisement, the baroness had her initials – A and P – worked into the elaborate

Doing the strip

At night, Bourbon Street looks like a cross between a Las Vegas show and a bus station. Girls in neon-hued boas and guys carting 'Huge Ass Beers' (purchased from thus-named beer stands) wander from bar to bar. Grifters and swindlers swirl among the tourists like bitters in a Sazerac cocktail, offering to read your palm, do you a gris-gris, sing you a song, guess your name, hug your girl... all while eyeing up your watch and wallet. The street is the best-known symbol of New Orleans' free-spirited attitude.

But that wasn't always the case. This was once one of the most sought-after addresses in the city for the upper class. No single building exposes the contradiction between Bourbon's past and present more than 327 Bourbon Street. The four-storey Greek Revival townhouse was once the residence of Judah P Benjamin, the Secretary of the Confederacy. Now it's the upscale strip bar, Temptations, where topless women twirl around brass poles in Judah's grand old living room.

Burlesque is largely to blame for the change in Bourbon's fortunes. As the wealthier citizens moved to the huge mansions in the Garden District in the early 20th century, the street began to go into decline. Rents dropped, and the French Quarter began to look to other industries to fill the gaps.

The first burlesque theatres opened on Bourbon in the 1920s, and, at first, they were vaudeville theatres with varied programmes of comedy and music. Over time, the variety shows added more and more dancers until there were no comics, singers or contortionists.

Just girls.

Burlesque in New Orleans hit its peak in the 1940s, when women like Kitty West came to town and fell for the easy money. West became one of the city's most famous strippers, doing her 'Evangeline the Oyster Girl' dance in a giant shell, using an enormous pearl to protect her... modesty. A generation of jazz musicians got their starts playing in strip clubs. Clarinettist Pete Fountain called it the 'conservatory of Bourbon Street'.

Along with the strippers, came other businesses to cater to the demands of the dancers' customers. Thus noisy bars, loud nightclubs and cheap restaurants began to push out the posh places (although a few still linger). That's why, even today, the street juxtaposes some of the city's finest old restaurants with some of its most egregious tourist traps.

By the 1960s, Bourbon Street's fate was sealed. Today, it has a worldwide reputation as a street of sleaze. A place where drinking until you throw up is not frowned upon. A place that Judah P Benjamin would surely never recognise.

ironwork on the balconies. The architecture on the square hasn't changed since then – nor has the use of the buildings, with ground-floor shops and upper storey flats – making this a particularly historically accurate section of the city. One of the apartments, the **1850 House**, is open to the public (*see below*).

The fairy-tale white church overlooking the square is **St Louis Cathedral**, the oldest continuously operating cathedral in the US. The present structure was built in the late 1700s, although it was altered considerably during the mid-19th century (*see p67*). This is the third church on this site – the first was a simple chapel built by settlers, later destroyed in a storm. The second church burned down in the Good Friday fire of 1788, when historians say it was largely responsible for its own destruction. After a small fire was discovered that day, priests in the cathedral refused to ring the church bell to call volunteers because it was a holy day. The fire razed the city to the ground.

The incongruous grey, blunt buildings on either side of the cathedral were built by the Spanish. The one to the left of the cathedral as you face it is the **Cabildo**, the former seat of government for the Spanish colony of Louisiana (or Casa Capitular). The one on the right is **Presbytère**. Planned as a residence for priests, it was gutted in the 1794 fire even before it was completed, and stood empty until the Americans finished it in 1813 for use as a courthouse. Both house sections of the Louisiana State Museum (*see p96*). The Cabildo holds good, interlocking exhibitions tracing the history of Louisiana, while the Presbytère has displays on Mardi Gras.

Between the cathedral and its flanking buildings are two mysterious-looking alleys leading to Royal Street. The one on the left is **Pirates Alley**, where William Faulkner lived in the 1920s (at No.624). Appropriately, his home has been converted into the excellent **Faulkner House** bookstore (*see p158*).

Away from Jackson Square, Chartres Street becomes mostly residential and quiet. It's a beautiful, shady stretch of street with lush balcony gardens where the hush is interrupted only by the occasional clip-clop of horse-drawn buggies in mid-tour. Two buildings in the 1100 block are tourist draws – the walled structure at No.1112 is the **Old Ursuline Convent**, built in 1753 (*see below*). This smooth, whitewashed building was one of few to survive the 1788 fire, and thus is one of the oldest buildings in the Quarter. Local lore dictates that it was spared the flames after the sisters placed an icon of the virgin in a window facing the fire and prayed for protection. The blaze, it is said, stopped at their doorstep. Across the street at No.1113 is the creamy yellow **Beauregard-**

Keyes House, with its gorgeous gardens. This was built in the 1820s and once served as home to Confederate General PGT Beauregard. It later belonged to that writer of breathless prose, Frances Parkinson Keyes (*see below*).

Beauregard-Keyes House & Garden

1113 Chartres Street, at Ursulines Street (523 7257). Bus 3 Vieux Carré, 55 Elysian Fields, 81 Almonaster, 82 Desire. **Open** *Tours on the hr 10am-3pm Mon-Sat.* **Admission** $5; $2 concessions; free under-6s. **No credit cards**. **Map** p282 C2.

This 1826 house reflects both the Creole and American building styles, with its American central hall and Creole veranda and courtyard. The house is furnished and decorated in the style of the late 19th century. Some of the furniture and items inside are from the family of Confederate general PGT Beauregard, who briefly lived in the house after the Civil War. In the 1940s, the bestselling novelist Frances Parkinson Keyes (1885-1970) took over the house, then in disrepair, gradually returning it to its old beauty. The back courtyard is very handsome and the side garden has been restored to a formal Creole garden. Keyes' doll and costume collections are on display in the courtyard buildings.

1850 House

523 St Ann Street, Jackson Square (568 6968/ 1-800 568 6968). Bus 3 Vieux Carré, 55 Elysian Fields, 81 Almonaster, 82 Desire. **Open** *9am-5pm Tue-Sun.* **Admission** $4; $3 concessions; free under-12s. **Credit** MC, V. **Map** p282 C2.

'House' is a little misleading for this museum as it's actually an apartment in the stately Pontalba. This makes a tour all the more interesting because it's the only chance you'll have to see the residential upper floors of the Pontalbas.

New Orleans Historic Pharmacy Museum

514 Chartres Street, at St Louis Street (565 8027/ www.pharmacymuseum.org). Bus 3 Vieux Carré, 55 Elysian Fields, 81 Almonaster, 82 Desire. **Open** *10am-5pm Tue-Sun.* **Admission** $2; $1 concessions; free under-12s. **Credit** AmEx, MC, V. **Map** p282 B2.

On the original site of the first pharmacy in the US, (circa 1823), the old wooden counters, cases and shelves here have been restored to jewel-like perfection, and on display are the beautiful handmade glass vessels that were the tools of the profession in the 19th century. Here, you return to a time when cocaine might have been dispensed over the counter for a toothache, a lithium potion for nervousness and live leeches swam in a porcelain bowl.

Old Ursuline Convent

1100 Chartres Street, at Ursulines Street (529 3040/www.accesscom.net/ursuline). Bus 3 Vieux Carré, 55 Elysian Fields, 81 Almonaster, 82 Desire. **Open** *Tours on the hour 10am-3pm Tue-Fri; 11.15am, 1pm, 2pm Sat, Sun.* **Admission** $5; $2-$4 concessions; free under-8s. **No credit cards**. **Map** p282 C2.

Grab some peace at the **Old Ursuline Convent**. *See p66.*

The grande dame of New Orleans architecture, this serene-looking convent was built between 1745 and 1750, replacing an earlier compound built in the 1720s. Having survived all of the fires that destroyed the rest of the city, this is the oldest surviving building in New Orleans. It even retains some details of the first structure: especially lovely are the hand-hewn cypress stairs. The Ursuline nuns first arrived in the city in 1727 from France and promptly set about their work of teaching and healing. The order was prosperous and shrewd, once owning vast swathes of land in what is now the lower French Quarter. It was notable for teaching not only the daughters of the bourgeoisie but black and Indian children as well. Today, the compound houses the archdiocese's archives. Visits are limited to tours.

St Louis Cathedral

725 Chartres Street, on Jackson Square (525 9585/ www.saintlouiscathedral.org). Bus 3 Vieux Carré, 55 Elysian Fields, 81 Almonaster, 82 Desire. **Open** 7am-6.30pm daily. *Tours* approx every 2hrs 9am-5pm Mon-Sat; 1-5pm Sun. **Admission** free. **Map** p282 C2.

Yes, St Louis Cathedral is modest in comparison to the cathedrals of Europe but it is quite rightly seen as the symbol of New Orleans. Its white, three-steepled façade looks almost too pretty as it crowns Jackson Square with an uncluttered elegance. Its exterior is more beautiful than its interior. Tours are arranged around masses and church activities, as this is the parish church for the French Quarter.

Decatur Street & the river

The last street before the wide brown expanse of the Mississippi River is Decatur Street. Originally called Rue de la Levée, for obvious reasons, it has had many personalities over the years. In the 19th century it contained rough sections such as the infamous Gallatin Alley (since demolished), which was said to be so dangerous that even the police refused to enter it. As the city fell into decay in the latter half of the 20th century Decatur suffered the worst among the Quarter's lanes until the hippies discovered it in the 1960s. After that it became the centre for New Orleans' counterculture, and it kept that bohemian bent for decades. In recent years, though, it has been gentrified along with much of the Quarter, and now has more of a tourist slant than ever before.

At the Canal Street end, Decatur Street divides into two streets for several blocks. The North Peter Street branch is dominated by the air-conditioned **Canal Place** shopping mall, with largely upscale shops (including Saks Fifth Avenue and Brooks Brothers, *see p151*), an occasionally arty, but sometimes mainstream cinema and the posh Westin Canal Place Hotel. Behind the shopping centre, the glossy glass angled **Aquarium of the Americas** glitters in the sunshine at the edge of the river. As aquariums go, this one is pretty

Get your alligator fix at the **French Market**.

cool; it includes a glass tunnel in which sharks and stingrays swim around you (*see below*). Across from Canal Place is the French Quarter branch of the popular Uptown music club **Tipitina's** (*see p212*) which features a mix of good local bands – with an emphasis on zydeco and blues – and touring acts. Directly behind Tipitina's, on the other branch of Decatur Street, is the touristy **House of Blues**, which has nightly performances by a wide variety of local and touring acts, as well as a noisy bar and restaurant (*see p203*).

Heading down Decatur past the statue of Jean Baptiste Le Moyne, Sieur de Bienville (who discovered south Louisiana and claimed it for the French in 1699) and his Indian guides, it's just one tourist shop after another. If it's a T-shirt you're after, this is the place for you. Canned Cajun music pours out of open shop doors and crowds of confused tourists wander by wondering where all the culture went. The

snowy white building on the river side is **Jackson Brewery**, once the place where Jax beer was made, but now a tourist-oriented shopping centre (*see p151*).

From the brewery you can see the hulaballoo in Jackson Square (*see p64*), while at the edge of the square on the river side, is the justifiably famous **Café du Monde**, an open-air café where a *café au lait* and a plate of *beignets* will only cost a couple of bucks (*see p131*).

At any point, you can walk behind the row of buildings on Decatur Street and make your way to the **Moonwalk**, which runs along the river at the top of the embankment (locally called a 'levee'), and offers lovely views of the Mississippi River. (Be careful at night, however, as it can be slightly dodgy after dark.)

Café du Monde is the first shop in the long and lean **French Market** building that stretches all the way to Esplanade Avenue (*see p167*). The first section is indoors, with shops where you can buy pralines, handmade clothes, toys, candles and other paraphernalia. Keep heading down to where Decatur Street branches off again at the glittering gold statue of Joan of Arc, mounted on a delicate steed. You'll pass a few outdoor restaurants with jazz bands, before reaching the open-air section of the market, which starts with a fruit and veg section, still favoured by Quarter residents, followed by an area where you can buy just about anything. It's very good for unusual souvenirs, and hand-blown glass trinkets.

Beyond the market is the **Old United States Mint**; another part of the Louisiana State Museum system (along with the Cabildo and the Presbytère), it holds an extensive collection of jazz memorabilia (*see p98*).

Aquarium of the Americas & IMAX Theater

1 Canal Street, at the Mississippi River (565 3033/ 1-800 774 7394; 581 IMAX/www.audubon institute.org). Bus 41 Canal. **Open** *Aquarium 9.30am-7pm daily; IMAX 10am-6pm Mon-Thur, Sun; 10am-8pm Fri, Sat; shows every hour.* **Admission** *Aquarium $14; $6.50-$10 concessions. IMAX $8; $5-$7 concessions.* **Credit** *AmEx, MC, V.* **Map** p282 A3.
Aquariums are all the rage, but it actually makes sense for New Orleans to have one. Located in a soaring glassy blue building on the banks of the Mississippi, it fittingly concentrates on places close at hand: the river, the Gulf of Mexico and the Caribbean. Authenticity extends to a replica of an offshore oil rig in the Gulf of Mexico section, which is, while fascinating, more than a little too forgiving of the ecological effects of oil exploration. Still, the Caribbean Reef installation is spectacular: visitors walk through a 30ft (9m) glass tunnel underneath the sea world. Next door is the IMAX Theater, with its constantly changing films (*see also p189*).

Faubourg Marigny & Bywater

Where the French Quarter's funky soul went.

If creeping commercialism and rising rents have squeezed out much of the French Quarter's bohemian flavour, the chief beneficiaries have been Faubourg Marigny and Bywater, the two neighbourhoods immediately downriver. The Marigny contains one of New Orleans' best entertainment and restaurant districts, while a diverse army of artists and urban pioneers has helped turn the Bywater, a historic but run-down working-class area, into a hotbed of renovation and revitalisation.

Both are largely residential, and though they contain few 'tourist' sites, both are pleasant places to stroll, browse interesting shops and observe one of the city's densest concentrations of 19th-century housing. One of the best ways to explore is on two wheels: you can rent a bike nearby at **Bicycle Michael's** (*see p223*) or join them for a 25-mile self-guided tour.

Visitors should be careful, though. These areas are generally safe to explore during the

day, but use caution, especially in the Bywater, where conditions can vary widely from block to block. In the evenings, bars and cafés light up much of Marigny, but Bywater should not be traversed on foot after dark.

Sightseeing

Faubourg Marigny

Day or night, a good place to begin exploring the Marigny is the tangle of streets at the French Quarter's edge, where Frenchmen and Decatur streets meet Esplanade Avenue. The surrounding blocks are filled with restaurants, cafés and nightclubs that have a neighbourhood feel. Food-wise, there's enough variety in the first few blocks of Frenchmen Street to suit any craving and budget, from fine dining at **Belle Forché** (*see p115*) to cheap Middle Eastern food at **Mona's Cafe** (*see p128*) and top veggie dishes at local fave **Old Dog New Trick Café** (*see p117*).

The lovely houses on Esplanade Avenue border the Marigny.

After dark, Marigny gets crowded, as fans pack in to hear jazz at **Snug Harbor** (*see p208*) and Latin and rock at **Café Brasil** (*see p205*). Check Frenchmen Street's flyer-encrusted telephone poles to find a concert or art event, or grab a pavement table at **PJ's Coffee & Tea** (*see p133*), which stays open late, and have an espresso and watch the action.

Often called New Orleans' first suburb, the Marigny was once a single plantation owned by the wealthy Marigny family. Bernard de Marigny began dividing up the farm and selling parcels in 1806, when land prices rose during a local population boom. The new neighbourhood filled up quickly with *les hommes de couleur libre* – free men of colour.

Marigny refused offers from American developers to turn his subdivision into a commercial centre with hotels, theatres and a gasworks, leading one to declare, 'Sir, I shall live by God to see the day when rank grass will choke up the gutters of your old faubourg.' The area did indeed fall into decline in the mid 1800s, as wealthy Creoles migrated to Esplanade Ridge, now in Mid City. Some early structures remain, including the **Claiborne Mansion** at 2111 Dauphine Street. Built in 1855 by WCC Claiborne, the son of Louisiana's first governor, the Greek Revival building is now a luxury guesthouse (*see p43*).

A few blocks east of leafy **Washington Square Park** stands the former home of Charles Laveau, a free man of colour said to have been the father of voodoo queen Marie Laveau (1801 Dauphine Street, at Kerlerec Street). Built between 1817 and 1833, the oddly shaped dwelling is listed on the National Register of Historic Places but is closed to the public.

Heading downriver on Frenchmen Street, you come to the thoroughfare with arguably the best name in the city, Elysian Fields. It is one of the many ironic elements of life in New Orleans that a boulevard named after heaven should be ugly, sparse and generally unsafe to walk down. *C'est la vie.* But if you make it this far, you might want to stop in at No.621, **American Aquatic Gardens** (*see p171*). It sells plants, fountains and statuary for New Orleans' elaborate patio gardens, and it's a pleasant place to grab some shade, gawk at lily pads the size of manhole covers, and maybe buy a quirky birdhouse.

A few businesses cluster near the intersection of Royal Street and Franklin Avenue. **Schiro's Community Café & Bar** (2483 Royal Street; 945 4425) has been around in one guise or another for decades; today, it's a grocery and restaurant, with daily plate-lunch specials, a full bar and a convivial atmosphere. Nearby,

the equally welcoming **Flora Coffee Shop & Gallery** (2600 Royal Street; 947 8358) serves coffee, juices, salads and sandwiches to an indie rock soundtrack.

In 2000, the **New Orleans Center for the Creative Arts** (2800 Chartres Street; 940 2787/1-800 201 4836), a state high school whose alumni include Harry Connick Jr and Wynton Marsalis, moved to stunning new digs in a renovated Marigny warehouse surrounded by a wasteland of old railway tracks and wharves at the edge of the river. Music fans who want to see part of the campus can take in art exhibitions during the academic year or attend events in the Center Stage series, which has recently included concerts by the Ahn Trio and soprano Fabiana Bravo.

Bywater

The Bywater runs from the railway tracks at Press Street to the aptly named Industrial Canal, at Poland Avenue. Also known as the Ninth Ward, Bywater was initially settled by German and Irish immigrants. It was hit hard by Hurricane Betsy in 1965 and fell into decline after that. Over the past few years, though, it's rebounded, with artists, musicians, and gay and lesbian homeowners paving the way, drawn by attractive houses and low prices.

It contains a wealth of modest historic buildings, mostly single-family houses and 'shotgun' duplexes, as well as a few churches and monuments. The 1866-built **St Vincent de Paul Catholic Church** (3053 Dauphine Street; 943 5566) is now known as Blessed Francis Xavier Seelos Parish, after a Bavarian-born priest who ministered to the area's German immigrants. Seelos died the year after the church was completed. In 2003, a fire destroyed its murals, but the stained-glass windows and a Seelos relic – part of his breastbone – were saved. It should be back open by late 2004.

Several blocks away, the tall arch that looms over the 3800 block of Burgundy Street is dedicated to soldiers who died in World War I. Directly across from it are three good examples of Bywater Victorian houses.

A few funky local bars draw patrons from all over town. Most notable are the strange and wonderful **Saturn Bar** and the legendary watering hole **Markey's** (*for both, see p141*). Both attract a friendly mix of hipsters, bohemians and curmudgeonly old-timers who've propped up the bar for donkey's years. Next door, the **Country Club** (*see p199*) is a good place for an afternoon swim. Nearby there are several restaurants worth seeking out; at the top of the list is the ever-packed

Sightseeing

Elizabeth's, which lures with its huge breakfasts, and **Bywater Barbecue**, with its creative cuisine (*for both, see p117*).

Though a sizeable population of artists calls the Bywater home, the area has few galleries. **Studio Inferno** (*see p192-93*) is a notable exception. This is considered to be one of the city's best galleries for handfired glassware. On the third Saturday of each month, from 9am to 3pm, there's more to look at when the **Bywater Art Market** (3301 Chartres Street, at Piety Street; 944 7900) goes live with painting, pottery, glass and photography by locals at bargain prices.

The studio/gallery of **Dr Bob** (3027 Chartres Street; 945 2225) is as far as can be from the chic, white-walled downtown gallery scene. Open, as the signs say, 'by chance or appointment', the doctor's gravel-paved compound is a technicolour riot of whirligigs and gewgaws. Inside, the proprietor shows his own folk-inspired creations, plus work by several 'outsider' artists (as in artists who are not him). Woodworkers turn out handcrafted furniture in an adjacent shop, and there's even a bar, the **Lampshade Lounge**, where bands occasionally play. It's the ultimate cooler-than-cool local scene.

You can always pray

If miracles do occur, why not in New Orleans? The chapel in **St Roch Cemetery** is dedicated to the idea that divine intervention works. Unlike many purveyors of miracles, St Roch (pronounced 'Rock') has proof. Of a sort. It is here that those who believe they have been healed through prayers to St Roch deposit cast-off crutches and other *milagro*-like symbols of their afflictions in a bizarre and yet somehow heartwarming manifestation of their faith. In a small, dank room in the cemetery chapel, hung to the walls, stacked on the floor, leaning against shelves, in fact everywhere are crutches, leg braces, back braces, even artificial limbs and objects representing hearts, lungs, livers, feet, heads, ears and eyes filling the walls and shelves and crowding around the statue of a rather glum-looking St Roch. The objects represent what was healed: a plaster hand = cured of arthritis. The chapel is paved with bricks inscribed with tributes like 'Thanks to St Roch for my eye,' or simply 'Thanks.'

The connection between New Orleans and St Roch – an obscure 14th-century saint who specialised in dealing with plague – dates back to 1867, when the city was gripped by its worst yellow fever outbreak in years. A young German priest, Peter Leonard Thevis, rallied his congregation to pray to St Roch for deliverance. If they were spared, he promised

to build a chapel in St Roch's honour. In fact, not a single parishioner died of yellow fever in 1867, nor in 1878, when, during another bout of disease St Roch was once again pressed into service.

Reverend Thevis, an energetic sort, set about building the chapel straight away. Constructed by parishioners after Thevis' design based on the Campo Santo dei Tedeschi in Rome, it's an odd sight, looking rather like the back side of a cathedral that's been sheared off and dropped in a cemetery. Inside, there are just the room with the altar and two side chambers, but nonetheless, the structure soars almost three storeys above the surrounding tombs. In 1895, Thevis added another cemetery, **St Roch No.2**, just across Music Street. Both have beautiful aboveground tombs and colourful tiling, as well as fountains and statues.

St Roch is in a blue-collar district across St Claude Avenue from the Bywater, on a relatively safe street. But drive or take a taxi, and don't stray far, as the area can be dicey.

St Roch Cemetery

1725 St Roch Avenue, at North Derbigny Street (596 3050/www.archdiocese-no.org). **Open** *Cemetery* 8am-4.30pm daily. *Chapel* 9am-3pm Mon-Sat.

CBD & the Warehouse District

There's not much left of the birthplace of jazz.

Jazz was born downtown, but you'd never know it from looking at the place. The blocks between the French Quarter and the start of Uptown are as historic as any other part of town, but they've been marred by modern developments. With so many competing elements, the area has no single overarching identity. Over the years, patches of it have been known as Faubourg St Mary, the American Sector and the Central Business District (or CBD) and by other more obscure names. Between Canal Street and the I-10 overpass (the beginning of Uptown), and between the river and Claiborne Avenue, you'll find all the city's skyscrapers, Harrah's Casino, galleries, museums, historic sites and the hub of the local legal community. But you won't find a common identity. Or any jazz, either, despite its historical roots in the area.

Rampart Street & around

This area's most important feature is all but hidden from view. Jazz was invented in the blocks around South Rampart and Perdido streets. A few historic buildings from that era still stand, but they're all in limbo, with no workable preservation plan. When the area was known as Back of Town, the **Eagle Saloon** (401 S Rampart Street) and the **Iroquois Theater** (413 S Rampart Street) were hopping with the new music. Louis Armstrong, who was born nearby, heard Buddy Bolden play at the Eagle Saloon and was inspired by it.

Also still standing is the building that once housed Karnofsky's tailor shop (427 S Rampart Street). The Karnofskys were surrogate parents to Armstrong. On New Year's Eve, 1912, Armstrong fired a pistol on a corner of Rampart Street. That landed him in the Colored Waifs' Home, where he learned to play cornet. He later bought his first horn at a pawnshop nearby.

None of these historic spots, though, has been marked. Preservationists' plans to save this little slice of history continually fail to materialise, often for want of funds, and

developers keep plodding ahead with their hotels and car parks. A couple of buildings Armstrong lived in as a boy were torn down when the remarkably unattractive **City Hall** complex was built at the corner of Poydras Street and Loyola Avenue.

Though City Hall is a depressing relic of 1960s architectural style, downtown boasts many worthier achievements. The area divides easily into several clusters. A wedge of skyscrapers stretches along Poydras Street. At the top of the Poydras Street strip are the Louisiana Superdome and the New Orleans Arena; at the bottom, the Ernest N Morial Convention Center stretches for half a mile down the Mississippi River. Between Poydras and Canal Street lies the CBD.

Between the convention centre and Loyola Avenue is the Warehouse District, which recently underwent a renaissance that saw its buildings converted into art galleries, trendy restaurants, flats and law offices. A growing cluster of museums – including the **D-Day Museum** and the **Ogden Museum of Southern Art** (*for both, see p76*) – is making this district more of a tourist destination than ever before.

St Charles Avenue & around

Uptown's grand St Charles Avenue begins humbly at Canal Street. The historic streetcar line runs up the avenue, with marked stops every few blocks. In the CBD, the street is studded with Greek Revival buildings which hark back to the architectural trend of the mid 19th century, the height of New Orleans' prosperity. In the first block after Canal Street, the massive **Crescent Billiard Hall** (115 St Charles Avenue), purpose-built in 1826, now houses the members-only Pickwick Club. Two blocks further is the Greek Revival-style **United Fruit Company Building** (321 St Charles Avenue); this notorious firm made a fortune in bananas in the 1940s and 1950s and meddled in Latin American politics with considerable help from the CIA. Down the street a bit stands **Gallier Hall** (545

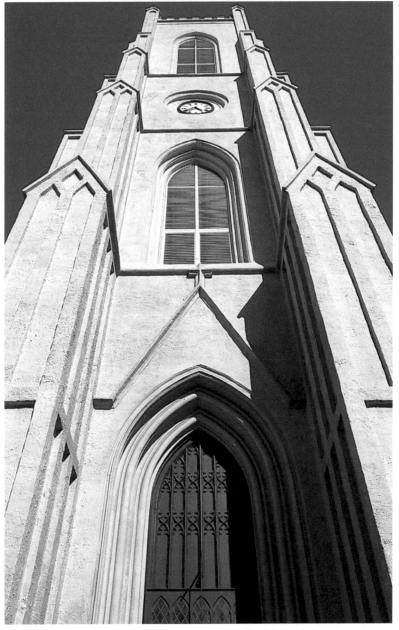

St Patrick's Cathedral, legacy of 19th-century Irish immigrants. *See p74.*

Sightseeing

The CBD stretches to the edge of the Mississippi River.

St Charles Avenue). Built in the 1850s, it served as City Hall for more than a century. Confederate President Jefferson Davis and Confederate General PGT Beauregard lay in state here. These days, it's used mostly for parties. The mayor watches Mardi Gras parades from the steps, where he is toasted by the king or queen of each passing procession.

Across the street from Gallier Hall is leafy **Lafayette Square**, one of New Orleans' oldest public plazas. In the 18th and 19th centuries, it was to the American Sector what Jackson Square is to the French Quarter. Free concerts are held here on Wednesday evenings in the spring. Across Camp Street from the square, the old Post Office now houses the United States Court of Appeals for the Fifth District. Other federal court buildings fill the block.

On Camp Street itself, the pearly white towers of **St Patrick's Cathedral** (724 Camp Street) are squeezed in between two taller, newer buildings, giving the church a somewhat breathless look. When waves of Irish immigrants flooded into New Orleans in the early 19th century, Catholic services in the city were virtually all conducted in French. So the Irish built their own church, St Patrick's, in 1838, in a Gothic style loosely (very loosely) based on that of York Minster. The vaulted ceilings, dramatic altar and elaborate murals by artist Leon Pomarade are impressive, but you have to go to mass to see them; the church is closed at other times.

A few blocks away, among the otherwise largely undistinguished buildings of Baronne Street (parallel to St Charles in the opposite direction from Camp), sits the **Church of the Immaculate Conception**, or Jesuit Church (130 Baronne Street). Its unique architecture mixes Arabian and Gothic styles with Moorish onion domes and horseshoe arches – elements found nowhere else in town. The original church was built by the Jesuits in 1857 and demolished in 1926 because of structural weaknesses. The current replica, built in the 1930s, has the original cast-iron pews and a gilt altar by local architect James Freret.

The American Sector

In 1791, a year after New Orleans was founded, the governing council awarded everything upriver of the city grid to Sieur de Bienville, who had explored and mapped much of the region. Thanks to that land grant, Bienville's plantation stretched for miles, from present-day Canal Street past Carrollton to the Riverbend. He eventually parcelled it into smaller plantations, selling the first of them in 1726. The strip that would ultimately become Canal Street was a swathe of dirt nearly 200 feet (61 metres) wide which marked the edge of the city and the start of farmland. As it was gradually developed, it became known as Faubourg St Mary.

As the city's population grew, Canal Street became a cultural dividing line and a meeting ground. By the 19th century, descendants of the French were living in the French Quarter. The new American residents took over everything above Canal Street, and the area became known as the American Sector. Canal Street became a meeting place for the respective governmental leaders of the two autonomous sections

of town. It was known as a 'neutral ground' – Napoleon's term for the space between two opposing armies. Today, grassy medians between opposing lanes of traffic are still called neutral grounds in southern Louisiana.

The antebellum wealth in the American sector largely came from river trading. Shipping magnates built the mansions visible today on St Charles Avenue and the massive warehouses and Greek Revival public buildings that still stand downtown.

The American Sector soon surpassed the French Quarter in size, as the Americans eclipsed the French in numbers. The occupation of New Orleans by Northern soldiers during the Civil War helped to break down divisions between the two groups, as they united against what they saw as a common enemy. By the end of the 19th century, the area between Canal and Poydras streets had become a regional banking centre, and the cultural gap had dwindled. In the 1920s, the first of the area's skyscrapers were built, and its future was sealed.

Heading towards Uptown, virtually all roads lead to **Lee Circle** (a hybrid roundabout with traffic signals), whose marble pillar and utterly sympathetic statue of Confederate General Robert E Lee were erected in 1884. It is said that Lee faces north so as never to have his back to his enemies. The piece was sculpted, however, by a New Yorker, Alexander Doyle.

Warehouse District

The Warehouse District's brick edifices were originally built to hold cotton, sugar and coffee. By the 1960s and 1970s, though, most shipping in the port of New Orleans had been diverted to other areas upriver, and the district became an ugly cluster of crumbling relics.

The 1984 Louisiana World's Fair turned all that around. The fair itself was a legendarily gaudy bust. A pair of 40-foot- (12-metre-) tall topless papier-mâché mermaids (which then-Governor Edwin Edwards famously described as having 'nipples as big as dinner plates') beckoned visitors to the riverfront attractions built among the massive, unused wharves and warehouses. But marketing efforts outside the city flopped: Louisiana's fair took place during a national recession, and though it was a hit with locals, it was the first World's

Fair to lose money. After it ended, developers took a new look at the area and saw that the warehouses were perfectly suited for conversion. Airy lofts with high ceilings and huge windows drew young professionals. Law offices opened in the blocks around the federal court buildings. Galleries blossomed on Julia Street. Trendy restaurants inevitably followed: in 1990, Emeril Lagasse opened **Emeril's** (800 Tchoupitoulas Street, *see p119*) in a converted warehouse, attracting others including **Cuvee** (322 Magazine Street; *see p119*) and **Restaurant August** (301 Tchoupitoulas Street; *see p120*).

Most tours start behind Lee Circle, where the rust-coloured, castle-like structure at 929 Camp Street has housed the **Confederate Museum** for more than a century (*see p98*). Its array of Civil War artefacts is impressive, but it gives no complete or general history of the war or its context, and it's a challenge not to see it as a shrine to the Confederacy. With its stars-and-bars souvenirs, the place is an interesting anachronism.

At 925 Camp Street, the new **Ogden Museum of Southern Art** (*see p100*) holds 2,700 pieces by respected Southern artists. The museum comprises the modernist five-storey Goldring Hall and the restored

Patrick F Taylor Library, though the latter won't open before 2004. It stands across the street from the **Contemporary Arts Center** (*see p98*) – the linchpin of the district. It was built in an abandoned warehouse in 1976, when the city had no contemporary arts scene to speak of; it helped the area to develop its current arty personality. The CAC suffers from something of an identity crisis, hosting both professional and community arts and theatre and lacking a permanent collection; it's really more a gallery than a museum.

Few people associate D-Day with New Orleans, but the **National D-Day Museum** (*see pp99-100*) around the corner at 945 Magazine Street was built here for a reason. The late historian Stephen Ambrose (who taught at the University of New Orleans) founded his efforts to create a D-Day museum on the achievements of local shipbuilder Andrew Jackson Higgins, who created the landing crafts used by the US Marines in Normandy, North Africa and the Pacific. The acclaimed museum's displays include timelines detailing the Normandy invasion and Pacific campaigns. Veterans, many of whom landed on the beaches in Higgins' boats, are on hand most days to talk about their experiences.

A block away at 420 Julia Street, the **Louisiana Children's Museum** (*see p98*) is crammed with interactive exhibits and educational games and activities. It has displays relating to science and nature, a play kitchen, a mini TV station and even a mini port. It's aimed at kids from toddlers to ten-year-olds (though the latter is stretching it a bit).

The Riverfront

Besides revitalising the Warehouse District, the World's Fair also brought people back to New Orleans' riverfront. The fair's legacy includes the development of the vast **Ernest N Morial Convention Center** stretching along the edge of the district, the busy **Riverwalk Marketplace** shopping centre (*see p151*) and a host of related shops and restaurants. The convention centre alone wanders for nearly half a mile, and it's still expanding. Riverwalk Marketplace is a three-tiered stretch of shops with a balcony over the river. At the end of the Riverwalk below the **World Trade Center** sits **Spanish Plaza**, one of the city's few monuments to its Spanish heritage. The plaza holds a massive fountain made of colourful tiles bearing the crests of regions of Spain.

Also close to the riverfront is the massive **Harrah's Casino**, which stretches from Canal Street down South Peters Street. It's the only land-based casino in the state, a fact

which might seem surprising considering that New Orleans' past is full of prodigious gamblers, including Bernard Marigny, who introduced craps to the New World. The establishment of Harrah's left a long, colourful trail of irregular legislative behaviour and deal-making, a couple of bankruptcies and a few people thrown in jail. Somehow, though, Harrah's managed to make the deal work, and now it's open 24/7, with a plush gaming arena worthy of Vegas. If you're unable to peel yourself away from the tables, at least drop by the central court to play slots under the gigantic fake oak tree and the canopy of fibre-optic stars.

Around the Superdome

For sports requiring a level playing field, the city's largest and most famous venue is the **Louisiana Superdome** (*see p214*). Built in 1975, it was once at the leading edge for multi-use stadiums, and it still has the world's largest continuous roof without interior supports. Though not exceptionally ugly as domed stadiums go, the 27-storey steel mushroom, which takes up 52 acres, is a fairly bland architectural achievement. It's complemented by the **New Orleans Arena** (*see p214*) just next door, where the boring green-tiled surface has been compared to a giant public toilet.

The Superdome has hosted everything from the local football team, the New Orleans Saints (which play in its environs each week), to the pope and the Rolling Stones. Depending on when you're in town, you might catch a rodeo, monster truck pull, carnival, religious revival or boat show in its spacious environs. The New Orleans Arena is home to the city's recently acquired basketball team, the New Orleans Hornets, and also hosts concerts.

The two stadiums are connected to the CBD by the **Hyatt Regency** (500 Poydras Plaza) and the **New Orleans Centre** shopping mall (1400 Poydras Street; *see p151*). The Hyatt is topped by a revolving restaurant and lounge offering panoramic views of the city.

Between the Hyatt and the Warehouse District is the city's most bizarrely placed monument. The **Richard & Annette Bloch Cancer Survivors Plaza** is a wildly eclectic series of sculpted pillars which fills the 'neutral ground' between the traffic lanes of busy Loyola Avenue. After Richard Bloch beat cancer twice, he and his wife devoted their money to erecting monuments to cancer survivors in 54 cities. New Orleans got its installation in 1995, and it's become justifiably popular.

Uptown

Where the master lives next door to the maid; this is both the city's wealthiest and poorest neighbourhood.

With vast mansions on broad boulevards lined with graceful old oak trees, were they anywhere else in America, sections of Uptown would be exclusive, gated and protected. But this is New Orleans, so Uptown is open to all.

While everyone in the city knows somebody who knows somebody who lives alone in a 25-bedroom Uptown mansion with only a maid and butler, many of the grand houses have been converted into affordable flats. Louisiana's colourful former governor Huey Long once called New Orleans the only city in the world where the master lived next door to the maid, and as un-PC as that statement is, he did have a point. Pricey streets filled with glorious monuments to the landed gentry bump up against broken-down blocks where nothing's been renovated since World War II. Uptown's beauty comes partly from its unpredictability, and that can be traced back to its early days.

After the Louisiana Purchase made New Orleans an American city, it was instantly flooded with new arrivals. The French Quarter simply couldn't hold them all. But that was fine with the Americans, who considered the Creoles insular and unfriendly. For their part, the Creoles saw the newcomers as brash, crude and interested only in money. So the Americans gravitated upriver from the Quarter, first near Canal Street and then towards the open spaces where plantations bordered the river. The pivotal event was the sale of the Livaudais Plantation in 1832 to a group of American entrepreneurs for $490,000. The sugar estate was soon carved up into lots of half an acre or more. Proving the Creoles right, the buyers built showy new houses and surrounded them with sweeping, lush tropical gardens. Faubourg Livaudais eventually became known as the Garden District.

Today, the whole area is known as Uptown, though under that umbrella fall a number of neighbourhoods, including the Garden District, the Lower Garden District, the Irish Channel and the Riverbend. St Charles Avenue and Magazine Street define Uptown, curving with the Mississippi River and ending when the river makes its sharp 90-degee bend. If you

The faded grandeur of the **Garden District**.

'I went on down to the Audubon Zoo...

...and they all asked for you'. Or so goes one of New Orleans' favourite Mardi Gras songs. Spread over 58 acres bordering the Mississippi River at the edge of Uptown, the **Audubon Zoo** is justifiably ranked as one of the nation's best, and it's much beloved by the locals.

Part of the zoo's success comes from the wealth of exotic wildlife just a few miles from the city limits. Its centrepiece is the Louisiana Swamp exhibit, a re-created bayou covering more than six acres which features a 1930s-style Cajun trapper village. It's not that difficult to create a swamp in New Orleans (just dig down a few feet), but this exhibit is particularly well done. Alligators laze in the dark pools and mud, coming to life with heart-stopping suddenness (usually when zookeepers bring out their next meal). Especially notable are the rare white alligators (for years, when trappers have come across one they've brought it here; by now, there are a fair few). Turtles, fish, raccoons and other south Louisiana wildlife fill the zoo's swamp. For anyone who finds the heat and humidity just a bit too authentic, the Cajun dance hall has air-conditioning, as well as food, drink and music.

The zoo also has your basic gorillas and monkeys, plus two gorgeous white tigers (it's fair to note that the zoo is a bit obsessed with white animals). There's also a fabulous butterfly exhibit, where you can wander among thousands of the pretty, fluttery creatures, and a good petting zoo for kids.

Wrapping around the zoo and extending all the way to St Charles Avenue, **Audubon Park** offers 400 acres of walking and running paths, lagoons, sheltering oaks and a recently upgraded golf course which was the subject of bitter controversy between Uptown residents and the Audubon organisation (*see p220*). Originally part of the De Bore sugar plantation, the park was sold to the city through some political chicanery which involved large profits for a 19th-century governor's cronies. In 1884 and 1885, it was the site of the massive World's Industrial and Cotton Centennial Exposition. No buildings from the fair survive, but the beaux arts philosophy of the day is reflected in the park's graceful design.

Audubon Park

From St Charles Avenue to Mississippi River, between Walnut Street & Exposition Boulevard (information 581 4629/1-800 774 7394/ Audubon Park Golf Course 865 8260/ Cascade Stables 891 2246/www.audubon institute.org). St Charles Streetcar/bus 11 Magazine. **Open** 6am-10pm daily. **Admission** free. **Map** p276 A/B9/10.

Audubon Zoo

6500 Magazine Street, Audubon Park (581 4629/1-800 774 7394/www.audubon institute.org). St Charles Streetcar/bus 11 Magazine. **Open** *Winter* 9.30am-5pm daily. *Summer* 9.30am-5pm Mon-Fri; 9.30am-6pm Sat, Sun. **Admission** $10; $5-$6 concessions; free under-2s. **Credit** AmEx, MC, V. **Map** p276 B9.

A free shuttle bus runs from the St Charles Streetcar to the Audubon Zoo, or you could take the Audubon riverboat back and forth between the zoo and Aquarium.

keep these two streets in mind as pole stars, navigating the Uptown-Garden District-Riverbend area will be easy. Remember that St Charles Avenue and Magazine Street are flanked by Lake Pontchartrain (above St Charles) and the Mississippi River (below Magazine) and you'll understand directions given to you by tour guides, bus drivers and helpful citizens. New Orleanians almost never say 'east', 'west', 'north' or 'south' but refer to all geography in relation to the river and lake. When they say 'head towards the river', that's just what you do. Multifaceted and beautiful though this neighbourhood is, this is also the one area where it is easiest to stumble from a tourist-friendly 'good' section into a dodgy 'bad' section. Most of Uptown is safe, but parts are not; use common sense and stay in the areas that look safest. If a block seems dangerous, it could well be; just don't go there.

Lower Garden District

The part of Uptown closest to downtown, the Lower Garden District – bordered by the interstate, Jackson Avenue, St Charles and the river – was the first section to be settled. In a nod to the classical sensibility prevalent in the 19th century, when most houses here were built, the Americans filled streets named after

Hellenic gods and muses with handsome Greek Revival mansions. But the area grew more working-class as industry along the river drew a flood of German and Irish immigrants to the city in the late 1800s; many mansions were carved up into flats to house them. So many Irish immigrants settled in the strip of land closest to the river that it became known as the Irish Channel (*see p82* **The Irish Channel**).

In the 1930s, dozens of blocks near Jackson Avenue and the river were razed to make room for the sprawling St Thomas public housing development. A generation later, a motorway access ramp bisected a wide, decaying stretch of once-grand Camp Street at Coliseum Square. The one-two punch of poverty and traffic plunged the entire area into a decline which has only recently begun to reverse.

Happily, today the Lower Garden District is unquestionably in the midst of a revival. The ramp finally came down in 1995, to the cheers of preservationists, and was replaced by a lovely tree-lined promenade. In 2001, the notorious St Thomas project was levelled. Proposed uses for the site included mixed-income housing and stores; one controversial plan was for a behemoth Wal-Mart mega-discount store, but it has been bitterly opposed by preservationists in the area (whence the 'No

Londoners take when they go out.

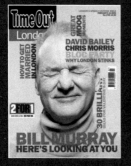

Sprawl-Mart' banners you'll see on Lower Garden District storefronts). Meanwhile, the closure of the old St Thomas Housing project, and the other changes in the area, have meant that professionals have begun filtering back into the district, taking advantage of low property prices and renovating old buildings while helping to foster a vibrant shopping and restaurant scene along Magazine Street (*see p149* **Magazine Street: get shopping**). Even the section of St Charles Avenue that runs through here, long the most blighted stretch of that otherwise grand thoroughfare, now holds several upscale restaurants and has seen increased pedestrian traffic.

Coliseum Square, with its shady park and mix of architectural styles, is a good place to begin touring the area. The art deco **Coliseum Theater**, at the intersection of Thalia Street and Coliseum Square, is now a video production studio. Nearby, but a century away in chronology, is the lovely **Goodrich-Stanley House** (1729 Coliseum Square). Built in 1837 for local businessman William Goodrich, the house was later the childhood home of the journalist and explorer Henry Morton Stanley. Stanley, whose original name was John Rowlands, was a Welsh cabin boy who jumped ship in New Orleans and had the good fortune to be adopted by cotton merchant Henry Hope Stanley. The younger Stanley made his name by tracking down the missing Scottish missionary and fellow explorer David Livingstone. He was later knighted and founded the Congo Free State.

An elaborate wrought-iron fence guards the **Grace King House** at 1749 Coliseum Square. King, a Louisiana historian and author, lived here from 1905 to 1932. The Greek Revival mansion was built in 1847. Coliseum Square ends at cobblestone-paved Felicity Street, which contains several buildings of note. The **Moore-Goldstein House** (No.1309), built in 1880, was designed by prominent local architect James Freret.

Rue de la Course (1500 Magazine Street, at Race Street; 529 1455; *see p133*), a quaint coffeeshop with a pressed-tin ceiling and a laid-back attitude, is a good place to take a break. Across Magazine Street stands the former **St Vincent's Infant Asylum**, an orphanage built in the aftermath of the Civil War. The building is now **St Vincent's Guesthouse** (1507 Magazine Street; 523 3411; *see p50*). The blocks around the junction of Magazine Street and Sophie Wright Place contain a colourful and well-preserved group of 19th-century buildings as well as a number of quirky antiques stores, vintage-clothing

Getting inside

It's hard to believe, but even with all the old mansions that line its streets, Uptown has no historic house museums. This is a disappointment, both for those keen on antebellum architecture and those who like to see the big picture.

So the desperate are forced to be creative. But, this being New Orleans, nobody is made to work too hard. One option is to visit the **Milton Latter Library** on St Charles Avenue (*see p86*). It's converted from a 1906 Italianate villa and provides a rare glimpse of the interior of a grand Garden District house. Though the building has been massively remodelled to serve its present function, its floor plan and much of its interior detailing remain intact.

Another idea is to attend one of the frequent open house events which are held in the area to raise funds for schools, churches and other worthy institutions. Private houses and gardens are opened to ticket holders. Check special-events listings in the daily *Times-Picayune* and weekly *Gambit*. Two of the biggest are the Preservation Resource Center's **Holiday Home Tour** in mid December and **Spring Fiesta**, held in late March or early April (*for both, see p104*).

shops and galleries. Towering over it all is the imposing Romanesque **St Alphonsus Art & Cultural Center** (2045 Constance Street, between Josephine and St Andrew streets; 524 8116). The former St Alphonsus Church, built in the 1850s to serve the area's Irish Catholic population, has an elaborate interior and exquisite stained-glass windows. These were neglected after it closed in 1979 until a volunteer group (www.stalphonsus.org) launched a restoration effort in the 1990s. In addition to lobbying for funds, the group operates a small museum and promotes the building's use as a venue for cultural and civic functions. The museum and church are open Tuesday, Thursday and Saturday from 10am to 2pm; private tours can be arranged.

The infamously crime-ridden St Thomas housing development used to abut the church's property, but it has since been knocked down and replaced with a more upscale development. The neighbourhood can still be a bit dodgy, though, so it's always best to visit when the cultural centre is open.

The Irish Channel

New Orleans' French, Spanish and American history is well known; less widely studied is its Irish history. It was the Irish immigrants who gave the city its distinctive 'N'awlins' accent – which sounds more Boston or Brooklyn than southern.

The large port was part of what brought them here. In the 19th century, 250,000 Irish entered America through the port of New Orleans, the country's second busiest harbour after New York's. Most moved on, but large numbers stayed.

In the early 1800s, many Irish immigrants to the city were well educated and had the business skills needed to make a good living. They were followed by a second, more blue-collar, wave of Irish immigrants. In 1831, the Canal and Banking Company began recruiting Irish labourers to dig New Orleans' New Basin Canal. This six-mile (15-kilometre) waterway, six feet (two metres) deep and 60 feet (18 metres) wide, was to link Lake Pontchartrain with the Mississippi River. The work was back-breaking, done under scorching sun, in stifling humidity, through swampland. It was so brutal that slaves were not used, as they were considered to be of too much monetary value to risk in such an endeavour.

Not knowing quite what they would face, tens of thousands of Irish were lured to New Orleans with the promise of money. What they found was brutal work in a hot climate. Plagued by disease, weakened by the toil, they died in droves. To this day, nobody knows precisely how many lost their lives on the canal project, but somewhere between 3,000 and 30,000 succumbed to cholera, yellow fever and malaria. The canal was used for a century before it became obsolete and was paved over with what is now West End Boulevard. In the 1990s, when work was done on the boulevard, numerous human bones were discovered beneath it, leading historians to conclude that many of the Irish labourers were buried where they fell. Rather than attempt to exhume the entire length of the canal, a Celtic cross made of Kilkenny stone was erected in 1990 at one end of the street, near what had been the head of the New Basin Canal.

A few years after the canal fiasco, in the 1840s and 1850s, the potato famine drove tens of thousands out of Ireland, and another wave of Irish immigrants arrived in New Orleans. An 1860 census counted 25,000 Irish-born residents in the city, or roughly one-sixth of the city's population.

So many Irish moved into the previously unused area between Magazine Street and the river Uptown that it became known as 'the Irish Channel', and it's still called that today. Constance and Annunciation streets were the main thoroughfares. In the middle of the neighbourhood, the Irish built a cathedral, **St Alphonsus** (pictured), where services were delivered in English and Gaelic rather than the usual French.

In the 1950s and 1960s, when racial integration became a divisive issue in New Orleans, most of the descendants of the original Irish families left the area as part of a widespread 'white flight' to the suburbs. There are still a few traditional Irish bars left around here, though; one is **Parasol's** (*see p144*). **O'Flaherty's** Irish pub in the French Quarter (*see p204*) is sub-named 'The Irish Channel' in a nod to the area. And the massive **St Patrick's Day** parade (*see p176*) still starts at St Alphonsus each year, as a sort of homage to the area where the city's now integrated and successful Irish community began.

The Garden District

Even if you have a car, even if you loathe exercise, even if it's July and you could fry oysters on the pavement – don't deprive yourself of a walk through the Garden District. Wandering through this gorgeous neighbourhood (bounded by Jackson and Louisiana avenues and St Charles and Magazine streets) and seeing its remarkable concentration of elaborate houses is one of New Orleans' great pleasures. Guided tours are worthwhile; their knowledgeable leaders provide history, anecdotes and context. But you don't really need them. The sensory delights of the houses and gardens provide a satisfying non-intellectual experience.

The most interesting and significant houses are not on St Charles Avenue but within the web of streets between Jackson and Louisiana avenues. A good place to start is at 2342 Prytania Street, the **Louise S McGehee School**, near the streetcar stop at St Charles Avenue and First Street. The school has been here since 1929; the lavish Renaissance/Second Empire-style villa was built in 1872.

It's notable for its Corinthian columns. The interior can be seen in the film *The Kingfish*, which stars New Orleans resident John Goodman as Governor Huey Long.

Across the street at 2340 Prytania Street, **Toby's Corner** is the oldest house in the Garden District. One of the first of the large Uptown houses, it was built for businessman Thomas Toby in 1839. When the raised Greek Revival mansion went up, the area was still rural, and 'Toby's Corner' was a significant landmark. He made a fortune here, but he unwisely loaned too much of it out to the nascent nation of Texas in the 1830s. When Toby's bills came due for the new house, Texas was broke, and he couldn't pay.

As it is in the French Quarter, intricate ironwork is a feature of many houses here. The cast-iron grillwork at 1331 First Street, designed by architect Samuel Jamison, is magnificent. This 1869 Italianate townhouse was one of the first in the district. The Jamison Greek Revival house a few doors down at No.1315 is virtually unchanged from when it was built in 1869, right down to the oak trees.

Walk this way Garden District

Duration: 30 minutes

The Garden District is still the closest thing New Orleans has to a posh neighbourhood. Its long streets of towering mansions stretch along the edge of the Mississippi River, and finding your way around it can be a bit daunting. One good way to get started is to take a short stroll along **Coliseum Street**, a shady, narrow street on the river side of St Charles Avenue. Named for a grandiose (and unfulfilled) scheme to build a dance and music hall similar to the 18th-century *Colisée de Paris*, Coliseum Street runs from the Warehouse District and dead-ends at Audubon Park. It's narrow even by New Orleans standards, and the looming trees and large houses that crowd it make it feel smaller still.

Start your walk at the corner of First and Coliseum streets and head Uptown, with the downtown skyline at your back. The beautiful 1850 Italianate villa you pass at **1331 First Street** was built for Michel Musson, who was a local cotton broker and an uncle of Impressionist painter Edgar Degas. A later owner, an iron merchant, was responsible for adding the spectacular cast-iron railings and elaborate detail. Nearby on Coliseum Street, the houses at **Nos.2305, 2307 and 2309** all date from 1868. Perhaps examples of post-Civil War austerity, they are relatively modest, but all are built on the same floor plan – the classic side hall layout.

A couple of blocks on, the **Robinson Mansion** at 1415 Third Street is one of the largest houses in the city, and it awes just by its sheer mass. The tobacco magnate Walter Robinson hired local architect James Gallier Jr in the late 1850s to make a statement, and Gallier obliged with a two-storey classical design. The double galleries with their rounded corners are particularly unusual.

Further down, the lovely house at **2618 Coliseum Street** was once a girls' boarding school called 'The Oaks'. This is one of the oldest houses in the district, dating to 1845.

A few houses down, and – whoa, where did that Swiss chalet come from? The 1870s confection at **2627 Coliseum Street** is evidence that even insular New Orleans get sucked into international trends – the elaborate scrollwork and other decorative detail were all the rage among Victorians.

The row of detached townhouses at **2700-2726 Coliseum Street** was built by esteemed local architect William Ferret, but construction was interrupted by the Civil War. The row was called 'Ferret's Folly' because of his lost investment; the houses are good examples of the late-antebellum Greek Revival style.

The ship-like blue and white monster of a building at the corner of Washington Street is **Commander's Palace**, one of the city's legendary restaurants. Now world-famous, this flagship of one branch of the fractious Brennan family dates to 1880. Famous as a bootleg saloon during Prohibition, it's now frequented by film stars, heads of state and Uptown ladies who lunch (*see p121*).

Just across the street from Commander's is **Lafayette Cemetery No.1**. Established in 1833, it is a showcase of New Orleans' obsession with death and its rituals. There are above-ground tombs, multi-generational vaults and society tombs. Many have lovely decorative elements, elaborate stonework and statuary. Even the humble burial vaults where members of mutual aid societies were laid to rest have an affecting beauty. It's understandably popular with filmmakers: Ashley Judd was almost killed here in *Double Jeopardy,* and John Woo let his assassin dogs out here in *Hard Boiled*.

From here, a quick walk down leafy Washington Street will take you to the little Rink shopping centre, where you can stop for an iced coffee before walking down Washington to the St Charles streetcar.

One of the most visited sites in the Garden District is the lovely, rambling 1857 Greek Revival/Italianate mansion at the corner of First and Chestnut streets (1239 First Street). Although she owns other houses, **Rosegate** is the primary home of novelist Anne Rice. She used to let fans tour it, but ended the practice after her husband Stan's death.

Pre-Rice, the most famous house around here was probably **1134 First Street**. The 1849 Greek Revival mansion has clean, simple lines and a beautiful garden, but its main claim to fame is that the first and only Confederate president, Jefferson Davis, died there in 1889 while visiting friends.

Michel Musson, uncle of the painter Edgar Degas, had James Gallier Sr build the Italianate villa at **1331 Third Street** for him in 1853. After the Civil War, Musson suffered financial reverses, and he sold the house and moved his family to a rented one on Esplanade Avenue, which his nephew visited in 1872-3. The latter now calls itself the **Degas House** (see p91).

The house at **1415 Third Street** is one of the largest in the Garden District. It's also one of the most elaborate, with a wide gallery and central parapet. This one was constructed in the late 1850s for the tobacco merchant Walter Robinson. A block over is another notable, **Colonel Short's Villa**, at 1448 Fourth Street. The 1859 Italianate house is handsome, but it's the rare cornstalk pattern on the cast-iron fence that people come to see. Make sure to look beyond the fence (similar to one in the French Quarter; see p61) at the remarkable ironwork on the house's columns.

After the houses, the great sight to see in the Garden District is the melancholy and beautiful **Lafayette Cemetery No.1**. Established in the 1830s for the American Protestants of Uptown (then a suburb called Lafayette), the cemetery is open only when a guard is on duty, and it's easiest to visit with a tour group; try **Save Our Cemeteries** (see p101) or **Historic New Orleans Walking Tours** (see p103).

Across Washington Avenue from the cemetery is **Commander's Palace**, one of the best restaurants in the US (see p121). Tenants of the **Rink** shopping centre include the cute **Garden District Book Shop** (with many autographed Anne Rice books; see p158) and a coffeehouse.

Finally, walk a bit further down leafy Washington Avenue and you'll come to the **New Orleans Fire Department Museum**, housed in an old brick fire station. It's friendly and fun, especially for kids.

Decaying beauty on Washington Street.

New Orleans Fire Department Museum

1135 Washington Avenue, at Magazine Street (896 4756/www.nofd.com). St Charles Streetcar/ bus 11 Magazine. **Open** 9am-2pm Mon-Fri. **Admission** free (reservations suggested). **Map** p279 A/B3.

A fire station since 1850, this two-storey building on a quiet stretch of Washington Avenue now houses an array of vintage firefighting equipment and memorabilia, including an 1838 hand pump and an 1860 hand-drawn truck. Visitors are welcome to wander at will, but friendly, knowledgeable firefighters are on hand to act as guides.

St Charles Avenue

Riding the St Charles streetcar up towards Carrollton Avenue is an ideal way to see Uptown. When something strikes your fancy, you can hop off and venture along the pavements and down backstreets to see a vast wealth of 19th-century houses.

As the most prominent and obvious street, St Charles Avenue was often the chosen site for buildings meant to make statements. Most of the biggest mansions along it were built after the Civil War, when the city's fortunes made a modest return. Lower down, the avenue gets calmer by the 3000 block. The **Columns Hotel**

(No.3811, *see p46*) was originally a mansion built for tobacco magnate Simon Hernsheim. The 1883 Italianate villa retains many of its original details, including stained glass.

The **Sully House** (at No.4010) is notable as the home of Thomas Sully, one of the city's most prominent architects, in the late 1800s. He built this modest Queen Anne house for his family. Though much of his work no longer stands, he was one of the architects who helped to create the look that St Charles Avenue is famous for. The grander **Castles House** (further along at No.6000), also built by Sully, is more typical of his style.

At Napoleon Avenue, take a detour in the direction of the river. At No.1314, **St Elizabeth's Orphanage**, founded by the Daughters of Charity of St Vincent de Paul, operated as a girls' home into the 20th century. Anne Rice bought it in the early 1990s, renovated it and used it to house her doll collection, but in 2003, she pared down her real estate holdings, and it went back on the market again.

Back on St Charles Avenue, the distinctive **Sacred Heart Academy** (No.4521) is lovely with its symmetrical three storeys and rows of louvred shutters. Built in 1900, it's the school of choice for the daughters of New Orleans' elite. Further along, on the left, at the junction with Soniat Street, is the sweet little **Milton Latter Memorial Library**, once the home of silent screen star Marguerite Clark. She gave up her career to marry pioneer Louisiana aviator Harry Williams, who was later killed in a plane crash. Inside, the chandeliers and beautiful decorative work are clues to the scale and style of other St Charles Avenue homes, though much of the interior has been massively remodelled to accommodate the library's needs.

One of the most famous mansions on the avenue is the frilly 1896 **Wedding Cake House** (No.5809). An exuberant mélange of Colonial Revival columns, Queen Anne decorative elements and Victorian excess painted sparkling white, it looks more like a film set than a real home.

Just beyond it, **Tulane University** (865 5000/www.tulane.edu) and **Loyola University** (865 2011/www.loyno.edu) are jammed next door to each other, and they feel like one giant campus. They were built at around the same time and have a sibling resemblance, but like real siblings, each rejects the comparison and asserts their differences.

Loyola, a Jesuit institution that traces its beginnings to 1849, has long been the South's leading Catholic university. Its grounds are dominated by the **Holy Name of Jesus Church**, a Gothic-style structure built in 1914. On its relaxed, friendly red-brick campus, you can find a quiet place to rest, get a caffe latte in the student centre or read in the splendid new high-tech Arts and Crafts-style **Monroe Library**.

Tulane is larger and more ambitious than Loyola, and it's eager to be regarded as a top national university, not just a regional star. Its students call it 'the Harvard of the South', but it's really a pricey party school – its social life is much more intense than its intellectual life. The school's history is a classic Louisiana smoke-and-mirrors tale. In 1883, wealthy New Orleans businessman Paul Tulane wanted to fund a technical school to train mechanics. Wily state politicians saw in his idea a way to revive the bankrupt University of Louisiana, the state school they had neglected and refused to fund. Somehow, the conservative Tulane was talked into making a deal, and the state university was rechristened after him and given a second chance. But Paul Tulane had his revenge. As part of the agreement, he was to leave his entire fortune to the university, but after his death no will was found, and his millions went to distant relatives. And they didn't give the university a dime.

Tulane's architecture is, by and large, undistinguished, but the campus has some interesting places to check out. The **Amistad Research Center** (*see p88*), one of the most important collections of African-American history in the world. The public can view changing displays and some of the significant art collection; the library is for scholars only.

Tulane also houses the **Howard-Tilton Memorial Library** (*see p88*), which boasts the Southeastern Architectural Archive and the William Ransom Hogan Archive of New Orleans Jazz. The **Newcomb Art Gallery** in the campus's Woldenberg Art Center hosts changing exhibitions (*see p88*).

Unlike many universities in US cities, Tulane and Loyola have not spawned their own village of beer-and-pizza joints, record shops, used bookstores and run-down group houses. The closest thing is probably **Maple Street**, which parallels St Charles Avenue and has coffeehouses, cafés, shops and one of the city's last few independent bookstores, the **Maple Street Bookshop** (*see p158*).

The area where the streetcar turns off St Charles Avenue onto Carrollton Avenue – known as the **Riverbend** – is green, leafy and rich with upscale shops, cafés and bars. Students tend to hang out around here, and it has a collegiate air. At the Riverbend's edge, the levee along the water is popular with cyclists, joggers and dog walkers.

Anne Rice's doll's house:
St Elizabeth's Orphanage.
See p86.

One of the many landmarks of the St Charles-Carrollton nexus is the **Camellia Grill**, perhaps the best-known diner in the city (*see p122*). Here, waiters in incongruous white jackets take orders without writing them down, while throwing out unintelligible instructions to the grill cook. Fans insist that no order is ever mixed up. Behind it, down Danté Street and other byways that head towards the Riverbend, the mixture of shops and little restaurants (including the famed **Brigsten's**; *see p123*) is worth a wander if you can find a parking space.

Amistad Research Center

Tilton Hall, Tulane University Campus, at St Charles Avenue (865 5535/fax 865 5580/www.tulane.edu/~amistad). St Charles Streetcar. **Open** 9am-4.30pm Mon-Sat. **Admission** free. **Map** p276 B/C8.
The ten million-plus documents here are available only to scholars, but the modest reading room has changing displays from the collection. The Amistad art collection includes major works by Jacob Lawrence, Henry O Tanner, Elizabeth Catlett and other important black artists. Some paintings and sculpture are on display, and visitors are free to walk through the offices and look at the work.

Howard-Tilton Memorial Library

7001 Freret Street, at Audubon Street (865 5605). Bus 15 Freret, 22 Broadway. **Open** *June-Aug* 8am-9pm Mon-Thur; 8am-4.45pm Fri; 10am-4.45pm Sat; noon-4.45pm Sun. *Sept-May* 8am-2am Mon-Thur; 8-10.45pm Fri; 8am-8.45pm Sat; 10am-2am Sun. **Admission** free. **Map** p276 B8.
This remarkable collection includes the impressive Southeastern Architectural Archive, dedicated to the buildings of New Orleans and the Gulf South, and the William Ransom Hogan Archive of New Orleans Jazz, devoted to preserving the history of the music.

Newcomb Art Gallery

Woldenberg Art Center, Tulane University, at Willow Street (865 5328/www.tulane.edu/~gallery). St Charles Streetcar. **Open** 10am-5pm Mon-Fri; noon-5pm Sun. **Admission** free. **Map** p276 B/C8.
Gallery director Erik Neil's speciality is Renaissance and baroque sculpture, but his interests also span African art and 18th-century French gardens, and his tenure promises a wide spectrum of themed exhibitions. Pieces of Newcomb pottery and 19th and early-20th-century art nouveau work by professors and students are on permanent display.

Magazine Street

Magazine Street is where commerce meets New Orleans funk. Running between the Mississippi River and St Charles Avenue, Magazine has always been a working-class area. For many years it was seamlessly connected to the riverfront, with workingmen's cafés, rooming houses and cheap shops lining it from top to bottom. The street's name evolved from the

French word *magasin*, meaning 'shop'. Today Magazine Street is a colourful stretch of second-hand stores, upscale antiques shops, comfortable coffeehouses and good restaurants (*see p149* **Magazine Street: get shopping**).

When exploring Magazine, remember that the businesses here tend to cluster together at long intervals, meaning it's not the best place for a stroll. It's better to park and walk.

In the 2000 block, just below Jackson Avenue, you'll find tempting little luxuries at **Belladonna** (*see p170*) and **Aidan Gill for Men** (*see p169*); charming, affordable folk art at **Simon of New Orleans** and heaps of dusty treasure at **The Quest** (*for both, see p156*), and several other antiques stores. For quick, cheap lunches, **Juan's Flying Burrito** (*see p121*) is a favourite.

Around the 3000 block of Magazine, near Louisiana Street, is a scattering of eateries and shops popular with underemployed twentysomethings, students and upmarket housewives. The friendly **Rue de la Course** coffeeshop at No.3128 (*see p133*) is artists-and-writers central, and an easy place to strike up conversations with locals. The huge notice board at the back is a great place to find out about music, meetings and cheap sublets. On weekend evenings there's often a street-party atmosphere around here, as people bar-and restaurant-hop. One of the anchors of the festivities is student favourite the **Bulldog**; the **Balcony Bar & Café** (*for both, see p144*) has a more diverse crowd. **Joey K's** restaurant (*see p127*) is good for casual dishes.

As Magazine Street heads Uptown, you'll find plenty of small, focused boutiques. Also on this route, entirely unmarked, is Trent Reznor's **Nothing Studio & Records**. Don't get excited, though – you're not getting inside. The offices are in a fortress-like grey masonry building at the corner of Magazine and Jena streets. It was formerly a mortuary (yawn). Now it has state-of-the-art security to keep the fans out, and one-way windows so Reznor and company can see those outside looking needy, and make fun of them.

North of here, the area gradually gets posher. Around the Magazine Street/Jefferson Avenue crossroads is another bustling group of upscale shops, including an outpost of **Earthsavers** (*see p170*), a couple of shoe stores, a massive **Whole Foods Market** (*see p167*) and enough caffeine for 100 all-nighters. In these four blocks, New Orleans' coffee culture goes mad: **PJ's Coffee & Tea** (*see p133*) is faced by **CC's**, while **Café Luna** (*for both, see p131*), one of the city's few independent coffeehouses, looks across at the daunting face of **Starbucks**.

Tremé & Mid-City

Find your way to one of the city's most beautiful overlooked neighbourhoods.

The area just across Rampart Street from the French Quarter is known as Tremé (pronounced 'truh-may'). Originally part of the Tremé family plantation, this is one of the nation's oldest black neighbourhoods. In antebellum times, Tremé was one of the few places in America where free people of colour were allowed to buy and own property, and it remains, to this day, a proudly black neighbourhood. All of its museums are dedicated to the lives and history of African-Americans in New Orleans.

Just beyond Tremé historic **Mid-City** begins. This is quite simply one of the city's prettiest areas. It's where New Orleans hides its biggest art museum and one of the nation's largest urban parks. It is also the home of Jazz Fest, so it is unsurprising that the area has been adopted by local artists, writers and musicians. Housing prices have rocketed here, however, so the newest residents are corporate types, who park their BMWs in front of trendy coffeeshops and dash inside to order skinny

lattes without taking a break from yapping into their mobile phones. Annoying though they are, it's easy to see what drew them here. With its oak-lined avenues, gorgeous tropical gardens and historic houses, this is a quietly beautiful place for a wander, and one that many tourists never discover.

Tremé

Although Tremé fell into disrepair decades ago – and has yet to fully recover – the city has begun to rediscover and honour this neighbourhood's heritage in ways that make it more accessible to outsiders. But although Tremé has several tourist draws and is home to many families, the area can still be unsafe, especially at night. Be alert and travel by car or taxi when possible.

The square facing the French Quarter on Rampart Street, between St Peter and St Ann streets, is **Congo Square**. In the earliest days of the colony, this area was designated by the French government as a place where slaves could congregate. French colonial law, as set down in the Code Noir, forbade owners to make slaves work on Sunday. Instead, they were to encourage them to go to church services. With a day off each week and a place to meet and interact, slaves here were able to retain much more of their African language, music, dance and religion than slaves elsewhere in North America. Here, they blended African and European styles into an early formation of jazz. And gumbo. And voodoo. In terms of the preservation of African culture in the New World, Congo Square is one of the most important sites in the nation. Sadly, most of the surrounding neighbourhood was levelled in the first half of the 20th century. To make amends, a section of the park was renamed after Louis Armstrong and a large arch was erected at St Ann Street with his name on it. Unfortunately, **Louis Armstrong Park** is a half-hearted effort that offers little beyond a statue of Armstrong and a bust of jazz pioneer Sidney Bechet. The park never caught on, and even Congo Square is little more than a bricked spot surrounded by benches.

The Spanish-looking church at Conti and Rampart streets is **Our Lady of Guadeloupe Chapel** (411 N Rampart Street; 525 1551),

Get lost in rambling **City Park**. See pp92-3.

Taking the Longue Vue

In publications that cater to the country-club crowd, you might see this place referred to as the 'Versailles of New Orleans'. Wildly hyperbolic though that is, it shows just how much some garden-crazy locals love this bucolic Xanadu at the outer edge of Mid-City.

Working with several noted architects from 1939 to 1942, a wealthy local family (the Sterns) created this oasis of classical revival-style beauty, and then later donated it all to charity. You can wander through 20 rooms filled with antiques and modern and contemporary art – what would have been the ultimate collection of a wealthy family of the time. The collections veer towards grandmother-friendly – needlework, chintz, period haute couture, porcelain and the like, but peeking into the mansion's art gallery,

dining room and drawing room, you can see where the Sterns entertained Eleanor Roosevelt, John and Robert Kennedy, Pablo Casals and many others.

For most people, the main attraction is the vast, lavish garden – ornately landscaped, lush and elegant, it is truly a local treasure. This nouveau-American garden is zealously preserved by a non-profit foundation as a kind of snapshot of the lifestyle of the rich and not-so-famous Americans of the time – a way of life that has all but disappeared.

Longue Vue House and Gardens

7 Bamboo Road, at Metairie Road (488 5488/www.longuevue.com). **Open** 10am-4.30pm Mon-Sat; 1-5pm Sun. **Admission** $10; $5 concessions. **Credit** MC, V.

Sightseeing

one of the oldest in the city. Now a very active Catholic parish church, it was built in 1826 on what was then the very edge of town as a mortuary chapel. It was distanced from the city because at that time malaria was thought to be caused by some sort of 'death gas' that escaped from dead bodies. To the rear of the chapel is a statue that has come to be known as 'St Expedite'. The much beloved St Expedite is sometimes referred to in whispers as 'the voodoo saint'. If you have never heard of St Expedite, don't rush for a copy of *Lives of the Saints*. The story is that a religious statue arrived from Europe in the 19th century with no labels or tags. The wooden crate was stamped only 'Expedite', and thus the saint received that name. Similar stories have been told in a number of contexts, though, and not only in New Orleans. But true or not, we like it.

The vast cemetery behind the chapel is **St Louis Cemetery No.1**, the oldest in New Orleans. While not the biggest, it is the most atmospheric and probably the scariest. This was the cemetery used in *Easy Rider* for some of its acid tripping scenes. Some tombs date from the 1760s, and it is fascinating to wander among the catacombs. While it makes for a gloomily wonderful solo wander, this place is best seen with a tour group, not least because it is not particularly safe – although the near-constant presence of tour groups means it is safer than it used to be – but also because its stories are told in-depth from someone well-versed in its history. Among its residents is **Homer Plessy**, who filed the 1892 Supreme Court case, Plessy v Ferguson, which resulted

in the 'Jim Crow' period of 'separate but equal' segregation in the southern US. Here and there among the winding, shady paths you'll find Xs marked out with coloured stones on the white tombs, and, at the bases of the tombs, coins, plastic flowers, buttons and all manner of odds and ends. The marks are made by people seeking some sort of intercession by voodoo spirits. The crumbling tomb that is most seriously marked is the one believed to belong to **Marie Laveau**, the legendary voodoo priestess, although the lettering on the tomb has worn away, so nobody is completely certain anymore. There are two other tombs that might house Laveau's remains, but oral history points to this one.

The neighbourhood beside the cemetery is where **Storyville**, the infamous red-light district, flourished from 1896 to 1917 (*see p9, **Pretty baby***). City councillor Sidney Story came up with the idea for a brothel community as a way of quarantining hookers, and it grew into a national scandal. The neighbourhood was demolished at the beginning of World War I, because too many sailors from the nearby naval base were contracting venereal diseases. Today, nothing remains of the grand brothels that provided a musical training ground for so many New Orleans musicians – Buddy Bolden, Jelly Roll Morton, Sidney Bechet, Louis Armstrong. Today, the grim Iberville Housing Projects stand where the buildings used to be.

The residential area around Armstrong Park deteriorated terribly during the mid- and late 20th century, although renovation and preservation efforts are beginning to make inroads into the section nearest Esplanade Avenue. Sadly, low funding levels affect all the museums in Tremé. Most are only open one or two days a week, have small, idiosyncratic collections and are, frankly, not terribly well run. For those with a particular interest in African-American culture and history this can be frustrating, but if you catch them when they're open, they're worth the effort. Foremost among them is the **New Orleans African-American Museum of Art, Culture and History**, which is filled with historical photos and art by African-American artists (see p98). Villa Meilleur, the restored 1828 Trème mansion in which the museum is located, is a stunner with lovely surrounding gardens. Across the street, the **Uphill Gallery** (1500 Governor Nicholls Street) holds a small collection of children's art. It's aimed largely at local, underprivileged kids, as part of an outreach effort to interest them in art. It's only open on Wednesdays. The small **Louisiana Museum of African-American History** is located in the gym on the second floor of **St Augustine's** (1210 Governor Nicholls Street, between N Rampart and St Claude Streets). It has a small collection of historic artefacts related to the city's black community but is only open at weekends. St Augustine's itself is remarkable for its Italianate frame design and for the fact that it was the first Catholic church to be built by an African-American congregation, in 1842. St Augustine's served New Orleans' freed people before the Civil War and was the first church where slaves were allowed to worship alongside freed men.

Across the street from St Augustine's, the **Backstreet Cultural Museum** is one of the neighbourhood's quirkiest sites. Its privately owned memorabilia is housed in a former mortuary. The collection of elaborate Mardi Gras Indian costumes, jazz funeral parade regalia and general bric-a-brac is as eccentric and interesting as the owner (see below).

Backstreet Cultural Museum

1116 St Claude Avenue, between Ursulines & Governor Nicholls streets (522 4806). Bus 88 St Claude. **Open** 10am-5pm Tue-Sat. **Admission** $3. **No credit cards. Map** p277 G6. A labour of love by mortuary worker Sylvester Francis, this is an odd collection of artefacts all devoted to several indigenous New Orleans traditions: jazz funerals, second line dancing and Mardi Gras Indians. This is not a traditional museum in any sense – the displays are not labelled and it all seems thrown together – but if you ask a few questions, it will all be explained by Francis himself, who still runs the place. Call before dropping by, as it's only open when he feels like opening it.

Mid-City & Bayou St John

There are two grand avenues in New Orleans. The most famous is St Charles, and the most under-appreciated is the similarly oak-lined Esplanade, which links the Mississippi River to beautiful Bayou St John in Mid-City.

The neighbourhood known as Mid-City stretches from Claiborne Avenue to Lake Pontchartrain. Although it starts only a mile or so from the Quarter, much of it is not safe to walk around at night. If you haven't got a car, take a bus or taxi (the most useful bus is 48 Esplanade, which goes from the French Quarter along Esplanade Avenue to City Park). By late 2004, you should also be able to take the revitalised streetcar line.

Several of Esplanade Avenue's grand houses are being restored, but many remain neglected, in particular, those between North Claiborne Avenue and North Broad Street. American townhouses, Creole cottages and French colonial mansions line the route, with touches of Greek Revival, Victorian and Italianate along the way. More than 190 of the houses on Esplanade Avenue were built before 1900, as compared to half that many on St Charles. One which is open to the public is the creamy yellow **Degas House**, where Edgar Degas stayed and painted while visiting relatives in New Orleans (see below).

Degas House

2306 Esplanade Avenue, at Tonti Street (821 5009/1-800 755 6730/www.degashouse.com). Bus 48 Esplanade. **Tours** by appointment only. **Admission** $10; $5 concessions. **Credit** MC, V. **Map** p278 F5. Built in 1852, this Italianate structure puzzled architectural historians for years, as it is substantially different from its representation in paintings. The answer seems to be that it was split in two at some point, and No.2306 is just one wing of the rambling villa that once housed an extended family. This was the home of the Mussons, distinguished French Creoles related to the painter Edgar Degas. Degas' mother was brought up in New Orleans but married in France, where she had her son. In 1872-3, Degas came to visit his American relatives. While here, he pined for Paris. He believed the semi-tropical sun was bad for his eyes and found the city's pleasures provincial. He seems to have been a bit of a whinger: he wrote plaintively to his dealer in Paris that there was too much to paint in here. Their mutual friend Manet, he said, would know what to do with this exotic place. Degas is believed to have painted his sister-in-law, Estelle Musson, while staying in this house; that piece is displayed at the New Orleans Museum of Art (see p100). The house is open to the public, but there's little to see directly connected to Degas' visit or even the Musson family.

Bayou St John

The area down Esplanade between North Broad Street and Claiborne Avenue is marked by pleasant coffeeshops, restaurants and small shops. If you fancy a picnic in the nearby park, check out the progressive health food shop **Whole Foods Market**, which has a good deli and an excellent cheese selection (*see p167*). For fresh breads and pastries, stop two doors down at **La Boulangerie**, a bakery run by two French brothers who've got the croissant and baguette thing down pat. The leafy patio at **Café Degas** across the street is a great place for a light lunch (*see p127*). Those with time on their hands can head up Grand Route St John (behind Café Degas) to the colourful **Fair Grinds Coffeehouse** – the baked goods are made here and the coffee beans are fair-trade. The mural uncovered when the building was renovated in 2002, and dates from the 1940s.

Behind all this trendy consumption is the vast **Fair Grounds Racecourse** (*see p222*). While most tourists know it best as the site of the New Orleans Jazz & Heritage Festival, held each spring in late April and early May (*see pp180-81*), the horse-racing season begins here on Thanksgiving Day. If you happen to be in town when the races are on, the Fair Grounds are an amusing place to while away an afternoon and spend a few bucks.

A few blocks down Esplanade Avenue, the city's largest cemetery district begins with **St Louis Cemetery No.3**. Established in 1835 on the site of a leper colony, this vast stretch of burial ground is strikingly beautiful. It's not even particularly gloomy, with thousands of white tombs lined up in neat rows and stretching as far as the eye can see. This is one of the safest cemeteries in the city to visit (as you'll be able to tell from the constant presence of tour buses out front), although it is a bit dull and whitewashed. At the office near the gates, you can pick up a brochure that will give you more history and a map.

From here you can walk down Esplanade to the attractive expanse of **Bayou St John**, which curves off to the right and left. The walk along the water to the left is prettiest, with big historic houses and footbridges over the water. It also passes **Cabrini High School** – today a girls' school, it was opened as an orphanage in 1902. The historic **Pitot House Museum**, near the bayou's bend, is a short stroll away. Constructed in the late 18th century in typical West Indies style, its period furnishings offer a realistic look at how the early French residents of New Orleans lived (*see p100*).

Just beyond the bayou on Esplanade Avenue, the large statue at the centre of the roundabout is of Confederate **General PGT Beauregard**, who died in a house on Esplanade Avenue.

City Park

Just beyond the statue of Beauregard, City Park sits on the former site of the Allard Plantation. It's a beautiful place – 1,400 acres of land shaded by enormous moss-draped oaks and laced with streams and bayous which are crossed by charming, arched bridges. Some of the trees are more than 1,000 years old, and their huge branches reach down so far that they touch the earth. Swans float languidly by, and wild geese roam – watch out; they'll nip if you get too close. This is one of the loveliest parks in the country.

City Park has relatively few services, so bringing a picnic lunch is a good idea. The museum has a café, and there are a few places to eat, but choice is limited. In summer, you'll want to use insect repellent, as the bayous are a breeding ground for mosquitoes. It's safe during the day, but at night it is deserted, except for a few parked cars that you wouldn't want to peek into, if you catch our drift.

The centrepiece is the **New Orleans Museum of Art**, with its white-columned front porch and small permanent collection

Beware of the geese in **City Park**.

The **New Orleans Museum of Art**.

of works that range from some 14th-century European paintings to a good photography collection and some decorative arts. It has a new gallery devoted to Louisiana artists, but its main draw is the excellent travelling exhibitions that pass through (for more, *see p100*). Ask the information desk inside NOMA for a map of the park.

As you stand in front of NOMA facing its front porch, the big oak trees to your left are known as the 'duelling oaks'; this is where Creole gentlemen settled *affaires d'honneur*. Duelling wasn't outlawed until 1890.

Just behind the museum is the most tourist-oriented section of the park, the **New Orleans Botanical Garden**. This lush garden dates back to the Depression, when much of the park was upgraded. Most of the work was done by artists and builders associated with the Works Progress Administration (a federal programme put into place by Franklin Delano Roosevelt). The workers created the art deco-inspired fountains, ponds, bridges and sculptures that make the park so delightful. The lush 12-acre gardens are filled with more than 2,000 native plants. Highlights are the arresting sculptures by Enrique Alferez, a Mexican-born sculptor. More of his work, also done under the auspices of the WPA, can be seen in the gardens and throughout the park. Nearby, a five-acre **Sculpture Garden** (scheduled to open in autumn 2003) will feature a significant collection of pieces of modern sculpture by artists including Henry Moore. *See p99* **A sculptural garden of Eden**.

Beyond the botanical and sculpture gardens lies a charming children's playground called **Storyland**. With its colourful storybook characters and small amusement park that features an antique wooden carousel, this place is a great favourite of children. Featuring the

work of famed carvers Looff and Carmel, the **William A Hines Carousel** is listed on the National Register of Historic Places and is glorious shape after a recent renovation. The adorable sculpted characters in Storyland were made by Mardi Gras float maker Blaine Kern Jr.

Further into the park are the **Bayou Oaks Golf Course** (*see p224*), with four 18-hole courses and a driving range, and the **City Park Stables**, which offer trail rides and riding lessons.

New Orleans Botanical Garden

Victory Avenue, southern end of City Park (483 9386/www.neworleans.com/garden). Bus 46 City Park, 48 Esplanade, 90 Carrollton. **Open** 10am-4.30pm Tue-Sun. **Admission** $3; $1 concessions; free under-5s. **No credit cards. Map** p278 D4.
The gardens stretch over ten acres and include a conservatory, gift shop and garden study centre. Visitors are free to walk about the grounds, where staff and volunteers will happily gab away about the greenery if you're at all interested. The garden's entrance is on Victory Avenue.

Storyland & William A Hines Carousel Gardens

Victory Avenue, southern end of City Park (483 9381/carousel 483 9356). Bus 46 City Park, 48 Esplanade, 90 Carrollton. **Open** *Storyland* 10am-2.30pm Mon-Fri; 10.30am-4.30pm Sat, Sun. *Carousel Gardens* 10am-2.30pm Wed-Fri; 11am-5.30pm Sat, Sun. **Admission** *Storyland* $2; free under-2s. *Carousel Gardens* $2; free under-2s; plus $10 for unlimited rides. **No credit cards. Map** p278 E4.
This pre-Disney children's playground, with its storybook characters and a small amusement park next door with a rare wooden carousel, will delight families with small children. The kiddie park hasn't been kept up as well as it might have been, but some people actually enjoy the shabbiness as a respite from theme-park perkiness.

Cities of the dead

'A New Orleans cemetery is a city in miniature, streets, curbs, iron fences, its tombs above ground... little two-story dollhouses complete with doorstep and lintel.' – Walker Percy

Mark Twain once said that New Orleans had no architecture to speak of except in the cemeteries. He was surely being sarcastic, for the cemeteries – or cities of the dead, as he dubbed them – are little more than a toy-town version of New Orleans itself.

The whitewashed tombs are about ten feet high – some small and simple like shotgun houses, others like elaborate little Garden District mansions – and aligned in neat rows along paths like lilliputian roadways stretching, sometimes, as far as the eye can see. Many of the tombs are surrounded by wrought-iron fences, and here and there the paths are dotted with old iron benches, where Creole widows would sit in the 19th century and greet well-wishers near their dead husbands' tombs.

While fascinating to see, the cemeteries are not here for aesthetic purposes. They were, instead, the results of centuries of trial and error, as early residents struggled to find a way to bury their dead so that they would stay buried. The problem is that New Orleans is below sea level, so the water table

'Little dollhouses' in **St Louis No.3**.

rises to a few inches below the topsoil. When holes were dug 6 feet deep, they tended to fill, almost immediately, with 5 feet 10 inches of water. Coffins placed deep in the holes were soon poking through the ground at spooky angles.

Early residents tried desperately to comeup with ways to solve the problem. For a while, rather horribly, they bored holes into the coffins before lowering them. Mourners standing around the grave could hear the water trickling in around the bodies of their dead relatives. And still the coffins rose with the first storm. However deep the graves were dug, whichever technique was used, the bodies always made their way out again. In heavy rains, coffins washed down the street.

It was the Spanish who introduced the idea of entombment, which was common in Spain at the time. The city took to it quickly, as it made the perfect solution to the problem. Soon crypts were being built instead of cemeteries.

Over time, it was discovered that the baking heat of the New Orleans sun combined with the oven-like qualities of the tombs meant most bodies decomposed down to nothing but dust and bones within a year. Thus the city came up with the thoroughly logical 'year-and-a-day law' (still in place today), under which, once a body is placed in a tomb, the tomb may not be opened until a year and a day have passed. After that point, if another family member has died, the tomb is opened and the remains are examined. If nothing is left but bones and hair, these are dumped from the coffin on to the ground at the back of the tomb. This creates room for a new

coffin to be installed. Thus it is common that small tombs hold generations of remains.

With all the names filling up the tomb fronts, there's little room for the creative and quirky comments, Bible verses and poems typically found in early American cemeteries elsewhere. Over time, then, the architecture of the tomb itself became the way in which families expressed their creativity. Some are gaudy and huge, like miniature Taj Mahals. Others are as simple and basic as bungalows. Some feature statues of the deceased, or of things the deceased loved (occasionally you'll see a tomb topped with a deer or a dog). No explanation is usually given for these idiosyncratic elements, and they become part of a cemetery's mystery, as generations down the line nobody can quite recall just why Grandpa Robichaux wanted a badger on top of his tomb.

Each cemetery has a distinctively different appearance from the others. The gaudiest tombs can be found in **Metairie Cemetery**, just off the interstate near Mid-City (at the Metairie Road exit). The darkest, most unusual and oldest tombs are in **St Louis No.1** near the French Quarter (see p90). The most beautiful marble angels are in **St Louis No.3** in Bayou St John (see p92), while the bodies of some of the earliest settlers are in **Lafayette Cemetery** in the Garden District (see p85).

All the cemeteries are open during daylight hours most days, and entry to all is free. One of the best tours in town is given by the local conservation group **Save Our Cemeteries** (1-888 721 7493, see also p103).

Museums

Guns, flags and war... and a little Henry Moore.

Given the age and historic oddities of New Orleans – scene of wars, occupations, transfers of power and the Louisiana Purchase – it's no surprise that the city is home to some fine historical museums. The fact that it also holds some strong art collections comes as a bit of surprise to those who think of it as a booze-and-guns kind of town. Still, there's no question that history is its strong suit, for here, history is everywhere – and it's especially well organised and labelled at the **Louisiana State Museum**, which is divided among several noteworthy buildings in and around the French Quarter. The cluster of museums in downtown's Warehouse District (which the city has been desperately and unsuccessfully trying to get everyone to call the 'Arts District') include the small but oh-so-modern **Contemporary Arts Center** (*see p98*) and the brand-new high-rise **Ogden Museum of Southern Art** (*see p100*), whose mandate is to redeem Southern art in the eyes of the world. No mean feat, if you ask us. After all, the wonderfully anachronistic **Confederate Museum** (*see p98*), next door to the Ogden, is more what people think of when they think of the US South.

Besides the Ogden, the other new kid on the block is the **National D-Day Museum** (*see pp99-100*), which was founded by one of the country's most beloved historians, the late Stephen Ambrose, and explores in fascinating detail the US contribution to World War II.

Finally, down in Mid-City, the city's premier arts venue is the **New Orleans Museum of Art** (*see p100*), which, even with its well-chosen small collection and gorgeous new sculpture garden, enjoys a setting that's more beautiful than most of the works inside.

French Quarter

The Cabildo & Louisiana State Museum

701 Chartres Street, at St Peter Street (568 6968/ http://lsm.crt.state.la.us). Riverfront Streetcar/bus 3 Vieux Carré, 5 Marigny/Bywater, 55 Elysian Fields. **Open** 9am-5pm Tue-Sun. **Admission** $5; $4 concessions; free under-12s. **Credit** MC, V. **Map** p282 C2.

The Cabildo is the Louisiana State Museum's flagship location. If you see only one historic museum, this should probably be it. The building it's in was

Enjoy Mardi Gras from the comfort of the **Presbytère Museum**. See p98.

'Southern art' is not an oxymoron

The Ogden Collection has come a long way from its modest genesis 30 years ago, when a Louisiana State University student named Roger Ogden persuaded his father to join him in giving his mother a painting for her birthday. The painting was a Louisiana landscape by the early 20th-century New Orleans impressionist Alexander Drysdale. Thus began an obsession with the region's art that would eventually drive Ogden, now a New Orleans business executive and philanthropist, to amass one of the nation's outstanding private collections.

Today, his extraordinary collection forms the nucleus of the nascent **Ogden Museum of Southern Art**'s holdings (*see p100*). It's the largest, most comprehensive of its kind in the US, with 2,700 paintings, watercolours, drawings, prints, sculptures, photographs and crafts reflecting the South's visual heritage from 1733 to the present.

The museum, affiliated with the Smithsonian Institution in Washington, DC, and operated by the University of New Orleans, was set to

open in late autumn 2003. The works will be spread through two buildings, with the 20th- and 21st-century collections in Goldring Hall, a new five-storey structure with a central atrium that rises the height of the building. The building will house 20 galleries, along with a shop and a rooftop terrace. Also here will be the **Center for Southern Craft and Design**, where regional artists and artisans can showcase their work.

The museum's featured selections include the Louisiana works that formed the heart of Ogden's original collection, and numerous special galleries such as those devoted to the work of the legendary Mississippi artist Walter Anderson and the creative legacies of the innovative modernist Will Henry Stevens and the African-American painter Benny Andrews, who was famed for his extraordinary collages.

Next to Goldring Hall, an imposing old library building will ultimately house the 18th- and 19th-century collections. It is scheduled to open in 2004 after extensive restoration work (but bear in mind that the whole project is already years behind. so don't book your tickets until the doors swing open). The library will also house the Institute for the Advancement of Southern Art and Culture and the Clementine Hunter Wing, showcasing works by the famed, self-taught painter of Louisiana plantation life (pictured).

When complete, the museum will be a place where visitors can 'experience the region's unique spirit, vitality and sense of place,' says Director Richard Gruber. 'What we are developing is a unique Southern experience, one based upon the region's rich and complex history and culture.'

Sightseeing

built as the Spanish government's headquarters; the Louisiana Purchase was signed here in 1795. Today, it houses thousands of artefacts and artworks reflecting Louisiana's historic and cultural legacy, including Napoleon's death mask. The medieval-looking Arsenal next door, with a separate entrance at 619 St Peter Street, is home to a changing array of special exhibitions. The Louisiana State Museum also operates the nearby 1850 House on St Ann Street (*see p66*), a historic residence, and Madame John's Legacy on Dumaine (*see p63*), one of the oldest houses in the city, now showing a long-running folk art exhibition. The Cabildo's sister facility, the Presbytère (*see p98*), and the Old US Mint (*see p98*) a few blocks away both host major exhibitions.

Historic New Orleans Collection

533 Royal Street, between Toulouse & St Louis streets (523 4662/www.hnoc.org). Riverfront Streetcar/bus 3 Vieux Carré, 5 Marigny/Bywater, 55 Elysian Fields. **Open** *Williams Gallery* 10am-4.30pm Tue-Sat. *Louisiana History Galleries & Trapolin House tours* 10am, 11am, 2pm, 3pm Tue-Sat. **Admission** *Williams Gallery* free. *Louisiana History Galleries & Trapolin House* (by guided tour only) $4. **No credit cards. Map** p282 B2.
Serious and low-key, the HNOC's free public gallery houses well-researched exhibitions on local history, complete with original maps, documents, pictures and artefacts. The maze of historic buildings, including the 1792 Merieult House (*see p60*), also houses a scholarly research facility. Private collectors General

and Mrs L Kemper Williams established the HNOC in 1966; you can tour their home, the 1889 Trapolin house, and the upstairs Louisiana History Galleries.

New Orleans African-American Museum of Art, Culture and History

1418 Governor Nicholls Street, at Villere Street (565 7497/527 0989/www.noaam.org). Bus 5 Marigny/Bywater, 88 St Claude. **Open** 10am-5pm Mon-Fri; 10am-2pm Sat. **Admission** $5; $2-$3 concessions. **No credit cards. Map** p277 G6.
Located in the restored Villa Meilleur in Tremé, next to the French Quarter, this museum hosts exhibitions interpreting African-American history and culture. While these have been inconsistent and unpredictable in quality, the house itself is a lovely example of Caribbean antebellum architecture which fits nicely in Tremé, one of the oldest African-American communities in the US. Built in 1828 and sequestered behind leafy gardens, it can seem like a throwback to 19th-century Haiti or Martinique.

Old US Mint

400 Esplanade Avenue, at Decatur Street (568 6968/ http://lsm.crt.state.la.us). Riverfront Streetcar/bus 3 Vieux Carré, 5 Marigny/Bywater, 48 Esplanade, 55 Elysian Fields. **Open** 9am-5pm Tue-Sun. **Admission** $5; $4 concessions; free under-12s. **Credit** MC, V. **Map** p282 D3.
Andrew Jackson reviewed his troops on this spot before the Battle of New Orleans; later, this block-long Greek Revival edifice did federal moneymaking duty from 1838 to 1909 (sample coins and notes are now sold in the shop). The building also houses an archive for French and Spanish colonial records. But overall, the focus is on the colourful history of jazz, and the related collection is impressive. Musical pilgrims come from around the world to see Louis Armstrong's first cornet, Dizzy Gillespie's modified horns, and the photos of bands on steamboats and in the Storyville bordellos where Jelly Roll Morton and so many other greats came of age, and where jazz was so gloriously born.

New Orleans Historic Pharmacy Museum

514 Chartres Street, at St Louis Street (565 8027/ www.pharmacymuseum.org). Riverfront Streetcar/ bus 3 Vieux Carré, 5 Marigny/Bywater, 55 Elysian Fields. **Open** 10am-5pm Tue-Sun. **Admission** $2; $1 concessions; free under-12s. **Credit** AmEx, MC, V. **Map** p282 B2.
Built in 1823 for Louis Dufilho, the first licensed pharmacist in America, this old apothecary has ceramic leech urns, beautiful handmade glass pill vessels and other 19th-century tools of the trade all on display. The sickroom and library, and the medicinal herb garden in the courtyard, will take you back in time and make you glad you don't live there.

The Presbytère

751 Chartres Street, at St Ann Street (568 6968/ http://lsm.crt.state.la.us). Riverfront Streetcar/bus 3 Vieux Carré, 5 Marigny/Bywater, 55 Elysian

Fields. **Open** 9am-5pm Tue-Sun. **Admission** $5; $4 concessions; free under-12s. **Credit** MC, V. **Map** p282 C2.
The Presbytère museum is now devoted to Mardi Gras, and it does an excellent job. Its permanent exhibition covers history, parades, masking, and the Cajun *Courir du Mardi Gras* (*see p239*). It traces Carnival from its ancient origins on to the bold, brash extravaganza of the present day.

Warehouse District

The Confederate Museum

929 Camp Street, at Andrew Higgins Boulevard (523 4522/www.confederatemuseum.com). St Charles Streetcar. **Open** 10am-4pm Mon-Sat. **Admission** $5; $2-$4 concessions. **Credit** MC, V. **Map** p279 B/C2.
Founded by Civil War veterans in the late 19th century, this museum is Louisiana's oldest. Today, with its archaic displays and utter lack of comment on whether the Confederacy might have been in the wrong, it stands out as what it is – a relic of an earlier time. It could even be seen as glorifying the Confederate cause. Still, if you can set aside indignation, the collection is truly fascinating if you have even a passing interest in the Civil War. The more unusual items on view include a crown of thorns given to Confederate President Jefferson Davis by Pope Pius IX and a variety of historic weapons, flags, uniforms and personal memorabilia.

Contemporary Arts Center

900 Camp Street, at St Joseph Street (528 3805/ www.cacno.org). St Charles Streetcar. **Open** *galleries* 11am-5pm Tue-Sun; *cybercafé* 11am-5pm daily. **Admission** $5; $3 concessions; free under 15s. Free to all Thur. **Credit** AmEx, MC, V. **Map** p279 C2.
This impressive visual and performing arts facility is the sun around which downtown's galleries orbit. It has little in the way of a permanent collection, though. Exhibitions change constantly: you might catch an electronic music concert, an opera, a digital graphics display, or any combination thereof.

Louisiana Children's Museum

420 Julia Street, between Magazine & Tchoupitoulas streets (523 1357/www.lcm.org). St Charles Streetcar/ bus 3 Vieux Carré, 10 Tchoupitoulas, 11 Magazine. **Open** *Sept-May* 9.30am-4.30pm Tue-Sat; noon-4.30pm Sun. *June-Aug* 9.30am-4.30pm Mon-Sat; noon-4.30pm Sun. **Admission** $6. **Credit** AmEx, Disc, MC, V. **Map** p279 C2.
This highly innovative and interactive 'please touch' museum makes science, maths, art, theatre and music fun. Hands-on activities include games, mazes and a scavenger hunt; permanent exhibits include Kidwatch Studio, the Lab and Cajun Cottage. It's all housed in a two-storey historic 1861 warehouse.

National D-Day Museum

945 Magazine Street, at Andrew Higgins Boulevard (527 6012/www.ddaymuseum.org). St Charles Streetcar/bus 3 Vieux Carré, 11 Magazine.

A sculptural garden of Eden

They used to be a local secret. The valuable sculpture collection at the K&B Corporation's headquarters on Lee Circle – a profusion of modernist works by artists like Henry Moore, Barbara Hepworth, Kenneth Snelson and Lynn Chadwick – filled an outdoor plaza and overflowed down to the street. Even the streetcar stop nearby was occupied by three of George Segal's life-size carved figures, waiting endlessly for their ride. It was the best sculpture collection in the city, and it was stuck on a concrete slab under the interstate. Inside the building, staff allowed the public to wander the halls in a kind of high-art hide-and-seek game, looking for more pieces of the 60-odd collection, which were tucked beside lift doors, behind wandering philodendron plants and near water coolers.

And then the K&B Corporation, a family-owned drugstore chain presided over by fervent arts supporter Sidney Besthoff, was bought in the mid-1990s by a national chain. The second thought everybody in town had upon hearing the news (after 'Where am I going to get pecan-and-maple ice-cream now?') was 'What the hell is going to happen to all those sculptures?'

For a while there, the future of the collection, valued at over $25 million, was uncertain. Then, in 1999, the family donated it all to the New Orleans Museum

of Art. NOMA couldn't believe its good luck and promptly began work on an outdoor sculpture garden on an island amid City Park's bayous and moss-draped waterways.

Scheduled to open in autumn 2003, the sculpture garden will be one of the most unusual art locales in the country. Traversed by meandering lagoons and bayous, City Park, one of America's largest urban green spaces, still retains a touch of swampy wildness (*see p91*). The park is actually no stranger to sculpture: in the 1930s, the Works Progress Administration extensively improved it, appointing legendary Mexican expatriate sculptor Enrique Alferez to preside over a team of artists who left their mark in the form of numerous art deco monuments and fountains still scattered across the park.

Today, those works are joined by Elizabeth Frink's *Riace Warriors* (pictured), who will now stride powerfully across the island, rather than across concrete, toward Kenneth Snelson's impossibly gossamer *Virlane Tower*, a gravity-defying isometric pylon composed only of metal tubes and steel cable, which now resides among moss-hung oaks rather than the glass towers of office buildings. And Henry Moore's *Reclining Mother and Child* look irresistibly beautiful and loving leaning together under the oaks.

Best of all, as was always the case, admission to see the sculptures is free.

The **National D-Day Museum**.

Open 9am-5pm daily. **Admission** $10; $5-$6 concessions; free under-5s, uniformed military. **Credit** AmEx, Disc, MC, V. **Map** p279 C2.

This shining new $21 million museum devoted to the soldiers who fought World War II has become wildly popular. The long-time passion of local historian Stephen Ambrose (bestselling author of *Band of Brothers*), it chronicles the Allied invasion of Normandy on 6 June 1944 with 3,500 artefacts, documents and photographs. There are also several short documentary films and a replica of the New Orleans-designed Higgins assault boat, the landing craft used in the invasion. General Eisenhower once called this boat the most important factor in winning the war. World War II veterans are almost always on hand to answer questions and talk about their own experiences.

Ogden Museum of Southern Art

925 Camp Street, at Andrew Higgins Boulevard (539 9600/www.ogdenmuseum.org). St Charles Streetcar/bus 3 Vieux Carré, 5 Marigny/Bywater, 55 Elysian Fields. **Map** p279 B2.

Scheduled to open in late 2003, this Smithsonian Institution affiliate will explore the history and culture of the American South through a varied range of art and memorabilia. Its impressive collection – which includes paintings, prints, ceramics, photography and sculpture from the 18th through the 21st centuries – is expected to vastly expand New Orleans' art offerings. The Ogden's opening hours and admission prices had not yet been decided as this guide went to press, so phone or check the website before you go. (*See also p97* '**Southern art' is not an oxymoron.**)

City Park & beyond

New Orleans Museum of Art

City Park, One Collins Diboll Circle (488 2631/ www.noma.org). Canal Streetcar/bus 46 City Park, 48 Esplanade, 90 Carrollton. **Open** 10am-5pm

Tue-Sun. **Admission** *Through 25 Feb 2004* $17; $10-$16 concessions. *From 26 Feb 2004* $6; $3-$5 concessions; free under-3s; free to Louisiana residents with ID 10am-noon Thur. **Credit** AmEx, MC, V. **Map** p278 E4.

Set among the ancient oaks of City Park, NOMA is the grand dame of New Orleans museums. It's known for its blockbuster travelling exhibitions – currently The Quest for Immortality: Treasures of Ancient Egypt – but it also holds a diverse collection of more than 40,000 works spanning the 15th to the 21st centuries. It has also gained attention for its strong African and Asian collections, its significant photography and Louisiana art holdings, and its Fabergé eggs, which once belonged to the Russian royal family. The latest addition is the truly impressive Sidney and Walda Besthoff Sculpture Garden, which features works by 20th-century masters including Henry Moore, Barbara Hepworth, Elizabeth Frink, Isamu Noguchi and Alexander Calder (*see* **A sculptural garden of Eden** *p99*).

Pitot House Museum

1440 Moss Street, between Esplanade Avenue and Grand Route St John (482 0312/www.pitot house-landmarks.org). Canal Streetcar/bus 46 City Park, 48 Esplanade, 90 Carrollton. **Open** 10am-3pm (last tour at 2pm) Wed-Sat. **Admission** $5; $2 concessions. **Credit** MC, V. **Map** p278 E4.

Built in the 1790s in a graceful West Indies style, featuring brick-between-post construction and a classical French colonial double-pitched roof, the Pitot House is one of the city's most graceful residences. Painted in soft Creole reds and yellows, it dates back to a time when Bayou St John was lined with plantations. Named for Jacques Pitot, a Haitian refugee who bought it in 1810 and later became mayor of New Orleans, the house was restored in the 1960s and is now furnished with early 19th-century antiques. This is the city's most respected historic house museum, and it's well worth a visit for its lovely location as well as its unusual architecture.

Guided Tours

Because it's easier than looking it up yourself.

New Orleans has been called one big outdoor museum for its marvellous architecture, historic sites and unusual traditions. Showing visitors the ins and outs of this 'museum' has become a mini industry, with walking, guided, bus and carriage tours. Specific tours come and go, but a corps of well-schooled, polished tour guides keep the overall quality high. Whether its a coach tour around town, a riverboat tour along the Mississippi or a walking tour of the French Quarter, there's much to learn from the guides.

Night-time tours that track ghost and vampire legends around the French Quarter have become so prevalent that it's led to an uproar, with residents complaining that they're too loud, too big and too invasive. As that pitched battle continues, so do the tours, causing pedestrian traffic jams as guides manoeuvre their groups to the spots with the juiciest stories.

French Quarter tours

Carriage tours

Mule-drawn carriage tours of the French Quarter are a staple of New Orleans tourism, but their allure is a mystery. The tours are smelly and slow, some of the mules wretched and the drivers notoriously inaccurate (though colourful) storytellers. If you want to see the Quarter by mule, there are several things to bear in mind. You're not required to take the first vehicle in line, so walk up and down, check out the driver and his beast, and ask about prices; these can vary widely, from $5 a person to $40 for a couple. The carriages park on Decatur Street in front of Jackson Square all day, every day. In summer, they are sometimes shut down when it's too hot and humid even for a mule.

Walking tours

Friends of the Cabildo French Quarter Walking Tours

Information 523 3939/fax 524 9130/www.friends ofthecabildo.org. Tour starts at the 1850 House Museum Store, 523 St Ann Street, on Jackson Square. **Tours** 1.30pm Mon; 10am, 1.30pm Tue-Sun (arrive 15 minutes before tour). **Rates** $12; $10 concessions; free under-12s. **Credit** AmEx, DC, Disc, MC, V. **Map** p282 C2.

Two-hour walks around the Quarter with trained volunteers, usually pensioners and/or long-time New Orleans residents with a wealth of detail to add to the facts. The emphasis is on architecture, historical accuracy and culture.

Haunted History Tours

Information 861 2727/www.hauntedhistory tours.com. Tours leave from Rev Zombie's Voodoo Shop, 723 St Peter Street, between Bourbon & Royal streets, French Quarter. **Tours** daily, at various times. **Rates** $18; $15 concessions; $9 under-12s. **Credit** AmEx, DC, Disc, MC, V. **Map** p282 B2.

Theatrical guides from this company are often dressed in black and accessorised with boots and capes, as they take their charges to the purported scenes of vampire and ghost sightings. Despite that, the tours can be very good. The same group also does cemetery and Garden District tours.
Branch: Tours also leave from Corner Bar & Restaurant, 500 St Peter Street, at Decatur Street, French Quarter.

Jean Lafitte National Historical Park & Preserve Tours

Information 589 2636/www.nps.gov/jela. Tours start at French Quarter Visitors Center, 419 Decatur Street, French Market. **Tours** 9.30am daily. **Rates** Free. **Map** p282 C3.

Universally called 'the ranger walks', these 90-minute tours of the Quarter are led by park rangers in uniform. These are some of the best tours in the city, and not just because they are free. Along with colourful stories, the tours are particularly good on the city's history and architecture. Each walk can accommodate 25 people. Passes are handed out at the office in the French Quarter Visitors Center from 9am every morning, and each person must collect his or her own ticket in person.

Le Monde Creole French Quarter Courtyard Walking Tour

Information 568 1801/www.lemondecreole.com. Tour starts at Le Monde Creole shop, 624 Royal Street, between St Peter & Toulouse streets. **Tours** *English* 10.30am, 1.30pm Mon-Sat; 10am, 1.30pm Sun. *French* 1pm Mon; 2pm Wed; 10am Fri; 12.30pm Sun. (Reservations suggested.) **Rates** $20; $15 concessions. **Credit** AmEx, MC, V. **Map** p282 B2.

This tour acquaints visitors with daily Creole life in New Orleans by following in the footsteps of the Locouls, a Creole family once based at Laura Plantation (*see p231*). The tour deals sensitively and insightfully with the 'shadow' Locouls – the white men's black mistresses and children.

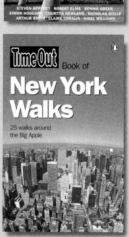

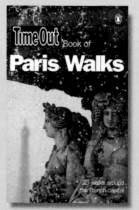

Nature just around the corner

Put off by the stuffed alligators for sale in
French Quarter souvenir shops? Want to
get up close and personal with the real thing?
Head for the Barataria, in the **Jean Lafitte
National Historical Park and Preserve**.
Just 15 minutes drive from downtown New
Orleans, it offers hikes among the flora and
fauna – 'gators included – plus free ranger-
led walks and Saturday morning canoe trips.

The preserve has nine Spanish-moss-
draped trails through palmetto groves and
along murky canals. Most are paved and
feature elevated boardwalks – a nice touch,
considering the creepy crawly things that call
the swamp home. Each season brings out a
different aspect of the preserve: summer, for
example, is the best time to see alligators
and butterflies, while migratory birds and
wild irises flood the park in spring.

Before hitting the trails, it's a good idea
to stop by the visitor centre (9am-5pm daily;
589 2330), where educational exhibits give
a sense of what life was like for the people
who settled in and made their livelihoods
from Louisiana's vast swamplands. Rangers
can also clue you in on trail hazards and
closures, which are frequent because of
flooding and other weather-related damage.

If you're short on time, opt for the Bayou
Coquille Trail, a 1.8-mile (4.6 kilometre)
hike which follows a path originally cut by
an oil company road. The trail ends rather
dramatically at an expansive vista of
marsh grasses and wetlands.

A full schedule of park activities and
free ranger-guided tours can be had at the
Barataria visitor centre or the Jean Lafitte
National Historical Park visitor centre in the
French Quarter (419 Decatur Street, French
Quarter, 589 2636). Space is limited for
most tours, so book in advance.

Garden District & cemetery tours

Historic New Orleans Walking Tours

*Information 947 2120/fax 947 2130/
www.tourneworleans.com. French Quarter tour
starts at Café Beignet, 1021 Decatur Street, at
Ursulines Street. Cemetery and Voodoo tour
starts in courtyard of Café Beignet, 334B Royal
Street, between Bienville & Conti streets. Garden
District Tour starts at Garden District Bookshop,
at the Rink Mall, Washington Street, at Prytania
Street.* **Tours** *French Quarter 10.30am daily.
Cemetery and Voodoo 10am, 1pm Mon-Sat;
10am Sun. Garden District 11am, 1.45pm daily.*
Rates *French Quarter tour* $12; $10 concessions;
free under-12s. *Cemetery and Voodoo tour* $15;
$13 concessions; free under-12s. *Garden District*
$14; $12 concessions; free under-12s.
No credit cards.

Ex-park ranger Rob Florence started this company,
and he runs some of the city's best tours. A cemetery historian and passionate preservationist, he
leads many walks himself. The Garden District tour
includes Lafayette Cemetery No.1. The Cemetery
and Voodoo tour takes you into St Louis No.1. Other
walk include a night-time ghost tour of the Quarter.

Save Our Cemeteries

Information 525 3377/1-888 721 7493/
www.saveourcemeteries.org. **Tours** *St Louis*
Cemetery No.1 10am Sun. *Lafayette Cemetery*
No.1 10.30am Mon, Wed, Fri, Sat. **Rates** *Lafayette*
Cemetery No.1 $6; $5 concessions; free under-12s.
St Louis Cemetery No.1 $12; $6-$10 concessions;
free under-12s. **Credit** (only for large groups
booking in advance) AmEx, MC, V.

Well-schooled volunteers lead tours in Lafayette
No.1 and St Louis No.1 to raise funds for the non-
profit conservation group protecting the graveyards.

River tours

Cajun Queen & Creole Queen

Information 529 4567/1-800 445 4109/
www.neworleanspaddlewheels.com. One-hour
harbour cruise, Chalmette Battlefield cruise
depart from wharf in front of the Aquarium
of the Americas. Jazz dinner cruise departs
from Riverwalk/Canal Street Dock.
Cruises *One-hour harbour cruise* 11.30am,
1pm, 2.30pm, 4pm daily. *Chalmette Battlefield*
10.30am, 2pm daily. *Jazz dinner cruise* 8pm daily.
Rates *One-hour harbour cruise* $14; $8 concessions;
free under-5s. *Chalmette Battlefield* $19; $11
concessions; free under-5s. *Jazz dinner cruise*
Without dinner $27; $18 concessions; free under-5s.
Including dinner $51; $27 concessions; free under-5s.
Credit AmEx, Disc, MC, V. **Map** p279 C1.

These two sister boats offer a range of short and
longish tours. The Creole Queen makes two daily
cruises to the Chalmette Battlefield, site of the 1815
Battle of New Orleans, where a park ranger leads a
short tour. It also does a nightly jazz dinner cruise.
The Cajun Queen takes passengers on one-hour
river tours four times a day.

New Orleans Steamboat Company

Information 586 8777/1-800 233 2628/
www.steamboatnatchez.com. Tours start at
Gray Line Ticket Booth, Toulouse Street Wharf,
at the Mississippi River. **Tours** phone for a schedule.
Rates $8-$45; $6-$23 concessions. **Credit** AmEx,
DC, Disc, MC, V. **Map** p282 B3.

Hear the calliope tooting out old songs? That's the
Natchez, the only steam-powered riverboat regularly plying the waters around New Orleans. No clichés
here, except that it always sails with a Dixieland jazz
band aboard. Its sister ship (not a steamboat), the
John James Audubon, makes four short trips daily
from the Riverwalk wharf to the Audubon Zoo dock
and back ($12.50-$16.50, $6.25-$8.25 concessions).

Other tours

Preservation Resource Center Tours

Information 581 7032/www.prcno.org. **Tours**
phone for details. **Rates** $25-$55. **Credit** MC, V.

The PRC, founded in 1974, is a hands-on, creative
force in New Orleans preservation. In addition to
innovative schemes, such as selling decrepit houses

to people who agree to fix them up, the PRC sponsors several high-profile annual architectural events,
including the Holiday Home Tour (in December),
which opens up showy private homes to public view;
Shotgun House Month (in March), which celebrates
the archetypal New Orleans dwelling with various
events; and the Stained Glass in Sacred Places tour
(in spring and autumn), which takes in the magnificent windows of some of New Orleans' churches.

Spring Fiesta Association Tour of Homes

Information 826 St Ann Street (581 1367).
Tours phone for details. **Rates** $12-$20.

Since 1937, this pioneering preservation group has
opened private homes to the public in order to spotlight New Orleans culture and raise funds. There are
usually three tours held in the third week of March
– one of French Quarter houses, one of Garden
District houses, and one that goes by bus to the
River Road plantations (*see pp229-32*). These pala-
tial piles are normally only seen in the pages of
Southern Living and *Architectural Digest* magazines,
so it's a big deal for house-worshippers.

Tour companies

Gray Line of New Orleans

Information 569 1401/1-800 535 7786/
fax 587 0742/www.graylineneworleans.com.
Tours start at Gray Line ticket booth, Toulouse
Street, at the Mississippi River. **Tours** phone for
a schedule. **Rates** $18-$47; $10-$24 concessions;
free under-6s. **Credit** AmEx, DC, Disc, MC, V.
Map p282 B3.

Always interesting, if rarely exciting, Gray Line
offers several comprehensive tours around New
Orleans on bus, boat and foot; phone for a full list.

New Orleans Tours

Information 592 0560/1-800 543 6332/
fax 592 0549/www.bigeasytours.com. Tours
pick up at hotels and at Tipitina's, 501 Napoleon
Avenue, at Tchoupitoulas Street. **Tours** phone
for a schedule. **Rates** $39-$54; $19-$29 concessions.
Credit AmEx, DC, Disc, MC, V.

Riverboat, bus, foot and combination tours – this
company does them all. It offers a variety of walking and bus tours of New Orleans, along with bus
trips to the plantations and several cruises, such as
a riverboat trip and tour of the Battle of New Orleans
site near Chalmette.

Tours by Isabelle

Information (391 3544/fax 391 3564/www.tours
byisabelle.com). **Tours** call to schedule. **Rates** $44-
$110; discount for under-12s. **Credit** Disc, MC, V.

While this local tour company offers riverboat and
bayou trips, its speciality is small-scale bus tours
(the maximum group size is 13 people) around New
Orleans and to the plantations of River Road.
Tours make pick-ups at hotels in the French
Quarter and the Garden District.

Eat, Drink, Shop

Restaurants	**106**
Coffeeshops & Cafés	**130**
Bars	**134**
Shops & Services	**148**

Features

Top ten Restaurants	111
How to Avoid tourist traps	112
The best Budget busters	114
The 'old school' restaurants	123
The new school	129
Still life alfresco	131
It's not food, it's a way of life	132
Top ten Bars	136
How to Drink in the French Quarter	145
The best Historic bars	147
Magazine Street: get shopping	149
Be nice or leave	153
Sparkle, made to order	164

Restaurants

Forget the bars, the bands, the wild nightlife… When you get down to it, in New Orleans, food is king.

Everything is simply perfect at **Dick & Jenny's**. *See p124.*

Before fusion was invented, and certainly before it became a dirty word in culinary circles, New Orleans had Creole. Embedded in this fact is everything that's important in the past, present and future of cuisine in this city. Sticklers to historical detail will tell you that Creole food originates in the city itself, a confluence of African and European influences converging on locally available ingredients, and that's true enough. But consider Creole in the broader sense – a continually evolving, mutable thing, irreverent about boundaries, playfully experimenting with what it finds. And that's why it's so damn fun to eat here.

The strongest element in local food is French. The ties between New Orleans and its French roots are inextricable, and they're found in the richness of local dishes. Creolised French cuisine thrives here, especially in the city's almost institutional restaurants – places such as **Antoine's**, **Galatoire's**, **Brennan's** and **Commander's Palace** – which maintain a reverence for the past in the menu and on the walls. History is thick there, and decadently well remembered. You'd do well to visit one of these virtual shrines while you're in town.

There is also, of course, Cajun food. To its critics, it's less refined than traditional Creole fare, picked up on the run by displaced French-Acadians from Canada, and improvisational, more rustic in nature. Cajun food came into its own on the prairies and bayous of Louisiana outside the city. It will always have an outsider status in New Orleans and thus it is a little harder to find, but at places such as **K-Paul's Louisiana Kitchen** and **Bon Ton Café** it has a time-honoured sanctuary. There are also many Creole places where Cajun food seems to slip on the menu with a rebel snicker – country boys charming their way on to the citified table.

All of this would be well and good if New Orleans contented itself with being a fondly considered culinary monument to the past. But Creole is not dead, at least not in the larger sense. A new generation of chefs, both from New Orleans and elsewhere, is taking the old standbys apart, expanding the boundaries and exploding them. Chefs like Susan Spicer (**Bayona**), Anne Kearney (**Peristyle**), Minh Bui (**56 Degrees**), John Besh (**August**), Donald Link (**Herbsaint**), Dick Benz (**Dick & Jenny's**) and Brack May (**Cobalt**) are complicating the mix and making local ingredients do ambitious new tricks. The next wave of Creolisation is already here with new, international influences, particularly Asian ones, asserting themselves on the plate. Punk irreverence is meeting up with haute cuisine. So far, they've been getting along fine, and the results continue to be interesting.

New Orleans might be one of the few American cities that can handle the tension of the new without throwing out the old. Chefs from around the world continue to train here and learn at the feet of old masters. But then they open their own restaurants. And that's when the party really starts.

French Quarter

American

Crescent City Brewhouse

527 Decatur Street, between Toulouse & St Louis streets (522 0571). Bus 3 Vieux Carré, 5 Marigny/ Bywater, 55 Elysian Fields. **Open** 11am-10pm Mon-Thur, Sun; 11am-11pm Fri, Sat. **Main courses** $18-$25. **Credit** AmEx, Disc, MC, V. **Map** p282 B3.
One of the country's best microbreweries is about 30 miles away in the town of Abita Springs, but in the likely event that you won't be crossing Lake Ponchartrain to the Abita Springs Brewery, this place offers a lovely consolation prize with its house-brewed selections. The hoppy Pilsner leads the pack of four to five constantly changing beers, and the menu complements it well, though it might be a touch more than you care to pay.

Dickie Brennan's Steakhouse

716 Iberville Street, between Bourbon & Royal streets (522 2467/www.dickiebrennanssteakhouse.com). Bus 3 Vieux Carré, 5 Marigny/Bywater, 55 Elysian Fields. **Open** 11.30am-2.30pm, 5.30-10pm Mon-Thur; 11.30am-2.30pm, 5-10pm Fri; 5-10pm Sat, Sun. **Main courses** $10-$15 lunch; $23-$35 dinner. **Credit** AmEx, DC, Disc, MC, V. **Map** p282 A2.
When you decorate a restaurant with weaponry, you're sending out a message to diners that they're not about to get a delicate, fussy little meal. And indeed, steaks here are seared on cast-iron skillets. Menu descriptions are light on adjectives and hyperbole. Potatoes come six different ways. The Brennan family's coat of arms sits over the restaurant, establishing a benchmark of quality a few storeys above your typical steakhouse.

House of Blues

225 Decatur Street, between Iberville & Bienville streets (529 2624/www.hob.com). Riverfront Streetcar/bus 3 Vieux Carré, 5 Marigny/Bywater. **Open** 11.30am-11pm Mon-Fri; 11.30am-midnight Sat; noon-11pm Sun. *Gospel Brunches* 9.30am, 11.45am, 2pm Sun. **Main courses** $8-$10 lunch; $8-$29 dinner. **Credit** AmEx, DC, Disc, MC, V. **Map** p282 A3.
Best known for its music club, House of Blues also does a decently priced lunch and dinner with a Southern accent. The menu runs just a tier above TGI Friday's booze-basted fare; the decor is dressed-up Delta; and the Sunday gospel brunch gives you a little religion. If you like a restaurant with a wide range of commemorative T-shirts, this is your place.

Rib Room

Omni Royal Orleans Hotel, 621 St Louis Street, at Royal Street (529 7045). Riverfront Streetcar/bus 3 Vieux Carré, 5 Marigny/Bywater, 55 Elysian Fields. **Open** 6.30-10.30am, 11.30am-2pm, 6-10pm Mon-Thur; 6.30-10.30am, 11.30am-2.30pm, 6-11pm Fri; 6.30-10.30am, 6-11pm Sat; 6.30-10.30am, 6-10pm Sun; *Jazz brunch* 11.30am-2.30pm Sat, Sun. **Main courses** $15-$24 lunch; $24-$39 dinner. **Credit** AmEx, Disc, MC, V. **Map** p282 B2.

Housed in the opulent Omni Royal Orleans Hotel, the Rib Room doesn't deviate much from the fare its name evokes. A Quarter mainstay for prime rib and steaks, there's also a rotisserie spinning out the chicken and Gulf shrimp, a smattering of Creole offerings and fried seafood. It's all a bit on the stodgy side, but there's a nice view of Royal Street.

Asian

Samurai Sushi

239 Decatur Street, between Iberville and Bienville streets (525 9595). Riverfront Streetcar/bus 3 Vieux Carré, 5 Marigny/Bywater, 55 Elysian Fields. **Open** 11.30am-10pm Mon-Thur; 11.30am-10.30pm Fri; 5-10.30pm Sat; 5-10pm Sun. **Main courses** $6-$11 lunch; $15-$26 dinner. **Credit** AmEx, DC, Disc, MC, V. **Map** p282 A3.
This place is a perpetual favourite among sushi lovers. Even Japanese tourists frequent it. Samurai's muted, minimalist decor features a tranquil wash-board fountain as a centrepiece, and extremely fresh ocean fish sashimi are standouts on its menu. The BBQ eel is a tangy winner.

Cajun

K-Paul's Louisiana Kitchen

416 Chartres Street, at Conti Street (524 7394/ www.chefpaul.com). Riverfront Streetcar/bus 3 Vieux Carré, 5 Marigny/Bywater, 55 Elysian Fields. **Open** 5.30-10pm Mon-Sat. **Main courses** $25-$35. **Credit** AmEx, DC, MC, V. **Map** p282 B2.
Since chef Paul Prudhomme basically introduced Cajun food to the world outside of Louisiana, his flagship restaurant has risen and fallen in the estimation of diners. Some swear by his blackened Louisiana drum and twin beef tenders with debris sauce; others scoff that the wait is too long and the experience overhyped and kitsch. Still, many mark K-Paul's as an essential stop on their pilgrimage to New Orleans, and those seeking voluminous portions will not be disappointed. Eat everything on your plate and the waiter may give you a gold star. And that might help you understand the detractors.

Contemporary

Bayona

430 Dauphine Street, at Conti Street (525 4455/ www.bayona.com). Bus 3 Vieux Carré. **Open** 11.30am-1.30pm, 6-9.30pm Mon-Thur; 11.30am-1.30pm, 6-10.30pm Fri; 6-10.30pm Sat. **Main courses** $15 lunch; $25 dinner. **Credit** AmEx, DC, MC, V. **Map** 282 B1.
Chef Susan Spicer's name is a byword for 'Damn, that's good!' in this town, and under her stewardship Bayona has earned just about every accolade that the press and the restaurant industry can bestow. Justly so. Spicer's cuisine has a Louisiana cadence without succumbing to the clichéd trappings of Creole and Cajun food. Her menu changes regularly

Eat, Drink, Shop

The queue stretches down the block at **Galatoires**. *See p112.*

and her wine list matches its worldly breadth. Try the cream of garlic soup, the sautéd salmon, the grilled duck breast, anything… You'll have to put your hand deep into your pocket once it's over, but for a meal this good you'll hardly mind.

The Bistro at the Maison de Ville

727 Toulouse Street, at Bourbon Street (528 9206/ www.maisondeville.com). Canal Streetcar/bus 3 Vieux Carré, 5 Marigny/Bywater, 55 Elysian Fields. **Open** 11.30am-2pm, 6-10pm Mon-Sat; 6-10pm Sun. **Main courses** $9-$15 lunch; $19-$27 dinner. **Credit** AmEx, DC, Disc, MC, V. **Map** p282 B2.

Dining at the Bistro, you'll be met with a two-pronged assault – first from maître d' Patrick van Hoorebeek's wry, inexhaustible charms; then from chef Greg Piccolo's gorgeously textured dishes. After that, there's the tiny restaurant's deceptively expansive wine list (many bottles are housed under the banquet seating in the close confines), not to mention the single malts and champagnes, which, given some nudging, van Hoorebeek might dramatically sabre open at tableside. Standing out from the solid French-inflected menu is the mussels Bruxelloise accompanied with a mayonnaise-topped jumble of crispy pommes frites.

Bombay Club

830 Conti Street, at Bourbon Street (586 0972/ www.thebombayclub.com). Canal Streetcar/bus 3 Vieux Carré, 5 Marigny/Bywater, 55 Elysian Fields. **Open** 5.30-10.30pm Mon-Wed, Sun; 5.30pm-1.30am Thur-Sat. **Main courses** $18-$26. **Credit** AmEx, DC, Disc, MC, V. **Map** p282 B2.

The Bombay Club runs a later kitchen than many places (until 1.30am at weekends), so it's a popular after-midnight spot in a town that just does not have enough of them. It's known equally well for its expansive battery of Martinis, but the menu offers reliable Creole fare including oyster and andouille fettucine and pancetta-wrapped salmon fillet.

Mr B's Bistro

201 Royal Street, at Iberville Street (523 2078/ www.mrbsbistro.com). Riverfront Streetcar/bus 3 Vieux Carré, 5 Marigny/Bywater, 55 Elysian Fields. **Open** 11am-3pm, 5.30-10pm daily. *Sunday brunch* Sept-May 10.30am-3pm; Jun-Aug 11am-3pm. **Main courses** $11-$15 lunch; $17-$27 dinner. **Credit** AmEx, DC, Disc, MC, V. **Map** p282 A2.

Popular with the business lunch set, and those in seach of a meal that is simultaneously posh and casual, Mr B's Bistro was opened by members of the Brennan family in the late 1970s. Here they refitted their trademark Creole fare for slightly more casual surroundings and softer prices. Dinner features nightly piano music and there's a Sunday jazz brunch. Under chef Michelle McRaney, the menu has taken an ambitious turn with offerings such as veal porterhouse topped with jumbo lump crabmeat, and the grilled shrimp risotto with white truffle oil.

Muriel's Jackson Square

801 Chartres Street, at St Ann Street (568 1885/ www.muriels.com). Riverfront Streetcar/bus 3 Vieux Carré, 5 Marigny/Bywater, 55 Elysian Fields. **Open** 5.30-10pm Mon, Tue; 11.30am-3pm, 5.30-10pm Wed, Thur; 11.30am-3pm, 5.30-11pm Fri, Sat; 11.30am-3pm Sun. **Main courses** $8-$13 lunch; $13-$32 dinner. **Credit** AmEx, DC, Disc, MC, V. **Map** p282 C2.

You can't ask for a better location than the corner Muriel's occupies on Jackson Square, augmented by a wraparound balcony. The owners spent buckets of money restoring this 19th-century building to its present eclectic splendour. Have a cocktail in the Seance Lounge before you eat (the room – awash in red lighting and strewn with sarcophagi, crystal balls and Ouija boards – is said to be haunted by a previous occupant), then tuck in the stuffed mirliton and the crawfish maque choux, or try the three-course table d'hôte menu. As much a visual experience as a culinary one.

Bayona: worth every penny. *See p107.*

NOLA

*534 St Louis Street, at Chartes Street (522 6652/
www.emerils.com). Riverfront Streetcar/bus 3
Vieux Carré, 5 Marigny/Bywater, 55 Elysian Fields.*
Open 11.30am-2pm, 6-10.30pm Mon-Thur; 11.30am-
2pm, 6-11pm Fri, Sat; 6-10.30pm Sun. **Main courses**
$15-$23 lunch; $20-$32 dinner. **Credit** AmEx, DC,
Disc, MC, V. **Map** p282 B2.
Damn, Emeril, how can you keep that high-energy,
spices-thrown-over-the-shoulder, cheers-from-the-
audience pitch in everything you do? Maybe the
answer is that you can't. The second ship to set sail
in TV chef Emeril Legasse's expanding restaurant
navy, NOLA tends to leave diners feeling one of two
ways after eating here: dizzy with awe over his complex dishes such as striped bass with gnocchi and
oysters or prosciutto-wrapped salmon; or wondering, 'how much did I pay for all that hype?'
Experiences tend to be wildly inconsistent here.
Some rave, others boo.

Palace Café

*605 Canal Street, at Chartes Street (523 1661/
www.palacecafe.com). Canal Streetcar/bus 3 Vieux
Carré, 5 Marigny/Bywater, 55 Elysian Fields.*
Open 11.30am-2.30pm, 5.30-10pm Mon-Fri;
10.30am-2.30pm, 5.30-10pm Sat, Sun. **Main
courses** $10-$17 lunch; $19-$27 dinner.
Credit AmEx, DC, Disc, MC, V. **Map** p282 A2.
Owner (and former chef) Dickie Brennan loves duck
so much that he insists on a trio of duckling perpet-
ually on the menu at Palace Café. Try any of them
and you'll share his sentiment. The pepper-crusted
duck breast with seared Hudson Valley foie gras is
the heavyweight, though those opting for the Gulf
fish, oysters or soft-shell crab won't be disappointed. Bright spots also include the Abita beer-battered
shrimp and crawfish Napoleon; and one would be
remiss to leave without trying the white chocolate
bread pudding, a house speciality.

The Pelican Club

*615 Bienville Street, at Exchange Alley (523 1504/
www.pelicanclub.com). Canal Streetcar/bus 3 Vieux
Carré, 5 Marigny/Bywater, 55 Elysian Fields.*
Open 5-10pm daily. **Main courses** $19-$38.
Credit AmEx, DC, Disc, MC, V. **Map** p282 B2.
The clubby entrance passes into a three-chambered
dining room; each room has its own aesthetic. Chef
Richard Hughes' style mirrors this, and it all works
gratifyingly well on the plate. Louisiana dishes get
an Asian infusion in the soft-shell crab in red curry
sauce with jumbo lump crabmeat; and the shrimp,
duck and shiitake mushroom spring rolls. Hughes'
creativity keeps inquisitive palates returning.

Peristyle

*1041 Dumaine Street, at N Rampart Street (593
9535). Bus 3 Vieux Carré, 5 Marigny/Bywater, 88
or 89 St Claude.* **Open** 6-9pm Tue-Thur; 11.30am-
1.30pm, 6-10pm Fri; 6-10pm Sat. **Main courses** $23-
$27. **Credit** AmEx, DC, MC, V. **Map** p282 C1.
Neither flames nor misfortune can hold back
indomitable chef Anne Kearney, whose original
Peristyle was gutted by fire in 1999. Happily, the
restaurant has recovered. Beloved by local gour-
mands, Peristyle has an international reputation.
After an aperitif of vin d'orange, a house special
made with dry white wine, brandy, oranges and
vanilla beans, try Louisiana crabmeat and roasted
beet salad. After that? Hell, what *can't* Kearney
cook? Colleagues around town are particularly
enamoured with her sweetbreads.

Creole

Antoine's

*713 St Louis Street, at Bourbon Street (581 4422/
www.antoines.com). Bus 3 Vieux Carré.* **Open**
11.30am-2pm, 5.30-9pm Mon-Sat. **Main courses**
$21-$38. **Credit** AmEx, DC, MC, V. **Map** p282 B2.

The best London bars & restaurants, just a click away.

Subscribe today and enjoy over 3,400 constantly updated reviews from *Time Out*'s acclaimed *London Eating & Drinking, Cheap Eats, Bars Pubs & Clubs* **Guides and** *Time Out London weekly*.

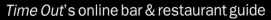

timeout.com/restaurants

Time Out's online bar & restaurant guide

Founded in 1840, Antoine's is the oldest continuously operated, family-run restaurant in the country. When you walk through its ten dining rooms, the history shows in memorabilia covering nearly every inch of available space. Its chefs have served presidents and popes, and while the prices reflect that heritage, few other restaurants in the city can match it for sheer spectacle – from its menu still written in *en français* (and barely altered in content since the doors first opened) to oysters Rockefeller (which were invented here). Note that jeans are never allowed and a jacket is required for evenings.

Arnaud's

813 Bienville Street, at Bourbon Street (523 5433/ www.arnauds.com). Bus 3 Vieux Carré, 41 Canal. **Open** 11am-2.30pm, 6-10pm Mon-Thur; 11am-2.30pm, 6-10.30pm Fri; 6-10.30pm Sat; 10am-2.30pm, 6-10pm Sun. **Main courses** $12-$30 lunch; $18-$40 dinner. **Credit** AmEx, DC, MC, V. **Map** p282 B2.
The Minotaur himself might well make his home among Arnaud's labyrinthine 12 buildings, an intricate maze of dining rooms and passageways. Founded by a self-proclaimed count in the early 20th century, there has always been a theatrical, gold lamé grandeur to Arnaud's. It has long enjoyed a reputation for its expansive Creole menu, which has been tweaked and updated over the years to keep it interesting for devoted regulars. The jazz brunch is one of the city's most popular and features such appealing options as the Creole cream cheese evangeline, eggs fauteaux (poached eggs with house-smoked Gulf pompano) and port-marinated strawberries Arnaud. Try to find the in-house Mardi Gras museum, hidden in the maze, before you leave.

Brennan's

417 Royal Street, between St Louis and Conti streets (525 9711/www.brennansneworleans.com). Riverfront Streetcar/bus 3 Vieux Carré, 5 Marigny/ Bywater, 55 Elysian Fields. **Open** 8am-2.30pm, 6-10pm daily. **Main courses** $16-$40 brunch; $30-$40 dinner. **Credit** AmEx, DC, MC, V. **Map** p282 B2.
Brunch at Brennan's is a meal of lustful, Caligulian proportions – one you will recall in specific detail years later. Start with a house special cocktail such as the brandy milk punch before moving on to Creole classics including eggs hussarde and sardou and oysters en brochette. The turtle soup is the best you may ever have, and bananas Foster, served flambé at tableside, was invented here. Pricey, but the doting service and the delirium it induces are worth it.

Broussard's

819 Conti Street, at Bourbon Street (581 3866/www.broussards.com). Bus 3 Vieux Carré. **Open** 5.30-10pm daily. **Main courses** $18-$35. **Credit** AmEx, MC, V. **Map** p282 B2.
Though Broussard's is a Creole mainstay, its owners are actually German and have a strong affinity with red meat. The sirloin of veal and rack of lamb speak well for those enthusiasms, though seafood dishes like the bouillabaisse excel as well.

Top ten Restaurants

In the best of all possible worlds, all your meals would happen in these restaurants.

Bayona

Ambitious but personal, and a wine list to match the menu's lofty achievements. *See p107.*

Belle Forché

Bucking the local wisdom that 'late night' and 'fine dining' are mutually exclusive terms. *See p115.*

Cobalt

Hearty and American in the best sense of both words. *See p119.*

Dick & Jenny's

Louisiana ingredients put to their best imaginable use. *See p124.*

The Grill Room

An experience that reminds you why symphonies, novels and perfect meals can really move us. *See p119.*

Herbsaint

A relative newcomer that hit the ground running and hasn't stopped since. *See p119.*

Pelican Club

South Louisiana meets Asian influences with delicious complexity. *See p109.*

Peristyle

Irrepressible, inventive and intimate; big-hearted but with all the right subtle charms. *See p109.*

Restaurant August

Assertive dishes with well-earned confidence. *See p120.*

Victor's

Playful, expressive and bold, plus you can pull back the curtains in a private booth. *See p120.*

Café Sbisa

1011 Decatur Street, at St Philip Street (522 5565/ www.cafesbisa.com). Riverfront Streetcar/bus 3 Vieux Carré. **Open** 5.30-10.30pm Mon-Fri, Sat; 10am-2.30pm, 5.30-10.30pm Sun. **Main courses** $17-$26. **Credit** AmEx, DC, Disc, MC, V. **Map** p282 C3.
In the past, Sbisa was a popular hangout for the ageing gay brunch crowd. These days the clientele is more general and touristy. The main dining room is

Eat, Drink, Shop

ringed by a mezzanine balcony with more seating, and brick walls and old ceiling beams are exposed throughout lending the place a very charming effect. There's a jazz band every night, and the Creole food can be excellent on a good night. Sunday brunch here is a great deal of fun.

Dickie Brennan's Bourbon House

144 Bourbon Street, at Iberville Street (522 0111/ www.bourbonhouse.com). Canal Streetcar/bus 3 Vieux Carré, 5 Marigny/Bywater, 55 Elysian Fields. **Open** 6.30-10am, 11.30am-2.30pm, 5.30-11pm Mon-Fri; 7.30-10am, 10.30am-2.30pm, 5.30-11pm Sat, Sun. **Main courses** $9-$22 lunch; $15-$28 dinner. **Credit** AmEx, DC, Disc, MC, V. **Map** p282 A2.
Bourbon House is actually two restaurants – a modestly priced oyster bar with limited table seating, and a more expansive (and expensive) dining room run by chef Jared Tees. The handblown, balloon-style chandeliers and wrought-iron details give it a Parisian feel, while the view of Bourbon Street's passing throng is free entertainment. Any oyster dish is a sure bet, and the three-course nightly prix fixe menu helps to minimise the financial damage. You can pick up a crêpe to go on the way out.

Galatoire's

209 Bourbon Street, at Iberville Street (525 2021/www.galatoires.com). Canal Streetcar/bus 3 Vieux Carré, 5 Marigny/Bywater, 55 Elysian Fields. **Open** *Bar* 11am-10pm Tue-Sat; 11.30am-10pm Sun.

Restaurant 11.30am-10pm Tue-Sat; noon-10pm Sun. **Main courses** $14-$27. **Credit** AmEx, DC, Disc, MC, V. **Map** p282 A2.
After the queue (no reservations are accepted), the rumours and the legends, what really remains at one of the city's best-known, see-and-be-seen society eateries? Well, damn good Creole food, actually. Not much has changed on the menu since Galatoire's opened in 1905 (any innovations have been battled back by diner uprisings), so it's best to come with a group, order a selection of the tried-and-true house specialities and pass your plates around. The oysters Rockefeller and en brochette are standouts, but don't leave without trying the stuffed aubergine. Finish with the banana bread pudding and a few flaming ladles of café Brulot and you'll understand why people will wait outside in all weather in hopes of getting to spend an hour at the table.

Gumbo Shop

630 St Peter Street, between Chartres and Royal streets (525 1486/www.gumboshop.com). Riverfront Streetcar/bus 3 Vieux Carré, 5 Marigny/Bywater, 55 Elysian Fields. **Open** 11am-11pm daily. **Main courses** $7-$18. **Credit** AmEx, DC, Disc, MC, V. **Map** p282 B2.
The French Quarter abounds with tourist traps peddling gumbo and crawfish éttouffée, so Gumbo Shop is an oasis among them. It's ever reliable for its gumbos (smoked duck and oyster gumbo and gumbo z'herbes – a vegetarian version – are favourites) and

How to avoid tourist traps

When you were little, your parents told you never to talk to a shifty-looking stranger, right? So why would you follow a man dancing with a menu in his hand into a restaurant? Be warned: for every good restaurant in New Orleans there's a bad one, and most of the worst are in the French Quarter, with a barker out front to lure you in.

The Quarter is the worst for two simple reasons: you're here, and you're from out of town. Elsewhere in the city restaurants tend to be more reliable because they depend on local business, and locals will not usually visit an inferior place more than once. In the CBD and the French Quarter, though, the odds of having a bad meal are much higher. Shady restaurateurs fork out high rents just to get the walk-in traffic, so don't think they're going to be generous with their food budgets. These places will throw anything in a cream sauce on to a plate, figuring that diners will never come back anyway.

You don't want to give them your money. We don't want you to give them your money. But how can you avoid them? Well, this

system isn't perfect, but here are a few tricks that can help you to pick out the bad ones before it's too late.

The most obvious warning is the guy out front. A barker huckstering customers is a sure sign of inferiority. Really, what kind of desperation are we talking about here? What kind of lowest common denominator is the restaurant trying to court? And what are people who actually do go inside *thinking*?

'Lookie! A dancing man! Let's eat there!' No. Keep walking.

Here are a few other warning signs:
● Waiters and kitchen staff milling around outside on the street.
● An absence of bona fide local reviews posted in the windows.
● A posted menu with a number of dishes listed 'in quotes' is a dead giveaway.
● Beware if the manager runs outside to greet you when he sees you peering in. Desperation is a dead giveaway.

Obviously, follow your instincts and go wherever you want. But you can't say we didn't warn you.

Classic food in a casual atmosphere is the house special at **Mr B's Bistro**. *See p108.*

simple dishes like redfish Creole, and it is beloved by locals and visitors who appreciate the fact that 'affordable' and 'good' need not be mutually exclusive concepts. An early 20th-century mural of Jackson Square is a centrepiece of the dining room, only steps away from the real thing.

Tujague's

823 Decatur Street, at Madison Street (525 8676/ www.tujagues.com). Riverfront Streetcar/bus 3 Vieux Carré, 5 Marigny/Bywater, 55 Elysian Fields. **Open** 11am-3pm, 5-10pm daily. **Main courses** $8-$16 lunch; $30-$36 dinner. **Credit** AmEx, DC, Disc, MC, V. **Map** p282 C3.

Tujague's is a more modest relation of places such as Antoine's and Galatoire's – equally historic but at a fraction of the price (and a fraction of the selection, it must be said). Having been around since 1856, the whole building has been slightly contorted by time and experience, like almost everything else in the Quarter. It works here to great effect. The bar is a wonderful place to have a cocktail and ponder history while gazing into oversized mirrors, and the four-course dinner menu is simple but good.

Italian

Bacco

W Hotel, 310 Chartres Street, at Bienville Street (522 2426/www.bacco.com). Riverfront Streetcar/ bus 3 Vieux Carré, 5 Marigny/Bywater, 55 Elysian Fields. **Open** 11.30am-2.30pm, 6-10pm daily. **Main courses** $10-$20 lunch; $10-$42 dinner. **Credit** AmEx, DC, MC, V. **Map** p282 A2.

The ubiquitous Brennan family goes Italian with handmade pasta and wood-fired pizza. Reserve a table in the Skylight Room and take your time with the hefty wine list. The chef is known for her black truffle fettucine and shrimp and lobster ravioli.

Café Giovanni

117 Decatur Street, at Canal Street (529 2154/ www.cafegiovannni.com). Canal or Riverfront Streetcar/bus 3 Vieux Carré, 5 Marigny/Bywater, 55 Elysian Fields. **Open** 5.30-10pm daily. **Main courses** $18-$26. **Credit** AmEx, DC, Disc, MC, V. **Map** p282 A3.

Chef Duke LoCicero calls his cuisine 'New World Italian', a kind of Italy-Louisiana mix of styles. Dishes such as oysters Giovanni, fried with a 'stained glass' of five sauces, helped to make his name, and those with lusty appetites surrender to his five-course 'feed me' menu with faith that the trip will be a hearty and interesting one. On Wednesday, Friday and Saturday nights, many of Café Giovanni's staff double as opera singers, belting out 'O Sole Mio' along with your duck classico.

Latin American

Country Flame

620 Iberville Street, between Chartres and Royal streets (522 1138). Canal or Riverfront Streetcar/ bus 3 Vieux Carré, 5 Marigny/Bywater, 55 Elysian Fields. **Open** 11am-10pm daily. **Main courses** $6-$10. **Credit** AmEx, MC, V. **Map** p282 A2.

The look is a little dodgy – pressed tin ceiling that's a bit too low, picnic table seating, tiny kitchen and

Budget busters

If money is no object, or if you're just pretending that it isn't, this is where you blow the bank account.

Bayona
A brilliant wine list and an extraordinary chef who's almost always in the kitchen. See p107.

Brennan's
Brunch here is terrifyingly decadent and worth every penny. See p111.

Commander's Palace
Benchmark-setting, eternally classic. See p121.

Galatoire's
Moneyed old New Orleans gathers here to regard itself – witness the spectacle. See p112.

The Grill Room
The decor might be a little intimidating, but the cuisine is simply arresting. See p119.

Herbsaint
One of the most ambitious restaurants to hit New Orleans in years. See p119.

Horinoya
The most discriminating sushi chefs in town are here, and the tasting menu is superb. See p118.

The Pelican Club
South Louisiana meets Asia – a historic and delicious event. See p109.

Peristyle
Cuisine as optimistic, energetic and generous as the chef behind it. See p109.

boxes of supplies that make you wonder exactly what the storeroom is used for – but don't let that put you off. In fact, this is the kind of place that attracts the suit-and-tie crowd along with the punkesses brimming with tattoos and piercings. All are lured by the tasty Mexican, Cuban and Spanish food. It's very fresh, and the daily specials are particularly good deals. Service is a bit lacklustre.

Neighbourhood

Acme Oyster House
724 Iberville Street, at Bourbon Street (522 5973/ www.acmeoyster.com) Canal Streetcar/bus 3 Vieux Carré, 5 Marigny/Bywater, 55 Elysian Fields. Open 11am-10pm Mon-Thur, Sun; 11am-11pm Fri, Sat. Main courses $6-$14. Credit AmEx, DC, Disc, MC, V. Map p282 A2.
Ignore the industrial-sized vent blowing the stench of fried fish to Iberville Street (judging by the crowds, it's not putting many people off) and step inside for what the Oyster House does best. By the half dozen, the dozen or the single salty shot, oysters are what's good here. Grab a frosty Abita beer, a side of red beans or jambalaya, and Bob's your uncle. The menu, for all its brevity, has some caution-raising selections (Cajun sushi? Red bean poopa?), but stick to the shells and you'll realise why this place has been around since 1910.

Angeli on Decatur
1141 Decatur Street, at Governor Nicholls Street (566 0077). Riverfront Streetcar/bus 3 Vieux Carré, 5 Marigny/Bywater, 55 Elysian Fields. Open 10am-4am Mon-Thur, Sun; 24hrs Fri, Sat. Main courses $6-$14. Credit AmEx, MC, V. Map p282 D3.

When the late-night munchies set in, you'll be grateful for Angeli's, where the oven stays on past 11pm. The Decatur Street location is a short stumble from some of the city's best bars. The food? Nothing that complicated – pizzas, salads, pitas – just what you need to cap a night out or to set you up for another couple of hours of alcoholic destruction.

Café Maspero
601 Decatur Street, at Toulouse Street (523 6250). Riverfront Streetcar/bus 3 Vieux Carré, 5 Marigny/ Bywater, 55 Elysian Fields. Open 11am-11pm Mon-Thur, Sun; 11am-midnight Fri, Sat. Main courses $5-$10. No credit cards (ATM on-site). Map p282 B2.
The queue outside can run half a block long, but that's because people seem to know that Maspero's is a good deal for lunch or dinner. The fried seafood plates are good, the fries are plentiful and the muffulettas (thick sandwiches piled with meat and olive salad) and veggie muffulettas are among the best in town. Skip the iffy wine list and grab a beer, then sit under the brick arches and scoff your bargain.

Central Grocery
923 Decatur Street, between Dumaine & St Philip streets (523 1620). Riverfront Streetcar/bus 3 Vieux Carré, 5 Marigny/Bywater, 55 Elysian Fields. Open 8am-5.30pm daily. Main courses $6-$10. Credit V. Map p282 C3.
First, there's the scent of olive oil perfuming everything inside. Then there are the imported groceries – pastas, risottos, olives. This is where people used to shop in the days before supermarkets. Still, even with all of that, the main attraction here is a sandwich. The muffuletta, to be precise. This bountiful

beast of a sandwich was invented here, stacked with ham, Genoa salami, pastrami, swiss and provelone, then a layer of salty olive salad. It's virtually all they serve here, but it's enough. It can get crowded, but patience is rewarded.

Clover Grill
900 Bourbon Street, at Dumaine Street (598 1010/ www.clovergrill.com). Bus 3 Vieux Carré, 5 Marigny/ Bywater, 55 Elysian Fields. **Open** 24hrs daily. **Main courses** $3-$7. **Credit** AmEx, MC, V. **Map** p282 C2.
The menu admonishes: 'We don't eat in your bed, so please don't sleep at our table' and adds sternly: 'No talking to yourself. Keep both hands on the table.' Clover Grill is that kind of place. The look is beaten-up 1950s; clocks inside offer the time at City Hall (the hands have stopped) and Chalmette, a boring suburb (the hands have given up and fallen off altogether). The countermen are blousy, bitchy and talkative. It's open 24 hours, and the scene at 3am is like an Edward Hopper automat painting dipped in strawberry ice-cream and sprinkled with playful transvestites and other colourful lost souls. Nothing on the breakfasts-and-burgers menu is more than $7. The perfect place to start your novel.

Napoleon House
500 Chartres Street, at St Louis Street (524 9752/ www.napoleonhouse.com). Riverfront Streetcar/ bus 3 Vieux Carré, 5 Marigny/Bywater, 55 Elysian Fields. **Open** 11am-midnight Mon-Thur; 11am-1am Fri, Sat; 11am-7pm Sun. **Main courses** $7 lunch; $17-$26 dinner. **Credit** AmEx, DC, Disc, MC, V. **Map** p282 A2.
According to rumour, this place was meant to be a sanctuary for Napoleon after a planned rescue from his exile in St Helena. It didn't work out, and what we're left with is a bar and restaurant with the most superior ambience in New Orleans. And that's saying something. Everything is dark, crumbling, vaguely sinister... It's everything that those songs about New Orleans warn you about. Get a Pimm's Cup and a seat by the ever-open, floor-to-ceiling windows, or else hide yourself somewhere deep in the shady recesses. Have a charcuterie or a cheese plate. Humbert Humbert might be sitting next to you. Now you're really in this city.

Port of Call
838 Esplanade Avenue, at Dauphine Street (523 0120). Bus 3 Vieux Carré, 5 Marigny/Bywater, 48 Esplanade. **Open** 11am-1am daily. **Main courses** $10. **Credit** AmEx, MC, V. **Map** p282 D1.
Port of Call will slap you with quite a few unusual contradictions on the way to your hamburger. The come-hither barbecue smell wafting on to the street? Fair enough, but what's this bayside, sea shanty decor all about? Fishnets over the air-conditioning ducts? Life preservers and wooden ship wheels? The menu tells a different story – burgers, steaks, pizzas; nothing with gills. The queue frequently spills out on to the street, and the service is more than just a touch relaxed, but here's to meat, cocktails and a sense of humour.

Quarter Scene Restaurant
900 Dumaine Street, at Dauphine Street (522 6533/ www.thequarterscene.com). Bus 3 Vieux Carré, 5 Marigny/Bywater. **Open** 8am-2pm, 5.30-10pm Mon-Fri; 8am-10pm Sat, Sun. **Main courses** $8-$9 lunch; $11-$20 dinner. **Credit** AmEx, DC, Disc, MC, V. **Map** p282 C1.
In the winter of his life, Tennessee Williams was a regular at this lower French Quarter café, popular with the gay community, although not exclusively so. The vibe is homey-urban, the kind of place *Friends* characters might hang around in if they lived in downtown New Orleans and harboured bohemian tendencies. Breakfast and lunch are more popular than the limited dinner menu, and the *pain perdu* (New Orleans-style French toast) with grilled bananas is a good choice.

Faubourg Marigny & the Bywater

Contemporary

Belle Forché
1407 Decatur Street, at Frenchmen Street (940 0722/www.belleforche.com). Riverfront Streetcar/bus 3 Vieux Carré, 5 Marigny/Bywater, 55 Elysian Fields. **Open** 5.30-10.30pm Tue, Wed, Sun; 5.30pm-1.30am Thur-Sat. **Main courses** $9-$14 cafe; $17-$28 dining room. **Credit** AmEx, DC, Disc, MC, V. **Map** p282 D3.
Among the many new eateries in the burgeoning neighbourhood known as the Marigny, Belle Forché (and chef Matt Yohalem) holds the crown. This two-part 'Criolle' restaurant has cuisine with all the attraction of a magnet turned up to 11. In one corner: a formal dining room with the city's most iconoclastic gumbo – thick with aubergine, crabmeat and hot pepper as well as the surprise of coconut and coriander. There's also such wide-ranging fare as cane syrup quail and pumpkin purée; and mahi mahi with plantain crust. In the other corner you'll find a café that's open 'till the wee hours. The food in here is a fraction of the price charged for items in the main restaurant – this may well be the best bargain in town. Try the flash-fried oysters and truffle sandwich, and feel the pull.

Marigny Brasserie
640 Frenchmen Street, at Royal Street (945 4472/www.marignybrasserie.com). Bus 3 Vieux Carré, 5 Marigny/Bywater, 55 Elysian Fields. **Open** 11am-2pm, 5.30-10pm Mon-Thur; 11am-2pm, 5.30-midnight Fri, Sat; 10.30am-3pm, 5.30-10pm Sun. **Main courses** $8-$12 lunch; $16-$26 dinner. **Credit** AmEx, DC, MC, V. **Map** p282 D2.
A former neighbourhood coffeehouse, Marigny Brasserie spills across a busy corner. The food here touches a number of bases – from paella to filet mignon – and the atmosphere is pleasant. The mood is very bistro, with large groups at the comfortable tables. The three-course early bird is a good deal.

Eat, Drink, Shop

Jamaican

Café Negril

606 Frenchmen Street, at Chartres Street (944 4744/www.cafenegril.com). Riverfront Streetcar/bus 3 Vieux Carré, 5 Marigny/Bywater, 55 Elysian Fields. **Open** 11am-3pm, 6pm-midnight Tue-Fri; 6pm-midnight Sat. **Main courses** $10-$15. **Credit** AmEx, Disc, MC, V. **Map** p282 D2.

Patience is rewarded at Café Negril, but you will need it. Even when this place is empty, service moves at an ethereal pace, still once the curry seafood soup arrives, you'll be most forgiving. There's not a wide drink selection (and the mixed drinks are generally ill-advised), so you'll need a few Red Stripes to wash away the sting of the jerk fish. But sometimes pain is good.

Neighbourhood

Bywater BBQ

3162 Dauphine Street, at Louisa Street (944 4445). Bus 5 Marigny/Bywater. **Open** 7am-10pm Mon-Fri; 11am-10pm Sat, Sun. **Main courses** $5-$10 lunch; $7-$15 dinner. **Credit** AmEx, MC, V.

Uncomplicated food and a local crowd mark Bywater BBQ, tucked into the residential neighbourhood beyond the Marigny. It is more well rounded than the name would suggest, with sandwiches, pastas and a good brunch spread available, and there's a small courtyard for outdoor dining.

Elizabeth's

601 Gallier Street, at Chartres Street (944 9272/www.elizabeths-restaurant.com). Bus 5 Marigny/Bywater. **Open** 7am-2.30pm Tue-Sat. **Main courses** $3-$10. **Credit** MC, V.

It's in the middle of nowhere, but that hasn't stopped anyone from discovering Elizabeth's homespun perfection. With its mismatched mugs and tacky plastic tablecloths, you'll feel as if you're in a friend's kitchen even before the generous portions appear. The 'Loula Mae' breakfast po-boy is a work of simple, spicy perfection; then there's the soft-shell crab meunière over cheese grits; the stuffed French toast with berries and cream cheese; and the coup de grace – praline pecan bacon. You'll likely be setting next to a raucous table of clean-cut folks from the Coast Guard barracks nearby. They come here every day.

Feelings Café

2600 Chartres Street, at Franklin Avenue (945 2222/www.feelingscafe.com). Bus 5 Marigny/Bywater, 57 Franklin. **Open** 6-10pm Mon-Thur; 11am-2pm, 6-11pm Fri; 6-11pm Sat; 11am-2pm, 6-10pm Sun. **Main courses** $14-$22 lunch; $17-$25 dinner. **Credit** AmEx, DC, Disc, MC, V.

Hidden from the Frenchmen Street crowds, this place predated the food renaissance in Marigny. It's loved for its piano bar (in a former slaves' quarters) and its pretty courtyard. The menu features Creole standards with Long Island duck thrown in for good measure. This is a romantic option.

Jack Dempsey's

738 Poland Avenue, at Dauphine Street (943 9914). Bus 5 Marigny/Bywater. **Open** 11am-1.30pm Tue; 11am-1.30pm, 5-8.30pm Wed, Thur; 11am-1.30pm, 5-9.30pm Fri; 4-9.30pm Sat. **Main courses** $11-$20. **Credit** AmEx, DC, Disc, MC, V.

At this Bywater classic just a few steps from the unsavoury-sounding Industrial Canal, you dine in bulk. Fried fish, shrimp, oysters, crab – it all seems to come by the pound, making Dempsey's the ideal venue for those with heroic appetites or a penchant for gluttony. There are no reservations, and no fuss – you arrive, you queue, you take your place at a simple table, and you eat like there's no tomorrow. The waitresses look, and act, as if they've just stepped out of 1955.

Soul food

Praline Connection

542 Frenchmen Street, at Chartres Street (943 3934/www.pralineconnection.com). Riverfront Streetcar/bus 3 Vieux Carré, 5 Marigny/Bywater, 55 Elysian Fields. **Open** 11am-10.30pm Mon-Thur, Sun; 11am-midnight Fri, Sat. **Main courses** $7-$12 lunch; $11-$20 dinner. **Credit** AmEx, DC, Disc, MC, V. **Map** p282 D2.

Soul gets a Louisiana accent at Praline Connection (which also boasts a cavernous gospel and blues hall at its CBD location). Despite a certain casualness toward service, the food here is reliably good and reasonably priced. Start with the BBQ oysters or fried chicken livers, move on to the stuffed bell pepper or stuffed crab (don't forget the sweet cornbread and tasty collard greens), then wrap it all up with bread pudding or sweet potato pie. The atmosphere is local and the music is righteous.

Branches: 907 South Peters Street, at Joseph Street, Warehouse District (523 3973); Louis Armstrong International Airport, Concourse B (466 7772).

Vegetarian

Old Dog New Trick

517 Frenchmen Street, at Decatur Street (943 6368/www.olddognewtrick.com). Riverfront Streetcar/bus 3 Vieux Carré, 5 Marigny/Bywater, 55 Elysian Fields. **Open** 11.30am-9pm Mon-Thur, Sun; 11.30am-9.30pm Fri, Sat. **Main courses** $7-$12. **Credit** AmEx, MC, V. **Map** p282 D3.

The dearth of vegetarian restaurants in New Orleans should clue you in to the suspicion, if not hostility, that locals have towards those who avoid the fleshy stuff. But ODNT, relocated and tweaked from its previous French Quarter location, is a creative and sustaining sanctuary for those who hold the moral high-ground when it comes to dinner. This is a beacon of health in the sinful Marigny, but the watermelon Martini offers a wink to those who think of this as the oral equivalent of the gym. The polenta pizza is rich and masterful, though just about anything on the menu will make your body feel good.

You either love 'em or you hate 'em, but the best are at **Acme Oyster House**. *See p114.*

CBD, Warehouse District & Central City

Asian

56 Degrees

Whitney Wyndham Hotel, 610 Poydras Street, at Camp Street (212 5658/www.56degrees.com). St Charles Streetcar/bus 11 Magazine. **Open** 6-10am, noon-2pm, 5-10pm Mon-Thur; 6-10am, noon-2pm, 5-11pm Fri; 6-11am, 5-11pm Sat; 6-11am, 5-10pm Sun. **Main courses** $13-$20 lunch; $17-$25 dinner. **Credit** AmEx, DC, MC, V. **Map** p279 C1.

Judging by frequent emptiness at peak meal times, 56 Degrees may not be around for much longer, and that would be a real shame. Then again, its cavernous setting – a partitioned, high-ceilinged section of an old bank lobby – may amplify the void. This design is engaging, as soon as you take notice of the myriad beautiful marble details. The menu is similarly intricate – a hybrid of Asian, European and Louisiana influences under chef Minh Bui. Diver scallops, wasabi-vodka poached mussels and an extraordinary manchego cheese salad are standouts. Reserve ahead and you can even have a table in a private bank vault.

Horinoya

920 Poydras Street, at O'Keefe Street (561 8914). St Charles Streetcar. **Open** 11.30am-2.30pm, 5-10pm Mon-Fri; 5-10pm Sat, Sun. **Main courses** $20. **Credit** AmEx, DC, Disc, MC, V. **Map** p277 F7.

Newcomer Horinoya has raised the bar for local sushi. The sashimi is best here – an unbelievably fresh celebration of texture and flavour – and the soybean paper roll is a house special. Take the chef's recommendations for what's freshest. Those willing to fork out a little more can reserve private, traditional Japanese dining rooms off the main room.

Lemon Grass Café

International House Hotel, 217 Camp Street, at Gravier Street (523 1200/www.lemongrassrest.com). St Charles Streetcar/bus 11 Magazine. **Open** 7.30-

10am, 11am-2pm, 6-10pm Mon-Fri; 7.30-10am, 6-10pm Sat, Sun. **Main courses** $10-15 lunch; $20-25 dinner. **Credit** AmEx, DC, MC, V. **Map** p279 C1.
Chef Minh Bui's flagship restaurant makes its home inside the trendy International House Hotel. There's a good deal of crossover with its sister restaurant, 56 Degrees (*see p118*), as well as unique dishes such as the Viet bird nest. Speaking pragmatically, of Bui's two spots, this one is the likely survivor.

Cajun

Bon Ton Café

401 Magazine Street, at Poydras Street (524 3386). St Charles Streetcar/bus 10 Tchoupitoulas, 11 Magazine. **Open** 11am-2pm, 5-9.30pm Mon-Fri. **Main courses** $13-23 lunch; $15-35 dinner. **Credit** AmEx, DC, MC, V. **Map** p279 C1.
The kitchen here has been serving up the same dishes for the past 50 years, including the crawfish bisque (served with a hard-boiled egg and a floating crawfish head – scoop out the insides with a fork; go on, be brave). You could try the crabmeat imperial or the soft-shell crab Alvin, which is served stuffed with even more crabmeat. This place tends to get very busy at lunchtime.

Contemporary

Cobalt

Hotel Monaco, 333 St Charles Avenue, at Poydras Street (565 5595/www.cobaltrestaurant.com). St Charles Streetcar. **Open** 7.30-9.30am, 11.30am-2pm, 6-9pm Mon-Fri; 8.30-10.30am, 5.30-9.30pm Sat; 5.30-9pm Sun. **Main courses** $9-$14 lunch; $16-$25 dinner. **Credit** AmEx, DC, Disc, MC, V. **Map** p279 C1.
With Susan Spicer stepping back from her consulting duties here, chef Brack May moves to the front with gusto. May calls his style 'Southern regional', a free approach to local ingredients along with bold experimentation that largely pays off. The crab gratin with gruyère commands attention, and May's hold never wavers in dishes such as red snapper and crawfish ravioli and the panéed pork tenderloin. The two-course blue plate specials at lunch and dinner are a steal, and even if you spend all of your time here sitting at the blue-tiled bar, you can have a charcuterie plate that's a meal in itself.

Cuvee

322 Magazine Street, at Natchez Street (587 9001/restaurantcuvee.com). Bus 11 Magazine. **Open** 11.30am-2pm, 6-10pm Mon-Thur; 11.30am-2pm, 6-11pm Fri; 6-11pm Sat. **Main courses** $18-$23 lunch; $22-$36 dinner. **Credit** AmEx, DC, MC, V. **Map** p279 C1.
Chef Bob Iacovone provides the heft Cuvee needs to square off its expansive wine cellar. The restaurant has more than 600 vintages, and most of the staff have some level of international wine certification. Prices are steep, but you can't exactly do foie gras burgers or sugarcane smoked duck breast on the cheap. If wine is something you hold dear, Cuvee is a smart, ambitious choice.

Emeril's

800 Tchoupitoulas Street, at Julia Street (528 9393/www.emerils.com). Bus 10 Tchoupitoulas. **Open** 11.30am-2pm, 6-10pm Mon-Thur; 11.30am-2pm, 6-11pm Fri; 6-11pm Sat; 6-10pm Sun. **Main courses** $18-$23, lunch; $22-$36 dinner. **Credit** AmEx, DC, Disc, MC, V. **Map** p279 C2.
Now that celebrity chef Emeril Lagasse is so ubiquitous, so hyperbolic, so (dare one say it aloud) overexposed, it's easy to forget that he was once just an inventive chef who was very hard to imitate. He has cloned himself all over the country, and the growth of his empire shows no signs of slowing, but if you want to see where it all began, head for this Tchoupitoulas Street corner. Seating overlooks an exposed kitchen, which turns out dishes such as corn cakes and caviar, barbecue shrimp and andouille sausage-crusted redfish.

The Grill Room

Windsor Court Hotel, 300 Gravier Street, at Tchoupitoulas Street (522 1992/www.windsorcourthotel.com). Bus 3 Vieux Carre, 10 Tchoupitoulas, 11 Magazine. **Open** 7-10.30am, 11.30am-2pm, 6-10pm Mon-Thur, Sun; 7-10.30am, 11.30am-2pm, 6-11pm Fri, Sat. **Main courses** $16-$24 lunch; $32-$36 dinner. **Credit** AmEx, DC, Disc, MC, V. **Map** p279 C1.
British chef Jonathan Wright takes the helm of the Grill Room with two Michelin stars under his belt, and he has done little less than awe diners here since his arrival. Wright's greatest facility is for crafting intricate dishes that unravel across the palate like the pages of a dense, canonical novel. His menu reflects seasonal and local ingredients, which he pairs in acrobatic and astonishing ways. Add to that an impeccable presentation and a masterful balance of textures and temperatures in each dish, and the Grill Room finally has a chef who is unquestionably the perfect fit for its commanding environs.

Herbsaint

701 St Charles Avenue, at Girod Street (524 4114/www.herbsaint.com). St Charles Streetcar. **Open** 11.30am-2pm, 5.30-10pm Mon-Fri; 5.30-10.30pm Sat. **Main courses** $10-$12 lunch; $18-$24 dinner. **Credit** AmEx, Disc, MC, V. **Map** p279 B1.
One of the highest compliments a restaurant can receive is the adulation of other chefs, so if you trust the experts, then Herbsaint sits in the top tier of New Orleans eateries. Chef Donald Link, with help from partner Susan Spicer, has been gathering in the awards in recent years – as well as the fervent loyalty of locals who flock to his side – with his take on nearly everything from rabbit to frogs' legs and braised pork belly. It all adds up to extremely nuanced dishes in an unpretentious but engaging CBD setting (its wide windows overlook the St Charles streetcar line). Save room for the chocolate beignets and banana brown butter tart.

Eat, Drink, Shop

Restaurant August

301 Tchoupitoulas Street, at Gravier Street (299 9777/www.rest-august.com). St Charles Streetcar/bus 10 Tchoupitoulas, 11 Magazine. **Open** 11am-2pm, 5.30-10pm Mon-Fri; 5.30-10pm Sat. **Main courses** $26. **Credit** AmEx, DC, Disc, MC, V. **Map** p279 C1.

August opened to great acclaim a couple of years ago, and has generated a steady buzz ever since. Starters are small but potent, especially the gnocchi with crab and truffle, and the salads with candied pumpkin seeds and warm, breaded goat cheese. Among main courses, the Moroccan spiced duck is rich with a decadent side of seared duck foie gras, and the chocolate three ways will slay any cravings you may have. The wine cellar is complementary to chef John Besh's cooking style.

Victor's at the Ritz-Carlton

Ritz-Carlton Hotel, 921 Canal Street, between Dauphine and Burgundy streets (524 1331/ www.ritz-carlton.com). St Charles or Canal Streetcar/bus 11 Magazine. **Open** 6.30-10.30pm Tue-Sat. **Main courses** $24-$34. **Credit** AmEx, DC, Disc, MC, V. **Map** p277 F7.

For sheer splendour, Victor's stands a foot above its competitors in the fine dining arena. Try to reserve one of the velvet-curtained 'cheater's booths' at the rear of the dining room, a throw-back to days when a man wanted a little privacy when dining out with his other lady. Chef Frank Brunacci's sensibility is at once playful and refined, French-focused but global in perspective. The cellar is formidable, and the sommelier first-rate, and the cheese cart is unrivalled. The chef's *degustation* menu is a particularly decadent route to take, but it's a road worth travelling.

Zoe Bistrot

W Hotel, 333 Poydras Street, at Tchoupitoulas Street (207 5018/www.zoebistrot.com). St Charles Streetcar/bus 10 Tchoupitoulas, 11 Magazine. **Open** 6.30am-2.30pm, 6-10pm. **Main courses** $12-$15 lunch; $20-$25 dinner. **Credit** AmEx, DC, Disc, MC, V. **Map** p279 C1.

Dining at this über-hip bistro in the W Hotel can be like eating in a library – everyone seems awed into silence, or just too trendy to talk. The minimalist design is better when lights are dim; then you may be less inclined to notice the lack of effort taken to separate the restaurant from the hotel lobby. The food, on the other hand, isn't so encumbered by image. At lunch, the lobster club on brioche with pommes frites is simply delicious. Dinner features bouillabaisse and pistachio-crusted chicken.

French

Rene Bistrot

817 Common Street, at Carondelet Street (412 2580/www.renebistrot.com). St Charles Streetcar/ bus 11 Magazine. **Open** 6.30-11am, 11.30am-2.30pm, 6-10.30pm daily. **Main courses** $10-$17 lunch; $15-$18 dinner. **Credit** AmEx, DC, Disc, MC, V. **Map** p279 C1.

Since departing his prestigious post at the Grill Room (*see p119*), chef Rene Bajeaux has been confirming his reputation at his namesake bistro. If the yen for good, largely un-Creolised French fare overtakes you, the menu offers a fitting battery of Gallic classics: escargots, onion soup with gruyère custard, bouillabaisse, steak frites... you know the drill. The decor is vibrantly hip, kind of an orange-y, plastic Paris style. Luckily, prices for mains rarely rise above the $20 range.

Neighbourhood

Mother's

401 Poydras Street, at Tchoupitoulas Street (523 9656/www.mothersrestaurant.com). St Charles Streetcar/bus 10 Tchoupitoulas, 11 Magazine. **Open** 6.30am-10pm Mon-Fri; 7am-10pm Sat, Sun. **Main courses** $4-$21. **Credit** AmEx, DC, MC, V. **Map** p279 C1.

Even in the most oppressive months of summer, the queue in front of Mother's will wrap around its shadeless corner in the pitiless heat. Such is the devotion and the curiosity it inspires. And for what? Well, the debris po-boy – beef bits drowned in the long-simmered house gravy – is a major part of the answer. The all-day breakfast with choices such as shrimp or crawfish étouffée omelets is another, then there's the freshly made southern-style biscuits, the gumbo, the soft-shell crab platter... What are you waiting for? Get in line.

Uglesich's

1238 Baronne Street, at Erato Street (523 8571). St Charles Streetcar. **Open** Oct-June 10.30am-4pm Mon-Fri. July-Sept closed. **Main courses** $10-$16. **No credit cards. Map** p279 B2.

The crowds can get dense at Uglesich's, a once-closeguarded secret long since leaked to every seafood lover in the West. Waiting is de rigueur, but once you're in, ahhh... where to begin? Maybe with the firecracker shrimp, fried pasta shells or the oyster shooters? Everything is made with love and dishes quake with flavour. The eponymous owner frequently threatens to retire, then stays open another year. When he finally does shutter these doors, there will be a black hole in the city's stomach.

Spanish

Rio Mar

800 South Peters Street, at Julia Street (525 3474/ www.riomarseafood.com). St Charles Streetcar/bus 10 Tchoupitoulas, 11 Magazine. **Open** 11.30am-2pm, 6-10pm Mon-Thur; 11.30am-2pm, 6-11pm Fri; 6-11pm Sat. **Main courses** $16-$20. **Credit** AmEx, DC, Disc, MC, V. **Map** p279 C2.

Acolytes say they feel like they're in a coastal Spanish village once they step into Rio Mar. The cuisine might prompt the mental trip but the decor – scattered blue tiles and patina-ed walls – doesn't do it. The menu features four different ceviches, which are undoubtedly the best in the city, as well as an ample array of Iberian dishes. The Gulf shrimp and saffron arroz is stocked with large, juicy shrimp.

Garden District

American

Houston's

1755 St Charles Avenue, at Felicity Street (524 1578/www.houstons.com). **Open** 11am-11pm Mon-Thur, Sun; 11am-midnight Fri, Sat. **Main courses** $8-$22. **Credit** AmEx, MC, V. **Map** p279 B2.

It amounts to something of a failure of the imagination to eat at a chain restaurant in New Orleans; but ask chefs where they like to go on their night off, and they'll admit to sneaking over here for a good steak. Expect a straightforward, red-blooded feed at this big restaurant – prime rib, double cut pork chop – along with BBQ shrimp or roast chicken. The quality is good, the portions ample, and there's a view of the St Charles streetcar rattling by outside.

Asian

Sake Café Uptown

2830 Magazine Street, between Washington Avenue & 6th Street (894 0033). **St Charles Streetcar/bus 11 Magazine.** **Open** 11.30am-10pm Mon-Thur; 11.30am-11pm Fri, Sat; noon-10pm Sun. **Credit** AmEx, DC, Disc, MC, V. **Map** p279 A3.

There probably isn't much similarity between authentic sushi and the gorgeous, oversized and hyperbolic roll offerings at Sake Café, and that is exactly why you should try it. Japanese nuance meets Louisiana largesse in things like the spicy tuna, avocado, BBQ eel and wasabi tobiko; another roll features tempura shrimp, snow crab, avocado, marble seaweed and eel sauce. They're large and a touch messy (a no-no for the real thing), but they have a way of sending beautiful bursts of disparate tastes rocketing round your mouth.

Contemporary

Eleven 79

1179 Annunciation Street, at Erato Street (299 1179). **St Charles Streetcar/bus 10 Tchoupitoulas, 11 Magazine.** **Open** 5.30-10.30pm Mon-Thur; 5.30-11.30pm Fri, Sat. **Main courses** $25-$32. **Credit** AmEx, MC, V. **Map** p279 C2.

The Italian-meets-Louisiana fare at Eleven 79 has inspired ferocious loyalty among diners, many of who convert to regulars midway through their first meal here. It helps to like veal – there are at least nine veal options on the menu – and a healthy love of pasta doesn't hurt. The grilled calamari with pecorino polenta is beloved by many, and the converted 19th-century cottage is a charmer, too.

Emeril's Delmonico

1300 St Charles Avenue, at Erato Street (525 4937/www.emerils.com). **St Charles Streetcar.** **Open** 11.30am-2pm, 6-10pm Mon-Thur; 11.30am-2pm, 6-11pm Fri; 6-11pm Sat; 6-10pm Sun. *Jazz brunch* 10.30am-2pm Sun. **Main courses** $13-$18 lunch; $21-$30 dinner. **Credit** AmEx, DC, Disc, MC, V. **Map** p279 B2.

Emeril Lagasse's most recent expansion in New Orleans is this Lower Garden District eatery. The setting is clubby and classic – an ample decorating budget well spent – and it's a good fit for dressed-up dishes that lean a little to the steakhouse side, along with better known Creole concoctions. Among Emeril fans, this is a consistent favourite.

Creole

Commander's Palace

1403 Washington Avenue, at Coliseum Street (896 7600/www.commanderspalace.com). **St Charles Streetcar.** **Open** 11.30am-2pm, 6-10pm Mon-Fri; 11.30am-1pm, 6-10pm Sat; 10.30am-1.30pm, 6-10pm Sun. **Main courses** $13-$15 lunch; $24-$39 dinner. **Credit** AmEx, DC, Disc, MC, V. **Map** p279 A3.

Since the untimely death of the late, great executive chef Jamie Shannon a few years ago, there's been a bit of a maelstrom in the kitchen at this venerable restaurant. It has settled down somewhat, now that a successor, Tory McPhail from the restaurant's Las Vegas branch, has been ensconced in the kitchen. This classic New Orleans restaurant has been festooned with almost every conceivable award including the James Beard Foundation's Lifetime Outstanding Restaurant distinction. Are you really going to argue with that? Take a long lunch or dinner, and don't forget to put your order in for the bread pudding soufflé early. This is one of the places where locals go to celebrate special occasions.

Mexican

Juan's Flying Burrito

2018 Magazine Street, between St Andrew and Josephine streets (569 0000/www.juansflying burrito.com). **Bus 11 Magazine.** **Open** 11am-11pm Mon-Sat; noon-10pm Sun. **Main courses** $5-$9. **Credit** AmEx, DC, Disc, MC, V. **Map** p279 B3.

This Cal-Mex Lower Garden District mainstay, beloved by folks from all walks of life, would be equally at home just about anywhere cool; think Brooklyn, Austin, San Francisco. The power chords of thrash metal growl overhead, and the intricately tattooed and pierced servers may at first seem a little intimidating. But there's a lot of love at Juan's. For starters, it has some of the city's best Margaritas. Then there's burritos with names such as the 'gutter punk' and 'the swifty', as well as tacos, quesadillas and enchiladas. You'll believe the house motto – 'we are all Juan' – before you go.

Branch: 4724 S Carrollton Avenue, at Canal Street (486 9950).

Neighbourhood

Parasol's

2533 Constance Street, at Third Street (899 2054/ www.parasols.com). St Charles Streetcar/bus 10 Tchoupitoulas, 11 Magazine. **Open** 11am-10pm daily. **Main courses** $6-$10. **Credit** AmEx, MC, V. **Map** p276 E9.

Every St Patrick's Day, this Irish favourite blocks off the street, pours out green beer to the masses and gets the neighbours grumbling. Every other day of the year, those neighbours get their bar and grill back to quaff Guinness and tuck into some of the most sublime po-boys around. The roast beef po-boy is the house Goliath, but the shrimp and oyster versions (spelled out in local vernacular 'shwimp' and 'erster' on the menu) are no wallflowers. Throw in a basket of fries and a few more pints, and you've got yourself a classic and inexpensive meal.

Sugar Magnolia

1910 Magazine Street, between St Mary & St Andrew streets (529 1110/www.sugarmagnolia restaurant.com). Bus 11 Magazine. **Open** 11am-4pm Mon; 11am-10pm Tue-Fri; 8am-10pm Sat; 8am-3pm Sun. **Main courses** $13-$20. **Credit** AmEx, Disc, MC, V. **Map** p279 B3.

Peculiarities are everywhere at Sugar Magnolia. Signs ask of your meal was 'everything delightful'? Beers are described: 'tastes great/you know the rest'. Who writes this stuff? But it still has much to recommend it. Its 1820s farmhouse location will keep you marvelling through the meal. The oysters bordelaise are, actually, kind of 'everything delightful' and the well-priced salads and sandwiches help to keep the tab at a reasonable level.

Surrey's Café and Juice Bar

1418 Magazine Street, at Terpsichore Street (524 3828). Bus 11 Magazine. **Open** 8am-3pm Wed-Sun. **Main courses** $2-$10. **No credit cards**. **Map** p279 B2.

There are few better cures for a night's excesses than brunch at Surrey's. First the organic juices – orange, carrot, beet, ginger – bring your energy levels back from the red zone, then the *migas* or the Costa Rican breakfast put you right on your feet. The three-cheese melt focaccia is excellent and the grilled aubergine muffuletta is a healthier (and no less delicious) way to enjoy one of New Orleans' more decadent sandwiches. Service is sometimes a little sleepy, and the wait can be excessive, but the grub is good.

Uptown

American

Bluebird Café

3625 Prytania Street, between Foucher & Anthony streets (895 7166). St Charles Streetcar. **Open** 7am-3pm Mon-Fri; 8am-3pm Sat, Sun. **Main courses** $6. **No credit cards**. **Map** p277 E9.

It's breakfast and lunch only at Bluebird, where huevos rancheros are the house favourite and long queues are common at weekends. Maybe the proximity to several area hospitals has something to do with the health-conscious menu that features buckwheat pancakes or eggs scrambled with nutritional yeast and tamari. On the other hand, the doctors probably won't be prescribing the chocolate chip pancakes or the ribeye steak and eggs.

Camellia Grill

626 S Carrollton Avenue, at St Charles Avenue (866 9573). St Charles Streetcar/bus 90 Carrollton. **Open** 9am-1am Mon-Thur, Sun; 9am-3am Fri; 8am-3am Sat. **Main courses** $3-$8. **No credit cards**. **Map** p276 A8.

Want to send your arteries down in a blaze of glory? This is the place. Camellia Grill adds a new dimension to the heart-stopping process with some of the fattiest, most wonderful burgers you could ever enjoy. Everything is perfect and perfectly bad for you – the chocolate freezes with ice-cream, the omelets made with fistfuls of eggs and cheese, the pecan pie… Sitting around the U-shaped counter you'll see all kinds praying at this altar of grease, shouting their orders to the bow-tied waiters. It's short-order heaven and hell rolled into one.

Martin Wine Cellar

3827 Baronne Street, at Napoleon Avenue (896 7380/www.martinwine.com). St Charles Streetcar/ bus 24 Napoleon. **Open** 9am-6.30pm Mon-Sat; 10am-4pm Sun. **Main courses** $7-$12. **Credit** AmEx, DC, Disc, MC, V. **Map** p276 D9.

In a city woefully short of delis, this wine store is manna from heaven. On one hand, it's arguably the city's best wine retailer, with an adventurous selection of cheeses and deli meats. On the restaurant side, it's routinely deluged with locals seeking the 'big Ben' (cold rare roast beef, BLT and horseradish mayo on an onion roll) or the Californian (turkey, havarti cheese, avocado and sprouts on wheat). The sandwiches and sides are equally fantastic, the Barq's rootbeers are cold and served in longneck bottles, just as they should be, and the service is fast and friendly, even at peak times.

Asian

Kyoto

4920 Prytania Street, between Robert & Upperline streets (891 3644). St Charles Streetcar. **Open** 11.30am-2.30pm, 5-10pm Mon-Thur; 11.30am-2.30pm, 5-10.30pm Fri; noon-10.30pm Sat. **Main courses** $8-$13 lunch; $11-$19 dinner. **Credit** AmEx, DC, Disc, MC, V. **Map** p276 C9.

Kyoto had been resting on its laurels a bit until it started getting some Uptown competition. In response to that, the decor has smartened up, the service has got a bit tighter and the *mise en place* is looking more precise. It's nestled into a charming little section of Prytania Street. Not the best sushi in the city, but still excellent if you're in the area.

The 'old school' restaurants

Making bananas Foster at **Brennan's**.

Egypt has its pyramids, Rome its Coliseum but, frankly, you can't get a good meal at either of them. Among New Orleans' most significant landmarks are restaurants that have operated for more than a century. Some have made the trip through the years with their menus almost entirely intact. One of these – **Antoine's** – has been in the same family since it opened in 1840. Its walls are papered in testaments to its past – early mentions in *The New Yorker*, photos of the half dozen US presidents who dined there, signed pictures of a phone book's worth of celebrities. One private room, the Mystery Room, did a brisk business in bootleg cocktails during Prohibition (*see p109*).

Founded in 1905, **Galatoire's** isn't nearly as old as Antoine's, but it remains the most densely concentrated daily re-enactment of local society's vanity fair (*see p112*). In one sense, Galatoire's is highly egalitarian: to get a table, everyone – landed names and commoners alike – must queue. For Galatoire's famous marathon Friday lunches, the line can stretch around the block. Regulars are so committed to having everything just as they like it that even the slightest change – the acceptance of credit cards, the use of ice-cubes instead of hand-shaved ice – is met with loud tantrums. Waiters are doting and have engendered almost fanatical loyalty among patrons.

Brennan's (*see p111*) is a child among these older peers (having opened in 1946), but it long ago established an old school attitude, launching a family dynasty that has since spread over several fractious branches across the city. Among the old guard, this is probably the friendliest, as it takes a laidback attitude to posh dining. It's also the home of another major Mardi Gras player, the krewe of Bacchus. Their photos remain enshrined in the Bacchus room, which adjoins the restaurant's wine cellar.

Ninja

8433 Oak Street, at Joliet Street (866 1119).
St Charles Streetcar. **Open** 11.30am-2.30pm, 5-10pm
Mon-Thur; 11.30am-2.30pm, 5-10.30pm Fri; noon-
3pm, 5-10.30pm Sat; noon-9pm Sun. **Main courses**
$5-$12 lunch; $10-$20 dinner. **Credit** AmEx, DC,
Disc, MC, V. **Map** p276 7A.

Many New Orleanians will profess that Ninja makes
their favourite sushi, and they gladly followed when
the restaurant relocated to this new, larger space on
Oak Street. Many of those same acolytes will admit
that the new digs are somewhat less than inspiring
(unless the sparse and underdecorated cafeteria look
is their bag). If you find bright fluorescent lighting
and fresh raw seafood to be adversarial concepts,
you'll probably want to pass on Ninja. But if sushi
is all you care about, you might just love this place.

Contemporary

Dick & Jenny's

*4501 Tchoupitoulas Street, at Jena Street (894
9880). Bus 10 Tchoupitoulas.* **Open** 5.30-10pm
Tue-Sat. Closed July. **Main courses** $12-$20.
Credit AmEx, Disc, MC, V. **Map** p276 C10.

There is some deception going on at Dick & Jenny's.
The beaten down exterior would suggest some
anonymous and avoidable sandwich shop. The
Tchoupitoulas Street address itself is decidedly
unfashionable. And yet this is another contender for
best restaurant in New Orleans. Chef Dick Benz
seems to have the Holy Grail of Louisiana cooking
in his kitchen. His menu reflects seasonal ingredients and changes every two months. His wine list is
expansive but surprisingly affordable. The only
caveat: no reservations, so take your bottle to the
patio and wait with the rest of those who've realised
that Benz is working on a level apart from his peers.

Gautreau's

*1728 Soniat Street, between Dryades & Daneel
streets (899 7397). St Charles Streetcar.* **Open**
6-10pm Mon-Sat. **Main courses** $17-$30.
Credit DC, Disc, MC, V. **Map** p279 A2.

Gautreau's has cycled through chefs over the past
few years, but regular diners say the essence
remains intact. Hidden in a residential neighbourhood, the menu rotates seasonally. More creative
offerings include roasted garlic and mascarpone
ravioli and curried cauliflower soup.

Mat & Naddie's

*937 Leonidas Street, at Freret Street (861 9600).
St Charles Streetcar/bus 15 Freret, 32 Leonidas.*
Open 11am-2pm, 5.30-9.30pm Tue-Fri; 5-9.30pm
Sat. **Main courses** $8-$13 lunch; $13-$24 dinner.
Credit AmEx, DC, Disc, MC, V. **Map** p276 A7.

The folk art that adorns Mat & Naddie's belies the
sophistication of its food. The paintings give you a
little wink – we know what this is all about – then
the servers start trotting out country pâté, wood-
grilled oysters, Indonesian tiger prawns. What the
hell is going on here? Tea-smoked lacquered duck?

Venison medallions with blackberry demi-glaze?
The apparent paradoxes work, and the building is
a nicely restored 19th-century specimen just a levee
away from the Mississippi River.

Upperline Restaurant

*1413 Upperline Street, between St Charles &
Prytania streets (891 9822/www.upperline.com).
St Charles Streetcar/bus 10 Tchoupitoulas,
11 Magazine.* **Open** 5.30-9.30pm Wed, Thur,
Sun; 5.30-10pm Fri, Sat. **Main courses** $17-$25.
Credit AmEx, DC, MC, V. **Map** p276 C7.

Owner JoAnn Clevenger is a stickler for detail and
Upperline clearly benefits from her attention. The
building is a bright yellow Uptown beacon, the
garden surrounding it meticulously maintained. A
three-course tasting meal, which compresses seven
different dishes, is a bargain.

Creole

Brigsten's

*723 Dante Street, at River Road (861 7610/
www.brigstens.com). St Charles Streetcar.* **Open** 5.30-
10pm Tue-Sat. Closed 2wks July. **Main courses**
$19-$26. **Credit** AmEx, DC, MC, V. **Map** p276 A8.

Chef Frank Brigtsen stays true to his Louisiana
roots in his use of local ingredients. A devoted shopper at local farmers' markets, he has developed a
menu that follows the seasons, and he's also got a
soft spot for local game. The house seafood platter
is recommended, as is virtually anything that has
come out of the water. And let's just say that rabbit
gets a special degree of love here.

Jacques-Imo's

*8324 Oak Street, at Cambronne Street (861 0886/
www.jacquesimoscafe.com). St Charles Streetcar.*
Open 5-10.30pm Mon-Sat. **Main courses** $12-$21.
Credit AmEx, DC, Disc, MC, V. **Map** p276 A7.

Owner-chef Jack Leonardi's garishly decorated
Uptown bungalow may have eclipsed every other
restaurant in town in terms of reputation over sub-
stance. Squillions of visitors come to New Orleans
thinking, 'I know this great little out-of-the-way spot
nobody's ever heard of…' only to find a great long
queue of other people with the same idea. Of course,
Jacques-Imo's is good at what it does – dishes that
frequently involve the deep-frying of seafood. It's
not perfect, and it's too crowded, but the flavour is
volcanic, and you've got to love the fact that you
walk through the kitchen to get to the dining room.
Still, it's the marketing coup of New Orleans.

French

Ciro's Cote Sud

*7918 Maple Street, between Fern & Short streets
(866 9551). St Charles Streetcar/bus 90 Carrollton.*
Open 5-10pm Mon-Thur, Sun; 5-11pm Fri, Sat. **Main
courses** $11-$18. **No credit cards. Map** p276 8A.

The Ciro's part of this restaurant's moniker harks
back to the days when old man Ciro made the city's

best pizzas. The pizzas remain – and they're still superior to any other in New Orleans – but the Cote Sud addition has been the real strength. The menu now has excellent southern French leanings (the *moules marinère*, onion soup and coq au vin are especially strong) reflecting the tastes of the friendly young French owner. And the decor is softer and more intimate than in its exclusively pizza days. The tarte tatin will make you long for the French grandmother you never had.

La Crepe Nanou

1401 Robert Street, at Prytania Street (899 2670/www.lacrepenanou.com). St Charles Streetcar. **Open** 6-10pm Mon-Thur, Sun; 6-11pm Fri, Sat. **Main courses** $7-$19. **Credit** AmEx, DC, MC, V. **Map** p276 C9.

Despite its name, this is not really a crêperie – in fact, it would probably be run straight out of France for its lofty prices. It is, however, awfully romantic – the kind of dark, cosy bistro there should be more of in this city. The savoury crêpe and seafood dishes are good if unremarkable, as are the overpriced dessert crêpes. There are a few outdoor tables, which afford an excellent view of the crowd waiting to dine, and that crowd is there every night.

Lilette

3637 Magazine Street, at Antonine Street (895 1636/www.cuisineofneworleans.com). Bus 11 Magazine. **Open** 11.30am-2pm, 6-10pm Tue-Thur; 11.30am-2pm, 6-11pm Fri, Sat. **Main courses** $13-$17 lunch; $18-$23 dinner. **Credit** AmEx, DC, Disc, MC, V. **Map** p277 E9.

Chef John Harris has been widely praised for his earthy French cuisine served in a beautifully renovated space. But while the wine-red walls and pressed tin ceiling are lovely, reports of Lilette's greatness have been exaggerated. The staff can be inattentive and are unfortunately apt to correct customers' pronunciations (*quel* drag). The food itself, though usually good and occasionally remarkable, is a bit steeply priced, scantily portioned and lacks bombast. You'll definitely have to put your hand in your pocket, and you may wonder if it was worth it.

Martinique Bistro

5908 Magazine Street, at Eleonore Street (891 8495). Bus 11 Magazine. **Open** 6-10pm Mon-Thur, Sun; 6-10.30pm Fri, Sat. **Main courses** $15-$23. **Credit** MC, V. **Map** p276 B9.

Chef Hubert Sandot's cuisine is as bright as the tangerine walls of his restaurant's exterior, an ebullient hybrid of his French and Martinique background. Then there's the courtyard, the city's most Edenic, secluded from busy Magazine Street by rustic brick walls. The menu changes frequently and reflects the seasonal rotation of fresh ingredients, but you might be lucky enough to catch shrimp sautéed with mango and curry, or the Caribbean jerk New Zealand lamb braised with Riesling and papaya. Vaguely amusingly, the chef has decorated the walls with photos of himself. Just so, we suppose, you know where the food's coming from.

Mexican

Taqueria Corona

5932 Magazine Street, at Nashville Street (897 3974). Bus 11 Magazine. **Open** 11am-2pm, 5-9.30pm daily. **Main courses** $4-$14. **Credit** AmEx, DC, Disc, MC, V. **Map** p276 A9.

There is a Mexican family behind Taqueria Corona, which immediately sets it apart from the largely Cal-Mex options peppered across the city. The Margaritas are decent but over-iced, and the real bargains are the very simply named numero uno, dos and tres: three combination plate specials piled with various mixtures of burritos, chimichangas and tacos, all fresh and made to order.

Branch: 857 Sulton Street, Warehouse District (524 9805).

Middle Eastern

Jamila's Café

7908 Maple Street, at Burdette Street (866 4366). St Charles Streetcar/bus 90 Carrollton. **Open** 11.30am-2pm, 6-10pm Tue-Thur; 11.30am-2pm, 6-11pm Fri, Sat; 6-10pm Sun. **Main courses** around $15. **Credit** AmEx, MC, V. **Map** p276 A7.

Jamila's is a Tunisian affair: the titular Jamila works the kitchen while husband Moncef Sbaa dotes over diners in the small dining room. The offerings are among the most dressed-up Middle Eastern fare in town – tajine of lamb, shrimp-stuffed calamari, couscous royal. Friday nights have the added bonus of flamenco guitarists, while Saturday nights are the real draw with gyrating belly-dancers.

Lebanon Café

1506 S Carrollton Avenue, at Jeanette Street (862 6200). St Charles Streetcar. **Open** 11am-10pm Mon-Thur; 11am-10.30pm Fri, Sat; noon-10pm Sun. **Main courses** $7-$14. **Credit** AmEx, DC, Disc, MC, V. **Map** p276 A7.

There is something inherently reliable, if slightly perverse, about restaurants that use numbers to designate their dinner offerings. So it is at Lebanon Café, well liked by its local regulars. There are a few tables outside when it's nice, so you can have your stuffed grape leaves under the moon. A young and informal crowd frequents this unassuming café.

Neighbourhood

Café Atchafalaya

901 Louisiana Street, at Laurel Street (891 5271). Bus 10 Tchoupitoulas, 11 Magazine. **Open** 11.30am-2pm, 5.30-9.30pm Tue-Fri; 8.30am-2pm, 5.30-9.30pm Sat; 9.30am-2pm Sun. **Main courses** $8-$15 lunch; $9-$22 dinner. **Credit** MC, V. **Map** p277 E9/10.

Just two blocks off Magazine Street, Café Atchafalaya recedes into the quiet of its borderline Uptown neighbourhood. Its modestly priced meals reflect both Creole and Southern enthusiasms: poached eggs on crab cakes for breakfast, or treacly

Mat and Naddie's: so much better than it looks. *See p124.*

praline Belgian waffles; calf's liver and onions or country fried steak for dinner. The blackboard specials change often and are usually your best bet.

Casamento's

4330 Magazine Street, between Napoleon Avenue & General Pershing Street (895 9761/www.casamentos restaurant.com). Bus 11 Magazine, 24 Napoleon. **Open** *Sept-May* 11.30am-1.30pm, 5.30-9pm Tue-Sun. *June-Aug* closed. **Main courses** $6-$12. **No credit cards. Map** p276 C9.

A favourite among tourists and the retired set, Casamento's is a throwback to the 1950s. Nearly every inch of it, including the kitchen, is covered in tile and awash in bright fluorescent light. Yet the oysters are remarkably good and fresh (the restaurant closes during the summer months when the

quality of local oysters drops) the service is homey and familiar and the fried dishes are satisfying. Prices have resisted post-'50s inflation, and there's a singular pleasure to be derived from knocking back a dozen bracing, salty oysters while sipping Dixie beer from the tiny house glasses.

Domilise Sandwich Shop & Bar

5240 Annunciation Street, at Bellecastle Street (899 9126). Bus 10 Tchoupitoulas, 11 Magazine. **Open** 10am-7pm Mon-Sat. **Main courses** $6-$9. **No credit cards. Map** p276 C10.

Domilise is so completely a neighbourhood restaurant that it's actually tucked into the middle of one, rather than at its commercial edges. Those in its Uptown environs know the potency of its po-boys, all of which come dressed (vernacular for lettuce, tomatoes, pickles, mayo). If you get stuck on your decision, you can go with a half-and-half seafood option, named 'the peacemaker'.

Franky & Johnny's
321 Arabella Street, at Tchoupitoulas Street (899 9146). Bus 10 Tchoupitoulas. **Open** 11am-10pm Mon-Thur, Sun; 11am-11.30pm Fri, Sat. **Main courses** $5-$9. **Credit** AmEx, Disc, MC, V. **Map** p276 E9.

If some Mulberry Street dive in Little Italy were washed in a bath of Louisiana swampwater, you'd probably end up with Franky & Johnny's. That's a good thing – the vibe is chummy and local; the building is broken down and ugly in the most beautiful way; and the food is inexpensive and brilliantly unhealthy. Order from menus tacked to the walls, get a beer, watch the football invariably playing on the house TVs and tuck in to bell pepper rings, boiled crabs or the oyster platter. Eating at Franky & Johnny's, even if it's your first time, is like putting on an old sweater – it fits perfectly right away.

Joey K's
3001 Magazine Street, at Dublin Street (891 0997). Bus 11 Magazine. **Open** 11am-10pm Mon-Fri; 8am-10pm Sat. **Main courses** $5-$15. **Credit** DC, MC, V. **Map** p276 D9.

Joey K's might be the easiest neighbourhood restaurant to find in New Orleans, situated in the heart of a busy commercial section of Magazine Street. Famous among locals for its all-you-can-eat catfish Fridays, it also does good shrimp and oyster po-boys and a nice Saturday breakfast with homemade biscuits. The beer comes generously dispensed in big frosty mugs, and it's worth saving room for the blackberry cobbler à la mode.

Pascal's Manale
1838 Napoleon Avenue, at Dryades Street (895 4877/www.pascalsmanale.com). St Charles Streetcar/bus 24 Napoleon. **Open** 11.30am-10pm Mon-Fri; 4-10pm Sat; 4-9pm Sun. **Main courses** $7-$13 lunch; $10-$24 dinner. **Credit** DC, MC, V. **Map** p276 D9.

As shown by the restaurant's moustached, accordion-wielding shrimp mascot, barbecue shrimp is the house speciality at this venerable old New Orleans favourite. Also popular are the raw oysters served by the dozen. The balance of the menu pairs up fried seafood and traditional Italian dishes, but if you're just coming here once, get the shrimp.

Mid-City

American

Ruth's Chris Steak House
711 N Broad Street, at Orleans Avenue (486 0810/www.ruthschris.com). Bus 46 City Park, 97, 98, 99 Broad. **Open** 11.30am-10pm Mon-Thur; 11.30am-11pm Fri; 5-11pm Sat; noon-9.30pm Sun. **Main courses** $11-$24 lunch; $18-$33 dinner. **Credit** AmEx, DC, Disc, MC, V. **Map** p277 E6.

Known across the country as a top-tier steakhouse chain, Ruth's Chris is actually a local joint. Everything begins somewhere, and this beef empire was founded on Broad Street. Broiled in an 1,800° (Fahrenheit) oven, these steaks are served with history (and fries), and this particular location is a favourite among local politicos, power brokers and their entourages. There are minor concessions on the menu for those who don't go the steak route, but nobody comes here for the shrimp.
Branch: 3633 Veterans Boulevard, Metairie (888 3600).

Contemporary

Gabrielle Restaurant
3201 Esplanade Avenue, at Mystery Street (948 6233/www.gabriellerestaurant.com). Bus 48 Esplanade. **Open** 5.30-10pm Tue-Thur; 11.30am-2pm, 5.30-11pm Fri; 5.30-11pm Sat. **Main courses** $16-$32. **Credit** AmEx, DC, Disc, MC, V. **Map** p278 E5.

Long the cornerstone of Mid-City's Esplanade Avenue eateries, Gabrielle is tiny but confident and always full of regulars who pledge their allegiance to chef/owners Greg and Mary Sonnier, while others shy away from its remarkably (too?) creative menu. Maybe it's the starters – barbecue shrimp pie, seared foie gras on a pig's ear with blueberry demiglace – or it might be the crabmeat-stuffed flounder or the Creole cream cheese-crusted lamb chops. The food here is inventive and filling, a remarkable performance all the way through to the dessert course. Both the peppermint patti and the apple upside-down bread pudding are wise ways to finish.

Creole & soul food

Dooky Chase's
2301 Orleans Avenue, at Miro Street (821 2294). Bus 46 City Park. **Open** 11.30am-9.30pm Mon-Thur, Sun; 11.30am-10.30pm Fri, Sat. **Main courses** $13 lunch; $11-$25 dinner. **Credit** AmEx, DC, Disc, MC, V. **Map** p277 F6.

Chef Leah Chase is one of the city's best-known and loved cooks (not to mention one of the lamentably few marquee African-American names in the local culinary world). Under her guidance, Dooky Chase's fuses Creole and a touch of soul memorably in dishes like *court bouillon* (red fish fillet in tomatoes and green peppers) and shrimp Clemenceau. The neighbourhood is iffy – best to cab it – but when Chase is in the kitchen it's worth the trip.

French

Café Degas
3127 Esplanade Avenue, at Ponce de Leon Street (945 5635/www.cafedegas.com). Bus 48 Esplanade. **Open** 5.30-10pm Mon; 11.30am-2.30pm, 5.30-10pm Tue-Sun. **Main courses** $9-$16. **Credit** AmEx, DC, Disc, MC, V. **Map** p278 E5.

Eat, Drink, Shop

Owing to a rather oppressive summer climate, there isn't nearly enough alfresco dining in New Orleans, but at Café Degas they've come up with a unique way to have your duck a l'orange and eat it too. The main dining room is a covered patio – complete with a giant tree growing through its centre – where clear plastic covers can be rolled down during more adversarial weather. The French menu is good, if a bit ordinary, but the atmosphere is among the city's most charming and romantic.

Chateaubriand

310 N Carrollton Avenue, at Bienville Street (207 0016/www.chateaubriandsteakhouse.com). Canal Streetcar/bus 90 Carrollton. **Open** 11.30am-2.30pm, 5.30-10.30pm Mon-Fri, Sun; 5.30-10.30pm Sat. **Main courses** $16-$23 lunch; $23-$30 dinner. **Credit** AmEx, Disc, MC, V. **Map** p278 D5.

This place bills itself as a French-accented steakhouse, a fact that undersells the quality of its traditional French fare. From its beautiful, Swiss cheese-topped French onion soup to its molten, buttery escargots and chillingly delicious profiteroles, you'll do as well following the Gallic route as trying the more loudly touted prime beef grilled fillet.

Middle Eastern

Mona's Café

3901 Banks Street, between Canal & Tulane streets (482 7743/www.shopno.com/monas). Bus 39 Tulane. **Open** 11am-9pm Mon-Thur, Sun; 11am-10pm Fri, Sat. **Main courses** $3-$13. **Credit** AmEx, DC, Disc, MC, V. **Map** p278 C5.

It has spawned locations across the city, but Mona's original Banks Street location marked the introduction of fresh, authentic Middle Eastern cuisine to New Orleans. The menu is inexpensive and reliable across the board. This is the place to hit when you've got a craving for houmous, baba ganuj, falafel or kebabs, all at very reasonable prices.
Branches: 504 Frenchmen Street, Marigny (949 4115); 4126 Magazine Street, Uptown (894 9800); 3151 Calhoun Street, Uptown (861 2124).

Neighbourhood

Liuzza's by the Track

1518 N Lopez Street, at Ponce de Leon Street (943 8667). Bus 48 Esplanade. **Open** *Restaurant* 11am-8.30pm Mon-Fri. **Main courses** $6-$11. **Credit** AmEx, DC, Disc, MC, V. **Map** p278 E5.

Just steps away from the New Orleans Fair Grounds, Liuzza's is the quintessential neighbourhood restaurant – run-down, stocked with regulars (themselves a little run-down, come to think of it) and without the slightest bit of self-consciousness. It is also, as it happens, home to one of the city's best gumbos and a masterful barbecue shrimp po-boy – French bread hollowed out and filled to brimming with buttery, spicy shrimp. Take in a few frosty mugs of locally brewed Abita beer and try to visit on Thursday night when local musicians bring their instruments and jam until morning.

Mandina's

3800 Canal Street, at N Cortez Street (482 9179). Canal Streetcar/bus 41, 42, 43 Canal. **Open** 11am-10.30pm Mon-Thur; 11am-11pm Fri, Sat; noon-9pm Sun. **Main courses** $8-$15. **No credit cards.** **Map** p278 B5.

Up to ten daily specials each day distinguishes Mandina's from its neighbourhood brethren. Trout meuniere, stuffed crab, shrimp étouffée, catfish almandine... maybe the offerings don't set the world on fire, but none of its many regulars are complaining about the generous portions, cosy ambience and doting service. There are no reservations, so belly up to the bar and get your name on the list, then sip a cocktail while you wait for your turn at a table.

Spanish

Lola's

3312 Esplanade Avenue, at Mystery Street (488 6946). Bus 48 Esplanade. **Open** 6-10pm Mon-Thur, Sun; 6-10.30pm Fri, Sat. **Main courses** $8-$22. **No credit cards.** **Map** p278 E4.

This place was a Mid-City hit almost immediately after opening, both for its paellas and its bring-your-own-booze policy (greatly facilitated by the strong wine selection at Whole Foods Market across the street). Crowds can be a little overwhelming (especially during Jazz Fest), you can't reserve a table and the dining room can get noisy, but regulars swear that the rich Spanish menu makes it worth the wait.

Further afield

While the best-known tourist restaurants are mostly in the city centre, some of the best restaurants not discovered by tourists are a short drive away in the near suburbs. Any cabbie can take you to most of these joints, or you can just get yourself a good map and strike out on your own.

Avondale

Mosca's

4137 Highway US 90W(436 9942). **Open** 5.30-9.30pm Tue-Sat. **Main courses** $12-$25. **No credit cards.**

Proving us wrong right at the get-go, this one is a bit too far for a cab ride, but if you've got a car, it's easy enough to find, and they'll happily give you directions to its location just outside the city limits. This stripped-down roadside restaurant is fascinating to experience. Portions are obscenely large and correspond to no straightforward (or even the most flexible) definition of either Italian or Creole (and they're all the better for it). Try the oysters bordelaise or the crabmeat salad, listen to the Avondale teenagers drag racing out on the highway, behold the waitresses of a bygone era… Mosca's isn't a restaurant; it's a phenomenon.

Jefferson

Crabby Jack's

428 Jefferson Highway, at Knox Road (833 2722/www.crabbyjacks.net). **Open** 10am-5pm Mon-Fri; 11am-4pm Sat. **Main courses** $8-$13. **Credit** AmEx, Disc, MC, V.

This lesser-known sister restaurant to Jacques-Imo's (*see p124*) sits just outside the city limits, but it's worth the cab or car ride. Crabby Jack's is open for lunch only, and it's really just the byproduct of Jacques-Imo's need for some extra kitchen space for off-site cooking, but it's also a great way to get a taste of the Oak Street location's food for a fraction of the price. The hot plate lunches – fried seafood with salad, toast and fries – are faves, but any of the sandwiches or the fried chicken will ruin you for dinner just as easily and thoroughly.

Drago's

3232 N Arnoult Road, at 17th Street (888 9254/ www.dragosrestaurant.com). **Open** 11am-9pm Mon-Thur; 11am-10pm Fri, Sat. **Main courses** $7-$16 lunch; $11-$23 dinner. **Credit** AmEx, DC, Disc, MC, V.

Many of the oystermen who supply the city are Croatian immigrants and their children, so Drago's, a second-generation Croatian restaurant in Metairie, taps into that vein with some of the area's freshest oysters. Of course, Drago's is also famous for its char-grilled oysters, a house recipe so tasty it seems to leave little exclamation points over diners' heads.

Lakeview/Bucktown

R&O Pizza Place

216 Metairie-Hammond Highway, Bucktown (831 1248). **Open** 11am-10pm Mon-Thur, Sun; 11am-11pm Fri, Sat. **Credit** Disc, MC, V.

This Bucktown classic is a favourite of Emeril Lagasse and that shows the man has taste. For you, this place represents as good a reason as any other to get yourself over to the scenic shoreline of lovely Lake Ponchartrain. You might be lucky enough to spy a pelican soaring above while you tuck into the thick and tasty seafood stew, or the fried crab claws and stuffed artichokes. All of which should serve as indications that the menu is a little more involved than the name would indicate.

Wolfe's

7224 Ponchartrain Boulevard, at Robert E Lee Boulevard (284 6004/www.wolfesofneworleans.com). **Open** 11.30am-2pm, 5.30-9.30pm Mon-Fri; 5.30-9.30pm Sat. **Main courses** $10-$14 lunch; $18-$24 dinner. **Credit** AmEx, DC, Disc, MC, V.

The lakefront area was once just a string of fried seafood and burger joints (albeit some very good

The new school

While the Creole heavyweights hone and perfect the classics, the next generation is challenging the accepted wisdom, lighting the fuse in fusion.

Lately some of the most promising new restaurants have sprouted up as part of new and refurbished guest spots. **Victor's at the Ritz-Carlton** is the most upscale of the lot (*see p120*). The real star here is the chef – Frank Brunacci – an Australian with a global sensibility and a sense of humour (is that a tomato sorbet on my plate?). His *degustation* menu is a wonder.

Former Windsor Court executive chef Rene Bajeaux goes solo at **Rene Bistrot** with classic French fare that has been winning noteworthy acclaim in the national press (*see p120*). After toying with a few tentative early identities, **Cobalt** has hit solid American ground with chef Brack May's lusty cuisine. It is housed in the cool Hotel Monaco, and the vibe here is relaxed, making it a more accessible dining experience (*see p119*).

Buoyed by partner Susan Spicer's track record, **Herbsaint** hit the ground running with no hotel attachments. Chef Donald Link has made his name with carefully assembled dishes that have drawn the respect of his peers around the city (*see p119*). Chef John Besh has done much the same in somewhat more formal digs at **Restaurant August** (*see p120*).

Finally, though it's not exactly new anymore, **Peristyle** must be credited with its rise like a phoenix from the flames. Having overcome a calamitous fire, chef Anne Kearney got right back on her feet with the reopened restaurant. She remains a chef who is setting the bar higher for others and may be the next super-chef in-the-making (*see p109*).

ones). That was until chef Tom Wolfe came along. Unencumbered by local expectations, Wolfe makes the most of local ingredients in a contemporary style that has no match in the city. Start with the sweetly potent lemon drop Martini before venturing over to the garlic-crusted oyster nachos and sweet potato-crusted duck sausage. The Steen's cane syrup slow roasted duck shouldn't be missed, nor the panko-crusted redfish. If there's any room left, the white chocolate butter bars will finish you off and make you glad you found one of the city's most surprising and ambitious restaurants.

Eat, Drink, Shop

Coffeeshops & Cafés

Get yourself a coffee, a croissant and a table in the sunshine. Now, *this* is living.

Iced coffee may not have been invented in New Orleans, but it's more popular here than anywhere else. Each café and coffeeshop has its own version, special blend or invention that makes it creamier, smoother or sweeter, because a long cold glass of coffee is just perfect for those afternoons when it's just too hot to do anything but sit in the shade. Whether you like your coffee hot or cold – or just prefer a nice cup of tea – this is the heart of café culture, and spending an afternoon stretched out in a courtyard under an umbrella talking about life, love and politics over a pastry and a cup of something is a local tradition. Whether it's café au lait and a plate of sugar-coated beignets at **Café du Monde**, or a jam-filled croissant at **Croissant d'Or**, this town encourages the leisurely consumption of decadent pastries and thick, chicory tinged coffee when, really, you should be doing other things.

Along with the inevitable Starbucks, there are a number of locally owned coffeeshop chains that have devoted followings. **Rue de la Course** (named after the street on which its first café opened) is beloved for its creamy flavoured iced coffee, big useful noticeboards where people peddle everything from flats to guitars, and sunny laid-back ambience. **PJ's** has fanatic groupies who swear by its cold-dripped iced coffee and sweet pastries. **CC's** is loved by trendy types for its bagels and big, comfy armchairs. Whatever your flavour, you'll be surprised how much time you can waste in any of them.

Angelo Brocato

214 N Carrollton Avenue, at Canal Street, Mid-City (486 0078). Canal Streetcar/Bus 41, 42, 43 Canal, 90 Carrollton. **Open** 9.30am-10pm Mon-Thur, Sun; 9.30am-10.30pm Fri, Sat. **Credit** Disc, MC, V. **Map** p278 D5.
A classic Italian bakery, Angelo Brocato's is also responsible for the city's best homemade gelatos and Italian ices – the strawberry and lemon in particular are legendary. Little of its classic charm was lost when it relocated to Mid-City from the French Quarter many years ago. Today, it's still the kind of place where kids moon over the display cases while their parents sip espressos and munch on sesame cookies and chocolate cannolis so good they would hold their own in New York.

Beignets and *café au lait* at **Café du Monde**.

Café du Monde
800 Decatur Street, at Jackson Square, French Quarter (581 2914/www.cafedumonde.com). Riverfront Streetcar/Bus 3 Vieux Carre, 5 Marigny/Bywater, 55 Elysian Fields. **Open** 24hrs daily. **No credit cards. Map** p282 C3.

Perched at the edge of the French Market and across from Jackson Square, Café du Monde's green-awninged patio is a local icon, and deservedly so. It's famous for its café au lait and hot beignets – little squares of fried dough, carpet-bombed with mounds of powdered sugar. It's a 24-hour haven, filled in equal parts by tourists and locals. Try the chicory coffee, get a table near the railing and watch the buskers spill over from the square through a sugary haze. You'll feel as saturated in history as in caffeine and fried sweetness.

Café Luna
802 Nashville Avenue, at Magazine Street, Uptown (269 2444). Bus 11 Magazine. **Open** 6.30am-7.30pm daily. **Credit** MC, V. **Map** p276 B10.

Things looked bleak when a certain international chain of predatory coffeehouses planted a branch across the street from Café Luna, which makes its home in a beautiful, crumbly old Victorian manse. The owners have hung in there, though. Needless to say, there's a far greater sense of personality here than across the street at the neighbours', from the handpainted tables on the wraparound porch (which is mercifully shaded by the draping branches of a live oak) to the paintings by local artists on the walls. There's nothing generic about Café Luna, which is why so many continue to appreciate it.

Café Marigny
640 Frenchmen Street, at Royal Street, Marigny (945 4472/www.cafemarigny.com). Bus 3 Vieux Carre, 5 Marigny/Bywater. **Open** 7am-10pm Mon-Thur, Sun; 7am-midnight Fri, Sat. **Credit** AmEx, DC, MC, V. **Map** p282 D2.

After you've spent the day walking amid the splashes of brightly coloured Marigny homes, Café Marigny is a cool and inviting place to duck into for a wedge of quiche, a small sandwich or an iced coffee, especially in the hotter months, when walking just a couple of blocks can be an extremely unpleasant, viscous experience. Toasted bagels and fruit juices are also available, and everything is freshly made on the premises.

CC's Coffeehouse
941 Royal Street, at St Philip Street, French Quarter (581 6996/www.communitycoffee.com). Bus 3 Vieux Carré. **Open** 6.30am-11pm Mon-Thur; 6.30am-midnight Fri, Sat; 7.30am-10pm Sun. **Credit** AmEx, MC, V. **Map** p282 C2.

New Orleanians are discerning coffee drinkers, and Community Coffee has long been successfully entrenched in most local households. When the company furthered its retail brand by opening the CC's Coffeehouse chain, they did so with the heft of tradition behind them. The interiors can be a touch homogeneous (Starbucks helped the company with early design ideas, and it shows), but the coffee is always good and the pastries are fresh and locally made. Try the red velvet cake and the Mochasippi, which now gives Starbucks a serious run for its money in these parts.
Branches: throughout the city.

Still life al fresco

When it comes to weather, it's always feast or famine, isn't it? New Orleans has endless sunny days firmly in its favour, but it's a case of too much of a good thing. Soaring summer temperatures and stultifying humidity mean that eating outdoors is more fun in theory than in practice. Still, give people the slightest encouragement (and a can of mosquito repellent) and they head outdoors. With the creative use of electric fans and big umbrellas, they find a way to make the unbearable pleasant. Whether or not the heat co-operates, this is a town made for al fresco dining.

A number of local restaurants and cafés recognise this fact. Most of the city's coffeehouses and cafés have patio or courtyard tables in addition to indoor space, and some – notably **Royal Blend** (*see p133*), **La Marquise** (*see p132*) and **Café du Monde** (*see above*) – are defined by them.

Restaurants do much the same thing. In the French Quarter, the courtyard at **Broussard's** (*see p111*) is a model of careful cultivation, while Uptown, diners clamour for tables in the lush tropical courtyard at **Martinique Bistro** (*see p125*). At **Mat & Naddie's** (*see p124*) on the Riverbend, you can hear the clamour of freight trains and the ships sounding their horns on the Mississippi River just over the levee, and few experiences offer as much misty Southern grandeur as having a cocktail on the sprawling balcony of the **Victorian Lounge** at the Columns Hotel (*see p144*). Is that the clatter of an old manual typewriter echoing percussively from an open window above you?

Somehow, dinner always tastes better under the stars. Where else in the US but New Orleans can you so realistically re-enact the romance of Van Gogh's *Night Café*?

Croissant d'Or

617 Ursulines Street, between Chartres &
Royal streets, French Quarter (524 4663). Bus 3
Vieux Carré. **Open** 7am-5pm daily. **Credit** MC, V.
Map p282 C2.

Situated in the old Angelo Brocato's building (tiled signs for sex-segregated entrances still remain outside), Croissant d'Or attracts a mix of French Quarter bohemians and European tourists who seem to have been given advance word about the quality of the pastries. Along with these, it serves excellent quiches, sandwiches and soups. But one of the biggest reasons so many return here might be the singular spectacle of its rather assertive counter ladies, who run things with a mixture of iron-fistedness and smiles. The drawback: no outdoor tables. Still, particularly on a rainy day, this is the perfect place to unfold your Sunday paper and settle in.

Fair Grinds Coffeehouse

3133 Ponce de Leon Street, at Esplanade Avenue,
Mid-City (948 3222/www.fairgrinds.com). Bus 48
Esplanade. **Open** 7am-11pm daily. **No credit**
cards. Map p278 E5.

There's something particularly inviting about Mid-City's small commercial pocket of restaurants, cafés and shops in the Bayou St John area. It has the feel of some quaint, liberal-leaning Vermont college town (with a bad case of acute humidity), and Fair Grinds steps easily into the groove with its peeling, wainscotted walls, hand-painted chairs and faded equestrian murals (a nod, along with its name, to the horse track just a few blocks behind it). Check out the old timey, belt-turned ceiling fans and eavesdrop on the vibrant conversations around you. It's a great place to while away an afternoon hour's lull.

La Boulangerie

625 St Charles Avenue, between Girod & Lafayette
streets, CBD (569 1925). St Charles Streetcar. **Open**
6am-7pm Mon-Sat; 7am-1pm Sun. **No credit cards.**
Map p279 B1.

When the Rizzo brothers opened the original La Boulangerie on Magazine Street, it was quickly acknowledged that they held the crown for the city's best bread (baked, incidentally, in an authentic French industrial oven). The croissants and pastries also took off, prompting expansion to a second storefront and finally this CBD café, which also serves coffee, homemade sandwiches and surprisingly tasty pizzas. The breadth of selection depends on demand that day – the Rizzos never quite seem prepared for the crowds they invariably attract – but even when the pickings are slim it's worth it. If you're here during Mardi Gras season, don't miss the *galette de roi*, the French take on the local king cake. While dramatically overpriced, it strikes just the right balance of flakiness and almondy moisture. Hey – you're on holiday, anyway.

La Marquise

625 Chartres Street, between Toulouse & St
Peter streets, French Quarter (524 0420). Bus 3
Vieux Carré, 5 Marigny/Bywater. **Open** 7am-7pm
Mon-Thur; 7am-8pm Fri-Sun. **No credit cards.**
Map p282 B2.

La Marquise shares most of its menu with Croissant d'Or but sports the added bonus of one of the French Quarter's most beautiful courtyards – long, shady and with plenty of tables. It's only steps away from Jackson Square, and it's the cheapest way to enjoy what some Quarterites pay tons of money for – a quiet little nook among the bustle.

It's not food, it's a way of life

Look, when you live in a place like New York, San Francisco, London or Paris, you've got a lot of creative outlets to occupy your energy. In a city as small as New Orleans, creativity tends to get channelled in a few directions, and along with music, food is the big one around here. You can't really appreciate how obsessed this city is until you find yourself sitting in a restaurant with a table of locals. Starters get passed around, and everybody has a nibble, buzzing with the discovery, all the while talking about other restaurants: 'Have you tried the duck at August?... Domilise's really does have the best po-boys in Uptown... I've heard that Susan Spicer's thinking about opening another restaurant...'

There would probably be a market for chef trading cards in this city. People gossip about the comings and goings of chefs, the openings and closings of restaurants, the latest *Food & Wine* or *Gourmet* magazine write-up, in the way that people elsewhere gossip about celebrities.

When Galatoire's restaurant (*see p112*) recently let one of its long-time waiters go after allegations of sexual harassment, the fury that ensued drew international attention. The restaurant was hit with an artillery of protest letters from regulars who were also some of the city's most prominent names. Those letters eventually became the subject of a long-running play, *The Galatoire's Monologues*, which played before sold-out audiences for weeks. All of which serves to illustrate the point that people develop ferociously strong attachments to restaurants here. And after you have a meal in some of them, you might understand why.

Eat, Drink, Shop

PJ's Coffee and Tea

634 Frenchmen Street, at Royal Street, Faubourg Marigny (949 2292). Bus 3 Vieux Carré, 5 Marigny/Bywater. **Open** 7am-11pm Mon-Thur, Sun; 7am-midnight Fri, Sat. **Credit** AmEx, MC, V. **Map** p282 D2.

Like CC's, PJ's began as a small local coffeehouse and burgeoned into a regional chain. While the decorator might be chided for all that mauve and formica, there's an expansive range of coffees and teas, decent bagels (the flavoured cream cheese is really good), assorted pastries and small sandwiches. The counters tend to be staffed by well-meaning but slow neo-hippies who cheerily banter with each other about club outings while (very) leisurely steaming the milk for your cappuccino.
Branches: throughout the city.

Royal Blend

621 Royal Street, between Toulouse & St Peter streets, French Quarter (523 2716/ www.royalblendcoffee.com). Bus 3 Vieux Carré, 5 Marigny/Bywater, 55 Elysian Fields. **Open** 6.30am-8.30pm Mon-Thur, Sun; 6.30am-11pm Fri, Sat. **Credit** AmEx, MC, V. **Map** p282 B2.

Like La Marquise, Royal Blend has both a great courtyard and a great location (beginning to see a trend in what makes for a good downtown café yet?) right in the middle of the French Quarter. Part of it also gives over to internet access – one of a dwindling number of such cafés downtown after they passed out of turn-of-the-century vogue. The standard selection of pastries, bagels and the like are here, and they're all fine, but the real draw is the ambience – a long, historic carriageway separates you from the madding crowd outside.

Rue de la Course

217 N Peters Street, between Iberville & Bienville streets, French Quarter (523 0206). Canal Streetcar/ Bus 3 Vieux Carré, 5 Marigny/Bywater, 55 Elysian Fields. **Open** 7am-10pm Mon-Thur, Sun; 7am-11pm Fri, Sat. **No credit cards. Map** p282 A3.

From the Vespas parked outside, you can tell Rue de la Course is somehow a bit cooler than your average café. Step inside and the flaking paint, pressed tin ceilings, smoky haze and jazz wafting (sometimes blasting) over the speakers will confirm your suspicions. All the Rue de la Courses ratchet up the hipness factor, but the two Magazine Street locations (affectionately called 'Little Rue' – the first location at Race Street – and 'Big Rue' – on Magazine Street Uptown) are the quintessential ones. Smoking is allowed – a rarity that helps to pack in the poets, musicians and artists. The coffees are good, the pastries are decent and you can play a game of chess or watch students and writers hammering away at their laptops. This is a favourite among those holding a torch for café society.
Branches: 3128 Magazine Street, Uptown (899 0242); 1140 S Carrollton Avenue, Uptown (861 4343); 401 Carondelet, CBD (586 0401); 1500 Magazine Street, at Race Street, Garden District (529 1455).

Chill in the shade at **Royal Blend**.

Still Perkin'

2727 Prytania Street, at Washington Avenue (899 0335). St Charles Streetcar. **Open** 7am-7.30pm Mon-Fri; 8am-7.30pm Sat, Sun. **Credit** Disc, MC, V. **Map** p279 A3.

Still Perkin' thrives largely because of its perfect location at the heart of the Garden District. Across the street is one of the city's loveliest (and safest) cemeteries, and it's surrounded by stately mansions in every direction. Serving sandwiches and pastries, it also brews its own brand of coffee. A great place to stop if you're doing a self-guided walking tour of the Garden District, and it's also part of an upscale mini mall that houses an excellent bookshop.

Bars

It's always cocktail hour in the Big Easy.

Fans of New Orleans who visit New York scoff at that city's assertion that it is the 'city that never sleeps'. As *if*. Any local will tell you that New Yorkers are amateurs when it comes to the 24-hour bar culture that is second nature around here. Indeed, this is the kind of town where you can walk into a bar at 8pm and step out a lifetime later to find the sun high in the sky, the street-sweepers busy at work, and others who have similarly just misplaced 10 hours of their lives blinking bewildered in the doorways of neighbouring bars, wondering what happened to the night before.

It is this sense that you could waste away whole days perched on a bar stool here, telling your life story to a new best friend and never quite noticing the time passing by, that gives this city its bar mystique. The world's greatest drinkers marvel at New Orleans. This is a town where the bars were so extraordinary they dazzled Truman Capote. There's a titillating element of near danger – as if you could be conscripted into a life of alcoholism merely by sitting down on a bar stool in the French Quarter – that fascinated writers like Tennessee Williams and William Faulkner. Places like **Napoleon House** and **Lafitte's Blacksmith Shop** in the French Quarter have been keeping people drunkenly happy for hundreds of years. Newcomers like **Snake & Jake's Christmas Club Lounge**, with its perpetual nightmare-before-Christmas ambience, and **Loa**, with its homage to posh voodoo, are following in the footsteps of the city's old bars, creating worlds where the clocks stop, the booze keeps flowing and anything – anything at all – can happen.

ON NOT GETTING ARRESTED

In the 1990s, Louisiana fought the national trend of moving from allowing 18-year-olds to drink towards a 21-and-over drinking rule. That rebelliousness came at a price: for years, the state lost millions in federal funding as the US government sternly guided it back to legal reality. Lesson learned. These days, the laws of this particular land prohibit drinking for anyone under 21. Those between 18 and 20 are legally allowed to go into bars, but they cannot drink alcohol. (You can lead a kid to booze, but you can't let him drink.)

Don't be fooled by this loophole, though. Bar owners can lose their liquor licences just as easily here as they can anywhere else, so they do an efficient job of carding. They check driver's licences, passports – any legal form of photo ID. So don't think that just because things are a little more relaxed down here that minors can sneak in and belly up to the bar. Also, just because you're over 21 and have the beard or wrinkles to prove it, don't think you won't get asked for ID. If you want a drink, take proof of age wherever you go.

The other important thing to remember while bar-hopping is the fluctuating 'go-cup' (or open-container) law. Don't listen to recent visitors who marvelled about being able to walk around with a bottle of beer in hand. That law, which briefly allowed glass bottles out and about, was recently changed *back* to allowing only plastic cups to be carried around with booze. Trust us – it's a good thing; the broken glass on the streets was lethal. Also, you're allowed to leave bars with open containers, but not to enter one. If you walk in with a cocktail, you will be asked to dump it. Apart from that, hey, this is a very easygoing place.

A final point: drinking the night away is encouraged – but stupid, rude and illegal behaviour is not. Though the police force is woefully understaffed, they nevertheless keep an eye out for drunk-and-disorderly behaviour. Anyone caught acting too rowdy – and yes, even flashing – will be dealt with accordingly. Acting cool, especially around and towards the police, is a very good thing. New Orleans cops have seen it all before. Don't bore them.

ON NOT GETTING ROBBED

This mix of permissiveness and alcohol makes many visitors prime candidates for all forms of violent crime: rapes, robbery, even murder. This may sound dramatic, but it's an issue. So it's important for visitors to be aware of their surroundings. Stay in groups as often as possible, keep an eye on your wallet, and if a side-street seems desolate or particularly dark, just don't go there.

While ATM fees are sometimes outrageous ($2.50 per transaction), it's a good idea not to carry too much cash on hand. And most importantly: **take taxis.** They're cheap and plentiful, and will take you right to the door. Some of the city's best bars are in dodgy neighbourhoods. They're perfectly safe to go to, but you wouldn't want to walk there.

The exquisitely decaying **Napoleon House**. They've seen your kind before. *See p139.*

French Quarter

Bombay Club
*830 Conti Street, at Bourbon Street (586 0972/
www.thebombayclub.com). Canal Streetcar/bus 3
Vieux Carré, 5 Marigny/Bywater, 55 Elysian
Fields.* **Open** 5.30-10.30pm Mon-Wed, Sun; 5.30pm-
1.30am Thur-Sat. **Credit** AmEx, DC, Disc, MC, V.
Map p282 B2.

When it comes to the elegant Martini, there's no
place like the Bombay Club. Owner Richard Fiske
is so obsessed with the drink that he boasts more than
115 different versions using everything in the alcohol arsenal: Absolut, Belvedere, Chopin, Grey Goose,
Ketel One, Stoli, Skyy, even (cough) Smirnoff. The
clientele is surprisingly eclectic, dropping in to hear
local jazz singers perform Wednesday through
Saturday. The bartenders are smart and polite, but
to a point: one recently had the gumption to do last
call in the wee hours despite the protestations of
singer and occasional customer Emmylou Harris.

Carousel Bar & Lounge
*Hotel Monteleone, 214 Royal Street, at Iberville
Street (523 3341/www.hotelmonteleone.com). Bus 3
Vieux Carré, 5 Marigny/Bywater.* **Open** 11am-1am
daily. **Credit** AmEx, DC, Disc, MC, V. **Map** p282 A2.
In 1949, the Hotel Monteleone bought itself a bar that
looks – and rotates – like an amusement park
carousel. The Carousel Bar has been one of the city's
curiosities ever since. Recently restored, it is beautifully painted but a bit disconcerting, as the bar and
bar stools constantly move, while the bartenders
stay in one place at the centre. Each complete revolution takes about 15 minutes. Lovely though it is,
this seems like *such* a bad idea (alcohol + spinning
= guess what?), and most people can only spin for a

brief period before, hand to mouth and green about
the gills, they choose to retire to one of the station-
ary tables nearby. Still it's a fun place. And think of
the drinking games…

Coop's Place
*1109 Decatur Street, at Ursulines Street (525
9053/www.coopsplace.net). Riverfront Streetcar/bus
3 Vieux Carré, 5 Marigny/Bywater.* **Open** 11am-3am
Mon-Thur, Sun; 11am-4am Fri, Sat. **Credit** AmEx,
Disc, MC, V. **Map** p282 C3.
There is something mildly intimidating but ultimately comforting about Coop's Place. The bartenders look curmudgeonly but are actually nice
enough; the beer selection is average – draughts and
bottles, foreign and domestic – and the cocktails are
strong. A pool table and a jukebox blasting anything
from The Clash to Tom Waits provide easy distractions. And as unlikely as it may seem, Coop's is
the city's most technologically innovative bar – its
website sports a webcam, so you can see who's there
before you head out, and it has the only free public
wireless port in town. Who'd of thunk it?

Cosimo's
*1201 Burgundy Street, at Governor Nicholls Street
(522 9715). Bus 3 Vieux Carré, 5 Marigny/Bywater.*
Open 4pm-6am daily; food served 5pm-1am.
Credit AmEx, MC, V. **Map** p282 D1.
A dark cool greets you in this bar. The jukebox is
turned down so low that Hendrix's guitar solos can
barely be heard over the pinging of the video poker
machine. There's a modest selection of beer, and
Hoegaarden on tap for a not-cheap $5.75 a pint. The
back bar looks like someone's living room, albeit one
with a pool table. And the food isn't bad; burgers
cooked over an open pit. Stephen Stills recently wan-
dered in and spent a night playing the piano here.

Bars

Carousel Bar

You spin me right 'round, baby. Take a seat and try to hold onto your drink. *See p135.*

Carrollton Station

Shoot the bear! Shoot the bear! We just can't stop saying it! *See p146.*

Circle Bar

One of the coolest bars in the world. Need we say more? *See p141.*

d.b.a.

Gorgeous place, great jukebox, dazzling booze selection. Get here. *See 139.*

French Quarter Bar (FQB)

Has a high IYDQ (Impress Your Date Quotient). *See p136.*

Loa

So many pretty people, so little time. *See p142.*

Molly's at the Market

Good local atmosphere and frozen Irish coffees. Mmmm. *See p137.*

R Bar

Fab jukebox, weird furniture and reasonable prices, just outside the Quarter. *See p139.*

St Joe's

Where God and booze meet on the other side. *See p147.*

Snake & Jake's Christmas Club Lounge

It's too weird for some – are you cool enough? *See p147.*

Coyote Ugly Saloon

225 N Peters Street, at Bienville Street (561 0003/ www.coyoteuglysaloon.com/neworleans). Bus 3 Vieux Carré, 5 Marigny/Bywater. **Open** noon-4am daily. **Credit** MC, V. **Map** p282 B3.

Some bars just try too damned hard. At Coyote Ugly you can smell the artifice. This is a branch of the Manhattan establishment, which was made infamous by the cheesy, perpetually-on-cable film of the same name. The attraction is the female bartenders who dance half-naked on the bar to blasting classic rock songs. They occasionally spray water on the crowd. If your idea of fun is taking a shot (for $20) from the belly or mouth of a bartendress with breasts of questionable authenticity, then this is the place for you. To give you an idea of the clientele, motorcycles always seem to line the front sidewalk.

The Dungeon (or Ye Original Dungeon Club)

738 Toulouse Street, at Bourbon Street (523 5530/ www.originaldungeon.com). Bus 3 Vieux Carré, 5 Marigny/Bywater. **Open** midnight-dawn Tue-Sun. **Credit** MC, V. **Map** p282 B2.

This is one bar that even the locals view with a tiny bit of anxiety. Regulars insist the Dungeon is all bark and only a little bite, but for years this late-night joint has maintained a reputation as a haunt of would-be vampires – courtesy, largely, of the notoriously claustrophobic pathway down to the gloomy basement bar. Just an upchuck away from Bourbon Street, this place doesn't even open until midnight, and it doesn't get busy until 3am, which only adds to its spooky reputation. Along with the nocturnal hours, other constants are the metal music blaring from the speakers and a leather-clad clientele who are sometimes friendlier than they look.

El Matador

504 Esplanade Avenue, at Decatur Street (569 8361). Riverfront Streetcar/bus 3 Vieux Carré, 5 Marigny/Bywater, 13 Esplanade, 57 Franklin. **Open** 9pm-3am Mon-Thur; from 5pm Fri-Sun. **Admission** free-$12. **Credit** AmEx, Disc, MC, V. **Map** p282 D3.

When El Matador became the Esplanade/Decatur corner post, many thrilled at the hip vibe created by owner Rio Hackford – son of Hollywood director Taylor Hackford of *An Officer and a Gentleman* fame. With its circular centre bar separating wall-side booths and warm red-and-black moodiness, this quickly became one of the city's trendiest bars. But because of what seems like a reflexive need to fill the schedule with live music, it's not a good place for a casual chat. That's not altogether a bad thing; local brass geniuses the Soul Rebels are Wednesday regulars. Sometimes, though, the volume can be ear-splitting. Still, the bartenders have far less attitude than their tattoos suggest and the prices are reasonable so El Matador retains a level of cool.

French Quarter Bar

Ritz-Carlton Hotel, 921 Canal Street, at Dauphine Street (524 1331/www.ritz-carlton.com). St Charles or Canal Streetcar/bus 11 Magazine. **Open** 11am-1am daily. **Credit** AmEx, DC, Disc, MC, V. **Map** p282 A1.

Let's get one thing straight from the start: if you come here, you're gonna pay. The good news is, it's (almost) worth it. Despite the price, this place is taking off on its own merits. It features an excellent wine list, a good (if expensive) menu and an upscale ambience with nods to local culture. There's even a Martini named after trumpeting crooner Jeremy Davenport. The service is great (mixed nuts greet you before your butt hits the stool).

The Hideout

1207 Decatur Street, at Governor Nicholls Street (529 7119). Riverfront Streetcar/bus 3 Vieux Carré, 5 Marigny/Bywater. **Open** 24hrs daily. **Credit** AmEx, MC, V. **Map** p282 D3.

Over the years, the Hideout has battled with the reputation of being too seedy for its own good. And yes, there's still the occasional biker with attitude, but these days the bartenders even wear make-up and don't mind calling you 'Baby' or 'Darlin'' while grabbing you a cheap bottle of beer. This is the kind of place where a woman can come in with a guy, watch him leave, then complain to anyone who will listen that she didn't know he was married when they left Tallahassee for New Orleans (true story).

Kerry Irish Pub

331 Decatur Street, at Conti Street (527 5954/ www.kerryirishpub.com). Riverfront Streetcar/bus 3 Vieux Carré, 5 Marigny/Bywater, 55 Elysian Fields, 57 Franklin. **Open** 2pm-2am daily. **Credit** AmEx, Disc, MC, V. **Map** p282 B3.

With its old brick walls and dimly lit stage, this friendly joint has a lot of loyal local fans, who come here not only for the laid-back, untouristy ambience, but also for the quality folk-based music played here nightly. One stage regular is former Alarm guitarist Dave Sharp. Put it all together and this is easily one of the best Irish pubs in the city. The prices are reasonable, there's a pool table right near the stage, and the T-shirt's a keeper (*see also p204*).

Lafitte's Blacksmith Shop

941 Bourbon Street, at St Philip Street (523 0066). Bus 3 Vieux Carré, 5 Marigny/Bywater. **Open** from noon daily. **Credit** AmEx, Disc, MC, V. **Map** p282 C2.

Proof that there are lamps designed specifically to make a place feel darker, Lafitte's is a French Quarter legend. You almost want to tiptoe in, as the exterior suggests the place is going to fall to one side, but in New Orleans everything looks as if it's in a state of decay. In the back a piano player (with a surrounding, semicircular bar) does all the old faves. On the downside, the beer selection is minimal, and the service rather brusque. But we like it anyway.

Lounge Lizards

200 Decatur Street, at Iberville Street (598 1500). Riverfront Streetcar/bus 3 Vieux Carré, 5 Marigny/ Bywater. **Open** 11am-3am daily. **Credit** AmEx, MC, V. **Map** p282 A3.

Just across the street from the House of Blues (*see p203*), Lounge Lizards runs in the opposite direction, booking a steady stream of quality local bands while keeping the food and drink prices fair and almost never charging cover. Even on Mardi Gras day, when tourists overrun the Quarter, this place sports a happy mix of locals and visitors singing arm in arm to local legends such as Walter 'Wolfman' Washington, Coco Robicheaux or Jeremy Lyons & the Deltabilly Boys. One of the best recent additions to the Quarter bar/live music scene.

Molly's at the Market

1107 Decatur Street, at Ursulines Street (525 5169/ www.mollysatthemarket.net). Riverfront Streetcar/bus 3 Vieux Carré, 5 Marigny/Bywater. **Open** 10am-6am daily. **Credit** AmEx, MC, V. **Map** p282 C3.

Pat O'Brien's fruity, deadly hurricane. You know you want one. *See p139.*

Even the dogs are cool at **d.b.a.**
See p139.

Rarely does a bar exude such a welcoming atmosphere while also seeming rather snobbish. Still, on any given night, you could see transplanted comedian Harry Anderson or poet and NPR contributor Andrei Codrescu cooling off with one of Molly's irresistible frozen Irish coffees. They'll be among a healthy mix of journalists, musicians and random hip twentysomethings. More local at night than it is during the day, Molly's rarely feels exclusive. Prices are reasonable and even with their occasional attitude problem, you might get a bartender to explain the late owner Jim Monahan's love of Yeats.

Napoleon House

500 Chartres Street, at St Louis Street (524 9752/ www.napoleonhouse.com). Riverfront Streetcar/bus 3 Vieux Carré, 5 Marigny/Bywater, 55 Elysian Fields. **Open** 11am-midnight Mon-Thur; 11am-1am Fri, Sat; 11am-7pm Sun. **Credit** AmEx, DC, Disc, MC, V. **Map** p282 B2.

One of the city's most storied bars, the Napoleon House was allegedly built to house the French general, whom a group of locals planned to spring from St Helena. True? Who knows. It's just another Quarter legend. Still, jailbreak or not, the Napoleon House has gained recognition as the city's best purveyor of the Pimm's Cup. With its big open windows, classical music and ambience of decaying grandeur, you could easily while away a day looking out at the street and soaking up the history.

Pat O'Brien's

718 St Peter Street, at Bourbon Street (525 4823/ 1-800 597 4823/www.patobriens.com). Bus 3 Vieux Carré, 5 Marigny/Bywater. **Open** 11am-3am Mon-Thur; 10am-4am Fri, Sat; 10am-3am Sun. **Credit** AmEx, MC, V. **Map** p282 B2.

Telling someone not to go to Pat O'Brien's while they're in New Orleans is sort of like telling someone not to go to Bourbon Street. Yes, it's cheesy, but why not just go ahead and get it over with? You know you want to. It may well be the most famous business in New Orleans, and we all know why: the fruity, syrupy, rum-laden concoction that is the Hurricane. (Drink at your own risk.) This vast bar is divided into three spaces. The main action is in the two adjoining courtyards, both with fountains, one topped by fire. Subtlety is absolutely dead here. Make your visit a drive-by, though, as the piped-in recorded music ignores local culture, and the helpful-to-the-point-of-peskiness staff constantly pepper patrons with cheery: 'Got a drink?! Need a drink?!' Buy one, then break free.

Port of Call

838 Esplanade Avenue, at Dauphine Street (523 0120). Bus 3 Vieux Carré, 5 Marigny/Bywater, 48 Esplanade. **Open** 11am-1am daily. **Credit** AmEx, MC, V. **Map** p282 D1.

The Port of Call has a dark, funky vibe that draws locals and tourists alike for the grill's enormous hamburgers and the bar's booze-loaded Monsoon cocktail (its take on the Hurricane). The place is a cramped affair either way and the queue virtually

constant, so you can expect to be shoved up against someone at the bar, where you may or may not get courteous service. (*See also p115.*)

Marigny

The Blue Nile

532 Frenchmen Street, between Decatur & Chartres streets (948 2583). Riverfront Streetcar/bus 3 Vieux Carré, 5 Marigny/Bywater. **Open** 7pm-2am daily. **Admission** free-$10. **Credit** AmEx, Disc, MC, V. **Map** p282 D2/3.

An expensive renovation here has resulted in a revamped music hall awash in cool blue tones enhanced by chic Egyptian decor. It's best known for the diverse acts who perform nightly, from trumpeter Kermit Ruffins to impish belly-dancers, but the bar is pretty well stocked with good stuff, too. The downside is that the large space can feel a bit cavernous when it's not full, which, unfortunately, happens a bit too often (*see also p205*).

d.b.a.

618 Frenchmen Street, between Chartres & Royal streets (942 3731/www.drinkgoodstuff.com). Riverfront Streetcar/bus 3 Vieux Carré, 5 Marigny/ Bywater. **Open** 4pm-4am Mon-Thur, Sun; 4pm-5am Fri, Sat. **Credit** AmEx, MC, V. **Map** p282 D2.

Though intended as a near-mirror image of its sister bar in NYC's East Village, d.b.a. is actually a lot nicer, with its floor-to-ceiling exposed wood surfaces, game room and double-wide space separating the nightly bands from the just-here-for-the-brilliant-whiskeys crowd. d.b.a. is unquestionably the city's most expansively stocked bar, with about 20 beers on draught and another 80 by the bottle, nearly 40 single-malt scotches and an extremely respectable number of wines by the glass and the bottle – not to mention rums, tequilas and gins… Prices are sensibly listed on big blackboards above the bar, in a nod to the patrons' relative literacy. The music can get a little loud late in the evening, but it's generally good music, and it rarely reaches the point where you find yourself annoyed. In fact, until the wee hours, you'll be able to hear your interior monologue, which will be a chatter of blissful enthusiasm.

R Bar

1431 Royal Street, at Kerlerec Street (948 7499/ www.royalstreetinn.com). Bus 3 Vieux Carré, 5 Marigny/Bywater. **Open** 3pm-5am Mon-Fri, Sun; 3pm-6am Sat, Sun. **Credit** AmEx, Disc, MC, V. **Map** p282 D2.

Most patrons of R Bar are likely to have a passing acquaintance with the burlesque revival, the latest Ben Sherman shirt patterns and the hot new young novelist everyone's reading. But mind you, it's not about affectation, and it does not put on pseudo-bohemian airs. The decor is timelessly cool – with old film posters and an antique barber's chair in one corner – and the crowd is the type that shuns other bars as soon as they become scenes. It's cooler than most places in town. And the jukebox kicks ass.

Maple Leaf Bar

MAPLE LEAF BAR

Open Every Day, 3pm-til

8316 OAK STREET
New Orleans LA • 70118

| Club | (504) 866-9359 |
| Leaf Line | (504) 866-5323 |

Shows start at 10:30pm

NEW ORLEANS' BEST ROOTS MUSIC

"There's a reason why locals and tourists alike flock to the Maple Leaf Bar…the history, character and steady stream of musicians triumph to make Maple Leaf the quintessential New Orleans club."
—*Digitalcity.com*

"The Maple Leaf is still the place to go if you're craving funky New Orleans music (brass bands, blues and funk, usually) that sometimes doesn't cease until sunrise."—*OffBeat Music Magazine*

"You haven't experienced real New Orleans music until you've worked up a sweat dancing your tootsies off at the Maple Leaf. The crowd is casual and eclectic—from college kids to burn-outs—but a love of can't-stand-still-music is the common thread that ties everyone together."—*CitySearch.com*

"…the Maple Leaf Bar, where the live music is legendary."—*TripAdvisor.com*

The Spotted Cat
623 Frenchmen Street, between Chartres &
Royal streets (943 3887/www.thespottedcat.com).
Riverfront Streetcar/bus 3 Vieux Carré,
5 Marigny/Bywater. **Open** 2pm-4am Mon-Thur,
Sun; noon-5am Fri, Sat. **Credit** AmEx, MC, V.
Map p282 D2.
The Spotted Cat is like a friend who doesn't add
much to the conversation, but without whom things
seem somehow incomplete. There are no beers on
draught – a major faux pas – and given the small
space the live music can get a little too close for comfort, yet it's still nice to have this old standby on the
block. Not a destination in itself, but a lovely place
to stop along the way.

Bywater

Markey's Bar
640 Louisa Street, at Royal Street (943 0785).
Bus 5 Marigny/Bywater. **Open** 2pm-3am Mon-Fri;
11am-2am Sat, Sun. **Credit** AmEx, MC, V.
The Bywater does not lack for casual neighbourhood bars; it's just that there aren't many that are
worth a trip. Markey's is different, thanks in part to
second-generation owner Roy Markey's ubiquity at
the place. It's officially an Irish pub, so there are
more than a few Pogues tunes on the jukebox. But
more importantly, the always-friendly bartenders
pour cheap pints, there's a free pool table and, during football season, Roy has been known to spring
for chicken wings for the house.

Saturn Bar
3067 St Claude Avenue, at Clouet Street (949 7532).
Bus 88, 89 St Claude. **Open** from 4pm Mon-Fri;
from noon Sat, Sun. **No credit cards.**
Once the hippest bar downriver from the Quarter,
the Saturn has lost some lustre over the years. But
loyal fans still brave the dodgy neighbourhood to
hang out at a bar roundly viewed as the most bizarre
in the city – think classy junk shop, with clusters of
clocks and photos of '50s icons. First-timers scratch
their heads as they search for the toilets behind the
owner's air-conditioner-repair room. No question at
all, this is a very unusually cool place. Still, the booze
is cheap, and the vibe is weird.

Mid-City

Finn McCool's
3701 Banks Street, at Telemachus Street (486 9080/
www.finnmccools.com). Canal Streetcar/bus 41, 42,
43 Canal. **Open** 11am-3am Mon-Thur, Sun; 11am-
5am Fri, Sat. **Credit** AmEx, DC, Disc, MC, V.
Map p277 E6.
This new Irish pub – owned by a young expat who
converted the old building himself – has become
seriously popular in record time since opening in
2002. Its diverse clientele is grounded by a nucleus
of Irish expats and their mates. This is no theme pub;
it's the real thing. Pints of Guinness and Harp line

the bar, and the jukebox is excellent and the atmosphere laid-back. Monday's pub quiz is a serious
affair that packs the room, but there's always more
to do than just drink at McCool's: you can play table
football, shoot some pool, get a game of chess going
or just shoot the breeze with the laconic Irish bartenders. In its own way, this is the most authentic
Irish pub in town.

Mick's Irish Pub
4801 Bienville Street, at N Bernadotte Street
(482 9113). Canal Streetcar/bus 41, 42, 43 Canal.
Open from 11am daily. **No credit cards.**
This small, noisy pub with its giant painted clover-
leaf window has been a favourite neighbourhood
watering hole for decades. The draught Guinness is
a popular choice, naturally, and the hamburgers
aren't bad. And if the cash flow dries up, more is on
tap at the on-site cashpoint. On the first Friday of
each month, the back room hosts a band and Irish
dancers (all locals, not necessarily Irish, who take
lessons nearby); they have a cracking time.

Nick's
2400 Tulane Avenue, at S Tonti Street (821 9128).
Bus 39 Tulane. **Open** from 3pm Mon-Thur; from
8pm Fri-Sun. **Credit** MC, V. **Map** p277 E6.
Hardly anybody graduates from a New Orleans
university without visiting Nick's at least once. The
bar is legendary among twentysomethings for its
potent drinks and its nonstop meat-market mental-
ity. The walls are packed with memorabilia, and the
bar itself seems to list to one side (or that could just
be us). It's a rite-of-passage, a place to let loose, even
if you've already graduated. Take a taxi, though, as
the area can be sketchy.

Pals
949 N Rendon Street, at St Philip Street (488
7257). Bus 48 Esplanade. **Open** from noon daily.
Credit AmEx, MC, V. **Map** p278 E5.
Hidden in a pretty and residential Bayou St John
neighbourhood about three blocks from the water,
this retro-designed bar is one of this area's few
stylish options. Big windows looking out on the
pavement and a back-lit bar give it pizazz. The beer
selection is limited, but the bartenders make good
cocktails, especially Martinis. Bands are known to
play now and again. The bar's trendiness factor isn't
hurt by the fact that its owner also owns the hip El
Matador in the French Quarter (*see p136*).

CBD

The Circle Bar
1032 St Charles Avenue, at Lee Circle (588 2616).
St Charles Streetcar. **Open** 4pm-4am Mon-Fri; 5pm-
4am Sat, Sun. **Credit** MC, V. **Map** p279 B2.
If you're heading for the cramped, scruffy building
that houses the Circle Bar, take plenty of quarters
for the jukebox – it's a *Who's Who* of New Orleans
music, from garage rock and rockabilly to R&B and
zydeco. It provides a mighty backing track for the

banter of regulars, who don't mind the modest beer selection or the ramshackle chairs that get pulled askew to allow more room for dancing, as long as they can keep feeding the juke. Live music cranks up most nights around 10.30pm (when there's often a cover), but things get livelier later when the night-crawlers flood in. They don't try too hard here, except to make you feel welcome, and that helps make the Circle one of the best bars in the city.

Club 360

33rd Floor, World Trade Center, 2 Canal Street, at the Mississippi River (522 9795). Canal or Riverfront Streetcar. **Open** from 11am daily. **Credit** AmEx, DC, Disc, MC, V. **Map** p279 C1.

Locals were ambivalent when the old, kitschy Top of the Mart untangled its tassels and folded its red velvet curtains for good, but they came round when the 33rd-floor revolving bar reopened as Club 360. The modern bar offers an inimitably stunning panorama of the city. That said, a full rotation takes about 90 minutes, and that's about how long you should stay. The management seems intent on encouraging a meat-market scene, and Corona is the only beer offered. On the other hand, this is one of the places celebrities hang out when they're in town, if you care about such things.

Doc Smith's Lounge

Inside Smith & Wollensky's, 1009 Poydras Street, at O'Keefe Street (561 0528/www.docsmiths.com). St Charles Streetcar. **Credit** AmEx, DC, Disc, MC, V. **Map** p277 F7.

Blokes could be forgiven for suffering a bit of 'shrinkage' when entering this new bar at the side of Smith & Wollensky's, what with all the testosterone in the air. The owners closed the grill that was here before, and sank nearly $400,000 into a lounge even more masculine than the adjoining steakhouse: it's all oak, brass and marble, with cigars for sale and 42-inch TVs strategically perched for sports viewing. This is a pricey affair – beer's cheap, but a glass of wine will set you back $6.50 to $21.50 and many cocktails knock on the $10 ceiling. But with upstairs balcony seating, a courtyard and a classic lounge, it's a good place for a night out.

Loa

International House Hotel, 221 Camp Street, at Gravier Street (553 9550/www.ihhotel.com). Bus 11 Magazine. **Open** 5pm-1am Mon-Fri; 1pm-3am Sat, Sun. **Credit** AmEx, DC, Disc, MC, V. **Map** p277 F7.

This is the one that started it all. Before entrepreneur Sean Cummings opened this simple but sophisticated bar inside his International House Hotel, there was little to do after dark in the CBD. After Loa became the place to see and be seen, everybody else followed. It's still one of the best-designed bars in town. Marble-top tables sit among black-striped chairs, soft lighting gleams and chill-out techno and R&B play. The steep prices are definitely a turn-off, but they do come with stiff pours – sometimes you almost get your money's worth.

Loft 523

523 Gravier Street, at Camp Street (200 6523/ www.loft523.com). Bus 11 Magazine. **Open** 5pm-1am Tue, Wed; 1pm-3am Thur-Sat. **Credit** AmEx, DC, Disc, MC, V. **Map** p279 C1.

Another initiative of Loa founder Sean Cummings, Loft 523, inside the bijou hotel of the same name, feels like an extension of the guest rooms. This place is so minimalist you ought to get a prize just for spotting the sign. Everything about the bar is a clash of ideas. Small yet open, with painted old brick alongside shiny new metallics, it's an arresting experience best enjoyed in smaller groups. Friday's R&B night packs in an upscale African-American crowd (despite the hefty $20 cover). Drinks prices are fine, considering the heavy pours.

Polo Lounge

Windsor Court Hotel, 300 Gravier Street, at Tchoupitoulas Street (523 6000/www.windsorcourt hotel.com). Bus 10 Tchoupitoulas. **Open** 10.30am-midnight Mon-Thur, Sun; 10.30am-1am Fri, Sat. **Credit** AmEx, DC, Disc, MC, V. **Map** p282 A3.

It would be tough to find a more popular high-end bar in New Orleans than the Polo. The Windsor Court Hotel's bar has a monstrous reputation to live up to; it's always lauded for its decor, service and general appeal. That's partly because the posh British expat vibe that runs through the rest of the place extends through to the bar. Everything here is top-notch, from booze to nuts, and you pay for it dearly. Dress to the nines and bring your credit card.

Sazerac Bar

Fairmont Hotel, 123 Baronne Street, at Canal Street (529 4733/www.fairmonthotel.com). Canal Streetcar. **Open** 10am-midnight daily. **Credit** AmEx, DC, Disc, MC, V. **Map** p282 A1.

There is posh, and then there is Old New Orleans posh. This place is the latter, and that's what makes it one of the best bars in town. It's named after the classic New Orleans drink invented here around the turn of the 19th century (made with rye whiskey and Pernod). The bar sits alongside the single most extraordinary hotel lobby in town.

Whiskey Blue

W Hotel, 333 Poydras Street, at S Peters Street (525 9444/www.whotels.com). Bus 3 Vieux Carré. **Open** 5pm-2am Mon-Wed, Sun; 5pm-3.30am Thur; 4pm-4am Fri, Sat. **Credit** AmEx, DC, Disc, MC, V. **Map** p279 C1.

This place is ultra-cool and ultra-chic – just ask the staff. Bars with a high snob factor always feel like paradoxes in laid-back New Orleans, but this slick place plods arrogantly along with its postmodern decor, fruity cocktails and attitude, attitude, attitude. The bartenders are model-pretty, and do they ever know it. What matters here isn't whether you win or lose, it's how good they think you look. Drink prices are a bit high, but they do make a mean Martini. If you've got the Prada skirt and a Gucci chip on your shoulder, come here. A place to show off your cheekbones in a town that couldn't care less.

The **Saturn Bar**. It doesn't get much weirder than this. *See p141.*

The Wine Loft

752 Tchoupitoulas Street, at Julia Street (561 0116/www.thewineloft.net). Bus 10 Tchoupitoulas. **Open** 5pm-2am Mon-Thur, Sun; from 5pm Fri, Sat. **Credit** AmEx, DC, Disc, MC, V. **Map** p279 C2.

Taking advantage of its proximity to an endless supply of Warehouse District yuppies in loft conversions and a surprising dearth of decent drinking spots, this place became one of the top bars in town quicker than you could say 'beaujolais'. Spacious and dimly lit, the Loft makes good on its name with an extensive selection of wines by the glass, with prices ranging from $4 (the Rabbit Ridge Montepiano Tuscan-style red) to $17 (the Verget Premier Cru Montée de Tonnerre). Be warned: it suffers horribly when crowded. The bar becomes overrun, the din gets almost unbearable and the service slows to a crawl. Reminds us of the old Yogi Berra line, 'Nobody goes there anymore; it's too crowded.'

Garden District

Balcony Bar & Café

3201 Magazine Street, at Harmony Street (895 1600). Bus 11 Magazine. **Credit** AmEx, DC, Disc, MC, V. **Map** p279 A4.

Neon beer signs smother the lower half of the front window of the Balcony Bar, highlighting the fact that this joint boasts 50 draught import, domestic and microbrew beers. In the spacious lower bar people generally watch sports or shoot pool; the action is upstairs, where early arrivals grab coveted balcony tables and student and Uptown professional regulars wait for them to leave so they can seize their moment in the sun.

Bridge Lounge

1201 Magazine Street, at Erato Street (299 1888). Bus 11 Magazine. **Open** from 3.30pm daily. **Credit** AmEx, MC, V. **Map** p279 B/C2.

This place greets you with a superb selection of wines and a snoozing Rottweiler sprawled on the floor. Owner Kate Briggs has covered the pea-green walls of this former punk club with photos of dogs (including her own); the blackboards tout reds, whites and bubblies. Prices run from $4 to $9 per glass; you could take a pass on the wine and try the key lime Martini. The attitude is relaxed during the week, though the place tends to fill with groups of raucous students at weekends.

The Bulldog

3236 Magazine Street, at Louisiana Avenue (891 1516/www.draftfreak.com). Bus 11 Magazine. **Open** from 2pm Mon-Thur; from 11am Fri-Sun. **Credit** AmEx, Disc, MC, V. **Map** p279 A4.

Not even its downtown counterpart d.b.a. (*see p139*), comes close to Bulldog's booze selection. Two blackboards constantly announce new beer arrivals (recent exotica include Chimay and Blue Bird Bitter on draught, along with Ayinger and Rogue Jazz Gun Ale). The kitchen turns out decent bar grub, but really this place is all about the beer – 50 on draught

and about twice as many bottled brews. The crowd tends towards hordes of still-hormonal twenty- and thirtysomethings.

The Half Moon

1125 St Mary Street, at Sophie Wright Place (522 0599). Bus 11 Magazine. **Open** 11am-4am daily. **Credit** AmEx, Disc, MC, V. **Map** p279 B3.

Once one of the hippest bars in the Garden District, the Half Moon suffered an identity crisis in recent years and today is only popular with its neighbours. The spacious interior is too spacious; too much respect is given to pool tables and very little to sitting and talking. You can tell that the long wooden bar served as an oyster bar in a former life. Despite the Half Moon's ragged state, though, it gets style points for its unpretentious servers and clientele.

Parasol's Restaurant & Bar

2533 Constance Street, at Third Street (897 5413/ www.parasols.com). Bus 11 Magazine. **Open** 11am-2am daily. **Credit** AmEx, MC, V. **Map** p279 B3.

There are two reasons to go to this Irish Channel legend: for the huge annual St Patrick's Day party and for the delicious roast beef po-boys. You'd be hard pressed to find a more laid-back boozer in the Garden District; the service here is friendly and the drinks are cheap and always generously poured. Still, you'd think they'd find a moment to wipe down the bar once in a while.

The Saint

961 St Mary Street, at Hastings Street (523 0050). Bus 11 Magazine. **Open** from 8pm daily. **No credit cards**. **Map** p279 B4.

The Saint is owned by the former bassist for the metal band White Zombie – who now plays (along with one of the bartenders) in the equally loud Rock City Morgue. For reasons not entirely clear, this is *the* late-night place in the Garden District. The lounge is a study in '70s frumpery: everything about it feels second-hand. But once 1am rolls around, it fills up. The later it gets, the louder the metal-heavy jukebox gets. What with all the head-banging going on, you might be surprised to find out how friendly everyone is. This place is a mystery. If you like it and decide to linger, there's an in-house cashpoint.

Victorian Lounge

The Columns Hotel, 3811 St Charles Avenue, between Peniston & General Taylor streets (899 9308/www.thecolumns.com). St Charles Streetcar. **Open** 3pm-midnight Mon-Thur; 3pm-2am Fri, Sat; 10am-midnight Sun. **Credit** AmEx, MC, V. **Map** p276 D9.

Housed in the historic Columns Hotel, the Victorian Lounge is perhaps the city's most opulent bar, but that doesn't mean it's inaccessible. Of course, you might want to change out of that torn Metallica T-shirt, but a little dusting off isn't too much to ask for a bar so beautiful it makes you want to be a better (or at least richer) person. The lofty wood-panelled ceiling inside lends the rooms an airy, expansive feel, though there are plenty of quiet nooks as well.

How to Drink in the French Quarter

First of all, let's get one thing straight. '*Laissez les bons temps rouler*' does not translate to 'Get drunk and throw up on the pavement in front of somebody's grandmother.'

There is something about coming to New Orleans, some little frisson of lawlessness, that seems to cause a certain segment of the travelling population to forget everything their mothers ever taught them. While you are encouraged to loosen up here in ways you might not do back home, you are not encouraged to climb the 300-year-old wrought-iron detail on the front of a historic building in a death-defying effort to grasp the breasts of a blonde from Omaha who is enjoying the dubious freedom of taking her top off in public for the first time.

OK?

Now, everybody gets a little stupid on their first trip to the Big Easy. But try and maintain some common sense. Don't hurt yourself or anybody else, and stay sober enough to have a little respect for others.

If you hail from a hamlet where liquor isn't sold on Sundays and all the pubs close while the night is still young, New Orleans' dazzling array of 24-hour bars, kerbside beer stands and jelly shots sold on street corners like lemonade at a village fair might make you lose your head, but remember that thousands of people actually live here. If you throw up on the pavement, they're going to have to step over your vomit on their way to work in the morning.

And that just isn't very nice.

Beyond respecting the locals, there's your own health to consider. With humidity that approaches 100 per cent in the summer, and temperatures that can reach 100 degrees Fahrenheit (38 degrees Celsius) for months at a time, you should be careful. Alcohol dehydrates you, and the combination is unpleasant, and potentially deadly. So pace yourself. If you're drinking during the day, alternate alcoholic drinks with glasses of water, and remember to eat.

Do this, and not only will you have a better time, but the locals will think you're a pro. Just like them.

Outside, the patio bar has the city's best view of the St Charles Avenue streetcar. Mint juleps were invented for places like this.

Uptown

The Kingpin

1307 Lyons Street, at Prytania Street (891 2373). St Charles Streetcar. **Open** from 3pm daily. **Credit** AmEx, Disc, MC, V. **Map** p276 9C.

Elvis and bowling are commemorated in equal measure at this nouveau rockabilly bar, which comes complete with its own miniature bowling lane. If things get a little crowded in the main bar – and they sometimes do – there's a second room with just as much character. There's a decent draught selection and a good mix among regulars – some genuine rapscallions find their way in among the kinds of guys who tuck their shirts into their shorts.

Le Bon Temps Roule

4801 Magazine Street, at Bordeaux Street (895 8117/www.lebontempsroule.com). Bus 11 Magazine. **Open** from 11am daily. **Credit** AmEx, Disc, MC, V. **Map** p276 C10.

Le Bon Temps Roule is like a roadside bar you might find somewhere in the Arkansas sticks or a dusty corner of Texas, but it happens to be in a tree-lined little stretch of Magazine Street. There's an excellent selection of beers on draught, a short-order kitchen that stays open late and a tiny stage wedged in the back for live music. Bartenders talk to you like

It's the nightmare before Christmas at **Snake & Jake's**. *See p147.*

you're a human being, and, for shellfish fans, there are free unlimited fresh oysters every Friday from 7 to 10pm (though you should tip the man with the shucking knife for karma's sake).

Carrollton Station
8140 Willow Street, at Dublin Street (865 9190/ www.carrolltonstation.com). St Charles Streetcar. **Open** from 3pm daily. **Credit** AmEx, MC, V. **Map** p276 B7.
Just a couple of blocks from the jumping Oak Street stretch that houses the Maple Leaf (*see p212*), Carrollton Station has a bounce all its own. Live music takes over at the long end of the bar's L-shaped layout, but if you don't care for the act, there's plenty of room to hang out with your friends and amuse yourself by playing a round or two of 'Shoot the Bear' – which, for many people is the real reason to come here. This vintage 1950s arcade game will instantly appeal to your inner hillbilly, as you drunkenly follow a circling bear from the business end of a pretend shotgun. Hit him 20 out of 20 shots and you'll earn the adulation of your barmates. When there's a gun in a bar and everything's actually alright, you know you're in New Orleans.

The Club/Ms Mae's
4336 Magazine Street, at Napoleon Avenue (895 9401). Bus 11 Magazine, 24 Napoleon. **Open** 24hrs daily. **No credit cards. Map** p276 D10.
Bikers line up their chromed Harleys outside, frat boys shoot pool with liquor-perfumed barflies who've seen their kind come and go, and at around 1.30am the after-concert crowd from Tipitina's (*see p212*) spills in for the pitchers of Dixie that sell here for the price of a single glass elsewhere. Ms Mae's is a night owl's delight that fits nicely into a sprawling evening of boozing. This bright little oasis of 24-hour drinking squats among genteel neighbourhood shops on one of the city's busiest corners, tempting many a drinker's weaker side. It won't hurt your wallet to relent (and there's an on-site cashpoint), but your conscience might have pangs in the morning.

Cooter Brown's Tavern
509 S Carrollton Avenue, between St Charles Avenue & River Road (866 9104/www.cooterbrowns.com). St Charles Streetcar. **Open** 11am-3am Mon-Thur, Sun; 11am-4am Fri, Sat. **Credit** AmEx, DC, Disc, MC, V. **Map** p276 A8.
When you serve 350 bottled beers and 65 more on draught, you're sending out a clear message to the hops-loving community. With almost every nation's brews represented, connoisseurs can drink their way around the world – in fact, they'll give you a T-shirt if you manage it. Sure, mistakes are made – Guinness served in pitchers? – and you might wonder if the cowboy boot-wearing fellows next to you appreciate all the place has to offer. But leave them to the big-screen TV and get a dozen raw oysters and a round of beers from nations you never knew brewed them. In a few nights the shirt will be yours.

Dos Jefes Uptown Cigar Bar
5535 Tchoupitoulas Street, at Joseph Street (891 8500/www.dosjefes.com). Bus 10 Tchoupitoulas. **Open** from 5pm daily. **Credit** AmEx, DC, Disc, MC, V. **Map** p276 B/C10.
Let the kids swill Bud Light and pick up first-year students down the road. You're grown up now, you know your scotches by name and you've got a taste for better things – single malts, wines of discernible origins and maybe a decent cigar. You can get all three at Dos Jefes, plus a nice selection of snacks and late-night music. The vibe is relaxed, and amenities like an in-house humidor are well thought out. And you can actually talk to your companions – it's the kind of place even non-bar lovers can get into.

F&M Patio Bar
4841 Tchoupitoulas Street, at Lyons Street (895 6784). Bus 10 Tchoupitoulas. **Open** 9pm-4am Mon-Wed, Sun; 8pm-6am Thur-Sat. **No credit cards. Map** p276 C10.
Arrive at F&M before midnight and you just might wonder where the hell everyone is, but put a few quarters in the Austin Powers pinball machine and

be patient. When the hours roll into the single digits, they'll be there – to dance, oddly enough. Drinks tend to be a bit pricey, which kind of makes you wonder how they manage to attract such a young crowd, but it's still a good place to have the night's last shout outside the Quarter. There's a cashpoint on site should it all go wrong.

Fat Harry's

4330 St Charles Avenue, at Napoleon Street (895 1045). St Charles Streetcar/bus 24 Napoleon. **Open** from 10.30am daily. **Credit** AmEx, DC, Disc, MC, V. **Map** p276 D9.

Like many places that keep long hours, Fat Harry's is really several different bars. At its best, during the day and early evening, it's a nicely priced bar and grill where you can get reliable burgers, decent beers and a good view from the tables outside. In the later hours, though, it becomes a mecca for extroverted undergraduates who lack the energy or funds to make the trip to the French Quarter. Mind the time and pick your crowd.

Monkey Hill Bar

6100 Magazine Street, at Webster Street (899 4800). Bus 11 Magazine. **Open** from 3pm daily. **Credit** AmEx, DC, Disc, MC, V. **Map** p276 B9.

If navy blazers with brass buttons and pinstriped trousers are your thing, and other bars just seem a bit too dirty, Monkey Hill Bar might be the place for you. There's no sign outside – the very ra-sha-sha Uptowners who frequent the place would never have it so. Once you step inside, you can't help being impressed by how well upholstered those sofas are, and look at those plush patterned pillows – not a single cigarette burn! There are no beers on draught, but the red lampshades, the Persian rugs and the mezzanine-level wine cellar are lovely. Ladies can wear their pearls here and feel perfectly safe.

Phillip's Restaurant & Bar

733 Cherokee Street, at Maple Street (865 1155/www.phillipsbar.com). St Charles Streetcar. **Open** from 4pm Mon-Fri, Sun; from 5.30pm Sat. **Credit** AmEx, Disc, MC, V. **Map** p276 B8.

A few bars line the Maple Street corridor in the Uptown university district, but Phillip's is the only one with any real panache. It might just be the dim lighting, or it could be the mirror over the bar that allows the discreet scoping out of attractive others. Of course, the fact that they screen the unwashed undergraduate masses at the door helps: you can get in a game of darts or pool here in peace.

St Joe's

5535 Magazine Street, at Joseph Street (no phone). Bus 11 Magazine. **Open** from 5pm daily. **Credit** AmEx, MC, V. **Map** p276 C9/10.

For some, a bar is a kind of holy place, and so it's fitting that St Joe's has decked out its interior with religious relics and icons. Sit on your bar stool and bask in saintly benevolence. The draught beers are upscale, as are the shelf liquors, attesting to the postgraduates and professionals that make up the regu-

lar crowd. The narrow, chummy main bar gives way to an expansive covered patio, so this is a good place to bring a large group. There's a pool table inside for quieter nights and thinner crowds. In the end, St Joe's doesn't need to try too hard, and thus seems to get things nearly perfect.

Snake & Jake's Christmas Club Lounge

7612 Oak Street, at Hillary Street (861 2802). St Charles Streetcar. **Open** from 9pm daily. **Credit** AmEx, MC, V. **Map** p276 B8.

You can almost hear the Angelo Badalamenti theme music playing as you pull up outside this bar in a seedy neighbourhood that even cats don't prowl the streets at night. Suddenly, there's a crumbling shanty decked with a giant, menacing, lighted Christmas wreath. Inside, more chipped and faded Christmas relics are strewn about like bad omens, and you half expect to find a gas-inhaling Dennis Hopper in a Santa hat glaring at you from a low-slung corner. Snake & Jake's is a late-late-night destination for the very cool. Ruined students arrive at 3am, many ready (though they don't yet know it) to remove their clothes for the bar's half-true promise: get naked, drink for free. Others have crawled out of the gutter just to witness the spectacle. There's a strong element of danger, depravity, degradation and despair here. For all those reasons, this just might be the best bar in the world.

Eat, Drink, Shop

The best Historic bars

Carousel Bar & Lounge

Housed in one of the French Quarter's grandest hotels and featuring a fully restored carousel over the rotating bar. *See p135.*

Napoleon House

Local home of Pimm's Cup cocktails, and said to have been planned as a hideout for Napoleon Bonaparte. *See p139.*

Lafitte's Blacksmith Shop

The oldest standing bar in the nation, and allegedly erstwhile home to a pirate. *See p137.*

Pat O'Brien's

After 70 years, this place is still pouring those head-swirling Hurricanes. Moves more booze than any other bar in the world, so they say. *See p139.*

Sazerac Bar

Gorgeous and tucked inside the glorious Fairmont Hotel, this is the birthplace of the famous Sazerac cocktail. *See p142.*

Shops & Services

From the very cheapest baubles to the most astonishingly expensive stores, this is a shopper's paradise.

Iconoclasts in true New Orleans style, the city's independent merchants seem to be winning the battle against big-name retailers and generic chains. The one-two punch of the French Quarter and Magazine Street generally offer the most titillating selection for shoppers of all types – the thrifty, the spendthrifts, the old, the young, the fashionistas and the fashion victims. Unless you plan on a shopping spree that covers the entire city, walking is the way to go, especially in the French Quarter and Warehouse District, where parking ordinances are fiercely and expensively enforced. Take a bus, taxi or streetcar to the Riverbend and Magazine Street shopping areas, then set out on foot. If you insist on visiting a suburban shopping mall, though, you'll need a car.

SALES TAX

A nine per cent sales tax is levied on top of the displayed price of most goods and services. Foreign visitors can recoup this by shopping in stores that display tax-free signs (there are more than 1,100). Be sure to get a voucher and a sales receipt when you buy, and get your tax back at the **Louisiana Tax Free Shopping Refund Center (LTFS)** at Louis Armstrong International Airport (568 5323) when you leave. Refunds of $500 or less are made in cash; larger ones are paid by cheque and posted to you. Phone 467 0723 for more information.

SHOPPING AREAS

It may be rife with tacky T-shirt and souvenir shops that supposedly target tourists (does anyone actually buy that stuff?), but if you bypass the **French Quarter** as a shopping area, you'll also miss out on fun foraging, cool goods and sweet deals. In fact, a diverse collection of shops and boutiques is nestled within this small area. **Royal Street**'s grand personality is as polished and lovely as the fine *objets d'art*, jewellery and antiquities that grace the windows of its shops. **Decatur Street** is rough-edged and bohemian by comparison, lined as it is with shops selling techno and grunge gear. **Chartres Street** is literally and figuratively somewhere in between, with its stylish clothing and jewellery boutiques, ultra-modern furniture shops and antiques galleries. The **French Market**, off Decatur Street at the back of the Quarter, is a fun and cheap place to

shop (*see p167*). The independent vendors expect you to bargain for their 'best' deals on imported clothing, jewellery, handbags, household adornments and plain old junk. Some vendors are out every day, but the best time to go is on Saturday and Sunday.

In the mid 20th century, **Canal Street** was the place to shop. Children in their Sunday best marched quietly alongside their behatted and begloved mothers as they visited the elegant independent department stores, places like DH Holmes, Maison Blanche, Krauss and Godchaux's, which generously lined the then-grand boulevard. Sadly, these places now exist only in local lore and literature and in the form of dusty hat and glove boxes at the back of Grandma's closet. One of the few old gems that remain is **Rubensteins** (*see p161*), which offers fine, mostly European designer clothing and accessories for men and women with a level of service and attention to detail harking back to a bygone era. **Adler & Sons** (*see p163*) has also survived the ages; it offers a distinguished selection of men's and women's jewellery and upscale personal effects as well as china, crystal and cutlery. Otherwise, the **Gallery of Shops** adjacent to the Ritz-Carlton (*see p151*) and the **Shops at Canal Place** (*see p151*) are the only other real retail options left on this formerly bustling thoroughfare. Today, Canal Street is dominated by shoe, electronics and souvenir shops which seem to be uniformly staffed by hostile purveyors of overpriced goods.

When it comes to fashionable dress, many well-dressed locals steer clear of the malls, heading instead for **Magazine Street**'s abundant clothing, shoe and accessory boutiques. Nearly every shop along that row is independently owned and offers its own unique items, often the work of local designers, jewellers, artists and craftspeople (*see next page* **Magazine Street: get shopping**).

The **Warehouse District** is indisputably the city's artistic epicentre. Fine art and craft galleries and glass-blowing studios satisfy an appetite for art whetted by the plethora of local museums. The adjacent **Central Business District** (CBD) is a bit more geared to the working class – albeit often the executive working class – and features the **Riverwalk** and **New Orleans Centre** (*for both, see p151*) shopping malls at its poles. Both are replete with branches of the usual national clothing and homeware chains.

At the junction of St Charles and South Carrollton avenues – easily reached by streetcar – the **Riverbend** is full of shops catering to stylish Garden District residents and Tulane University students. This is the best area to get what you need for an evening out on the town. On the river side of South Carrollton Avenue, the emphasis is on upscale clothing and jewellery, such as the dazzling array of finery found at **Yvonne LaFleur**'s boutique (*see p165*). If you need opera-length black kid gloves, this is the place. On the side of the avenue away from the river, the more intimate

shops on tree-lined **Maple Street** appeal to the collegiate set. **Gae-tana's** is a favourite for casual clothes and accessories at occasionally reasonable prices; its sales rack is also locally famous. Nearby **Hemline** serves up great date outfits (*for both, see p160*).

One-stop

Department stores

In a city that seems to offer shoppers endless opportunities to score something truly unique, it's disconcerting to think of hordes of people milling about in climate-controlled environments perusing mass-manufactured goods. If you must

Magazine Street: get shopping

Magazine Street begins at the Canal Street edge of the French Quarter and rambles all the way up to Audubon Park. Downtown, it's lined with office buildings, but just beyond the interstate, it gives way to the shops suggested by its name (translated from the French *magasin*). It holds mile after mile of snazzy clothing boutiques, glittering jewellery shops and stores selling antiques of all types: fine furniture and dusty old junk.

It's impossible to tackle it all in one day. Even if your wallet could survive the onslaught, your feet likely wouldn't. Plan to target a single section of the street instead. The Magazine Street Merchants Association (1-800 387 8924) puts out a helpful free leaflet that lists the shops and groups them by location, and most Magazine Street shops keep stacks of these near the till.

Whatever you do, when it comes to the street's many antiques shops, don't think that if you've seen one you've seen them all. There's a wide diversity here. Designer and artist **Chris Guarisco**'s eponymous digs at No.3615, for instance, may be touted as an antiques store, but when his and others' wacky creations – such as a massive chandelier crafted entirely of oyster shells, mortared with construction cement and hung from a Victorian ceiling medallion – is placed next to roughed-up old spindle benches, the effect is definitely out there.

Every place on Magazine Street has its own personality. If you expect a place with a name like the **Garden District NeedleWork Shop** (No.2011, 558 0221) to be serene and homely, think again. It's housed in an interesting old building on a grand old block,

but its mission is cutting-edge: to reinvigorate a dying art. All the resources you need to get creative with needle and thread are right here. They offer classes, too.

Down the block at **The Quest** (No.2039, *see p156*) Coddy Parkerson has run a shop on Magazine Street since 1979. He is a one-man-library when it comes to the area's military history, which is handy when you're browsing his shop full of antique military paraphernalia and weapons.

If you're more into making love than war, you'll have no trouble getting in the mood after a visit to **House of Lounge** (No.2044, *see p165*). Visiting Hollywood types pop in here to stock up on retro glamour and hip contemporary lingerie.

Unlike most of its neighbours, **Cameron Jones For Your Home** (No.2127, 524 3119) focuses on the contemporary, with accent furniture – bar stools, gifts, lighting – and a smattering of good local art. The mood is sleek and sexy throughout.

There's nothing sexy about **Joey K's Restaurant** (No.3001, *see p127*), but it's an excellent, affordable place to stop for a meal or a giant frosted chalice of cold beer. It's a true New Orleans neighbourhood restaurant, with locals and shop owners crowding in for flavourful Creole dishes and fried seafood.

A block or so down, cabinetmaker Shaun Wilkerson showcases his extensive range of handmade aged cypress tables, beds and armoires at his gallery/studio, **Wilkerson Row** (No.3137, 899 3311). The upscale rustic mood kind of makes you want to drag off one of those massive beds and move it into the woods.

All that glitters is silver at **As You Like It**. *See p152.*

venture into a one-stop shopping arena, there are several to choose from – just don't make a habit of it. And do appreciate the air-conditioning while you're there; you won't find air that frigid in the Quarter.

Dillard's

Lakeside Shopping Center, 3301 Veterans Memorial Boulevard, at N Causeway Boulevard, Metairie (833 1075/www.dillards.com). St Charles Streetcar/bus 16 S Claiborne, 39 Tulane, 90 Carrollton, then E5 Causeway. **Open** 10am-9pm Mon-Sat; noon-6pm Sun. **Credit** AmEx, DC, Disc, MC, V.

Dillard's stocks everything from lipstick to leather furnishings and tends towards the conservative side in its selection of men's, women's and children's clothing. Prices are moderate, though some higher-end collections (Ralph Lauren, DKNY) have been tossed in for good measure.

Branches: The Esplanade (*see p151*, 468 6050); Oakwood Shopping Center, 197 West Bank Expressway, at Terry Parkway, Gretna (362 4800).

JC Penney

Lakeside Shopping Center, 3301 Veterans Memorial Boulevard, at N Causeway Boulevard, Metairie (837 9880/www.jcpenney.com). St Charles Streetcar/bus 16 S Claiborne, 39 Tulane, 90 Carrollton, then E5 Causeway. **Open** 10am-9pm Mon-Sat; noon-6pm Sun. **Credit** AmEx, Disc, MC, V.

It's the same everywhere you go, and this branch is no exception: JC Penney is America's original mainstream clothing and homeware emporium, selling at what some like to call 'value-driven' prices. In other words, it's cheap. A phone ordering service is also available. Jokingly called 'Jacques Pené' by locals.

Macy's

New Orleans Centre, 1400 Poydras Street, next to the Louisiana Superdome, CBD (592 5985/ www.macys.com). Bus 16 S Claiborne. **Open** 10am-8pm Mon-Sat; noon-6pm Sun. **Credit** AmEx, MC, V. **Map** p279 B1.

Macy's is reliable for moderate to high-end clothing, shoes and cosmetics. Frequent sales taking 20% to 40% off homeware and men's, women's and children's clothing have made it a workhorse for locals in need of necessities.

Branch: The Esplanade (*see p151*, 465 3985).

Saks Fifth Avenue

Shops at Canal Place, 333 Canal Street, at Decatur Street, French Quarter (524 2200/www.s5a.com). Bus 41 Canal. **Open** 10am-7pm Mon-Sat; noon-6pm Sun. **Credit** AmEx, DC, Disc, MC, V. **Map** p279 C1.

Saks stocks delicious desirables you may not be able to find elsewhere in New Orleans. Searching for Annick Goutal fragrances, a Vera Wang gown, Prada pumps or an Armani suit? This is your place. Its location in the French Quarter is a real plus.

Shopping malls: downtown

Most of the inner city malls are smaller than the behemoths out in the suburbs. Still, you can find much of what you need in the way of national chains at the five downtown malls. Most are within walking distance of hotels and tourist attractions. Their size makes them easier to access than their suburban cousins, and the purveyors inside vary considerably, giving each mall a distinct personality of its own.

Eat, Drink, Shop

Gallery of Shops

Ritz-Carlton Hotel, 921 Canal Street, at Burgundy
Street, French Quarter (524 1331). Canal Streetcar/
bus 3 Vieux Carré. **Open** 11am-7pm Mon-Sat;
11am-6pm Sun. **Map** p282 A1.

Located next to the Ritz-Carlton Hotel on Canal
Street, this new one-storey retail centre houses an
intimate collection of upscale shops and boutiques,
several flogging goods bearing the Ritz insignia.
The Ritz-Carlton Home Collection sells signature
bedding, and the Ritz-Carlton Spa Too has spa and
fitness gear. At the back, the space opens on to the
ultra-posh Spa at the Ritz, which includes a fitness
centre and salon where you could steam away your
worries after spending all your money (provided you
haven't maxed out your credit card). Other shops
include Asia Antiques and Stacie Boudousque, a chi-
chi women's boutique packed with designer labels.

Jackson Brewery

600 Decatur Street, at the river, French Quarter
(566 7245/www.jacksonbrewery.com). Bus 3 Vieux
Carré. **Open** 9am-8pm Mon-Sat; 10am-7pm Sun.
Map p282 B3.

More a self-contained group of touristy shops than
a mall (much less a brewery) this place (universally
called 'Jax Brewery' by locals) has a few aces up its
sleeve: 1. The view from the balcony is unbeatable.
2. The mall has clean public loos which are open to
all, bless its little heart. And 3. It offers the only food
court in the French Quarter. You probably didn't
come to New Orleans to eat at a food court, but it's
a sensible way to feed a family in the middle of the
day, and it includes some local outlets as well as a
bank of internet terminals where you can check
email for free. You can also pick up good indigenous
foodie gifts at Bayou Country General Store and
visit the Jax Collection, a free museum devoted to
the beloved beer once brewed on this spot.

New Orleans Centre

1400 Poydras Street, next to the Louisiana
Superdome, CBD (568 0000). Bus 16 S Claiborne.
Open 10am-8pm Mon-Sat; noon-6pm Sun.
Map p279 B1.

Built in the late 1980s and surrounded by office
buildings, this mall caters to businesspeople and visitors to the Superdome, which links to it via an open-
air walkway. Macy's and Lord & Taylor department
stores anchor it at each end. Otherwise, there are the
usual suspects, like Gap and Victoria's Secret.

Riverwalk

1 Poydras Street, at the Mississippi River, CBD
(522 1555/www.riverwalkmarketplace.com).
Riverfront Streetcar/bus 3 Vieux Carré, 10
Tchoupitoulas. **Open** 10am-9pm Mon-Sat;
11am-7pm Sun. **Map** p279 C1.

Right on the Mississippi and worth visiting just for
the view of the river, the Riverwalk is best known
as the mall that was hit by an out-of-control Chinese
merchant ship in December 1996. In between watching for runaway boats, you can browse 100 stores,

including Banana Republic, Gap, Gap Kids and
Abercrombie & Fitch. Curiosity value apart, though,
the linear layout and frequent crowding make it less
than pleasant. Also, the shops cater to tourists, so
souvenir and gift prices tend to be high.

Shops at Canal Place

333 Canal Street, at Decatur Street, French Quarter
(522 9200). Bus 41 Canal. **Open** 10am-6pm
Mon-Wed; 10am-7pm Thur-Sat; noon-6pm Sun.
Map p279 C1.

This is home base for shoppers seeking high-end
designer goods. With Saks Fifth Avenue as its
anchor (*see p150*), Canal Place has attracted 60 top-
notch tenants, including Pottery Barn, Betsey
Johnson, Kenneth Cole, Williams-Sonoma, Banana
Republic, Gucci, Brooks Brothers and St Germain, a
locally owned women's shoe store boasting an
exceptional selection of *au courant* footwear. As
malls go, this one is rather pleasant. It's not too large,
and the small third-floor cinema specialises in foreign and limited release films.

Shopping malls: suburban

If you're planning a major shopping spree,
the suburban malls in Metairie (about 20
minutes' drive away) offer abundant free
parking and choice of stores, all wrapped
up in enclosed, climate-controlled, generic
environments. Another attraction is the fact
that, at 8.75 per cent, sales tax in Jefferson
Parish is slightly cheaper than in the city.

Clearview Shopping Center

4436 Veterans Memorial Boulevard, at Clearview
Parkway, Metairie (885 0202). **Open** 10am-9pm
Mon-Fri; noon-6pm Sat, Sun.

Built in the early 1970s and once a popular suburban destination, a few years ago this mall was
struggling to hold on. It looked like a goner until
2002, when saviours arrived in the forms of huge
chain stores Target and Bed Bath & Beyond, a cinema megaplex and a bevy of casual eateries. Sears
anchors one end; the even cheaper Target pins down
the other. The restaurants, unexpectedly, are the
stars. Each is a regional franchise, but all are quite
good and affordable. Dinner and a movie are possible here, but beware: every teenager for miles
around has the same thing in mind every weekend.

The Esplanade

1401 W Esplanade Boulevard, near Williams
Boulevard, Kenner (465 2161/www.mallibu.com).
Open 10am-9pm Mon-Sat; noon-6pm Sun.

This is the largest mall in the New Orleans area, and
also the furthest from downtown, almost all the way
to the airport. Anchors are Macy's and regional
department stores Dillard's and Mervyn's; the last
is cheapest, with nary a designer item in sight. You
can find just about everything but hardware in the
135 stores here. If you're driving, head west on
Interstate 10 and take the Williams Boulevard exit.

Eat, Drink, Shop

Lakeside Shopping Center

3301 Veterans Memorial Boulevard, at N Causeway Boulevard, Metairie (835 8000). St Charles Streetcar/bus 16 S Claiborne, 39 Tulane, 90 Carrollton, then Causeway North. **Open** 10am-9pm Mon-Sat; noon-6pm Sun.

One of the oldest in the country, this mall was refurbished in the 1990s and has become the area's most popular. Department store giants Dillard's and JC Penney are the big players; otherwise Lakeside is packed with the popular names. Head here if you crave goods from J Crew, Gap, Banana Republic, Eddie Bauer, The Sharper Image and Nine West.

Antiques

New Orleans' strong European heritage, coupled with its status as a port city and relative old age, converge to make it a premier destination for antiques collectors from around the world. In New Orleans, there's a bar or church on every corner – and an antiques store in between. Most of the established shops are concentrated on Magazine Street and in the French Quarter; those on Royal Street are highly reputable, often run by third and fourth generation family members. The personalities of the stores are diverse; some are cavernous, highbrow institutions offering polished pieces of perfect pedigree, others are dusty storefronts overseen by chatty grandmothers hawking, we suspect, the contents of their attics.

Auction houses

Those seeking more than just one or two antique pieces might want to visit auction houses, where entire suites – and sometimes entire housefuls – of fine furnishings, art and doodahs are available in one fell swoop. Great bargains on real treasures are as common as crazy bidding wars over vintage chamberpots. Even if you're not interested in buying, auctions are great fun, giving you a chance to check out the estates of wealthy Southern families. Be careful, though, it's so much fun that you could lose perspective. Do you really need a spittoon?

Hampshire House Auctions Ltd

920 Oxiety Street, Kenner (469 6744). **Open** 9am-5pm Mon-Fri. **Credit** AmEx, DC, Disc, MC, V.

An auction here is almost worth the trip way out to the suburbs near the airport. They take place about once a month in a cavernous old no-frills building in an obscure industrial neighbourhood. Sit on mismatched office and folding chairs for a chance at great deals on jewellery, fine art, silver, pottery, collections, even entire estates. The atmosphere is friendly, casual and focused on the goods on the block, just like the members of the Rosato family, who own and run the place.

Neal Auction Company

4038 Magazine Street, at Marengo Street, Uptown (899 5329/www.nealauction.com). Bus 11 Magazine. **Open** 9am-5pm Mon-Fri. **Credit** Disc, MC, V. **Map** p276 D10.

New Orleans' oldest auction house is particularly strong on American and English furniture, as well as porcelain, paintings, prints, sculpture, jewellery and oriental rugs. A tip: items that don't sell at the Magazine Street showroom are warehoused on Carondolet Street, where no-minimum-bid auctions are occasionally held. Call for details.

New Orleans Auction Galleries

801 Magazine Street, at Julia Street, CBD (566 1849/www.neworleansauction.com). Bus 11 Magazine. **Open** 9am-5pm Mon-Fri. **No credit cards. Map** p 279 C2.

One of the city's most popular auction houses, this gallery places an emphasis on formal French and European antiques, including its lovely cypress linen presses and lots of silver.
Branch: 1330 St Charles Avenue, at Erato Street, Warehouse District (586 8733).

Talebloo Auction & Antique Gallery

2015 Magazine Street, at Jackson Avenue, Lower Garden District (581 9700). Bus 11 Magazine. **Open** 9am-5pm Mon-Sat. **Credit** MC, V. **Map** p279 B3.

Talebloo, which opened in mid 2002, may be the new kid on the block, but proprietor and Persian rug authority Lou Talebloo has been a player on the New Orleans auction scene for 23 years. Talebloo hosts four or five auctions a year in addition to operating a massive retail space, mostly dedicated to French antiques with a few English pieces mixed in. Since Talebloo is also an importer of fine Persian rugs, they're strong on those as well.

Top Drawer Auction & Appraisal, Inc

4310 & 4318 Magazine Street, at Napoleon Avenue, Uptown (897 1004/www.topdrawerantiques.net). Bus 11 Magazine. **Open** 10am-5pm Tue-Sat. **Credit** Disc, MC, V. **Map** p276 D10.

Aaron Jarabinca, a third generation auctioneer, maintains an informal atmosphere in his massive antiques emporium. Downstairs at No.4318, French antiques are up for retail sale; upstairs, auctions are held (four each year). All of No.4310 is dedicated to the retail sale of American antiques. Jarabinca claims his is the only local auction house that buys entire estates – not just antiques and art. As a result, Top Drawer's pieces date from the early 1800s through the late 1950s.

Antiques shops

As You Like It

3033 Magazine Street, at 7th Street, Uptown (897 6915/1-800 828 2311/www.asyoulikeitsilver shop.com). Bus 11 Magazine. **Open** 10am-5pm Mon-Sat. **Credit** AmEx, Disc, MC, V. **Map** p279 A3.

Be nice or leave

Blue dogs and red cats have worn out their welcome among long-time collectors of New Orleans folk art, but one figure has broken out of the mass-replicable (and copyrightable) image grind. Simon Hardeveld, a native of Cannes, France, has a buoyant, bright-eyed sensibility that has captured the playfulness of the city without creating another cliché.

For the past several years, Simon's images have been popping up in local restaurants, bars and homes. The vibrant works, done in oil-based enamel paint on plywood and pressed tin, reflect his wry sense of humour in ways that are alternately direct and incomprehensible. Many are signs featuring bold, colourfully underscored messages: one welcome sign exclaims, 'Oh No! Not You Again!' while another begs, 'Please God, Don't Sue Me.' Easily a dozen restaurants and shops in New Orleans have signs made by Simon that say simply, 'Be Nice Or Leave.'

Simon, who resembles a paint-splattered Willie Nelson, speaks with a bouillabaisse-thick accent in grammatically flexible English. He begins painting early each morning at his home studio, but most days he can be found at the back of his Magazine Street shop, **Simon of New Orleans** (*see p156*), putting finishing touches on a new work or taking a commission from a patron, the number of whom has vastly grown since his work has been featured in publications like *The New York Times*, *Travel & Leisure* and *USA Today*.

All his paintings are hallmarked by the presence of little firecracker-like explosions of colour wallpapered across the background, which he calls 'energy'.

'I know the painting is finished when there's nearly no more space to put energy,' he says.

As both a painter and a retailer of his own work, Simon is decidedly proletarian. He uses found objects – oyster shells, discarded musical instruments, Mardi Gras beads, the odd metal bracelet or playing card – right down to the wood and tin that he uses as canvases, which he picks up around town. Around his studio, snakes made of beer bottlecaps spring from paintings, Zulu coconuts dangle from vivid mobiles; a mounted railroad nail is accompanied by the cryptic message 'From the Cross'.

Simon's prices – some pieces can be had for under $100 – have made his work widely accessible, and he has no plans to change that. 'I don't try to make my prices more complicated,' he says. That hasn't stopped more ambitious collectors from snapping up his work, which hangs everywhere from art galleries and consulates to local restaurants and Las Vegas casinos.

For his part, Simon is just happy to be painting full time, after more than a decade as a chef and restaurateur. He now works alongside his wife Maria each day, as she tends to her own brisk business selling 19th- and 20th-century European antiques. The only way you'll find Simon in the kitchen is in the form of one of his paintings, where he says many patrons are apt to hang his work. 'When you're having a glass of wine with some friends, people often stay in the kitchen, and my painting is a conversation piece,' he says. 'My paintings still match the po-boy more than the sofa.'

An entire storeful of quality silver cutlery, serving pieces, hollowware, goblets, trays, candlesticks and tea services in hundreds of active, inactive and obsolete patterns. Pieces are sold singly and in sets.

Avignon House Antiques
3426 Magazine Street, at Delachaise Street, Uptown (899 2844). Bus 11 Magazine. **Open** 10am-5pm Tue-Sat. **Credit** MC, V. **Map** p277 C8.
The cottage housing this shop, with its brilliant blue shutters, brings you close to Provence, as does the selection of 18th- and 19th-century French antiques inside. The offering of furniture, mirrors, lighting, art and accessories is comprehensive.

Bep's Antiques
2051 Magazine Street, at Josephine Street, Uptown (525 7726/www.bepsantiques.com). Bus 11 Magazine. **Open** 9.30am-5pm Mon-Sat. **Credit** AmEx, Disc, MC, V. **Map** p279 B3.
This small, charming store is packed with rural American and European pine and oak furniture, china, medicine bottles, brass – and, inexplicably, New Age, rock and world music CDs.

Bush Antiques
2109 & 2111 Magazine Street, between Josephine & Jackson streets, Uptown (581 3518/ www.bush antiques.com). Bus 11 Magazine. **Open** 10am-5pm Mon-Sat. **Credit** AmEx, Disc, MC, V. **Map** p279 B3.
The speciality at Bush Antiques is fantastic, elaborate antique beds fit for royalty, but general French and Belgian antiques, religious artefacts, ironwork and lighting are also mixed in.

Charbonnet & Charbonnet
2728 Magazine Street, at Washington Street, Uptown (891 9948). Bus 11 Magazine. **Open** 9am-5.30pm Mon-Sat. **Credit** MC, V. **Map** p279 A/B3.
Charbonnet & Charbonnet's collection of antique pine and cypress cupboards and tables is complemented by bespoke furniture crafted in-house from old Louisiana pine or cypress wood. Headboards made from old pocket doors start at $375.

Christopher's Discoveries
2842 Magazine Street, at Sixth Street, Uptown (899 6226). Bus 11 Magazine. **Open** 10am-10pm daily. **Credit** AmEx, DC, Disc, MC, Visa. **Map** p277 E9.
Set aside a bit of time for this one. The sheer volume of unusual antiques, accessories and sleek modern furnishings means Christopher's takes a while to wander through. It's stylish and fun, with the added attraction of surprisingly reasonable prices.

Civil War Store
212 Chartres Street, at Iberville Street, French Quarter (522 3328). Bus 3 Vieux Carré, 41 Canal, 55 Elysian Fields, 81 Almonaster, 82 Desire. **Open** 10.30am-6.30pm daily. **Credit** AmEx, Disc, MC, V. **Map** p282 A2.
This quirky store sells anything you can think of associated with the American Civil War – from Confederate money to swords to musket balls. Your new collection obsession starts here.

Keil's Antiques
325 Royal Street, at Conti Street, French Quarter (522 4552). Bus 3 Vieux Carré, 55 Elysian Fields, 81 Almonaster, 82 Desire. **Open** 9am-5pm Mon-Sat. **Credit** AmEx, MC, V. **Map** p282 B2.
This elegant store with friendly staff and diverse prices specialises in 18th- and 19th-century French and English antiques. New Orleans families have shopped here since 1899. You can blow the budget or spend carefully: fine gifts for under $100.

Lucullus
3932 Magazine Street, between Napoleon & Louisiana streets, Uptown (894 0500). Bus 11 Magazine. **Open** *June-Aug* 10am-5pm Tue-Sat. *Sept-May* 10am-5pm Mon-Sat. **Credit** AmEx, MC, V. **Map** p276 D10.
From dining tables to porcelain fruit and veg, everything here is connected to food and eating. A clever concept and an imaginative collection of culinary antiques, art and objects.
Branch: 610 Chartres Street, between Wilkinson & Toulouse streets, French Quarter (528 9620).

Magazine Street Oak & Cypress Company, Etc
5831 Magazine Street, at State Street Drive, Uptown (895 3748). Bus 11 Magazine. **Open** 10am-5pm Mon-Sat. **Credit** MC, V. **Map** p276 B9.
Most of New Orleans' abundant historic houses were built using Louisiana swamp cypress, a beautiful fine-grained wood which is prized because it is as hard as rock and naturally resistant to the mould, decay and other miseries associated with the south Louisiana climate. Cypress furniture has the same marvellous qualities. Look here for restored antique furnishings such as Hoosier cabinets and oak ice-boxes. Bespoke work is also available.

Manheim Galleries
409 Royal Street, at Conti Street, French Quarter (568 1901). Bus 3 Vieux Carré, 55 Elysian Fields, 81 Almonaster, 82 Desire. **Open** 9am-5pm Mon-Sat. **Credit** AmEx, Disc, MC, V. **Map** p282 B2.
This fourth generation, family-owned business is housed in a building designed by Benjamin Henry Latrobe, one of the architects of the US Capitol building. There are five expansive floors filled with oil paintings, exquisite porcelain and furniture. There's also a famous jade room that attracts collectors from around the country. The in-house cabinet shop's master carvers have produced bespoke furniture in walnut and mahogany since 1898.

Moss Antiques
411 Royal Street, at Conti Street, French Quarter (522 3981). Bus 3 Vieux Carré, 55 Elysian Fields, 81 Almonaster, 82 Desire. **Open** 9am-5pm Mon-Sat. **Credit** AmEx, MC, V. **Map** p282 B2.
A sister store to Keil's Antiques (*see above*), Moss is one of the city's best-loved antiques stores with a large collection of high-quality (and high-priced) antique and estate jewellery as well as elaborate and beautiful French and English furniture.

Get your love amulets and gambling beans at **F&F Botanica Company.** *See p157.*

The Quest

2039 Magazine Street, at Josephine Street, Lower Garden District (410 2039). Bus 11 Magazine. **Open** by appointment. **No credit cards. Map** p279 B3.

Author, historian, know-it-all and generally fine bloke Codman 'Coddy' Parkerson has been a dedicated Magazine Street merchant since 1979 – about 10 years before 'antiquing' on the street became all the rage. The Quest is filled with unusual dust-covered finds with a strong emphasis on antique military paraphernalia, weapons and medical devices – some of which Coddy unearths on weekend forays into the Louisiana swamps in his search for sunken boats and lost treasure.

MS Rau

630 Royal Street, at St Peter Street, French Quarter (523 5660). Bus 3 Vieux Carré, 55 Elysian Fields, 81 Almonaster, 82 Desire. **Open** 9am-5.15pm Mon-Sat. **Credit** AmEx, MC, V. **Map** p282 B2.

This third generation, family-owned store has been in business since 1912. It's best known for its impressive and extensive cut glass collection.

Robinson's Antiques

329 Royal Street, at Conti Street, French Quarter (523 6683). Bus 3 Vieux Carré, 55 Elysian Fields, 81 Almonaster, 82 Desire. **Open** 10am-5pm Mon-Sat. **Credit** AmEx, DC, Disc, MC, V. **Map** p282 B2.

Owned by locally famous antiques dealer Henry Stern until his death in 1993, this shop is committed

to the high-quality merchandise and service he was known for. You'll find pretty much everything here, including French and English furniture, silverware, paintings, chandeliers and rugs.

Silk Road Collection

3714 Magazine Street, at Amelia Street, Uptown (894 8540/www.silkroadcollection.com). Bus 11 Magazine. **Open** 10am-5pm Mon-Sat; noon-4pm Sun. **Credit** AmEx, Disc, MC, V. **Map** p276 D9.

An absolute must for enthusiasts of rare luxuries, Silk Road seeks out exotic treasures from the camel-driven trade caravans that, for 1,000 years, made their way from China to India, Arabia and Europe. Look for freshwater, cultured, South Sea and Tahitian pearl jewellery, Chinese folk art and artefacts from the Manchu Dynasty (1644–1925).

Simon of New Orleans

2126 Magazine Street, at Jackson Avenue, Lower Garden District (561 0088). Bus 11 Magazine. **Open** 10am-5pm Mon-Sat. **Credit** AmEx, MC, V. **Map** p279 B3.

Nothing short of delightful, in his eponymous hotch-potch of a shop, folk artist Simon sells his own brightly painted signs (most bearing humorous or thought-provoking messages) as well as antiques, primitive furniture and lighting. Signs can be designed to order and taken home as a playful, artistic reminder of your time in New Orleans. *See also p153* **Be nice or leave.**

Astrology & the occult

Shops and businesses catering to those who believe in the supernatural are scattered throughout the city; many are operated out of people's back rooms or front parlours. Most of New Orleans' alternative belief systems can be traced back to the days of slavery, when a myriad of faiths amalgamated into what is commonly called voodoo. Fortune-telling is also popular here; the commonest forms are palmistry and tarot card reading. Anyone who buys a city licence can offer readings; since there's no exam for psychic ability, you won't be able to tell beforehand whether your chosen reader is an intuitive type or a complete huckster. Readings can be uncannily accurate or completely off the mark. Expect to pay $10 to $30 for a reading that can last from 10 to 30 minutes; agree on a price before you start.

Psychic readings & spiritual supplies

Bottom of the Cup Tea Room

732 Royal Street, at St Ann Street, French Quarter (523 1204). Bus 3 Vieux Carré, 55 Elysian Fields, 81 Almonaster, 82 Desire. **Open** 10am-7pm daily. **Credit** AmEx, Disc, MC, V. **Map** p282 C2.
Offering tarot and tea leaf readings in the French Quarter since 1929, this place is friendly and not the least bit spooky. Private audiotaped readings are available; it's best to book these in advance. They also sell tarot cards, crystals and accessories. **Branch**: 327 Chartres Street, at Conti Street, French Quarter (524 1997)

Esoterica Occult Goods

541 Dumaine Street, at Chartres Street,French Quarter (581 7711/1-800 353 7001/www.one witch.com). Bus 3 Vieux Carré, 55 Elysian Fields, 81 Almonaster, 82 Desire. **Open** noon-10pm daily. **Credit** MC, V. **Map** p282 C2.
This place is a one-stop shopping solution for crystal balls, candles, incense, oils and bespoke gris-gris bags (for holding voodoo charms). Its self-styled witches give tarot readings and spiritual consultations. It's best to book in advance. Bring your own tape recorder if you wish.

F&F Botanica Company

801 N Broad Avenue, at Orleans Avenue, Mid-City (482 9142). Bus 46 Canal. **Open** 7.30am-6pm Mon-Sat. **Credit** AmEx, DC, Disc, MC, V. **Map** p277 E6.
This comprehensive spiritual supply house has everything from statues of saints to a floor wash guaranteed to clean out evil spirits. There are fabulous candles with purposes handprinted on the side like 'Going to court' and the kind of scary 'Destroy Everything'. There's a 'Go Away Evil' amulet, and 'Love drawing' potion. Cook up your own concoctions from the ancient herbs and roots.

Island of Salvation Botanica

835 Piety Street, at Burgundy, Bywater (948 9961/www.feyvodou.com). Bus 82 Desire. **Open** 10am-5.30pm Wed-Sat, 12.30-5.30pm Sun. **Credit** AmEx, MC, V.
The proprietress here, Sallie Ann Glassman, is New Orleans' most visible high priestess of voodoo. Sallie's intelligence and logic shine out from under her soothing demeanour, engaging manner and ceaseless public advocacy for peace. Her tarot readings are highly personal. The shop carries a small but thorough amount of spiritual supplies, plus a good selection of books, including works by Sallie herself. She'll make a believer out of you.

Bookshops

New Orleans has served as a beacon to writers throughout its history, so it's no surprise that bookstores are numerous here. Most sellers of used, rare and collectable volumes are located in the French Quarter; all are independently owned. If you're after new books, you'll take in more of the local literary culture if you patronise locally owned shops. But despite their charms, independent bookstores usually can't offer the kinds of discounts on bestsellers and recent releases the big boys can. So which is best depends on your priorities. Note that many museum gift shops often have well chosen selections of books about New Orleans.

Afro-American Book Stop

New Orleans Centre, 1400 Poydras Street, next to the Louisiana Superdome, CBD (588 1474). Bus 16 S Claiborne. **Open** 10am-8pm Mon-Sat; noon-6pm Sun. **Credit** AmEx, Disc, MC, V. **Map** p279 B1.
This place offers an excellent selection of African-American and African books. Author-related events are held frequently, and staff are knowledgeable. **Branch**: Plaza Shopping Center, 5700 Read Boulevard, New Orleans East (243 2436).

Barnes & Noble

3721 Veterans Memorial Boulevard, near Lakeside Shopping Center, Metairie (455 4929/ www.barnesandnoble.com). **Open** 9am-11pm daily. **Credit** AmEx, DC, Disc, MC, V.
This is the area's largest bookstore, stamped from the same mould as any of its sister branches anywhere else. It's considered a good meeting spot for bookish, straight singles who prefer coffee and pseudo-intellectual conversation over booze and idle banter. Weekend nights here can get a bit steamy.

Beaucoup Books

5414 Magazine Street, at Jefferson Avenue, Uptown (895 2663). Bus 11 Magazine. **Open** 10am-6pm Mon-Sat; noon-5pm Sun. **Credit** AmEx, Disc, MC, V. **Map** 276 C9/10.
This classic neighbourhood bookstore is known for frequent readings by popular, respected local and national authors. The stock is small but carefully

Eat, Drink, Shop

chosen, and heavy on literary fiction and New Orleans and Louisiana authors. This is the kind of bookstore that writers love.

DeVille Books & Prints

344 Carondelet Street, at Perdido Street, CBD (525 1846). St Charles Streetcar. **Open** 10.30am-5.30pm. **Credit** MC, V ($5 min). **Map** p279 B1.
This is the city of New Orleans distilled into a bookstore: urbane, charming, eclectic and easygoing. The very knowledgeable staff oversee a comfortable shop stocked with local favourites, a particularly excellent history section and a very good collection of second-hand regional and local books.

Faulkner House Books

624 Pirate's Alley, between St Peter & Orleans streets, French Quarter (524 2940). Bus 3 Vieux Carré, 55 Elysian Fields, 81 Almonaster, 82 Desire. **Open** 10am-6pm daily. **Credit** AmEx, MC, V. **Map** p282 B/C2.
This intimate shop was once the home of the titular writer. It was while living here, in 1925, that he gave up poetry and decided to become an author. He penned *Soldier's Pay* here during his lengthy stay in New Orleans. As one would expect, the shop specialises in his books, including some rare and first editions. But there's also a good selection of other literature and poetry, with a strong emphasis on local and Southern writers.

Garden District Book Shop

2727 Prytania Street, at Washington Avenue, Garden District (895 2266). St Charles Streetcar. **Open** 10am-6pm Mon-Sat; 11am-4pm Sun. **Credit** Disc, MC, V. **Map** p279 A3.
This small but comprehensive little shop is consistently the place chosen by spooky author Anne Rice for the unveiling of her new works. In a way that's strange, as this place is not spooky itself, but the fact is that she lives just around the corner, so it's actually her neighbourhood bookshop. Here you will find autographed copies, special editions and, sometimes, Rice herself, and also a good collection of new books, best sellers, gardening tomes and the like.

Maple Street Bookshop

7523 Maple Street, at Cherokee Street, Riverbend (866 4916/www.maplestreetbookshop.com). St Charles Streetcar. **Open** 9am-9pm Mon-Sat; 10am-6pm Sun. **Credit** MC, V. **Map** p276 B8.
When you cross the rickety wooden porch to the threshold of Maple Street Bookshop, you half expect to find a pipe-smoking, turtleneck-wearing old professor gazing at you over pince-nez – and you very well might. Since 1964, Maple Street has been a haven and gathering place for characters of just this sort. It cultivates and maintains this image with its ubiquitous bumper sticker: 'Fight the stupids'. The shop has an excellent selection of fiction and nonfiction; many works are autographed. Next door at No.7529 is Maple Street Children's Bookshop (861 2105), a charming spot that stages popular weekend readings for the junior set.

Octavia Books

513 Octavia Street, at Annunciation Street, Uptown (899 7323) Bus 10 Tchoupitoulas. **Open** 10am-6pm Mon-Sat. **Credit** AmEx, Disc, MC, V. **Map** p276 C10.
We love this little shop nestled in a residential Uptown neighbourhood. Its contemporary architecture – complete with patio waterfall – has won awards, and the staff are both interested and interesting. It all just makes book shopping more fun.

Second-hand, rare & collectable books

Beckham's Book Shop

228 Decatur Street, at Iberville Street, French Quarter (522 9875). Bus 3 Vieux Carré, 55 Elysian Fields, 81 Almonaster, 82 Desire. **Open** 10am-6pm daily. **Credit** Disc, MC, V. **Map** p282 A3.
Not as in David. As in … oh, who knows? This dusty old place is two wonderfully shabby floors of books, prints and pamphlets. A book lover's haven.

Great Acquisitions Books

8200 Hampson Street, at S Carrollton Avenue, Riverbend (861 8707). St Charles Streetcar. **Open** 10.30am-6pm Mon-Sat. **Credit** AmEx, Disc, MC, V. **Map** p276 A8.
Great Acquisitions is the place to go for first editions and rare books. It has sections on art, photography, music, travel and history, and it's heavy on Louisiana and Southern literature. The helpful staff provide a free search service.

Kaboom Books

901 Barracks Street, at Dauphine Street, French Quarter (529 5780/kaboombks@aol.com). Bus 3 Vieux Carré, 48 Esplanade. **Open** 11am-6pm daily. **No credit cards. Map** p282 D1.
This is one of our favourite used bookstores in the world. The owner is a droll sweetheart who – and we're not kidding about this – really does know everything about literature. You can wander for hours among the massive shelves stacked with a consistently good assortment of classic and contemporary fiction, politics, philosophy and drama. Prices are better than reasonable; some of them are steals. We have never forgotten buying a first edition copy of John dos Passos' *Prospects of a Golden Age* here for about $5. Pull up a chair in front of the big picture windows and read for a while as you watch the French Quarter go by. Shop here. Give them your money. They're wonderful.

Librairie Bookshop

823 Chartres Street, between Dumaine & St Ann streets, French Quarter (525 4837). Bus 3 Vieux Carré, 55 Elysian Fields, 82 Desire. **Open** 10am-6pm daily. **Credit** Disc, MC, V. **Map** p282 C2.
The shopkeeper here is a born jazz lover, as you'll be able to see fairly quckly by taking a quick glance at the shelves. Browse for books on just about any subject to the strains of Miles Davis' trumpet. It's all so very New Orleans.

Even dogs know that **Kaboom Books** is one of the city's best bookstores. *See p158.*

Computer parts & repair

The Computer Shoppe
2125 Veterans Memorial Boulevard, between Bonnabel & N Causeway boulevards, Metairie (833 5100/www.computer-shoppe.com). St Charles Streetcar/bus 16 S Claiborne, 39 Tulane, 90 Carrollton, then E5 Causeway. **Open** 8am-6pm Mon-Thur; 8am-5pm Fri; 10am-4pm Sat. **Credit** AmEx, Disc, MC, V.

It's hard to find shops that sell or repair Macs in New Orleans, but this shop in inner suburbia is probably the best place; it's been an Apple dealer since 1976.

Prompt Computer Center
58 West Bank Expressway, at Stumpf Boulevard, Gretna (362 3922). Bus W-2 West Bank Expressway. **Open** 9am-5.30pm Mon-Fri. **Credit** AmEx, Disc, MC, V.

This place offers a 24-hour repair service for IBM-compatibles. Rentals are also available.

Dry-cleaning & laundry

There are laundrettes everywhere in town. One not listed here (because it is only sort of a laundrette) is **Igor's Checkpoint Charlie** (at the corner of Esplanade Avenue and Decatur Street in the French Quarter). This is a 24-hour music club with laundry facilities. You can hear a band and grab a burger, all while your clothes spin and dry. Laundry day was never such fun!

Hula Mae's Tropic Wash
840 N Rampart Street, at Dumaine Street, French Quarter (522 1336). Bus 3 Vieux Carré, 48 Esplanade, 55 Elysian Fields, 57 Franklin, 81 Almonaster. **Open** 7am-10pm daily. **Credit** AmEx, MC, V. **Map** p282 C1.

This laundrette is located on the former site of a recording studio which was used by Cosimo Matassa, a local legend who produced the likes of Little Richard and Fats Domino. It does laundry and delivers within the French Quarter. Colourful and about as much fun as a laundrette can be.

Washing Well Laundryteria
841 Bourbon Street, at Dumaine Street, French Quarter (523 9955). Bus 3 Vieux Carré, 55 Elysian Fields, 81 Almonaster, 82 Desire. **Open** 7.30am-6pm Mon-Fri; 7.30am-2pm Sat. **Credit** AmEx, Disc, MC, V. **Map** p282 C2.

Offers same-day pick-up and return of laundry and dry-cleaning throughout the city. Laundry is charged by the load.

Fashion

New Orleans was once a very formal city. Everyone dressed to go downtown, dressed for dinner, dressed for church and dressed for parties. And they did so while adhering to rigid little rules: no white before Easter or after the first of September, handbags and shoes must match, a lady never wore red, blah, blah, blah. Formality died when common sense took over: it's impossible to feel comfortable or look fresh in this climate when garbed to within an inch of passing out. The city's small boutiques cater to a myriad of personal styles, and are generally known for their selections, discernible personalities and enhanced service levels.

ah-ha
3129 Magazine Street, at Ninth Street, Garden District (269 2442). Bus 11 Magazine. **Open** 11am-6pm Mon-Sat. **Credit** AmEx, DC, Disc, MC, V. **Map** p279 A4.

Ah-ha! Just what we've been looking for. This fun, trend-conscious emporium targets the youngish women that its parent company, the venerable Rubensteins (*see p161*), just can't reach with its stodgier collection. Recently relocated to larger quarters but still in the same funky neighbourhood, ah-ha is the area's largest seller of the hot Urban Outfitters range. It also has shoes, clothing, accessories, jewellery and a smattering of groovy knick-knacks for the home at prices that'll make you smile.

Beauvoir

3632 Magazine Street, at Antonine Street, Uptown (895 5581). Bus 11 Magazine. **Open** 11am-5.30pm Mon-Sat. **Credit** AmEx, MC, V. **Map** p279 A4.
This Magazine Street newcomer stocks chic, up-to-date dresses, jeans, handbags and accessories from unique and inspired brands to the idle rich with money to burn. SoHo fashions, oh so inaccessible to all but a wealthy few. Bummer.

Fairy

3634 Magazine Street, near Jackson Avenue, Lower Garden District (269 2033). Bus 11 Magazine. **Open** 11am-6pm Tue-Fri. **Credit** AmEx, Disc, MC, V. **Map** p279 B4.
As you might imagine from the name, this shop's speciality isn't boring suits destined for the boardroom. Instead, women of all ages come here for the kind of sweetly sexy, whimsical clothing and accessories you pull on when it's time to sparkle. Proprietress Elizabeth is as personable and appealing as her shop. And she makes it a goal to keep the prices fair, so as not to ruin the party.

Frock Candy

3336 Magazine Street, near Jackson Avenue, Lower Garden District (891 9230). Bus 11 Magazine. **Open** 10am-6pm Mon-Thur; 10am-7pm Fri, Sat; noon-6pm Sun. **Credit** AmEx, Disc, MC, V. **Map** p279 B3.
It has our favourite name in the whole chapter, and this shop prides itself on offering the newest, edgiest street looks to the desperately hip. It targets teens and barely-twentysomethings travelling with either their parents' credit cards or, better yet, their whole wallets in hand.

Funky Monkey

3127 Magazine Street, near Jackson Avenue, Lower Garden District (899 5587). Bus 11 Magazine. **Open** 11am-6pm Mon-Sat; noon-5pm Sun. **Credit** AmEx, Disc, MC, V. **Map** p297 B3.
At adorable, affordable Funky Monkey, the lines blur between eclectic everyday street gear, mild-mannered masquerade garb, and full-blown, ill-mannered, cover-your-face costumes. Looking for a bra covered in silk sunflowers with a teeny skirt to match? Look no further. Yearning to let out your inner Elvis in a white jumpsuit with sequins? Ditto. Just seeking a beaded handbag or a pair of cat-eye glasses? They're here, too. There's a mixture of new and vintage clothing here, along with lots of accessories you'll never wear to the office, great costume jewellery and little odds and ends.

gae-tana's

7732 Maple Street, between Adams & Burdette streets, Riverbend (865 9625). St Charles Streetcar. **Open** 9.30am-6pm Mon-Sat; noon-5pm Sun. **Credit** AmEx, Disc, MC, V. **Map** p276 B8.
This place in the university area focuses on upscale, flattering, unusual but comfortable clothing for twenty- and thirtysomethings. They also have a few interesting pairs of shoes you won't find elsewhere in town and a nice, inexpensive jewellery selection.

The Grace Note

900 Royal Street, at Dumaine Street, French Quarter (522 1513). Bus 3 Vieux Carré, 55 Elysian Fields, 81 Almonaster, 82 Desire. **Open** 10am-6pm Mon-Sat; 11am-5pm Sun. **Credit** AmEx, MC, V. **Map** p282 C2.
This is one of our absolute favourite New Orleans shops, with an environment as soft and sensual as the name implies. Plush velvet and silk pillows, throws and hangings make the space feel a bit like a harem. The store carries a careful mix of eclectic clothing and jewellery by local designers as well as vintage pieces. Of particular interest are unique cloche hats by local designer Libby Brighton and luxe jackets made from vintage fabrics and *chibori* (Japanese tie-dye) velvet. Sadly, you get what you pay for, and treasures such as these don't come cheap. But if you're drawn to the unusual, this may be the place to splurge.

Harold Clarke Designs

5234 Magazine Street, at Jefferson Avenue, Uptown (897 0770/www.haroldclarke.com). Bus 11 Magazine. **Open** 10am-6pm Mon-Sat; by appointment at other times. **Credit** AmEx, DC, Disc, MC. **Map** p276 C10.
Jamaican-born designer Harold Clarke, who now calls New Orleans home, has a worldwide reputation for designing graceful, inspired bridal dresses and glamorous ball gowns guaranteed to turn heads. All dresses are made in-house. This is elegant personal service from another era, and Clarke's chic clientele includes celebrities and socialites. While the Magazine Street store deals only in bespoke pieces, the French Quarter boutique sells one-of-a-kind and limited edition gowns.
Branch: 901 Iberville Street, French Quarter (568 0440).

Hemline

7916 Maple Street, at Adams Street, Riverbend (862 0420/www.hemlinenola.com). St Charles Streetcar/bus 34 Carrollton. **Open** 10am-6pm Mon-Sat. **Credit** AmEx, DC, Disc, MC, V. **Map** p276 B8.
Pretty. Sexy. Will stretch the budget but not stomp it dead. These are clothes you wear on a special date. This store is one of the most popular in town with women of all ages. It's the kind of place you go to when you need a party dress, or that perfect top, and you want to splurge a little but not go completely crazy. Absolutely worth a visit.
Branches: 605 Chartres Street, French Quarter (568 0111); 3025 Magazine Street, Uptown (269 4005); 838 Royal Street, French Quarter (522 8577).

Le Fleur de Paris

712 Royal Street, at Pirate's Alley, French Quarter (525 1899). Bus 3 Vieux Carré, 55 Elysian Fields, 81 Almonaster, 82 Desire. **Open** 10am-6pm daily. **Credit** AmEx, Disc, MC, V. **Map** p282 C2.

The fabulously garbed plastic beauties gracing the picture window set the stage for a sensual experience even before you even enter this store. This is a paradise for the woman who dresses to be noticed. In the unlikely event that you cannot find your heart's desire amid the fine gowns, suits and lingerie in every hue and texture, a staff designer is on hand to create something for you. While bespoke work is as expensive as you'd expect, many stunning off-the-rack numbers are surprisingly affordable.

Ms Spratt's

4537 Magazine Street, at Cadiz Street, Uptown (891 0063). Bus 11 Magazine. **Credit** AmEx, Disc, MC, V. **Map** p276 D10.

Ms Spratt's takes a fresh approach to outfitting women in large sizes, with clothing and accessories from a variety of national brands including Jones New York, Liz & Jane and Coco & Juan.

Perlis

6070 Magazine Street, at State Street, Uptown (895 8661). Bus 11 Magazine. **Open** 9am-6pm Mon-Sat. **Credit** AmEx, DC, Disc, MC, V. **Map** p276 B9.

A New Orleans institution, Perlis is the only place many Uptown men shop. The clothing, which evidences fine craftsmanship, is undeniably conservative and bears no sign of any sort of newfangled influence. Service is exemplary, and Perlis keeps 'em coming back with its guarantee of free lifelong alterations to suits, jackets and formalwear bearing its label. The store recently expanded to offer more selection for women and boys. The women's department is also conservative but leaves room for a few fun handbags and frivolous, colourful, easy-to-wear resort pieces. Everything's a bit pricey, but sales racks can be awesome. Distinctive shirts and ties bearing Perlis' red crawfish logo make for gifts that are unmistakably New Orleans.

Rubensteins

102 St Charles Avenue, at Canal Street, CBD (581 6666/www.rubensteinsfashion.com). St Charles Streetcar/bus 41, 42, 43 Canal. **Open** 10.30am-5.30pm Mon-Wed; 10am-5.45pm Thur-Sat. **Credit** AmEx, DC, Disc, MC, V. **Map** p279 C1.

For decades this legendary, family-owned clothier catered only to men, but it now offers a limited though carefully stocked women's department. Casual-, career- and formalwear are available from largely European houses including Gucci and Armani. Service is excellent and personable.

Trashy Diva

829 Chartres Street, at St Ann Street, French Quarter (581 4555). Bus 3 Vieux Carré, 41 Canal, 55 Elysian Fields, 81 Almonaster, 82 Desire. **Open** noon-6pm daily. **Credit** AmEx, DC, Disc, MC, V. **Map** p282 C2.

This place aims to dress the woman who yearns for the yesteryear of high style. The carefully chosen and well preserved vintage items include silk coats and dresses and elegant wool suits with matching hats and handbags, most from the 1930s to 1960s. The Uptown branch sells labels including Anna Sui and the Trashy Diva line.
Branch: 2048 Magazine Street, Uptown (299 8777).

Uptown Costume & Dancewear

4326 Magazine Street, at Milan Street, Uptown (895 7969). Bus 11 Magazine. **Open** 10am-6pm Mon-Fri. **Credit** MC, V. **Map** p276 D10.

It's always acceptable to wear a costume in New Orleans – why wait for Mardi Gras or Halloween? The selection at this Uptown institution is the best around. Even if you don't plan to buy, it's a fun place to pop in for a look around.

Weinstein's

4011 Magazine Street, at Marengo Street, Uptown (895 6278). Bus 11 Magazine. **Open** 10pm-6pm Mon-Sat. **Credit** AmEx, DC, MC, V. **Map** p279 C1.

Loyal customers followed Weinstein's to its new digs from its old location in the Shops at Canal Place for its exclusive collections of women's and men's Italian and Belgian designer clothing. Prices are high, but so is the quality.

Children's clothing

Giggleberries

5509 Magazine Street, at Jefferson Avenue, Uptown (899 5509/www.giggleberrieskids.com) Bus 11 Magazine. **Open** 10am-6pm Mon-Sat; noon-5pm Sun. **Credit** MC, V. **Map** p276 C10.

This fun little shop on a chic strip of Magazine Street caters for infants and toddlers (boys and girls up to size 4) and older girls (sizes 5 to 16). The selection is limited but well chosen and tends to the ickle trendy, hip and unusual. These clothes would suit kids with lots of personality and style. Many of the shoes here are also available in adult sizes, and the accessories appeal to girls of all ages.

Mignon

2727 Prytania Street, at Washington Avenue, Garden District (891 2374). St Charles Streetcar. **Open** 10am-5pm Mon-Sat. **Credit** AmEx, MC, V. **Map** p279 A3.

This Garden District store carries the kind of kids' clothing you either love or hate: heavy on the lace, appliqués and ruffles and the Little Lord Fauntleroy look. It has sizes for ages from toddler to four (boys) and ten (girls). Prices are high – dresses start at $100, and they're only going to get them dirty.

Pippen Lane

2929 Magazine Street, at 7th Street, Uptown (269 0106/www.pippenlane.com). Bus 11 Magazine. **Open** 10am-6pm Mon-Fri; 10am-5pm Sat. **Credit** AmEx, Disc, MC, V. **Map** p279 A3/4.

Pippen Lane has expensive, high-quality clothing, shoes, accessories, furnishings and small toys for

timeout.com

The online guide to the world's greatest cities

babies and children. The choices range from frilly and traditional to screamingly hip. It's terrifyingly expensive, but there's always a sales rack, and it has blow-out sales twice a year.

Fashion accessories

Hats

Kabuki Design Studio

1036 Royal Street, at Ursulines Street, French Quarter (523 8004). Bus 3 Vieux Carré, 41 Canal, 55 Elysian Fields, 81 Almonaster, 82 Desire. **Open** 10am-5pm Mon-Sat; by appointment at other times. **Credit** AmEx, MC, V. **Map** p282 C2.
Home to the theatrical Tracy Thompson and her inspired collection of adornments for the head. The fabulous Thompson designs, sews and shapes each hat herself, and all are worth the money.

Meyer the Hatter

120 St Charles Avenue, at Canal Street, CBD (525 1048/1-800 882 4287). St Charles Streetcar/bus 41 Canal. **Open** 10am-6pm Mon-Sat. **Credit** AmEx, DC, Disc, MC, V. **Map** p279 C1.
At this dishevelled family-run shop with its 1950s decor, men have been buying top labels such as Dobbs and Stetson since 1894. The old-timers here provide expert help and can tell a good story to boot: ask about the time the Marx Brothers shopped here.

Jewellery

Down the ages, Southern women have tended to deck themselves out in jewels as a means of displaying just how valuable they are to their men. It's idiotic and archaic – but so entrenched as to be almost compulsory – even today. Spread this out over a few centuries and you have a glut of fantastic heirloom bling-bling (called 'estate jewellery') floating about the many second-hand stores alongside abundant fine contemporary pieces. Prices are generally competitive here, a result of the supply and demand unbalance. Particularly when it comes to antique platinum and diamond jewellery, this is a great place.

Adler & Sons

722 Canal Street, at St Charles Avenue, CBD (523 5292). St Charles Streetcar/bus 41 Canal. **Open** 10am-5.45pm Mon-Wed, Fri, Sat; 10am-7pm Thur. **Credit** AmEx, DC, Disc, MC, V. **Map** p279 C1.
Just the sight of an Adler's box is enough to make a New Orleans debutante woozy. This venerable and highly reputable institution has been ringing southern fingers for over a century and stocks everything from little gold earrings to hubcap-sized rocks and Elvisian pinkie rings for men. It's neither cheap nor cutting edge. It's New Orleans' Tiffany's.
Branches: Lakeside Shopping Center (*see p152*, 523 5292); Oakwood Shopping Center, 197 West Bank Expressway, at Terry Parkway, Gretna (523 5292).

Anne Pratt Designs

3937 Magazine Street, at Austerlitz Street, Uptown (891 6532). St Charles Streetcar. **Open** 11am-5.30pm Mon-Sat. **Credit** MC, V. **Map** p279 B4.
This noted designer works with gold, silver and precious and semiprecious stones in creating her whimsical pieces. Pratt also carries handmade iron furniture, gorgeous fixtures and accessories.

The Bead Shop

4612 Magazine Street, at Cadiz Street, Uptown (895 6161). Bus 11 Magazine. **Open** 10am-5.30pm Mon-Sat; noon-5.30pm Sun. **Credit** AmEx, MC, V. **Map** p276 D10.
This sweet little shop holds thousands of different beads, stones and other small objects you can use to make your own jewellery. If you are a doofus when it comes to putting things together, they will assemble your selected components for you for a fee, or you can choose from prefabricated items.
Branch: 800 Metairie Road, Metairie (837 0371).

Dominique Giordano Jewelry Design

5420 Magazine Street, between Jefferson Avenue and Octavia Street, Uptown (895 3909). Bus 11 Magazine. **Open** 10am-6pm Tue-Sat. **Credit** AmEx, Disc, MC, V. **Map** p276 C10.
Dominique sells her own original pieces made using sterling silver and precious and semiprecious stones. A catalogue is available on request.

Hoover Watches & Jewels

301 Royal Street, at Conti Street, French Quarter (522 7289). Bus 3 Vieux Carré. **Open** 10.30am-6.30pm Mon-Sat; noon-5pm Sun. **Credit** AmEx, DC, MC, V. **Map** p282 B2.
Specialises in vintage wrist and pocket watches for men and women from Rolex, Hamilton, Ben Russ and Patek Philippe, as well as antique, vintage and modern women's jewellery including an array of wedding and engagement rings.

Katy Beh Contemporary Jewelry

3701 Magazine Street, at Amelia Street, Uptown (896 9600). Bus 11 Magazine. **Open** 10am-5pm Mon-Sat. **Credit** AmEx, Disc, MC, V. **Map** p276 D/E9.
Fine jewellery of silver, gold and gemstones from an international coterie of celebrated designers: Michael Good, Barbara Heinrich and Rubenstein/Ross. Not the stuff your grandmother wore.

Mignon Faget

710 Dublin Street, at Maple Street, Riverbend (865 7361/www.mignonfaget.com). St Charles Streetcar. **Open** 10am-5pm Mon-Sat. **Credit** AmEx, Disc, MC, V. **Map** p276 A8.
New Orleans' most popular jewellery designer is known and loved for her original and comprehensive nature- and New Orleans-themed collections in silver and gold. Shotgun house necklace, anyone?
Branches: Shops at Canal Place (*see p151*, 524 2973); Lakeside Shopping Center (*see p152*, 835 2244).

Eat, Drink, Shop

Sparkle, made to order

Though designer Mignon Faget has been creating her distinctive New Orleans jewellery for 30 years, she had few local competitors until the early 1990s, when **The Bead Shop** (*see p163*) first opened its Magazine Street location. As it established itself, its range of classes and materials grew, and soon it had the effect of freeing the inner jewellery designer in more than a few people.

New Orleans native Robin Zenker is the most recent newcomer to the scene. Her experience with interior architecture in San Francisco, coupled with an innate sense of style and rare eclecticism, is expressed in bold, colourful designs for earrings, necklaces, chokers and bracelets in sterling and semiprecious stones. Zenker's **Zen Den** studio Uptown is open by appointment only (895 6982).

Mignon Faget.

Not far away, **Molly McNamara** executes contemporary handcrafted designs from inside her eponymous studio and gallery (2128 Magazine Street, Uptown; 566 1100). Inspirations for her silver and freshwater pearl adornments include the heavens, Picasso, Marie Laveau and the common oyster.

Like Mignon Faget, designer **Ruby Ann Bertram-Harker**'s designs (*see below*) are inspired by local life and culture, and though her work is now carried in national galleries and boutiques, her inspiration remains decidedly down-home. She uses unusual materials in her one-of-a-kind jewellery, accessories and clothing.

Mary Viola Walker (3652 Magazine Sreet, Uptown; 891 4122) uses rare semiprecious stones like strawberry obsidian and iridescent blue-green angel pearls to create her distinctive jewellery. Walker's hallmark is a bold but thoughtful touch in designs intended to flatter. Her handmade pieces come in very limited editions.

Though silver is the favoured metal among most New Orleans designers, both **Mignon Faget** and **Anne Pratt** (*for both, see p163*) also work with gold.

Ruby Ann Bertram-Harker
3005 Magazine Street, at 7th Street, Uptown (897 0811/1-800 826 7282/www.rubyonline.com). Bus 11 Magazine. **Open** 10am-5pm Mon-Sat. **Credit** AmEx, MC, V. **Map** p279 A3/4.
Formerly Ruby Ann Toblar-Blanco (don't ask) – call her what you will, this local designer creates elegant, feminine designs with an antique feel using freshwater pearls, gemstones, coral and sterling silver.
Branch: 304 Chartres Street, at Bienville Street, French Quarter (525 1050).

Sabai
3115 Magazine Street, between Washington and Louisiana avenues, Uptown (899 9555). Bus 11 Magazine. **Open** 10am-6pm Mon-Sat; 11am-5pm Sun. **Credit** AmEx, Disc, MC, V. **Map** p279 A3/4.
This shop has unusual handcrafted jewellery from all over the world featuring rare and interesting

stones. The ambience is somewhere between a harem and an upmarket opium den. The jewellery collection – mostly in silver with semi-precious stones – is affordable. The Asian-inspired gifts and tchotchkes add to the feeling. Very cool.
Branch: 924 Royal Street, French Quarter (525 6211).

Symmetry
8138 Hampson Street, at Dublin Street, Riverbend (861 9925/www.symmetryjewelers.com). St Charles Streetcar. **Open** *Summer* 10am-5pm Tue-Sat. *Winter* 10am-5pm Mon-Sat. **Credit** AmEx, Disc, MC, V. **Map** p276 A8.
Handcrafted jewellery by local designers is sold here at prices ranging from the almost reasonable to the absolutely staggering. The staff will also work with you to create your own design, which they will then execute for you at great cost.

Lingerie

Basics Underneath

802 Octavia Street, at Magazine Street, Uptown (894 1000). Bus 11 Magazine. **Open** 10am-6pm Mon-Sat. **Credit** AmEx, DC, Disc, MC, V. **Map** p276 C9/10.

This tiny little shop is stuffed with bits of fine lingerie, much of it European. Italian thongs abound. Swimsuits are also for sale in warmer months.

House of Lounge

2044 Magazine Street, between Josephine & St Andrew streets, Uptown (671 8300/www.houseof lounge.com). Bus 11 Magazine. **Open** 10am-6pm Mon-Sat; noon-5pm Sun. **Credit** AmEx, Disc, MC, V. **Map** p279 B3.

The styles here range from retro glamour to hip sex-kitten numbers. Visitors looking for local wares will appreciate Tracy Thompson's whimsical hats as well as Rosemary Kimble's delicate butterfly wings. Custom-made HoL offerings run to elegant smoking jackets and glamorously kinky corsets.

Yvonne LaFleur

8131 Hampson Street, at Dublin Street, Riverbend (866 9666/www.yvonnelafleur.com). St Charles Streetcar. **Open** 10am-6pm Mon-Wed, Fri, Sat; 10am-8pm Thur. **Credit** AmEx, Disc, MC, V. **Map** p276 A8.

Expensive off-the-rack and bespoke silk lingerie, including a decent selection in larger sizes, is sold in surroundings that vaguely suggest a classy bordello. This glamorous shop also has an extensive hat department that will delight brides and ultra-girlies; lavish bespoke creations feature veils, flowers and feathers from all over the world.

Luggage

Rapp's Luggage & Gifts

604 Canal Street, at St Charles Avenue, CBD (568 1953). St Charles Streetcar/bus 41 Canal. **Open** 10am-6pm Mon-Sat. **Credit** AmEx, Disc, MC, V. **Map** p279 C1.

One of the city's oldest stores – in business since 1865 and located on busy Canal Street since the 1920s – Rapp's Luggage & Gifts has a wide collection of travelling bags and briefcases as well as smaller goods. A handy leather and luggage repair service is also available.

Branch: New Orleans Centre (*see p151*, 566 0700).

Shoes

In addition to the speciality and designer shoe stores listed below, **Canal Street** is positively overrun with stores selling athletic shoes, tennis shoes, trainers… There you can find everything from basic Keds and Converses to the kinds of blinking, bouncy moon shoes that made some basketball players millions.

Aerosoles

510 St Peter Street, between Decatur & Chartres streets, French Quarter (529 7463). Bus 3 Vieux Carré, 41 Canal, 55 Elysian Fields, 81 Almonaster, 82 Desire. **Open** 10am-7pm daily. **Credit** AmEx, DC, Disc, MC, V. **Map** p282 B2/3.

Tending toward deeply uncool practical styles, Aerosoles shoes are known for their high comfort factor but not for their looks. When you've been schlepping around town all day and your feet are killing you, however, perhaps you won't really care what your shoes look like.

Feet First

4119 Magazine Street, at Octavia Street, Uptown (899 6800). Bus 11 Magazine. **Open** 10am-6pm Mon-Sat; noon-5pm Sun. **Credit** AmEx, Disc, MC, V. **Map** p276 C9/10.

Name-brand shoes for women (Kenneth Cole, 9 West and the like) at discount prices, but the selection offered here can be a bit spotty.

Branch: 518 Chartres Street, at St Louis Street, French Quarter (566 7525).

Haase's Shoe Store & Young Folk's Shop

8119 Oak Street, at S Carrollton Avenue, Carrollton (866 9944). St Charles Streetcar. **Open** 9.30am-5pm Mon-Sat. **Credit** AmEx, Disc, MC, V. **Map** p276 B7.

This family-owned store has been around for about a zillion years and has been outfitting youngsters in Stride Rite shoes from the very beginning. The children's clothing is well made and very traditional.

Johnston & Murphy

The Shops at Canal Place, 333 Canal Street, at Decatur Street, French Quarter (524 4039). Bus 41 Canal. **Open** 10am-7pm Mon-Sat; noon-6pm Sun. **Credit** AmEx, Disc, MC, V. **Map** p282 A3.

Looking for mainstream upscale men's shoes at mainstream upscale prices? Look no further.

Pied Nu

5521 Magazine Street, at Octavia Street, Uptown (899 4118). Bus 11 Magazine. **Open** 10am-6pm Mon-Fri; 10am-5pm Sat. **Credit** AmEx, Disc, MC, V. **Map** p276 C9/10.

Pied Nu stocks a small but meticulously chosen collection of shoes by the likes of Calvin Klein, Sigerson Morrison and Robert Clergerie, plus upmarket accessories, linens and lamps. It's easy to fall head over stiletto heels in love with these little treasures, but the outrageous prices and famously snooty staff (who act as if they don't need your business) may leave you shaking in your Italian leather boots.

Saint Germain

Shops at Canal Place, 333 Canal Street, at Decatur Street, French Quarter (522 1720). Bus 41 Canal. **Open** 10am-6pm Mon-Wed; 10am-7pm Thur-Sat; noon-6pm Sun. **Credit** AmEx, DC, Disc, MC, V. **Map** p282 A3.

Sassy shoes from hot designers including American Donald J Pliner and Frenchman Luc Berjen, along with handmade bridal shoes by Brit star Emma

Eat, Drink, Shop

Exotic **Sabai** is where you'll find your new bracelet. *See p164.*

Hope, are all here. There is also a small but brilliantly edited selection of accessories, including some adorable beaded evening bags. Faith, the proprietress, is a darling who knows entirely too much about fabulous shoes.

Victoria's Uptown

7725 Maple Street, at Adams Street, Riverbend (861 8861). St Charles Streetcar. **Open** 10am-6pm Mon-Sat. **Credit** AmEx, MC, V. **Map** p276 B8.
A good range of snazzy labels like Zeitgeist NY, Cynthia Rowley and Enrico Antinori – brought to you at discounted prices. Hurrah!
Branch: 532 Chartres Street, at St Louis Street, French Quarter (568 9990).

Florists

Magazine Flowers & Greenery

737 Octavia Street, at Magazine Street, Uptown (891 4356). Bus 11 Magazine. **Open** 10.30am-5.30pm Tue-Sat. **Credit** AmEx, MC, V. **Map** p276 C9/10.
This attractive store offers natural and unpretentious flower arrangements, both dried and fresh. You'll also find lots of orchids and flowering plants.

Tommy's Flower Shop

1029 Chartres Street, between Phillip & Ursulines streets, French Quarter (522 6563). Bus 55 Elysian Fields. **Open** 10am-6.30pm Mon-Sat; 10am-5pm Sun. **Credit** AmEx, MC, V. **Map** p282 B2.
It's a pleasure to shop at this sweet little spot. Tommy's selections include the usual suspects as well as some uncommon varieties. And the propri-

etor is quirky and unpredictable. Along with its flower selection, Tommy's is also famous locally for its quirky, hand-lettered adverts in local papers.

Urban Earth

1528 Jackson Avenue, at St Charles Avenue, Garden District (524 0100). St Charles Streetcar. **Open** 10am-5pm Tue-Sat. **Credit** Disc, MC, V. **Map** p279 B3.
This place is totally out there, with floral designs that incorporate the oddest elements. You'll find no common daisies or carnations here. Call Urban Earth when you care enough to send… well, something really weird. Sure to make a lasting impression.

Food & drink

Central Grocery Company

923 Decatur Street, at St Philip Street, French Quarter (523 1620). Bus 3 Vieux Carré, 55 Elysian Fields, 81 Almonaster, 82 Desire. **Open** 8am-5.30pm daily. **No credit cards. Map** p282 C2/3.
One of the few remaining traditional Italian groceries in the city, this place is packed to the rafters with imports. The deli sells the best muffuletta sandwich (a gigantic New Orleans original containing ham, cheese, Genoa salami and olive salad on thick Italian bread) in town for a couple of bucks per quarter (a whole sandwich would feed a family of four). Grab a section and have a picnic by the river.

Langenstein's

1330 Arabella Street, at Pitt Street, Uptown (899 9283). St Charles Streetcar. **Open** 8am-7pm Mon-Sat. **Credit** MC, V. **Map** p276 C9.

Get the floaty peignoir of your dreams at **Yvonne LaFleur**. *See p165.*

This posh Uptown grocery has the best meat market in the city, dahlin'. The deli stocks a selection of high-quality but pricey home-made local favourites like crawfish bisque and shrimp Creole. A good place to stock up for a picnic.
Branch: 800 Metairie Road, Metairie (831 6682).

Martin Wine Cellar

3827 Baronne Street, at Peniston Street, Uptown (899 7411/www.martinwine.com). Bus 15 Freret Street. **Open** 9am-7pm Mon-Sat; 10am-4pm Sun. **Credit** AmEx, DC, Disc, MC, V. **Map** p276 D9.
This Uptown place has a huge selection of excellent wines and imported beers, plus a good deli, trays of party food and an assortment of gourmet treats (try the grapes encased in Roquefort and chopped pecans). Staff are friendly and knowledgeable.
Branch: 714 Elmeer Street, Metairie (896 7300).

Vieux Carré Wine & Spirits

422 Chartres Street, at St Louis Street, French Quarter (568 9463). Bus 3 Vieux Carré, 55 Elysian Fields, 81 Almonaster, 82 Desire. **Open** 10am-10pm Mon-Sat; 10am-7pm Sun. **Credit** AmEx, Disc, MC, V. **Map** p282 B2.
This place offers the French Quarter's largest selection of wines and spirits, sold with quirky Quarter personality. The wines are well-chosen and interesting, and staff will deliver to hotels.

Whole Foods Market

3135 Esplanade Avenue, at Ponce de Leon Street, Mid-City (943 1626/www.wholefoods.com). Bus 48 Esplanade. **Open** 8am-9pm Mon-Sat; 8am-8pm Sun. **Credit** AmEx, Disc, MC, V. **Map** p278 E5.

This small store on Esplanade Avenue was the city's first full-service natural foods supermarket. It sells organic fruit and veg, cheeses, fresh breads, herbal teas, herbal remedies, food supplements and skin care products. It has a fab deli as well. And it sells very good meats, so it's not just for veggies. Healthy living doesn't come cheap, though – the prices are crazy. Still, it's fun to shop with the posh hippies and gather goods for a lunch under the oaks in City Park. The gorgeous new Uptown location dwarfs the original and is an excellent place to shop for a picnic in beautiful Audubon Park – even if it is jammed with snobby Uptown housewives demanding to know just how organic everything really is.
Branch: 5600 Magazine Street, at Jefferson Avenue, Uptown (899 9119).

Farmer's markets

Sadly, these days the **French Market** (on Decatur Street in the French Quarter; *see p68*) is a shadow of its former self, with souvenir stands now outnumbering the food stalls. However, a few of the vendors stick around all night, and you can still get fresh fruit and veg, as well as New Orleans spices, a million kinds of hot sauce and packaged seasoned red beans. Touristy or not, it's still a great deal of fun.

Another market is the **Crescent City Farmers' Market** (700 Magazine Street, at Girod Street, Warehouse District), which operates on Saturday mornings from 8am to noon. This stellar farmers' market has become outrageously popular among locals, as it offers locally grown flowers, plants, fruits, vegetables and herbs, artisan breads and fresh seafood in season to an urban population desperate for a taste of the countryside. Around 10am, a local chef (a different one each week) gives a free culinary demonstration with samples. The same market is also held on Tuesdays at the Uptown Square shopping area at 200 Broadway from 10am to 2pm (rain or shine), while a Thursday version is held at the American Can Company (3700 Orleans Avenue, Mid-City) from 4pm to 6pm.

Speciality & gift foods

If you want to take home the flavour of New Orleans, Cajun and Creole spices, sugary pralines, dark chicory coffee, beignet mix and packaged red beans all travel well. You can find many of these at reasonable prices in standard local grocery stores, but a number of speciality shops offer a wider selection.

Cafe du Monde Shop

800 Decatur Street, at St Ann Street, French Quarter (525 4544). Bus 3 Vieux Carré, 55 Elysian Fields, 81 Almonaster, 82 Desire. **Open** 24hrs daily. **Credit** AmEx, Disc, MC, V. **Map** p282 C3.
Across the street from the famous café of the same name (*see p131*), this shop sells its brand of coffee and *beignet* mix and will ship overseas.

Creole Delicacies Gourmet Shop

533 St Ann Street, at Chartres Street, French Quarter (525 9508). Bus 3 Vieux Carré, 55 Elysian Fields, 81 Almonaster, 82 Desire. **Open** 9am-5pm daily. **Credit** AmEx, DC, Disc, MC, V. **Map** p282 C2.
Specialises in gift baskets containing all the mixes and spices you need to cook Creole and Cajun. **Branch**: 3rd Floor, Riverwalk, CBD (*see p151*, 523 6425).

Health & beauty

Most area drugstores stock basic, moderately priced cosmetics. For higher-end beauty products and a larger selection head for a department store. Day spas also sell imported and designer cosmetic supplies.

Hairdressers

Eclipse Salon

536 Bienville Street, at Royal Street, French Quarter (522 3318). Bus 3 Vieux Carré, 55 Elysian Fields, 81 Almonaster, 82 Desire. **Open** 9am-6pm Mon, Wed, Fri, Sat; 9am-8pm Tue, Thur. **Credit** AmEx, MC, V. **Map** p282 B2.
This full-service salon in the French Quarter provides haircuts for men and women, as well as makeovers and nail and body treatments. It carries Aveda and Paul Mitchell products.

Twisted Hair Salon

4826 Magazine Street, at Napoleon Avenue, Uptown (891 9998). Bus 11 Magazine. **Open** 11am-6pm Tue-Sat. **Credit** AmEx, MC, V. **Map** p276 D10.
This is the place to go if you're looking for a bit more go-ahead-and-add-a-bit. The folks at Twisted Hair specialise in extensions for all hair types; they offer human and synthetic hair as well as dreadlocks, braids, colour and plain old haircuts.

Opticians

St Charles Vision

138 Carondelet Street, at Common Street, CBD (522 0826). St Charles Streetcar. **Open** 9am-5pm Mon-Fri. **Credit** AmEx, Disc, MC, V. **Map** p279 B/C1.
This optician has a same-day service and a large selection of designer frames. The Carrollton Avenue branch is especially good.
Branches: 624 S Carrollton Avenue, Uptown (866 6311); 3200 Severn Avenue, Metairie (887 2020).

Perfume

Department stores' cosmetics sections all carry a good number of famous-name fragrances, while pharmacies stock many less expensive brands. For something more in the spirit of the city, try these small shops in the French Quarter for scents like vetiver, oleander and sweet olive.

Bourbon French Parfums

525 St Ann Street, at Decatur Street, French Quarter (522 4480/www.neworleansperfume.com). Bus 3 Vieux Carré, 55 Elysian Fields, 81 Almonaster, 82 Desire. **Open** 9am-5pm daily. **Credit** AmEx, Disc, MC, V. **Map** p282 C3.
In business since 1843, this locally owned shop in the French Quarter makes custom-blended fragrances for men and women.

Hové Parfumeur

824 Royal Street, at St Ann Street, French Quarter (525 7827). Bus 3 Vieux Carré, 55 Elysian Fields, 81 Almonaster, 82 Desire. **Open** 10am-5pm Mon-Sat. **Credit** AmEx, MC, V. **Map** p282 C2.
A New Orleans landmark. The sweet olive scent is the quintessential New Orleans fragrance, capturing the sweet smell of the trees that bloom all over the city in spring and autumn. Also look out for the vetiver perfumes and soaps for men and women, made from a scented root found in Louisiana. This is the shop that inspired Tom Robbins to write the novel *Jitterbug Perfume*.

Pharmacies

There are chain pharmacies all around town. Several branches of **Rite Aid** are open 24 hours daily, including one in the Garden District (3401 St Charles Avenue, at Louisiana Avenue, 895

Eat, Drink, Shop

Why shouldn't guys be pampered too? They are at **Aidan Gill for Men**.

0344, prescriptions 896 4575) and one Uptown
(4330 S Claiborne Avenue, at Napoleon Avenue,
895 6655, prescriptions 896 4570). The Mid-City
Walgreens branch (3311 Canal Street, at
Jefferson Davis Parkway, 822 8070) is open
from 7am to 11pm daily. The only pharmacy
left in the French Quarter is the **Royal
Pharmacy** (1101 Royal Street, at Ursulines
Street, 523 5401); it's open from 9am to 6pm
Monday to Saturday.

Shops & spas

Aidan Gill for Men

*2026 Magazine Street, at St Andrew Street,
Lower Garden District (587 9090/www.aidangillfor
men.com). Bus 11 Magazine.* **Open** 10am-6pm
Tue-Thur, Sat; 9am-5pm Fri. **Credit** AmEx, MC, V.
Map p279 B3.
'Unisex is a dead word,' proclaims Aidan Gill, proprietor of this decidedly masculine enclave in the
Lower Garden District. Stepping into the shop, one
is immediately put in mind of those bygone men's
salons where a gentleman would while away his
afternoon with a cigar, a whiskey and some lively
banter. Antique barber chairs and other memorabilia make for a clubby 19th-century atmosphere,
and no one getting a hot towel shave (the house speciality) or a haircut is without a pint of Guinness or
something a bit stronger. On the retail side, Gill
offers handmade men's shaving gear, soaps, neck-
ties and other accessories, most of which you'd be
hard-pressed to find elsewhere this side of the pond.

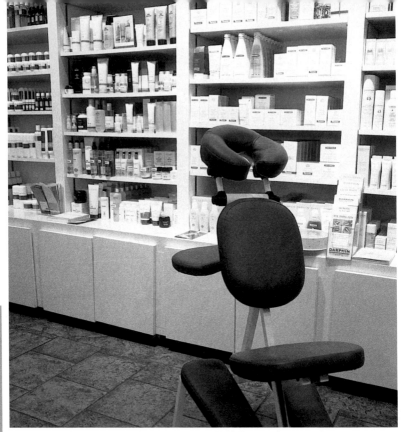

With shelf after shelf of skin and hair products, **Belladonna** is heaven, of a sort.

Belladonna

2900 Magazine Street, at Sixth Street, Uptown (891 4393/www.belladonnadayspa.com). Bus 11 Magazine. **Open** 9am-8pm Mon-Fri; 9am-6pm Sat. **Credit** AmEx, MC, V. **Map** p279 A3.

This Japanese-style day spa offers comprehensive services and a fine selection of cosmetics. Between treatments, relax in the Japanese garden with a cup of herb tea or enjoy the jacuzzi, steam room or sauna. Appointments can be hard to come by, so book a bit ahead. Even if you don't get a facial or massage, you can indulge in expensive scented candles, soaps, perfumes and the like in the big, sprawling shop.

Earthsavers

434 Chartres Street, at Conti Street, French Quarter (581 4999/www.earthsaversonline.com). Bus 3 Vieux Carré, 55 Elysian Fields, 81 Almonaster, 82 Desire. **Open** 10am-6pm Mon-Wed, Fri; 10am-8pm Thur; noon-5pm Sun. **Credit** AmEx, Disc, MC, V. **Map** p282 B2.

Earthsavers has dozens of complete lines of eco-friendly products for bath and body (all are free of things like mineral oil, and the store promises that none are tested on animals). It carries names like Kiehl's as well as quite a few more expensive posh brands. Services offered range from a basic shoulder rub to a $160 day of relaxation that includes the works: manicure, pedicure, facial, one-hour massage and a light, healthy lunch. Also has a good range of skin care products and cosmetics for men.

Branches: 5501 Magazine Street, at Joseph Street, Uptown (899 8555); 3301 Veterans Boulevard, Metairie (885 5152); 528 North Columbia Street, Covington (1-985 875 0300).

Fifi Mahoney's

828 Chartres Street, between St Ann & Dumaine streets, French Quarter (525 4343). Bus 3 Vieux Carré, 55 Elysian Fields, 81 Almonaster, 82 Desire. **Open** noon-6pm daily. **Credit** MC, V. **Map** p282 B2.

One thing is certain: things are never dull at Fifi's. Though it is largely geared towards transvestites, many women shop here as well, and anyone looking for an experience (or a fuchsia wig) is welcome. They do custom make-up services for men and women and sell extravagant nail varnishes and lipsticks, but their forté is definitely the array of astonishing wigs in vainglorious colours. Who's up for an aquamarine bob? This is strictly for the glam.

Tattooing & body piercing

This port city has long been graced with tattoo parlours, which originally catered to sailors looking for fun. Talented tattoo artists and piercers still flourish in small studios scattered around town: **Electric Expressions** (3421 S Carrollton Avenue, at Bienville Street, Mid-City, 488 1500); **Electric Ladyland Tattoo** (8106 Earhart Boulevard, at Carrollton Avenue, Central City, 866 3859); and **Rings of Desire** (1128 Decatur Street, at Governor Nicholls Avenue, French Quarter, 524 6147).

Household, furniture & gifts

American Aquatic Gardens

612 Elysian Fields Avenue, between Royal & Chartres streets, Marigny (944 0410). Bus 55 Elysian Fields, 81 Almonaster, 82 Desire. **Open** 9am-5pm daily. **Credit** Disc, MC, V. **Map** p277 G6.
This is an absolutely stellar place to shop. All the staff are friendly and knowledgeable, and no wonder; if you could spend every day here, you would be, too. The unique adornments for the home and garden are wonderful, and the prices come as a pleasant surprise. The outdoor selection includes benches, sculptures, statuary, fountains and wall plaques, as well as everything you need to create and maintain your own aquatic garden. Interior items include lamps, wall hangings, paintings, mirrors and vases. Ask about the Sacred Pond.

Big Life Toys & Gifts

3117 Magazine Street, between Washington & Louisiana streets, Uptown (895 8695/www.biglife toys.com). Bus 11 Magazine. **Open** 10am-6pm Mon-Sat; noon-4pm Sun. **Credit** AmEx, Disc, MC, V. **Map** p276 C9/10.
Big Life is a unique toy store, with a strong bent toward the basics for children up to 8, has a big stock of infant playthings from Lamaze and Tomy. The gift shop down the block at No.3109 offers distinctly retro housewares, furniture, glassware and adornments to make your world a little funkier. A sampling: tiki lamps, goofy clocks, wind-up nuns, kitschy jewellery and Martini glasses. The branch up the road at 5430 Magazine Street has toys and character items for people aged eight to adult from names like Sanrio and Paul Frank. You probably won't find any Fur Real kitties here, but you will find such classics as Slinky, Curious George, Silly Putty, Magic Rocks and Hello Kitty.
Branch: 5430 Magazine Street, at Octavia Street, Warehouse District (899 8697).

Creative Concrete

1700 Benefit Street, at Gentilly Boulevard, Gentilly (949 5195). Bus 90 Carrollton. **Open** 9am-5pm Mon-Sat. **Credit** Disc, MC, V. **Map** p278 F4.
You'll need directions to find this place tucked under the interstate in old Gentilly, but if you can, and

you're in the market for reasonably priced yard art and statuary, you'll be ecstatic. The stock includes a collection of Gentilly balls. Now back in fashion, these decorative glass spheres, which come in silver, gold and blue, first got their name in the 1950s, when they could be found perched in gardens all over this neighbourhood at the edge of Mid-City. Everything here is made on the premises.

Derby Pottery and Tile

2029 Magazine Street, at Jackson Avenue, Garden District (586 9003). Bus 11 Magazine. **Open** 10.30am-5pm Mon-Sat. **Credit** AmEx, DC, Disc, MC, V. **Map** p279 B3.
Handmade pottery, tiles and sculpture created on the premises by proprietor Mark Derby. The images redolent of New Orleans which grace many of these elegant, inspired ceramics make lovely souvenirs.

Eclectique Antiques/Shades of Light

2116 Magazine Street, at Josephine Street, Lower Garden District (524 6500). Bus 11 Magazine. **Open** 10am-5pm Mon-Sat. **Credit** AmEx, DC, Disc, MC, V. **Map** p279 B3.
Designer David Donovan creates impressive one-of-a-kind lamps and lampshades. There's also a good selection of antique light fixtures and chandeliers.

Mystic Blue Signs

2212 Magazine Street, at Jackson Avenue, Garden District (525 4691). Bus 11 Magazine. **Open** 9am-5pm Mon-Fri. **No credit cards. Map** p279 B3.
One of the few of its kind left these days, this shop rejects computer-generated images in favour of classic hand-painted signs that are real works of art. Decide what you want and Eve, the shop's painter, will create it. She is best at lovely, old-fashioned, whimsical signs. Her work is much sought after and is commissioned by businesses worldwide.

Relics

2010 Magazine Street, at Josephine Street, Lower Garden District (524 9190/www.relics neworleans.com). Bus 11 Magazine. **Open** 9am-5pm Mon-Fri. **Credit** AmEx, DC, Disc, MC, V. **Map** p279 B3.
This aptly named store has a wide range of elegant, stylish decorative items, some with local histories. It is fabulous for vintage furniture, textiles, art, estate jewellery and religious articles.

Scriptura

5423 Magazine Street, at Jefferson Avenue, Uptown (897 1555). Bus 11 Magazine. **Open** 10am-5pm Mon-Sat. **Credit** AmEx, MC, V. **Map** p276 C9/10.
This is the place to find sophisticated, high quality paper products from Italy, England and France, including fine stationery, leatherbound journals and exquisite wrapping paper. Venetian glass pens, personalised wax seals made by a local bronze foundry and unusual paper lampshades are just a few of the items available. Scriptura is gift central for your posh friends with literary pretensions.

Big fun at **Big Life Toys & Gifts**. *See p171.*

Branches: 328 Chartres Street, French Quarter (299 1234); Lakeside Shopping Center (*see p152*, 219 1113).

Utopia

5408 Magazine Street, at Jefferson Avenue, Uptown (899 8488). Bus 11 Magazine. **Open** 10am-6pm Mon-Sat; noon-5pm Sun. **Credit** AmEx, DC, Disc, MC, V. **Map** p276 C9/10.
Spend an hour rummaging around this cluttered shop to discover clothing, including simple cotton and linen designs from the family-run Flax label, as well as jewellery, photo frames and a big selection of fanciful painted furniture by talented Texan designer David Marsh.

Music

Musical instruments

International Vintage Guitars of New Orleans

1011 Magazine Street, at Howard Avenue, CBD (524 4557). Bus 11 Magazine. **Open** noon-6pm Mon-Sat. **Credit** AmEx, Disc, MC, V. **Map** p279 C2.
The colours and shapes of the beautiful vintage guitars here mean that simply walking in to this big, noisy shop is a bit of a treat. Local and visiting musicians visit to check out the ever-changing inventory, so while browsing you may run into Eric Clapton or Willy DeVille doing the same thing.

New Orleans Music Exchange

3342 Magazine Street, at Louisiana Avenue, Uptown (891 7670). Bus 11 Magazine. **Open** 10.30am-7.30pm Mon-Sat; 1-5pm Sun. **Credit** AmEx, Disc, MC, V. **Map** p279 A4.
Local musicians flock here to buy, sell and trade every type of instrument under the sun. If you don't see what you're looking for, just ask Jimmy to find it for you and he'll scare it up in a couple of days. The nicest guys in the world run this place, while musicians hang out here, windowshopping and trying out the new equipment as it comes in.

Werlein's

214 Decatur Street, at Iberville Street, French Quarter (883 5080). Bus 3 Vieux Carré, 41 Canal, 55 Elysian Fields, 81 Almonaster, 82 Desire. **Open** 10am-6pm Mon-Sat. **Credit** AmEx, Disc, MC, V. **Map** p282 A3.
Family-owned and operated since 1842, this is a New Orleans institution. The store in the Quarter has steel washboards and squeezeboxes for Cajun and zydeco musicians, while the Metairie superstore covers everything from new and used instruments and sheet music to software and sound systems.
Branch: 3750 Veterans Memorial Boulevard, Metairie (883 5060).

Records, tapes & CDs

Along with those listed here, **Beckham's Book Shop** (*see p158*) is also worth visiting for second-hand classical vinyl.

Borders

3131 Veterans Memorial Boulevard, at N Causeway Boulevard, Metairie (835 1363/www.borders.com). St Charles Streetcar/bus 16 S Claiborne, 39 Tulane, 90 Carrollton, then E5 Causeway. **Open** 9am-11pm Mon-Sat; 9am-9pm Sun. **Credit** AmEx, Disc, MC, V.
The second storey of this chain bookstore has a wide selection of CDs and is especially strong in world music. It's not cheap, though.

Jim Russell Records

1837 Magazine Street, at St Mary Street, Uptown (522 2602). Bus 11 Magazine. **Open** 10am-7pm Mon-Sat; 1-6pm Sun. **Credit** AmEx, MC, V. **Map** p279 B3.
This eccentric shop has an extensive, if curious, collection of old 45s and LPs, including albums by the Neville Brothers and other local musicians. There's also a large selection of rap, soul, R&B, jazz and blues. Jim Russell Sr is a walking music encyclopaedia, especially when it comes to local artists. He's usually around on Sundays; Jim Russell Jr mans the store the rest of the time.

Louisiana Music Factory

210 Decatur Street, at Bienville Street, French Quarter (586 1094/www.louisianamusicfactory.com). Bus 3 Vieux Carré, 41 Canal, 55 Elysian Fields, 81 Almonaster, 82 Desire. **Open** 10am-10pm daily. **Credit** AmEx, Disc, MC, V. **Map** p282 B3.

Art is anything but modern at **Mystic Blue Signs**. *See p171.*

This French Quarter store is widely viewed as the best place in town to find music by local and regional artists. It has extensive jazz and blues selections, along with bountiful bins of music by Cajun, zydeco, R&B and gospel artists. Things are made even easier by its helpful, knowledgeable staff of music lovers. If they haven't heard of it, it probably doesn't exist. Rickety stairs lead vinyl collectors up to an attic paradise full of second-hand LPs. Top local musicians frequently host live weekend performances here to celebrate new releases. The scene is lively, fun and very local.

Magic Bus
527 Conti Street, at Decatur Street, French Quarter (522 0530). Bus 3 Vieux Carré, 55 Elysian Fields, 81 Almonaster, 82 Desire. **Open** 11am-7pm daily. **Credit** AmEx, MC, V. **Map** p282 B3.
The cool British blokes who run this little place offer some 15,000 titles in new and second-hand CDs and some rare vinyl – mainly rock and pop, but with a good local bin and quite a bit of jazz.

Mushroom
1037 Broadway, at Zimple Street, Uptown (866 6065). Bus 22 Broadway. **Open** 10am-midnight daily. **Credit** AmEx, Disc, MC, V. **Map** p276 B8.
This shop just at the edge of Tulane University is as packed with university students as it is with music. Shop here for 'import' (never say 'bootleg') CDs of live performances.

Musica Latina
4714 Magazine Street, at Valmont Street, Uptown (895 4227). Bus 11 Magazine. **Open** 10.30am-7pm Mon-Sat; 3-6pm Sun. **Credit** AmEx, Disc, MC, V. **Map** p276 D10.
If your taste is for Latin sounds, you'll be thrilled with Musica Latina, which stocks mainstream and hard-to-find salsa, merengue, boleros and flamenco.

Peaches
3129 Gentilly Boulevard, at Elysian Fields, Gentilly (282 3322). Bus 55 Elysian Fields. **Open** 10am-9pm Mon-Thur; 10am-10pm Fri, Sat; noon-9pm Sun. **Credit** AmEx, Disc, MC, V.
This is quite simply the best place in town to find the latest rap, soul and gospel recordings.

Rock & Roll Collectibles
1214 Decatur Street, at Governor Nicholls Street, French Quarter (561 5683/www.rockcollectibles.org). Bus 3 Vieux Carré, 48 Esplanade, 55 Elysian Fields, 81 Almonaster, 82 Desire. **Open** 10am-10pm daily. **Credit** AmEx, MC, V. **Map** p282 D3.
This place stocks rock vinyl galore, along with plenty of blues, soul and jazz, including local musicians.

Tower Records
408 N Peters Street, at Conti Street, French Quarter (529 4411/www.towerrecords.com). Bus 3 Vieux Carré, 55 Elysian Fields, 81 Almonaster, 82 Desire. **Open** 9am-midnight daily. **Credit** AmEx, Disc, MC, V. **Map** p282 B3.

The big daddy of music retail, with two floors offering an impressive selection in most categories, including a surprisingly good array of works by local musicians. The video section on the ground floor is pretty thorough, too.

Virgin Megastore

Jackson Brewery, 600 Decatur Street, at the river, French Quarter (671 8100/www.virginmega.com). Bus 3 Vieux Carré, 55 Elysian Fields, 81 Almonaster, 82 Desire. **Open** 10am-midnight daily. **Credit** AmEx, Disc, MC, V. **Map** p282 B3.
Even bigger and better than the other chain monsters in the scope and depth of its selection. If it's not here, it's probably out of print, and you're out of luck.

Pets

Dr Mike's Animal House

1120 N Rampart Street, at Governor Nicholls Street, French Quarter (523 4455). Bus 3 Vieux Carré, 57 Franklin. **Open** 8am-6pm Mon-Fri; 8am-noon Sat. **No credit cards. Map** p282 D1.
Expect to pay $40 for a check-up for your pet and $25 for grooming at this vet's office. They make house calls, too, and staff are the sweetest.

Three Dog Bakery

827 Royal Street, at Dumaine Street, French Quarter (525 2253). Bus 3 Vieux Carré, 55 Elysian Fields, 81 Almonaster, 82 Desire. **Open** 10am-6pm daily. **Credit** AmEx, DC, Disc, MC, V. **Map** p282 C2.
This shop looks like a classic old-fashioned bakery, but the goodies are strictly for the dogs. Infamous among non-dog owners for its animal indulgence factor. They're just dogs, after all.

Photography

New Orleans doesn't have a great selection of camera equipment, so don't hold out hope for a great buy. Camera shops are usually small, with limited stock, and are scattered all over the city. Do not get sucked in by the camera and electronics stores on Canal Street – if you're desperate, get a disposable camera from a drugstore, and buy something from a familiar source when you get home. If your camera needs mending, visit **AAA Camera Repair** (1631 St Charles Avenue, at Terpsichore Street, Lower Garden District, 561 5822).

Shop

Liberty Camera

337 Carondelet Street, at Poydras Street, CBD (523 6252). St Charles Streetcar. **Open** 9am-5.30pm Mon-Fri; 9am-2.30pm Sat. **Credit** AmEx, DC, Disc, MC, V. **Map** p279 B1.
This shop is stuffy but knowledgeable, with the usual brands – Nikon, Pentax, Minolta and Olympus – plus darkroom equipment.

Film processing

Along with the places listed here, one-hour photo processing is available at most drugstores in town, including **Eckerd, Rite Aid** and **Walgreens** (*see p168*).

Fox Photo

220 Baronne Street, at Common Street, CBD (523 4672/www.wolfcamera.com). St Charles Streetcar/ bus 41 Canal. **Open** 8am-5.30pm Mon-Fri. **Credit** AmEx, Disc, MC, V. **Map** p279 B1.
One-hour photo developing within walking distance of the French Quarter. In addition to the usual photo developing/copying services, this branch is one of few places in town other than professional labs to process black-and-white film on the premises.

Sport & fitness

For bicycle and in-line skate shops, *see p223*. Other than that, come on, why fool yourself? Your chances of exercising while you're here are pretty slim. For the truly committed, though, there is **Oshman's Supersports** (5300 Tchoupitoulas Street, Uptown, 895 7791), a large, mainstream sports store with a good price range and a decent sale rack. Just in case you have a swimming costume or jogging shorts emergency while you're here.

Ticket agencies

Ticketmaster (or 'Ticketmonster', as it is occasionally known) sells tickets for all major sporting and entertainment events. Locations are scattered around town (522 5555/ www.ticketmaster. com).

Video rental

The video selection at **Tower Records** is more diverse than at many other chain rental stores, and it has a good stock of foreign titles.

Blockbuster Video

5330 Tchoupitoulas Street, at Valmont Street, Uptown (897 9426). Bus 10 Tchoupitoulas. **Open** 10am-midnight daily. **Credit** AmEx, Disc, MC, V. **Map** p276 C10.
This nationwide chain, with branches all over town, stocks the latest video and DVD releases as well as many of the classics. Check the phone book for its many branch locations.

Video Alternatives

4725 Magazine Street, at Valence Street, Uptown (891 5347). Bus 11 Magazine. **Open** 11am-10pm daily. **Credit** AmEx, Disc, MC, V. **Map** p276 D10.
This little Uptown shop specialises in rentals of obscure, foreign and classic films. It's good for weird, wacky and strange US films, too.

Eat, Drink, Shop

Arts & Entertainment

Festivals & Events	176
Children	182
Film	186
Galleries	190
Gay & Lesbian	197
Music	202
The Performing Arts	215
Sport & Fitness	219

Features

Are you experienced?	179
Jazz Fest	180
Top Ten New Orleans films	189
Encouraging art	191
Hot shops	194
Southern decadence	200
Frenchmen love good music	207
The best local music	209
When the saints go marching in	213
The theatrical alternative	216
From rags to riches	220
Play ball	225

Festivals & Events

You missed Mardi Gras? So what? You're never far from a party in this town.

New Orleans rocks. Year-round, non-stop, all the time. Every imaginable type of festival is on the calendar, from the **Tennessee Williams Festival** to **Jazz Fest** (*see pp180-1*) and from **Southern Decadence** to a **St Patrick's Day** celebration so crazy it puts Boston's to shame – let there be no doubt that this town loves a party. The wonders of strawberries, the beauty of song, the fact that some people are gay, the mere existence of the French Quarter – in New Orleans *anything* is an excuse for a celebration of some sort. So who cares if you didn't make it to Mardi Gras? This town rocks all year long.

ABOUT THE LISTINGS

We've included an address and phone number for each event wherever possible – but some are so loosely organised that there is simply no overarching group to phone. For more information on seasonal events, contact the **New Orleans Convention and Visitors Bureau** (2020 St Charles, 566 5011/1-800 672 6124/www.neworleans cvb.com), or for events that happen outside town, try the **Louisiana Department of Culture, Recreation & Tourism** (1-800 334 8626).

Spring

St Patrick's Day

Date the week of 17 Mar.
St Patrick's Day in New Orleans often feels like Mardi Gras painted green. Like Carnival, the Irish holiday is celebrated with street parties and parades, bead-throwing and general out-of-control frolicking. Parasol's (*see p144*) Irish bar has the most famous get-together. Paddy's Day attracts thousands of dressed-up party-goers to the Irish Channel, where they drink and dance in the street. There's also a raucous parade on the Saturday closest to the 17th; it starts at 1pm at the corner of Magazine and Race streets and heads down Magazine through the Irish Channel. There are bands, floats and dangerous 'throws' – along with beads, riders toss the hefty ingredients of Irish stew to the eager crowds. Potatoes, cabbages and onions fly overhead (and occasionally *into* heads). Molly's at the Market (*see p137*) hosts a party on the Friday night closest to the 17th, with a more subdued walking parade through the Quarter. At both parades, strolling males bestow paper carnations and kisses upon women who fail to run away quickly enough.

St Joseph's Day

Information: American-Italian Renaissance Foundation (522 7294/www.airf.com). **Date** 19 Mar.
Some people might be surprised to learn that New Orleans has a massive Italian-American community, but you'll never doubt it if you've ever been in town on St Joseph's Day. Local Italian heritage is strongly Sicilian, thus the importance of St Joseph, a major figure in Sicilian culture. The historical antecedents are murky, but the local tradition has evolved into the assembly of massive altars of food. The altars, often made of stacked breads and Italian sweets, have become a public phenomenon, moving out of private homes into churches and schools. They're usually on view for the two days before the 19th. One place to see these towering monuments to good eating is Angelo Brocato's ice-cream parlour (*see p130*). There's a parade on the Saturday nearest the 19th, though the route changes annually.

Tennessee Williams New Orleans Literary Festival

Information: 581 1144/www.tennesseewilliams.net. **Date** end Mar.
This four-day festival is the city's biggest literary event, with writers, wannabe writers and hangers-on who spend hundreds of dollars for passes to attend dozens of seminars and readings held around town. It's the city's own Hay-on-Wye, with the inevitable 'N'awlins' flavour. Its hilarious Stella Shouting Contest has earned national attention.

French Quarter Festival

Information: 522 5730/www.frenchquarter festivals.org. **Date** early Apr.
Some regular attendees swear they'd rather get their music fix here than at the much more famous Jazz Fest (see *p180*). And they have a point. The trad jazz, food and atmosphere here are superb, and the Quarter is less crowded and hot than the racetrack. This festival gets more popular every year as more tourists discover that it's good and free.

Crescent City Classic

Information: 861 8686/www.ccc10K.com. **Date** 2nd Sat in Apr.
This 10km (6-mile) marathon wends its way from Jackson Square through the city. World-class runners and casual athletes who train for months relish the challenge. Those with more sense skip the race and head to City Park for the after-party.

Ponchatoula Strawberry Festival

Information: 1-800 542 7520/1-985 542 7520/ www.lastrawberryfestival.com. **Date** 2nd weekend in Apr.

Arts & Entertainment

The **French Quarter Festival** is like Jazz Fest with more bars and less mud. *See p176.*

Yes, a festival in honour of a berry might sound boring, but don't be fooled. You can make Daiquiris out of these babies. And pies. And a surprising array of other edible and drinkable products. Let's put it this way: this festival is enough fun that thousands of New Orleanians make the trek every year to the tiny bayou town of Ponchatoula, 30 minutes north-west of the city, to stuff themselves silly on strawberries, enjoy carnival rides and watch the rural locals do amusingly bucolic things.

Festival International de Louisiane

Information: 1-337 232 8086/www.festivalinter national.com. **Date** last week in Apr.
You haven't lived until you've seen 10,000 Cajuns get together for a party. We're talking all-night dancing, several stages of music, accordions-o-rama, crawfish pie, fillet gumbo… the whole shebang. Held in Lafayette, self-proclaimed capital of Cajun Louisiana (about two hours' drive away; *see pp235-40*), this four-day event features hundreds of dancers, musicians and artisans. Excellent music is guaranteed, as is outrageously good food. Son of a gun, they know how to have big fun on the bayou.

Summer

International Arts Festival

City Park, 1 Palm Drive, Mid-City. Bus 48 Esplanade. Information: 367 1313/ www.international artsfestival.com. **Date** 2nd weekend in June. **Map** p278 D/E2-4.

Much Red Stripe beer is consumed during this three-day celebration of Caribbean culture. Formerly the Reggae Riddums festival, it's changed in name but not in spirit. The reggae never stops pumping, so the people never stop dancing. There are good crafts, cool T-shirts and excellent jerk chicken to be had. This is one of the city's smallest festivals, but everyone has a good time. There are also Latin music and a little R&B, but most big acts are reggae.

Go 4th on the River

Information: New Orleans Convention and Visitors Bureau (566 5011/1-800 672 6124/www.neworleans cvb.com). **Date** 4 July.
Patriotism New Orleans-style is a small but pleasant thing. Independence Day means jazz bands on Bourbon Street, food sold hither and yon, lots of happy tourists – *plus ça change,* really. But it all comes together in the evening, when a massive fireworks display above the river fills the Moonwalk with locals and tourists who *ooh* and *aah* like little kids before trooping back to the bar.

Essence Music Festival

Louisiana Superdome, Sugar Bowl Drive, at Poydras Street, CBD. Bus 16 S Claiborne. Information: New Orleans Convention and Visitors Bureau (566 5011/ 1-800 672 6124); Essence magazine (www.ess ence.com). **Date** early July. **Map** p279 A/B1.
Organised by *Essence,* a slick magazine for African-American women, this festival celebrates black American culture with several days of performances by top-selling international bands before huge

Stars like Bonnie Raitt perform at the **Festival International de Louisiane**. *See p177.*

crowds in the Superdome. Bestselling writers and famous personalities also give talks, and there are panel discussions on political and social issues and book signings by top authors. The event is very popular locally and regionally.

White Linen Night

Information: Contemporary Arts Center (528 3805/ www.cacno.org). **Date** 1st Sat in Aug.
Map p279 C2.

Art for style's sake, you might call this soirée, as artists, those who want to be artists, and those who want to hang out with artists (and those who like a free glass of wine, really) all turn out to celebrate the New Orleans art scene over many glasses of chardonnay at the Contemporary Arts Center (*see p98*) and the surrounding galleries in the Warehouse District. The dress code is a play on Tennessee Williams-style southernness, with everybody in white, especially linen. Bands play, the bars are crowded with people looking even more southern than usual, the night is sultry, and some people even look at the paintings.

Original Southwest Louisiana Zydeco Music Festival

Southern Development Foundation Farm, 457 Zydeco Road, Plaisance, near Opelousas (1-337 942 2392/www.zydeco.org). **Date** Sat before Labour Day (1st Mon in Sept).

About three hours from New Orleans, the little Cajun town of Opelousas is a world unto itself, and during this event that world is ruled by zydeco. For any fan of the genre, this is *the* festival to attend. More than a dozen of the top zydeco bands around take to the

stage at this one-day outdoor extravaganza in front of crowds of more than 15,000. Food booths serve Cajun and Creole dishes, while arts and crafts stalls demonstrate basket-weaving and storytelling. A different, enjoyable and ultra-rural experience.

Southern Decadence

Information: www.southerndecadence.com.
Date weekend before Labour Day (1st Mon in Sept).

One of the city's largest gay events, this festival's Sunday afternoon parade – and we mean the whole afternoon – is a spectacle not to be missed. Some consider it to be basically a French Quarter-wide drag show, but others find the range and attention to detail in the costumes astonishing. All through the weekend, the city's gay bars are in high fever, and the dancing continues until everyone passes out. Decadence has been a bit controversial of late for its full-on nudity, but it remains hugely popular. *See also* **Southern Decadence** *p200.*

Autumn

Words & Music: A Literary Feast in New Orleans

Locations around the city. Information: 586 1609/ www.wordsandmusic.org. **Date** late Sept.

Evolving from the annual birthday party held for William Faulkner in his old home by Faulkner House Books (*see p158*), this small literary festival often involves premieres of new literary and musical works. Well-known writers – local and national – teach classes and take part in informative panels between cocktail parties.

New Orleans Lesbian & Gay Pride Festival

Louis Armstrong Park, between Orleans Avenue & N Rampart Street, Tremé. Bus 57 Franklin. Information: New Orleans Alliance for Pride (943 1999/www.neworleans gaypride.org). **Date** end Sept/early Oct. **Map** p277 F/G6.

A small but constantly expanding celebration of gay life, this event features music by gay-friendly bands, food from gay-friendly restaurants, booze from gay-friendly bars… you get the picture. It's an all-day party, and it's always a blast.

Art for Art's Sake

Information: Contemporary Arts Center, 900 Camp Street, at Howard Avenue (528 3805/ www.cacno.org). **Date** 1st Sat in Oct.

Essentially White Linen Night without the poncey clothes, this event is when all the galleries around town open their doors to wandering crowds of chablis-and-brie hounds. It's one of the biggest art events in town, and a great deal of fun. Free food and drink can be had in the galleries, and bands play in the streets. Focal points are the Warehouse District around the Julia Street/CAC axis and Magazine Street between Antonine and Napoleon.

New Orleans Film & Video Festival

Information: New Orleans Film & Video Society (523 3818/www.neworleansfilmfest.com). **Date** 2nd wk in Oct.

Sundance it ain't, but this festival brings in dozens of independent and documentary films and filmmakers ever year. It's a good chance to see films months before they appear in a cinema near you. You never know who you might see; the leading actors from *Easy Rider* recently attended the event to discuss the film, which was partly filmed here. Held at Canal Place Cinema and around the city.

Halloween

Date 31 Oct and nearest Sat.

New Orleans was made for Halloween. The centre of the action is in the French Quarter, where costumes abound and the bars are packed. For many years, the main party was an annual event at Anne Rice's house called the 'Gathering of the Coven', for which thousands of fans travelled from all over the country. But that ended after her husband, Stan, died several years ago. Rumours always abound that she'll start it up again, but we wouldn't count on it. If you're one of the hopeful ones, keep an eye on her website (www.annerice.com). The largest Halloween event these days is the Julia Street Wharf party and fund-raiser for the local AIDS hospice Lazarus House (www.halloweenneworleans.com). As many as 10,000 people show up every year for this event, one of the biggest in the local gay community. The partying actually stretches out over four days. Costumes are outrageous.

Opening Day at the Fair Grounds

Fair Grounds Racecourse, 1751 Gentilly Boulevard, near Esplanade Avenue, Gentilly (944 5515/ 1-800 262 7983/www.fgno.com). Bus 48 Esplanade. **Tickets** $1-$4. **Date** Thanksgiving Day (4th Thur in Nov). **Map** p278 E/F4/5.

Only in New Orleans is the Thanksgiving holiday, symbolic anniversary of the Pilgrims' first year on the continent, celebrated at a racetrack. Following century-old tradition, the local horse-racing season

Are you experienced?

Seeing Royal Street clogged with party-goers is not an unusual sight in the French Quarter, but if it's late May and they're all wandering around with small, engraved wine glasses, that means it's time for the **New Orleans Wine & Food Experience**.

Originally dreamed up by restaurateurs and tourism types to pull in travellers during the slow summer season, over time the Experience has become a major US wine event. It's spread out over five days in late May, with a jammed schedule of tastings, seminars, dinners and parties. In 2004, it will take place from 26 to 30 May.

The Royal Street Stroll sets the tone for the event: each ticketholder receives an empty wine glass to be filled, over and over again, at dozens of antiques shops, art galleries and boutiques along Royal Street, where winemakers from around the world set up pouring stations. Jazz bands play on the street, turning it into one big party zone.

On subsequent evenings, restaurants pair with wineries for spectacular dinners; the chefs design high-stakes menus and the vintners bring out their more interesting bottles. With more than 250 wineries participating in the festival, more than a little competitiveness can be seen in the showcasing of unusual and impressive wines.

The festival is on the pricey side ($395 for the full event, though partial tickets are available for much less – the Royal Street party is $49) but oenophiles fork out for the chance to preview important new wines and mingle with some of the country's top winemakers. Tickets can be purchased online (www.nowfe.com), by phone (529 9463) or by fax (596 3663).

Jazz Fest

When the New Orleans Jazz & Heritage Festival – better known as Jazz Fest – debuted in 1969 in Armstrong Park, it was so sparsely attended that kids from a nearby school were invited to come help eat the food. These days, a daily turnout of 75,000 is considered disappointing, and 100,000 is common.

For eight days, a who's who of Louisiana musicians and top international acts play on half a dozen stages spread across the Fair Grounds in Mid-City (the festival outgrew its old Congo Square location long ago). The name isn't entirely appropriate – only two of the ten stages are dedicated to jazz – but only purists complain. The variety of roots-related musical offerings keeps everyone else happy.

To locals, Jazz Fest – held on the last weekend in April and the first weekend in May each year – marks the beginning of summer. In 1991, the second weekend was expanded to Thursday to give locals a day without huge tourist crowds. It was so successful that the other Thursday was added in 2003.

The stages have been enlarged recently, and the BellSouth/WWOZ Jazz Tent, the Rhodes Gospel Tent and the Popeye's Blues Tent moved on to the pavement next to the track. The downside of this is that the days when you could sit in the grass or lean against a tree while listening to the biggest bands are over. It's also harder to drift between stages than it used to be.

These days, the Acura Stage is the main one. It accommodates crowds of up to 25,000 (though you won't see a thing if you're more than about 30 rows back). To many, this stage represents the height of commercialisation. Still, with the biggest names playing there, fans set up camp right in front at the start of the day, armed with chairs, blankets and, in extreme cases, flowerbed fencing. Those who come later are forced to stand behind them. And people who go to that kind of effort tend to stay put all day (which seems like a waste with everything else going on so close by).

Jazz Fest is loved almost as much for its food as it is for its bands; restaurants and vendors from all over the region sell their specialities here. Favourites include seafood po-boys, crawfish étoufée, *cochon du lait* (pork sandwiches with gravy) and boudin (mild Cajun sausage with rice). You can also try quail, pheasant and andouille gumbo. Some people claim to buy tickets to Jazz Fest just for the crawfish bread – fresh loaves stuffed with crawfish tails, cheese and spices and then baked. In a word: heaven.

If you come to Jazz Fest, remember that New Orleans is hot, humid and sunny in the spring. Hats, sunscreen and sunglasses are crucial. Sandals or trainers are advisable – but bear in mind that if it rains, the racetrack infield gets muddy, and you don't want horse dung between your toes. And rain, along with

---

opens on Thanksgiving Day, and family groups turn out by the thousands. The mood is festive, the track is beautiful, and a good time is had by all. It beats the hell out of bad television, dry turkey and quarrelling with the family all afternoon.

Winter

Celebration in the Oaks

City Park, 1 Palm Drive, Mid-City (482 4888/ www.neworleanscitypark.com). Canal Streetcar/ bus 48 Esplanade. **Date** Fri after Thanksgiving-1st Sun in Jan. **Map** p 278 D/E2-4.

Bucolic City Park (*see pp92-3*) is transformed into a winter wonderland, with millions of tiny fairy lights draping the big oak trees and swaying out over the bayous, luminous displays afloat on the lagoons, and Christmas music filling the air. It's essentially a drive-through experience, but you can get closer by parking and walking through the Christmas-tree forest or riding the historic Carousel.

Christmas Eve bonfires along the levee

Fires begin in Gramercy and continue upriver to Convent, along US 44. Information: St James Welcome Center, Gramercy (1-800 367 7852/ www.stjamesla.com). **Date** 24 Dec; fires lit 7pm-midnight.

The charming south Louisiana custom of lighting fires along the levees to light the way for Santa Claus's progress has been attributed to the French and the Germans. Whatever its true derivation, residents of the River Parishes (St James, St Charles and St John the Baptist) just outside New Orleans are devoted to the tradition, spending weeks building elaborate structures shaped like castles and animals that they then set ablaze all at once. The atmosphere is festive, and the fires burning along the slow-moving river under the night sky are a beautiful sight. The heaviest concentration of bonfires can be seen in the towns of Gramercy, Lutcher, Vacherie and Convent, about 35 miles up the Mississippi River from New Orleans.

heat and humidity, is a regular feature of Jazz Fest, so plan accordingly. There's precious little cover from sun or rain on the field, so the clubhouse is a godsend. With air-conditioning, seats and clean toilets, the grandstands are a good place to cool off, rest your feet and plan your next move. There are performance areas in the clubhouse, so you can enjoy Jazz Fest even as you recover from it.

Performance schedules are available on the festival website, in programmes sold at the event, and in the daily *Times-Picayune* and the free magazine *OffBeat*, which also has stories about performers and club listings, as does the free weekly newspaper *Gambit*.

New Orleans Jazz & Heritage Festival

Held at Fair Grounds Racecourse, 1751 Gentilly Boulevard, near Esplanade Avenue, Mid-City (information 522 4786/www.no jazzfest.com). Bus 48 Esplanade.
Date last Thur in Apr-1st Sun in May.
Map p278 E/F4/5.

New Year's Eve

In the French Quarter and locations throughout the city. **Date** 31 Dec.
Strangely enough, New Orleans doesn't do New Year's Eve all that well. Perhaps a city used to partying like it's New Year's Eve all year long is bound to see one night of self-conscious merrymaking as anticlimactic. Still, the streets do get packed – this is one of the busiest tourist periods in New Orleans – and there are parties everywhere. A lighted ball is dropped down the side of the Jackson Brewery to signify the waning seconds of the old year (a custom occasionally given a run for its money in the gay section of Bourbon Street with a 'drop the drag queen' ceremony). At midnight, a massive fireworks display lights up the Mississippi River (if the weather cooperates). Despite the lack of local interest, the event has become such a tourist draw that it's now shown on national television, along with festivities in places like New York's Times Square. Get ready for a lot of drunk college students.

Sugar Bowl

Louisiana Superdome, 1500 Sugar Bowl Drive, at Poydras Street, CBD (525 8573/www.nokiasugar bowl.com). Bus 16 S Claiborne. **Date** on or near 1 Jan. **Map** p279 A/B1.
American football season isn't over until the Sugar Bowl is played on New Year's Day. Each year, two of the leading university teams vie for post-season glory at the Supderdome. Fans arrive in the city awash in their respective school colours, and sing their school songs as they stagger through the French Quarter. Tickets to the game are virtually impossible to get for non-students. But you can always join the party on the street.

Mardi Gras

Date 24 Feb 2004, 8 Feb 2005, and 47 days before Easter each year.
And finally – we've saved the best for last – this citywide blowout justifiably calls itself the biggest free party on Earth. We've devoted a chapter to it – a paragraph could never do it justice. *See pp22-8.*

Children

Everyone's a kid in New Orleans.

In New Orleans, the Inner Child rules. This freedom is what gives the city much of its charm, but it creates challenges for parents accustomed to predictable adult behaviours. When you can't depend on the grown-ups around you to act any more mature than your average nine-year-old when it comes to leaping for beads tossed from Mardi Gras floats, things get a little exciting. And the city's notoriously lax liquor laws mean not only that you'll see people enjoying cocktails as they walk down the street, but that you can't depend on clerks to refuse to sell liquor to kids who could pass for 14.

The best way to enjoy New Orleans if you're travelling with children is to communicate to them clearly what the boundaries are and keep them under close supervision. Do that, and you could all have the time of your life here.

Babysitting

Neither the city nor the state impose any rigorous licensing requirements on babysitting, so you'll have to trust your chosen agency. Both of the agencies listed below claim they only employ people aged over 21 with no criminal records and with prior experience. Nevertheless, careful screening of the sitter is advised. Alternatively, some hotels have childminding services or will recommend them. Families generally fare best by either staying together or travelling with other families and sharing childcare duties.

Accent on Children's Arrangements

Information 524 1227/fax 524 1229/www.accent oca.com. **Open** 8.30am-5pm Mon-Fri; on call 24hrs daily. **Cost** varies; call for more information. **Credit** AmEx, MC, V.
A range of services for kids from daycare to city tours, for large groups only (it's geared to events planners) and by prior arrangement.

Dependable Kid Care

Information 486 4001/fax 486 5008/www.depend ablekidcare.com. **Open** 8am-5pm Mon-Fri; on call 24hrs daily. **Cost** from $39 for the first 3 hrs, plus hotel parking (usually $10-$20); call for more information. **Credit** AmEx, MC, V.
This firm will send a babysitter to your hotel or lodging, even if your child is ailing – they'll bring games with them, too. Half- and full-day outings to fun sites can also be arranged.

Eating out

Children should be encouraged to sample New Orleans' justly famous cuisine. It's not all raw oysters and fiery Cajun spices – though many adults are stunned when their kids take with great zeal to oddities such as boiled crawfish and andouille sausage. If the 'Try it, you might like it' approach fails, many restaurants have menus to please all palates. Happily, New Orleans affords plenty of ways for families to get fresh, memorable meals on a budget.

In the French Quarter, sample the fluffy beignets at **Café du Monde** (*see p131*). If your kids won't brave the half-shells at **Acme Oyster House** (*see p114*), they might go for the fried-oyster or shrimp po-boy.

For a more formal occasion, indulge in dinner or weekend brunch at the **Palace Café** (*see p109*). The children's menu isn't bad, but if all else fails, give up and order the white chocolate bread pudding.

In the CBD, **Taqueria Corona** (*see p125*) and **Mother's** (*see p120*) are good bets. The Southwestern food at Taqueria is cheap, fresh and inspired, and the cheese taco is quite child-friendly. Mother's cafeteria line gives finicky eaters a chance to look at all the food before committing to anything.

Uptown, step into the 1950s diner **Camellia Grill** (*see p122*) for the best burgers in the city. At fast, casual **Crabby Jack's** (*see p129*), the fried chicken should please all palates, and the po-boys are inspired.

Entertainment

General

Blaine Kern's Mardi Gras World

233 Newton Street, at Brooklyn Street, Algiers (361 7821/1-800 362 8213/www.mardigras world.com). Bus 108 Algiers Local/Canal Street Ferry, then shuttle bus. **Open** 9.30am-5pm daily (tours every 30min; last tour 4.30pm). **Admission** $13.50; $6.50-$10 concessions; free under-4s. **Credit** AmEx, DC, Disc, MC, V. **Map** p277 H8.
Visit the warehouse where artists work all year round to create the floats for Mardi Gras parades. Exhibits are fantastic, and in the absence of the usual Mardi Gras hubbub, kids can look at the spectacular floats instead of diving under the wheels in search of goodies thrown from them.

Along with scary rides there are warm fuzzies at **Six Flags**. *See p184.*

The hands-on **Aquarium of the Americas**.

IMAX Theatre

For listings, see p68.

The five-storey screen and booming digital sound system combine to help the adult viewer forget that all the films are about animals and the environment. Kids love it, and it's next door to the Aquarium of the Americas (*see below and p68*).

Louisiana Children's Museum

420 Julia Street, between Magazine & Tchoupitoulas streets, Warehouse District (523 1357/www.lcm.org). Bus 3 Vieux Carré, 10 Tchoupitoulas, 11 Magazine. **Open** *9.30am-4.30pm Tue-Sat; noon-4.30pm Sun.* **Admission** $6. **Credit** AmEx, Disc, MC, V. **Map** p279 C2.

The well-conceived interactive exhibits here teach maths and science concepts without preaching. Kids can create their own news broadcasts, encase themselves in giant bubbles and watch the interplay of bones as a skeleton rides a bike. The toddler room is like a very large, locked and padded cell filled with toys and tot-friendly playground equipment. Parents will be bored to tears, however.

Rivertown

Williams Boulevard at the Mississippi River, Kenner (468 7131).

This historic district 20 minutes' drive from downtown New Orleans houses a collection of small museums, many geared towards children. Choices include the Science Complex, which has a planetarium and a high-tech observatory, the Children's Castle, the Louisiana Toy Train Museum, the Louisiana Wildlife Museum and Aquarium, the Mardi Gras Museum and the Saints Hall of Fame.

Six Flags (formerly Jazzland Park)

12301 Lake Forest Boulevard, near the intersection of I-10 and I-510, Eastern New Orleans (253 8100/ www.sixflags.com). **Open** *Spring, autumn* 10am-8pm Sat; 11am-7pm Sun. *Summer* daily; call or check website for hours. **Admission** $32.99; concessions $22.99 (kids under 48in/122cm tall); free under-2s. **Credit** AmEx, MC, V.

The Six Flags chain has taken over the ailing Jazzland and spent tens of millions of dollars on additions and improvements – new shaded spaces are the most welcome. The new Looney Tunes characters and amusements may lack local charm, but they keep children smiling. A live stunt show with fireworks stages a battle between Batman and the Joker and other assorted bad guys. Rides include Catwoman's Whip, a high-speed nausea-inducing spinner; the Jester, which runs entirely backwards; and Batman: The Ride, one of those diabolical ski-lift-style roller coasters that does back flips, hairpin turns, vertical loops, corkscrews and a 'zero heart-line spin' (no thanks). Some Winn-Dixie grocery stores sell tickets at an $11 discount.

Animals & nature

Aquarium of the Americas

For listings, see p68.

The aquarium features several hands-on exhibits and continually runs special events, such as parent/ child sleepovers and mini camps. The Caribbean Reef exhibit, which encases the viewer in a clear tunnel, makes for a dramatic entry into the aquarium.

Audubon Zoo

For listings, see p78.

Some 1,500 animals live in natural habitats on beautifully landscaped grounds in Audubon Park. Good exhibits currently include the Louisiana Swamp Exhibit, Jaguar Jungle, African Savanna, Australian Outback and Asian Domain, but the zoo strives to keep things interesting with regular new and visiting attractions. Up-close and hands-on experiences include the Swamp Nursery and Embraceable Zoo. Wagons and pushchairs can be hired at the entrance.

Global Wildlife Center

26389 Highway 40, Folsom (1-504 624 9453/ www.globalwildlife.com). **Open** *Summer* 9am-4pm daily. *Winter* 9am-3pm daily. Call for check-in times. **Admission** $10; $9 over-65s; $8 2-11s (includes wagon tour). **Credit** Disc, MC, V.

This is about a 75-minute drive from the city and worth every second. A wagon tour takes you round hundreds of acres populated by over 3,000 animals, including giraffes, zebras and antelope. It's enhanced exponentially if you buy plenty of feed for the animals, who'll eat right from your hands.

Audubon Zoo: it's got 'gators and, evidently, dragons. *See p184.*

French Quarter

Although it's most famous for 24-hour adult entertainment, by day the French Quarter is great for kids. On weekends, and most days in fair weather, street performers abound in **Jackson Square** (*see pp64-6*). A walk around its perimeter can occupy hours if you enjoy the mimes, balloon artists, psychics, musicians, tap dancers and portraitists to the full. On the Decatur Street side of the square, **mule-drawn carriages** offer 35-minute tours of the Quarter for about $40 per party (*see p101*).

Climb the steps to the **Moon Walk**, a promenade which overlooks the Mississippi River. From here, you can walk through **Woldenberg Riverfront Park**, where 17 green acres stretch along the water between the French Quarter and Canal Street, offering great views all the way to the excellent **Aquarium of the Americas** and the **IMAX Theatre** (*see p184 for both*).

Musée Conti Wax Museum of Louisiana

For listings, see p59.
The Musée Conti takes the usual tabloid approach to history, with tableaux depicting Napoleon signing away Louisiana while in the bath, frenzied voodoo dancers and slaves being whipped.

New Orleans Historic Pharmacy Museum

For listings, see p66.
This 19th-century apothecary shop has been preserved on its original site. The collection of jars, voodoo powders, gris-gris potions and containers for leeches will appeal to budding scientists, doctors and horror film directors.

Parks & play

Celebration Station

5959 Veterans Memorial Boulevard, at I-10, Metairie (887 7888/www.celebrationstation.com).
Open 10am-11pm Mon-Thur; 10am-midnight Fri, Sat; 11am-10pm Sun. **Admission** free; arcade tokens 25¢; outside games day pass $18.99.
Credit Disc, MC, V.
Video games, pizza, miniature golf, go-karts and batting cages are a few of the fun distractions on offer at this indoor-outdoor amusement centre.

City Park

For listings, see p93.
City Park covers 1,500 lovely acres. Storyland playground, with its nursery rhyme and fairy tale scenes, is great for small children, who can sit in Cinderella's pumpkin coach. Nearby, there are scaled-down rides, a stunning old-fashioned carousel, a miniature train, and canoes and boats for hire.

Film

More people make movies here than watch them.

New Orleans is not a great city in which to see a film, and it's no big secret why. There are so many other things to do here that spending two hours sitting in a cinema can seem like a waste of good drinking time. In a city known for its food, music, architecture and sights, why see a film you can see anywhere? Even the locals feel this way. So there are hardly any cinemas within the city limits. Worse yet, the invasion of the suburban multiplexes has consolidated the cinema scene to the point that there are only three viable non-multiplex places left in town. Uptown, the Prytania is one of the oldest cinemas, and still has only one screen, while Canal Place, in the French Quarter, has a handful of small screens and frequently shows art-house flicks, and Zeitgeist, in a dodgy area at the edge of the Garden District is the artiest of all, showing very arthouse films in a thrown-together cinema with uncomfortable seats. It's very Tribeca, dahhhling. There's also the **IMAX Theatre** (*see p189*), in the French Quarter, with the usual nature films.

New Orleans is really better at making films than showing them. The city has a long history as a film set – and it was particularly popular for filmmaking in the 1990s with *Interview with a Vampire, The Pelican Brief* and *Lolita* all filmed here. But by 2000 it had fallen behind places like Florida and North Carolina, whose political savvy and tax incentives caused Hollywood to turn away from Louisiana, which was seen as greedy and plagued by demanding unions. That is beginning to change, however. The city received a shot in the arm in 2002 when Gary Fleder came here to direct Dustin Hoffman, John Cusack and Rachel Weisz in a $60 million adaptation of John Grisham's *The Runaway Jury*. In 2003, with a renewed commitment to economic development, the state legislature introduced tax incentives that immediately attracted interest from other major filmmakers. Part-time New Orleanian Taylor Hackford (*An Officer and a Gentleman*) came back to town to direct Jamie Foxx in the Ray Charles biopic *Unchain My Heart*. Other, smaller films followed, and filmmaking in New Orleans now appears to be on the upswing.

Unfortunately, there have been grumblings that the tax incentive programme is flawed, and kinks are still being worked out, and there also remains a problem with a local film labour

shortage. Many filmmakers complain that the production pool here is only one-and-a-half crews deep, meaning that if two films are being shot simultaneously, one crew is going to be out of luck. But, for the most part, the city's word of mouth in the film industry is good. New Orleans and the rural areas around it are photogenic – director Marc Forster proved as much when he filmed Billy Bob Thornton and Oscar winner Halle Berry in 2001's *Monster's Ball* in and around the city. In addition, the city's unusual architecture has stood in for Europe in a number of films.

Also growing is the post-production scene here. The most prominent outfit is **Swelltone Labs** (299 0082/www.swelltonelabs.com), which is co-owned by local Larry Blake, who handles all director Steven Soderbergh's sound editing, recording and mixing. The smaller **Storyville Post** (522 2232/www.story-ville.com) specialises in big commercial productions but has handled smaller independent and documentary films.

While the area has yet to produce another major director like Soderbergh (who hails from Baton Rouge), promising indie filmmakers like Glen Pitre (*Belizaire the Cajun, The Scoundrel's Wife*) and Pat Mire (*Dirty Rice*) have shown a flair for making films with a south Louisiana flavour. And keep an eye out for up-and-coming screenwriters-turned-directors like Henry Griffin (*Mutiny*) and Mari Kornhauser (*Zandalee, Housebound*).

Cinemas

With cinemas, as with many other things, New Orleans' present does not live up to its past. Gone the way of the dinosaur are most of the grand movie houses that once graced the city – including Vitascope Hall, the country's first film-only cinema.

A few of the old cinemas are still standing, however, but virtually none of them show films anymore; these include **State Palace** (*see p214*) and the **Orpheum** (*see p216*) downtown. Only the truly magnificent **Saenger Theatre** (*see p216*) at the edge of the French Quarter still shows the occasional film on the big screen. But that's rare, and more's the pity, given its grand architecture. But the cineplex invasion that started in the 1990s, has long since turned into a full-scale filmland

Arts & Entertainment

The Clint Eastwood thriller **Tightrope** was filmed in New Orleans.

occupation, and no one sees any change in the near future. The massive modern cineplexes are all to be found in the suburbs. The popular, expansive AMC Palace chain has set up shop in adjacent Jefferson Parish, about 15 minutes drive from downtown, with two massive cinemas: **AMC Palace 20** and **AMC Palace 12**. Across the river on the West Bank it has another, **AMC Palace 16** (*for all, see p189*).

The last old cinema still showing films on a single screen is the 80-year-old **Prytania Theatre** Uptown. Unfortunately, the cineplex revolution has forced the Prytania to chuck its art-house ways in recent years and focus on mainstream blockbuster fare.

This has put pressure on two smaller venues. **Canal Place Cinema** shows independent, foreign and documentary films on four screens inside The Shops at Canal Place in the French Quarter. Another very different site is **Zeitgeist Multi-Disciplinary Arts Center**, (*for both, see p189*), which helped to launch a kind of mini arts renaissance in its Garden District neighbourhood a couple of years ago. Zeitgeist, a low-budget venue which also hosts

musical performances and shows visual and performance art, has been active in showing politically charged work (*see also p218*).

Film-goers can get listings from the daily newspaper, the *Times-Picayune* (which also features a Friday preview tabloid, *Lagniappe*), and from the free alternative weekly newspaper *Gambit Weekly* which can be found in most coffeeshops and restaurants around town.

The latter is a staunch supporter of October's **New Orleans Film and Video Festival** (523 3818/www.neworleansfilmfest.com), which in recent years has grown exponentially. It's still not a national player, but attendance has surged, and members hope to join forces with the growing production scene to keep the momentum going. NOFF does an excellent job of providing quality indie fare and helpful seminars for aspiring filmmakers over the course of several days (*see p179*).

Finally, local filmmaker Jeremy Campbell has founded a New Orleans chapter of the nationwide **Flicker** film festival network, which sponsors sporadic showings of smaller films throughout the city (www.ten18.org).

The most famous movie that was sort of filmed here: **A Streetcar Named Desire**.

Top ten New Orleans films

Angel Heart (1987)
One of the best New Orleans films, this underrated noir thriller stars a young Mickey Rourke as a private detective working for evil client Robert De Niro and getting some crazy chicken love from Lisa Bonet.

The Big Easy (1987)
This film was bad on so many levels, yet, to this day, few movies have attracted as much attention to the city as this one. The sexual chemistry between crooked Cajun NOPD cop Dennis Quaid and Assistant DA Ellen Barkin is steamy, and New Orleans looks good.

Dead Man Walking (1995)
The true story of Sister Helen Prejean, who lives in New Orleans and counsels death-row inmates, by husband-and-wife team Tim Robbins and Susan Sarandon, with the remarkable Sean Penn as the tormented bad guy about to learn what the title means.

Down By Law (1986)
Jim Jarmusch's New Wave homage to New Orleans features Tom Waits, John Lurie and Roberto Benigni as believable losers.

King Creole (1958)
By far Elvis' best film (even he said as much), with Casablanca's Michael Curtiz directing The King as a singing tough in the French Quarter battling gangster Walter Matthau.

New Orleans (1947)
Well-meaning if pat exploration of the early days of jazz with Louis Armstrong and Billie Holiday (singing the classic 'Do You Know What it Means to Miss New Orleans?').

Panic in the Streets (1950)
Director Elia Kazan's intense first film features health inspector Richard Widmark chasing plague-infected hood Jack Palance (in his big-screen debut) along the wharves of the French Quarter.

Pretty Baby (1977)
Louis Malle's controversial portrait of Storyville and photographer EJ Bellocq includes Brooke Shields' screen debut as a juvenile hooker-in-training, with Susan Sarandon as mum.

A Streetcar Named Desire (1951)
This was almost all shot on a soundstage, but still, Tennessee Williams' classic story features Marlon Brando, Vivien Leigh, Kim Hunter and Karl Malden caught in a web of New Orleans-style lust and mendacity.

Tightrope (1984)
A surprisingly strong early Clint Eastwood performance as a pervy cop forced to call the kettle black while investigating an equally pervy killer on a spree. Geneviève Bujold supplies the bondage equipment.

AMC Palace Theatre 12
Clearview Mall, 4436 Veterans Memorial Boulevard, at Clearview Parkway, Metairie (734 2020/www.amctheatres.com). Tickets $7; $5 concessions. **Credit** MC, V.

AMC Palace Theatre 16
1151 Manhattan Boulevard, Harvey (734 2020/www.amctheatres.com). Tickets $7; $5 concessions. **Credit** MC, V.

AMC Palace Theatre 20
1200 Elmwood Park Boulevard, at Citrus Boulevard, Jefferson (734 2020/www.amctheatres.com). Tickets $7; $5 concessions. **Credit** MC, V.

IMAX Theatre
1 Canal Street, at Audubon Aquarium, French Quarter (581 4629/www.auduboninstitute.org) Riverfront Streetcar, Canal Streetcar/Bus 3 Vieux Carré, 5 Marigny/Bywater, 11 Magazine. Tickets $8; $5-$7 concessions. **Credit** AmEx, MC, V. **Map** p283 B3.

Landmark's Canal Place Cinema
Third floor, The Shops at Canal Place, 333 Canal Street, at North Peters Street, French Quarter (581 5400/www.landmark theatres.com). Canal Streetcar, Bus 3 Vieux Carré, 5 Marigny/Bywater, 11 Magazine. Tickets $7; $5 concessions. **Credit** MC, V. **Map** p282 A3.

Prytania Theatre
5339 Prytania Street, at Leontine Street, Uptown (891 2787/www.theprytania.com). St Charles Streetcar, then walk several blocks. Tickets $6.50; $5.50 concessions. **Credit** MC, V. **Map** p276 C9.

Zeitgeist Multi-Disciplinary Arts Center
1724 Oretha Castle Haley Boulevard, at Felicity Street (525 2767/www.zeitgeistinc.org). St Charles Streetcar/Bus 15 Jackson. Tickets $6; $5 concessions. **No credit cards.**

Arts & Entertainment

Galleries

Believe it or not, this city has an arty side.

When it comes to galleries, New Orleans is unpredictable, especially in the French Quarter, where galleries appear, merge and morph, and where many have changed names or locations over the past few years. Things are more stable in the **Warehouse District**, where many of the city's serious galleries are located, especially along **Julia Street**, the de facto Gallery Row.

As a rule of thumb, the pricier **French Quarter** galleries are found along the 200 to 700 blocks of **Royal Street**, while the more whimsical and affordable – and no less interesting – ones are found on the 800 to 1200 blocks of Royal, as well as along **Chartres Street** and on the numerous cross streets. But this is a city that likes to break the rules, so a rule of thumb is just that.

You might notice that along some stretches of Royal Street there are more galleries than are mentioned here – including some places that proclaim themselves galleries but sell only cigars, ice-cream or T-shirts. Generally, the real galleries look the part, with art carefully arranged along the walls and not mingled in with baseball caps and instant *beignet* mix. This is less of a problem **Uptown**, though on **Magazine Street** antiques shops and even junk stores sometimes declare themselves to be 'galleries'.

For the sake of consistency, most galleries listed here have a track record or pedigree that roughly translates into an established following. Still, feel free to meander, to venture into any place that catches your fancy, for some of the most novel and appealing items are found in those ephemeral unknown places. Remember, art is among the more personal pleasures, a pastime that appeals not only to the eye and mind, but also to the heart. Enjoy.

French Quarter

A Gallery for Fine Photography

241 Chartres Street, at Bienville Street (568 1313/ www.agallery.com). Riverfront Streetcar/bus 3 Vieux Carré, 5 Marigny/Bywater. **Open** 9.30am-6pm Mon-Sat; 10.30am-6pm Sun. **Credit** AmEx, Disc, MC, V. **Map** p282 B2.

This is a world-class emporium of photographic greats of the past and present, from the Wild West of Edward Curtis to the steamy boudoirs of Helmut Newton. Rare 19th-century photographs and hard-to-find books make this gallery a must for serious collectors and photography buffs.

Axelle Fine Arts

709 Royal Street, at St Peter Street (299 1666/ www.axelle.com). Riverfront Streetcar/bus 3 Vieux Carré, 5 Marigny/Bywater. **Open** 10am-6pm daily. **Credit** AmEx, MC, V. **Map** p282 B2.

Based in New York, San Francisco and New Orleans, Axelle specialises in the work of serious contemporary French artists such as Elisabeth Estivalet, Andre Bourrie and Michel Delacroix.

Bassetti Fine Art Photographs

233 Chartres Street, at Bienville Street (529 9811). Riverfront Streetcar/bus 3 Vieux Carré, 5 Marigny/ Bywater. **Open** 11am-5.30pm Tue-Sat. **Credit** AmEx, MC, V. **Map** p282 B2.

This sleek gallery offers fine contemporary photographs by leading American artists, specialising in the Southern imagery of contemporary masters like Keith Carter, Jack Spencer and Shelby Lee Adams.

Bee Galleries

509 Royal Street, at St Louis Street (587 7117/ www.beegalleries.com). Riverfront Streetcar/bus 3 Vieux Carré, 5 Marigny/Bywater. **Open** 10am-6pm daily. **Credit** AmEx, DC, MC, V. **Map** p282 B2.

This gallery keeps some of New Orleans' most popular artists, such as Martin 'the Magician' Laborde, Jim 'Red Cat' Tweedy, Steve Martin and Ray Cole., in the Royal Street spotlight.

Bergen Putman Gallery

730 Royal Street, at Orleans Street (523 7882/ www.bergenputmangallery.com). Riverfront Streetcar/bus 3 Vieux Carré, 5 Marigny/Bywater. **Open** 9am-9pm daily. **Credit** AmEx, Disc, MC, V. **Map** p282 C2.

Collectable poster art including landscapes, French Quarter scenes, Mardi Gras prints and Jazz Fest posters. Probably the largest poster selection in the region: 'over 10,000 items in stock'.

Bryant Galleries

316 Royal Street, between Bienville & Conti streets (525 5584/www.bryantgalleries.com). Riverfront Streetcar/bus 3 Vieux Carré, 5 Marigny/Bywater. **Open** 10am-6pm Mon-Fri; 10am-9pm Sat, Sun. **Credit** AmEx, DC, Disc, MC, V. **Map** p282 B2.

A French Quarter institution, this place features international artists such as Leonardo Nierman, Juan Medina, as well as accomplished local painters such as Alan Flattmann.

Callan Fine Art

240 Chartres Street, at Bienville Street (524 0025/ www.callanfineart.com). Riverfront Streetcar/bus 3 Vieux Carré, 5 Marigny/Bywater. **Open** 10am-5pm daily. **Credit** AmEx, DC, Disc, MC, V. **Map** p282 B2.

Arts & Entertainment

This gallery offers a range of 19th- and early 20th-century European and American paintings and sculpture, including artists of the British Royal Academy as well as examples from the Barbizon and impressionist schools.

Crescent Gallery
628 Toulouse Street, between Royal & Chartres streets (525 5255/www.crescentgallery.net). Riverfront Streetcar/bus 3 Vieux Carré, 5 Marigny/Bywater. **Open** 10am-6pm Mon, Tue, Thur-Sat; 1pm-6pm Sun. **Credit** AmEx, Disc, MC, V. **Map** p282 B2.
The domain of Rolland Golden and other painters working in the realistic, impressionistic and figurative traditions. Golden is a long-standing local painter known for his stylised realism, and the artists around him reflect the same concern for design within formal traditions.

Dixon & Harris
237 Royal Street, at Bienville Street (524 0282/www.dixonandharris.com). Riverfront Streetcar/bus 3 Vieux Carré, 5 Marigny/Bywater. **Open** 9.30am-5.30pm daily. **Credit** AmEx, DC, MC, V. **Map** p282 B2.
Formerly Dixon and Dixon, this Royal Street landmark, primarily a purveyor of antique furnishings, still carries a selection of 18th- and 19th-century paintings amid the rare porcelains, grandfather clocks, antique rugs and estate jewellery.

Elliott Gallery
540 Royal Street, at Toulouse Street (524 8696/www.elliottgallery.com). Riverfront Streetcar/bus 3 Vieux Carré, 5 Marigny/Bywater. **Open** 10am-5.30pm daily. **Credit** AmEx, DC, Disc, MC, V. **Map** p282 B2.
The long-established and locally owned Elliott Gallery exhibits and sells the works of contemporary European artists such as Theo Tobiasse, Max Pappart and James Coignard. Formerly called the Nahan Galleries, it is still operated by the same family at the same location.

Frenchy Gallery
319 Royal Street, between Bienville & Conti streets (561 5885/www.frenchylive.com). Riverfront Streetcar/bus 3 Vieux Carré, 5 Marigny/Bywater. **Open** daily; call for hours. **Credit** AmEx, MC, V. **Map** p282 B2.
The 'performance painter' Randy Leo 'Frenchy' Frenchette is a local artist whose popular works tend to centre on local musicians. His gallery also features similarly themed works by other artists.

Hanson Gallery
229 Royal Street, between Iberville & Bienville streets (524 8211/www.hansongallery-nola.com). Riverfront Streetcar/bus 3 Vieux Carré, 5 Marigny/Bywater. **Open** 10am-6pm Mon-Sat; 11am-5pm Sun. **Credit** AmEx, Disc, MC, V. **Map** p282 A2.
Hanson features light, lively contemporary art in various media, ranging in style from Pop to surreal, and from impressionism to photorealism, including cityscapes, landscapes, figurative and abstract paintings by artists such as LeRoy Neiman, Adrian Deckbar and Peter Max.

Kurt E Schon, Ltd
510 St Louis Street, between Decatur & Chartres streets (524 5462/www.kurteschonltd.com). Riverfront Streetcar/bus 3 Vieux Carré, 5 Marigny/Bywater. **Open** 9am-5pm Mon-Fri; 9am-3pm Sat. **Credit** AmEx, MC, V. **Map** p282 B2.
A longstanding landmark, this gallery is a cornucopia of landscapes and genre works from the 17th through the 20th centuries, including 19th-century academy and salon painters. Knowledgeable staff navigate more than 400 works on six floors.

La Belle Galerie
309 Chartres Street, at Bienville Street (529 5538/www.labellegalerie.com). Riverfront Streetcar/bus 3 Vieux Carré, 5 Marigny/Bywater. **Open** 10am-7pm daily. **Credit** AmEx, DC, Disc, MC, V. **Map** p282 B2.
The paintings and other works of art at La Belle Galerie celebrate the African-American experience. The gallery's Black Art Collection features posters, African artefacts and works devoted to jazz by local and national artists.

Encouraging art

From Edgar Degas on down, artists have almost always slaved in anonymity and poverty in New Orleans. They come here for the creative atmosphere and cheap rents – and then leave to get discovered.

Now, local arts supporters are trying to change all that. Stephen Lanier, director of the ambitious new visual arts complex **Louisiana ArtWorks**, hopes the non-profit 'arts incubator' will enhance collaboration, support and exposure. He believes it will become a national model.

The heart of the $26 million project will be a massive complex containing four large studios. A series of catwalks will allow the public to watch the artists at work below. Visitors will be able to indulge their own artistic leanings in hands-on demonstration areas.

The five-storey facility will also include small, affordable private studios for local artists. These will only occasionally be open to the public, but works made there will be displayed in an on-site gallery.

Louisiana ArtWorks is set to open in March 2004 at the corner of Howard and Carondelet streets downtown, a block from Lee Circle on the St Charles streetcar line. For information call 523 1465 or see www.artscouncilofneworleans.org.

Arts & Entertainment

Martin Lawrence Gallery

*433 Royal Street, between Conti & St Louis streets
(299 9055/www.martinlawrence.com). Riverfront
Streetcar/bus 3 Vieux Carré, 5 Marigny/Bywater.*
Open 10am-6pm daily. **Credit** AmEx, Disc, MC, V.
Map p282 B2.
Specalises in original paintings and drawings,
along with sculptures and graphics by big names
including Picasso, Erté, Chagall, Warhol, Haring,
Lichtenstein, Francis, Kondakova, McKnight,
Hallam, Ricker and Miro.

Michalopoulos

*617 Bienville Street, between Royal & Chartres
streets (558 0505/www.michalopoulos.com).
Riverfront Streetcar/bus 3 Vieux Carré, 5
Marigny/Bywater.* **Open** 10am-6pm Mon-Sat;
11am-6pm Sun. **Credit** AmEx, Disc, MC, V.
Map p282 B2.
Here, the local artist James Michalopoulos presents
his own vision of deliriously levitating, perilously
leaning, helter-skelter New Orleans architecture,
street scenes and portraits, captured in his highly
popular oil paintings and lithographs.

Peligro

*305 Decatur Street, at Bienville Street (581 1706).
Riverfront Streetcar/bus 3 Vieux Carré, 5 Marigny/
Bywater.* **Open** 10am-6pm Mon-Thur; 10am-8pm
Fri, Sat; noon-6pm Sun. **Credit** AmEx, Disc, MC, V.
Map p282 B3.
This classic New Orleans folk art gallery specialises in funky visionary and outsider art by
untrained as well as faux-naïf artists. Emerging
local and international maestros turn up in the mix
as well. Offers a lively collection of folk, outsider
and primitive arts and crafts.

Rodrigue Studios

*721 Royal Street, at Orleans Street (581 4244/
www.georgerodrigue.com). Riverfront Streetcar/
bus 3 Vieux Carré, 5 Marigny/Bywater.*
Open 10am-6pm Mon-Sat; noon-5pm Sun.
Credit AmEx, MC, V. **Map** p282 C2.
This gallery showcases the popular phenomenon
(or mystery, depending on your perspective) that
is the ubiquitous Blue Dog, and other works by
Louisiana artist George Rodrigue. There are oil
paintings, serigraphs and iris prints, ranging in
price from a few hundred for prints up to a few
hundred thousand for some paintings.

Stone and Press Galleries

*238 Chartres Street, between Iberville & Bienville
streets (561 8555/www.stoneandpress.com).
Riverfront Streetcar/bus 3 Vieux Carré, 5
Marigny/Bywater.* **Open** Sept-June 10am-6pm
daily. *July, Aug* 10am-6pm Mon-Sat. **Credit**
AmEx, Disc, MC, V. **Map** p282 A2.
Stone and Press Galleries feature works on paper
in various media. The etchings, lithographs, wood
engravings and mezzotints include works by some
of the best-known names among American,
European and Louisiana printmakers.

Vincent Mann Gallery

*713 Bienville Street, at Royal Street (523 2342).
Riverfront Streetcar/bus 3 Vieux Carré, 5
Marigny/Bywater.* **Open** 10am-5pm Mon-Sat.
Credit AmEx, MC, V. **Map** p282 B2.
One of the older French Quarter galleries, this place
features serene, colourful works by 19th- and 20th-
century impressionists and post-impressionists.

Windsor Fine Art

*313 Royal Street, at Bienville Street (586 0202/
www.windsorfineart.com). Riverfront Streetcar/
bus 3 Vieux Carré, 5 Marigny/Bywater.* **Open**
10am-6pm Mon, Tue, Sun; 9am-9pm Wed-Sat.
Credit AmEx, MC, V. **Map** p282 B2.
Three floors of paintings, works on paper, glass-
works, limited-edition graphics and sculpture by a
mixture of popular contemporary artists such as
Royo and Alexandra Nechita as well as masters
including Rembrandt, Picasso, Chagall and Renoir.

Warehouse District

Ariodante Contemporary Craft Gallery

*535 Julia Street, between Camp & Magazine streets
(524 3233). St Charles Streetcar/bus 11 Magazine.*
Open 11am-5pm Mon-Sat. **Credit** AmEx, MC, V.
Map p279 C2.
Specialising in the useful arts and artful crafts,
Ariodante has a light, decorous touch, fair to the eye
yet not too heavy on the wallet, all located in a nice-
ly appointed jewellery box of a space.

Arthur Roger Gallery

*432 Julia Street, between Constance & Magazine
streets (522 1999/www.arthurrogergallery.com).
St Charles Streetcar/bus 11 Magazine.* **Open** 10am-
5pm Mon-Sat. **Credit** AmEx, MC, V. **Map** p279 C2.
One of the best-known and arguably the leading
local gallery for contemporary art by regionally and
nationally known artists ranging from Lin Emery,
Jacqueline Bishop and Willie Birch to edgy film
director John Waters. Check out the back room,
where works by many gallery artists are on display.

d.o.c.s. Gallery

*709 Camp Street, at Girod Street (524 3936/
www.docsgallery.com). St Charles Streetcar/
bus 11 Magazine.* **Open** 11am-6pm Tue-Sat;
by appointment at other times. **Credit** AmEx,
MC, V. **Map** p279 C1.
Gallery director Richard Nesbitt keeps a sharp eye
out for the lesser-known artists he hopes will emerge
into art-world prominence much in the way that a
butterfly emerges from its cocoon. A neatly compact
space, slightly off the beaten path but worth watching for the surprises it may offer.

George Schmidt Gallery

*626 Julia Street, between Camp Street & St Charles
Avenue (592 0206/www.georgeschmidt.com).
St Charles Streetcar.* **Open** 12.30-4.30pm
Tue-Sat. **Credit** MC, V. **Map** p279 B2.

Face up to contemporary art at the
Arthur Roger Gallery. *See p192.*

Works by George Schmidt, whose bailiwick is 'history painting, narrative art and other reactionary work', are showcased in this space. Ranging from small monotypes to mural-size depictions of the more momentous – or at least colourful – occurrences in local history, Schmidt's lively canvases are feats of visual storytelling.

Heriard-Cimino Gallery
440 Julia Street, between Constance and Magazine streets (525 7300/www.heriard-cimino.com). St Charles Streetcar/bus 11 Magazine. **Open** 10.30am-5.30pm Tue-Fri; 10am-5pm Sat. **Credit** AmEx, Disc, MC, V. **Map** p279 C2.
The Heriard-Cimino Gallery is known for sparse, typically minimalist and often abstract paintings and sculpture, with an occasional foray into expressionism or even surrealism, all rendered with a strong sense of colour, space and humour by local and national artists.

John Stinson Fine Arts
900 S Peters Street, at St Joseph Street (566 1944/ www.johnstinsonfinearts.com). Bus 10 Tchoupitoulas. **Open** 10am-7pm Mon-Fri; noon-5pm Sat. **Credit** AmEx, MC, V. **Map** p279 C2.
Reflecting the eclectic and unpredictable tastes of its antiques-appraiser namesake, this gallery bounces from the vintage to the contemporary and then back again with unusual dexterity. Cutting-edge photographs of nude New Yorkers alternate with 19th-century French still lifes and landscapes.

Jonathan Ferrara Gallery
841 Carondelet Street, between St Joseph & Julia streets (522 5471/www.jonathanferraragallery.com). St Charles Streetcar. **Open** noon-6pm Tue-Sat; by appointment at other times. **Credit** AmEx, MC, V. **Map** p279 B2.

This is no locals gallery – Jonathan Ferrara Gallery features works by an eclectic stable of painters, sculptors and glass artists from all over the world. You might well find works from the Havana arts underground sharing wall space with paintings by New Orleans university instructors. It's a good idea to expect the unexpected here.

LeMieux Gallery
332 Julia Street, at Tchoupitoulas Street (522 5988/www.lemieuxgallery.com). Bus 10 Tchoupitoulas. **Open** 10am-6pm Mon-Sat. **Credit** AmEx, MC, V. **Map** p279 C2.
LeMieux showcases 'Third Coast art' – work by artists based on the Gulf Coast, from Louisiana to Florida. Works here range from surreal urban landscapes to elegant floral still lifes. The gallery also offers works by Paul Ninas, an early New Orleans modernist famed for his impressions of the Caribbean and French Quarter of yore.

Marguerite Oestreicher Fine Arts
720 Julia Street, at St Charles Avenue (581 9253). St Charles Streetcar. **Open** 10am-5pm Tue-Sat; by appointment at other times. **Credit** AmEx, MC, V. **Map** p279 B2.
Marguerite Oestreicher Fine Arts is housed in what is perhaps the most unusual gallery space in the Warehouse District – the former carriage house of a large, but long-demolished, mansion. Inside, you'll find distinctively humanist and finely crafted paintings, prints and sculptures from around the world.

Soren Christensen Gallery
400 Julia Street, at Constance Street (569 9501/ www.sorengallery.com). St Charles Streetcar/ bus 11 Magazine. **Open** 10am-5.30pm Tue-Fri; 11am-5pm Sat; by appointment Mon, Sun. **Credit** AmEx, MC, V. **Map** p279 C2.

Hot shops

Two of New Orleans' signature qualities –
intense heat and wild creativity – have
found visual expression in a thriving art
glass movement which has swept the city
in the past decade. Glass-making studios
– or 'hot shops', as they're called in the
vernacular – stud the city's artscape, from
the Warehouse District to hidden corners
of residential neighbourhoods.

How this came about is a chicken-and-egg
question. Instructor Gene Koss at Tulane
University regularly nurtures new glass
artists, and the plethora of art glass present
in the city attracts glassworkers and buyers
from around the world.

New Orleans' glassblowers work in the
European tradition, inflating glass on the
tips of blowing rods, while glass casters
ladle the molten material directly into carved
carbon moulds. Using these methods, artists
create all manner of objects, from huge and
elaborate sculptures to chandeliers and
wacky neon creatures.

If you want to learn more about the making
of glass art – or even take a lesson in doing
it yourself – there are plenty of places in New
Orleans willing to help. You can take classes,
observe the pros in the act or just buy the
fruits of their overheated labour.

Lighthouse Glass Gallery

*742 Camp Street, at Julia Street, CBD (529
4494). Bus 11 Magazine.* **Open** noon-6pm
Mon-Sat. **Credit** AmEx, MC, V. **Map** p279 C2.
In a Warehouse District building shaped like
a lighthouse, Martha Robbins' eclectic gallery
features fine contemporary glass, paintings
and sculpture by local and national artists,
with an emphasis on everyday art for the
home. Call first to make sure it's open.

Mercury Injection

*727 Louisa Street, at Dauphine Street,
Bywater (723 6397). Bus 5 Marigny/
Bywater.* **Open** By appointment or chance.
No credit cards.
Glass artist Michael Cain creates neon flights
of fancy in his Bywater atelier, where bizarrely
shaped, stylised light sculptures form glowing
multicoloured forests. He's also branched out
recently into traditional glass techniques,
painting and sculpture.

New Orleans School of GlassWorks & Printmaking

*727 Magazine Street, at Julia Street (529
7277/www.neworleansglassworks.com).
Bus 11 Magazine.* **Open** 10am-5pm Mon-Sat.
Credit Disc, MC, V. **Map** p279 C2.

This is the only glass shop in town offering public classes (sign up in person or by phone). It also allows spectators in its air-conditioned hot shop. Staff also teach metalwork and lamp-making and exhibit stylish, ornate creations in a gallery, which also hosts shows by visiting artists.

Nuance Gallery

728 Dublin Street, at Maple Street, Riverbend (865 8466). St Charles Streetcar/bus 34 Carrollton Express. **Open** 10.30am-5pm Wed-Sat. **Credit** AmEx, Disc, MC, V. **Map** p276 A8.
Glassblower Arden Stuart hosts an exciting array of Louisiana crafts artists at her gallery, which displays pottery, clothing and woodwork. A visit here could accompany a streetcar journey and a walk in Audubon Park (*see p78*).

Rosetree Glass Studio and Gallery

446 Vallette Street, at Eliza Street, Algiers (366 3602/www.rosetreeglass.com). Canal Street ferry, then 15min walk/bus 101 Algiers Loop. **Open** 9am-5pm Mon-Fri; 10am-3pm Sat. **Credit** MC, V.
Make an outing of a visit here by taking the free ferry to Algiers and walking the last seven blocks through historic Algiers Point. Mark Rosenbaum won awards for renovating a cinema into this gallery for Italian-style blown glass. The studio makes items like perfume bottles, paperweights and bowls ($15-$800); the gallery exhibits unique pieces and lighting.

Studio Inferno

3000 Royal Street, at Montegut Street, Bywater (945 1878). Bus 5 Marigny/ Bywater. **Open** 9am-5pm Mon-Fri; 10am-5pm Sat. **Credit** AmEx, MC, V. **Map** p277 H6.
This historic warehouse, painted fiery orange and red, houses two open studios. Downstairs is one of the city's few cast glass shops; upstairs, glassblowers put final touches to their airy creations. After the hot shops, you can cool down in the air-conditioned gallery (pictured) and see the unique cast-glass *milagros* (good luck charms), colourful vases and inventive Martini glasses. The labyrinthine structure also houses artists working in other media.

A notable newcomer in the Warehouse District, the design- and decor-oriented Soren Christensen Gallery focuses on contemporary painting, sculpture and photography.

Stan Rice Gallery

861 Carondelet Street, between St Joseph & Julia streets (586 9495/www.stanrice.com). St Charles Streetcar. **Open** 11am-4pm Wed-Sun. **Credit** AmEx, MC, V. **Map** p279 B2.
Poet and painter Stan Rice, the late husband of novelist Anne Rice, strived for vividness in all things. He never sold his paintings, though he occasionally gave them away, and this gallery is his legacy.

Stella Jones Gallery

201 St Charles Avenue, between Gravier & Common streets (568 9050/www.stellajonesgallery.com). St Charles Streetcar. **Open** 11am-6pm Mon-Fri; noon-6pm Sat; by appointment Sun. **Credit** AmEx, DC, Disc, MC, V. **Map** p279 C1.
Located just outside the Warehouse District in the lobby of a tall office block, Stella Jones is one of America's leading purveyors of contemporary and vintage African-American art. The gallery has a sense of history and a mission to educate.

Steve Martin Studio

624 Julia Street, between Camp Street & St Charles Avenue (566 1390/www.stevemartinstudio.com). St Charles Streetcar. **Open** noon-5pm Tue-Sat; by appointment at other times. **Credit** AmEx, MC, V. **Map** p279 B/C2.
This gallery, in a classic townhouse, features lively contemporary works by regional and national artists – including proprietor Steve Martin's elaborate linear extrapolations in paint, pigment and wire.

Sylvia Schmidt Gallery

400A Julia Street, at Tchoupitoulas Street (522 2000). St Charles Streetcar/bus 11 Magazine. **Open** 11am-4.30pm Tue-Sat; by appointment Mon, Sun. **Credit** AmEx, MC, V. **Map** p279 C2.
Contemporary painters and sculptors, including modern masters such as Robert Warrens and Robert Hausey, are featured here. The emphasis is on wry, surreal imagism as well as realism and figurative work with a whimsical touch.

Uptown

Academy Gallery

5256 Magazine Street, at Valmont Street (899 8111/www.nofa.com). Bus 11 Magazine. **Open** 9am-4pm Mon-Fri; 10am-4pm Sat. **No credit cards. Map** p276 C10.
The Academy Gallery belongs to the New Orleans Academy of Fine Arts – the Uptown bastion of European academic art traditions – and it lives up

Arts & Entertainment

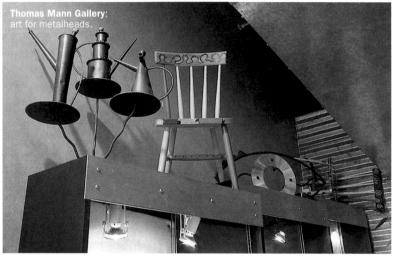

Thomas Mann Gallery: art for metalheads.

to its name. Realism in the vein of founder Auseklis Ozols is featured, along with works by accomplished local and national artists.

Anton Haardt Gallery

2858 Magazine Street, at 6th Street (891 9080/ www.antonart.com). Bus 11 Magazine. **Open** 11am-5pm Tue-Sat. **Credit** AmEx, Disc, MC, V. **Map** p277 E9.

Southern folk and outsider art are the house specialities here. Offerings range from the primordial Louisiana mysteries of David Butler to the zany metaphysics of Georgia's Reverend Howard Finster.

Barrister's Gallery

1724 Oretha Castle Haley Boulevard, at Felicity Street (525 2767/www.barristersgallery.com). St Charles Streetcar/bus 15 Jackson. **Open** 10.30am-5pm Tue-Sat. **Credit** AmEx, MC, V. **Map** p277 F8.

Long known for showing funky folk, outsider and tribal art, Barrister's – now housed in a former Central City supermarket – also exhibits contemporary art by a mixture of alternative and established artists, including some whose work might not be shown elsewhere. Always colourful; a gallery for the adventuresome.

Carol Robinson Gallery

840 Napoleon Avenue, at Magazine Street (895 6130/www.carolrobinsongallery.com). Bus 11 Magazine, 24 Napoleon. **Open** 10am-5.30pm Tue-Fri; 10am-5pm Sat. **Credit** AmEx, MC, V. **Map** p276 D10.

Located in a late-19th-century two-storey house, this gallery features works in all media, with an emphasis on Southern contemporary artists. Included are high-intensity figurative paintings by Jere Allen and Masahiro Arai's meditations on light and shadow.

Cole Pratt Gallery

3800 Magazine Street, at Peniston Street (891 6789/www.coleprattgallery.com). Bus 11 Magazine. **Open** 10am-5pm Tue-Sat. **Credit** AmEx, Disc, MC, V. **Map** p276 D9.

This gallery offers work by local and national contemporary artists. It's known for decorous elegance in works of figurative realism and designer abstraction, and for its pleasantly informal atmosphere.

Gallery I/O/Thomas Mann Gallery

1812 Magazine Street, between Felicity & St Mary streets (581 2113/www.thomasmann.com). Bus 11 Magazine. **Open** 11am-6pm Mon-Sat. **Credit** AmEx, MC, V. **Map** p277 F9.

Gallery I/O and the adjacent Thomas Mann Gallery showcase the work of numerous well-known metal artists, including, of course, Mann himself, as well as a variety of unusual items for the home.

Lionel Milton Gallery

1818 Magazine Street, between Felicity & St Mary streets (522 6966/www.lionelmiltongallery.com). Bus 11 Magazine. **Open** 11am-6pm Tue-Sat. **Credit** AmEx, MC, V. **Map** p277 F9.

Milton, of MTV fame, mixes a cartoon and graffiti approach to vibrantly coloured paintings of New Orleans scenes in this Lower Garden District gallery.

Poet's Gallery

3113 Magazine Street, between 8th & Harmony streets (899 4100). Bus 11 Magazine. **Open** 11am-6pm Mon-Sat. **Credit** AmEx, Disc, MC, V. **Map** p277 E9.

This small, colourful alternative space is a favourite venue for trendy underground artists doing unusual, provocative and typically affordable work. While it is very unlikely that you'll have heard of them yet, the emerging artists showcased here, along with those at Barrister's (*see above*) are ones to watch.

Gay & Lesbian

With parties, bars and shopping galore, you'll have a gay old time.

In most cities in the conservative South, the gay scene keeps a low profile. Not in New Orleans. In this town, The Love That Dare Not Speak Its Name practically shouts it from the wrought-iron balconies. Rather than try to be inconspicuous, bars hang out rainbow flags and open their doors to the street; same-sex couples walk hand in hand through the French Quarter and nobody raises an eyebrow. Maybe it's the European influence, or the city's historic role as a port of entry for foreign products and attitudes. More likely, it's simply that New Orleans' general tolerance for unconventional behaviour extends to homosexuality as it does to just about everything else.

That's not to say that the Crescent City has always been blissfully free of bigotry. Queers of a certain age can tell stories of mass arrests at gay Mardi Gras balls in the 1960s, and police have been known to launch raids on a handful of 'back room' bars. Verbal attacks on gay men, lesbians and the transgendered do occasionally happen; physical attacks are less common, but they, too, occur. Recently, a right-wing backlash against **Southern Decadence** attempted to fan the flames of anti-gay sentiment (*see p200*).

Still, gay men and lesbians enjoy protections here that are relatively rare in other Southern cities. In 1991, the New Orleans City Council passed an ordinance banning discrimination based on sexual orientation; six years later, spousal benefits for city employees were extended to same-sex partners. Although the gay community here is not as politically active or organised as those in some other US cities, its numbers are too great for local elected officials to ignore – as are the economic benefits that gay travellers bring.

And in New Orleans, those travellers will find some of the best gay clubs anywhere. Proximity encourages mixing; sidle up to any given bar and you're likely to end up sharing drinks with a businessman, a waiter and the odd drag queen. And though the city has its share of muscle queens and trendoids, the attitude level tends to be low. Southerners in general are friendly and sociable, and the gay community combines that natural gregariousness with irony and a measure of camp – evident in the gay Mardi Gras balls and celebrations like Southern Decadence and the Gay Easter Parade.

INFORMATION

Several free publications provide extensive bar listings, maps and information about special events all along the gay Gulf Coast. The tabloid *Ambush* is the oldest and fattest. *The Whiz* has a good bar map along with the occasional theatre review. *Eclipse* is a cheeky glossy with event calendars and escort ads. A monthly magazine for lesbians, *Sisterhood,* has recently been launched as well. All can be found in gay bars and in the shops listed in this section, as well as in mainstream coffeeshops in the Quarter.

Faubourg Marigny Book Store (600 Frenchmen Street, at Chartres Street; 948 9845) is one of the country's oldest gay and lesbian bookshops.

Bars & clubs

New Orleans' peculiar drinking laws, which allow patrons to carry alcoholic beverages on the street, encourage a lot of bar-hopping. Fortunately, the city's most popular gay bars (several of which literally never close) are all within easy walking distance of each other, with the heaviest concentration along St Ann and Bourbon streets (a stretch local wags have dubbed the 'Fruit Loop'). There are a few neighbourhood bars scattered elsewhere in the Quarter and along Rampart Street, and a number in the Faubourg Marigny.

Although women will feel welcome at all but the most testosterone-fuelled places, only one lesbian bar proper, **Kim's 940**, is located near the French Quarter (*see p199*). Otherwise, it's a trip to the suburbs, unfortunately.

French Quarter

Bourbon Pub & Parade Dance Club

801 Bourbon Street, at St Ann Street (529 2107/ www.bourbonclub.com). Bus 3 Vieux Carré, 48 Esplanade. **Open** *Pub* 24hrs daily. *Dance club* from 10pm Mon-Sat; from 4pm Sun. **Admission** *Parade* $5-$10. **No credit cards. Map** p282 C2.

Happy hour at this ultrapopular pub often spills out into the street. Nights feature muscled-up go-go boys on the bar in various stages of undress, music videos on big screens and a state-of-the-art sound system blasting everyone's favourite screaming diva hits. Cover includes admission to the upstairs dance club and legendary wraparound balcony.

Café Lafitte in Exile

901 Bourbon Street, at Dumaine Street (522 8397/www.lafittes.com). Bus 3 Vieux Carré, 48 Esplanade. **Open** 24hrs daily. **No credit cards. Map** p282 C2.

Friendly and unpretentious, Lafitte's (not to be confused with the largely straight Jean Lafitte's Blacksmith Shop up the street) draws a mostly male crowd in their 30s and 40s. The upstairs lounge is a little quieter, with a pool table and cruisey balcony. Sunday afternoon happy hour is a big draw, as rowdy patrons toss napkins into the ceiling fans to the strains of vintage disco.

Corner Pocket

940 St Louis Street, at Burgundy Street (568 9829/www.cornerpocket.net). Bus 3 Vieux Carré. **Open** 24hrs daily. **Admission** $3 Mon, Fri, Sat; free Tue-Thur, Sun. **No credit cards. Map** p282 B1.

Hats off (and just about everything else, too) to the Corner Pocket for allowing the skinny, tattooed youth of New Orleans an opportunity to express itself artistically through interpretive dance. Patrons of the art show their appreciation by stuffing dollars into G-strings – a perfect, symbiotic relationship. When it's crowded – usually on weekend nights – few places offer as much sleazy fun.

Golden Lantern

1239 Royal Street, at Barracks Street (529 2860/ www.goldenlantern.com). Bus 3 Vieux Carré. **Open** 24hrs daily. **Admission** free. **No credit cards. Map** p282 D2.

One of the Quarter's last 'neighbourhood' gay bars, the Lantern – ground zero for Southern Decadence (*see p201*) – was once known as one of the city's wildest bars. Now, like many of its patrons, it's seen better days. But the drinks are strong, the bartender makes you feel like a regular, and it's one of the few gay bars where you can hear music that didn't come off an assembly line. There's an ATM on-site.

Good Friends Bar

740 Dauphine Street, at St Ann Street (566 7191/ www.goodfriendsbar.com). Bus 3 Vieux Carré, 48 Esplanade. **Open** 24hrs daily. **Credit** MC, V. **Map** p282 C1.

An air of gentility and a relatively low music volume encourage conversation at this laid-back spot. The downstairs bar attracts a diverse crowd – young and old, men and women – while the upstairs pub, open Thur-Sun, features good Martinis and a Sunday afternoon piano sing-along.

Oz

800 Bourbon Street, at St Ann Street (593 9491/ www.ozneworleans.com). Bus 3 Vieux Carré, 48 Esplanade. **Open** 24hrs daily. **Admission** $3-$5 Fri, Sat and during shows. **No credit cards. Map** p282 C3.

'This is a gay bar', proclaims a sign at the entrance to this popular dance club, reminding straight kids and tourists to be nice if they want to party with the pretty boys (and girls). Oz is about high-energy techno played at ear-splitting volume, plus beefy bar dancers and weekly events like drag bingo and talent contests. It really gets cooking late and sometimes doesn't let up until daybreak. Many a relationship has been forgotten here.

Rawhide 2010

740 Burgundy Street, at St Ann Street (525 8106/ www.rawhide2010.com). Bus 3 Vieux Carré, 48 Esplanade. **Open** 24hrs daily. **Admission** varies. **No credit cards. Map** p282 C1.

A mechanic-shop theme and pulsating techno draw the leather-and-Levis crowd to Rawhide. Things used to get hot and heavy in the club's darker recesses, and although the scene appears to have calmed down considerably, it's still a cruisey place with friendly bartenders and lots of locals.

Rampart Street

Despite repeated predictions of an eminent 'Renaissance on Rampart', the French Quarter's Northern boundary still remains mostly seedy and can be a little scary at night. Of course, that makes the handful of gay bars here just that much more interesting. Use caution, though, especially late at night, and don't walk around here alone.

Ninth Circle at Congo Square

700 N Rampart Street, at St Peter Street (524 7654/www.9thcircleatcongo square.com). Bus 5 Marigny/Bywater, 88, 89 St Claude. **Open** 24hrs daily. **Admission** free. **No credit cards. Map** p282 B1.

Craving a cocktail at breakfast? You could seek help, or give in and head to the 4-to-8am happy hour at funky Ninth Circle. A popular gathering place for local nightcrawlers. Has an on-site ATM.

The Seventh Circle

820 N Rampart Street, at St Ann Street (523 6588). Bus 5 Marigny/Bywater, 88, 89 St Claude. **Open** 11am-2am daily. **Admission** free. **No credit cards. Map** p282 C1.

High ceilings make this little place feel much bigger than it is and offer plenty of headroom for the uninhibited male dancers who grace the bar at weekends.

VooDoo at Congo Square

718 N Rampart Street, at Orleans Street (527 0703). Bus 5 Marigny/Bywater, 88, 89 St Claude. **Open** 24hrs daily. **Admission** free. **No credit cards. Map** p282 C1.

This small but colourful bar draws an almost exclusively local crowd. It's a laid-back and friendly place to meet the locals. It has its own ATM.

Faubourg Marigny & Bywater

Several gay bars cater to the Faubourg Marigny and Bywater neighbourhoods; a few – including downtown's only lesbian bar, **Kim's 940** (*see* *below*) – may interest out-of-towners. Note that the streets around here can be confusing and some are just a bit too dangerous for our liking after dark, so take a taxi.

Cowpokes
2240 St Claude Avenue, at Marigny Street (947 0505/www.cowpokesno.com). Bus 5 Marigny/Bywater, 88, 89 St Claude. **Open** 4pm-2am daily. **Admission** varies. **Credit** MC, V. **Map** p277 H6.
Kick up your boot heels at country-themed Cowpokes, which offers free line-dancing lessons on Tuesdays and women's nights on Thursdays. It also hosts comedy shows and theatrical productions; call for the schedule or check one of the bar mags.

The Phoenix & The Eagle
941 Elysian Fields Avenue, at N Rampart Street (945 9264/www.phoenixbar.com). Bus 5 Marigny/Bywater, 55 Elysian Fields, 88 St Claude. **Open** *Phoenix* 24hrs daily. *The Eagle* from 9pm Tue-Sun. **Admission** free. **No credit cards**. **Map** p277 G6.
It might be the headquarters of the hardcore leather crowd, but with weekly bring-your-own-meat barbecues and special events like the annual Easter bonnet contest, the Phoenix is less intimidating than one might expect. The second-storey Eagle, however, is strictly for the adventurous.

Women's bars

Kim's 940
940 Elysian Fields Avenue, at N Rampart Street, Marigny (944 4888/www.kims940.com). Bus 5 Marigny/Bywater, 55 Elysian Fields, 88, 89 St Claude. **Open** from 5pm Tue-Thur; from 8pm Fri-Sun. **Admission** free; shows $5. **Credit** MC, V. **Map** p277 G6.
With a dancefloor and DJ along with weekly karaoke and once-a-month drag king shows, Kim's is a cheeky place that takes gay men's bars on at their own game. Men are welcome at both the downstairs bar and the upstairs guesthouse.

Rainbow's Lounge
3536 18th Street, at N Arnoult Street, Metairie (454 3200/www.rainbowslounge.com). **Open** from 8pm Thur-Sun. **Admission** free Thur, Sun; $5 Fri, Sat. **Credit** AmEx, MC, V.
It's a darn shame when you find yourself going out to the 'burbs to find a lesbian bar, but that's how it is. The girls shake it, along with more than a few guys, at this cheerful, laid-back joint. Boiled crawfish and beer are served on Sundays during mudbug season.

Saunas & gyms

The Club New Orleans
515 Toulouse Street, between Decatur & Chartres streets, French Quarter (581 2402/www.the-clubs.com). Bus 3 Vieux Carré. **Open** 24hrs daily.

Just **Good Friends**... *See p198.*

Admission $8 8-hour pass; $13-$18 lockers and changing rooms; discounts Tue-Thur. **Credit** MC, V. **Map** p282 B 2/3.
A 24-hour men-only spa with gym equipment, video rooms and a handy rooftop sundeck.

Flex
700 Baronne Street, at Girod Street, CBD (598 3539/www.flexbaths.com). St Charles or Canal Streetcar. **Open** 24hrs daily. **Admission** $5-$10. **Credit** AmEx, MC, V. **Map** p279 B1.
Fitness equipment, sauna, steam and some serious cruising – not necessarily in that order – are the centres of attention at this place in the CBD.

Swimming

The Country Club
634 Louisa Street, at Royal Street, Bywater (945 0742/www.countryclubneworleans.com). Bus 5 Marigny/Bywater. **Open** 11am-1am Mon-Thur; 10am-1am Fri-Sun. **Admission** $8 Mon-Thur; $10 Fri-Sun; $5 after 5pm daily. **Shows** $10-$20. **Credit** AmEx, Disc, MC, V.
Sun worshippers can bare it all at this popular, coed, clothing-optional Bywater institution. The large pool helps you beat the New Orleans heat, and the club hosts frequent shows and events, including films on Thursday nights. Bar, workout equipment and pool table on the premises.

Southern Decadence

Gay New Orleanians have a knack for adding a queer twist to any holiday, from Easter to Halloween. But Southern Decadence is an exclusively gay phenomenon. Held during the week leading up to Labour Day (the first Monday in September), Decadence lives up to its name. It's made up of several days of intense partying, exhibitionism so eye-popping that even some locals have raised their eyebrows, and more tacky drag than RuPaul

ever dreamed of. It culminates in a Sunday afternoon parade that combines all three with Caligula-like indulgence.

The whole immodest shindig began modestly enough in 1972, as a simple going-away party among a group of friends. The following year, the gathering was repeated with costumes and a short procession. By the third year, the parade had a Grand Marshal – to this day a highly coveted,

Accommodation

Gay travellers will feel welcome at just about any New Orleans hotel or French Quarter B&B. Some of the gay-operated guesthouses and B&Bs, however, can provide intimate surroundings and a little more insight into the local queer community. Book early for Mardi Gras, Decadence and other special events; summer is usually the best time to get a bargain.

Bourgoyne Guest House

839 Bourbon Street, between Dumaine & St Ann streets, French Quarter, New Orleans, LA 70116 (524 3621/525 3983). Bus 3 Vieux Carré, 48 Esplanade. **Rates** $93-$191. **Credit** AmEx, DC, MC, V. **Map** p282 C2.
If being near the bars of the French Quarter is a must, you can't do much better than this 1830s Bourbon Street townhouse, whose rooms are filled with antiques. The charming courtyard offers a pleasant respite from the craziness outside.

French Quarter Quartet

1-800 367 5858/www.fqquartet.com. **Rates** $49-$199. **Credit** AmEx, Disc, MC, V.
This is a group of four historic, cosy, gay-friendly properties in and around the Quarter.

Lafitte Guest House

1003 Bourbon Street, at St Philip Street, French Quarter, New Orleans, LA 70116 (581 2678/ 1-800 331 7971/fax 581 2677/www.lafitte guesthouse.com). Bus 3 Vieux Carré. **Rates** $99-$189. **Credit** AmEx, DC, Disc, MC, V. **Map** p282 C2.
This place has 14 guest rooms close to the heart of New Orleans gay nightlife. One of its central attractions is the social hour held each afternoon, when guests can mingle over wine and hors d'oeuvres.

Royal Street Courtyard

2438 Royal Street, at Spain Street, Marigny, New Orleans, LA 70117 (943 6818/1-888 846 4004/ fax 945 1212/email Royalctyd@aol.com). Bus 3 Vieux Carré, 5 Marigny/Bywater. **Rates** $55-$135; prices rise dramatically during special events. **Credit** AmEx, Disc, MC, V. **Map** p277 H6.

subjectively chosen position subject to much envy – and a small but enthusiastic following. It had also developed its own set of rituals: revellers, mostly unshaven and in motley drag, would begin assembling around noon on Sunday outside the **Golden Lantern** (*see p198*). From there, the parade would wind through the Quarter, making frequent cocktail stops along the way.

Decadence grew in size and notoriety over its first two decades but remained a mostly local phenomenon. That changed in the 1990s, when the holiday came to the attention of the national gay press. In 2001, more than 100,000 people converged on the French Quarter for the event. Some residents felt the celebration had become too big and too, well, decadent. There were complaints about public nudity and pleas to the local community to rein in badly behaving visitors.

Still, city officials, respecting Decadence's economic impact, were mostly content to look the other way.

Until 2002, that is. That year, a crusading Christian minister armed with a video camera hit the streets in order to document what he described as 'public orgies'. The resulting tape was distributed to evangelical church leaders throughout the city, as well as to influential politicians sympathetic to the

cause. Embarrassed by the hubbub, many politicos vowed to enforce public decency laws, and several bars banned cameras and discouraged public sex. But it wasn't enough for the anti-Decadence movement, which continued to push for it to be shut down.

In May 2003, a state legislator from a conservative New Orleans suburb won passage of a bill that imposed a minimum ten-day jail term for acts of 'vaginal, oral or anal sexual intercourse... for the purpose of gaining the attention of the public'. Supporters insisted the bill wasn't meant to single out gay men – though it went to the trouble to make sure to exempt the kind of breast-baring popular at Mardi Gras.

The evangelicals are still on the warpath, but it seems unlikely that many steps will be taken against Decadence. Once a tradition is established in New Orleans, it's all but impossible to dislodge. But the police might feel obligated to be more aggressive with arrests; in any event, visitors would be wise to keep their amorous pursuits private. The days of open-air blowjobs in broad daylight are over, at least for now.

And not everybody in the gay community thinks that's such a bad thing. Many believed the party needed toning down a bit, lest it stray too far from its playful local roots.

This 1850s mansion lies several blocks from the action on a nice stretch of residential Royal Street in the Faubourg Marigny.

Ursuline Guest House

708 Ursulines Street, at Royal Street, French Quarter, New Orleans, LA 70116 (525 8509/1-800 654 2351/fax 525 8408). Bus 3 Vieux Carré. **Rates** $85-$125. **Credit** AmEx, MC, V. **Map** p282 C2.
This is an adults-only inn on a quiet Lower Quarter street. Rates include breakfast, afternoon wine and access to the lush courtyard and whirlpool.

Shopping & services

Postmark New Orleans (631 Toulouse Street, French Quarter; 529 2052) has a good selection of cards and gifts along with upscale crafts, lamps and vintage furs. Not far away, **Alternatives** (909 Bourbon Street, French Quarter; 524 5222) squeezes an awful lot of merchandise – including candles, adult toys and flashy, skintight clubwear – into a tiny Bourbon Street shop. The **Gay Heritage**

Tour (945 6789; reservations required; *see also p253*) departs from here every Wednesday and Saturday for a spin around the city's gay landmarks. At **Hit Parade** (741 Bourbon Street, French Quarter; 524 7700) you'll find a bigger selection of skimpy clothing and more attitude than just about anywhere else in town. **Rab-Dab Clothing and Gifts** (508 St Philip Street, French Quarter; 529 3577) specialises in hip gear for gay club kids. Across the street, **Second Skin Leather** (521 St Philip Street, French Quarter; 561 8167) has outfits and accoutrements for almost any fetish, as well as a wide selection of adult magazines and videos, all sold in a laid-back, unthreatening environment. At the other end of the scale, think pink at **Fifi Mahoney's** (*see p170*), where they can and will crown your beautiful self in a bespoke wig in any colour known to man. They also have cosmetics, to bring out the roses in your cheeks.

For gay publications, gay helplines and other information, *see p253*.

Arts & Entertainment

Music

Louis Armstrong, Fats Domino, the Neville Brothers, Dr John, Wynton Marsalis, Professor Longhair... need we say more?

While there is no definitive, must-see act playing regularly that captures the spirit of New Orleans as Dr John, Professor Longhair, Ernie K-Doe and the Neville Brothers once did, the New Orleans scene is arguably healthier than ever, with more talent in more genres than ever before. One characteristic that pervades the city's live music scene is its informality. Shows aren't performances; they're extensions of lives, and approached with casualness, as if the bands were hanging out with a big group of their closest friends. It's an approach that has its pros and cons (shows start whenever they start, and end when the band want to go home) – but understanding will help you to have a better time here. Relax. The band will play, and they will probably be good.

In the end, though, we can promise you only one thing: whatever the time of year, whatever the day of the week, there'll be a band playing somewhere in town that you'll be glad you saw, and that you'll brag about when you go home.

Music clubs

For reasons of both space and taste, our list is selective rather than comprehensive; most noticeably absent are venues on Bourbon Street, because they usually book cover bands and are so close together that the requisite tourist stroll will give you a taste of what's to be heard. All clubs listed are accessible by streetcar, bus or taxi from anywhere in New Orleans. Don't overlook smaller, out-of-the-way places; these are the gems of the local music scene and often provide the most lasting memories of New Orleans as a *sui generis* city for live music.

French Quarter

Crescent City Brewhouse

527 Decatur Street, between Toulouse & St Louis streets (522 0571/www.crescentcitybrewhouse.com). Bus 3 Vieux Carré, 5 Marigny/Bywater, 55 Elysian Fields. **Open** 11am-10pm Mon-Thur, Sun; 11am-11pm Fri, Sat. **Credit** AmEx, Disc, MC, V. **Map** p282 B3.
A rare local brewpub, this place offers jazz and Latin combos in the early evening and oldies cover bands later, alongside good, moderately priced food. The bands play on the ground floor, so the best seats are at the front of the main bar. Because of its French

Quarter location, it draws more tourists than locals, but the good beer makes it worth an hour's visit and the music isn't bad either.

Donna's Bar & Grill

800 N Rampart Street, at St Ann Street (596 6914/www.donnasbarandgrill.com). Bus 3 Vieux Carré, 5 Marigny/Bywater, 48 Esplanade, 89 St Claude. **Open** from 8.30pm Mon, Thur-Sun. **Admission** $5. **Credit** MC, V. **Map** p282 C1.
This is the city's hotspot for brass bands, and it hosts performances nightly. Across from Louis Armstrong Park on the north edge of the French Quarter, it draws a local crowd. You can order food from the bartenders until late. The cover charge is reasonable, but don't forget to tip the band if the hat is passed around. A word of caution: though the lights make Armstrong Park look inviting at night, don't be tempted to visit it or the surrounding Tremé district after dark – both can be a bit dodgy.

El Matador

504 Esplanade Avenue, at Decatur Street (569 8361). Riverfront Streetcar/bus 3 Vieux Carré, 5 Marigny/Bywater, 13 Esplanade, 57 Franklin. **Open** 9pm-3am Mon-Thur; from 5pm Fri-Sun. **Admission** free-$12. **Credit** AmEx, Disc, MC, V. **Map** p282 D3.
Every city has a home for the downscale groove-ocracy, and in New Orleans, it's the Matador. Patrons are hipper than you, thinner than you and more rock 'n' roll than you. Fortunately, they aren't aggressively so, which makes it a pleasant exception to the rule. The music varies from Friday night flamenco shows to gigs by touring underground rock bands, usually with a glam/punk edge. The sound is passable if you're on the spot the size of a manhole cover right behind the bar; otherwise, the stage volume can drown out the vocals.

Funky Butt at Congo Square

714 N Rampart Street, at Orleans Avenue (558 0872/www.funkybutt.com). Bus 5 Marigny/Bywater, 89 St Claude. **Open** 7pm-3am daily. **Admission** $5-$15. **No credit cards.** **Map** p282 C1.
This place rivals Snug Harbor (*see p208*) as the city's top spot for contemporary jazz. Named after the home club of jazz legend Buddy Bolden, the Butt serves up hot music and Creole cooking in swanky surrounds with a laid-back feel. Cover charges can be high, but the talent is top-notch and the setting puts spectators a few feet from some of the world's greatest jazz players.

Get your brass over to **Donna's Bar & Grill**. *See p202.*

House of Blues

225 Decatur Street, between Iberville & Bienville streets (529 2624/www.hob.com). Riverfront Streetcar/bus 3 Vieux Carré, 5 Marigny/Bywater. **Open** 8pm-3am daily. *Box office* 10am-9pm daily; 10am-midnight on show nights. *Shop* 10am-10pm Mon-Thur, Sun; 10am-midnight Fri, Sat. *Restaurant* 11.30am-11pm Mon-Fri; 11.30am-midnight Sat; noon-11pm Sun. *Gospel brunches* 9.30am, 11.45am, 2pm Sun (phone for reservations). **Admission** $6-$25. **Credit** AmEx, DC, MC, V. **Map** p282 A3.

The House of Blues' corporate atmosphere can clash with the city's *laissez les bons temps rouler* attitude, and that has kept many locals from embracing it. Still, there's no denying its stature as the premier small venue for national acts. Despite its name, the booking policy is very broad, taking in funk, world beat, alt rock and pretty much anything that will attract a crowd. When big names such as Willie Nelson and Marilyn Manson feel like doing a club date, they do it here, but the club also books middle-to-upper-echelon New Orleans bands. The House of Blues complex is also home to the Parish, a homely, intimate venue often used for acoustic acts and rock bands on the way up. Though the sound can be dodgy, it's more comfortable than the main room.

Jimmy Buffett's Margaritaville Café & Storyville Tavern

1104 Decatur Street, at Ursulines Street (592 2565/ www.margaritavillecafe.com). Riverfront Streetcar/ bus 3 Vieux Carré, 5 Marigny/Bywater, 55 Elysian Fields, 57 Franklin. **Open** 11am-midnight daily. *Restaurant* 11am-10.30pm daily. **Admission** free. **Credit** AmEx, DC, Disc, MC, V. **Map** p282 C3.

The best House bands

ReBirth Brass Band
These funky shows are more than just shows – they're little pieces of New Orleans. *Tuesdays at the Maple Leaf, see p212.*

John Fohl
Fohl is known to adapt unlikely songs, including Hendrix numbers, into his repertoire of acoustic blues. *Mondays at Dos Jefes, see p211.*

Alex McMurray
Between jazzy blues tunes, McMurray wisecracks about the woozier side of life in New Orleans. *Wednesdays at the Circle Bar, see p209.*

Bingo!
This act combines Tom Waits-ish songs of loss with games of bingo. *Thursday nights in the back room of Fiorella's, 1136 Decatur Street.*

Papa Grows Funk
This is a band's band. They tour regularly, but if you catch them when they're in town, you'll be glad you did. *Mondays at the Maple Leaf, see p212.*

Arts & Entertainment

Fruity cocktail fanatic and pop musician Jimmy Buffett opened this club to replicate a similar place in his hometown of Key West, Florida. It once had two stages operating day and night, but now the big room is devoted to private convention parties and to special occasion gigs, while the small front bar continues to host good folk singers and blues guitarists playing solo every night. Admission is free. For Buffett fans, there's a gift shop around the corner next to the French Market.

The Kerry Irish Pub

331 Decatur Street, at Conti Street (527 5954/ www.kerryirishpub.com). Riverfront Streetcar/ bus 3 Vieux Carré, 5 Marigny/Bywater, 55 Elysian Fields, 57 Franklin. **Open** 2pm-2am daily. **Admission** free. **Credit** AmEx, Disc, MC, V. **Map** p282 B3.

The Kerry Irish Pub offers traditional Irish music, although with each passing year, a little more country sneaks into the line-up. This is a good place to see local country singer Kim Carson playing informally with a few friends. During the day and on into the early evening, the Kerry is first and foremost a place to find a reliable pint of Guinness, but as the evening wears on, the balance of the crowd shifts towards those who are there for the music.

Lounge Lizard's

200 Decatur Street, at Iberville Street (598 1500). Riverfront Streetcar/bus 3 Vieux Carré, 5 Marigny/ Bywater. **Open** 11am-3am daily. **Admission** free-$6. **Credit** AmEx, MC, V. **Map** p282 A3.

This space across the street from the House of Blues is wide and shallow: if you don't know how many fillings the singer has when the show starts, you will by the time you leave. Lounge Lizard's hasn't developed much personality yet, with a generic French Quarter bar space, a clientele that changes with the acts and a booking policy that has so far generally focused on second-tier New Orleans musicians with no obvious genre preference. Then again, the bar also brought in hillbilly legend Hasil Adkins not long ago, so there's promise.

O'Flaherty's Irish Channel Pub

514 Toulouse Street, between Chartres & Decatur streets (529 1317). Riverfront Streetcar/bus 3 Vieux Carré, 5 Marigny/Bywater, 55 Elysian Fields, 57 Franklin. **Open** noon-1.30am Mon-Fri; noon-3am Sat, Sun. *Ballad Room* 7.30pm-midnight Thur-Sat. **Admission** *Ballad Room* $5-$10. *Informer Room* free. **Credit** AmEx, DC, Disc, MC, V. **Map** p282 B2.

O'Flaherty's is in the French Quarter, not the Irish Channel, but it's the largest and most genuine Irish-influenced music club in New Orleans, drawing a crowd of expats and visitors. Housed in a large complex containing three bars, a small courtyard and a gift shop, it offers a wide selection of English, Irish and Scottish beers and stouts, a number of Irish and Scotch whiskies, and Irish food. Traditional Irish ballads are performed for dancers at 8pm in the Informer Room (where talking is allowed), while the larger Ballad Room features Irish bands later in the evening (and quite fiercely discourages conversation).

Smokin' hot jazz, but no cold brews, at **Preservation Hall**.

Palm Court Jazz Café

1204 Decatur Street, at Governor Nicholls Street (525 0200/www.palmcourtjazz.com). Riverfront Streetcar/bus 3 Vieux Carré, 5 Marigny/Bywater, 55 Elysian Fields, 57 Franklin. **Open** 7-11pm Wed-Sat (music from 8pm). **Admission** $5 with meal, free at the bar. **Credit** AmEx, DC, Disc, MC, V. **Map** p282 D3.

Second only to Preservation Hall (*see below*) as the best place for traditional jazz, the Palm Court (unlike the Hall) has the added attraction of a full menu and bar as well. You'll find more tourists than locals here, but this isn't a cheesy tourist joint, as the high-quality live music attests. An adjoining warehouse also sells trad jazz recordings.

Preservation Hall

726 St Peter Street, at Bourbon Street (523 8939/ www.preservationhall.com). Bus 3 Vieux Carré, 42 Canal. **Open** 8pm-midnight daily. **Admission** $5. **No credit cards. Map** p282 B2.

As old as the traditional jazz that's played inside, Preservation Hall serves as a living testament to the old-style New Orleans music scene. Bands play two sets (9pm and 11pm), and a queue usually starts forming outside at 8 every night. Inside, the amenities are kept to a minimum: there is no bar, there is also no air-conditioning, food or toilets, and seating is (very) limited. But that doesn't prevent the musicians – some of them well over 80 years old – from playing hot sets. Yes, the crowd is almost exclusively made up of tourists, but to miss this place is to miss a part of New Orleans history.

Marigny, Bywater & Tremé

The Blue Nile

532 Frenchmen Street, between Decatur & Chartres streets, Marigny (948 2583). Riverfront Streetcar/ bus 3 Vieux Carré, 5 Marigny/Bywater. **Open** 7pm-2am daily. **Admission** free-$10. **Credit** AmEx, Disc, MC, V. **Map** p282 D2/3.

This club has been through many hands and many names – it's been the Dream Palace, Café Istanbul, and the Dream Palace again, in between bouts of sitting empty. It was up for sale again at press time and could close, but fingers crossed that the Blue Nile stays around. It's become the city's most comfortable venue for avant-garde music, with Thursday performances by the Improvisational Arts Council, and it also features live Latin American, soul and funk acts, all of which are laced with more than a touch of jazz.

Café Brasil

2100 Chartres Street, at Frenchmen Street, Marigny (949 0851/http://station-terra.com). Riverfront Streetcar/bus 3 Vieux Carré, 5 Marigny/ Bywater, 55 Elysian Fields. **Open** 8pm-2am Mon-Thur, Sun; 8pm-4am Fri, Sat. **Admission** free-$10. **No credit cards. Map** p282 G6.

Located in the heart of Faubourg Marigny, three blocks from Esplanade Avenue and the edge of the French Quarter, Café Brasil hops on weekend nights with one of the hippest crowds in New Orleans. Friday nights usually feature Latin bands, while funk, rock, jazz and hip hop bands take to the stage

Frenchmen love good music

There was a time in the past when the corner of Frenchmen and Chartres was the home of Saturday night. In the 1990s, at the Faubourg Marigny end of the French Quarter, traffic at the intersection regularly ground to a halt as a crowd formed between **Café Brasil** (*see p205*) on one side of the street and the now defunct Café Istanbul on the other. Along with the usual scenemakers, there were old hippies, suburban secretaries, tourists and people from just about every ethnic and sexual subcategory.

At the end of the 1990s, though, the Frenchmen scene took a downturn, possibly because some of the bars changed hands. The more popular bands outgrew Café Brasil, and the Latin bands that replaced them didn't attract such an eclectic audience.

All this changed in 2000, when the opening of **d.b.a.** (*see below*) kicked off a period of renewal for the area. Since then, the **Spotted Cat** (*see p208*) has opened, and the renovated **Dragon's Den** (*see below*) and **Blue Nile** (*see p205*) have opened, creating new haunts.

Sanely, people stay out of the traffic now, but the party is still as much outdoors as in. Listeners on the pavement can hear whoever's playing at the Spotted Cat about as well as the crowd inside can, and bands across the street at d.b.a. are about as loud.

Frenchmen Street really comes to life at weekends. On a normal Friday or Saturday night, it's not unusual to find fire-twirlers or people spinning maces on lengths of chain in intricate patterns. That's not to say it's dead during the week; in fact, many prefer it then – bands play to less packed rooms and the crowds on the street aren't as thick. But the vibe is still there. And so is the music.

the rest of the week. On more popular nights, the crowd spills out on to Frenchmen Street, creating a block-party atmosphere. There's a bar next door for those unwilling to pack into the main room or pay the cover charge, if there is one (they range up to $10). The beer choice is limited, and there's no food, but if you're in the mood to dance to live music you'd be hard pressed to find a better crowd than this one.

d.b.a.
618 Frenchmen Street, between Chartres & Royal streets, Marigny (942 3731/www.drinkgood stuff.com). Riverfront Streetcar/bus 3 Vieux Carré, 5 Marigny/Bywater. **Open** 4pm-4am Mon-Thur, Sun; 4pm-5am Fri, Sat. **Admission** free. **Credit** AmEx, MC, V. **Map** p282 D2.
d.b.a. is a shrine to alcohol. Not booze – alcohol. The chalkboards list chi-chi scotches, vodkas, cognacs and beers, all at prices that'll eat up your trust fund in no time. In a back corner, a postage-stamp stage accommodates small bands. The music tends towards eclectic jazz, blues and country, and the bar is home to 007, featuring members of the Iguanas and G Love & Special Sauce, which plays Jamaican rock steady music. *See also p139.*

Dragon's Den
435 Esplanade Avenue, at Frenchmen Street, above Siam Restaurant, Marigny (949 1750). Riverfront Streetcar/bus 3 Vieux Carré, 5 Marigny/Bywater, 48 Esplanade. **Open** from 5pm daily. **Food served** 5pm-midnight Mon-Thur, Sun; 5pm-1am Fri, Sat. **Admission** free Mon-Thur; $5-$10 Fri-Sun. **Credit** AmEx, Disc, MC, V. **Map** p282 D3.
The Dragon's Den has opened and closed again a few times now, always because of fire safety

concerns. At the time of writing, it was open again, but who knows whether it will still be there when you get here? What makes it exciting is its alluring covertness, which starts with the walk down the alley to the dubious, curved staircase leading up to the bar space. The room is small, it can get warm, and the music is reliably funky and exotic. The bands are almost always danceable. A visit here can make for a very sexy night.

Ernie K-Doe's Mother-in-Law Lounge
1500 N Claiborne Avenue, at Columbus Street, Tremé (947 1078/www.kdoe.com). Bus 50, 51, 52 St Bernard, 82 Desire. **Open** from 5pm daily. **Admission** free. **No credit cards. Map** p277 G6.
Since Ernie himself passed away in 2001, this club's main attraction is no more. The small room was owned and run by the R&B singer, whose 'Mother-in-Law' was a hit 30 years ago. Today, his widow, Antoinette, keeps the bar open, and it serves as much as a shrine to K-Doe now as it did when he was alive. There are still occasional gigs by garage soul/rock bands true to the K-Doe spirit. In a town filled with eccentrics, he was in a league of his own. Those who want to connect to another side of the New Orleans legend should make a pilgrimage here.

The Hi-Ho Lounge
2239 St Claude Avenue, at Marigny Street, Bywater (947 9344/www.hiholounge.com). Bus 5 Marigny/ Bywater, 88, 89 St Claude. **Open** from 6pm daily. **Admission** free-$5. **Credit** MC, V. **Map** p277 H6.
When the Hi-Ho first opened, it was little more than a living room with a bar, tables (some with board games) and a space that served as a stage. The door

The grande dame of the local music scene is definitely **Tipitina's**. *See p212.*

was barred when guests were safely inside. It wasn't a terribly comforting atmosphere, and the club closed. Now it's open again, with an improved stage and PA, but it remains one of the city's most marginal venues. The acts, too, tend to be marginal, with a preponderance of indie and underground rock bands that are just starting their careers (and we use the word with caution).

Snug Harbor

626 Frenchmen Street, at Royal Street, Marigny (949 0696/www.snugjazz.com). Riverfront Streetcar/ bus 3 Vieux Carré, 5 Marigny/ Bywater. **Open** 5pm-1am daily. **Shows** 9pm, 11pm daily. **Food served** 5-10.30pm Mon-Thur, Sun; 5-11.30pm Fri, Sat. **Admission** $10-$25. **Credit** AmEx, MC, V. **Map** p282 D2.

Still New Orleans' leading jazz club, Snug Harbor offers the city's best contemporary jazz, seven nights a week. The cover charge can be high, but it's worth it: this is the way jazz should be seen and heard. It's a sit-down venue, with tables and benches right up to the stage. Crowds are generally quiet and respectful. It's not uncommon for unscheduled players to join the band on stage, leading to some of the best impromptu jam sessions in the world.

The Spotted Cat

623 Frenchmen Street, between Chartres & Royal streets, Marigny (943 3887/www.thespotted cat.com). Riverfront Streetcar/bus 3 Vieux Carré, *5 Marigny/Bywater.* **Open** 2pm-4am Mon-Thur, Sun; noon-5am Fri, Sat. **Admission** free. **Credit** AmEx, MC, V. **Map** p282 D2.

The Spotted Cat is an intimate joint with a stage the size of a hedgehog's shadow. The band sets up by the front window and is surrounded by the audience, who lounge on chairs, lean on the bar and stand around outside. Given all of that, the room ought not to work – the bar consumes far too much floor space, for starters – but the Spotted Cat has a great vibe nonetheless. There is a one-drink minimum, and tipping the band is a must since there's no cover.

Sweet Lorraine's

1931 St Claude Avenue, at Touro Street, Bywater (945 9654/www.sweetlorrainesjazzclub.com). Bus 5 Marigny/Bywater, 88, 89 St Claude. **Open** from 8pm Mon, Tue, Thur-Sun. **Admission** $5-$15. **Credit** AmEx, MC, V. **Map** p277 G6.

This Ninth Ward joint often has jazz on the weekends. A small bar opens on to a main room filled with polished metal tables and comfortable chairs. The sound system is small but adequate, given the intimate size of the room and the kinds of bands that play here. The club attracts a genial crowd of hip, professional African-Americans and middle-aged white bohemians from the surrounding Marigny and Bywater areas. The audience is knowledgeable and appreciative of the music. Drinks can be pricey, but the cover charge is reasonable.

Vaughan's Lounge

4229 Dauphine Street, at Lesseps Street, Bywater (947 5562). Bus 5 Marigny/Bywater. **Open** from 11.30am daily. **Admission** free Mon-Wed, Fri-Sun; $10 Thur. **No credit cards.**

A Thursday night at Vaughan's is as much a happening as a musical experience. Located way down in the Bywater neighbourhood and best reached by taxi or car, this was a small bar that became a music lover's haven when it started booking trumpeter Kermit Ruffins and his Barbecue Swingers on Thursday nights. At first, there was no cover charge, and free red beans and rice were served between sets. Now there's a $10 admission charge, but the place still jumps every Thursday.

CBD

The Circle Bar

1032 St Charles Avenue, at Lee Circle (588 2616). St Charles Streetcar. **Open** 4pm-3am Mon-Fri; 5pm-3am Sat, Sun. **Admission** free Mon-Thur, Sun; $10-$25 Fri, Sat. **Credit** MC, V. **Map** p279 B2.

Before and after live shows, the Circle Bar is quite simply one of the best places to hang out in New Orleans. The jukebox is top-notch – maybe the best in the city – with smart, semi-obscure soul, rockabilly, garage, country, punk and pop. And since this is a place people pass through on their way out or home for the evening, it always has a warm feel. Early in the week, the live acts tend towards the small and the solo, but in a room as small as the Circle Bar, that's enough to charge the atmosphere. When there are rock bands here, as there are at weekends, it's a hip-to-haunch crush, which can be great in a rock 'n' roll way, or it can just feel crowded. Soul legends periodically play here.

Le Chat Noir

715 St Charles Avenue, between Girod & Julia streets (581 5812/www.cabaretlechatnoir.com). St Charles Streetcar. **Open** 7pm-2am Tue-Sat. *Box office* 3-6pm Mon; 1-6pm Tue-Sat. **Shows** call or see website for details. **Admission** varies. **Credit** AmEx, MC. **Map** p279 B1/2.

This classy venue on St Charles Avenue fills a niche for a crowd too old to hang out at music clubs until the wee hours and too young to spend night after dreary night at home. One of only two locations that feature regular cabaret, Le Chat Noir's bar is cleanly decorated in black and white and looks out on to the avenue. The performance room is small but not crowded, with cocktail tables around a stage and small dancefloor. In addition to cabaret shows, Le Chat Noir hosts local theatre productions and the occasional jazz performance.

Michaul's Live Cajun Music Restaurant

840 St Charles Avenue, at Julia Street (522 5517/ www.michauls.com). St Charles Streetcar. **Open** 6-9.30pm daily. **Admission** $5; free with dinner or drinks. **Credit** AmEx, DC, Disc, MC, V. **Map** p279 B2.

The best Local music

In New Orleans, one thing you can count on is that everybody's in a band. No, seriously, *everybody* is in a band. Pick up a copy of the free local magazine *OffBeat,* and the sheer number of gigs each night can be dizzying. To help you choose, here are some of our favourites.

Blues
John Mooney, Jumpin' Johnny Sansone

Brass
ReBirth Brass Band, Bonerama

Cajun
Steve Riley and the Mamou Playboys, Bruce Daigrepont

Eclectic
Quintron, Electrical Spectacle

Folk/acoustic
Jeff and Vida, John Fohl

Funk
Papa Grows Funk, The Funky Meters

Jazz
Astral Project, Naked on the Floor

Rock
Supagroup, The Iguanas

Zydeco
Nathan and the Zydeco Cha-Chas, Geno Delafose, Sunpie and the Sunspots

There's not much Cajun music in New Orleans, but Michaul's offers a taste. The restaurant's attempt to re-create authentic Cajun surroundings – wooden rafters, stuffed and mounted animals, swamp decor – is as transparent as its plate-glass windows. Though Cajun bands play nightly, the patrons are mainly here to eat. Frankly, the best Cajun music experience in town is the very good Sunday afternoon *fais do-do* at Tipitina's (*see p212*).

Warehouse District

The Howlin' Wolf

828 S Peters Street, at Julia Street (522 9653/ www.howlin-wolf.com). Bus 3 Vieux Carré, 10 Tchoupitoulas. **Open** from 3pm Mon-Sat, show nights. **Admission** $5-$20. **Credit** AmEx, Disc, MC, V. **Map** p279 C2.

Long one of the city's top venues for national touring bands, Howlin' Wolf is successful because of the way it satisfies as many different audiences as

Let the good times roll at
Mid City Lanes Rock 'n' Bowl.
See p212.

possible. That kind of eclectism usually spells disaster for a music club, but the Wolf's hospitable policy means you might see the Strokes there one week and an emerging alternative punk rock band from East Jesus the next. Since the Wolf recently changed ownership, it has gone through some changes, retaining its reputation for adventurous booking but also starting to carve a niche for itself supporting local heavy commercial bands and indie acts that are outgrowing the smaller venues in town. It aims for a younger, often suburban audience, and so features quite a bit of rap.

Mermaid Lounge

1100 Constance Street, at John Churchill Chase Street (524 4747/www.mermaidlounge.com). Bus 10 Tchoupitoulas, 11 Magazine. **Open** from 9pm Tue-Sat. **Admission** varies. **No credit cards.** **Map** p279 C2.

Perhaps the most out-of-the-way club in New Orleans, this hole in the wall is a haven for young urban hipsters. When the bar opened, it was in the middle of nowhere; now that the neighbouring warehouse has been converted into flats, things have changed. In the old days, you could stand outside the front door and hear the music without paying cover, but now the stage is where that door used to be. The place isn't as subversive as it once was, but it's still run like a clubhouse for the owners and their friends. The booking is eccentric and favours indie rock bands. Punctuality is a bourgeois trait, so don't hurry. Nothing starts on time at the Mermaid. Ever.

Mulate's Cajun Restaurant

201 Julia Street, at Convention Center Boulevard (522 1492/www.mulates.com). Bus 3 Vieux Carré, 11 Tchoupitoulas. **Open** 11am-11pm daily. *Music* 7-10.30pm daily. **Admission** free. **Credit** AmEx, DC, Disc, MC, V. **Map** p279 C2.

Like Michaul's (*see p209*), Mulate's caters to an almost exclusively tourist crowd, lured inside by the Cajun cuisine and music. This place feels more authentic than Michaul's, though, and it usually has higher-calibre bands, good enough to keep the small dancefloor busy. (There are dance instructors on hand to help out novices.) There's no cover charge, but both restaurant and bar prices are pretty high. And generally, what you get here is a thoroughly sanitised version of Cajun culture.

Garden District

Pontchartrain Hotel

2031 St Charles Avenue, at Andrews Street (524 0581/www.thepontchartrainhotel.com). St Charles Streetcar. **Open** 4.30-11pm Mon-Thur; 10am-2am Fri, Sat; 10am-11pm Sun. **Admission** free. **Credit** AmEx, DC, Disc, MC, V. **Map** p279 B3.

One of the few true piano bars in New Orleans is in the lobby of this grande dame of a hotel looking out on to St Charles Avenue. There's no cover charge, and the bar is a comfortable, intimate, warm space, usually filled with hotel guests and friends and fans

of the piano players. The music gets going early in the evenings (starting at 5pm) from Tuesday to Saturday, but the best times to visit are weekend nights, when Philip Melancon performs his witty songs about New Orleans characters and celebrities. The drinks prices here are a little steep, but really still reasonable considering the lack of cover. Don't forget to tip the piano player.

Twi-Ro-Pa

1544 Tchoupitoulas Street, at Orange Street (587 3777/www.twiropa.com). Bus 11 Tchoupitoulas. **Open** for shows. **Admission** varies. **Credit** MC, V. **Map** p279 C3.

Shows at this renovated warehouse space have a pleasantly subversive feel, with the beats ringing out across a mechanical wasteland. It isn't particularly close to anything, and the car park behind it is surrounded by industrial detritus. The room is only open when promoters need a large space, and the sound quality depends on the equipment that gets brought in for each individual gig. Twi-Ro-Pa's relative isolation and size have made it popular for big party shows during Jazz Fest.

Uptown

Carrollton Station Bar & Music Club

8140 Willow Street, at Dublin Street (865 9190/www.carrolltonstation.com). St Charles Streetcar. **Open** 3pm-3am daily. **Admission** $5-$10 Fri, Sat. **Credit** AmEx, Disc, MC, V. **Map** p276 B7.

Carrollton Station is under new management these days, but it has maintained its soul – good roots music in a comfortable room. This relaxed, small venue hosts rock, funk and folk bands from Thursday to Sunday, and it boasts one of the better beer selections among the city's music clubs. It caters more to the college crowd than it used to, but older regulars don't seem to feel out of place. You can stand in the front half of the bar and get lost in the band. Or you can hang out at the back and shoot the shit – or shoot the bear: the classic 'Bear Hunt' shooting game is still here and still working. Also check out the 'Chicken Drop' rules on the wall. The game was real, and it didn't end as long ago as you might think. *See also p146.*

Dos Jefes Cigar Bar

5535 Tchoupitoulas Street, at Joseph Street (891 8500/www.dosjefes.com). Bus 11 Tchoupitoulas. **Open** 5pm-3am Mon-Fri; 7pm-3am Sat, Sun. **Admission** free. **Credit** AmEx, DC, Disc, MC, V. **Map** p276 C10.

Dos Jefes began as an extension of an uptown cigar store which bore the same name, but these days, only the bar remains. This place is a stogie smoker's heaven, but it's also an intimate spot to hear solo and duo blues and jazz. Lil' Queenie regularly sings jazz standards accompanied by a pianist, while John Fohl effortlessly creates finger-twisting acoustic blues on Monday nights.

Arts & Entertainment

Le Bon Temps Roule

4801 Magazine Street, at Bordeaux Street
(895 8117). Bus 11 Magazine. **Open** 11am-3am
Mon-Thur, Sun; 24hrs Fri, Sat. **Admission** $3-$5.
Credit AmEx, Disc, MC, V. **Map** p276 C10.

The small back room of this popular Uptown bar
(*see p145*) has a roadhouse feel. Regulars drop by
most nights to check out the bands, and college students slip in from the front room, curious about
who's playing in the back. On crowded nights, the
whole thing gets pretty hot and sticky, so leave your
finery at home. The sweat adds to the vibe from the
rockin' blues, rockin' R&B and rockin' damn rock.
The Bon Temps also is known for having one of the
best late-night grills in town.

Maple Leaf Bar

8316 Oak Street, at Dante Street (866 9359).
St Charles Streetcar. **Open** 3pm-3am daily.
Admission $5-$16. **Credit** AmEx, Disc,
MC, V. **Map** p276 A7.

The New Orleans music magazine *OffBeat* once
claimed that 'no musical tour of New Orleans would
be complete without a stop at the Maple Leaf', and
this is still true. Early in the evening, hard-core
drinkers congregate along the long bar, knocking
them back. The real action takes place one room
over, where red walls surround a long, narrow
dancefloor that's rarely empty after 9pm. At the
back, there's another bar with tables for chess and
pool, plus an outdoor patio for cooling off. The place
jumps when the city's top brass, funk, R&B and
zydeco bands play late into the night. Tuesday
nights, when the ReBirth Brass Band plays, is
magical and not to be missed. There is nothing else
like this on earth. And that's a promise.

Neutral Ground Coffeehouse

5110 Danneel Street, at Soniat Street (891 3381/
www.neutralground.org). St Charles Streetcar.
Open 7pm-1am daily. **Admission** free.
No credit cards. Map p276 C9.

This is the top spot in town for acoustic folk music,
drawing younger kids (who can't get into bars) and
a number of ageing folkies. You can play chess and
backgammon over coffee when there's no band playing, but on most nights there are performances by
three different acts – usually local acoustic musicians and performance poets. When national folk
acts come to town, this is where they play.

Tipitina's

501 Napoleon Avenue, at Tchoupitoulas Street
(tickets 895 8477/www.tipitinas.com). Bus 11
Tchoupitoulas, 24 Napoleon. **Open** Box office
11am-6pm daily. **Admission** $5-$20. **Credit**
AmEx, DC, MC, V. **Map** p276 D10.

Prior to the opening of the House of Blues in 1995
(*see p203*), Tipitina's was New Orleans' premier club
for local greats and nationally touring acts. It still
offers some of the best live music in the city,
although its star has fallen slightly. Recent additions
to this legendary venue (including a fantastic new

PA system and – at long last – air-conditioning)
make it a must on any music lover's itinerary.
Everyone from local brass bands to international
reggae stars plays at Tip's. A large balcony overlooks the stage and dancefloor, and on Sundays
there's usually a Cajun *fais do-do* dance which
provides the best, most authentic Cajun music and
all-round experience in the city.

Mid-City

The Dixie Taverne

3340 Canal Street, at Jefferson Davis Parkway
(822 8268/www.dixietaverne.com). Canal Streetcar/
bus 41, 42, 43 Canal. **Open** from 6pm daily.
Admission $5. **Credit** MC, V.

The Dixie Taverne is the home of anti-establishment
music in New Orleans, and, given that, it's just about
everything you'd expect. This loud and sweaty joint
was a gritty neighbourhood saloon before it got into
the punk and metal business. It takes hard, heavy
music seriously and books both local bands and
international acts without promising futures.

Mid City Lanes Rock 'n' Bowl

4133 S Carrollton Avenue, at Tulane Avenue
(482 3133/www.rockandbowl.com). Bus 34
Carrollton Express, 39 Tulane. **Open** 10am-2am
daily. **Admission** $3-$10. **Credit** AmEx, DC,
Disc, MC, V. **Map** p276 D5.

Checkpoint Charlie's (*see p159*) may be the only
music venue in town with its own launderette, but
Rock 'n' Bowl ups the ante. This is the only club in
town with its own bowling alley – ten glorious lanes.
Located off the beaten track, in a strip of shops in
the shadow of the interstate, Rock 'n' Bowl is a hidden gem with a musical spirit and a heart of gold.
As well as organising the hottest zydeco night in
town (on Thursdays), it books rockabilly, R&B and
blues bands just about every night. The club has
expanded to include the floor below the bowling
alley, so for one cover charge (usually $5), you can
go back and forth between the two stages and catch
up to six bands in one night.

Sandbar

The Cove, University of New Orleans, off Elysian
Fields Avenue (835 5277). Bus 55 Elysian Fields,
56 Elysian Fields Express, 60 Hayne. **Open** Feb-
May, Sept-Dec 8-11pm Wed. *Jan, June-Aug* closed.
Admission $5. **No credit cards.**

The University of New Orleans has one of the best
jazz studies courses in the world, so it's no surprise
that on Wednesday nights its Sandbar club plays
host to some of the hottest young performers in contemporary jazz – most of whom are students at the
university. The Sandbar's student-pub ambience is
nothing special, but the music cranked out inside is
stellar, making the club worth the trek to the campus, at the north end of town near Lake
Pontchartrain. The best way to find the Sandbar is
to get to the UNO, look on a campus map for the student centre and then ask someone.

When the saints go marching in

'As the family and people went to the graveyard to bury one of their loved ones, we'd play a funeral march. It was pretty sad, and it put a feeling of weeping in their hearts and minds, and when they left there, we didn't want them to hear that going home. It became a tradition to play jazzy numbers going back to make the relatives and friends cast off their sadness, and the people along the streets used to dance to the music. I used to follow those parades myself, long before I thought of becoming a drummer. The jazz played after New Orleans funerals didn't show any lack of respect for the person being buried. It rather showed their people that we wanted them to be happy.'

Baby Dodd, Louis Armstrong's drummer, was describing a typical jazz funeral in New Orleans in the 1920s when he wrote that. Today, the general philosophy is much the same, and the practice of playing the dead to rest is alive and well in the New Orleans black community. Though not as common as they once were, musical funeral processions are still familiar sights, mostly in the French Quarter, Uptown and in the Ninth Ward.

The roots of jazz funerals lie in the 'benevolent societies' that formed in the 19th century, before insurance companies took on their modern role. Members paid dues to these organisations, and if they became ill, they were given financial help. When they died, the societies paid for burial. They also provided brass bands to perform at weddings and funerals.

The concept of the jazz funeral was fully developed by the 1920s. Then, as now, band members dressed in dark trousers, white shirts, dark ties and matching caps. A grand marshal dressed in a black tuxedo and white gloves, holding a black hat in his hand, led the procession. On the way to the grave, he marched at a slow, dignified pace to mournful music. On the way back, he moved to the beat of celebratory music, with a horde of second-liners (dancers with umbrellas) following behind. Today, brass bands – made up of a younger generation of musicians who aren't necessarily well-versed in the tradition – have been known to deviate from the script of yesteryear. Many opt for a sad song or two and then rush straight into all-out celebration.

Anyone can hire a band and a police escort and have a jazz funeral, though it's usually relatives of musicians and industry folk who do so nowadays. The only kicker is: somebody's got to die first.

The music never stops on Bourbon Street.

Larger venues

Tickets for these venues can also be purchased through Ticketmaster (522 5555/www.ticketmaster.com).

Contemporary Arts Center

900 Camp Street, between Andrew Higgins Boulevard & St Joseph Street, Warehouse District (information 523 1216/box office 528 3800/ www.cacno.org). St Charles Streetcar/bus 10 Magazine. **Open** *Box office 11am-5pm daily.* **Admission** varies. **Credit** AmEx, MC, V. **Map** p279 C2.

Used as a music venue during Mardi Gras and Jazz Fest, the warehouse space adjoining the Contemporary Arts Center is a hotspot for big names in jazz, funk and rock. Amenities are limited to whatever is set up for each show, but usually include a few full-service bars, food from local caterers and portable toilets in the car park. *See also p98.*

Louisiana Superdome

Sugar Bowl Drive, at Poydras Street, CBD (box office 587 3800/tour information 587 3808/ www.superdome.com). Bus 16 S Claiborne. **Open** *Box office 9am-4.30pm Mon-Fri; for special events Sat, Sun.* **Admission** varies. **Credit** MC, V. **Map** p279 A/B1.

With a seating capacity close to 80,000, the Superdome is one of the largest concert venues in the country. Accordingly, where music is concerned, it hosts only the most massive international acts, such as the Rolling Stones and U2. (The iconic image of Bono opening his jacket to reveal an American flag came from a performance here). Unfortunately, the cavernous dome can make for some of the worst-sounding shows in the city.

New Orleans Arena

Poydras Street, at the Louisiana Superdome, CBD (tickets 587 3800/24hr information 846 5959/ www.superdome.com). Bus 16 S Claiborne. **Open** *Box office 9am-4.30pm Mon-Fri and 2hrs before performances.* **Admission** varies. **Credit** AmEx, MC, V. **Map** p279 B1.

Next door to the immense Superdome and second to it in size, this new arena is home to the New Orleans Hornets and local college basketball teams, and it's also replaced the Lakefront Arena as the city's top venue for large concerts. Its construction was completed rather hastily, and the lack of polish is obvious to anyone who focuses on the structure rather than the stage. But with the likes of Bruce Springsteen, Britney Spears, Kiss and Nine Inch Nails gracing the stage, it's unlikely fans will pay too much attention to the soft furnishings.

Saenger Theatre

143 North Rampart Street, at Canal Street, French Quarter (524 2490/www.saengertheatre.com). Canal Streetcar/bus 3 Vieux Carré, 41, 42, 43 Canal. **Open** *Box office 10am-5pm Mon-Fri.* **Admission** varies. **Credit** AmEx, MC, V. **Map** p282 A1.

Located almost directly across Canal Street from the State Palace Theatre (*see below*), the Saenger is a more refined, classier version of its neighbour. However, while more genteel performances are regularly staged here, the Saenger also hosts rock, jazz and funk bands too popular for local clubs but not big enough for the arenas and stadiums. Whatever the performance, with its Romanesque interior, this exquisitely restored old theatre is almost worth a visit for its ornate decor alone.

State Palace Theatre

1108 Canal Street, at N Rampart Street, French Quarter (522 4435/tickets 482 7112/www.state palace.com). Canal Streetcar/bus 3 Vieux Carré, 41 Canal. **Open** *Ticket line 9am-5pm Mon-Fri. Box office night of the show.* **Admission** varies. **Credit** AmEx, Disc, MC, V. **Map** p282 A1.

This beautiful old theatre reinvented itself several years ago as a mid-size music venue for concerts by nationally touring rock and rap artists. The State Palace seats about 4,000 on its floor and in its many gilded balconies. Recently it has emerged as the premier venue for multi-band gigs by ska and punk tours making stops in New Orleans.

UNO Lakefront Arena

6801 Franklin Avenue, at Leon C Simon Drive, Gentilly (280 7222/http://arena.uno.edu). Bus 57, 58 Franklin, 60 Hayne. **Open** *Box office 9am-5pm Mon-Fri.* **Admission** varies. **Credit** AmEx, MC, V.

The original New Orleans home of arena rock, the Senator Nat G Kiefer University of New Orleans Lakefront Arena (its full name, not that anybody cares) is similar to most other sports arena-cum-music venues in the US. In other words, the vast expanses of cement can make the sound ear-piercingly bright, and the capacity of 9,000 makes the setting anything but intimate.

Arts & Entertainment

The Performing Arts

When you need culture of a different sort. But put the beer down first.

Over the top: The **Saenger Theatre**
See p216.

See p216.

It seems as if performance of some kind is happening on just about every street corner in the city. Locals are natural hams – even visitors, once acclimatised, tend to follow suit. But when it comes to the classical performing arts, the city has less to offer. There are a few outlets, but, aside from music, where New Orleans unsurprisingly excels, there are few dance events and only occasional plays that are worthwhile. Still, if you're in the mood, or in town at the right time, you just might find a production to entertain you.

Theatre

New Orleans' theatre scene is a tightly knit club which favours mostly the tried and tested. Touring Broadway shows are the main draws, but only a few pass through town each year.

Contemporary Arts Center
900 Camp Street, between Higgins Boulevard & St Joseph Street, Warehouse District (528 3805/ www.cacno.org). St Charles Streetcar. **Tickets** prices vary; phone for details. **Credit** AmEx, MC, V. **Map** p279 C2.
Housed within a four-storey converted warehouse at the edge of downtown, the CAC wears many hats; one of its best roles is as a modern art gallery, but it's also the main local outpost for alternative theatre. Don't be fooled by the minimal look of the exterior; there's plenty of action inside, with a 200-seat theatre used mainly for music and dance and another 150-seater for intimate plays. The city's most cutting-edge quality theatre often takes place here. (*See also p98.*)

Loyola University
Marquette Theatre & Lower Depths Theatre, 6363 St Charles Avenue, at Calhoun Street, Uptown (box office 865 3824/Department of Drama & Speech

The theatrical alternative

Some New Orleans theatre venues play the role even though they lack the costume: no curtain to drop, and nothing resembling traditional theatre seating. In these alternative spaces, the show goes on all the same, and the provocative entertainment suits the uncompromising surroundings.

Le Chat Noir

715 St Charles Avenue, between Girod & Julia streets, Warehouse District (581 5812/www.cabaretlechatnoir.com). St Charles Streetcar. **Tickets** *$12-$20.* **Credit** *AmEx, MC, V.* **Map** *p279 B2.*
White-clothed tables ring the narrow semicircular stage at Le Chat Noir, which resembles nothing so much as a kind of slumming Copacabana. The productions here tend to vary in format from one-act play competitions to small musicals and full-blown three-act shows. Performances here are unusually refreshing, perhaps because of the versatility demanded by the tiny sliver of a stage. Be aware that the house typically adds $6 to the ticket price to cover a drink. So you might as well have one.

True Brew Theatre

200 Julia Street, at Fulton Street, Warehouse District (box office 524 8440/ www.truebrew.com). Bus 11 Magazine. **Tickets** *$3-$26.* **Credit** *MC, V.* **Map** *p279 C2.*
This cosy coffeehouse has made a back room into a theatre; plays sometimes spill out into the shop itself. Don't let the low-fi folding chairs set on risers fool you into assuming the theatre is slipshod. Expect an edgy local menu peppered with politics and parodies. Some very good productions are put on here, to small but fervent crowds.

Zeitgeist Alternative Arts Center

For listings, see p218.
The city's best alternative theatre, this place looks as if it's just been thrown together, and, to an extent, it has, but it's been hurled into being by people who are zealous about theatre. Zeitgeist's staff are dedicated, and performances are creative, unpredictable and cutting-edge. You never know what you might see here, but whatever it is, Zeitgeist always deserves your attention.

865 3840/www.loyno.edu). St Charles Streetcar. **Tickets** *prices vary; average $5-$15.* **No credit cards.** *Map p276 B/C8.*
While it stages fewer performances than does Tulane University (*see p217*), Loyola nonetheless has a vigorous theatre department. Student productions at its two venues are often New Orleanians' best chance to see work by popular playwrights like Wendy Wasserstein and Tom Stoppard.

Mahalia Jackson Theater of the Performing Arts

Louis Armstrong Park, entrance on Basin Street or N Rampart Street, at St Ann Street, Tremé (565 7470). Bus 88, 89 St Claude. **Tickets** *prices vary; phone for details.* **Map** *p282 C1.*
This would be a good place to get another wearing out of that black-tie gala outfit. It's got all the gilt and red carpet in the city, essentially. It's the home of the opera (see p218) and the frequent site of national ballet performances. The sweeping multi-tiered lobby is great for people-watching at the interval.

Orpheum Theatre

129 University Place, at Common Street, CBD (524 3285/www.orpheumneworleans.com). Canal Streetcar/bus 3 Vieux Carré. **Tickets** *prices vary; phone for details.* **Credit** *AmEx, Disc, MC, V.* **Map** *p282 A1.*

Though it's noted for hosting a variety of musical events, this dramatic Gothic-style building, with its grand old lobby, is best known as the home of the Louisiana Philharmonic Orchestra (*see p218*). Acoustics are superb, whether the orchestra's going posh or taking a casual turn with its popular Blue Jeans series. The building feels far older than its years, which only adds to its faded charm.

Le Petit Théâtre du Vieux Carré

616 St Peter Street, at Chartres Street & Jackson Square, French Quarter (522 2081/www.lepetit theatre.com). Bus 3 Vieux Carré, 55 Elysian Fields, 57 Franklin. **Tickets** *prices vary; average $10-$25.* **Credit** *AmEx, MC, V.* **Map** *p282 B2.*
One of the oldest amateur theatres in the country, the French Quarter's clubhouse-like Le Petit was founded by a bunch of theatre lovers who were producing plays in their living rooms in the 1920s. Today, the theatre is still a catalyst. A new orchestra pit is expected to enhance its established role as a reliable venue for seriously shopworn but largely enjoyable musicals.

Saenger Theatre

143 N Rampart Street, at Canal Street, French Quarter (524 2490/www.saengertheatre.com). Canal Streetcar. **Tickets** *prices vary; phone for details.* **Credit** *AmEx, MC, V.* **Map** *p282 A1.*

When it opened in 1927 as a cinema palace, the Saenger was a world-class venue. Today, the building is still in remarkably good shape, though the neighbourhood on Canal Street at the edge of the French Quarter has deteriorated dramatically. Inside, opulent Renaissance Florence-inspired (read: gaudy) details include Greek and Romanesque sculptures, cut-glass chandeliers and a Hogwarts-like special-effects ceiling that mimics the night sky with twinkling stars and moving clouds. Virtually the only thing you'll see here these days is touring mainstream Broadway shows and some mid-sized regional productions. *Cats, Nunsense, 42nd Street* and *Oklahoma!* are the kinds of big hits this place promotes to drag the suburbanites in to town for a day of 'culchah'. Occasionally you'll catch a rock concert here – the Cure played three nights here in 2000. Once in a blue moon a slightly alternative theatrical production (of the *Rent* variety) will have a run here, but it won't last long.

Southern Repertory Theater

3rd Floor, The Shops at Canal Place, 333 Canal Street, at N Peters Street, French Quarter (835 6002/www.southernrep.com). Canal Streetcar/bus 55 Elysian Fields, 57 Franklin. **Tickets** prices vary; average $6-$20. **Credit** MC, V. **Map** p282 A3.
As the name indicates, this company specialises in showcasing Southern talent – both playwrights and actors – in a space on the third storey of a posh shopping centre at the edge of the French Quarter. Thanks to the venue, plenty of parking (not to mention shopping) are among the perks of a visit here. Work tends to be raw and original, as the year-round theatrical season sizzles with new play readings, workshops and competitions.

Summer Stages

Information 598 3800. **Tickets** prices vary; average $5-$20. **No credit cards.**
Telescoped into a short season from June to August, Summer Stages' forte is creative renderings of Shakespearean plays staged in unusual venues – a favourite is City Park (*see pp92-3*). Imagine *Julius Caesar* performed against the huge columns of the Peristyle, with the nearby lagoon adding to the atmosphere.

Tulane University

6823 St Charles Avenue, at Audubon Boulevard, Uptown (865 5106/www.tulane.edu). St Charles Streetcar/bus 15 Freret, 22 Broadway. **Tickets** prices vary; average free-$20. **Credit** MC, V. **Map** p276 B7/8.
Intrepid arts lovers will uncover Tulane's lively schedule of touring and university-produced theatre performances, although they aren't well publicised. For the diligent, though, good theatre is here

for the taking: over the course of summer, the Tulane Shakespeare Festival offers three plays performed by an excellent professional cast supplemented by student interns. The well-respected Summer Lyric Theatre (865 5269/865 5271) also produces plays throughout the summer months.

Zeitgeist Multi-Disciplinary Arts Center

1724 Oretha Castle Haley Boulevard, at Felicity Street, Garden District (525 2767/www.zeitgeist inc.org). St Charles Streetcar/bus 15 Jackson. **Tickets** prices vary; average free-$25. **No credit cards. Map** p279 B2.
Zeitgeist means 'spirit of the age', and that's an appropriate name for this adaptive venue that changes its offerings in chameleon-like fashion. Founder and indefatigable arts booster Rene Broussard fills the centre's schedule with an all year-round ultra-counterculture roster of events. Zeitgeist is settled down after an itinerant existence that has led it to four venues since it was established in 1993. This is the edgiest theatre in New Orleans. *See also p216* **The theatrical alternative.**

Dance

Newcomb Dance Program

Newcomb College of Tulane University, Audubon Boulevard, at Freret Street, Uptown (314 7761/ summer dance workshop 314 7742/www.tulane.edu). St Charles Streetcar/bus 15 Freret. **Tickets** prices vary; average free-$20. **No credit cards. Map** p276 B7/8.
Newcomb College and Tulane University share an Uptown campus, where Newcomb's inventive dance department puts on only one generally respectable student performance each year. In addition, the school also holds a jazz dance conference and workshop each June, which draws scholars, choreographers and fans. There are several shows a year by touring dance groups.

New Orleans Ballet Association

Performances at Mahalia Jackson Theater of the Performing Arts, Armstrong Park, 801 N Rampart Street, at St Ann Street, Tremé (information 522 0996/www.nobadance.com). Bus 88, 89 St Claude. **Tickets** $26-$72. **Credit** AmEx, Disc, MC, V. **Map** p282 C1.
As much as the city's music might inspire spontaneous dancing, precious little professional dance makes it to the stage in New Orleans. The ballet season is very short, usually comprising just four productions, and the palette is somewhat varied, from traditional ballet to ethnic and contemporary dance. Look for Ballet Folklorico de Mexico's *Navidades* Christmas show and the George Balanchine Centennial Celebration put on by the excellent Miami City Ballet, back by popular demand. Don't blink between performances: there are usually only two per production, sometimes on consecutive evenings, or even in the same day.

Classical music & opera

Performance groups

Louisiana Philharmonic Orchestra

Information 523 6530/www.lpomusic.com. **Tickets** $13-$60. **Credit** AmEx, Disc, MC, V.
A decade ago, the musicians of the New Orleans Symphony rebelled against the board of directors – composed mainly of local business leaders – over pay and budget structures. The board wouldn't back down, so, after an extraordinary public battle of wills, the symphony disbanded. Within a few months they regrouped, and the Louisiana Philharmonic was born. The musician-owned and -run organisation struggled for a few years, but it's now fiscally sound and holding its own. Programming is conservative, but visits by international artists like Pinchas Zukerman liven things up. Most performances are at the Orpheum Theatre (*see p216*), but the free outdoor concerts in places like City Park are favourites with locals. Bring a picnic and a blanket and enjoy.

Musica da Camera

Information 865 8203/www.nomdc.org. **Tickets** prices vary; average free-$12.
Musica da Camera perform medieval music on original instruments, providing an unusual and beautiful alternative to the city's other classical offerings. They play in churches and halls all over the region; for dates and venues, check local listings or phone.

Newcomb College

Information 865 5267/www.tulane.edu/music.
Tulane's Newcomb College regularly stages high-quality performances by students, faculty and guest professionals on the Tulane and Newcomb campuses. The Music at Midday classical concerts series takes place weekdays at noon during term time. Annual concert piano and classical guitar series run from August to May, along with a long list of performances by visiting players. Check local newspapers for listings, or phone.

New Orleans Opera

Information 529 2278/tickets 529 3000/ www.neworleansopera.org. **Tickets** $30-$120. **Credit** AmEx, Disc, MC, V.
Opera and New Orleans go way back. The city had its first company in the early 1800s, and by the 1890s, the genre was so popular that the glorious French Opera House was built. Sadly, the building burned down in 1919, effectively ending local opera production until the 1940s, when the Opera Association was formed. It's a testament to the city's love of the art form that in these days of astronomical costs and shrinking audiences, it continues to stage full-scale productions (at the Mahalia Jackson Theater; *see p216*). Emerging and fading stars are usually cast in leading roles, and programming tends to be predictable, though a new administration is attempting to gently lead things in a more adventurous direction.

Sport & Fitness

The Saints suck, but they're not alone – there are lots of bad teams in the City That Victory Forgot.

New Orleans understands parties. With Mardi Gras, Jazz Fest and countless other littler fests every year, the city turns almost any public get-together into an event. Well, that goes double for sport. In the hour before a New Orleans Saints home game, you'd think the football team was Super Bowl-bound, even though it has only won one play-off game in its 35-year existence. How long the party continues into the game, though, depends on the team's performance. Which is often dismal. Still, the city has become one of the preferred locations for the Super Bowl, hosting nine so far, and even though it only recently acquired a basketball team of its own, the Superdome has already been the site of four national championship games. An event-friendly business climate and a wealth of hotel rooms help to make New Orleans an appealing host city for sporting events, but the most important feature is that, in sport as in most other facets of life here, people just know how to have fun.

INFORMATION

The *Times-Picayune* is the most reliable source of information on local sports and schedules of events. It is not, however, the most comprehensive source, since events not played in New Orleans receive little coverage. Sport junkies will probably want to supplement their reading with *USA Today*'s sports page.

Perhaps the number one source for Saints news is Buddy Diliberto, who hosts a nightly sports radio talk show (6.15-10pm) on **WWL** (870 AM). Buddy D, as he is known, has been intimately associated with the Saints since he was inspired by yet another loss to suggest that fans at games wear paper bags over their heads to show they were ashamed to be seen there. His joke took off, people wore bags and the 'Aints' were born. Buddy D could only be a celebrity in New Orleans, where his speech impediment and overeager delivery have made him a beloved hero.

TICKETS

Ticketmaster (522 5555/www.ticketmaster. com) is the giant here just as it is everywhere else in the US, so tickets for most sporting events can be bought via its ticket line (a service charge is added to the price). Tickets are also generally available from the teams' ticket offices, usually at no extra charge.

If you want to get tickets through less official channels, talk to hotel concierges, many of whom act as unofficial brokers. You can also buy tickets from touts (or 'scalpers'), but tread carefully and make sure the tickets you are being offered are for the right date and game before you hand over any money. Also, scalping is illegal in the US, so if you don't want police attention, don't do it. But if you must, always haggle a little first.

LOUISIANA SUPERDOME

This is the giant home of the Saints football team, and it also hosts other major events, sporting and otherwise. Tours of the building were suspended after 11 September 2001. There's a website with more information at www.superdome.com. *See also p222.*

Spectator sports

Baseball

Despite the lack of a major league franchise, New Orleans is a baseball city. The **New Orleans Zephyrs**, a Triple A farm team for the National League's Houston Astros, play at Zephyr Field in Metairie, and even though summer isn't a great time to be out of doors in New Orleans, the Zephyrs attract a healthy crowd. The field is as pleasant a place to watch a game as it is possible to find this far from an air-conditioner. In 1998 the Zephyrs won the first-ever Triple A World Series, giving New Orleans its dreamed-of number one team, albeit in a minor league. The team sank like a stone the next season, but the city has clutched the Z's to its breast nevertheless.

In most of America, college baseball isn't much of a spectator sport. It doesn't have the immediacy of basketball or football, nor does it have the star power. **Louisiana State University**, however, draws a crowd unlike any other team in the nation. In a 2000 College World Series play-off game, when the Tigers played the UCLA Bruins, there were more people in **Alex Box Stadium** for one game

From rags to riches

For 103 years, generations of duffers and hackers have worked on their games on the par-68 course in Audubon Park. Its Uptown location and cheap green fees made it an appealing option for golfers with little time, skill or money, but the course itself had become something of a cow pasture. The holes had few defining features beyond a tee box and a green, so playing the course was a little hazardous – the inexperienced could suddenly find themselves playing fairways that didn't belong to the hole they were on. The sprinkler system had long ago given up, and greens were either shaggy or bare. Two trees on the ninth hole, intended to force golfers to decide whether to hit their tee shots around or over them, had grown so tall and wide that the choice became lobbing a short iron over them or trying to slap a ball under them. In short, the course bordered on unplayable.

A facelift in October 2002 changed all that. It has always been easy to feel you're somewhere apart from the city in Audubon Park, where the old oaks are so dense that they shut out the rest of the world. Now, new sprinklers keep the grass green and lush. The new layout has shortened the course by 2,000 yards, and it's now a par 62.

This is a surprisingly complex course that requires golfers to use most clubs in their bags. The par-5 ninth hole requires a wood off the tee and invites big hitters to try to clear a lake to set up a short second shot. This has gone down well. Since it reopened, the course has become so busy that tee times frequently must be reserved more than a week in advance.

The renovations have not, however, met with universal approval. Preservationists and nearby residents opposed the plans, concerned about the demolition of the park's 40-year-old conservatory and about the effect of a planned clubhouse on the park's oaks. A bike and jogging path borders part of the golf course in its circuit around the park, and some critics feared the effect of the renovations on it. Underlying the protest was the concern expressed by one opponent that the renovations would 'subordinate the values of free green space and the oak trees to the wishes of golfers'.

The reality, typically, lies somewhere in between. In the face of protest, plans for the controversial clubhouse have been scaled back, while some say the landscaping cut into the new course make it more attractive. *For tee information 865 8260. See also p78.*

than attended UCLA's entire season at home. Obviously, LSU baseball is a very big deal here. LSU is in Baton Rouge, an hour north of New Orleans, but since the team have won five College World Series championships since 1990, everybody's willing to make the drive. Home games are played at Alex Box Stadium in Baton Rouge. It's a comfortable place to watch a game, but as the Southeastern Conference doesn't allow beer at its games, thirsty fans may prefer to wait until LSU comes here to play the University of New Orleans (UNO) or Tulane University, both of which regularly field competitive teams.

The professional season runs from mid April to early September, the college season from early February to early June.

Louisiana State University

Alex Box Stadium, S Stadium Drive, Baton Rouge (information 1-225 578 3202/box office 1-800 960 8587). **Open** *Box office* 8am-5pm Mon-Fri. **Tickets** $7; $5 concessions; free under-2s. **Credit** AmEx, MC, V.

New Orleans Zephyrs

Zephyr Field, 6000 Airline Highway, between Transcontinental & David drives, Metairie (734 5155). Bus E2 Airport. **Open** 9am-5pm Mon-Fri and game days. **Tickets** $5-$10; concessions $4-$9. **Credit** AmEx, D, MC, V.

Tulane University

Turchin Stadium, Tulane University, at Claiborne Avenue, Uptown (box office 861 9283/ www.tulane.edu). St Charles Streetcar. **Open** 8.30am-5pm Mon-Fri and game days. **Tickets** $5-$10. **Credit** AmEx, MC, V. **Map** p276 C8.

University of New Orleans

Privateer Park, at Leon C Simon & Press drives, Gentilly (box office 280 4263). Bus 58 Franklin Express. **Open** Box office 9am-5pm Mon-Fri. **Tickets** $5-$6. **Credit** AmEx, MC, V.

Basketball

2002 saw the return of professional basketball when the **Hornets** relocated to New Orleans from Charlotte and became the team so many local sports fans had longed for. The NBA season lasts from September to April, and the team plays its home games in the **New Orleans Arena**. *See p225* **Play ball**.

At university level, **LSU** dominates the landscape in New Orleans simply because so many locals attended the university. LSU's basketball programme has produced stars such as 'Pistol' Pete Maravich and Shaquille O'Neal. In recent years, though, the Tigers have been hampered by a reduced number of scholarships for players because of recruiting violations. But with the penalty period over,

the team has shown signs of recovery, and in 2003 they made the NCAA tournament. Their weekend games at **Maravich Assembly Center** in Baton Rouge are usually sold out, but closer to home, **Tulane** and **UNO** also have strong teams. Both make it to the NCAA Tournament every so often, and that's an impressive feat considering that UNO is a commuter school whose players are often transfers from junior colleges.

Women's basketball is growing nationwide, and in some places it draws as big a crowd as the men's game. In the past few seasons, both Tulane's and LSU's women's teams have been doing well, and double-headers (featuring a women's and a men's game) are good deals.

The basketball season runs from early November to early March.

New Orleans Hornets

New Orleans Arena, Louisiana Superdome, Sugar Bowl Drive, at Poydras Street, CBD (box office 525 4667/www.hornets.com). Bus 16 S Claiborne. **Open** *Box office* 9am-5pm daily; later on game nights. **Tickets** $7-$250. **Credit** AmEx, MC, V. **Map** p279 A/B1.

Louisiana State University

Pete Maravich Assembly Center, N Stadium Drive, Baton Rouge (information 1-225 578 3202/box office 1-800 960 8587/www.lsusports.net). **Open** *Box office* 8am-5pm Mon-Fri. **Tickets** $10-$15. **Credit** AmEx, MC, V.

Tulane University

Foggelman Arena, Tulane University, at Freret Street, Uptown (box office 861 9283/ www.tulane.edu). St Charles Streetcar. **Open** *Box office* 9am-5pm Mon-Fri, game days. **Tickets** $12-$16. **Credit** AmEx, MC, V. **Map** p276 B8.

University of New Orleans

UNO Lakefront Arena, 6801 Franklin Avenue, at Leon C Simon Boulevard, Gentilly (arena box office 280 4263/UNO athletics box office 280 4263). Bus 58 Franklin Express, 60 Hayne. **Open** Box office 9am-5pm Mon-Fri. **Tickets** $5-$20. **Credit** AmEx, MC, V.

Football

American football's vise-like grip on the nation is as strong in New Orleans as it is everywhere else. Highlights from high school games are considered important enough to make the TV news on Friday nights. Of course, the New Orleans **Saints** are the primary object of football obsession, but that obsession is tinged with a dose of fatalism and dark humour as a result of the team's history of heroically avoiding success. Saints games are played at the Superdome, and they can be raucous, depending on how the team's doing. The Dome is fairly friendly, though the longtime rivalry with Atlanta has caused the ribbing to rise above the good-natured at matches between the two. **Tickets** can be bought from the Superdome or from the Saints box office in the Superdome (on ground level, facing Poydras Street).

The most complete local football experience is an **LSU** game in Baton Rouge. Pick-up trucks, tents and barbecue grills start to collect on LSU's grounds on the night before a game, and by the next morning, they're strewn all over campus, surrounded by people. Exactly why watching a game requires five or ten hours of preparation is unclear, but beer and hamburgers seem crucial to the process. Eventually a football game is played. Tickets are often sold out, but if you can snag one, it's a hell of a show.

At the other end of the spectrum are **Tulane** Green Wave home games. Tulane is the only local university that fields a team, and it does so in the Louisiana Superdome. The quality of Tulane football has improved lately, so much that in 2002 the team played the University of Hawaii in the Hawaii Bowl. Their conference – Conference USA – is a fairly new one, though, and they have no established tradition of football or rivalries. As a result, games are often underattended, played in front of a group of fans small enough to learn each other's names.

Football is also, of course, big business in New Orleans. The **Sugar Bowl** is a part of the Bowl Championship Series, a number of college football games that are played around 1 January every year to determine the champion team. Since the Sugar Bowl combines New Year celebrations with excited football fans, the atmosphere is as giddy as you'd expect it to be.

The professional season runs from the end of August to the end of December, the college season from September to December.

Louisiana State University

Tiger Stadium, N Stadium Drive, Baton Rouge (campus information 1-225 578 3202/box office 1-800 960 8587/www.lsusports.net). **Open** *Box office* 8am-5pm Mon-Fri. **Tickets** $36. **Credit** AmEx, MC, V.

New Orleans Saints

Louisiana Superdome, Sugar Bowl Drive, at Poydras Street, CBD (Superdome box office 587 3800/ Saints box office 731 1700/www. neworleanssaints.com). Bus 16 S Claiborne. **Open** *Superdome box office* 9am-4.30pm Mon-Fri; weekends for special events. *Saints box office* 8am-5pm Mon-Fri; 8am-1pm Sat. **Tickets** $25-$150. **Credit** *Superdome box office* AmEx, MC, V. *Saints box office* MC, V. **Map** p279 A/B1.

Tulane University

Louisiana Superdome, Sugar Bowl Drive, at Poydras Street, CBD (Superdome box office 587 3800/Tulane box office 865 5810/www.tulane.edu). Bus 16 S Claiborne. **Open** *Superdome box office* 9am-4.30pm Mon-Fri; weekends for special events. *Tulane box office* 8.30am-5pm Mon-Fri, game days. **Tickets** $20-$25. **Credit** AmEx, MC, V. **Map** p279 A/B1.

Horse racing

The attractive Fair Grounds in Mid-City make a pleasant place to spend an afternoon watching the horses do all the work while you sip a cold beer. Those who have been to Jazz Fest (also held here) will be amazed at how different the grounds look without tents, food booths and tens of thousands of people. Racing season opens on Thanksgiving day, and for many, going to the track is as much a part of the Thanksgiving tradition as turkey and pecan pie. The season ends at the end of March.

Fair Grounds Racecourse

1751 Gentilly Boulevard, near Esplanade Avenue, Mid-City (944 5515/1-800 262 7983/ www.fgno.com). Bus 48 Esplanade. **Open** Mon, Thur-Sun (hours vary; phone for details). **Tickets** $1-$4. **Map** p278 E/F4/5.

Louisiana car licence plates announce the state as a 'Sportsman's Paradise'. Archaic, gender-specific name aside, there's a lot for the outdoor-inclined to do in and around New Orleans. The city's tropical locale means year-round golf or tennis is not out of the question; the flipside of the weather coin, though, is that the summer's heat and humidity demand respect. During July, August and September it gets hot early, peaks near 100 degrees Fahrenheit (38 Celsius) in the midafternoons, then stays hot into the late evenings. This is hard to take for people who aren't used to it; if you're participating in any high-exertion activities, take sensible precautions: wear a hat, drink plenty of water and keep a reasonable perspective.

Cycling

New Orleans is not a particularly good city for riding a bicycle. Its flat terrain is appealing, but the potholes and narrow streets make cycling risky. Those who wish to cycle must be safe or else head to **City Park** (*see p92*) or **Audubon Park** (*see p78*), both of which are safely out of traffic's way. Those wishing to work up a sweat against a backdrop

Not quite worshipped: **the New Orleans Saints**. *See p221.*

of more attractive scenery can try the path on top of the levee that runs from Carrollton Avenue west towards Kenner, which offers a good view of the river.

You can rent bikes from **Joe's Bike Shop** in Central City. In the French Quarter, there is **French Quarter Bicycles,** and **Bicycle Michael's** (which also organises tours) is in nearby Marigny.

Bicycle Michael's

622 Frenchmen Street, between Royal & Chartres streets, Marigny (945 9505/www.bicycle michaels.com). Bus 3 Vieux Carré, 5 Marigny/ Bywater, 48 Esplanade, 55 Elysian Fields. **Open** 10am-7pm Mon-Sat; 10am-5pm Sun. **Rates** $20 per day, plus $5 helmet. **Credit** AmEx, Disc, MC, V. **Map** p282 D2.

French Quarter Bicycles

522 Dumaine Street, at Decatur Street, French Quarter (529 3136/www.fqbikes.com). Riverfront Streetcar/bus 3 Vieux Carré, 5 Marigny/Bywater, 55 Elysian Fields. **Open** 11am-7pm Mon-Fri; 10am-6pm Sat, Sun. **Rates** $5 per hr; $20 per business day; $25 per 24hrs; $200 deposit (cash or credit). **Credit** MC, V. **Map** p282 C3.

Joe's Bike Shop

2509 Tulane Avenue, at N Rocheblave Street, Tremé (821 2354). Bus 39 Tulane. **Rates** $15 per day; $50 per wk; $25 per weekend. **Credit** Disc, MC, V. **Map** p277 E6.

Laid Back Tours

625 Hagan Avenue, at Moss Street, Mid-City (488 8991/www.laidbacktours.com). Canal Streetcar/bus 46 City Park. **Open** 10am-6pm Mon-Sat; call ahead. **Rates** $17 per day. **Map** p278 E5.

Fishing

The world is divided into four kinds of people: those who find fishing cruel, those who find it a colossal bore, those who find the boredom therapeutic, and those who find every element of fishing absolutely fascinating. Those who fear their float going under because it means they'll have to stop drinking and start reeling will not want to fish in Louisiana, where the bayous and the Gulf of Mexico provide a variety of game fish and a fair amount of action. In the inland waters, it's possible to catch largemouth bass, striped bass, flounder, speckled trout and redfish; in the mouth of the Mississippi, you'll find red snapper, amberjack, grouper, copia, tarpon, shark, white trout, barracuda and trigger fish.

Fishing charters are easily arranged: look in the Yellow Pages or ask your hotel concierge. Prices range from $135 to $150 per person per day, depending on the size of the party, services offered, length of the journey and demand. Two reputable charter companies are **Captain Nick's** (361 3004/ 1-800 375 3474/www.captnicks.com) and the family-run **Bourgeois Charters** (341 5614/www.neworleansfishing.com).

For information on fishing licences, call the **Louisiana Department of Wildlife & Fisheries** (1-888 765 2602/www.wildlife license.com). A three-day non-resident licence usually costs $13, but prices vary depending on the kinds of fishing.

Golf

During the 1970s oil boom, it was thought that the unconscionably wealthy didn't have quite enough ways to spend their money, so new golf courses were built for them. When the boom ended and all the money went to Texas, New Orleans was left with a number of fine golf courses and not enough people to play them. The courses aren't always in the best condition, owing to lack of money for maintenance and the effect of the long, hot summers. Also, because of the amount of land golf courses require, most of them are outside the city centre.

Golfers who don't want to pay a lot to discover that their swings are no better in New Orleans than they were back home will enjoy the **Bayou Oaks Golf Course** in City Park. The prices are very reasonable, and both the West and East courses present a fair challenge; East is a bit more interesting. There isn't any rough, and each hole could use one more sand trap, but shots that drift too far right or left will end up under very large oaks, forcing players to take shots that call to mind Wayne Gretzky more than Tiger Woods. Duffers and those with time constraints might prefer the North course, which is shorter and more open.

For years, the golf course in **Audubon Park** was a rough, divot-scarred pasture of a course, but renovations have made it one of the most in-demand courses in the city (*see p220* **From rags to riches**).

English Turn, a Jack Nicklaus-designed course on the West Bank, hosts an annual PGA event and is the Cadillac of the area's courses. It's a private club, but resourceful concierges can usually get a tee time for those willing to pay the $155 green fees. The fairways are playable for the average club member, but the tricky two- and three-tiered greens will embarrass all but the best.

In New Orleans East, **Eastover** is generally kept in good condition and is slightly more moderately priced than English Turn. The club has had a major facelift recently: using nearby land, the attractive course

was rebuilt into two to accommodate both the club's own members and its lucrative tournament business. Both courses are fairly challenging; 'The Teeth of the Gator' is the tougher of the two. Unfortunately, the new holes aren't as attractive as the older ones, because their young greenery hasn't yet grown enough to give them that mature, impressive look.

Out of town, if you don't mind a 30-minute drive to Slidell, **Oak Harbor** has one of the most interesting layouts around; few tee shots are as simple as they look. It's near Lake Pontchartrain, and consequently the wind is often strong and unpredictable.

Bayou Oaks Golf Course
City Park, 1040 Filmore Avenue, near Wisner Boulevard, Mid-City (483 9397). Canal Streetcar/ bus 43 Canal, 48 Esplanade. **Open** 7am-7pm Mon-Fri; 5.30am-8pm Sat, Sun; hours vary according to season; usually dawn to dusk. **Rates** *Non-residents* $10-$18 per round; concessions for over-65s. **Credit** AmEx, MC, V. **Map** p278 E2.

Eastover
5889 Eastover Drive, at Lake Forest Boulevard, New Orleans East (245 7347/www.eastovercc.com). **Open** 7.30am-5pm Mon-Fri; 6.30am-5pm Sat, Sun; hours vary according to season. **Rates** *mid June-Jan* $85 per round. *Feb-mid June* $109 per round. **Credit** AmEx, DC, Disc, MC, V.
Rates include golfing cart, green fees and taxes.

English Turn Golf & Country Club
1 Clubhouse Drive, off English Turn Parkway, West Bank (391 8018/www.englishturn.com). **Open** 8am-dusk daily; hours vary according to season. **Rates** $155 per round; $85 per round for guests of members. **Credit** AmEx, MC, V.
Note that you must be a guest of a member or book a tee time through a hotel concierge or your local golf pro to play at this exclusive club.

Oak Harbor
201 Oak Harbor Boulevard, at Pontchartrain Drive, Slidell (254 0830/www.oakharborgolf.com). **Open** 7am-6pm daily. **Rates** *Non-residents* $79 per round. *Louisiana residents* $39-$59 per round. **Credit** AmEx, Disc, MC, V.

Running

Considering the behaviour of New Orleans' drivers, there's something appropriate about residents of the city referring to the grassy traffic islands in the middle of the road as 'neutral grounds'. Not only do they keep the cars safely separated, but they provide a pleasant place for runners who want to get a feeling for the city. One of the busiest neutral grounds for joggers is on St Charles Avenue, heading Uptown from Lee Circle

Play ball

On 10 May 2002, New Orleans re-entered the National Basketball Association after 23 years. In 1979, the city lost the New Orleans Jazz to Utah, of all places, and since then, for a long time the best it was able to do was to flirt with acquiring a replacement. The closest it came was in 1994, when it nearly acquired the Minnesota Timberwolves, but that deal fell through at the last minute, dashing hoop fans' dreams.

In early 2002, the Charlotte Hornets were looking at New Orleans and Norfolk, Virginia, as possible new homes. After months of study, the decision to move to New Orleans was made, and thus the New Orleans Hornets were born.

The team's move to the Big Easy had many doubters in the NBA and the pro sporting community. The city lacks the kinds of prominent businesses that have become integral to the financial success of professional franchises, and there were worries about the potential fan base, too. There is a substantial economic disparity between the haves and the have-nots in Louisiana, and solidly middle-class families are in the minority.

Nonetheless, New Orleans sold 8,000 season tickets; not only did the fans come, but the team made it to the play-offs in its inaugural season. The Hornets have yet to be adopted by the city and become a part of its identity in the way that the Saints have, but they've been well received despite daunting ticket prices – $7 to sit in the rafters, $250 to sit courtside. Most games have been sell-outs, and local fans of basketball are starting to believe the team just might stay around.

past Audubon Park and on to Riverbend and Carrollton Avenue. Twice a year, New Orleans hosts the **Crescent City Classic**, a ten-kilometre (six-mile) road race from the French Quarter to City Park. The race is usually held on Easter weekend (see p176).

For competitive runners, the **New Orleans Track Club** (482 6682/www.runnotc.org) administers races and provides info on upcoming events. For more detailed listings of running and walking organisations and events, pick up the free monthly *Health & Fitness*, distributed around town.

Tennis

Most tennis clubs in New Orleans are private, but the well-kept and well-lit **City Park Tennis Center** and the **Audubon Park** courts are open to the public.

Audubon Park Tennis Courts

6320 Tchoupitoulas Street, at Calhoun Street, Uptown (895 1042). Bus 19 Nashville Express, or 11 Magazine then 10min walk. **Open** 8am-7pm Mon-Fri; 8am-6pm Sat, Sun. **Rates** $6 per hr. **No credit cards. Map** p276 B10.

City Park Tennis Center

City Park, between Victory Avenue & Dreyfous Drive, Mid-City (483 9383). Canal Streetcar/ bus 48 Esplanade. **Open** 7am-10pm Mon-Thur; 7am-7pm Fri-Sun. **Rates** $5.50 Mon-Fri; $6.50 Sat, Sun. **No credit cards. Map** p278 D4.

Watersports

Although boat-owning locals crowd the flat, polluted waters of Lake Pontchartrain, there are a few options for visitors wanting to get out on the water. **Murray Yacht Sales/ Boat Rentals** (283 2507/www.murrayyacht sales.com), on the lake's edge, charters 26-foot (eight-metre) sailing boats and runs weekend sailing courses ($39 per two-hour weekday class, $225 per full weekend with three hours during the week). Otherwise, at weekends you can rent a canoe or pedalo and explore the lagoons of **City Park** (see p92) or try one of the canoe treks at **Jean Lafitte National Historical Park & Preserve** (see p103). Or rent a kayak or book a tour on one from **Laid Back Tours** (see p223).

Fitness

Gyms

The following gyms offer day memberships. For spas, see p169.

Downtown Fitness Centers

One Canal Place, 3rd floor, at Decatur Street, French Quarter (525 2956/www.downtownfitness center.com). Canal Streetcar/bus 3 Vieux Carré, 41 Canal. **Open** 6am-9pm Mon-Fri; 9am-6pm Sat, Sun. **Rates** $12 per day; $30 3-day pass. **Credit** AmEx, Disc, MC, V. **Map** p282 A3.

This trendy downtown gym has free weights, weight machines, treadmills and tanning beds, and lots of flirting twentysomethings.

Elmwood Fitness Center Downtown

701 Poydras Street, at Carondelet Street, CBD (588 1600). St Charles Streetcar/bus 16 S Claiborne. **Open** 5.30am-9pm Mon-Fri; 8am-4pm Sat. **Rates** $10 per day; $35 per wk. **Credit** AmEx, MC, V. **Map** p279 B1.

This city branch of a Metairie gym offers weights, cardiovascular equipment, a sauna, a whirlpool and aerobics classes to thrill its business-suited clientele.

Mackie Shilstone Pro Spa

Avenue Plaza Hotel, 2111 St Charles Avenue, at Josephine Street, Lower Garden District (566 1212/www.avenueplazahotel.com). St Charles Streetcar. **Open** 6am-9pm Mon-Fri; 8am-5pm Sat, Sun. **Rates** $9 per day; personal training from $50 per session. **Credit** AmEx, DC, Disc, MC, V. **Map** p279 B3.

The legendary Shilstone's sport-specific workouts have pushed boxers to championship level and reha-bilitated pro athletes. Coaches lead first-rate sessions on a drop-in basis, or you can work out on your own at the impressively equipped gym.

Rivercenter Racquet & Health Club

6th floor of parking garage, New Orleans Hilton, Poydras Street, at Convention Center Boulevard, CBD (556 3742/www.hilton.com). Bus 3 Vieux Carré. **Open** 5.30am-9pm Mon-Fri; 7am-7pm Sat; 7am-5pm Sun. **Rates** $10 1-day pass; $18 2-day pass; $27 3-day pass; $36 4-day pass; $45 5-day pass. **Credit** AmEx, Disc, MC, V. **Map** p279 C1.

This hotel centre has indoor tennis, racquetball and squash courts, weight machines, cardio equipment, a sauna and aerobics classes, but no pool.

Salvation Studio

2nd Floor, 2917 Magazine Street, at 6th Street, Garden District (896 2200/www.salvation studio.com). Bus 11 Magazine. **Open** first class at 6am, last class at 7pm; call for daily schedules. **Rates** $11 per class. **Credit** AmEx, MC, V. **Map** p279 A4.

This trendy classes-only fitness club has enthusias-tic trainers and open, clean spaces above a small shopping centre. Call for info on the varied classes.

Superdome YMCA

1500 Poydras Street, near the Louisiana Superdome, CBD (412 9622/www.ymcaneworleans.com). Bus 16 S Claiborne. **Open** 5am-8pm Mon-Fri; 8am-1pm Sat, Sun. **Rates** $8 per day. **Credit** MC, V. **Map** p279 B1.

Primarily a workout facility, with weight machines, free weights, cycles, treadmills and stair machines.

Trips Out of Town

Getting started	228
Plantation Country	229
Cajun Country	235
Beaches	241

Features

This isn't Tara	230
Courir du Mardi Gras	239
Houses of cards	244

Getting Started

Get out of town.

Virtually everybody gets to New Orleans, thinks about heading out of town for some swamp action, and then somehow never quite gets around to it. Another late night in the bar, another late start the next morning… It's easy to find things to amuse you in the Big Easy, but here's what you're missing if you never step beyond the city border: Cajuns, baby alligators sunning themselves on a log amid lush lotus flowers, the mist rising above a vast swamp in the heat of the day, enormous plantation houses, zydeco played in the towns where it was invented by the people who love it most, long white-sand beaches at the edge of an emerald green sea. Etc.

All of this is anywhere from a 20-minute drive (the swamps) to a three-hour drive (the beach) from central New Orleans. Now, we're not criticising anybody for choosing to spend as much time in the city as they can. But if you've got a day to spare, and you need some fresh air, we've got some ideas on just where you can go.

GETTING AROUND

It is unfair but true, you really need a car to see the area properly. Even if you just rented one for a couple of days, it's hard to do it by public transport. On the other hand, if you have no option except public transport, there is some service to the larger communities. The most useful **Amtrak** service is the Sunset Limited. It departs every couple of days for **Lafayette** (headed west) and, in the other direction, to the beaches of **Pensacola**, Florida.

By coach, **Greyhound** has much more extensive services in the area, and travels to those cities daily, as well as to many smaller communities such as Opelousas, Louisiana, and Fort Walton Beach, Florida (*for both, see p248*).

CALLING AHEAD

Phone numbers in this section are given as they would be dialled from New Orleans. If you are already in the area being written about, drop the prefix and dial only the last seven numbers.

► For tour companies, see **Guided Tours** *pp101-4*.
► For details of New Orleans' airport and its train and bus stations, see *p248*.
► For the Trips out of Town map, see *pp272-3*.

Plantation Country

Oh, fiddle-dee-dee. So *this* is how Louisiana's Scarletts lived.

The Great River Road

In its prime, the River Road, which runs on either side of the Mississippi River, was one of the most opulent stretches in the country, populated by planter families striving to out-*nouveau-riche* each other with bigger and bigger houses. The wealth came from sugar cane, tobacco and, on the northern reaches of the road, cotton. The levee banking the river is a recent addition, as are the dozens of petrochemical plants – both spoil the views. No longer is a drive down River Road a step back in time. Today, it's more of an occasion to worry about the fumes you're inhaling.

More than a dozen plantations on the river are open to the public. But they're rather scattered, and each tour costs about $10, so seeing more than three in a day can be time-consuming, pricey and repetitive, so make a plan before you set out.

One note about visiting plantations: high-stakes farming required masses of cheap labour, and this was supplied by slaves until the Civil War, but you'd never know it from some of the tours. Little remains today of the tiny houses that housed the dozens, sometimes hundreds, of black people who were owned by each planter. Only recently did tour guides even start to refer to these people as what they really

were – slaves – rather than as 'servants', which has become a common euphemism. Most of the tours whitewash things to some extent. For the exceptions, *see* **This isn't Tara** *p230*.

The closest plantation to New Orleans is also the oldest one intact, though not the most impressive. **Destrehan Plantation**, built in 1787, is unusual in that its builder-contractor, Charles Pacquet, was a free man of colour. It shows strong colonial and West Indian influences. The tour here is one of the most historic in the area.

About a mile from Destrehan, **Ormond Plantation** is another 18th-century West Indian colonial-style house. Notice the *garçonnieres*, side wings built for the young men of the family, who came and went as they wished. Though relatively small, the house has a restaurant and B&B.

About 30 minutes' drive on is the fanciful **San Francisco** (it has no numbered address, so watch for the signs). It's painted in a vivid Victorian azure, and its onion-dome-topped cisterns lend it a Moorish look.

The house's name is believed to be a corruption of the moniker given it by its first owner, who was said to have been so impoverished by the expense of building the house that he dubbed it *Sans Frusquin,* French slang for 'penniless'. The structure

Nottoway Plantation, the 'White Castle' of River Road. *See p231*.

This isn't Tara

On many of the River Road plantation tours, it's not unusual to see an African-American guide dressed in an antebellum hoop skirt. The black guides tell the same stories as the white ones – tales of splendid mansions and rich estates carved out of wilderness. Hardly mentioned are the enslaved Africans whose work made all the wealth and luxury possible. The cultural myopia which has led to the slaves' descendants explaining history from the masters' point of view is emblematic of the American, and the southern, attitude toward slavery. Half a generation after the modern civil rights movement, the ghost of slavery still haunts the plantations. In preservation and tourism-industry circles, it is sometimes referred to as 'the rattle of slave chains', and it unnerves just about everybody.

Change has been in the wind for some time, though. The National Park Service has been re-evaluating and retooling its presentation of antebellum properties, while individuals like Norman Marmillion have been blazing their own trails. Marmillion, proprietor of **Laura Plantation** (pictured), has cast the plantation story in a new light.

A descendant of an aristocratic Creole family (owners of San Francisco plantation), Marmillion opened Laura to the public in 1995 with the aim of telling the full story of life on the plantations. While describing the lives of the Creole family who owned Laura, tour guides refer constantly to the estate's 200 enslaved workers. This inclusion of the slaves' history has proved so popular that Laura now offers two tours every day, one emphasising the owners' lives and the other told from the slaves' point of view. Laura, a commercial venture owned by Marmillion and a small group of dedicated preservationist investors, has become one of the most popular plantation houses in Louisiana.

Recently, other plantations on River Road have begun making noises about adding slave cabins (**San Francisco**, see p232) and expanding tour guides' commentary on the lives of the slaves (**Destrehan**, see p231). Given the general preference for fantasy over fact, overalls probably won't be outnumbering hoop skirts on River Road any time soon – but *Roots* is gaining on *Gone With the Wind*.

was gorgeously and authentically renovated in the 1980s after being bought by Marathon Oil, which operates a massive refinery nearby.

Since a fire in 2002 reduced the lovely Tezcuco Plantation to ashes, **Houmas House** is the lone survivor on the east bank of River Road open to the public; it was closed for renovation recently but was expected to reopen in late 2003. The mansion – which starred alongside Bette Davis and Olivia de Havilland in *Hush, Hush Sweet Charlotte* – is stunning, especially the gardens, covered carriageway and Spanish-flavoured rear house. The Greek Revival main house dates from 1840.

After Houmas House, cross the river at the Sunshine Bridge to **Oak Alley**, the most famous of River Road's showplaces. Featured in many a film and magazine layout, the 1839 Greek Revival house is approached via a sweeping lane of trees that arc overhead; most are a century older than the house. Oak Alley harvests sugar cane and is thus considered a working plantation. You can have a fine time just lounging about outside, but if you go in, you'll get an exhaustive tour of the antiques-furnished rooms, and a chance to take in the view from the balcony. Afterwards, grab a mint julep and rest a spell. There are cabins for overnight stays and a small restaurant that's one of the few places to eat on River Road.

Laura Plantation, just three miles (five kilometres) downriver from Oak Alley, offers an interesting contrast to its neighbour. Though its main house is relatively modest, this Creole sugar cane plantation founded in the late 18th century offers the most interesting experience on River Road. First, it played a role in the development of the US folk tale. The West African slaves here used the French they learned in captivity to recount traditional tales from their homeland. These stories were written down in the late 19th century by folklorist Alcee Fortier and used by his friend Joel Chandler Harris as the basis for the Uncle Remus books. He wrote them in black dialect, so that *Compair Lapin* became Br'er Rabbit. Laura is also unusual in that a few of its slave cabins and other outbuildings have been preserved. Knowledgeable guides give tours emphasising day-to-day plantation life, with proper weight given to the slaves' lives (*see p230* **This isn't Tara**). Finally, Laura differs from most of the plantations in the area, in that it was run by three generations of women. The Locoul family owned Laura for more than 150 years and named it after a daughter, the last Locoul to run it, in the mid 19th century.

Madewood Plantation is off the main track (follow the signs from River Road) on Bayou Lafourche, which straggles south off

the Mississippi. Built in 1846, the columned Greek Revival house was saved from decay in 1964 by current occupant Naomi Marshall. It's now a museum and B&B, with 21 rooms decorated in period antiques.

You're almost to Baton Rouge when you reach **Nottoway Plantation**, a gaudy 53,000-square-foot (4,924-sq-metre) house which took ten years to build and was completed on the eve of the Civil War. Two storeys of sparkling white Italianate verandas have earned it the nickname 'the White Castle' (also the name of the nearest town). The interior is notable for its lavish details, including 365 windows and doors, one for each day of the year. A gash in one front column shows where a Union gunboat aimed and hit while patrolling the river – 108 years later, the shell fell out on its own. Nottoway offers accommodation in the plantation house and has a restaurant (*see below*).

Destrehan Plantation

13034 River Road, Destrehan (1-985 764 9315/www.destrehanplantation.org). **Open** 9am-4pm daily. **Admission** $10; $3-$5 concessions; free under-6s. **Credit** AmEx, MC, V.

Houmas House

40136 Highway 942/River Road, Darrow (1-888 323 8314/www.houmashouse.com). **Open** 10am-5pm daily. **Admission** $8; $3-$6 concessions. **Credit** MC, V. Closed for renovation until late 2003; call before visiting to make sure it's open.

Laura Plantation

2247 Highway 18, Vacherie (1-225 265 7690/www.lauraplantation.com). **Open** 9am-5pm daily (last entry 4pm). **Admission** $10; $5 concessions. **Credit** *Gift shop only* MC, V.

Madewood Plantation

4250 Highway 308, Napoleonville (1-504 369 7151/1-800 375 7151/fwww.madewood.com). **Open** 10am-4pm daily. **Admission** $8; $4 concessions. **Credit** AmEx, MC, V.

Nottoway Plantation

30970 Highway 405, White Castle (1-225 545 2730/www.nottoway.com). **Open** 9am-5pm daily. **Admission** $10; $4 concessions; free under-5s. **Credit** AmEx, Disc, MC, V.

Oak Alley

3645 Highway 18/River Road, Vacherie (1-225 265 2151/1-800 442 5539/www.oakalley plantation.com). **Open** *Nov-Feb* 9am-5pm daily. *Mar-Oct* 9am-5.30pm daily. **Admission** $10; $3-$5 concessions. **Credit** *Restaurant & gift shop only* AmEx, Disc, MC, V.

Ormond Plantation

13786 River Road, Destrehan (1-504 764 8544/www.plantation.com). **Open** 10am-4pm daily. **Admission** $5. **Credit** AmEx, MC, V.

Trips Out of Town

San Francisco

535 Highway 44/River Road, Garyville (1-504 535 2341/1-888 322 1756/www.sanfrancisco plantation.org). **Open** 9.40am-4.40pm daily. **Admission** $10; $3-$5 concessions; free under-6s. **Credit** Disc, MC, V.

Where to stay, eat & drink

One of the best places to spend the night is **Madewood**. It's slightly off track but worth the detour. Dinner and breakfast are included; guests eat with the hostess, in a nod to plantation hospitality (rates $165-$259 for two).

Guests at **Nottoway** can sleep in the main house's high-ceilinged bedrooms but must be up and out of the guides' way by 9am. Rooms in newer outbuildings have later wake-up calls (rates $135-$250 including dinner).

You can also eat at **Oak Alley** (breakfast 8.30-10am, lunch 11am-3pm, main courses $5-$25). A cottage acts as a B&B (rates $100-$140).

Near Houmas House, the lovely **Cabin Restaurant** (Highway 22 at Highway 44, in Burnside, 1-225 473 3007, main courses $5-$20), is housed in original Monroe Plantation slave quarters. The food is good but Southern-heavy, starting with a heap of cornbread. People drive from New Orleans just to eat here.

Just upriver from San Francisco, on the north edge of tiny Convent, is one of the area's best seafood restaurants and a great place for lunch. **Hymel's Restaurant** (8740 Highway 44/River Road, 1-225 562 7031, closed all Mon & dinner Tue, Wed, main courses $3-$28) is extremely casual and usually packed with locals. The raw oysters are the biggest and freshest you're likely to see – short of a nuclear accident – and are a house speciality, as is all the fried seafood.

If you're looking to splurge, you can have an excellent (if pricey) dinner at **Lafitte's Landing Restaurant** (404 Claiborne Avenue, Donaldsonville, 1-225 473 1232, closed dinner Sun, all Mon & Tue, main courses $18-$28). Owner/chef John Folse has a fanciful way with local produce and seafood. Nearby **Bittersweet Plantation** offers upscale B&B accommodation (1-225 473 1232, rates $175-$295).

Getting there

By car

From New Orleans, head west on I-10 and take the Geismar/Lutcher Bridge exit. Follow the road to Highway 44 and the Great River Road. Destrehan Plantation is about 25min from New Orleans.

By bus

Forget public transport for River Road; there isn't any. Commercial bus tours are an option if you have no car, and they actually work out as a good deal. You see two

to four houses and are spared the headaches of driving narrow, twisting, two-lane roads with confusing and contradictory signs. For details, *see p104.*

By water

Several of the riverboat tours out of New Orleans include plantation stops. Most only stop at one house, but you get a pleasant trip on the river and glimpses of quite a few houses in places where the levee dips a bit. For details, *see p104.*

St Francisville

A 45-minute drive north from Baton Rouge, the town of St Francisville is made picturesque by rolling hills, winding country roads and bluffs – a landscape much different from New Orleans' flat vista. Once a centre of farming life, today St Francisville is a quiet country town whose principal trade is tourism. The plantations that once thrived on crops of indigo or cotton now serve as museums and inns, or private homes. While River Road's plantations are largely part of the state's French history, St Francisville is where the English settled, and the history, architecture and antiques here differ considerably from those downriver.

So varied is the area's wildlife that naturalist and artist John James Audubon spent nearly two years here sketching the flora and fauna and painting at least 80 of his famous folios. The **Audubon Pilgrimage**, held the third weekend of every March, commemorates him with a festival and a tour of buildings and areas related to his time here.

If you approach St Francisville via Highway 1, the scenic route from Baton Rouge, you'll land up first at the tucked-away village of **New Roads** in Pointe Coupee Parish, on the bank of the False River. Once part of the Mississippi, the river became separated from it when the Mississippi changed its course. One of the state's oldest plantations, French colonial **Parlange**, is located here. Built in 1750, it's still a working farm owned by a descendant of the original family. For a contemplative retreat, take a walk around the vast gardens.

From Parlange, head north toward the Mississippi River, passing the minuscule **Pointe Coupee Parish Museum**, where you can pick up informative brochures about the area, and Main Street, with its antiques stores, waterfront restaurants and small inns.

The only way to get to St Francisville from here (other than a long highway detour) is to cross the Mississippi River by car ferry. The crossing takes ten minutes and costs $1. Roll off the ramp and drive down the peaceful, tree-lined stretch of road to downtown St Francisville. Ferdinand Street, the main thoroughfare of the town's charming historic district, takes you to the helpful **West Feliciana Historical Society** museum, which doubles as a tourist office. Drop by to stock up on free maps and brochures guiding you to the area's plantations.

Generally, you can follow the clear signs to the plantations, which are scattered about away from the town centre. If you like 'em large, stop at **Rosedown Plantation**. Its 28 acres of sculpted gardens frame an enormous white-columned house stocked from floor to ceiling with antiques, china and silver. It is generally considered to be the most complete of the area's plantations. Slaves' staircases are left intact, so visitors can see how they moved through the house – on dangerously steep steps in the dark.

If size doesn't matter, head back up the road to **Catalpa Plantation** (but call first to make an appointment). This graceful small house stands at the end of a long tree-shaded drive under gnarled oaks draped in Spanish moss. Today, it's home to descendants of the original owners of Rosedown. In its day, the focal point was not the brick main house but its 30-acre grounds; people longed for invitations to Catalpa, with its renowned fountains, island, shady nooks and greenhouses which produced cinnamon, guava, tea and coffee.

Another plantation not to miss is **Oakley House**, where Audubon briefly made a living teaching the family's daughter, Eliza Pirrie, in 1821. When Eliza became ill and was unable to take lessons for several months, her father refused to pay the artist and tutor, so he quit. Oakley House was built after the pattern of houses in the West Indies – raised to catch every breeze, with a sleeping porch and wide gallery. It is filled with antiques and portraits, and there are many pleasing paths to walk.

If you're in St Francisville in the spring or summer, don't miss the celebrated classical **Afton Villa Gardens**, beautifully restored around the scant ruins of a mansion. If you're lucky enough to visit in March, you can catch Daffodil Valley at its best: that's when 100,000 of the yellow flowers burst into bloom.

The most advertised, and supposedly most haunted, house around is the **Myrtles Plantation**. Built in 1796, the place is said to have been the scene of many murders. It's renowned for its exquisite plaster frieze work, which is more than 200 years old and matches the blue colour of the lacy wrought ironwork on the porch, contributing to the house's atmosphere of eerie perfection. There are two tours, one historical and one haunted (weekend nights only). Visitors can stay overnight in the house, but the scariest lodging is rumoured to be the caretaker's

cottage, where no one has been able to last through the night. Don't bring your Ouija board, though – they're forbidden.

Further south, nothing can prepare you for **Butler-Greenwood**'s elaborate landscape. As you wind up the driveway, you're greeted by 200-year-old oaks dripping with Spanish moss. At night, deer and armadillos wander alongside the oaks. Anne Butler, a member of the original family, still lives on the property. (Given her history here, she might one day haunt it: Butler has written a book recounting how she was shot multiple times by her former husband.) Built in 1795, Butler-Greenwood features a Victorian parlour with nearly all of its original contents intact, from the 12-piece rosewood furniture set and Sèvres vases to the floral Brussels carpet and window dressing of lambrequins and lace curtains with porcelain calla lily tie-backs. The B&B here is one of the best around; each cottage is different.

Take US 61 to Highway 66 to get to the **Greenwood Plantation**, whose restoration so impressed Hollywood types that they filmed the *North and South* miniseries here. Walton Barnes bought the ruins of the house in 1968 and painstakingly restored it to its former glory with the help of his son, Richard, working from historical documents and photos. The younger Barnes now owns the mansion and runs the working plantation, while his father is proprietor of the B&B.

If you continue on Highway 66, you'll end up at the gates of the infamous **Angola Louisiana State Prison Farm**. The prison, which is surrounded on three sides by swamp and river and on the fourth by massive fences, is said to be inescapable. In the 20th century the prison was one of the nation's most brutal and became known as 'the bloodiest prison in the South' because of violence by inmates and guards. The situation was alleviated under federal court order, but inmates are still made to work in the fields, escorted by mounted guards armed with rifles. The prison was used in the Susan Sarandon/Sean Penn film *Dead Man Walking* (1995) and Oliver Stone's *JFK* (1991). On weekends in April and Sundays in October, inmates compete in the Angola Prison Rodeo, which is open to the public. For an indirect but informative look at the prison, visit the **Angola Museum**, just outside the prison gates. It houses everything from 1940s logbooks listing prisoners' crimes and sentences to the actual electric chair used in the prison until several years ago, when it was replaced by lethal injections. The prison's dark history is outlined in startlingly honest fashion. The fascinating records on display include the admission papers for the blues singer Leadbelly, with a notation indicating he was arrested for manslaughter and released after writing a song for the prison warden.

Afton Villa Gardens
9247 US Highway 61 North, St Francisville (1-225 635 6773). **Open** *Mar-June, Oct-Nov* 9am-4.30pm daily. *July-Sept, Dec* closed. **Admission** $5; free under-12s. **No credit cards.**

Angola Museum
Louisiana State Prison Farm, Highway 66, Angola (1-225 655 4411/www.angolamuseum.org). **Open** 8am-4.30pm Mon-Fri; 9am-5pm Sat; 1-5pm Sun. **Admission** free.

Butler-Greenwood
8345 US Highway 61, St Francisville (1-225 635 6312/www.butlergreenwood.com). **Open** 9am-5pm daily. **Admission** $5. **Credit** AmEx, MC, V.

Catalpa Plantation
9508 Highway 61 North, St Francisville (1-225 635 3372). **Open** by appointment. **Admission** $6; $3 concessions; free under-6s. **No credit cards.**

Greenwood Plantation
6838 Highland Road, St Francisville (1-225 655 4475/1-800 259 4475/www.greenwood plantation.com). **Open** *Mar-Oct* 9am-5pm daily. *Nov-Feb* 10am-4pm daily. **Admission** $7; $2 concessions. **Credit** AmEx, Disc, MC, V.

Myrtles Plantation
7747 Highway 61, St Francisville (1-225 635 6277/www.myrtlesplantation.com). **Open** 9am-5pm daily. *Evening tours* 6pm, 7pm, 8pm Fri, Sat. **Admission** $8; $4 concessions; evening tour $10. **Credit** AmEx, MC, V.

Oakley House Plantation
11788 Louisiana Highway 965, St Francisville (1-225 635 3739/www.crt.state.la.us). **Open** 9am-5pm daily. **Admission** $2; free concessions. **No credit cards.**

Rosedown Plantation
12501 Highway 10, St Francisville (1-225 635 3110). **Open** 9am-5pm daily. **Admission** $10; $4-$8 concessions; free under-5s. **Credit** AmEx, MC, V.

Where to stay

This area has some of the best B&Bs in the state, but they're pricey; contact the **West Feliciana Parish Tourist Commission** (at the **West Feliciana Historical Society**, *see below*) for a complete list, and expect to pay at least $100 for a double room. One of the most unusual and relaxing B&Bs is the **Shadetree Inn** (1818 St Ferdinand Street, 1-225 635 6116, www.shadetreeinn.com, rates $95-$195). Owner KW Kennon has restored this once-abandoned house, which is set on a tree-covered bluff, to an eccentric, rustic beauty. The three suites

are decorated in a simple style, with polished wooden floors and comfortable furnishings. The **Butler-Greenwood** plantation's B&B (rates $125-$175, *see above*) has seven cottages scattered around the grounds and a peaceful pond with ducks and peacocks.

At **Wisteria**, a B&B in the heart of St Francisville's historic district, you can stay in a lavishly decorated 1902 Colonial Revival house with a sunken bathtub and veranda (11808 Ferdinand Street, 1-225 635 2262, www.wisteria getaway.com, rates $199-$350). In charming, quieter New Roads, the 1835 **Samson House** offers B&B accommodation in a Creole plantation house (405 Richey Street, 1-225 638 6254, www.manornetworks.com, rates $100-$125). **Mon Rêve** is an 1820 plantation house with B&B accommodation, a boat dock and a fishing pier (9825 False River Road, 1-225 638 7848, www.monreve-mydream.com, rates $75-$150).

Where to eat

Despite its many tourists, St Francisville offers few eating opportunities. Locals gather for lunch at **Magnolia Café** at the corner of Ferdinand and Commerce streets (1-225 635 6528, closed dinner Sun, Mon & Tue, main courses $6-$12), which has friendly, no-frills service and freshly made comfort foods such as soups, meat loaf and burritos. If you're after something more upmarket, try the **Oxbow Carriage House** restaurant (1-225 635 6276, closed dinner Sun, all Mon, main courses $17-$22) at the Myrtles Plantation. Near Bayou Sara in the historic district, **Hodge Podge** (11429 Ferdinand Street, 1-225 635 2663, closed dinner, all Mon, main courses $4-$9), offers deli sandwiches, soups and salads.

Getting there

By car
From New Orleans, take I-10 to Baton Rouge, then exit on to Highway 61 north and follow it directly to St Francisville. Or, for a more adventuresome route, take Highway 1 north; the junction is just west of Baton Rouge proper, off Interstate 110. Highway 1 quickly gets scenic and takes you to New Roads, from which you can catch a ferry across the river to St Francisville.

Tourist information

West Feliciana Historical Society
11757 Ferdinand Street, at Feliciana Street, St Francisville (1-225 635 6330/www.stfrancisville.us). **Open** 9am-5pm Mon-Sat; 9.30am-5pm Sun. Houses a small museum and the tourist commission.

Cajun Country

Join the *rendezvous avec des Cajuns* in the place where a washboard is a musical instrument.

It's summertime, and just beyond the sugar cane fields off Highway 3212 in New Iberia, near the bottom of Louisiana's so-called Cajun Triangle, the pulsating sounds of Keith Frank and the Soileau Zydeco Band are filling the air. Hundreds of people are gathered around a makeshift stage and plywood dancefloor, clapping, stomping and grinding to the beat. It's the annual Cajun Hot Sauce Festival – just another opportunity to eat too much, drink too much and get carried away by the rhythms.

But don't sweat it if you missed out, because depending on which weekend you pick, you could still catch the Crawfish Festival, or the Catfish Festival, or the Alligator Festival, or the Cajun Joke-Telling Festival, and on and on and on. The people of south Louisiana, particularly in the 22 parishes that make up Acadiana, or Cajun Country, have a powerful, shameless love for life, or, as they would surely put it, a *joie de vivre*. And now more than ever, their distinct regional culture is being celebrated in one festival after another.

Approximately 700,000 Acadians live in south Louisiana; they comprise the largest French-speaking minority in the country. The people now known as Cajuns are descendants of French colonists who first settled in Nova Scotia in the 1600s. In 1713, Britain acquired the region, and the colonists were told to pledge allegiance to the Crown or get the heck out. After decades of debate, thousands – estimates range from 6,000 to more than 10,000 – were deported in 1755. Roughly 3,000 ended up in south Louisiana. The exodus was tragic, families were divided and never reunited, and it has marked the Cajuns ever since.

Culturally, Cajuns dominate Acadiana, but they're far from the only group here. Although it's referred to (and marketed as) Cajun Country, Acadiana is actually an ethnically diverse place, where the cultures have borrowed liberally from one another over the centuries. Take the example of the music. Cajun music – the slightly twangy sound of Acadiana's white French-speaking people – has German, Spanish, Scottish, Irish and Afro-Caribbean influences. Cajun two-steps and waltzes are driven by fiddles, triangles ('ti-fers') and, perhaps most distinctively, accordions – the last introduced to south Louisiana by German immigrants.

Zydeco is Cajun-influenced rhythm and blues played on accordions, electric guitars, *frottoirs* (corrugated metal washboards worn like vests and struck with bottle openers or thimbles) and the occasional fiddle. It's immediately identifiable as a south Louisiana product, but it's sometimes wrongly labelled as Cajun. In fact, the high-energy music is mainly associated with south-west Louisiana's black Creoles, a group whose ethnicity is difficult to define. The *Encyclopedia of Cajun Culture* describes a Creole as 'a native of south Louisiana whose ancestry is black, white or mixed-race (black-

Grant Street Dancehall. *See p236*.

Try out your Cajun French at **Vermilionville**.

white, black-indian, black-white-indian), usually of French-speaking heritage'. When you mix in Native Americans from the Chitimacha, Coushatta and Houma tribes, non-Creole African-Americans and the descendants of other European countries, then you have the cultural hotchpotch that is Acadiana.

Most visitors who want to explore the area head towards Lafayette, about two-and-a-half hours from New Orleans. Considered the Cajun capital, it's the largest city in Acadiana, with a population of 110,000. Though the exiles settled over a large area, people in these parts tend to view Lafayette and the seven surrounding parishes – Acadia, Iberia, St Landry, St Martin, Vermilion, Evangeline and St Mary's – as the true keepers of the Cajun flame. Now, Cajuns elsewhere might argue with that, but there's no debating the fact that a trip to Lafayette and its expanses of rice fields and crawfish farms, is essential to any Cajun experience.

Lafayette

A good way to start any trip is by learning a bit about Cajun history at the **Acadian Cultural Center** near the airport. It houses exhibits, artefacts and photographs on life in south Louisiana. A video played on the hour tells the story of the 'Great Derangement', as the Acadian banishment was known, and of the French colonists' settlement of Louisiana.

The learning can continue next door, with a bit more entertainment, at **Vermilionville**, a 23-acre folklife park set on the banks of the Vermilion River. Seventeen replica structures, including a plantation house, cotton gins and a schoolhouse, are used to re-create a 19th-century Cajun/Creole village. Craftspeople in costume demonstrate skills like blacksmithing and sewing; cooking demonstrations are held three times a day. Everybody there wants to speak to you in the nearly incomprehensible Cajun French (like regular French only faster, with archaic verbiage and a southern accent; good luck). There's also a restaurant, **La Cuisine de Maman**, which hosts live music on Sundays.

Even *more* learning is yours, if you can bear it, at **Acadian Village**, a replica of a late-19th-century settlement with mostly authentic buildings that were moved here, restored and furnished with period pieces.

By now, you're surely an expert on the fall and rise of the Cajuns, so feel free to leave them behind for a while and head to the **Acadiana Park Nature Station and Hiking Trail** in the north-east section of the city (East Alexander Street, at Teurlings Drive, 1-337 291 8448, admission free), a peaceful park filled with picnic tables, tennis courts and miles of nature trails snaking past towering oaks and sweet gum trees.

In the evening, you can learn about Cajun culture the best way we know, by going dancing at the **307 Jazz Club** (307 Jefferson Street, 1-337 262 0307) or at **Grant Street Dance Hall** (113 W Grant Street, 1-337 237 8513), one of the state's most famous music clubs for Cajun, country and rock.

A number of events in Lafayette draw in tourists from both outside and inside the state. The **Festival International de la Louisiane** in April celebrates the music, food and crafts of French-speaking communities all over the world. Hundreds of musicians and artists from more than a dozen countries join with their Louisiana brethren for concerts, theatre and dance (*see also p177*). Then, every September, more than 100,000 people attend the three-day **Festivals Acadiens**. The party kicks off with a Cajun music concert and continues until the wee hours with a *fais-do-do* (literally a 'go to sleep', a dance that goes into the night). There's the best Cajun and zydeco music around, along with local food like crawfish fettuccine, crawfish beignets and home-made boudin.

For more on all Lafayette festivals, see www.lafayettetravel.com and click on events and festivals.

Acadian Cultural Center

501 Fisher Road, Lafayette (1-337 232 0789/ www.nps.org). **Open** 8am-5pm daily. **Admission** free.

Acadian Village

200 Greenleaf Drive, Lafayette (1-337 981 2364/ www.acadianvillage.org). **Open** 10am-5pm daily. **Admission** $7; $4-$6 concessions; free under-6s. **Credit** MC, V.

Vermilionville

300 Fisher Road, Lafayette (1-337 233 4077/www.vermilionville.org). **Open** 10am-4pm Tues-Sun. **Admission** $8; $5-$6.50 concessions; free under-6s. **Credit** AmEx, Disc, MC, V.

Where to stay

This area is not known for its good hotels, and outside of Lafayette, you could find yourself in an old-fashioned 1960s roadside motel out of sheer necessity. Because of this, most people choose to stay in Lafayette. Options include the **Best Western Hotel Acadiana** (1801 W Pinhook Road, 1-337 233 8120, rates $69) and **Best Suites** (125 E Kaliste Saloom Road, 1-337 235 1367, rates $79-$87). B&Bs include the quiet **T'Srere's House** (1905 Verot School Road, 1-800 984 9347, rates $85-$100), and the **Bois des Chenes** (338 N Sterling Street, 1-337 233 7816, rates $100-$150), a classic columned mansion built in 1820. In the town of Sunset, about 10 miles from Lafayette, the beautiful **Chretien Point Plantation** (665 Chretien Point Road, 1-800-880-7050, rates $150-$250) offers a taste of antebellum southern living.

If you head to New Iberia, pickings are slim. Options are the **Best Western** (2714 Highway 14, 1-337 364 3030, rates $56-$62), **Comfort Suites** (2817 Highway 14, 1-337 367 0855, rates $79-$182) and the **Holiday Inn** (2915 Highway 14, 1-337 367 1201, rates $67).

Where to eat & drink

Head out early and grab breakfast at **Dwyer's Café** (323 Jefferson Street, 1-337 235 9364, closed dinner, main courses $3-$6) in central Lafayette. It has a small-town feel and serves hearty breakfasts and fried-catfish sandwiches.

At **Randol's Restaurant and Cajun Dance Hall** (2320 Kaliste Saloom Road, 1-800 962 2586, closed lunch, main courses $8-$16) in south Lafayette, you can eat crabcakes and two-step to live Cajun music every night. Similarly, **Prejean's** (3480 Interstate 49 North, 1-337 896 3247, main courses $15-$25), on the Interstate 49 access road, features a band and lively Cajun dancing every night. You can dine there on elk and venison or crab and crawfish enchiladas. Don't need a dance hall with your meal? Try **Dwight's Restaurant** (4800 Johnston Street, 1-337 984 3706, closed Sat, main courses $6-$10) for boiled crawfish and seafood platters.

Resources

Hospitals

Lafayette General Medical Center, 1214 Coolidge Street (1-337 289 7991/911 in an emergency). **Open** 24 hrs daily.

Police

Lafayette Police Headquarters, 900 East University, (1-337 291 8600/911 in an emergency). **Open** 24 hrs daily.

Trips Out of Town

Tourist information

Lafayette Convention & Visitors Bureau, 1400 NW Evangeline Thruway, off I-10, Lafayette (1-800 346 1958/www.lafayettetravel.com). **Open** 8.30am-5pm Mon-Fri; 9am-5pm Sat, Sun.

Getting there

By car

From New Orleans, follow I-10 west through Baton Rouge, and over the spectacular Atchafalaya Swamp Freeway. Take Exit 103A, which will deposit you on the Evangeline Thruway into town. The Lafayette Convention & Visitors Bureau is a couple of minutes down the road.

By bus

Greyhound (1-800 229 9424/www.greyhound.com) runs frequent daily services to Lafayette from New Orleans. A return ticket costs approximately $35 and the journey takes 3-4 hrs.

By train

For the generally infrequent **Amtrak** service (1-800 872 7245/www.amtrak.com), *see p248.*

Around Lafayette

Avery Island & Breaux Bridge

Avery Island, home of Tabasco sauce, is a short drive away from Central Lafayette on a barrier island in the Louisiana wetlands. It has long been the home of the McIlhenny and Avery families, creators of Tabasco sauce and collectors of unusual animals. The areas of Avery Island that are open to the public actually represent a tiny percentage of the space and activity on the island. The rest is home to the family and its pepper farms and factories. The island itself is an oddity, sitting as it does on a salt mountain (known as a salt dome) hundreds of feet deep. The public cannot visit the salt mines on the island, which are said to contain tunnels more than 100 feet (30.5 metres) high and a mile (1.6 kilometres) wide, but you can tour the factory and see the process by which Tabasco is made – bushels of salted peppers are mashed and set in oak barrels to age, as they have been since 1791. The lush **Jungle Gardens**, where the snowy egret was saved from extinction, is also on Avery Island. The gardens are refuge to hundreds of species of birds – another fixation of early 20th-century patriarch Edmund McIlhenny. The park is walled with bamboo, and features alligator ponds and bird-nesting platforms crowded with endangered species.

Just six miles east of Lafayette, via winding country roads through swamps and small towns, is **Breaux Bridge**, the self-proclaimed (and generally accepted) Crawfish Capital of the World. This town of 8,000 is Cajun hip, with good food, lively music and antiques stores in its renovated downtown. **Café des Amis** (140 E Bridge Street, 1-337 332 5273, closed all Mon, dinner Sun, main courses $9-$21) has a friendly atmosphere and wonderful, fattening foods in glorious sauces. In the colourful dining room, the walls are lined with work by area artists. It holds a raucous zydeco breakfast every Saturday morning. The best option for dinner is the world-famous **Mulate's** (325 Mills Avenue, 1-800 422 2586, main courses $13-$19), where you can hear live music seven nights a week and at lunch on weekends. Folks like Robert Duvall, Paul Simon and Dennis Quaid have watched the Cajun two-step in this building, which is supported by cypress beams that were cut in a nearby swamp.

Jungle Gardens

Highway 329, Avery Island (1-337 369 6243). **Open** *Summer* 8am-5.30pm daily. *Winter* 9am-4pm daily. **Admission** $6; $4.25 concessions; free under-6s. **Credit** MC, V.

Tabasco Plant

Highway 329, Avery Island (1-337 365 8173). **Open** 9am-4pm daily. **Admission** free.

St Martinville

St Martinville, about 15 miles (24 kilometres) south of Breaux Bridge, is the home of the **Evangeline Oak**, which was made famous by Henry Wadsworth Longfellow's 1847 epic poem *Evangeline*. The poem tells of the story of two lovers separated when they are forced to leave Nova Scotia. The tree, on the banks of Bayou Teche, is said to mark the spot where Evangeline waited for her love. The poem ends with Gabriel dying in Evangeline's arms, but it has been so popular that the line between fiction and reality has been erased, and everyone in St Martinville will tell you that the 'real' Evangeline and Gabriel met at last under the Evangeline Oak in the middle of St Martinville. It's the town's main tourist attraction, and nearby is a statue of Evangeline, modelled on early Hollywood film star Dolores del Rio, who played the Acadian heroine in the 1928 silent film *The Romance of Evangeline*.

It's all set around the picture-perfect white towers of the lovely **St Martin de Tours Catholic Church**, which dates from 1765 and is one of the oldest churches in Louisiana. Also nearby is the **Acadian Memorial** honouring Acadian exiles. Here, a large mural depicts the arrival of Cajuns in Louisiana, while a wall is inscribed with the names of the original 3,000 Acadian settlers, and an eternal flame burns on Bayou Teche.

Courir du Mardi Gras

When a culture's rite of passage to manhood comes at Mardi Gras, you have to believe that culture knows how to have a good time. That's how the *Courir du Mardi Gras* works in Cajun Country. All a young man needs to do is not drink so much that he can't ride a horse, follow a mob to a farmhouse and then be the first to catch a live chicken.

How hard is that?

The point of the *Courir du Mardi Gras* (or 'Mardi Gras Run') is for a posse (which is traditionally all men) colourfully costumed as beggars and pranksters to go from farm to farm collecting ingredients for a communal gumbo. Farmers typically offer a chicken, which they throw into the fields where the group must catch it. Symbolically, to catch the chicken is to provide, and thus to become a man in the community's eyes. Some towns now have separate women's runs (Tee Mamou) or mixed gender runs (Eunice and Basile).

The run is probably one of the wildest community events you'll see in all of Louisiana, and that's saying something. Heavy drinking adds a macho element, so wild and dangerous stunts like standing in the saddle while riding become part of the show. If being the first person to the chicken means running through swamps and muck, climbing trees or roofs or whatever it is that stands in the way, so be it.

Cajun Mardi Gras is very different from New Orleans Mardi Gras, but its traditions are equally time-honoured. It, too, draws on medieval French customs. Fat Tuesday here looks like a society of beggars and clowns run amok. The captain of the ride may carry a whip as a symbol of his control, and of Lent and the period of atonement. Cajun costumes typically mock authority: a traditional hat worn by riders is akin to a bishop's mitre, but is worn with ragtag jumpsuits and a vividly painted mask. The most common hat is the colourful, towering, cone-shaped *capuchon*, which looks like a crazily painted dunce's cap.

Begging is a central theme, and the riders on the run solicit money from everyone, from the farmers they visit down to the spectators. They point to their open palms and ask for 'five little pennies' or chant 'where's the chicken' in French. Just as at Halloween, refusing them can subject one to pranks and pestering. Granting them something, on the other hand, should result in an invitation to the party at the end of the day, where the communal merrymaking culminates with Cajun music and dancing.

Towns with Mardi Gras runs include Eunice, Duralde, Mamou, Tee Mamou, Basile, Church Point and Elton.

Opelousas & around

North of Lafayette, Cajun country continues in the tiny rural towns of Opelousas, Eunice and Mamou. **Opelousas** is the birthplace of the late zydeco great Clifton Chenier, and thus to many it's seen as the birthplace of zydeco itself.

The legendary local honkytonk known as **Slim's Y-Ki-Ki Club** (8393 Highway 182, 1-337 942 9980) was featured in the film *Passion Fish* and is a mandatory stop for all zydeco enthusiasts, but it's open only at weekends. In nearby Lawtell, **Richard's Club** (11178 US Highway 190, 1-337 543 8233), is known

Friendly **Café des Amis**. *See p238.*

as 'the Grand Ole Opry of zydeco' among its many fans around the world. It has live music on weekends and a large dancefloor.

Not far away, in the small, battered downtown section of **Eunice**, at the corner of South Second Street and Park Avenue the 1924 **Liberty Theater** stands as a connection between the town's past and present. This was originally a vaudeville and silent film house; nowadays the famed **Rendezvous des Cajuns** is held here every Saturday night (6pm to 7.30pm); it features 'Cajun and zydeco music, local recipes and Cajun humour'. The whole thing is broadcast live on a number of radio stations. So small is the town that to find out who's playing, you are advised to call the mayor's office (1-337 457 7389). This is the boudin capital of Louisiana, so discover the mild, fresh sausage at **Johnson's Grocery** on Maple Street, where it is made every day.

If you want to learn more about the 'prairie Cajuns' – as the dry-land Cajuns around here are called – you can do so at the folksy **Acadian Cultural Center** directly behind the theatre. The tiny but oh-so-friendly **Eunice Museum** and the **Cajun Music Hall of Fame** are both a short walk away. You can meet the locals if you stop in for lunch at **The Pelican** (1501 W Laurel Avenue, 1-337 457-2323, main courses $5-$8), because that's where just about everybody here eats.

This is the true Cajun music capital of the state, so around here it's all about the accordion. At **Savoy's Music Center** (4413 US Highway 190 East, 1-337 457 9563; look for the billboard) you can catch weekly Cajun music jam sessions with the renowned accordion player and maker Marc Savoy. Or you can go to nearby **Mamou** (one town would be the suburb of the other if either was of any size), where the justifiably storied **Fred's Lounge** (420 Sixth Street, 1-337 468-5411; open 8pm-2am Sat only) has hosted a raucous Cajun music radio programme (KVPI, 1050AM) on Saturdays for more than 40 years.

Both Mamou and Eunice are well known for their *Courir du Mardi Gras* celebrations, (*see p239*) which are nothing at all like New Orleans' Mardi Gras. In this Carnival tradition, masked men gallop across the countryside on horseback, collecting chickens and the other ingredients for a community gumbo.

For more information about any of these places, upcoming events and all things Cajun, try www.eunice-la.com/interest.html, or ask at the Eunice Museum.

Acadian Cultural Center
250 W Park Avenue, Eunice (1-337 262 6862/ www.nps.gov/jela). **Open** 8am-5pm Tue-Sat. **Admission** free.

Cajun Music Hall of Fame
240 S CC Duson Drive, Eunice (1-337 457 6534). **Open** *Summer* 9am-5pm Tue-Sat. *Winter* 8.30am-4.30pm Tue-Sat. **Admission** free.

Eunice Museum
220 S CC Duson Drive, Eunice (1-337 457 6540). **Open** 9am-5pm Tue-Sat. **Admission** free.

Tourist information

Opelousas Tourist Information Center
828 E Landry Street, Opelousas (1-800 424 5442). **Open** 8am-4pm daily.

Getting there

By car
From Lafayette, take Interstate 10 west to Exit 80, at Crowley. Follow Louisiana Highway 13 about 25 miles (40 km) north to Eunice. Mamou and Opelousas are both a few miles further on; follow the signs.

By bus
Greyhound (1-800 229 9424/www.greyhound.com) runs a regular service to Opelousas.

Beaches

If it's sand and sea you're after, head east to the Redneck Riviera.

New Orleans is surrounded by water, but, let's face it, it's horrible. Brown and mucky, polluted and grim; and there's no beach, only swamp. So when they long for a day by the seaside, the locals head east.

Decades ago, popular seaside destinations were scattered along the Mississippi Gulf Coast in places like Gulfport and Biloxi, but these have one distinct disadvantage: ugly brown water. A few hours drive away, though, the Florida Panhandle – the thin finger of land that points towards Alabama – has some of the best beaches in the country. These are picture postcard places with white sand and clear, turquoise water, only a few hours drive from the French Quarter.

This is America's Ibiza, with all that implies: beautiful scenery, drunken idiots, hormonal university students, unhealthy food, sunstroke and the sea, the beautiful sea. New Orleanians have a love/hate relationship with this area, so

much so that they've dubbed it the 'Redneck Riviera' – a name that sums up its glories and miseries to delicious perfection.

It's really too far for a one-day trip, so you should plan on spending the night, but you could easily leave New Orleans first thing one morning and return the next night, sunbaked, sandy, and glad you took the time.

Pensacola

Tourist tacky, filled with fried-food restaurants and souvenir tat and very popular with country bumpkins from Alabama and Georgia, the fact is that Pensacola is still a great beach town. Gorgeous and vast but always crowded **Pensacola Beach** is located on **Santa Rosa Island**, the barrier island in the bay, about eight miles (13 kilometres) from downtown. (Take US 98 east across the three-mile (five kilometre) Pensacola Bay Bridge to

Hit the water in **Pensacola.**

Join the crowds on **Pensacola Beach**.

Gulf Breeze, then look out for the landmark sign: a 40-foot (23-metre) neon billfish, circa 1955. Take the bridge to the tollbooth plaza, where $1 gets you across).

Alongside the bridge is the Pensacola Beach Pier, the longest in the Gulf of Mexico. It's open for fishing 24 hours a day, but who cares? The beach calls, with creamy sand and azure water.

If the omnipresent crowds on the beach cause your heart to sink, just keep driving. Further down the island, **Navarre Beach** is much less crowded and even more beautiful, while on the western tip, **Fort Pickens** is sometimes almost completely deserted and is always drop-dead gorgeous. Fans swear this is the most beautiful beach in the country. As it is a protected park, there are no hotels at Fort Pickens, but it has legendary camping spots. The fort itself is famous as the prison of Geronimo, the Native American chief. The jetties off Fort Pickens are a prime spot for snorkelling.

Fort Pickens

1400 Fort Pickens Road, Santa Rosa Island, Pensacola (1-850 934 2600/reservations 1-800 365 2267/www.nps.gov). **Open** 7am-10pm daily. **Admission** $8 per car; camping $20. **Credit** Disc, MC, V.

Where to stay

Once the home of sea captain William Hazard Northup, the **Pensacola Victorian Bed & Breakfast** (203 West Gregory St, 1-850 434 2818, rates $75-$110) rents four spacious, antiques-decorated rooms. Owners Chuck and Barbee Major are in the process of building a custard stand and café on the property.

The 1905 **Noble Manor** (110 W Strong Street, 1-850 434 9544, www.noblemanor.com, rates $69-$99), located in the shady older section of Pensacola, has decent rooms and the added benefit of a swimming pool. It's also within hobbling distance of **Hopkins Boarding House** (*see below*), and near the friendly Queen Anne-style **Springhill Guesthouse** (903 N Spring Street, 1-850 438 6887, www.springhillguesthouse.com, rates $89-$99), which has two rooms for rent with breakfast at the Boarding House included, though the turret suite has a full kitchen.

Pensacola Beach is lined with massive hotels, and skyscraper condos owned by chains. Your condo choices are endless here as long as you don't mind places like the **Clarion Suites Resort** (20 Via De Luna Drive, 1-850 932 4300, rates $169). For a bargain, look to **Five Flags Inn** (299 Fort Pickens Road, 1-850 932 3586, www.fiveflagsinn.com, rates $99) and **Tiki House Motel** (17 Via De Luna Drive, 1-850 934 4447, www.tikibeach.net, rates $39-$85).

Where to eat & drink

Check out all the fish the South has to offer at **Joe Patti's Seafood Company** (South A Street, at Main Street, 1-850 432 3315, restaurant 1-850 434 3193, closed dinner, all Sun, Mon, main courses $6-$11). If you wonder how fresh the seafood is, this place has its own fleet of shrimp boats tied up alongside a vast retail fish market behind the restaurant. While the **Fish House** (600 Barracks Street, 1-850 470 0003, main courses $7-$20) appears slightly intimidating because of its weathered façade and sheer size, the food is excellent. Order a fresh catch meal and pick the fish you want: pompano or amberjack. The restaurant is as widely known for its rich, smoked gouda grits as it is for its harbour view.

Hopkins Boarding House (900 North Spring Street, at West Street, 1-850 438 3979, closed Mon, main courses $8) is an institution in Pensacola, and is famous throughout the south. Patrons sit in a 19th-century boarding house around half a dozen tables and eat enormous plates of food that just keep on coming. The fried chicken is particularly beloved. Even the mayor comes here.

If money is no object, splurge at **Jackson's** (400 S Palafox Street, 1-850 469 9898, closed lunch, all Sun, main courses $25-$34), which has a phenomenal wine list and a long line of awards for its seafood and steaks.

Resources

Hospital

Baptist Hospital, 1000 W Moreno Street (1-850 434 4011/911 in an emergency). **Open** 24 hrs daily.

Police station

711 N Hayne Street (850 435 1900/911 in an emergency/www.pensacolapolice.com). **Open** 24 hrs daily.

Tourist information

Pensacola Convention & Visitor's Information Center, 1401 E Gregory Street (1-800 874 1234/ www.visitpensacola.com). **Open** 8am-5pm daily.

Getting there

By car

Pensacola is on I-10 225 miles (362 km) east of New Orleans. Quite literally, get on the interstate in downtown New Orleans, and get off at the beach. Follow the signs to the ocean.

By bus

Greyhound (1-800 229 9424/www.greyhound.com) runs several buses a day between New Orleans and Pensacola. The journey takes just over 5hrs. A return ticket costs approximately $50.

Houses of cards

Once sleepy seaside destinations, **Gulfport** and **Biloxi**, Mississippi, thundered into the 1990s with a new marketing tool to promote tourism: Gulf-front casinos. The biggest building on US Highway 90 used to be Beauvoir, the last home of Jefferson Davis, first and only president of the Confederacy; now the **Grand Casino Biloxi**, at 137,000 square feet (41,757 square metres), takes that honour. And there are 11 other glitzy gambling palaces to go with it, detracting from the antebellum homes along Beach Boulevard (US Highway 90). If you can't make it to Vegas, you wouldn't go far wrong checking out its coastal counterpart. Biloxi claims ten casinos; Gulfport has two.

Along with slot machines, baccarat and blackjack, the casino operators have also managed to introduce glitzy live entertainment to the area. If you sift through the Osmonds, Don Rickleses and Tony Orlandos, you'll sometimes find some more worthwhile entertainment, such as Cirque du Soleil and, er, Andrew Lloyd Webber shows.

The area heavy is **Beau Rivage Resort & Casino** (875 Beach Boulevard, Biloxi, 1-228 386 7111/www.beaurivage.com). It's got the highest snazz factor on the coast, having brought Cirque du Soleil to the region. It also has 12 restaurants and a 1,780-room hotel which was named as one of the best places to stay in the area by *Conde Nast Traveller*.

The **Grand Casino** (265 Beach Boulevard, Biloxi, 1-228 436 2946) has a sister casino in Gulfport, and both are comprehensive coastal complexes. It's anyone's guess how people manage to find the time – much less the money – to gamble, with ten restaurants, a Jack Nicklaus-designed golf course, a spa, a swimming pool and a nightclub.

By train

There are relatively infrequent **Amtrak** services (1-800 872 7245/www.amtrak.com).

Destin & around

From Santa Rosa Island to Panama City, the coast is a tacky stretch of condos, resorts, strip malls, golf courses and water parks. It's hard to see the beauty through all the concrete. **Fort Walton Beach**, **Okaloosa Island** and **Destin** are legendary beach towns that all seem to blend into one giant boardwalk. The attraction here is behind it all, where there are beautiful beaches and clear water, which the local tourism offices have hopefully dubbed 'the Emerald Coast'. These places are particularly popular with spring breakers and the 18-30 crowd.

We could argue all day about which has the nicest beach, but suffice it to say you can probably go from one to another without noticing too much of a difference, so find a spot of sand you like and relax. Pick up brochures about fishing charter companies and dolphin cruises at the Visitors Bureau (*see p245*), or drive to the harbour and meet the captains in person. (To get there, take US 98, also called Miracle Strip Parkway, cross the East Pass Bridge from Okaloosa Island into Destin, and take the first right at the stoplight).

Besides suntanning, there isn't much else in Destin that is low-key. People come here to bungee-jump, parasail, jet-ski, kayak and get tattoos and piercings. Beer is the fashionable thirst quencher, and young women wear red-white-and-blue bikinis to show their patriotism. Oh, and you can forget walking, unless it's on the sand. The noisy, busy, four-lane US 98 runs alongside the water and is inhospitable to pedestrians. Seriously, if it weren't for the beach, nobody would ever come here.

Henderson Beach State Park, farther east but still in Destin, is not as frenzied, blessedly, and is sort of like a less beautiful, less quiet version of Fort Pickens.

Where to stay, eat & drink

Abbott Realty/Resort Quest (1-888 909 6807, www.abbott-resorts.com) in Destin rents many of the thousands of condos along the beach. The charming **Henderson Park Inn**, which looks like a New England inn on steroids, is a comfortable place to gaze at the beach, with welcoming rocking chairs and a veranda (2700 Old Highway 98, Destin, 1-800 336 4853, www.hendersonparkinn.com, rates $95-$189). It's best in the off-season as rates skyrocket in the summer. No children are allowed.

If you're saving money, there's a primitive campsite at **Henderson Beach Park** (1700 Emerald Cove Parkway, Destin, 1-850 837 7550, reservations 1-800 326 3521, rates $18-$20), which also has a small nature trail.

When it's time to eat and drink, get ready to get fat. The **Boathouse Oyster Bar** (in Destin Harbor, 1-850 837 3645) is a good place to chill, at least until people start pulling off their underwear and stapling them to the wall (we did mention rednecks earlier…). Don't ask us, it's some sort of drunk tradition.

The **Donut Hole** is a local institution where hefty breakfasts and home-made doughnuts are consumed by people who've never heard the word 'cholesterol'. The 'diet plate', as marked on the menu, is home-baked buttermilk biscuits with sausage patties, cheese and fried eggs all smothered in gravy, served with home fries. No lie. If you're watching your waistline, it might be a good idea not to eat around here.

Tourist information

Emerald Coast Convention & Visitors Bureau
1540 Miracle Strip Parkway SE, Fort Walton Beach (1-850 651 7131/www.destin-fwb.com). **Open** 8am-5pm Mon-Fri; 10am-4pm Sat, Sun.

Getting there

By car
From Pensacola, take US 98 east. Follow the signs to Fort Walton Beach, Okaloosa Island and Destin.

Along Scenic Highway 30A

Away from the madness of Destin, the towns and beaches along Scenic Highway 30A have a more laid-back atmosphere. The age range is higher, and that's probably because the prices are, too. Forget chilli fries: this is the crostini-and-crustacean crowd.

Approximately 40 per cent of the 56,000 acres along 30A is state-owned and protected. With its many state parks, trails and lakes, the whole area is popular with cyclists, canoe and kayak enthusiasts. A Walton County ordinance forbids buildings taller than four storeys, this law has kept the condos from building here, and kept the spectacular beach in view.

There are ten towns along 30A; signposts will tell you when you leave one and enter another – otherwise, they're so similar you'd hardly notice. In the westerly community of **Santa Rosa Beach**, **Topsail Hill Preserve State Park** has white quartz sand beaches, towering dunes and several freshwater coastal dune lakes, as well as cabins to hire.

Further east is **Grayton Beach**, a sleepy little town of 19th-century cottages, beach houses and shacks. It has somehow managed to avoid the modern development curse. A couple of miles away, **Grayton Beach State Park** offers cabins, a campground and several miles of perfect white beaches and endless beautiful blue-green waters.

Soft sand awaits at **Grayton Beach**.

Put your feet up on **Santa Rosa Beach**.

Just south of Grayton Beach, also on 30A, is the most influential beach town in America, **Seaside**. Begun in the 1980s as a revolt against high-rise condoism, it's a 'planned community' that keeps a firm grip on design. A kind of hyper-19th-century look is the mandate, but as you approach the thickets of pastel neo-Victorian houses and picket fences it's more as if you are driving into the 1950s. The area is walkable, and the shops, cafés and services are excellent, but it's all a little Stepford for us.

Another creation of Seaside's developers, **Rosemary Beach**, is about five miles east on 30A, where there is a lovely beach and stylish cottages for hire.

Grayton Beach State Park

357 Main Park Road, US 30A, Santa Rosa Beach (1-850 231 4210/www.floridastateparks.org). **Open** 8am-dusk daily. **Admission** $3.25 per vehicle (up to 8 people). **Rates** *Camping* $16-$18. *Cabins* $110. **No credit cards.**

Where to stay

Grayton Beach State Park now has cabins as well as campsites (*see above*), as does **Topsail Hill Preserve State Park** (7525 W Scenic Highway 30A, Santa Rosa Beach, 1-850 267 0299, rates $32-$38). Topsail Hill park also has a swimming pool, as well as tennis and shuffleboard courts, paved cycling and walking trails and a clubhouse.

Perhaps unsurprisingly, staying in stylish Seaside, Rosemary Beach or WaterColor will cost you, but for a less expensive option within Seaside, try the **Seaside Motor Court** (4730 Highway 30A, Seaside, 1-888 732 7433, www.seasidefl.com, rates $142-$249). This is a simulacrum of a 1950s motel.

Just a walk away is the quaint and colourful **Sugar Beach Inn** B&B (3501 E Highway 30A, Seagrove Beach, 1-850 231 1577, rates $110-$200). While, in Rosemary Beach, there's the **Pensione** (78 Main Street, Rosemary Beach, 1-850 231 1790, rates $118-$178).

Where to eat & drink

There's no going hungry on 30A: all sorts of foodie splurges are available. **Sandor's**, a six-table restaurant, is run by Sandor Zombori, who has cordon bleu training (2984 S Highway 395, Seagrove Beach, 1-850 231 2858, closed lunch, all Sun, main courses $29-$35). Other pricey but worthwhile eateries are **Fish Out of Water** (34 Goldenrod Circle, Seagrove Beach, 1-850 534 5050, closed lunch, main courses $25-$34) and **Bud & Alley's** (2236 E Highway 30A, Seaside, 1-850 231 5900, main courses $18-$30). Cheapish eats can be had at **Angelina's Pizzeria** (4005 E Highway 30A, Seagrove Beach, 1-850 231 2500, main courses $7-$18), an Italian joint often overrun by families; **Market Café** (3004 S Highway 395, Seagrove Beach, 1-850 231 5736, closed Sun, main courses $7-$18) is known for its fried-grouper sandwiches; and the immensely popular and funky **Red Bar** (70 Hotz Avenue, Grayton Beach, 1-850 231 1008, main courses $10-$17), has music at weekends and a lively brunch on Sundays.

Getting there

By car

From Destin, take Scenic Highway 30A, directly off US 98 east, towards Grayton Beach.

Directory

Getting Around	**248**
Resources A-Z	**252**
Further Resources	**262**
Index	**264**
Advertisers' index	**270**

Features

Useful buses and streetcars	249
Average monthly climate	260
Travel advice	263

Directory

Getting Around

By bus

Greyhound buses to and from destinations throughout the US arrive and depart from the **Union Passenger Terminal** (528 1610) at 1001 Loyola Avenue in the CBD.

Greyhound Lines
524 7571/customer service
525 6075/1-800 231 2222/
www.greyhound.com.

By train

Three **Amtrak** (1-800 872 7245/www.amtrak.com) services also arrive at and depart from the rather cool, 1950s-era **Union Passenger Terminal** (528 1610; 1001 Loyola Avenue) at the edge of downtown New Orleans. The fabled 'City of New Orleans' service runs daily between Chicago and New Orleans, a journey of 19 hours; the 'Crescent' runs daily from New York City to New Orleans by way of Washington DC, a journey that takes 29 hours. If you want to explore Louisiana and the surrounding regions, though, you will probably find the 'Sunset Limited' the most useful route, even though departures are only three times a week. This service between Miami and Los Angeles stops along the way in New Orleans, Lafayette, and Pensacola, Florida.

By air

The recently renamed **Louis Armstrong New Orleans International Airport** (464 0831/www.flymsy.com) is finally named after somebody everybody's heard of. For years it was named after an obscure local politico from the 1960s, but now it's named after Satchmo. Located about 20 minutes drive to the west of the city in the monumentally unattractive suburb of Kenner, the airport has expanded considerably over the past decade, and is poised to do the same again. A $41 million concourse expansion, with construction to start in late 2003, is on the books. The airport is also considering adding additional runways, but the plans are being fought by neighbours.

The airport is served by major airlines, but, despite its optimistic name, its primary international connection is to Latin America. The airport's runways are not long enough to handle most longhaul planes.

This is a list of airlines that operate out of New Orleans:
AirTran 1-800 825 8538/ www.airtran.com.
American Airlines 1-800 433 7300/www.aa.com.
America West 1-800 327 7810/ www.americawest.com.
Continental Airlines 1-800 523 3273 www.continental.com.
Delta Air Lines 1-800 221 1212/ www.delta.com.
Frontier Airlines 1-800 432 1359/ www.frontierairlines.com.
JetBlue 1-800 538 2583/ www.jetblue.com.
Northwest Airlines *Domestic* 1-800 225 2525/*International* 1-800 447 4747/www.nwa.com.
Southwest Airlines 1-800 435 9792/www.southwest.com.
USAirways (USAir) 1-800 428 4322/www.usairways.com.
United Airlines 1-800 241 6522/ www.ual.com.

By bus

Getting from the airport into town by public transport isn't particularly easy. One option is **Jefferson Transit** (818 1077/ www.jeffersontransit.org) which provides a bus that runs from the airport to the CBD (at least a 45-minute ride). The good news is it's cheap: the fare is $1.60 (drivers do not provide change, although they will issue a credit voucher for use on your return trip if you do not have exact change, but for heaven's sake don't give them a twenty). The bad news is: only carry-on luggage is allowed. The other good news is that buses depart about every 15 minutes from 6am to midnight daily. The other bad news is that the bus takes you to Tulane Avenue and Elk Place in the CBD, which is, quite some distance from most major hotels and from the French Quarter. After 6.30pm, the bus stops miles away at Carrollton and Tulane avenues, where you must transfer to an RTA bus (39 Tulane-CBD). This is just bad news all around. The transfer point is inconvenient, it's not in the nicest area of town and the process is all but guaranteed to delay your journey, since the connecting bus can often be infrequent and late.

Heading the other way, buses to the airport from Tulane and Elk run from 6am to 6.30pm. From 6.30pm to midnight, the bus picks up at Carrollton and Tulane, again an inconvenient transfer,

Useful buses and streetcars

Visitors to New Orleans will find these routes especially helpful in getting around town to sights, parks, museums and to the city's more interesting neighbourhoods.

3 Vieux Carré

A small faux trolley, the Vieux Carré bus covers more ground in the French Quarter than any other form of public transport. The route loops around the Quarter and also hits the Convention Centre and the edge of the Marigny.

5 Marigny Bywater

Sometimes called 'the boho Express', as it often carries artists and performers to work and play in the Quarter from their homes in the Marigny and Bywater neighbourhoods.

10 Tchoupitoulas

Pretty much a straight shot from the CBD along Tchoupitoulas Street to Audubon Park.

11 Magazine

Faithfully follows Magazine Street, a favourite with shoppers and gallery-hoppers.

41, 42 & 43 Canal

All are good for getting from downtown to the cemeteries at the end of Canal Street. The routes also loop through upscale Lakeview and go to the edge of Lake Pontchartrain.

48 Esplanade

Running from the edge of the French Quarter, this route is a good window on beautiful Esplanade Avenue. It also goes to the Fair Grounds Racetrack and City Park.

St Charles Streetcar

It's a fun ride just for the vintage streetcar ambience, but it's also the only public transport along St Charles Avenue. In addition to the sights, the streetcar takes you to Tulane University and Audubon Park.

---

especially if you have luggage, which come to think of it, you won't, as it's not allowed. So... on to Plan B then.

By shuttle

The airport provides an excellent shuttle service (522 3500/1-866 596 2699/ www.bigeasy.com), which costs $10 (cash or credit card) per person one-way to most downtown hotels. The service is available as soon as planes arrive at the airport, and runs until the last plane of the day has arrived. The modern, pleasant shuttles depart from the airport every fifteen minutes. It's a good idea to book ahead, just for that little touch of comfort.

If you want the shuttle to collect you from your hotel and take you to the airport, phone the day before your departure and make a reservation. Even if you are not staying at a hotel serviced by the shuttle, you can make an arrangement to be picked up in front of one.

By taxi

There is always a long queue of taxis at the airport waiting to whisk you into the city. Expect to pay $28 from the airport to most locations in New Orleans for up to two passengers. For three or more passengers, the cost is $12 per person ($36 for three people, $48 for four people). Taxis are probably the quickest and most efficient way of getting to and from the airport, although, obviously, they're also the most expensive. And the quality of cabs is, shall we say, unpredictable. Air-conditioning is definitely not guaranteed. And sometimes you wonder if the car will get you where you're going. It's all very third world.

Public transport

The public transport system in New Orleans is run by the **Regional Transit Authority** (www.norta.com). RTA operates all the Orleans Parish buses and streetcars, including the famous St Charles Streetcar, the longest continuously operating railcar line in the nation. A new Canal Streetcar line is scheduled to open late in 2003, and will include a 5-mile run to City Park and the Mid-City cemeteries, connecting to the St Charles Streetcar line at Carrollton. While much that can be said about the RTA is far from complimentary, it is the only transit system in the nation to build its own streetcars – those for the new line are being manufactured in the Streetcar Barn off Carrollton Avenue Uptown. Also, the famed 'Streetcar named Desire' is being planned to return to city streets by the end of the decade (*see p21*).

Public transport here is fairly dependable, although if there is a breakdown you might have to wait 30-60 minutes for a bus, even on a heavily used route. Also, some bus lines run infrequently at night and on weekends.

Directory

Astonishingly, bus stops often do not list route numbers, and none of them post lists of schedules or stops, so, in the end, they offer little more than a place to stand and hope. If you really intend to traverse the city by bus, arm yourself with schedules. They can be obtained at the RTA website (www.norta.com) or you can pick one up at the main branch of the city's public library (219 Loyola Avenue at Tulane Avenue – *see p255*). You can also phone the Regional Transit Authority's **RideLine** (248 3900), but be prepared for long waits on hold.

The fare for all lines, except for express buses and the Riverside Streetcar, is $1.25, plus 25¢ for a transfer (the fare for those over 65 or disabled is 40¢, and they also get free transfers). Transfers must be purchased when you board the bus or streetcar, at the same time as you purchase a ticket, and they cannot be used on the same bus route from which they are purchased. The fare for express buses and for the Riverfront Streetcar is $1.50.

Travel passes

Travel passes, known as **VisiTour Passes**, can be used in place of tickets and transfers on any RTA vehicle, and are an excellent bargain if you plan on being out and about most of the day. The one-day pass ($5), and the three-day pass ($12) are both available from most hotel concierges and from tourist information booths. The 30-day pass ($55) is available at banks and grocery stores throughout the city.

Ferries

As a river city, New Orleans does have a workhorse ferry system that is generally scheduled for the convenience of cross-river commuters. For

visitors the trip alone is a marvelous way to get on the river for free. (Pedestrians pay nothing for the ferry.) From the ferry you can see the New Orleans skyline and get a feel for the city's water-dictated geography. It is also a fun way to extend a bicycle tour of downtown to the West Bank. There are three ferries: all are free to pedestrians and bicyclists. There is a charge of $1 for motor vehicles, which is collected on the West Bank side as you exit the ferry.

Canal Street–Algiers Ferry

Departs from the foot of Canal Street, between the Aquarium of the Americas and Riverwalk Mall, every 15 mins from 5.45am to midnight daily.

Chalmette–Algiers Ferry

Departs from Chalmette at the intersection of Parish Road and St Bernard Highway (about a mile and a half east of the Chalmette Battlefield) and runs to Patterson Road in east Algiers every 15 mins, 5.45am to 9.15pm daily.

Jackson Avenue–Gretna Ferry

Departs from the foot of Jackson Avenue, at the intersection of Tchoupitoulas Street, and runs to Huey P Long Avenue and First Street in Gretna every 15 mins, 5.45am to 9.30pm daily.

Taxis & limos

Taxis are a great way to get around New Orleans if you don't have a car. They are also the safest way to travel late at night, and as a rule the quickest. It's one of those best of times/worst of times things, though, as taxi drivers can be either friendly and helpful, providing a wealth of local knowledge, or abrasive and sullen, even downright rude. You pays your money, and you takes your chances. Although there are city regulations for fleet maintenance and for

things like cleanliness, taxi quality still varies widely. You wonder how some of the cars keep from rattling apart.

If you are downtown during the day, you won't have any problem finding a cab. You can flag one down on Decatur Street, in other parts of the Quarter and on Canal Street near the larger hotels; otherwise, your best bet is to find a big hotel and go to the first taxi in the queue outside. If you're in an outlying neighbourhood, call one of the cab companies listed here. They'll usually give you an estimate on how long the cab will take. If you're in a bar, restaurant or shop, ask the staff to call one for you. Regular meter fares begin at $2.50 and increase by 20¢ every one-eighth of a mile or 40 seconds. There is also an additional charge of $1 for each extra passenger. A tip of 10 per cent is the norm; if you have luggage, tip an extra dollar per piece. In the event that you have a complaint about a cab, a driver or the service provided, phone the Taxicab Bureau (565 6272).

Local taxis

United Cabs *522 9771.*
White Fleet *948 6605.*
Checker-Yellow Cabs *943 2411.*

Limousine services

New Orleans Limousine Service *529 5226.*
Orleans Limousines *288 1111.*

Driving

Driving a car in New Orleans can be a thrill, especially if you come from a place where driving rules are obeyed and enforced. Few local drivers even pay much heed to traffic lights, so always look both ways before pulling into an intersection, even if your light is green. There will almost always be some fool blasting through the red light at the last second, or even seconds after the last second. To add to the mayhem, most left turns at major intersections are illegal, thus requiring drivers to go beyond the intersection, make a U-turn and then follow that with a right turn on to the cross street. Check street signs carefully. And maybe pray.

American Automobile Association (AAA)

3445 N Causeway Boulevard, at 14th Street, Metairie (838 7500/1-800 222 7623/www.aaa.com). **Open** 8.30am-7pm Mon, Wed; 8.30am-5.15pm Tue, Thur, Fri.
The AAA has heaps of maps and state-by-state guidebooks, plus a treasure trove of travel tips – all free to members, including those belonging to affiliated clubs such as the British AA.

Car rental

Renting a car for a day provides an excellent way to escape into the surrounding countryside or see sights a bit further afield. You will need a valid driver's licence and a major credit card (American Express, Discover, MasterCard or Visa). The business is very competitive, so it's worth phoning two or more agencies to compare prices. Most should offer unlimited mileage. Be sure to ask about discounts for AAA and frequent flyer programme members.

National rental companies

Alamo Rent A Car 08705 994000 www.alamo.co.uk
Avis 1-800 831 2847/ www.avis.com.
Budget 1-800 527 7000/ www.budget.com.
Enterprise 1-800 736 8222/ www.enterprise.com.
Hertz 1-800 654 3131/ www.hertz.com.
National 1-800 227 7368/ www.nationalcar.com.

Breakdown services

AAA Emergency Road Service

1-800 222 4357. **Open** 24hrs daily.
Members – including those of affiliated clubs such as the British

AA – receive free towing and roadside service. There's also maps and other services for members.

The Auto Clinic

3520 Westbank Expressway (349 0800) **Open** 9am-6pm Mon-Sat.
Offers a tow and delivery service included in the price of repairs.

Doody & Hank's

719 O'Keefe Street (522 5391/524 0118). **Open** 7.30am-5pm Mon-Fri.
Doody & Hank's not only has an amusing name, it also provides road service in and around the city.

Expert Auto Service

895 4345. **Open** 9am-5pm Mon-Fri.
Offers car service Uptown.

Parking

Although finding a parking space is fairly easy – except in the CBD and French Quarter, where the opposite is usually the case – there are countless rules about parking in New Orleans, and the city makes a tidy profit from issuing tickets to and impounding the cars of the confused.

If you park on any street near downtown or the Quarter, look carefully for signs and pavement markings telling you when and where you can park: even if you don't see them, the authorities know where they are and they will tow your car away in a heartbeat. Never waste your time or energy arguing with a meter maid; they are made of stone.

Parking meters accept nickels, dimes and quarters and require payment from 8am to 6pm Mon-Fri.

The bad habits of New Orleans drivers mean your vehicle will be much safer in an off-street car park; there are plenty of them, even during high season. There are several parking lots in the French Quarter where you can expect to pay around $5 an hour or $20 for 12 hours – reasonable compared to many congested US cities. During the hot months, consider paying a bit more for indoor parking.

At the edge of the French Quarter and the CBD, you can find easy parking in the Canal Place shopping complex at the foot of Canal Street.

Louisiana Superdome

Sugar Bowl Drive, at Poydras Street (587 3805/www.superdome.com). **Map** p279 A/B1.
There are four parking garages at the Superdome. Some offer a flat rate of $5 if you enter between 5.30am and 2pm. After that, an hourly rate applies until 9pm.

Cycling

Cycling around New Orleans gives you the flexibility to explore neighbourhoods that are beyond walking distance, and the flat terrain makes for easy pedalling. But beware: not only do many local cyclists complain of drivers' attitude toward the rules of the road, the huge potholes don't help either. Keep your head up and your eyes open. Maps with suggested bike routes are available from bike shops, though these routes are designed more for recreational biking than for helping you get somewhere. For more bicycle options, *see p223.*

Bicycle Michael's

622 Frenchmen Street, between Royal & Chartres streets, Marigny (945 9505/www.bicycle michaels.com). Bus 3 Vieux Carré, 5 Marigny/Bywater, 48 Esplanade, 55 Elysian Fields. **Open** 10am-7pm Mon-Sat; 10am-5pm Sun. **Rates** $20 per day, plus $5 helmet. **Credit** AmEx, Disc, MC, V. **Map** p282 D2.
Within easy walking distance of the French Quarter, Bicycle Michael's bike rental rate is $7.50 an hour for the first two hours, with a $20 daily rate applied after that.

Laid-Back Tours

625 Hagan Avenue, at Moss Street, Mid-City (488 8991/www.laidback tours.com). Canal Streetcar/bus 46 City Park. **Open** 10am-6pm Mon-Sat; call ahead. **Rates** $17 per day. **Map** p278 E5.
This company conducts bike tours (by appointment) and also rents cycles for $17 per day and up, helmet included. Located on beautiful Bayou St John, it stocks recumbent bikes and provides kayak rentals.

Resources A-Z

Convention Centre

Ernest N Morial Convention Center

900 Convention Center Boulevard, at Julia Street, Warehouse District (582 3027/www.mccno.com). Bus 10 Tchoupitoulas. **Map** p279 C2.
With 1.1 million square feet of space so far and growing like the glass-covered beast that ate New Orleans. This ever-expanding complex is the fourth largest of its kind in the US.

Courier services

DHL
1-800 225 5345/www.dhl-usa.com.
The best option for international express shipments.

Federal Express
1-800 463 3339/www.fedex.com.
Especially good for US deliveries. Phone for opening hours and pick-up locations around town.

Trax Express Deliveries
804 Perdido Street, CBD (525 9917).
Open 7.45am-5.15pm Mon-Fri.
The go-to courier express among local businesses, prized for its 24-hour service and dependability.

United Cab
522 9771.
A taxi company with reliable package delivery 24 hours a day.

UPS
1-800 742 5877/www.ups.com.
Packets and larger shipments are UPS' specialities. Phone for hours and pick-up information.

US Postal Service
1-800 222 1811/www.usps.gov.
Priority mail service to 27 countries. The express part is limited to the US segment of the delivery, though. Nobody guarantees speedy delivery in Outer Mongolia.

Office services

Kinko's
762 St Charles Avenue, at Julia Street, CBD (581 2541/ www.kinkos.com). St Charles Streetcar. **Open** 24hrs daily.
Map p279 B2.

There are five full-service Kinko's in the metro area (all listed in the phone book). This is the most central and the coolest, with lots of late-night singles dropping by to copy their poetry and pick up concert flyers. There are self-service copiers and a battery of computers with internet access (20 cents per minute). Typesetting, printing, faxing and passport photos are also available.

All embassies in the US are located in Washington, DC, but UK nationals visiting New Orleans can contact the Honorary British Consulate here for information and advice. The nearest consular offices for all other English-speaking countries are in Washington, DC.

Honorary British Consulate
10th Floor, 321 St Charles Avenue, between Union & Perdido streets, CBD, New Orleans, LA 70130 (524 4180). St Charles Streetcar.
Open 9.30am-2.30pm Mon-Fri.
Map p279 C1.
In case of emergency outside office hours, British passport holders should contact the Consulate General in Houston, Texas (1-713 659 6270/www.britainusa.com/houston). All visa enquiries should be directed to the Consulate General in Los Angeles, California (1-310 481 2900/www.britainusa.com/la).

Better Business Bureau
24hr information line 581 6222/www.neworleans.bbb.org.
The BBB has information on almost every company in the city. If you have a complaint about a product or service, call the BBB and it will make a report, although it won't do much more than that. If you want to know if a complaint has already been registered against a business or corporation, the BBB will tell you.

Consumer Product Safety Commission
1-800 638 2772/www.cpsc.gov.

Louisiana Attorney General's Office of Consumer Protection
1-800 351 4889/www.ag.state.la.us.
Call this office to make a complaint regarding consumer law enforcement or any other agency.

New Orleans has an indifferent attitude toward the disabled. Many federally mandated accessibility laws seem to have been ignored here, and the historic status of many buildings precludes structural changes. More restaurants and hotels are becoming sensitive to people with disabilities (especially as they travel in greater numbers), but as many are located in old buildings, it's always wise to phone ahead to check on accessibility. When booking a hotel room, anyone with impaired mobility should choose one of the newer hotels, most of which have been designed with accessibility.

Getting around the city is also problematic. The cracked, buckling sidewalks and streets of New Orleans are tough on everyone, but especially on those with disabilities. Public transportation makes an effort, but it requires planning ahead. All regional city buses on fixed routes are equipped with lifts, can 'kneel' to make access easier and have handgrips and spaces designed for wheelchair users. But the lifts are out of order more frequently than they should be, so you may have to wait at a bus stop through one or more buses. RTA technically provides mobility-impaired customers with a special pick-up service, Paratransit (827 7433/ www.regionaltransit.org). But the conditions of use make it difficult for short-term visitors: you must book two weeks in advance and provide medical certification of your condition to be eligible to use it. Its availability is best during non-rush hours (10am-3pm weekdays). For full details of the Paratransit system, as well as information on just about any aspect of navigating New Orleans if you have a disability, it's a good idea to contact the Advocacy Center for the Elderly and Disabled.

Advocacy Center for the Elderly & Disabled
Suite 2112, 225 Baronne Street (522 2337/1-800 960 7705/ www.advocacyla.org.
Open 9am-5pm Mon-Fri.
This umbrella agency is a good starting place for referrals and information.

Deaf Action Center
Catholic Charities (523 3755/ 24hr TDD line 525 3323).
Phone line 8am-4.40pm Mon-Fri.
The best source of information on local resources for the deaf.

Lighthouse for the Blind
123 State Street (897 3456/ www.lhb.org)
In addition to an excellent referral and information centre, this non-profit group has a shop that carries unusual and hard-to-find equipment and aids for the blind and the visually impaired.

WRBH (88.3 FM)
899 1144/www.wrbh.org.
A 24-hour radio station devoted to the needs of the blind and visually impaired. Volunteers read books, magazines, children's stories and other information. Each day's newspaper is read between 7 and 10am and repeated from 6.30 to 8pm daily. On Saturdays from 11am to 12.30pm, the *Times-Picayune's* Friday entertainment guide, *Lagniappe*, is read.

Electricity

United States uses a 110-120V, 60-cycle AC voltage. Except for dual-voltage, flat-pin plug shavers, Europeans will need to run any small appliances they bring via an adaptor, available at airport shops, some large pharmacies and department stores. Bear in

mind that most US VCRs and televisions use a different frequency from those in Europe: you will not be able to play back camcorder footage during your trip. However, you can buy and use blank tapes.

Gay & lesbian

Resources

Ambush
522 8049/www.ambushmag.com.
The primary conduit of gay, lesbian, bisexual and transgendered news, *Ambush* comes out every other week. It's an amateurish effort, though fat with ads: serious news is ignored in favour of grainy snapshots from clubs. Still, it's the best print source for information about gay events and nightlife. Its distributed free at gay bars and most coffeehouses, cafés and other meeting places in the French Quarter.

Gay Heritage Tour
Meets at Alternatives shop, 909 Bourbon Street, at Dumaine Street, French Quarter (information 945 6789/Alternatives 524 5222/ nolabienville@aol.com). Bus 3 Vieux Carré, 48 Esplanade. **Rates** $20. **Credit** AmEx, MC, V.
Map p282 C2.
Ideal for orienting yourself to gay New Orleans, this two-and-a-half hour tour blends history, sightseeing with club reviews and an insider's perspective. Advance reservations are required. Founder Roberts Batson also occasionally does a one-man stand-up version of the tour, 'Amazing Place This New Orleans', at the True Brew Coffeehouse, 200 Julia Street (details 945 6789).

Gay New Orleans
www.gaynewworleans.com.
This website is operated by Ambush and leans heavily towards their advertisers, but it's still a handy source of key information about gay and lesbian life and events.

Lesbian & Gay Community Center of New Orleans
2114 Decatur Street, at Frenchmen Street, French Quarter (945 1103/ fax 945 1102). Bus 3 Vieux Carré, 5 Marigny/Bywater, 82 Desire.
Open noon-7pm Mon-Fri; 9am-5.30pm Sat, Sun. **Map** p282 D3.
This volunteer-run centre provides details on social, cultural, health, religious and political activities.

Health

The NO/AIDS Task Force
Suite 500, 2601 Tulane Avenue, at Dorgenois Street, Tremé (821 2601/statewide hotline 1-800 992 4379/www.crescentcity.com). Bus 39 Tulane. **Open** *Centre* 8.30am-5pm Mon-Fri. *Phone line* noon-8pm daily.
Provides information and a full range of educational, preventive, testing and client services.

Health & medical

Emergency care

If you need an ambulance, dial **911**. It can be dialled for free from local payphones.

In New Orleans, the **Charity Hospital** system provides access to medical care in almost every imaginable area. Charity's Trauma Care Unit is rated the best in the country, which is good news considering that this is where you will probably end up in the unlikely event that you are on the receiving end of a gunshot. You must pay for emergency treatment, so if you're a foreign national, try to contact your insurers before you seek treatment and they will direct you to a hospital that will deal directly with them. For referral to a local doctor, contact the **Tulane University Professional Physicians Referral Group** (588 5800).

Charity Hospital Campus
Louisiana State University Medical School, 1532 Tulane Avenue, CBD (903 7154/www.lsuhsc.edu). Bus 39 Tulane. **Open** *Emergency room* 24hrs daily. **Map** p279 B1.

Daughters of Charity Health Center
3900 S Carrollton Avenue, at Palmetto Street, Central City (482 0084). Bus 90 Carrollton. **Open** 8am-6.30pm Mon-Thur; 10am-2pm Fri; 9am-2pm Sat. **Map** p276 C6.
The closest thing New Orleans has to a free clinic, this centre offers care for the entire family, including counselling and an on-site pharmacy. There is a sliding fee scale.

Directory

Dentists

NO Dental Association

834 6449/www.nodental.com. **Open** *Phone line* 9am-5pm Mon-Fri.
The place to call for referrals to a dentist; outside office hours, a recorded message will direct you to an emergency number.

Pharmacies

For pharmacies, including those open 24 hours daily, *see p168.*

Helplines & agencies

AIDS/HIV

See p253 **NO/AIDS Task Force.**

Alcohol/drug abuse

Alcoholics Anonymous Central Office

779 1178/www.aa-neworleans.org.
Open *Phone line* 24hrs daily.
The helpline is run by volunteers, and there are occasional gaps when you'll get voice mail, requesting that you leave a number; a counsellor will call you back as soon as possible.

Narcotics Anonymous

899 6262. **Open** *Recorded information* 24hrs daily.
Call for a recorded list of meeting times and locations.

Child abuse

Child Protection Hot Line

680 9000. **Open** *Phone line* 24hrs daily.

Psychiatric emergency services

DePaul-Tulane Behavioral Health Center

Tulane University, 1040 Calhoun Street, Uptown (899 8282). Bus 11 Magazine. **Open** 24hrs daily.
Map p276 B8.
This excellent psychiatric hospital provides outpatient and evening treatment. Fees on a sliding scale.

Rape

Rape Crisis Line

483 8888. **Open** *Phone line* 24hrs daily. An answering service connects callers to a rape counsellor.

Suicide prevention

Suicide/Crisis Line

523 2673. **Open** *Phone line* 24hrs daily.
Counsellors work with callers or refer them to services, depending on the situation. The line is open all night, but you may have to wait on hold for several minutes.

Immigration & customs

Few international flights arrive in New Orleans; you'll usually have to transfer to a domestic flight at another US airport and go through immigration and customs there. This will mean reclaiming your baggage at the transfer airport, taking it through customs and then checking it in again. The airlines try to make this process painless by having a transfer check-in desk just outside customs at most major transfer airports, but you'll have to make your own way to the domestic departures terminal. Connection times do take account of this, and of the fact that you may have to queue at immigration, but we recommend that you get through the transfer process and check in for your New Orleans flight before taking any time to relax.

Standard immigration regulations apply to all visitors. During your flight, you should be given an immigration form (which you may find deeply curious, as some of the questions have not, apparently, changed since the McCarthy era) along with a customs declaration form to be presented when you land. Fill them in very carefully, and ask for another if you make a mistake – nothing less than perfection will do. Be prepared to wait for up to an hour when you first arrive at immigration. Expect to explain the nature of your visit (business and/or pleasure). If you don't have a return ticket and are planning a long visit, you will probably be questioned closely. As this book was going to press, the current US administration was considering tightening its rules on arrivals from all foreign countries, and had plans to extensively interview each traveller. This could make the process much longer.

Unless something goes wrong, you will be granted an tourist visa to cover the length of your stay. For information on visas, *see p260.*

US Customs allows visitors to bring in $200 worth of gifts ($400 for returning Americans), 200 cigarettes or 50 cigars, and one litre of spirits (liquor) duty free. No plants, fruit, meat or fresh produce can be taken through customs. For more detailed information, check out the US Customs website at www.customs.ustreas.gov or contact your nearest US embassy or consulate.

UK Customs & Excise allows returning travellers to bring in $145 worth of gifts and goods and an unlimited amount of money, as long as they can prove it's theirs.

Insurance

It's advisable to take out comprehensive travel insurance cover before arriving in New Orleans – it's almost impossible to arrange once you are already there. Make sure you have adequate health cover, since medical expenses can be very high. If you are American, your own insurance is likely to cover you during your stay. *See p253* for a list of New Orleans hospitals and emergency rooms.

Internet access

Cyber Bar & Café
At the Contemporary Arts Center, 900 Camp Street, Warehouse District (523 0990/www.cacno.org). St Charles streetcar. **Open** 10am-5pm Mon-Fri, 11am-5pm Sat-Sun. **Map** p279 C2.
The ground floor café attached to the arts centre is a relaxed spot for checking email or going online. More coffeehouse than café. Eagle-eyed staffers keep crumb-prone foods away from the machines.

Kinko's
All five New Orleans area shops have computers with 24-hour internet access (*see p252*).

New Orleans Public Library
Main Branch, 219 Loyola Avenue, at Tulane Avenue, CBD(596 2570/ www.nutrias.org). Bus 39 Tulane. **Open** 10am-6pm Mon-Thur, 10am-5pm Sat. **Map** p279 B1.
With 18 computers and no fee, the main library is the cheapest option. There are often long waits, especially right after schools let out in the afternoons, and on Saturdays.

Royal Access Internet Café
621 Royal Street, at Toulouse, French Quarter (525 0401/ www.royalaccess.com). **Open** 9am-8pm Mon-Thur; 9am-10pm Fri-Sat; 9am-6pm Sun. **Map** p282 B2.
Upstairs from the pleasant Royal Blend Coffee & Tea House (*see p133*), this is a well-maintained, well-run place to go online. Large-screen PCs are $8 an hour, $5 for 30 minutes and $3 for 15 minutes.

Libraries

The New Orleans public library system is unbelievably underfunded, but a creative, dedicated workforce gives the city better libraries than it pays for. Besides the main library in the CBD, there are 13 branches (see Yellow Pages or www.nutrias.org for all addresses and information). For visitors, the two most useful branches are the main one and the Latter branch, which is located inside a historic mansion on St Charles Avenue in the Garden District.

New Orleans Public Library (main branch)
219 Loyola Avenue, at Tulane Avenue, CBD (596 2570/ www.nutrias.org). Bus 39 Tulane. **Open** 10am-6pm Mon-Thur; 10am-5pm Sat. **Map** p279 B1.
The well-informed, helpful staff, free computers, changing art and history exhibitions and occasional speakers make the main library useful and interesting for almost everyone.

Latter Memorial Library
5120 St Charles Avenue, at Soniat Street, Uptown (596 2625/ www.nutrias.org). St Charles Streetcar. **Open** 11am-6pm Mon-Thur; 11am-5pm Sat. **Map** p276 C9.
Previously home to millionaires and a film star, this elaborate 1907 neo-Italianate villa has all the basic library services plus a lively, steady schedule of events.

Media

New Orleans is not a media-intensive city. It has only one daily newspaper and a smattering of magazines and weekly publications. If you want to keep up with the outside world while you're here, pick up the *New York Times,* which is available in coin-operated boxes all over town and in newsstands. *USA Today* and the *Wall Street Journal* are also easy to find. Foreign and UK newspapers are difficult to find, although Tower Records often has a good collection (*see p173*).

Newspapers & magazines

City Business
www.neworleans.com/citybusiness.
Fortnightly tabloid devoted to the wholehearted promotion of New Orleans and regional businesses. Bland and uncritical, useless to tourists and, for that matter, locals.

Gambit Weekly
www.bestofneworleans.com
The primary weekly alternative newspaper, *Gambit* is distributed free at cafés, coffeehouses and music stores. Its political reporting is respected and award-winning. It tends to be more left-of-centre than other local publications. It can be

noncommittal in some reviews, but the entertainment and events listings are the most comprehensive in town.

New Orleans Magazine
This glossy monthly delivers mostly uncritical stories on local personalities. It has good restaurant reviews and interesting snippets of little-known local history. Otherwise, this one is for local rich people to read about one another.

OffBeat
www.offbeat.com.
This is a comprehensive monthly magazine on New Orleans music with a detailed calendar of gigs plus interviews, album reviews and lively columns. Distributed free at cafés, bars, clubs and other likely spots.

Times-Picayune
www.nolalive.com.
The cock of the walk. The *Times-Picayune* not only has no major competition, it doesn't even have any small suburban dailies to worry about. It's professionally written and well edited but takes a complacent, even wilfully obtuse attitude towards New Orleans' enduring problems of race, crime and political malfeasance. It also tends to be a very thin paper – in fact some Monday editions barely line the bird cage – that brushes the surface of national and international events. It periodically pours massive resources into high-profile series in transparent attempts to win big awards such as the Pulitzer Prize for journalism. And, sadly, it succeeds. In a just world, mediocrity would never be so rewarded.

Radio

WRBH (88.3 FM)
Radio for the blind and 'print impaired'. *See also p253.*

WTUL (91.5 FM)
Tulane University's student-run station is unpredictable, cutting edge, award winning and almost always interesting. No hits are played here.

WWNO (89.9 FM)
This public radio station broadcasts National Public Radio's stellar news programmes, 'All Things Considered' and 'Morning Edition'. It's light on local news but a crucial pipeline to intelligent reporting on national and world events. The majority of airtime is devoted to classical music, with spots for jazz and opera.

WWL (870 AM)
Talk radio in which the airtime is usually filled with people who should shut the heck up. Yada yada yada.

Directory

WWOZ (89.9 FM)

This is music heaven. WWOZ is a public station devoted to New Orleans and roots sounds. Its staff of incredibly knowledgeable volunteer DJs broadcast programmes about jazz (in all its varieties), '50s R&B, zydeco, Cajun, blues, gospel, Latin, Caribbean, world beat and almost everything else that isn't Top 40. Local musicians are regularly interviewed and the music scene is discussed in detail.

WYLD (98.5 FM & 940 AM)

The city's largest African-American station has mainstream music and popular DJs who invite comments from the community.

TV

In New Orleans, as in most US cities, national networks dominate the airwaves. Public access channels tend to be the preserve of boring political drones. It's interesting to note that, in one of America's wildest cities, out of six local stations, two are religious.

WGNO, Channel 26, ABC
WDSU, Channel 6, CBS
WWL, Channel 4, NBC
WYES, Channel 12, PBS
WLAE, Channel 32, PBS and Catholic programming
WHNO, Channel 20, religious programming

Money

The US dollar ($) equals 100 cents (¢). Coins range from copper pennies (1¢) to silver nickels (5¢), dimes (10¢), quarters (25¢) and half dollars (50¢).

In 2000 the US Mint issued a new 'golden' dollar coin. Embossed with a portrait of Sacagawea, a Native American woman who acted as a guide to early 19th-century explorers Lewis and Clark, the coin has been so popular with collectors that very few have made their way into general circulation. Most vending machines are not yet equipped to take them.

Paper money 'bills' come in denominations of $1, $5, $10, $20, $50 and $100, which, are all the same size and colour.

In 2000 the US Treasury redesigned the bills with larger portraits, so you may well end up with bills of the same denomination that look slightly different. Fear not: all are still legal tender.

Since counterfeiting of $50 and $100 bills is a booming business, many small shops will not accept them. If you have to use a $50 or $100 bill, ask first, especially if you're only spending a few dollars. On the whole, it's best to restrict your paper money to denominations of $1, $5, $10 and $20.

Banks & bureaux de change

Most banks are open from 9am to 3pm Monday to Friday; although some stay open until 6pm. Most are also open from 9am to noon on Saturdays. You will need some kind of photo identification, such as a passport, to transact any business such as cashing travellers' cheques or for obtaining cash from a credit card. Note that there aren't as many bureaux de change in New Orleans as in other tourist meccas such as San Francisco and New York. If you arrive in New Orleans after 5pm, change money at the airport or, if you have US dollar travellers' cheques, buy something in order to get some change.

If you want to use your travellers' cheques at a shop, ask first if a minimum purchase is required. Most banks and shops in New Orleans accept travellers' cheques in US dollars. You can also obtain cash on a credit card from certain banks. Check with your credit card company before you leave.

Hibernia National Bank

313 Carondelet Street, at Gravier Street, CBD (533 5471/ www.hibernia.com). St Charles Streetcar. **Open** *9am-4pm Mon-Thur; 9am-5pm Fri.* **Map** *p279 B1.*

Regions Bank

541 Chartres Street, at Toulouse Street, French Quarter (584 2185/ www.regionsbank.com). Bus 3 Vieux Carré, 55 Elysian Fields, 81 Almonaster, 82 Desire. **Open** *9am-4pm Mon-Fri; 9am-noon Sat.* **Map** *p282 B2.*

Travelex America

465 9647. **Open** *6am-7pm daily.* Located in the lobby of the airport, this bureau de change is handy when you arrive and leave.

Western Union

1-800 325 6000/ www.westernunion.com Western Union has been around forever, but it still works if you're in need of quick cash. Any of the dozen or so locations in New Orleans will tell you how to get money wired to you and where to pick it up. You can also wire money to anyone outside the state over the phone using a Visa or MasterCard. Phone the number above or check the phone book for the nearest branch.

ATMs

Automated Teller Machines (ATMs or cashpoints) are everywhere – and that includes shops, bars, casinos and late-night cafés. Most accept major credit cards such as American Express, MasterCard, Visa and selected international debit and cash cards – tap in your usual PIN number. There is a fee, of course – cash on demand has its price. You can find the nearest ATM location by phoning **Plus System** (1-800 843 7587) or **Cirrus** (1-800 424 7787). If you have forgotten your PIN number or your card has been demagnetised, most banks will dispense cash to card holders; try **Bank One**, which offers advances at all its branches. You can also get cash back at supermarkets if you pay with a card bearing the Cirrus or Plus logo (with your usual PIN).

Credit cards

Credit (as opposed to debit) cards are required by almost all hotels, car rental agencies and airlines; they're also less disastrous if you're robbed, and are accepted almost everywhere. Restaurants, petrol stations, many taxis and, of course, shops take them. Without a doubt, your stay will be made much more pleasant if you 'don't leave home without them'. The five major credit cards most often accepted in the US are American Express, Discover, Diners Club, MasterCard and Visa. If you lose your credit card (or your travellers' cheques), call the appropriate number below.

Lost or stolen credit cards
American Express *1-800 992 3404*. **Discover** *1-800 347 2683*. **MasterCard** *1-800 307 7309*. **Visa** *1-800 336 8472*.

Lost or stolen travellers' cheques
American Express *1-800 221 7282*. **Thomas Cook** *1-800 223 7373*. **Visa** *1-800 227 6811*.

Postal services

Most post offices are open from 8.30am to 5pm Monday to Friday, with limited hours on Saturday. Contact the **US Postal Service** (1-800 275-8777/www.usps.com) for information on your nearest branch and mailing facilities. Stamps can be bought at all post offices as well as at many hotels, grocery stores and convenience stores. **Western Union** (*see p256*) will take a telegram over the phone and charge it to your phone bill (not available from payphones). For information on how to transfer money, *see p256* **Money**.

Main Post Office
701 Loyola Avenue, at Girod Street, CBD (1-800 275 8777/ www.usps.com). **Open** 7am-8pm Mon-Fri; 8am-5pm Sat; noon-5pm Sun. **Map** p279 B1. The main branch is open more hours than any other post office in the city, though its schedule was trimmed considerably in 2002. It's far and away the best post office for sending

foreign mail. If you need to receive mail in New Orleans and you're not sure where you'll be staying, have it marked General Delivery and posted to the Main Post Office, where it will be kept for ten days. You'll need a photo ID to collect it.

Vieux Carré Post Office
1022 Iberville Street, between Burgundy & N Rampart streets, French Quarter (1-800 275 8777/www.usps.com). Bus 3 Vieux Carré, 40 Canal. **Open** 8.30am-4.30pm Mon-Fri. **Map** p282 A1.

Royal Mail & Parcel
828 Royal Street, between St Ann & Dumaine streets, French Quarter (522 8523). Bus 3 Vieux Carré. **Open** 8.30am-6.30pm Mon-Fri; 9.30am-5.30pm Sat. **Map** p282 C2. This French Quarter shop is experienced in packing and shipping objects large and small worldwide.

The Wooden Box
816 S Peters Street, Warehouse District (568 0281). Bus 10 Tchoupitoulas, 11 Magazine. **Open** 9am-5.30pm Mon-Fri. **Map** p279 C2. For antiques, glass, computers and furniture. They aren't cheap, but they are meticulous and reliable.

Public toilets (restrooms)

For a city so dependent on tourism, New Orleans has been slow to acknowledge the need for public toilets. During Mardi Gras, hundreds of people, male and female, are arrested for public urination. This is partly explained by the fact that, in the French Quarter, you'll see signs in almost every establishment stating that only customers can use the toilets. If you buy a drink in a café or restaurant, you'll be able to avail yourself of the facilities. Otherwise, there are public ones at the tourist information windows opposite Jackson Square on Decatur Street.

Here's an insiders tip: every large French Quarter hotel has big, clean loos near the lobby; walk in like you belong and you'll rarely be challenged.

Religion

New Orleans is a predominantly Catholic city – its fixation on Mardi Gras is the easiest evidence of that – but there's no lack of places to worship whatever your faith or beliefs. For a more complete list, check the *Yellow Pages* and read the religion page in the Saturday *Times-Picayune*.

Buddhist

Zen Center of New Orleans
748 Camp Street, at Julia Street, Warehouse District (523 1213). St Charles Streetcar. **Map** p279 C2.

Christian (Catholic)

St Louis Cathedral
725 Chartres Street, on Jackson Square, French Quarter (525 9585/ www.stlouiscathedral.org). Bus 55 Elysian Fields, 82 Desire. **Map** p282 C2. The mother of New Orleans churches, dating from 1783.

St Patrick's Catholic Church
724 Camp Street, at Julia Street, Warehouse District (525 4413). St Charles Streetcar. **Map** p279 C2. This French Quarter church is particularly popular for its regular weekday masses attended by local businesspeople, and for its weekend weddings.

Christian (other)

First Unitarian Universalist Church
5212 S Claiborne Avenue, at Jefferson Avenue, Uptown (866 9010). Bus 16 S Claiborne, 32 Carrollton. **Map** p276 C8. Cerebral, intellectual, friendly.

Greater St Stephen Full Gospel Baptist Church
2308 S Liberty Street, at Simon Bolivar Avenue, Uptown (244 6800/www.gssbc.net). Bus 15 Freret. **Map** p279 A2. One of the largest churches in the country, Greater St Stephen is a powerhouse with three locations and several thousand members. Its mostly African-American congregation welcomes all visitors.

Directory

St Mark's United Methodist Church

1130 N Rampart Street, between Governor Nicholls & Ursulines streets, French Quarter (523 0450). Bus 57 Franklin, 88 St Claude. **Map** *p282 D1.*
With a location on the edge of the French Quarter, this modern congregation strives for racial integration and pursues an agenda of social justice.

Jewish

Congregation Anshe Sephard

2230 Carondelet Street, at Jackson Avenue, Central City (522 4714). St Charles Streetcar. **Map** *p279 B3.* Orthodox/traditional.

Touro Synagogue

4238 St Charles Avenue, at General Pershing Street, Uptown (895 4843). St Charles Streetcar. **Map** *p276 D9.*

The once-staggering crime rate in New Orleans has been steadily declining over the last decade, but, as in most US cities, problems remain. This is a particularly difficult city to gauge, because the cityscape can change from one block to the next. Locals speak of 'good blocks' and 'bad blocks' like people in other cities talk about 'good neighbourhoods' and 'bad neighbourhoods'. The touristy areas are generally safe, but you can quite easily stumble into a not-so-safe area. Just be aware of your surroundings, and always retreat from any situation that makes you feel in the least uncomfortable.

Never wander off the beaten pack after dark, especially if you aren't completely sure where you are or where you're going. (Happily, the exception is during Mardi Gras, when the maxim of 'safety in numbers' is writ large on the streets.) And never take all your wealth with you: take small amounts of cash; use the hotel safe for the rest of your money, or just bank on your credit card.

The most unstable areas are, of course, the poorest places. Public housing projects are often the epicentres of high-crime districts, and they are liberally scattered throughout the city, not just at the urban edge. The Lafitte Housing Projects, surrounding the ancient St Louis Cemeteries Nos.1 and 2, for example, are just a couple of blocks from the French Quarter.

Some travellers, perhaps lulled into a false sense of security by the declining crime statistics and by the general friendliness of New Orleans, have been lured to public housing to buy drugs. Setting aside all questions about the legality of drug use, the foolhardiness of doing a drug deal with strangers on their home ground cannot be overemphasised. Just say no to scary drug deals.

The French Quarter, with its 24-hour timetable and police protection for tourists, is arguably the safest area in the city. But that doesn't mean crime isn't a problem here. The tourist-thronged Quarter provides rich pickings for pickpockets, muggers and car thieves, who are alert to the straggler alone on an empty street in the wee hours. Both St Charles Avenue and Magazine Street are usually cheerful places, but there are dicey neighbourhoods within a few blocks of these streets, and it's not always easy for an outsider to recognise them. If you're veering more than a block or two off the main road, ask a shop clerk, a passer-by or a bus driver for the best route.

Crime in the city tends to be woefully low-tech and impressively deadly. The basic approach is the old-fashioned armed robbery: sticking a gun in someone's face and demanding the goods. Should you be confronted by an armed thief, just give up everything immediately and with no

protest. No camera, passport or cash is worth your life. Always dial **911** and report the crime to the police immediately. You will need a police report for any insurance claims (and it's even possible the cops might actually find the perpetrators).

For details of safety issues particularly relevant to women travellers, *see p261* **Women**.

According to anecdotal evidence, the citizens of New Orleans smoke a lot of tobacco. Except in hospitals, federal buildings, large shopping malls and a few upmarket restaurants, you are free to light up at will. Most small restaurants have smoking and no-smoking sections.

With five well-known universities, New Orleans has a large and diverse student population. While downtown universities don't have typical campuses, Uptown, around Loyola and Tulane, it has the kind of campus life you might expect, with music clubs, coffeehouses, shops and a laissez-faire attitude. The city is also a favourite destination for vacationing students.

Delgado Community College

501 City Park Avenue, at Bienville Street, Mid-City (483 4216/ www.dcc.edu). Bus 46 City Park. **Map** *p278 C5.*
The mostly adult working-class students here follow two-year technical programmes. The college also offers non-credit courses in areas like pottery, local history, ballroom dancing and even barbecuing.

Dillard University

2601 Gentilly Boulevard, at Elysian Fields, Gentilly (283 8822/ www.dillard.edu). Bus 97 Broad.
Founded in 1869 to educate former slaves, Dillard is one of the old-line African-American universities. Its green, relaxed campus in Gentilly is populated by some of the South's top black students.

Loyola University

6363 St Charles Avenue, at Broadway, Uptown (865 2011/ www.loyno.edu). St Charles Streetcar. **Map** p276 B8.

Located next to Tulane on St Charles Avenue, Loyola is known for its law school, business school and sociology and theology faculties. Its Jesuit heritage is apparent in its students' strong bent towards social justice and activism.

Southern University at New Orleans

6400 Press Drive, between Chef Menteur & Leon C Simon streets, Gentilly (286 5000/www.suno.edu). Bus 57 Franklin, 59 Congress.

Developed as a branch of Baton Rouge's Southern University, SUNO opened in 1959, when Louisiana colleges were still segregated by race. It's primarily a black institution but has become slightly more multiracial. Strong on evening courses.

Tulane University

6823 St Charles Avenue, at Calhoun Street, Uptown (865 5000/ www.tulane.edu). St Charles Streetcar. **Map** p276 B8.

Rich, old and social, Tulane is the uni of choice for Eastern students who think it will be easier than Ivy League institutions and Southerners who want to spend their student years in New Orleans. Tulane's law school is sought after for its networking opportunities, while the business, Latin American studies and architecture faculties are all nationally recognised.

University of New Orleans

Lakefront, between Elysian Fields & Robert E Lee Street, Gentilly (280 6000/www.uno.edu). Bus 55 Elysian Fields.

A classic 'commuter school' success story, UNO was originally a branch of Louisiana State University but is now the largest college in New Orleans, with 16,000 enrolled. It's popular with adult students, people who work full time and non-New Orleanians who want a Big Easy degree on the cheap. Over the years, UNO has developed some first-class departments, including the jazz studies faculty and the World War II research centre.

Xavier University

1 Drexel Drive, between Carrollton Avenue & Washington Street, Mid-City (486 7411/www.xula.edu). Bus 34 Carrollton, 39 Tulane.

Xavier is the only Catholic university (as opposed to college) founded for African-Americans in the US. It has found a niche in the healthcare field, with a very competitive pharmacy programme and a hugely successful pre-med programme. The small campus hosts many African, Third World and black cultural events.

Telephones

Dialling & codes

The area code for the city of New Orleans, Orleans Parish, Jefferson Parish and St Bernard (Chalmette) Parish is 504. If you are making a local call within this area, you don't need to dial the area code. The listings in this guide do not include the 504 area code, so if you're phoning from outside New Orleans but within the US, dial 1 504 before the seven-digit numbers listed. All other area codes are included in the listings where appropriate.

Further afield but still part of the metropolitan area, the North Shore, Grand Isle and surrounding areas now have the area code 985. These numbers are charged at the local rate, and you need not dial 1 first – just dial the area code and number.

Toll-free numbers within the US traditionally began with 1-800, but new prefixes have now been added, including 1-888 and 1-866. Numbers beginning with 1-900 or 1-976 usually charge high by-the-minute rates. Many hotels add a surcharge on all calls.

Making a call

The telephone system in New Orleans is cheap and reliable. A local call costs 35¢, and operator and emergency calls are free. Public payphones only accept nickels, dimes and quarters – not ideal for long-distance calls. To make a call from a public phone, pick up the receiver and check for a dial tone before parting with your money; some phones require you to dial the number first and wait for an operator or recorded message to tell you how much change to deposit. To make a collect (reverse charge) call, dial 0 for the operator followed by the area code and phone number. For help, dial 0 for an operator.

Hotels are colossally greedy when it comes to telephone charges. Almost all charge for local calls, 800 calls and collect calls, and find ways of adding 'service charges' when you use a phone card. You're usually better off using the pay phone in the lobby.

One of the most convenient ways of making a call is to use a phone card. These can be purchased at almost any retail outlet and range in price from $5 to $50; the cost of a call can work out as low as 3¢ per minute. Read the card info carefully before buying; some deduct a 'connection charge' up to 75¢ every time you use your card. To use a phone card, dial the 1-800 number given on your card, and follow the recorded instructions.

Telephone directories are available at some public phones (although they have often been stolen) and in hotel rooms. If you can't find one, dial directory assistance (411) and ask for your listing by name – there is a charge for this service, except from a payphone.

Useful numbers

Operator assistance 0.
Emergency (police, fire, ambulance) 911.
Directory assistance 411.

International calls

To dial a number outside the US, dial 011, then the country code, followed by the city code and the phone number. The process is fully explained in the residential telephone book (the white pages, not in the commercial *Yellow Pages*). If you have any problems getting through, dial 00 for an international operator.

Directory

Average monthly climate

	High temp	Rainfall	% Sunshine	Relative humidity
Jan	69°F (20°C)	4.97in (11.9cm)	49%	67%
Feb	65°F (18°C)	5.23in (13.3cm)	51%	64%
Mar	71°F (21°C)	4.73in (12cm)	57%	60%
Apr	79°F (26°C)	4.50in (11.4cm)	65%	59%
May	85°F (29°C)	5.07in (12.9cm)	69%	59%
June	90°F (32°C)	4.63in (11.8cm)	67%	60%
July	91°F (32°C)	6.73in (17.1cm)	61%	62%
Aug	90°F (32°C)	6.02in (15.3cm)	63%	63%
Sept	87°F (31°C)	5.87in (14.9cm)	64%	62%
Oct	79°F (26°C)	2.66in (6.8cm)	72%	59%
Nov	70°F (21°C)	4.06in (10.3cm)	62%	60%
Dec	64°F (18°C)	5.27in (13.4cm)	48%	66%

Country codes include 44 for the UK, 353 for Ireland, 61 for Australia and 64 for New Zealand.

Mobile phones

Whereas in Europe mobile phones work on the GSM network at either 900 or 1800mHz, the US has no standard mobile phone network covering the whole country. Some of the major urban centres such as New York and Los Angeles offer access to the GSM network at 1900mHz, but the rest of the country, including New Orleans, uses a variety of other digital and analogue networks. This means European handsets will not work in New Orleans, and travellers from Europe will have to hire a handset with service once they arrive. Try **Cellular Rentals** (2601 Tulane Avenue, at S Dorgenois Street, Tremé, 822 7770) or else **Solid Communications** (710 Poland Avenue, at Dauphin Street, Bywater, 943 1888), both of which rent phones on a daily, weekly or monthly basis. US visitors should ask their service provider whether their mobile phones will work here.

Thunderstorms often disconnect both land lines and mobiles for hours at a time.

Time & date

New Orleans is on Central Standard Time, which is one hour behind Eastern Standard (New York and Washington, DC) and six hours behind GMT. It is one hour ahead of Mountain Time (Denver and the Rocky Mountains) and two hours ahead of Pacific Standard Time (California). Daylight Savings Time (which is almost concurrent with British Summer Time) runs from the first Sunday in April to the last Sunday in October. During this period, clocks are put forward one hour.

In the US, dates are written in the order of month, day, year; therefore, 2.5.03 is the fifth of February 2003, not the second of May.

Tipping

In New Orleans, the tourism industry is the biggest game in town for local workers, but the pay is rubbish. Most of the city's working class residents work in restaurants, hotels and bars. Many of them earn less than minimum wage; bartenders and waiters are payed between $2 and $3 an hour. Hotel maids generally earn the minimum wage. They all depend on tips in order to make a living.

Bellhops & baggage handlers $1-$2 per bag
Hotel maids $1 a night
Hotel concierges $3-$5
Bartenders 15% of the bill
Cabbies, hairdressers & food delivery staff 15%-20% of the bill
Valets, counter staff $1-$3, depending on the size of the order and any special arrangements
Wait staff 15%-20%.

Visas

Under the Visa Waiver Program, citizens of the UK, Japan, Australia, New Zealand and all Western European countries (except Portugal, Greece and Vatican City) do not need a visa for stays in the United States that last less than 90 days (business or pleasure) – as long as they have a passport valid for the full 90-day period and a return ticket. An open stand-by ticket is acceptable. Canadians and Mexicans do not need visas but must have legal proof of their residency. All other travellers must have visas.

Full information and visa application forms can be obtained from any US embassy or consulate.

If you require a visa urgently, apply via the travel agent when you book your ticket. For more information, you can always check the US State Department website: http://travel.state.gov/travel.

Directory

US Embassy Visa Information Line

0891 200 290. Recorded information for callers in the UK.

When to go

New Orleans seems to offer an endless summer, and that's not exactly a good thing. The conventional wisdom is that summer lasts from Mardi Gras (in February or March) to Thanksgiving (in late November). Even in the dead of winter, temperatures rarely drop below 50°F (10°C), except during usually brief and rare cold snaps. .

In April, temperatures are around 80°F (27°C), and, with humidity factored in, during July, August and September they can hover well above 100°F (38°C). Suddenly, you understand why Tennessee Williams's characters are so neurotic and grumpy.

Mosquitoes appear as soon as the weather gets warm; they're worst from about 5pm until dark. Use insect repellent regularly if you're vulnerable, especially on outdoor forays such as swamp tours.

Despite these annoyances, for those who can cope with the heat, summer is still an excellent time to visit. It's the low season: tourist and convention business is so slow that hotel rates are rock bottom, and clubs, shops and restaurants practically pay you to come inside. Besides, a steamy summer night here is sensual and oppressive, almost physically heavy. It's hard to breathe, to think, and that's sort of what it's all about. On a night like that, with a long, cold cocktail in your hand, you'll really be experiencing the city the way locals know it. When it's really hot, New Orleans is in its element.

On the down side, hot weather can make you ill if you're not used to it or don't take it seriously. Hats and sunglasses are a good idea during the day, and sunblock is essential. During the hottest months, try to avoid being outdoors between 11am and 3pm except for short bursts. The heat and humidity will sap your energy more quickly than you can imagine. The locals pace themselves, moving slowly, drinking constantly (water, even); follow their lead.

For the best weather, stick to autumn (fall) and spring. Even winter is comfortable most of the time, as it rarely gets very cold. In spring, the days are warm and breezy and the city blooms with tropical flowers.

Public holidays

New Year's Day 1 Jan
Martin Luther King Day third Mon in Jan
Presidents' Day third Mon in Feb
Mardi Gras Day Feb or Mar
Memorial Day last Mon in May
Independence Day 4 July
Labour Day first Mon in Sept
Columbus Day second Mon in Oct
Thanksgiving Day last Thur in Nov
Christmas Day 25 Dec

Women

New Orleans is a comfortable city for women, retaining enough of its old-fashioned manners to soften the edges of its mostly unapologetic male supremacy. While, feminist consciousness may not be a major element here, the cult of the Scarlett O'Hara-style Southern belle with a will of iron persists. New Orleans has consistently elected strong women to represent it in Washington, including former US Representative Lindy Boggs and current US Senator Mary Landrieu, and it has several female city councillors. Yet New Orleans retains a definite masculine feel; as if Stanley Kowalski still glowers at its Blanche DuBois frills.

In terms of crime and safety, the usual caveats apply, of course, but women seem to be no more at risk than men, and despite the high crime rates, reported incidents of rape are relatively low. Women going to bars and clubs alone or in groups will find it easy to blend in. Women alone at a bar are not often harassed.

Newcomb College Center for Research on Women

200 Caroline Richardson Hall, Tulane University, at Audubon Boulevard, Uptown (865 5238/ www.tulane.edu/~wc). St Charles Streetcar. **Open** *Sept-May* 9am-9pm Mon-Sat. *June-Aug* 9am-5pm daily. **Map** p276 B8.
One of the leading academic centres for women's studies, Newcomb has a fascinating library, changing exhibits, and a full schedule of talks and meetings. The friendly staff welcome visitors.

Planned Parenthood

4018 Magazine Street, between Napoleon & Louisiana avenues, Uptown (897 9200). Bus 11 Magazine. **Open** 8am-5pm Mon; 10am-7pm Tue, Wed; 9am-5pm Thur; noon-5pm Fri; 9am-noon Sat. **Map** p279 D9.
Long under siege in Catholic Louisiana, Planned Parenthood is still the best source of birth control and abortion info. Appointments are required every day except Wednesday, when walk-ins are welcome from 10am to noon.

Rape Crisis Center

Information 482 9922. **Open** *phone line* 24hrs daily.

Work

The employment situation in New Orleans is unstable at best. There is little in the way of a middle-income population, and decently paid employment is scarce. To work legally, non-US citizens must obtain a 'green card' from a US embassy while still in their home country. Under-the-table (illegal) work is not unknown but is low-paying and insecure.

UK students might want to check out **Study Abroad** (020 7801 9699/www.study abroad.com) to see if they qualify for a US-based work-study programme.

Directory

Further Reference

Books

Non-fiction

Christopher Benfey:
Degas in New Orleans
Degas' stay on Esplanade Avenue
in 1870s New Orleans.

**Jason Berry, Jonathan Foose
& Tad Jones**: *Up From the
Cradle of Jazz: New Orleans Music
Since World War II*
Insights into the succeeding
generations of musicians such
as Fats Domino and the Neville
Brothers who took New Orleans
music in new directions.

John Churchill Chase:
*Frenchmen, Desire, Good Children
and Other Streets of New Orleans*
Definitive and delightful history
(written in the 1950s) of the city
through its streets.

Josh Clark (ed): *French Quarter
Fiction (The Newest Stories of
America's Oldest Bohemia)*
A brilliant collection of works
by the new generation of New
Orleans writers like Richard Ford,
Poppy Z Brite and Josh Russell.

Randolph Delahanty: *New
Orleans: Elegance and Decadence*
A satisfying examination of New
Orleans through its houses and
cultural history.

Joy Dickinson: *Haunted City:
An Unauthorized Guide to the
Magical, Magnificent New
Orleans of Anne Rice*
The who, what, when and where
of New Orleans in Rice's books.

Robert Florence: *New Orleans
Cemeteries: Life in the Cities of
the Dead*
History, myth, culture and the
present are interwoven in this
beautifully illustrated volume.

James Gill: *Lords of Misrule:
Mardi Gras and the Politics of
Race in New Orleans*
British transplant Gill turns a
sharp yet not unsympathetic eye
on the intertwined history of Mardi
Gras and New Orleans' identity.

Lillian Hellman: An *Unfinished
Woman; Pentimento*
A New Orleans native, Hellman's
memoirs tell the colourful tale of
her upbringing on Prytania Street
in the Garden District.

Walter Johnson: *Soul by Soul:
Life Inside the Antebellum Slave
Market*
Johnson presents New Orleans as
a fulcrum for the slave trade in an
impeccable cultural history.

John R Kemp: *New Orleans:
An Illustrated History*
Large illustrated overview of New
Orleans' history.

Jon Kukla: *A Wilderness so
Immense: The Louisiana Purchase
and Destiny of America*
An excellent recounting of why
Napoleon and Jefferson both
thought selling half the continent
for 4¢ an acre was a brilliant deal.

Judy Long (ed): *Literary
New Orleans*
The city as those who love it
have written about it; from Louis
Armstrong to Mark Twain and
Tennessee Williams. A brilliant
collection of poetry and prose.

Kerri McCaffety:
Obituary Cocktail
Affecting and affectionate
photographic documentation
of New Orleans bars.

Henri Schindler: *New Orleans
Mardi Gras*
Lavishly illustrated discussion
of the Carnival tradition by one
of the most knowledgeable Mardi
Gras historians.

Michael P Smith: *Mardi Gras
Indians*
The first book to examine the
culture of the black Indians of
New Orleans. Superb photos.

Mary Ann Sternberg: *Along
the River Road: Past and Present
of Louisiana's Historic Byway*
Useful for visitors exploring the
River Road and its plantations.

Jerry E Strahan: *Managing
Ignatius: The Lunacy of Lucky
Dogs and Life in the Quarter*
A real-life 'Confederacy of
Dunces', by the over-educated
manager of the Lucky Dog
hotdog carts. It's very funny
and rings painfully true.

Roulhac Toledano: *National
Trust Guide to New Orleans
Architectural and Cultural
Treasures*
Toledano's 1996 guide is small
and portable. An excellent
companion to walks and
rides around the city.

Fiction

Nelson Algren: *A Walk on
the Wild Side*
Wonderfully tawdry American
novel set in the French Quarter.

Poppy Z Brite: *Exquisite Corpse*
Fantasy writer Brite's vivid tale of
a French Quarter serial killer.

Robert Olen Butler: *A Good
Scent From a Strange Mountain*
The New Orleans of immigrant
Vietnamese, told in short stories.

George Washington Cable:
Old Creole Days
Cluttered with Creole and black
dialect, slowed down by the
elaborate descriptive style of the
Victorian era, Cable's 1879 stories
are nevertheless entertaining tales.

Kate Chopin: *The Awakening*
Chopin's overwrought 1899
novel of a sexually and spiritually
frustrated Creole wife is told
with dreamlike softness but is
still contemporary in its
understanding of gender roles.

Tony Dunbar: *Shelter from
the Storm*
The best of a series of mysteries
by a New Orleans attorney,
featuring hapless lawyer-cum-
gourmand Tubby Dubonnet.

William Faulkner: *Pylon;
Absolom, Absolom!; The Wild
Palms; Mosquitoes*
New Orleans is a marginal but
significant setting for many of
Faulkner's books. *Mosquitoes* is
a satiric account of the lives of
artists and writers in the French
Quarter in the 1920s.

Ernest Gaines: *A Gathering
of Old Men*
The old men are black, and they
gather on decrepit porches in rural
Louisiana to recount stories shot
through with wisdom.

Shirley Ann Grau: *Keepers
of the House; The House on
Coliseum Street*
A Pulitzer Prize winner delves
into post-World War II, pre-Civil
Rights movement New Orleans.

Michael Ondaatje: *Coming
Through Slaughter*
The much lauded fictionalised
story of the life of trumpeter
Buddy Bolden and the birth of
jazz in New Orleans.

Directory

Walker Percy: *The Moviegoer*
Troubled Catholic Bix Bolling
retreats to lower-middle-class
Gentilly while he searches for
meaning in movies.
Anne Rice: *Lasher*; *The Feast
of All Saints*; *Interview With
the Vampire*
New Orleans is the stage for Anne
Rice's fertile imagination.
John Kennedy Toole: *A
Confederacy of Dunces*
The definitive and hilarious tale
of New Orleans that won the
author a posthumous Pulitzer
Prize. Quite simply the best book
ever about the city and its people.
Tennessee Williams:
A Streetcar Named Desire
Read the play or watch a
production, but don't miss the
Marlon Brando/Vivien Leigh film.

Music

Albums are in italics, tracks in
inverted commas.
Louis Armstrong:
The Hot Fives, Vol 1 (1988)
Satchmo's earliest work from
1925 and 1926; *Let's Do It* (1995),
a collection of his later vocal
work, much of it with Ella
Fitzgerald.
Sidney Bechet: *New Orleans
Jazz*; *Spirits of New Orleans*
Freddy Cannon: 'Way Down
Yonder in New Orleans' (1957)
Fats Domino: 'Walking to New
Orleans' (1960)
Dr John: *Gris Gris* (1968); *The
Night Tripper (The Sun, Moon
and Herbs)* (1971); *Gumbo* (1972);
'I Thought I Heard New Orleans
Say' (1979)
Gottschalk: *Classics of the
Americas Vol 4: Piano Works*
(Georges Rabol, piano).
Donald Harrison Jr: 'Indian
Blue: featuring the Guardians of
the Flame Mardi Gras Indians
and Dr John'
John Kay: 'Down in New
Orleans' (1978)
The Meters: *Funkify Your Life:
The Meters Anthology* (1995)
Jelly Roll Morton: *The
Complete Jelly Roll Morton
1926-1930*
The Neville Bros:
*Treacherous: A History of
the Neville Bros Vols 1 & 2*
(1986, 1990)

Travel advice

For up-to-date information on travel to a specific country –
including the latest news on safety and security, health
issues, local laws and customs – contact your home
country government's department of foreign affairs.
Most countries have websites packed with useful
advice for would-be travellers.

Australia
www.dfat.gov.au/travel

Canada
www.voyage.gc.ca

New Zealand
www.mft.govt.nz/travel

Republic of Ireland
www.irlgov.ie/iveagh

UK
www.fco.gov.uk/travel

USA
http://travel.state.gov

Professor Longhair: 'Mardi
Gras in New Orleans' (1950);
New Orleans Piano (1972);
Crawfish Fiesta (1980); *The Last
Mardi Gras* (1982); *Rock 'n' Roll
Gumbo* (1985)
**Michael Ray & the Cosmic
Krewe**: *Michael Ray & the
Cosmic Krewe* (1994)
Shirley and Lee: *The Legendary
Masters Series* (1990)
Swingin' Haymakers: *For Rent*
(1995)
Tom Waits: 'I Wish I was in
New Orleans' (1977)
Wild Magnolias: *They Call
Us Wild* (1975)
Wild Tchoupitoulas: *The
Wild Tchoupitoulas* (1976)
Compilations: *Cajun Dance
Party: Fais Do-Do* (1994); *The
Mardi Gras Indians Super
Sunday Showdown* (1992)

Websites

City of New Orleans
www.new-orleans.la.us.
The official city website was
redesigned and pumped up under
the new mayor, Ray Nagin; it now
offers a wealth of information
about the city, municipal offices
(such as how to pay traffic tickets
online) and government.
Eccentric New Orleans
www.eccentricneworleans.com.
Filmmaker and ad-hoc sociologist
Rick Delaup's homage to the
French Quarter characters. His
website documents New Orleans'
kinky, quirky and bizarre bits.

Gambit Weekly
www.bestofneworleans.com.
Online version of the weekly
entertainment/arts/lifestyle
newspaper.
**Unofficial Louisiana
Travel Guide**
www.seelouisiana.com.
A funky compendium of facts and
links concerning Louisiana, from
plantation house museums to info
about the profusion of toxic
chemical plants.
**New Orleans Convention &
Visitors Bureau**
www.neworleanscvb.com.
Good source for info on upcoming
events, institutions, daily weather
and tips for visitors. It also takes
bookings, but remember that it's
not comprehensive – it only lists
businesses that are dues-paying
members of the CVB.
Offbeat magazine
www.offbeat.com.
Online version of New Orleans'
band and club bible. Great for
listings.
RTA
www.regionaltransit.com.
The New Orleans Regional
Transit site has bus and
streetcar schedules and maps.
Times Picayune
www.nola.com.
Online version of the daily
newspaper.
WWOZ
www.wwoz.org.
The sounds of New Orleans from
the city's best radio station, with
excellent links to other sources.

Directory

Index

Numbers in **bold** indicate the key entry for the topic; numbers in *italics* indicate photographs.

a

Acadian Cultural Center 236, 237, 240
Acadian Village 236, 237
Acadians 235
African-American Experience Tour 10
African-American history 10, 16-17, 91
accommodation 36-52
  gay & lesbian 200
Afton Villa Gardens **233**, 234
AIDS/HIV helpline 254
airport 248
Alex Box Stadium 219
Alferez, Enrique 93, 99
Ambrose, Stephen **34**, 76, 100
American Aquatic Gardens 70, **171**
American Sector 75
Amistad Research Center 86, **88**
Anderson, Sherwood 17, 29, **30**
Angola Louisiana State Prison Farm 233
Angola Museum **233**, 234
antiques shops 152-156
Aquarium of the Americas 67, **68**, 184, *184*, 185
aquariums *see* zoos, wildlife parks & aquariums
Armstrong, Louis 16, 20, 72, 89, 90, 263
art
  Southern 97
  see also Museums *and* galleries
  Art for Art's Sake 179
arts & entertainment **175-226**
arts, performing **215-218**
astrology & the occult shops 157
ATMs 256
auction houses 152
Audubon, John James 15
Audubon Park **78**, *79*, 220, 222, 226
Audubon Park Golf Course 220, *220*, 224
Audubon Pilgrimage 232
Audubon Zoo **78**, 184, *185*
Avery Island 238

Avondale, restaurants 128-129
Awakening, The **30**, 262

b

babysitting 182
Bacchus 23
Backstreet Cultural Museum 91
Bajeaux, Rene 120, 129
ballet 218
bamboula 14
bands, local 209
banks 256
'Baratarians' 13
bargain hotels 51
bars **134-147** *see also* *p269* bars index
  gay & lesbian 197-199
baseball 219
basketball 18-19, **221**, 225
Battle of New Orleans *6*, 13
Bayou St John 92
beaches 241-246
Beauregard, General PGT 66, 92
Beauregard-Keyes House & Garden 66
beauty salons 168-170
bed & breakfasts 52
Benjamin, Judah P 65
Benz, Dick 106, 124
Besh, John 106, 120, 129
Besthoff, Sidney 99
bicycle hire 69
Bienville, Sieur de **7**, 68, 75
Big Daddy's 57, 60
Big Easy, The 189
Biguenet, John 34
Biloxi 244
Bingo! 203
Blaine Kern's Mardi Gras World 28, **182**
Blessed Francis Xavier Seelos Parish 70
Bloch, Richard 76
'Bloody O'Reilly' 11
Bolden, Buddy 16, 72, 90, 202
books
  by New Orleans writers 262
  literary New Orleans 29-34
  shops 157-158
Bosworth, Sheila 34
Bourbon Street 27, **57-59**, 60, 65
boutique hotels 45
breakdown services 251
Breaux Bridge 238
Brennan family 106, 107, 109, 111, 112, 113, 114, 123
Bridges, Ruby 17

Brigtsten, Frank 124
Brinkley, Douglas 34
Brite, Poppy Z **34**, 262
Brunacci, Frank 120, 129
Bucktown 129
buddhist centres 257
Buddy D 219
Buffett, Jimmy 203-204
Bukowski, Charles 33
bureaux de change 256
Burke, James Lee 56
burlesque 65
Burroughs, William 33
bus
  arriving by 248
  getting around by 228, **249-250**
  business services 252
Butler, Benjamin F 15
Butler-Greenwood **233**, 234
Bywater The **69-71**
  accommodation 43-44
  bars 141
  gay & lesbian 197-199
  music clubs 205-209
  restaurants 115-117
Bywater Art Market 71

c

Cabildo, The 14, 66, **96**
Cable, George Washington 18, 30, 63, 262
Cabrini High School 92
cafés **130-133**
Cajun country 11, **235-240**
Cajun Hot Sauce Festival 235
Cajun Music Hall of Fame 240
Canal Street 54
'Cancer Corridor' 17
Capote, Truman 17, 29, **31**
car rental 251
carriage tours 101
Cartier Bresson, Henri 32
casinos, seaside 244
Cassady, Neil 33
Castles House 86
Cat on a Hot Tin Roof 33
Catalpa Plantation **233**, 234
Cavelier, René-Robert 7
CBD (Central Business District) 54, **72-76**
  accommodation 44-48
  bars 141-144
  music clubs 209
  restaurants 118-121
CD shops 172-173
Celebration in the Oaks 180
Celebration Station 185
cemeteries **94-95**
  Lafayette Cemetery 84, 85, **95**

Metairie Cemetery 95
St Louis Cemetery No.1 90, 95
St Louis Cemetery No.3 92, *94*, 95
St Roch Cemetery 71
Center for Southern Craft and Design 97
Chandler, Joel 231
Chartres Street **64**, 190
Chase, Leah 127
Chenier, Clifton 239
child abuse helpline 254
children **182-185**
  clothes shops 161-163
Children's Castle 184
Chopin, Kate **30**, 262
Christmas Eve Bonfires along the levee 180
Church of the Immaculate Conception 74
churches 257-258
  Blessed Francis Xavier Seelos Parish 70
  Church of the Immaculate Conception 74
  First Unitarian Universalist Church 257
  Greater St Stephen Full Gospel Baptist Church 257
  Holy Name of Jesus Church 86
  Old Ursuline Convent 66, *67*
  Our Lady of Guadeloupe Chapel 89
  St Alphonsus 82, *83*
  St Augustine's 14, **91**
  St Louis Cathedral 11, 61, 66, **67**, **257**
  St Mark's United Methodist Church 258
  St Patrick's Cathedral 14, *73*, **74**, 257
  St Vincent de Paul Catholic Church 70
cinemas 186-189
City Hall 14, **72**
City Park *89*, **92-93**, *92*, 180, 185, 222, 226
Civil War 15, 75, 98
Claiborne Mansion 36, 43, **70**
Claiborne, WCC **13**, 70, 43
classical music 218
climate 260, 261
clubs
  gay & lesbian 197-199
  music 202-213
cocktails, origin of 60
Code Noir 10, 11, 14, 89
Codrescu, Andrei 29, **34**
coffee shops **130-133**
Coliseum Square 81
Coliseum Theater 81
Colonel Short's Villa 85

Colored Waifs' Home 16, 72
Columbus, Christopher 7
Company of the Indies 7-8
Company of the West 7
computer parts & repair
159
Comus 23, 25
Confederacy of Dunces, A
34, 263
Confederate Museum 75,
96, **98**
Congo Square 89
Connick Jr, Harry 20, 23, 70
consulates 252
consumer information 252
Contemporary Arts Center
76, 96, **98**, **214**, **215**
conventions 252
'cornstalk fences' 61
courier services 252
Courir de Mardi Gras **239**,
240
credit cards 256
Creoles 11, 13
Crescent Billiard Hall 72
Crescent City Classic 176
crime 18
Crozat, Antoine 7
customs 254
cycling 222-223, 251

d

dance 218
De la Salle, Sieur 7
De Soto, Hernando 7
Dead Man Walking 189,
233
Decatur Street 67
Degas, Edgar 60, 84, 85, 91
Degas House 85, 91
Delgado Community
College 258
dentists 254
department stores 149-151
Destin 244
Destrehan Plantation **229**,
230, 231
Diliberto, Buddy 219
Dillard University 258
disabled access &
information 252
Dr Bob 71
Dr John 20, 263
Dodd, Baby 213
Domino, Fats 17
Dos Passos, John 31
Double Dealer 30-31
Double Jeopardy 84
Down By Law 189
Doyle, Alexander 74
drink shops 166-167
driving in New Orleans 250
dry-cleaning 159

e

Edwards, Edwin 75
1850 House 66
Emerald Coast 245
emergency care 253
Endymion 23
entertainment
for children 182-185

see also arts &
entertainment
Ernest N Morial
Convention Center 72,
76, **252**
Esplanade Avenue 54
Essence Music Festival
177
Eunice 240
Eunice Museum 240
Evangeline Oak 238

f

Fair Grounds Racecourse
92, 222
fashion accessory shops
163-166
fashion shops 159-163
Faubourg Livaudais 77
Faubourg Marigny 54,
69-71
accommodation 36, **43-44**
bars 139-141
bars, gay & lesbian
197-199
music clubs 205-208
restaurants 115-117
Faubourg St Mary 75
Faulkner, William 17, **31**,
61, 66, 178, 262
Faulkner Words & Music
Festival 31, **179**
Ferlinghetti, Lawrence 33
ferries 250
Festival Acadiens 237
Festival International de
Louisiana 177, *178*, 237
festivals & events **176-181**
film **186-189**
film processing 174
First Unitarian
Universalist Church 257
fishing 223-224
fitness *see* sport & fitness
Fitzgerald, F Scott 31
flashing at Mardi Gras 27
florists 166
Fohl, John **203**, 209, 211
food & drink shops 166-168
football, American 221
Ford, Richard 34
Fort Pickens 243
Fort Walton Beach 244
Fortier, Alcee 231
Francis, Sylvester 91
French and Indian War 11
French Quarter 11, 14, 54,
56-68
accommodation 36,
37-43
bars 135-139
bars, gay & lesbian
197-199
for children 185
drinking in the 145
Festival 176
galleries 190
music clubs 202-205
restaurants 106-115
tours, guided 101
walk 60
Frenchmen Street 207
Freret, James 74, 81

Freret, William 84
funerals, jazz 213
furniture shops 171-172

g

Gallatin Alley 67
Gallier Hall 14, **72**
Gallier House 10, 62, **63**, 72
Gallier Jr, James 10, 62, 63
galleries, art **190-196**
see also museums
Garden District 14, 54, *77*,
82-88
accommodation 36,
48-51
bars 144-145
music clubs 211
restaurants 121-122
tours, guided 103-104
walk 84
see also Lower Garden
District
gardens *see* parks &
gardens
gathering of the drummers
28`
Gautreaux, Tim 34
gay & lesbian 59, **197-201**
accommodation 200
bars & clubs 197
bookshop 197
Mardi Gras 28
resources 253
saunas & gyms 199
shopping & services 201
gift shops 168
Gilchrist, Ellen 34
Ginsberg, Allen 33
glass-making studios 194
Global Wildlife Center 184
Go 4th on the River 177
golf 220, **224**
Goodrich, William 81
Goodrich-Stanley House 81
Grace King House 81
Grau, Shirley Ann 34
Grayton Beach 245, *245*
Grayton Beach State Park
245
Great River Road 229-232
Greater St Stephen Full
Gospel Baptist Church
257
Greenwood Plantation
233, 234
guided tours 101-104
Gulf Breeze 243
Gulfport 244
gyms 226
gay 199

h

hairdressers 168
Halloween 179
Hard Boiled 84
Hardeveld, Simon 153
Harrah's Casino 76
Harris, John 125
hat shops 163
health & beauty shops
168-171

health & medical 253-254
Hearn, Lafcadio 17, **30**
Hellman, Lillian 29, **33**, 262
helplines & agencies 254
Henderson Beach State
Park 244
Hennessey, David 16
Henry, O 29, **30**
Hermann-Grima Historic
House 59
Higgins, Andrew Jackson
76
Historic New Orleans
Collection 60, 64, **97**
history **6-17**
Holiday Home Tour 81,
104
holidays, public 261
Holy Name of Jesus Church
86
horse racing 222
'hot shops' 194
hotels
gay & lesbian 200
see also accommodation
Houmas House 231
House of Blues 68, **203**
household, furniture & gift
shops 171-172
Howard-Tilton Memorial
Library 86, **88**
Hughes, Richard 109
hurricanes 18
Hurston, Zora Neale 31
*Hush, Hush Sweet
Charlotte* 231

i

Iberville, Sieur de 7
IMAX Theatre **68**, 184,
185, 186, **189**
immigration 254
insurance 254
International Arts Festival
177
internet access 255
Interview with the Vampire
34, 186, 263
Irish Channel 79
Irish immigrants 14, 74, 79,
82
Italian immigrants 16

j

Jackson, Andrew *6*, 13, 64
Jackson Brewery 68
Jackson Square 61, **64-66**,
185
jazz 9, 14, 59, 180
birth of 16
Jazz Fest 176, **180**
jazz funerals 213
Jean Lafitte National
Historical Park and
Preserve 102, **103**
Jefferson, restaurants 129
Jefferson, Thomas 6, 11, 13
jewellery shops 163-164
'Jim Crow' segregation
laws 17, 33, 90
Jungle Gardens 238
Julia Street 190

k

Karnofsky family 72
Kearney, Anne 106, 109, 129
Kerouac, Jack 29, **33**
Keyes, Francis Parkinson 66
King Creole 189
King, Grace 30, 81
Kingfish, The 83
'Know-Nothing Party' 14
Komunyakaa, Yusef 34
Kowalski, Stanley 29
Krewe of Muses 24
Krewe du Vieux 24, 27
krewes 15, 23-24

o

L'Overture, Toussaint 13
Labranche House 61
Lafayette 14, 177, 228, **236-238**
Lafayette Cemetery 84, 85, **95**
Lafayette Square 74
Lafitte, Jean 13, 59
Lafitte's Blacksmith Shop 59, **137**
Lakeview, restaurants 129
Lalaurie House 63
Lalaurie, Marie Delphine McCarty 63
Lardner, Ring 31
LaRocca, Nick 16
Larry Flynt's Hustler Club 57, 60
laundry 159
Laura Plantation 230, *230*, **231**
Laveau, Marie 14, 70, 90
Law, John 7
Le Moyne, Jean Baptiste **7**, 68
Le Moyne, Pierre 7
Lee Circle 74
Lee, Robert E 74
Legasse, Emeril 75, 109, 119, 121, 129
Lemann, Nicholas 34
lesbian *see* gay & lesbian
Lewis, Michael 34
libraries 255
limos 250
lingerie shops 165
Link, Donald 119, 129
literary New Orleans **29-34**
festivals 176, 177, 178
'Little Palermo' 16
LoCicero, Duke 113
Locoul family 231
Lolita 186
Longfellow, Henry Wadsworth 238
Longue Vue House and Gardens 90
Louis Armstrong New Orleans International Airport 248
Louis Armstrong Park 89
Louis XIV 7, 64
Louis XV 7
Louise S McGehee School 82

Louisiana ArtWorks 191
Louisiana Children's Museum 76, **98**, 184
Louisiana Department of Culture, Recreation & Tourism 176
Louisiana Museum of African-American History 91
Louisiana Philharmonic Orchestra 218
Louisiana Purchase 6
Louisiana State Museum 14, 66, **96**
Louisiana State University 219-220, 222
Louisiana Superdome 72, 76, 214, 219, **222**
Louisiana Territory 6
Louisiana Toy Train Museum 184
Louisiana Wildlife Museum and Aquarium 184
Love Potion No.9 14
Lower Garden District 78-81
Loyola University 86, **259**
theatre 215
luggage shops 165

m

Madame John's Legacy 62, **63**
Madewood Plantation 231
Magazine Street 81, **88**, 190
magazines 255
Mahogany Hall 9
Maison LeMonnier 60
malls, shopping 151-152
Maple Street 86
Mardi Gras 7, 15, **22-28**
accommodation during 36
Museum of 184
Marigny *see* Faubourg Marigny
Marigny, Bernard de 70, 76
markets
farmer's markets 167-168
French Market **68**, *68*, 167
Marmillion, Norman 230
Marsalis, Branford & Wynton 17, 20, 70
Martin, Valerie 34
May, Brack 106, 119, 129
McCarty, Louis 63
McIlhenny, Edmund 238
McMurray, Alex 203
McPhail, Tony 121
McRaney, Michelle 108
media 255
Merieult House 60
Metairie Cemetery 95
Mid-City 54, 89, **91-93**
accommodation 51-52
bars 141
music clubs 212
restaurants 127-128
Millay, Edna St Vincent 31
Mills, Clark 64

Milton Latter Memorial Library 81, 86, **255**
Mississippi River 14, **67-68**
Mistick Krewe of Barkus 28
mobile phones 260
MOMS Ball 28
Momus 23
money 256
Monroe Library 86
Monster's Ball 186
Moonwalk 68
Moore-Goldstein House 81
Morial, Dutch 19
Morial, Marc 19
Morton, Jelly Roll 9, 90, 263
mule-drawn carriages 185
Musée Conti Wax Museum of Louisiana **59**, 185
museums **96-100**
Backstreet Cultural Museum 91
Beauregard-Keyes House & Garden 66
The Cabildo 14, 66, **96**
Confederate Museum 75, 96, **98**
Degas House 91
1850 House 66
Gallier House 10, 62, **63**, 72
Hermann-Grima Historic House 59
Historic New Orleans Collection 60, 64, **97**
Longue Vue House and Gardens 90
Louisiana Children's Museum 76, **98**, 184
Louisiana Museum of African-American History 91
Louisiana State Museum 14, 66, **96**
Louisiana Toy Train Museum 184
Louisiana Wildlife Museum and Aquarium 184
Madame John's Legacy 62, **63**
Mardi Gras Museum 184
Musée Conti Wax Museum of Louisiana **59**, 185
National D-Day Museum 72, 76, 96, **98**, *100*
New Orleans African-American Museum of Art, Culture and History 91, **98**
New Orleans Historic Pharmacy Museum **66**, 98, 185
New Orleans Historic Voodoo Museum 62, **63**, *63*
New Orleans Museum of Art (NOMA) 92, 96, 99, **100**
Newcomb Art Gallery 86, **88**
Ogden Museum of Southern Art 72, 75, 96, 97, **100**

Old US Mint 98
Pitot House Museum 92, **100**
The Presbytère 66, *96*, **98**
Saints Hall of Fame 184
Science Complex 184
music **202-214**
classical & opera 218
clubs 202-213
festivals 177, 178, 180
related to New Orleans 263
shops 172-174
musical instrument shops 172-173
Musson, Michael 84, 85
Myrtles Plantation **233**, 234
Mystick Krewe of Comus 23, 25

n

Nagin, Mayor Ray 18, 19
Napoleon 11, 13, 64
National D-Day Museum 72, 76, 96, **98**, *100*
Native Americans 7
Navarre Beach 243
New Basin Canal 14
New Orleans 189
New Orleans African-American Museum of Art, Culture and History 91, **98**
New Orleans Arena 72, 76, **214**, 221
New Orleans Botanical Garden 93
New Orleans Center for the Creative Arts 70
New Orleans Centre 76, **151**
New Orleans Convention and Visitors Bureau 176
New Orleans Film and Video Festival **179**, 187
New Orleans Historic Pharmacy Museum **66**, 98, 185
New Orleans Historic Voodoo Museum 62, **63**, *63*
New Orleans Hornets 19, *19*, **221**, **225**, *225*
New Orleans Jazz & Heritage Festival 92, **180-181**
New Orleans Lesbian & Gay Pride Festival 179
New Orleans Museum of Art (NOMA) 92, 96, 99, **100**
New Orleans Opera 218
New Orleans Saints 219, **221-222**, 223
New Orleans Wine & Food Experience 179
New Orleans Zephyrs 219-220
New Roads 232
New Year's Eve 180

Index

Newcomb Art Gallery 86, **88**
newspapers 255
NOMA *see* New Orleans Museum of Art
Nottaway Plantation *229*, 231
Nouvelle Orleans 9

O

O'Reilly, General Alejandro 11
Oak Alley 231
Oakley House Plantation **233**, 234
occult shops 157
office services 252
Ogden Museum of Southern Art 72, 75, 96, 97, **100**
Ogden, Richard 97
Okaloosa Island 244
Old United States Mint 68
Old Ursuline Convent 66, *67*
Old US Mint 98
On The Road 33
Opelousas 239-240
Opening Day at the Fair Grounds 179
opera 218
opticians 168
Original Southwest Louisiana Zydeco Music Festival 178
Orleans Ballroom 61
Orleans, Duke of 7
Ormond Plantation **229**, 231
Orpheus 23
Our Lady of Guadeloupe Chapel 89
outdoor eating 131

P

Pacquet, Charles 229
Pakenham, General Edward 13
Panic in the Streets 189
Papa Grows Funk 203
parking 251
parks & gardens
    American Aquatic Gardens 70, **171**
    Audubon Park **78**, *79*, 220, 222, 226
    City Park *89*, **92-93**, *92*, 180, 185, 222, 226
    Louis Armstrong Park 89
    New Orleans Botanical Garden 93
    Sculpture Garden 93
Parlange 232
Paschal, Dean 34
Passion Fish 239
Pauger, Adrien de 56
Pelican Brief, The 186
Pennington, Richard 19
Pensacola 228, **241-243**, *241*, *242*
Percy, Walker 17, 29, **34**, 94, 263

performing arts **215-218**
perfume shops 168
pet shops 174
Peychaud, AA 60
pharmacies 168-169
photography shops 174
Piccolo, Greg 108
Pirates Alley 60, 66
Pitot House Museum 92, **100**
plaçage 17
Plantation Country **229-234**
Plessy, Homer 90
Pointe Coupee Parish Museum 232
Pointe de Mardi Gras 7
Pomerade, Leon 74
Ponchatoula Strawberry Festival 176
Pontalba Buildings 64
Porter, Katharine Anne 30
post offices 257
postal services 257
Presbytère, The 66, *96*, **98**
Preservation Hall 59, **205**, *205*
President Zachary Taylor House 60
Pretty Baby 189
prostitution 9
Proteus 23
Prudhomme, Paul 107
Prytania Theatre 187
psychiatric emergency services 254
psychic readings & spiritual supplies 157
public holidays 261
public toilets 257

Q

Quadroon Ballroom **17**, 62
quadroons 9, **17**

R

racial politics 16-17
Rampart Street 72
gay bars on 198
rape helpline 254
ReBirth Brass Band **203**, 209, 212
Reconstruction 16
record shops 172
reference, further 262
religion 257
reservation services 52
restaurants **106-129**
    for children 182
    by cuisine
        American 107, 121, 122, 127
        Asian 107, 118-119, 121, 122
        Cajun 107, 119
        Contemporary 107-109, 115, 119-120, 121, 124, 127
        Creole 109-113, 121, 124, 127
        French 120, 124, 127-128

Italian 113
Jamaican 117
Latin American 113-114
Mexican 121, 125
Middle Eastern 125, 128
Neighbourhood 114-115, 117, 120, 122, 125, 128
Soul food 117, 127
Spanish 120-121, 128
Vegetarian 117
restrooms 257
Rex, krewe of **23**, 25, 28
Rice, Anne **34**, 85, 86, 263
Richard & Annette Bloch Cancer Survivors Plaza 76
River Road 229-232
river tours 104
Riverbend 86
Riverfront, the 76
Rivertown 184
Riverwalk Marketplace 76, **151**
Robinson Mansion 84
Robinson, Walter 85
Rosedown Plantation **233**, 234
Rosemary Beach 246
Royal Street **59**, 190
Runaway Jury, The 186
running 224

S

Saenger Theatre 214, *215*, **216**
safety 258
St Alphonsus 82, *83*
St Alphonsus Art & Cultural Center 81
St Anthony's Close 61
St Augustine's 14, **91**
St Charles Avenue 54, 72, **85-88**
St Charles Avenue streetcar 14, 85, 249
St Domingue 13, 14
St Elizabeth's Orphanage 86, *87*
St Expedite 90
St Francisville 232-234
St Joseph's Day 176
St Louis Cathedral 11, 61, 66, **67**, **257**
St Louis Cemetery No.1 90, 95
St Louis Cemetery No.3 92, *94*, 95
St Mark's United Methodist Church 258
St Martinville 238
St Patrick's Cathedral 14, *73*, **74**, 257
St Patrick's Day 82, **176**
St Roch Cemetery 71
St Thomas project 79, 81
St Vincent's Infant Asylum 81
St Vincent de Paul Catholic Church 70
Saints Hall of Fame 184

San Francisco (Plantation) **229**, 230, 232
Sandot, Hubert 125
Santa Rosa Beach 245, *246*
Santa Rosa Island 241
Saturn 24
Saxon, Lyle 31
Scenic Highway 30A 244
Science Complex 184
sculpture 99
Sculpture Garden 93
Seaside 246
services *see* shops & services
Seven Years War 11
sex shops 57
Shannon, Jamie 121
shoe shops 165-166
shops & services **148-174**
    gay & lesbian 201
    on Magazine Street 88
sightseeing **53-104**
Simon of New Orleans 153, **156**
Six Flags *183*, 184
smoking 258
Soderbergh Steven 186
Soldiers Pay **31**, 61
Somerset Maugham, W 31
Sonnier, Greg and Mary 127
Southern Decadence 176, 178, 197, **200**
Southern University at New Orleans 259
Spanish Plaza 76
Spanish rule in Louisiana 11
spas 169-170
speciality shops 168
Spectacle, Le 59
Spicer, Susan 106, 107, 119, 129
Spratling, William 31
sport & fitness **219-226**
    events 176, 179, 181
    shops 174
Spring Fiesta 81, **104**
Stanley, Henry Morton 81
State Palace Theater 214
Stern family 90
Story, Sidney 9, 90
Storyland & William A Hines Carousel Gardens 93
Storyville 9, 90
Streetcar Named Desire A **33**, *188*, 189, 263
streetcars 21, **249**
Studio Inferno 71
study 258-259
Sugar Bowl **181**, 222
suicide prevention helpline 254
Sully House 86
Sully, Thomas 86
Summer Stages 217
Superdome *see* Louisiana Superdome
Supreme Court Building 60
swimming, gay & lesbian 199
synagogues 258

Index

Tabary Theatre 59
Tabasco Plant 239
Tara 230
tattooing & body piercing 171
taxis 249, 250
Taylor, Zachary 60
telephones 259
Tennessee Williams New Orleans Literary Festival 176
tennis 226
theatre 215-218
theme parks & attractions Blaine Kern's Mardi Gras World 28, **182**
Six Flags *183*, 184
ticket agencies 174
tickets, for sporting events 219
Tightrope 187, 189
time & date 260
Times-Picayune 255
Tipitina's 68, **212**
tipping 260
Toby, Thomas 83
Toby's Corner 83
toilets, public 257
Toole, John Kennedy **34**, 263
Topsail Hill Preserve State Park 245
tour companies 104
tours, guided 101-104
trains
  arriving by 248
  getting around by 228
travel advice 263
travel passes 250
Tremé **89-91**
  music clubs 205-208
trips out of town **227-246**
Tulane, Paul 86
Tulane University 86, 221, 222, **259**
  theatre 217
TV 256
Twain, Mark 14, 29, **30**, 94
Twelfth Night Revelers 25

Ulloa, Antonia de 11
Unchain My Heart 186
Uncle Remus books 231
Unfinished Woman, An 33
Unification Movement 16
Union Passenger Terminal 248
United Fruit Company Building 72
universities 258-259
University of New Orleans 221, **259**
UNO Lakefront Arena 214
Uptown 54, **77-88**
  accommodation 36, **48-51**
  bars 145-147
  galleries 190, **195-196**
  music rooms 211-212
  restaurants 122-127

V

Villa Meilleur 91
Vermilionville **236**, *236*, 237
video rental 174
Vieux Carré 56
visas 260
vodou *see* voodoo
voodoo 9, **14**, 62, 63, 89-90

W

walks
  French Quarter 60
  Garden District 84
War of 1812 13
Warehouse District **72-76**
  accommodation 44-48
  galleries 190, **192-195**
  music clubs 209-211
  restaurants 118-121
Washington Square Park 70
watersports 226
weather 260, 261
websites 263
Wedding Cake House 86
West Feliciana Historical Society 233, **234**
White League 16
White Linen Night 178
White, Lulu 9
Whitman, Walt 29, **30**
Wilde, Oscar 30
wildlife parks *see* zoos, wildlife parks & aquariums
Williams Research Center 64
Williams, Tennessee 17, 29, *32*, **33**, 176, 263
Williamson, Kimberly 20
Woldenberg Riverfront Park 185
Wolfe, Tom 129
women 261
Words & Music: A Literary Feast in New Orleans 178
work 261
World Fair 75
World Trade Center 76
Wright, Jonathan 119

X

Xavier University 259

Y

Yohalem, Matt 115

Z

zoos, wildlife parks & aquariums
  Aquarium of the Americas 67, **68**, 184, *184*, 185
  Audubon Zoo **78**, 184, *185*
  Global Wildlife Center 184
  Louisiana Wildlife

Museum and Aquarium 184
Zulu **23**, 25
zydeco 178, **235**, 239, 240

Accommodation
Audubon Cottages 37
Avenue Plaza Hotel 49
Bienville House 39
Bourbon Orleans Hotel 62
Bourgoyne Guest House 200
Chateau Hotel **41**, 51
The Chimes Bed & Breakfast **49**, 51
Le Cirque Hotel 47
Claiborne Mansion 36, **43**, 70
Columns Hotel 36, **49**, 85
Cornstalk Hotel **41**, 51
Cotton Brokers Houses Bed & Breakfast 51
Degas House Bed & Breakfast 51
Elysian Fields Inn 44
Fairmont Hotel 44
French Quarter Quartet 200
The Frenchman Hotel 44
Hampton Inn Garden District 49
Hotel Maison de Ville 37
Hotel Monaco 47, *48*
Hotel Provincial 40
Hotel St Marie 43
Hotel Ste Helene 40
Hotel Villa Convento 43
Hubbard Mansion 48
India House 52, *52*
International House 36, 45, *45*, **47**
Lafitte Guesthouse **40**, 200
Loft 523 36, 45, *46*, **47**
Maison Orleans at Ritz-Carlton 37, **39**
Marquette House **49**, 51
Mazant Guesthouse **44**, 51
McKendrick-Breaux House Bed & Breakfast **49**, *50*
Monteleone Hotel 40
Old World Inn 50
Olivier House Hotel 41
Omni Royal Orleans Hotel 60
Le Pavilion Hotel 47
Place d'Armes 43
Prince Conti Hotel 41
Le Richelieu Hotel *40*, 41
Ritz-Carlton Hotel 36, 37, 39
Royal Sonesta Hotel 39
Royal Street Courtyard 36, **44**, 200
St Charles Guesthouse 50
St Charles Inn 50
St James Hotel 48
St Vincent's Guest House **50**, 51, 81
Sonlat House 36, 37, **39**
Sun Oak Bed & Breakfast 44
Ursuline Guest House **43**
W Hotel 45, **48**
W Hotel French Quarter 39

Bars
Balcony Bar & Café 88, **143**
The Blue Nile 139
Bombay Club 135
Le Bon Temps Roule 145
Bridge Lounge 144
Bourbon Pub 59, **197**
The Bulldog 144
Café Lafitte in Exile 198
Carousel Bar & Lounge **135**, 136, 147
Carrollton Station 136, **146**, 211
The Circle Bar 136, **141**
The Club/Ms Mae's 146
Club 360 142
Coop's Palace 135
Cooter Brown's Tavern 146
Corner Pocket 198
Cosimo's 135
Coyote Ugly Saloon 136
d.b.a. 136, *138*, **139**, 207
Doc Smith's Lounge 142
Dos Jefes Uptown Cigar Bar **146**, 211
The Dungeon (or Ye Original Dungeon Club) 136
Eagle Saloon 72
F&M Patio Bar 146
Fat Harry's 147
Finn McCool's 141
French Quarter Bar 136
Golden Lantern **198**, 201
Good Friends Bar **198**, *199*
The Half Moon 144
The Hideout 136
Kerry Irish Pub 137
Kim's 940 197, 198 **199**
The Kingpin 145
Lafitte's Blacksmith Shop 134, **137**, 147
Loa 136, **142**
Loft 523 142
Lounge Lizards 137
Markey's Bar 70, **141**
El Matador 136
Mick's Irish Pub 141
Molly's at the Market 136, **137**
Monkey Hill Bar 147
Napoleon House 60, 64, 115, 134, *135*, **139**, 147
Nick's 141
Ninth Circle at Congo Square 198
O'Flaherty's 82, **204**
Oz 59, **198**
Pals 141
Parasol's Restaurant & Bar 82, **144**
Pat O'Brien's 59, *137*, **139**, 147
Phillip's Restaurant & Bar 147
Polo Lounge 142
Port of Call 115, **139**
R Bar 136, **139**
Rainbow Lounge 199
The Saint 144
St Joe's 136, **147**
Saturn Bar 70, **141**, *143*

Sazerac Bar **142,** 147
The Seventh Circle 198
Snake & Jake's Christmas
  Club Lounge 134, 136,
  146, **147**
The Spotted Cat 141
Victorian Lounge 131, **144**
VooDoo at Congo Square
  198
Whiskey Blue 142
The Wine Loft 143

Restaurants & Cafés

Acme Oyster House **114,**
  118, 182
Angeli on Decatur 114
Angelo Brocato 130
Antoine's 61, 106, **109,** 123
Arnaud 111
August 106
Bacco 113
Bayona 106, **107,** 109, 111,
  114
Belle Forché 69, **111,** 115
The Bistro at the Maison
  de Ville 108
Bluebird Café 122
Bombay Club 108
Bon Ton Café 106, **119**
La Boulangerie 92, **132**
Brennan's 60, 106, **111,**
  114, 123, *123*
Brigtsen's 88, **124**
Broussard's **111,** 131
Bywater BBQ 71, **117**
Café Atchafalaya 125
Café Degas 92, **127**
Café Giovanni 113
Café Luna 88, **131**
Café Marigny 131
Café Maspero 114
Café du Monde 61, 68, *130,*
  131, 182
Café Negril 117
Café Sbisa 111
Camellia Grill 88, **122,** 182
Casamento's 126
CC's Coffeehouse 88, **131**
Central Grocery 114
Chateaubriand 128
Ciro's Cote Sud 124
Clover Grill 115
Cobalt 106, 111, **119,** 129
Commander's Palace 84,
  85, 106, 114, **121**
Country Flame 113
Crabby Jack's **129,** 182
Le Crepe Nanou 125
Crescent City Brewhouse
  107
Croissant d'Or 132
Cuvee 75, **119**
Dick & Jenny's 106, *106,*
  111, **124**
Dickie Brennan's Bourbon
  House 112
Dickie Brennan's
  Steakhouse 107
Domilise Sandwich Shop &
  Bar 126
Dooky Chase's 127
Drago's 129

Eleven 79 121
Elizabeth's 71, **117**
Emeril's 75, **119**
Emeril's Delmonico 121
Fair Grinds Coffeehouse
  132
56 Degrees 106, **118**
Feelings Café 117
Franky & Johnny's 127
Gabrielle Restaurant 127
Galatoire's 31, 57, 66, 106,
  108, **112,** 114, 123, 132
Gautreau's 124
The Grill Room 111, 114,
  119
Gumbo Shop 112
Herbsaint 106, 111, 114,
  119, 129
Horinoya 114, **118**
House of Blues 107
Houston's 121
Jack Dempsey's 117
Jacques-Imo's 124
Jamila's Café 125
Joey K's 88, **127**
Juan's Flying Burrito 88,
  121
K-Paul's Louisiana Kitchen
  106, **107**
Kyoto 122
Lebanon Café 125
Lemon Grass Café 118
Lilette 125
Liuzza's by the Track 128
Lola's 128
Mandina's 128
Marigny Brasserie 115
La Marquise 131, **132**
Martin Wine Cellar 122
Martinique Bistro **125,** 131
Mat & Naddie's **124,** *126,*
  131
Mona's Café 69, **128**
Mosca's 128
Mother's **120,** 182
Mr B's Bistro 108, *113*
Muriel's Jackson Square
  108
Napoleon House **115,** 139
Ninja 124
NOLA 109
Old Dog New Trick 69,
  117
Palace Café **109,** 182
Parasol's 122
Pascal's Manale 127
The Pelican Club **109,** 111,
  114
Peristyle **109,** 111, 114,
  129
PJ's Coffee and Tea 70, 88,
  133
Port of Call **115,** 139
Praline Connection 117
Quarter Scene Restaurant
  115
R&O Pizza Place 129
Rene Bistrot **120,** 129
Restaurant August 75, 111,
  120, 129
Rib Room 107
Rio Mar 120
Royal Blend 131, **133,** *133*
Royal Café 61, *62*

Rue de la Course 81, 88,
  133
Ruth's Chris Steak House
  127
Sake Café Uptown 121
Samurai Sushi 107
Still Perkin' 133
Sugar Magnolia 122
Surrey's Café and Juice Bar
  122
Taqueria Corona **125,** 182
Tujague's 113
Uglesich's 120
Upperline Restaurant 124
Victor's at the Ritz-Carlton
  111, **120,** 129
Wolfe's 129
Zoe Bistrot 120

Advertisers' Index

Please refer to relevant sections for addresses and telephone numbers

Louisiana Office of Tourism	**IFC**

Bars

Maple Leaf Bar	**140**

In Context

OffBeat	**4**
The National D-Day Museum	**8**

Shops & Services

Louisiana Music Factory	**154**

Mardi Gras

Mardi Gras World	**24**

Music

Tipitina's	**206**

Sightseeing

Louisiana Office of Tourism	**58**

Maps

DirectLine Travel Insurance	**274**

Restaurants

eatdrink.timeoutny.com	**110**
TONY Eating & Drinking Guide	**116**

Time Out City Guides Series	**IBC**

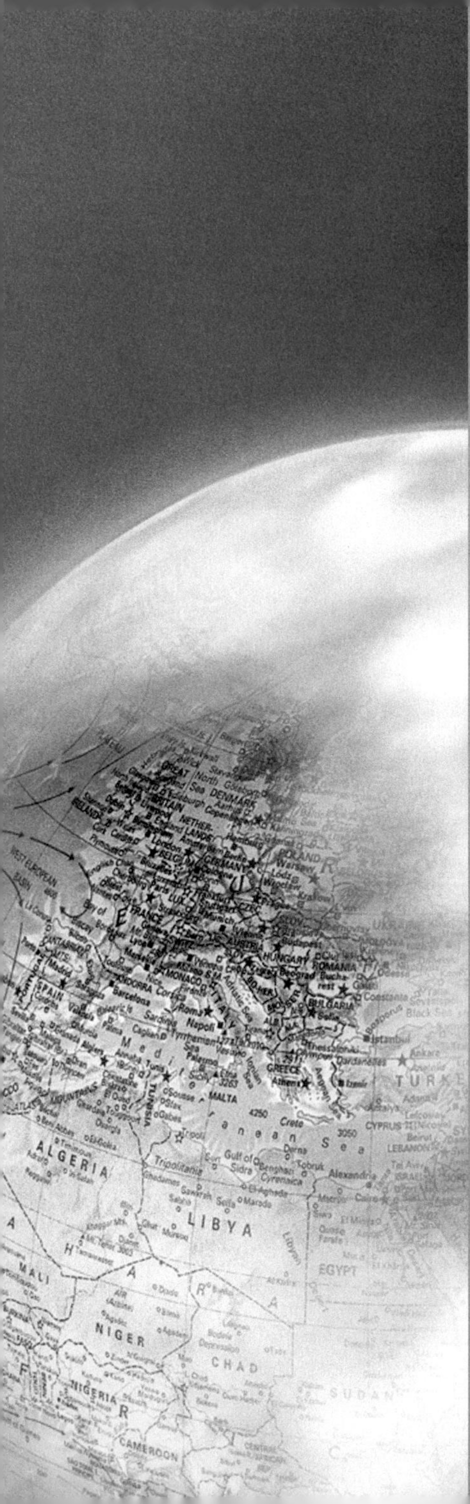

Maps

Trips Out of Town 272
Greater New Orleans 275
Uptown 276
Mid-City 278
Garden District & CBD 279
Transport 280
French Quarter 282
Street index 283

Trips Out of Town

† To Jackson & Memphis

Brookhaven

MISS

McComb

Amite

Hammond

Ponchatoula

Natchez

Catahoula Lake

Saline Wildlife Area

Larto Lake

Saline Lake

Homochitto National Forest

Mansura

Woodville

Angola

St Francisville

BATON ROUGE

Lake Maurepas

Opelousas

Grand Coteau

Breaux Bridge

Rayne

LAFAYETTE

St Martinville

White Castle

Gramercy

Convent

Vacherie

Reserve

New Orleans International Airport

Live Oaks Gardens

Jefferson Island

New Iberia

Grand Lake

Jungle Gardens & Bird Sanctuary

Avery Island

Weeks Bay

Vermilion Bay

Napoleonville

Lake Verret

Six Mile Lake

Raceland

Lockport

Larose

Cut O

Marsh Island

Morgan City

Houma

Galliano

Lake Boudreaux

Golden Meadow

US interstate

US federal

State and provincial

Places of interest

Parks or forests

GULF

OF

MEXICO

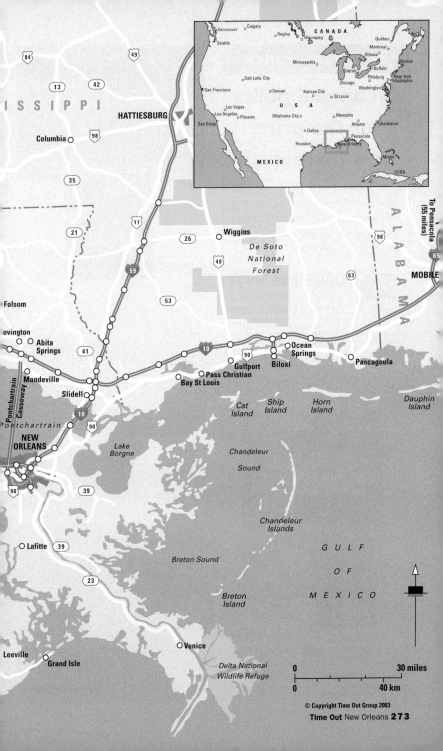

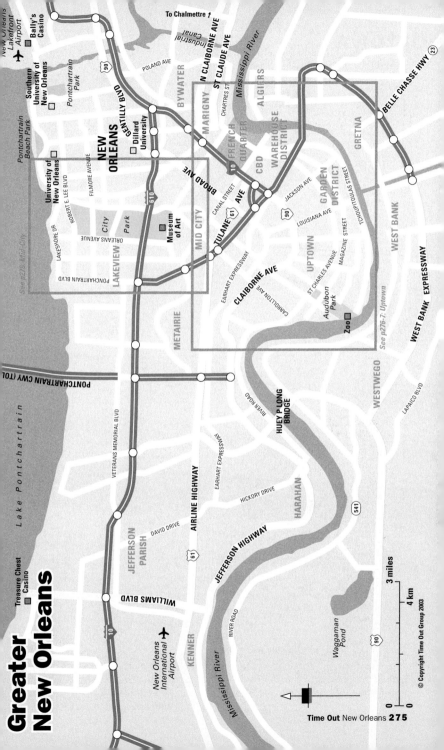

Greater
New Orleans

© Copyright Time Out Group 2003

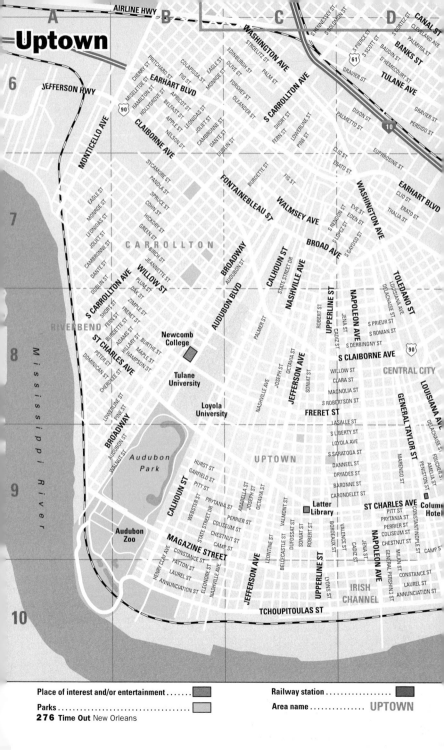

Uptown

Place of interest and/or entertainment . . . .

Parks . . . .

Railway station . . . .

Area name . . . . **UPTOWN**

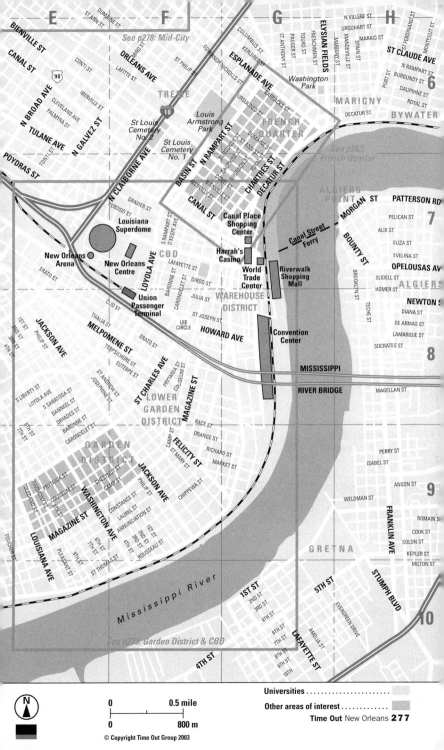

© Copyright Time Out Group 2003

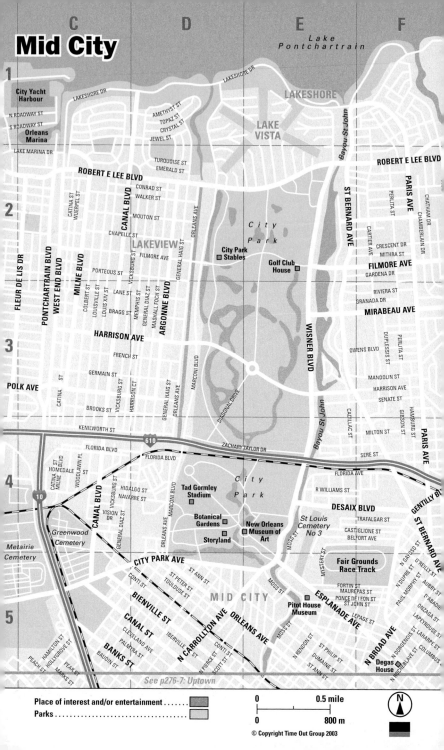

Garden District & CBD

© Copyright Time Out Group 2003

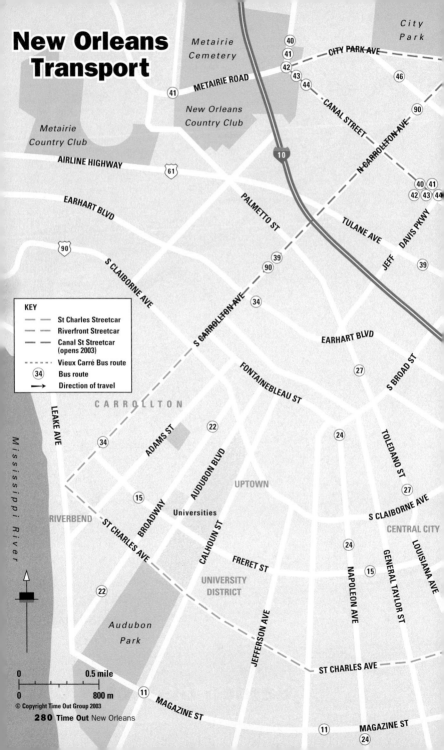

New Orleans
Transport

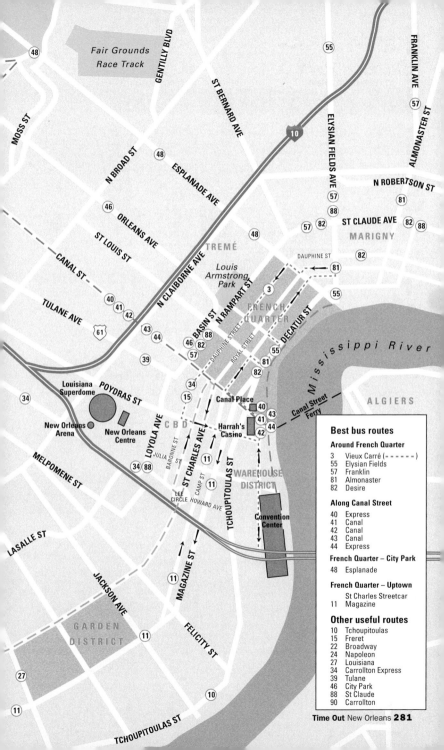

Fair Grounds
Race Track

GENTILLY BLVD

FRANKLIN AVE

ST BERNARD AVE

MOSS ST

48

55

57

ALMONASTER ST

10

ELYSIAN FIELDS AVE

N BROAD ST

48

ESPLANADE AVE

N ROBERTSON ST

57

88

81

46

ORLEANS AVE

57

82

ST CLAUDE AVE

82

88

ST LOUIS ST

MARIGNY

CANAL ST

48

DAUPHINE ST

82

TREMÉ

Louis
Armstrong
Park

81

TULANE AVE

40
41
42

N CLAIBORNE AVE

BASIN ST

N RAMPART ST

3

55

FRENCH
QUARTER

DECATUR ST

Mississippi River

61

43
44

88
46 82
57

DAUPHINE STREET

ROYAL STREET

55

81
82

39

34

15

34

Louisiana
Superdome

POYDRAS ST

Canal Place

40

ALGIERS

Canal Street Ferry

New Orleans
Arena

New Orleans
Centre

LOYOLA AVE

CBD

ST CHARLES AVE

Harrah's
Casino

43
41
44
42

MELPOMENE ST

34 88

JULIA

BARONNE ST

CAMP ST

34

11

11

TCHOUPITOULAS ST

WAREHOUSE
DISTRICT

LASALLE ST

LEE
CIRCLE

HOWARD AVE

Convention
Center

JACKSON AVE

MAGAZINE ST

11

11

GARDEN

DISTRICT

11

FELICITY ST

27

10

11

TCHOUPITOULAS ST

Best bus routes

Around French Quarter

3   Vieux Carré (– – – – – –)
55 Elysian Fields
57 Franklin
81 Almonaster
82 Desire

Along Canal Street

40 Express
41 Canal
42 Canal
43 Canal
44 Express

French Quarter – City Park

48 Esplanade

French Quarter – Uptown

    St Charles Streetcar
11 Magazine

Other useful routes

10 Tchoupitoulas
15 Freret
22 Broadway
24 Napoleon
27 Louisiana
34 Carrollton Express
39 Tulane
46 City Park
88 St Claude
90 Carrollton

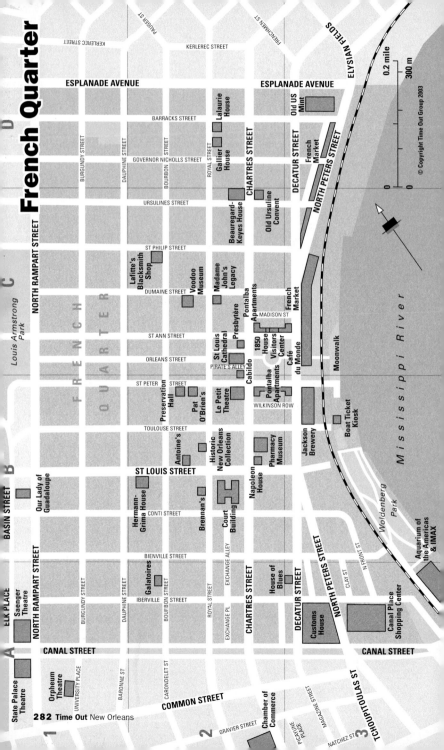

French Quarter

Louis Armstrong Park

F R E N C H   Q U A R T E R

Mississippi River

Woldenberg Park

0 | 0.2 mile

0 | 300 m

ELYSIAN FIELDS

Streets

KERLEREC STREET

ESPLANADE AVENUE

BARRACKS STREET

GOVERNOR NICHOLLS STREET

URSULINES STREET

ST PHILIP STREET

DUMAINE STREET

ST ANN STREET

ORLEANS STREET

ST PETER STREET

TOULOUSE STREET

ST LOUIS STREET

CONTI STREET

BIENVILLE STREET

IBERVILLE STREET

CANAL STREET

COMMON STREET

GRAVIER STREET

PAUGER ST

FRENCHMEN ST

KERLEREC STREET

ESPLANADE AVENUE

PICAYUNE PLACE

NATCHEZ ST

TCHOUPITOULAS ST

BASIN STREET

NORTH RAMPART STREET

BURGUNDY STREET

DAUPHINE STREET

BOURBON STREET

ROYAL STREET

CHARTRES STREET

DECATUR STREET

NORTH PETERS STREET

CLAY ST

N FRONT ST

EXCHANGE ALLEY

EXCHANGE PL

MADISON ST

WILKINSON ROW

PIRATE'S ALLEY

ELK PLACE

UNIVERSITY PLACE

BARONNE ST

CARONDELET ST

MAGAZINE STREET

Landmarks

State Palace Theatre

Orpheum Theatre

Saenger Theatre

Our Lady of Guadaloupe

Hermann-Grima House

Brennan's

Court Building

Galatoires

House of Blues

Customs House

Canal Place Shopping Center

Aquarium of the Americas & IMAX

Boat Ticket Kiosk

Jackson Brewery

Moonwalk

French Market

Café du Monde

Pontalba Apartments

Presbytère

St Louis Cathedral

Cabildo

1850 House Visitors Center

Le Petit Theatre

Pharmacy Museum

Napoleon House

Historic New Orleans Collection

Antoine's

Preservation Hall

Pat O'Brien's

Voodoo Museum

Madame John's Legacy

Lafitte's Blacksmith Shop

Beauregard-Keyes House

Old Ursuline Convent

Gallier House

Lalaurie House

Old US Mint

Chamber of Commerce

Street Index

1st St - p276 E8/9/F9,
p279 A1/2/B3/4
1st St (Gretna) - p276-7 G10
2nd St - p276-7 E8/9/F9,
p279 A2/3/B3/4
2nd St (Gretna) - p276-7 G10
3rd St - p276-7 E8/9/F9,
p279 A2/3/B3/4
3rd St (Gretna) - p276-7 G10
4th St - p276-7 E8/9/F9/10,
p279 A2/3/B3/4
4th St (Gretna) - p276-7 G10
5th St - p276-7 G10/H10
6th St - p276-7 E8/9,
p279 A3/B4
6th St (Gretna) - p276-7
G10/H10
7th St - p276-7 E8/9,
p279 A3/4
7th St (Gretna) - p276-7
G10/H10
8th St - p276-7 E8-10,
p279 A3/4
8th St (Gretna) - p276-7
G10/H10
9th St - p276-7 E9/10,
p279 A3/4
9th St (Gretna) - p276-7
G10/H10
10th - p276-7 G10/H10

Adams St - p276-7
A8/B7/8/C7
Airline Hwy - p276-7 A5/B5
Aline St - p279 A4
Alix St - p276-7 H7
Amelia St - p276-7 D8/9
Amelia St (Gretna) - p276-7
G10
Amethyst St - p278 D1
Annunciation St - p276-7
B10/C10/D10/E9/10/G9,
p279 A4/B3/4/C2/3
Anson St - p276-7 H9
Apple St - p276-7 B6/C7
Apricot St - p276-7 B6
Arabella St - p276-7 B10/C9
Argonne Blvd - p278 D2/3
Aubry St - p278 F5
Audubon Blvd - p276-7
B8/C7/8
Audubon St - p276-7
A9/B7/8/C7

Banks St - p276-7 D6,
p278 C5/D5
Baronne St - p276-7
C9/D9/E9/9/F7/8,
p279 A3/B1-3, p282 A1
Barracks St - p276-7 G6,
p282 D1-3
Basin St - p276-7 F7,
p282 B1
Baudin St - p276-7 D6,
p278 C5
Belfast St - p276-7 B6/C7
Belfort Ave - p278 E4/F4
Bellecastle St - p276-7 C9/10
Bienville St - p276-7
E6/F6/F7/G7, p278 D5,
p282 B1-3
Birch St - p276-7 A7/B7/8
Bordeaux St - p276-7 C9/10
Bounty St - p276-7 H7

Bourbon St - p276-7 F7/G6/7,
p282 A2/B2/C2
Bragg St - p278 C3/D3
Breakwater Dr - p278 C1
Broad Ave - p276-7 C7
Broadway - p276-7 B8/9/C7
Brooks St - p278 C3/D3
Burdette St - p276-7
A8/B7/8/C7
Burgundy St - p276-7 7/G6/H6,
p282 A1/B1/C1
Burthe St - p276-7 A7/8/B8

Cadillac St - p278 E3/4
Cadiz St - p276-7 D8-10
Calhoun St - p276-7 C7-10
Cambronne St - p276-7
A7/B6/7/C6
Camp St - p276-7
B9/C9/D9/E9/F9,
p279 A3/4/B3/C1/2
Canal Blvd - p278 C2-5/D1
Canal St - p276-7
D6/E6/F6/7, p278 C5/D5,
p279 B1/C1 A1-3
Carondelet St - p276-7
C9/D9/E9/9/F7/8,
p279 A3/B1-3, p282 A2
Cartier Ave - p278 F1-3
Castiglione St - p278 E4/F4
Catina St - p278 C2-4
Chamberlain Dr - p278 F2/3
Chapelle St - p278 C2/D2
Chartres St - p279 C1,
p282 A2/B2/C2/D2
Chatham Dr - p278 F2
Cherokee St - p276-7 A8/B8
Cherry St - p276-7 B6
Chestnut St - p276-7
B9/C9/D9/E9/F9,
p279 A3/B2
Chippewa St - p276-7
E9/10/F9, p279 A4/
B3/4/C3
City Park Ave - p278 C5/D5
Claiborne Ave - p276-7
B6/7/C7/8/D8/E7/8/F6/7
Clara St - p276-7 C8/D8/E9,
p279 A2
Clay St - p282 A3
Cleveland Ave - p276-7
D6/E6/F7, p278 C5/D5
Clio St - p276-7
C6/D7/E7/8/F8,
p279 A1/B2
Cohn St - p276-7 B7
Colapissa St - p276-7 B6
Colbert St - p278 C2/3
Coliseum St - p276-7
B9/C9/D9/E9/F8/9,
p279 A3/B2/3
Columbus St - p276-7 G6
Commerce St - p279 C1/2
Common St - p279 B1/C1,
p282 A1-3
Conrad St - p278 C2/D2
Constance St - p276-7
B9/10/C10/D10/
E9/10/F9,
p279 A4/B3/C2
Constantinople St - p276-7
D9/10
Conti St - p276-7 E6/F6/7/G7,

p278 C5/D5, p282 B1-3
Convention Center Blvd -
p279 C1/2
Cook St - p276-7 H9
Crescent Dr - p278 F2
Crystal St - p278 D1

D'Abadie St - p278 F5
D'Hemecourt St - p276-7 D6
Danneel St - p276-7
C9/D9/E8/9, p279 A2/3
Dante St - p276-7 A7/B6/7/C6
Dauphine St - p276-7
F7/G6/7/H6, p282
A1/B1/C1
De Armas St - p276-7 H8
Decatur St - p276-7 G6/7/H6,
p279 C1, p282 A3/B3/
C3/D3
Delachaise St - p276-7
D7-9/E9/10, p279 A3/4
Desaix Blvd - p278 E4/F4
Diagonal Dr - p278 D3/4
Diana St - p276-7 H8
Dixon St - p276-7 D6
Dominican St - p276-7 A8
Dryades St - p276-7
C9/D9/E8/9, p279 A2/3
Dublin St - p276-7 A7/8/B7/C6
Dufossat St - p276-7 C9/10
Dumaine St - p276-7 F6/G6,
p278 D5/E5, p282 C1/2
Duplessis St - p278 F3

Eagle St - p276-7 A7/B6/7/C6
Earhart Blvd - p276-7
B6/C6/7/D7
Earhart Blvd - p279 A1
Earhart Expwy - p276-7 A6/7
Eden St - p276-7 D7
Edinburgh St - p276-7 B6/C6
Eleonore St - p276-7 B9/10
Eliza St - p276-7 H7
Elk Pl - p282 A1
Elysian Fields - p276-7 G6,
p282 D3
Emerald St - p278 D2
Erato St - p276-7
C6/7/D7/E7/F8,
p279 A1/B2
Esplanade Ave - p276-7
F6/G6, p278 E5/F5,
p282 D1-3
Euphrosine St - p276-7 D6/7
Euterpe St - p276-7 E8/F9,
p279 B2/C3
Eve St - p276-7 D7
Evelina St - p276-7 H7
Evergreen Dr - p276-7 H10
Exchange Alley - p282 A2/B3
Exchange Pl - p282 A2

Felicity St - p276-7 E8/F8/9
p279 A2/B2/3/C3
Fern St - p276-7 A8/B7/8/C6
Fig St - p276-7 B6/C7
Filmore Ave - p278
C2/D2/E2/F2
Fleur de Lis Dr - p278 B3/C2
Florida Ave - p278 E4/F4
Florida Blvd - p278 C4/D4
Fontainebleau St - p276-7 D7
Forshey St - p276-7 B6/C6
Fortin St - p278 E5/F5

Foucher St - p276-7 D9/E9/10
Franklin Ave - p276-7 H8-10
French St - p278 C3/D3
Frenchmen St - p276-7 G6
Frenchmen St - p282 D2
Freret St - p276-7
A7/B8/C8/D8, p279 B1
Front S - p279 C2

Gardena Dr - p278 E3/F3
Garfield St - p276-7 B9/C9
General Diaz St - p278
C4/D2/3
General Haig St - p278 D2-4
General Pershing St - p276-7
D7-10
General Taylor St - p276-7
D7-10
Gentilly Blvd - p278 F4
Germain St - p278 C3/D3
Gibson St - p278 F3/4
Girod St - p276-7 F7/G8,
p279 B1/C1/2
Governor Nicholls St -
p276-7 F6/G6, p282 D1-3
Granada Dr - p278 E3/F3
Gravier St - p276-7 D6/E7/F7,
p279 A1/B1/C1,
p282 A2/3
Green St - p276-7 B7

Hamburg St - p278 F3/4
Hamilton St - p276-7 B6
p278 C5
Hampson St - p276-7 A8/B8
Harmony St - p276-7 E8-10
p279 A3/4
Harrison Ave - p278
C3/D3/E3/F3
Harrison Ct - p278 D3
Henry Clay Ave - p276-7
B9/10
Hickory St - p276-7 B7
Hidalgo St - p278 C4/D4
Hillary St - p276-7 A8/B7/8/C7
Hollygrove St - p276-7 B6
p278 C5
Homedale St - p278 C4
Homer St - p276-7 H8
Howard Ave - p276-7 F8/G8,
p279 C2
Hurst St - p276-7 B9/C9

Iberville St - p276-7
E6/F6/7/G7, p278 C5/D5,
p279 B1/C1, p282 A1-3
Isabel St - p276-7 H9

Jackson Ave - p276-7 E8/F9,
p279 A2/B3
Jeannette St - p276-7 A7/B7/8
Jefferson Ave - p276-7 C8-10
Jefferson Hwy - p276-7 A6
Jena St - p276-7 D7-10
Jewel St - p278 D1
Joliet St - p276-7 A7/B6/7/C6
Joseph St - p276-7 C7-10
Josephine St - p276-7
E8/F8/9, p279 A2/B2/3
Julia St - p276-7 F8/G8,
p279 B2/C2
Kenilworth St - p278
Kepler St - p276-7
Kerlerec St - p27

p282 D1/2

Lafayette Sq - p279 C1
Lafayette St - p276-7 F7/G7
Lafayette St (Gretna) - p276-7 G10
Lafitte St - p276-7 E6/F6
Laharpe St - p278 F5
Lake Marina Dr - p278 B2/C2
Lakeshore Dr - p278 C1/D1/E1
Lamarque St - p276-7 H8
Lane St - p278 C3/D3
Lapeyrouse St - p278 F5
Lasalle St - p276-7 C8/D8, p279 A2/B1
Laurel St - p276-7 B10/C10/D10/E9/10/F9
Laurel St - p279 A4/B3
Lee Circle - p276-7 F8, p279 B2
Leonidas St - p276-7 A7/B6/7
Leontine St - p276-7 C9/10
Lepage St - p278 E5/F5
Louis XIV St - p278 C2/3
Louisiana Ave - p276-7 D7/8/9/E9/10, p279 A3/4
Louisville St - p278 C2/3
Lowerline St - p276-7 A9/B7/8/C6/7
Loyola Ave - p276-7 C9/D9/E8/F7, p279 B1
Loyola St - p279 A2/3
Lyons St - p276-7 C10/D10

Madison St - p282 C2/3
Magazine St - p282 A3
p276-7 A9/B9/C10/D10/E9/F9/8, p279 A3/4/B2/3
Magellan St - p276-7 H8
Magnolia St - p276-7 C8/D8/E9, p279 A2
Mandeville St - p276-7 H6
Mandolin St - p278 F3
Maple St - p276-7 A7/8/B8
Marais St - p276-7 G6/H6
Marconi Blvd - p278 D2-4
Marengo St - p276-7 D8-10
Marigny St - p276-7 H6
Market St - p276-7 F9/G9, p279 C3
Marks St - p278 C5
Mashall Foch St - p278 D2-4
Maurepas St - p278 E5/F5
Melpomene St - p276-7 E8/F8 p279 A2/B2
Memphis St - p278 C3/D2
Milan St - p276-7 D8-10
Milne Blvd - p278 C2-4
Milton St - p276-7 H10, p278 E4/F5
Mirabeau Ave - p278 E3/F3
Miro St - p276-7 F6
Mistletoe St - p276-7 B6
Mithra St - p278 F2
Monroe St - p276-7 A7/B6/7/C6
Montegut St - p276-7 H6
Monticello Ave - p276-7 A6/7/B6
Morgan St - p276-7 H7
Moss St - p278 E4/5
Mouton St - p278 C2/D2
Mystery St - p278 E4/5
N Broad Ave - p276-7 E6, p278 F5
N Carrollton Ave - p278 D5

N Dorgenois St - p278 F5
N Dupré St - p278 F5
N Front St - p282 A3/B3
N Galvez St - p276-7 E6/7/F6
N Gayoso St - p278 F4/5
N Peters St - p282 A3/B3/C3/D3
N Pierce St - p278 D5
N Rampart St - p276-7 F7/G6/H6, p279 B1, p282 A1/B1/C1/D1
N Rendon St - p278 E5
N Roadway St - p278 B1/C1
N Rocheblave St - p278 F5
N Villere St - p276-7 G6/H5
Napoleon Ave - p276-7 D7-10
Nashville Ave - p276-7 B10/C7-9
Natchez St - p282 A3
Navarre St - p278 C4/D4
Nelson St - p276-7 B6/7/C7
Newton St - p276-7 H8

O'Keefe Ave - p276-7 F7
O'Reilly St - p278 F5
Oak St - p276-7 A7/B7/8
Octavia St - p276-7 C7-10
Oleander St - p276-7 B6/C6
Olive St - p276-7 B6/C6
Onzaga St - p278 F5
Opelousas Ave - p276-7 H7
Orange St - p276-7 F9/G9, p279 B3/C3
Orleans Ave - p276-7 E6/F6, p278 D2-5/E5
Orleans St - p282 C1/2
Owens Blvd - p278 E3/F3

Palm St - p276-7 C6
Palmer St - p276-7 C8
Palmetto St - p276-7 C6/D6
Palmyra St - p276-7 D6/E6/F7, p278 C5/D5
Panola St - p276-7 B7
Paris Ave - p278 F1/4
Patterson Rd - p276-7 H7
Patton St - p276-7 B9/10
Pauger St - p276-7 G6, p282 D2
Paul Morphy St - p278 F5
Peach St - p278 C5
Pear St - p278 C5
Pelican St - p276-7 H7
Peniston St - p276-7 D8/9
Perdido St - p276-7 D6/E7/F7, p279 A1/B1
Perlita St - p278 F2/3
Perrier St - p276-7 B9/C9/D9
Perry St - p276-7 H9
Peter St - p276-7 A8/B8
Philip St - p276-7 E8/F9, p279 A2/3/B3
Picayune Pl - p282 A3
Pine St - p276-7 A9/B7/8/C6/7
Pirate's Alley - p282 C2
Pitt St - p276-7 B9/C9/D9
Pleasant St - p276-7 E9/10, p279 A3/4
Plum St - p276-7 A7/B7/8
Polk Ave - p278 C3/D3
Polymnia St - p279 B2
Ponce de Leon St - p278 E5/F5
Pontchartrain Blvd - p278 C2/3
Port St - p276-7 H6
Porteous St - p278 C2/D2
Poydras St - p276-7 E7/F7, p279 A1/B1/C1
Pratt Dr - p278 F2
Pritchard St - p276-7 B6

Prytania St - p276-7 B9/C9/D9/E9/F8/9, p279 A3/B2/3

R Williams St - p278 E4
Race St - p276-7 F8/9/G9, p279 B3/C3
Richard St - p276-7 F9/G9, p279 C3
Riviera St - p278 E3/F3
Robert E Lee Blvd - p278 C2/D2/E2/F2
Robert St - p276-7 C7-10
Romain St - p276-7 H9
Rousseau St - p276-7 F9, p279 B4/C4
Royal St - p276-7 G6/7/H6, p282 A2/B2/C3

S Carrollton Ave - p276-7 A8/B7/C6
S Cortez St - p276-7 D6
S Derbigny St - p276-7 D8
S Galvez St - p279 A1
S Gayoso St - p276-7 D7
S Hennessey St - p276-7 C6/D5
S Liberty St - p276-7 C9/D9/E8 p279 A2
S Lopez St - p276-7 D7
S Pierce St - p276-7 D6
S Prieur St - p276-7 D8
S Rampart St - p276-7 F7
S Rendon St - p276-7 C7/D7
S Roadway St - p278 B1/C1
S Robertson St - p276-7 C8/D8/E9
S Robertson St - p279 A2
S Roman St - p276-7 D8, p279 A1
S Saratoga St - p276-7 C9/D9/E8/9, p279 A2/3
S Scott St - p276-7 D6
S Solomon St - p276-7 C6/D5
Scott St - p278 D5
Senate St - p278 E3/F3
Sere St - p278 E4/F4
Short St - p276-7 A8/B7/8/C6
Simon Bolivar St - p279 A2/B2
Slidell St - p276-7 H7
Socrates St - p276-7 H8
Solon St - p276-7 H9
Soniat St - p276-7 C8-10
Sophie Wright Pl - p279 B3
Soraparu St - p279 B3/4
S Peters St - p279 C1/2
Spain St - p276-7 H6
Spruce St - p276-7 B7
St Andrew St - p276-7 E8/F8/9 p279 A2/B3/C3
St Ann St - p276-7 F6/G6/7, p278 D5/E5, p282 C1/2
St Anthony St - p276-7 G6
St Bernard Ave - p278 E1-3/F4/5
St Charles Ave - p276-7 A8/B8/9/C9/D9/E9/F8, p279 A3/B2/3/C1
St Claude Ave - p276-7 H6
St Ferdinand St - p276-7 H6
St John St - p278 E5/F5
St Joseph St - p276-7 F8/G8
St Louis St - p282 B1-3
St Mary St - p276-7 F8/9, p279 B3/C3
St Peter St - p278 D5/E5, p282 B1-3
St Philip St - p276-7 F6/G6, p278 D5/E5, p282 C1/2
St Thomas St - p276-7 E10/F9, p279 A4/B3/4/C3

State Street Dr - p276-7 B9/10/C6-9
Stroelitz St - p276-7 C6
Stumph Blvd - p276-7 H10
Sugar Bowl Dr - p279 A1/B1
Sycamore St - p276-7 B7

Tchoupitoulas St - p276-7 B10/C10/D10, p279 A4/B4/C2/3, p282 A3
Terpsichore St - p276-7 E8/F8, p279 B2/C3
Thalia St - p276-7 D7/E7/8/F8, p279 A1/B2
Toledano St - p276-7 D7/8/E9/10, p279 A3/4
Tonti St - p276-7 E6/7/F6
Topaz St - p278 D1
Toulouse St - p278 D5/E5, p282 B1/2
Touro St - p276-7 G6
Trafalgar St - p278 E4/F4
Tulane Ave - p276-7 D6/E6/7/F7, p279 B1
Turquoise St - p278 D2

Union St - p279 B1
University Pl - p282 A1
Upperline St - p276-7 C8-10
Urquhart St - p276-7 G6/H6
Ursulines St - p276-7 F6/G6
Ursulines St - p282 C1-3

Valence St - p276-7 C8/9/D9/10
Valmont St - p276-7 C8-10
Vicksburg St - p278 C3/4/D2
Vision Dr - p278 C4

Walker St - p278 C2/D2
Walmsey Ave - p276-7 C7
Walnut St - p279 A4/B9
Washington Ave - p276-7 C6/D7/E8/9/F10, p279 A2/3/B4
Webster St - p276-7 B9
Weldman St - p276-7 H9
West End Blvd - p278 C2/3
Wilkinson Row - p282 B2/3
Willow St - p276-7 A7/B7/8/C8/D8, p279 A2
Wisner Blvd - p278 E2-4
Woodlawn Pl - p278 C4
Wuerpel St - p278 C2/3

Zachary Taylor Dr - p278 D4/E4
Zimple St - p276-7 A7/B8